RACES OF MANKIND
THEIR ORIGIN AND MIGRATION

Races of Mankind
Their Origin and Migration

All recognized ancient tribes and nations
identified and their migrations traced.

By

CALVIN KEPHART, LL.M., D.C.L., Ph.D.

Author of *Origin of the Conjugal Community* (or
Community Property Law) *and Other Ancient Laws, The
Swedes and Swedish Goths, Herr Volcnant von Erlach,
Minnesinger, Origin of Heraldry in Europe* (*Also of
Miscellaneous Surnames and Insignia*), *Sanskrit Language
— Its Origin, Composition and Diffusion,* and other his-
torical publications and articles.

PHILOSOPHICAL LIBRARY, INC.
15 East 40th Street
New York 16, N. Y.

© 1960, Calvin Kephart

Library of Congress catalogue card number 60-13647

PHILOSOPHICAL LIBRARY, Inc., Publisher
15 East 40th Street, New York 16, N. Y.

Printed in the United States of America

PREFACE

This treatise in ethnography is an outgrowth of research by the writer for a publication on the origin of the principle of the *Conjugal Community* (or *Community Property Law*), which appears in the legal system of our southwestern and far western states. This principle of law entered our country from Spanish and French sources and in modified form governs the income and disposition of property acquired by married couples in those states.[1]

By the process of elimination in that study, the principle was isolated to the codes of the ancient Welsh (Kymry) and Irish, the Visigoths of Sweden and Spain, and the far earlier Babylonian King Hammurabi (c. 2100 B.C.). On the assumption that the last-named code must have been the original source, the manner in which the principle was transmitted to peoples of western Europe became the problem to be solved and it obviously required an investigation of the antecedents of the Kimmeric and Gothic divisions of the Nordic race. Upon recourse to the works of Herodotus, the author found surpassing aid there. His appellation of the "Father of History" is well deserved. But his works, like the Bible, must be read with interpretation and discrimination; "the wheat must be separated from the chaff."

Since both the Kimmeric and the Gothic subraces anciently inhabited successively the region then known as Western Scythia,[2] the probable course of transmission of this principle of law was at once fairly apparent. However, the solution of the problem necessitated the achievement of a feat that has not been accomplished hitherto, namely, the lifting of the Scythian veil. It presented a rough and

---

1 Calvin Kephart, *Origin of the Conjugal Community (or Community Property Law) and other Ancient Laws* (1938).

2 Roughly, the region between the Vistula and Ural Rivers and north of the Carpathian and Caucasian Mountains and the Black and Caspian Seas, now Poland proper and southern European Russia.

v

rugged task, one beset with numerous conflicting historical and ethnological reports and inferences, but the
challenge to scholarship was too alluring to forgo.

Each step forward presented expanding ethnological
ramifications, many of which were highly inviting to a
student of racial migrations. Eventually, the interaction
of fundamentally different races was encountered in widely-separated regions, so that the investigation assumed
far broader aspects than those of tracing the path of transmission of a single principle of law. The only commend-
able alternative was to follow out each clue to its uttermost limits. The results presented in the following pages
are believed to solve problems of racial relationships and
migrations touching every recognized race on the earth's
surface.

Someone has said that the value of any history depends
on the sources relied upon by the writer and the manner
in which he has used those sources. Both original and secondary sources have been utilized here, the latter only
when the facts or conclusions found seemed in the light
of other known facts to be free from doubt. The distinction between ancient primary and secondary sources is
quite thin at times because ancient writers put down both
what they saw and what they heard. Conclusions contrary
to some reached here can be cited from other books. That
is freely recognized. No apology is offered for this procedure. It may be said to be an application of inductive
reasoning in historical research, and, as in many other
cases, it has been singularly fertile of results. As said by
Bury, "in dealing with such fragmentary material, reconstructions and hypotheses are inevitable. In ancient * * *
history, as in physical science, hypotheses, founded on a
critical examination of the data, are necessary for the
advancement of knowledge. The reconstructions may fall
tomorrow, but, if they are legitimate, they will not have
been useless." Originality of solution is claimed only in
those instances in which the conclusion actually is original.
The reader will have to determine for himself which
conclusions are such.

This production is intended to be chiefly a factual

rather than a philosophical work, in order to facilitate the portrayal of the various racial origins and migrations as clearly as possible. No assertion is made that all authoritative sources have been investigated. The books are glutted with unconnected facts of ethnology and history and with many conflicting statements and inferences. Perhaps the greatest need of scholarship today is the perspective and capability to analyze and synthesize the available facts of a given subject and to integrate them chronologically in the hazy stream of human events. When the conclusion reached here in any one phase of the subject seemed to be soundly supported by related and cumulative data and to be correct, that aspect was pursued no further. The conclusions on controverted subjects are advanced in no dogmatic spirit but rather in a tentative, though highly confident, manner; however, that attitude cannot always be conveniently stated in the text and it must be understood by the reader to persist throughout.

The different tribes and nations did not reside in vacuo but always within variable distances of or in contact with other tribes or nations. It was their relationship with or knowledge of others that usually impelled them to exchange various customs, ideas, words, or goods or to quarrel and emigrate or cause their opponents to emigrate elsewhere. Consequently, different peoples are mentioned repeatedly in several chapters of the book in connection with the consideration of other peoples. It may constitute a form of repetition, but, for the above reason, it could not well be avoided; in fact, such repetition of names of tribes or nations or places should tend to impress them on the mind of the reader.

It is suggested that a satisfactory map of Asia, Europe, and Africa be kept before the reader when reading this book, so that his attention may be properly oriented at all times and confusion of races and events may be avoided. Frequent reference to the table of glacial chronology and corresponding races of man also will aid in gaining and retaining the proper perspective of events as they occurred in the distant past.

In the light of human nature, the author does not

assume that various interested professions will accept with avidity all of the original or revised findings announced herein, but he is serenely confident that Father Time will aid in the suitable appraisal of all such deductions, which he believes to be correct. He will welcome any positive evidence of error, but must decry merely captious attitudes of critics whose earlier knowledge of the subject may be disturbed.

A signal challenge here has been the evident intention of various professors, acting as authorities but with apparent racial bias, to confuse this subject in the minds of the general public by such assertions as these, which have come to the writer's notice: (1) No relatively pure races can be named (despite that the component races of presently mixed peoples are determinable), (2) there has been no Turanian, or Aryan, or Negro, or Hebrew race or racial subdivision, but only bombastic claims of such, (3) there are no superior or inferior races, and so on. The facts are to the contrary. Such utterances usually confuse race with language, in disregard of the fact that, while languages change constantly, races remain substantially unchanged through long periods in the absence of intermarriage with dissimilar races. All kinds of changes of tribal and national names and racial dialects have occurred and will recur throughout the ages. The two ideas should be carefully distinguished. Such assertions ordinarily result largely from superficial study of the subject, as will be demonstrated in subsequent pages.

Especial acknowledgment is gratefully made here of the encouragement extended to the author by his late good friend and mentor, Honorable Charles S. Lobingier, jurist, author, educator, and editor of the Civil Law Section of *Corpus Juris*, and of the faithful and accurate service performed by his amanuensis, Mrs. Bernice (Belmore) MacArthur.

More specifically, gratitude is expressed to the following scholars for their careful review of and suggestions for improvements in the sections named, viz., Dr. William C. Alden, retired geologist, U. S. Geological Survey, for the sections pertaining to *Geological Considerations* and *The*

Ice Ages, Rev. George S. Duncan, Ph.D., retired professor of Assyriology and Egyptology, American University, for the section on *Social Emergence of Primordial Man,* and W. E. Crouch, B. S., former chief of the Section of Game Management, U. S. Fish and Wildlife Service, for the section on *Origin of Man.* And last, but not least, was the critical review of the manuscript and the verification of citations by a friend and kinsman, Milton Rubincam, F.A.S.G., past-president of the National Genealogical Society, Washington, editor of its *Quarterly Magazine,* contributing editor of *The American Genealogist,* and author of numerous articles on genealogy, biography, and history, including monographs on Dr. David Rittenhouse, the eminent American scientist and statesman, Lord Cornbury, first royal governor of the colonies of New York and New Jersey, and Samuel Witham Stockton, one of the negotiators of the secret treaty between the new American government and the city of Amsterdam in 1778. His suggestions have been most helpful.

The consummation of the volume is due largely to the constant aid and encouragement of the author's devoted wife (Olga Ahlson von Zweigbergk) and to the availability of the facilities of the Library of Congress and its co-öperative staff.

CALVIN KEPHART, *Erlach Villa, Shady Side, Maryland.*

AN ADAPTATION

Tell me not in mournful slumbers
    'Life is but an empty dream!'
For the soul is dead that slumbers,
    And things are not what they seem.

Life is real! Life is earnest!
    And the grave is not its goal.
Dust thou art, to dust thou returnest,
    Was not spoken of the soul.

Lives of great men all remind us
    We can make our lives sublime
And, departing, leave behind us
    Footprints on the sands of time.

—From *A Psalm of Life,* by
    Henry Wadsworth Longfellow

CONTENTS

xi

CHAPTER III. *MAN'S PROGRESS AND DISPERSION*

CHAPTER IV. *EUROPEAN CONQUESTS BY KELTS AND TURANIANS*

CHAPTER V. *DISPERSION OF KIMMERIANS AND OTHERS*

CHAPTER VI. *KIMMERIC INVASIONS OF WESTERN EUROPE*

CHARTS AND MAPS

RACES OF MANKIND

THEIR ORIGIN AND MIGRATION

CHAPTER I. MAN'S EMERGENCE

1. *Introduction.* In comparison with the most recent estimates of roughly 4.5 billion years as the age of this earth,[1] man is a relatively late phenomenon of nature. The humanoid stem from which he sprang probably arose on the earth only one or two million years ago, although much higher estimates have appeared recently. Numerous branches have come and gone, but apparently only the one branch known as *Homo sapiens,* modern man, remains. It has truly been a case of the stern survival of the fittest, but modern man must still prove his capability to survive perpetually.

The leading authorities agree that all of the existing races of mankind had a common origin.[2] Not only is the unity of man proved by the test of fertility, but his early works everywhere afford the most significant resemblances. Moreover, in their physical construction all present races are identical fundamentally. This similarity of development hardly could have occurred at more than one time or place or in more than one line of descent from humanoid precursors. It follows, therefore, that modern man must have descended from a single ancestral stock at a single place of origin, a single cradle-land, whence the populating of the earth was done by migration. The questions as to his probable manner and place of origin are discussed subsequently.

---

1 Stated by Doctors F. R. Houtermans, of the University of Bern, G J. Wasserburg, of California Institute of Technology, and G. H. Weatherell, of Carnegie Institute of Washington on September 10, 1957, at the opening of a symposium on the earth's age before the International Union of Geodesy and Geophysics at Toronto, Ontario. Prior estimates were lower.

2 Eminent European naturalists, such as Prichard, Cuvier, Blumenbach, Humboldt, Pickering, Owen, Latham, De Quatrefages, and others, early reached this conclusion.

Man roamed over the surface of the earth so many thousands of years before the beginning of recorded history, which goes back scarcely beyond 5000 B. C., that we cannot be certain as to what happened in his evolution during those ages. His cultural progress during the last 25,000 years has exceeded that made during the entire previous time of his existence. His death-rate was great and his numbers were relatively small until the beginning of historical times. The effectiveness of the study of history, whether in general or in particular, is markedly enhanced as we learn more about the ethnic relation of the various races of the earth today. To this end, scientists endeavor to interpret and correlate the assembled geographical, geological, anthropological, ethnological, historical, and linguistic[3] data, with the result that the scope of our knowledge regarding early man and his activities, customs, and movements is constantly being broadened. This work aims to coördinate further the extant data concerning the early races, to the end that a clearer perspective of their relationships and movements may be had. Any such clarification should have a directive effect in the pursuit of other phases of knowledge relating to early man.

The establishment of historical fact is always a matter of applied logic. Certain materials are presented, be they carved stone, bronze implements, or writings; the task of the historian is to construct the explanation of the production and preservation of these materials which will be most logically consistent with the total body of accumulated fact, including other historical facts and the facts we call scientific. The conclusions of history, therefore, are in fact hypotheses, and these hypotheses change from time to time as the mass of accredited facts with which the hypotheses must square is changed. What is legend to-

---

3 For example, the Indo-European family of languages embraces the Indian, Iranian, Keltic, Sanskrit, Hellenic, Romanic, Slavonic, Suebic, Kimmeric, Gothic, Lithuanian, and Sarmatian.

day may be history tomorrow, just as what is history today may be legend tomorrow.[4]

It is hoped that the new or little-known conclusions presented here in the light of the available and assembled data may stimulate thought and research in directions hitherto not followed in any great degree, if at all. We cannot study man inductively as we study physical nature but must depend upon the historical method and our knowledge of the laws of the human mind. The phenomena of nature are governed by constant laws — Divine principles — that operate everywhere and forever alike, whereas the workings of the human mind cannot be explained by laws of nature. Any arbitrary action of natural laws would immediately hurl the world into chaos. A man's desires affect his attitude toward life. The accumulated personal experience of each individual determines the character of his reaction to any new set of circumstances. Consequently, the racial soul or mind of each branch of the human stock is the product of thousands of years of experience with and reaction to the multifarious phases of its environment (whether hot or cold, for example) and relations with other races. Freedom, both physical and mental, reason, human emotions, and environment are continually producing racial variations from age to age. As Dr. G. Elliot Smith says, "The career of mankind has not been the inevitable result of the action of natural causes, but has in large measure been shaped by accidents and catastrophes, by the actions of dominating personalities who have deliberately provoked great movements, peaceful and warlike, which have shaped the destiny of the world."[5] All events of history are relationships of individuals; they are thoughts in action. Dr. Smith quotes from Sir Edward Tylor's *Primitive Culture* (1871) thus:

4 Knight Dunlap and Robert Sutherland Gill, *The Dramatic Personality of Jesus* (Williams & Wilkins Co., Baltimore, 1933), page 3.
5 G. Elliot Smith, *Human History* (W. W. Norton & Co., New York, 1929), pp. 36-40.

The notion of the continuity of civilization is no barren philosophical principle, but is at once made practical by the consideration that they who wish to understand their own lives ought to know the stages through which their opinions and habits have become what they are. . . .

History, taken as our guide in explaining the different stages of civilization, offers a theory based on actual experience. This is a development theory, in which both advance and relapse have their acknowledged places. But, so far as history is to be our criterion, progression is primary and degradation is secondary. Culture must be gained before it is lost. Moreover, in striking a balance between the effects of forward and backward movement in civilization, it must be borne in mind how powerfully the diffusion of the culture acts in preserving the results of progress from the attacks of degeneration. A progressive movement in culture spreads and becomes independent of the fate of its originators.[5]

But modern theories of ethnology fail to give due consideration to the obvious facts of the continuity of history (despite its relapses) in cultural progress.

Thus, the continuity of history and the diffusion of culture are the essential instruments for the explanation of man's behavior. Not only has the mind of man operated in substantially the same general way down through the ages, but recent research has demonstrated that both prehistoric man and animals were subject to much the same ills that prevail today. It is not surprising, therefore, that ever since man first gained the ability to examine the conditions of his existence his chief occupation has been the conscious search for the means of safeguarding his own life, says Smith, who adds that "the never-ending pursuit of this elusive aim was responsible for the creation of civilization, with most of its arts and crafts, its essential customs and beliefs." Moreover, man always has sought to prolong his existence after what we call death, and this striving, which is common to all races, is a phase of religion. Since every human being is dependent on his fellows for the knowledge of speech and for the customs and ideas that he learns or adopts, clearly his mode of behavior involves participation in the diffusion of culture. And he adds thereto his own modest contribution. Hence, it is essential that we should study the historical antecedents of each important group of people and ascertain as nearly as possible its early racial relationships.

All life apparently has had a purpose from the beginning; else why the struggle for advancement? If the principle of continuity in the evolution of animal life and of man and his cultural growth exists, are we in a position to assail the views of those philosophers who contend that this continuity includes both the inorganic and the organic, the inanimate and the animate, under supreme laws of the universe? The negative view is expressed by Guyot in the following words: "It is, in fact, the universal law of all that exists in finite nature not to have in itself either the reason or the entire aim of its own existence. Every being exists not only itself but forms necessarily a portion of a great whole, of which the plan and the idea go infinitely beyond it and in which it is destined to play a part. . . . The superior being then solicits, so to speak, the creation of the inferior being and associates it to his own functions; and it is correct to say that inorganic nature is made for organized nature and the whole globe for man as both are made for God, the origin and end of all things."[6]

Accordingly, he conceives the earth to be the abode, the theater of action, and the means of education of man, that his functions may be increasingly exalted and ennobled, for the Divine purposes beyond the capability of man fully to comprehend, since the finite never can comprehend the Infinite or Absolute. The inexplicable tendency of the human races as a whole to ascend to higher levels of existence, to evolve from within, despite its difficulties, false starts, and apparent failures, seems to indicate

---

[6] Arnold Guyot, *The Earth and Man* (Scribner, New York, 1890), pp. 10-11.

a supreme and infinite Divine plan in which man has a substantial part to fulfill, whatever it may be. Despite impressions to the contrary, we can only surmise about our status before and after this life.

It is said that reverence for God is the beginning of wisdom. The mission on earth of Jesus of Nazareth was to teach mankind that the prime desideratum in life is to learn how to live in harmony with the immutable Divine laws — the laws of God — physically, mentally, morally, and spiritually. A steam power plant is no better than the fuel supplied to it; the same with man. The laws of God embrace such subjects as diet, physical and mental activities, rest, sleep, moral behavior toward one's fellow-man, spiritual attitude, and so on. On these premisses, it may be inferred that the achievement of true happiness, in its broadest sense, including exercise of the creative faculty, is the fundamental object of life as we proceed along our respective pathways. In this aim, we necessarily must co-operate with our fellow beings under the moral laws.

It may be that man is at the end of the long procession of organized beings, but the probability is that there are still higher phases of life in the Divine plan that are beyond his powers of conception or comprehension. Consequently, the greater the success attained in learning how to live in harmony with the Divine laws and in achieving true happiness in life, the more complete should be our preparation for whatever future status may befit each of us, regardless of the form that it may assume. One cannot long counteract the laws of nature successfully.

2. *Geological Considerations.* In studying the formation of the earth, the geologist divides past time into eras and each of the eras into periods. Each period is represented by certain classes of rocks, the thickness of which is fairly well-known. Therefore, making due allowance for different rates of formation at different times, the geologist can determine roughly the length of each era as compared with the others. Prehistoric time also is reckoned by means of paleontology, anatomy, and human skill.

The following brief geological and cultural table of the earth and its inhabitants will be helpful in the consideration of the subject of racial origins and dispersion throughout the surface of the earth. It shows at a glance the periods of development of animal and human life. The lengths of the different eras are not absolute, inasmuch as there is considerable variation in the estimates of the authorities.

Era	Period	Epoch and Principal Form of Life	Millions of Years since beginning of each Epoch[7]
Azoic		Cooling of the earth and rock formation. Lifeless rocks; fundamental gneiss.	About 3350
Archeozoic		Sedimentary rocks; primordial life, soft living matter, without shell, skeleton, or other structure that persisted as recognizable fossil after death.	1000 (?)
Proterozoic		Traces of simple life forms, such as seaweeds (algae) and microscopic creatures, crustaceans, brachiopods.	790

7 Based largely on the minimal figures of Barrell quoted in United States Geological Survey Bulletin No. 769, by M. G. Wilmarth, 1925, page 5, and later data.

Paleozoic	(Cambrian ((	First traces of plant and water-animal life, trilo- bites, sponges, protozoa.	540
	(Ordovician ((	Cryptogam plants, inver- tebrates, and earliest verte- brate types.	470
	(Silurian ((	Mollusks, sea scorpions, fish types, reef-building corals.	380
	(Devonian (	Fishes, mollusks, turf, tree ferns, land plants.	340
	(Carboniferous ((	Amphibia, insects, ar- chaic forms of reptiles, and forests, nearly all in swamps.	290
Mesozoic	(Triassic (	Reptiles and amphibia, in water and on land.	190
	(Jurassic ((	Giant reptiles, fish, first mammals, crocodiles, bird- like creatures.	155
	(Cretaceous ((	Modern fish, birds, flowering plants, chalk formation.	120
Cenozoic	(Tertiary (	(Eocene) Ancestors of (Oligocene) modern animals,	55 35
	((	(Miocene) plants, grass, (Pliocene) land forests, and of man.	19 7
	(Quaternary (	(Pleistocene) Modern types. (Recent)	1-

The Pleistocene epoch is that of the great series of glaciations, during which the successive branches of mankind evolved from the primordial human stem, modern man being the latest. The Recent epoch began about 20,000 years ago with the return of warmth after the Achen glaciation and the retreat of large glacial ice fronts, though there were subsequent minor glaciations and diminishing periods of coldness for some thousands of years.

3. *Ice Ages.* Each of the great geological eras was preceded by extensive movements in the earth's crust that caused large areas to rise above the surrounding ground or water, forming vast plains, plateaus, and mountain ranges. This may have resulted from a condition of unstable equilibrium between the body of land and the mass of water in the ocean with its underlying rocks. Changing atmospheric conditions at certain times also resulted in the covering of large parts of the earth with a succession of huge glaciers, which were thousands of years in developing to their maximal extent and required thousands of years more for their disappearance. The glacial and interglacial epochs known to us comprise what is termed the great Ice Age of Pleistocene time.

When a large area of the earth's surface, perhaps formerly flat and covered with water, is forced upward in the readjustment of masses of the earth, it exerts a disturbing effect on the water distribution and the atmosphere of the whole region. The water drains off such areas and not only may ocean currents be modified but winds are created by the inequality of temperature between mountain and plain. Snowfall is dependent upon the presence of moisture and low temperature in the air. The moisture may come from the evaporation of water from the plains or from warm ocean currents near the land. Moisture from the ocean may be carried over the continent in the paths of cyclonic storms unobstructed by lofty mountain ranges. The air on the warm plain expands and is forced upward by chilled air from the mountains. The warm moist air from the ocean currents replaces the cold air on the higher elevations and is chilled, in consequence of which its moisture condenses into rain or snow, which turns into ice as it piles up and hardens on the plains and mountains. The development of great ice sheets depends on an excess of snowfall over the evaporation, thawing, and outward drift of dry snow from the central glacial mass.

With recurrent rises of the temperature, melting of the snow and ice begins and may continue for thousands of years. Thus, we have the gradual disappearance of glaciers as apparently is occurring today. Glacial ice on the mountains advances slowly down the valleys and at places onto the adjacent plains. If it blocks valleys, large bodies of water may be impounded where none previously existed, so that large marshy areas may be formed. The water level in the oceans also will be raised markedly. In time, the mountains may be considerably worn down by glacial erosion caused by the moving ice.

The poles of the earth were not always covered with ice. Preceding Pleistocene time there were ages of world-wide warmth apparently without marked temperature zones, when subtropical vegetation is known to have grown in the polar regions, as proved by warm-climate fossil remains found there. Plant remains of the Silurian period, which accumulated in the coal beds at the poles, were the same as those that grew at the equator. Similarly, the trilobites and other animal life were identical in their species in America, Europe, Africa, and Australia. In fact, the present epoch is not normal. We appear to be in an epoch of glacial retreat or in an interglacial period, since it is decidedly colder than it was prior to the inception of the Pleistocene ice age. Each glaciation of large parts of the earth's surface, where animal life existed and was adapted to warmth, resulted in the migration or annihilation of practically all such forms of life in those regions.

We are concerned here with only the *last* great ice age, that of Pleistocene time in the Quaternary Period from about 1,000,000[8] years ago or less to about 20,000 years ago, with its periods of advance and retreat. At their maximum, the great ice sheets covered approximately 4,000,000 square miles of North America, extending as far south as New York and St. Louis and as far west as the Pacific Ocean. The outer limit of the ice in the Missis-

---

8 The estimates of geologists vary widely as to the duration of the Pleistocene ice age, some being as low as 300,000 years (Obermaier) and others as high as 1,290,000 years (Pilgrim). The turn toward warmer weather began apparently 40,000 or more years ago and continued with alternating periods of warm weather and cold weather into the so-called Recent epoch, apparently the beginning of another interglacial stage.

sippi Basin is very largely marked by the courses of the Ohio and the Missouri Rivers. Ice also covered approximately 2,000,000 square miles of Europe, extending as far south as the Thames River and the Carpathian Mountains, with additional heavy glaciations on the Pyrenees and the Alps and various other mountain heights. It did not extend into Asia except to cross the northerly end of the Ural Mountains and cover the northwesterly corner of Siberia. Local glaciations occurred in Washington, Oregon, California, Idaho, Montana, Wyoming, Utah, and Colorado, on the Andes Mountains in South America, on the Atlas Mountains in Africa, on Mount Lebanon in the Near East, on the Caucasus Mountains,[9] and on various mountains in Manchuria, in relatively small areas in northeastern Siberia, and on the Himalaya and other mountains of Tibet. The mountains of Australia, New Zealand, and Tasmania also appear to have been glaciated during Pleistocene time. Including the polar regions, more than 12,000,000 square miles, one-fifth of the land surface of the globe, were covered with ice, but not all at any one time. Because of the great distance of the plains of interior Asia and Siberia from the warm ocean currents and the existence of intervening high mountain ranges, the moisture gathered from the oceans was dissipated on the mountains before reaching those regions.

This ice age was not continuous, but consisted of four major glacial advances and four major retreats of the ice fronts, each of thousands of years' duration, with three interglacial stages of warmth, also thousands of years long, a later secondary glaciation and retreat, and two or three subsequent minor ones. They are believed to have been more or less contemporaneous on the different continents. Below is a tentative correlation by name of these Pleistocene stages:

---

9 During the fourth glaciation, the British Isles supported a separate ice sheet. The Baltic glacier extended southeastward toward Moscow, nearly reached Warsaw, and from the Elbe River the margin extended northward along the Danish Peninsula and over Scandinavia. It was severe on the Caucasus, Alps, Pyrenees, and other mountain ranges.

Stage	Alps	North Germany	North America
1st Glacial	Günz	Elbe	Nebraskan
Interglacial	Günz-Mindel	Elbe-Elster	Aftonian
2nd Glacial	Mindel	Elster	Kansan
Interglacial	Mindel-Riss	Elster-Saale	Yarmouth
3rd Glacial	Riss	Saale	Illinoian
Interglacial	Riss-Würm	Saale-Weichsel	Sangamon
4th Glacial	Würm I	Weichsel	Wisconsin
Interglacial	Laufen	Laufen	——
5th Glacial	Würm II		(Secondary)
Post Glaciations.[10]			

The second major interglacial period is believed to have endured much longer than the first and third. The last (Würm II) glaciation[11] terminated with two or three minor temporary advances at the beginning of the post-glacial period. The accompanying sketch portrays these glacial movements[11] along with the known races of man and their cultures. It is schematic only, chiefly as a guide by the use of the Alpine nomenclature of glacial stages. The chronology and correlation of race and culture there-with are still unsettled.

Each Pleistocene glaciation possibly was accompanied, if not caused, by the rising of large areas of land in the continents affected, and the snow accumulated over the glaciated areas in thicknesses of thousands of feet and hardened into ice. The temperature of the entire world slowly sank until the summer's sun was not warm enough to melt much of the winter's snow. For hundreds of miles beyond the outer limits of the ice, there was a margin of territory subject to the cold winds that moved toward the warmer region, as in Siberia today. That condition

---

10 This post-glaciation includes two minor glacial advances and retreats, the Achen and the Bühl, and subsequent oscillations to the present time, as shown on a later graphical outline.

11 See *Old and New Standards of Pleistocene Division in Relation to the Pre-history of Man in Europe*, Bull. Geological Society of America, vol. 33, pp. 411-490, July 3, 1922, by H. F. Osborn and C. A. Reeds.

ICE AGE CHART

Type of Man	Type of Culture	Glacial Chronology (years B.C.)
Pithecanthropus	Eolithic	600,000
		550,000
Sinanthropus	Pre-Chellean	
	Pre-Chellean	500,000
Soloensis	Pre-Chellean	450,000
Rhodesian	Chellean	400,000
Heidelberg	Chellean	350,000
(Eoanthropus, modern man's ancestral line concurrent with these races in southeastern Asia, not yet discovered.)		300,000
Neanderthal	Acheulean	250,000
		200,000
Neanderthal	Mousterian	150,000
Homo Sapiens well developed in southeastern Asia		125,000
		100,000
Black, Yellow, and Brown races already distinguishable		75,000
Aryan (Brown) tribes up Indus River valley and on Iranian plateau		50,000

Günz glaciation

Günz-Mindel interglacial period

Mindel glaciation

Mindel-Riss interglacial period

Riss glaciation

Riss-Würm interglacial period

Würm I glaciation

Laufen interglacial period

(Continued)

continued for thousands of years until the maximal extension of ice had been reached. This condition persisted with
varying degrees of intensity for several thousand years
more, until a marked rise of temperature began to show
its effect. The ice on the slopes of mountain ranges then
sluggishly flowed in deep rivers or in glacial form down
the valleys and over adjacent plains to spread itself like
a vast cake or cap over large parts of the continents. Ice
sheets that did not head in mountains, as in North America, merely spread over adjacent plains. Finally, under
the effect of higher temperature, the ice fronts gradually
were melted back. Large rivers were formed on the earth's
surface by the melting ice, a conspicuous example of
which is the Missouri. Each advance and retreat during
the Pleistocene age may have embraced one or more sizeable intermediate advances and retreats.

The most common varieties of glaciers are those named
below.[12]

(1) Mountain glaciers, formed in fields of almost
perpetual snow, which flow down some valley
until melted by the rise of temperature at lower
levels;

(2) Piedmont glaciers, which are formed by mountain glaciers reaching beyond the end of their
valleys and spreading out like lobes on the adjacent lowlands;

(3) Continental ice sheets, which are not dependent on mountains and may originate at low
levels, spreading widely over the adjacent plains.

The thickest ice sheets were formed on the low ground
and not on the mountains or table-lands. Thus, the Baltic
region was heavily glaciated whereas the Tibetan plateau
was not. The higher mountains were not completely
covered by the glaciers, but their peaks projected above
like islands in a sea of white.

Our most splendid mountain ranges, with their sharp

12 A. P. Coleman, *Ice Ages, Recent and Ancient* (Macmillan, 1926), pp. xxv-
xxvi.

peaks, their deeply hollowed U-shaped valleys and their rockbound lakes, owe their shapes in large part to erosion by ice; and in much of northern Europe and North America large parts of the lowlands received their smoothly swelling or hilly forms from the shaping of the rocky surfaces and the spreading of the loose materials by ice. The thousands of years of later influences have not greatly modified the impress of ice sheets left upon the continents,[13]

The rate of movement of glaciers varied with the nature of the terrain, being rapid where it was hilly and mountainous and slow where the surface was approximately level. It may have been only a few inches or a few feet daily and yet the whole mass was in constant slow motion, due to the force of gravity. The glaciers at present found in Switzerland move from 1 inch to 4 feet daily. Those in Alaska move about 7 feet daily, while those in Greenland move 50 to 60 feet or more daily and even more rapidly in summer. The ice of mountain glaciers ordinarily is covered by debris, boulders, or finer material, broken loose by its wearing along the sides of its course. The continental ice also transported much drift material derived from the overridden rocks.

During the various interglacial epochs, primitive men and animals advanced northward from eastern Mediterranean and western African regions into Europe, only to be largely annihilated or gradually forced southward again by the next glaciation. In thus moving southward, such peoples were either exterminated by or forced to amalgamate with the peoples who had remained in the south, toward whom they slowly retreated. In Asia during the glacial epochs man was confined by the cold winds of Siberia and the high mountain ranges mainly to the southern regions, chiefly the archipelagos, India, lower China, and the southerly shores of the Pacific Ocean. The effects of the cold were seriously felt even in the Mediterranean Basin because of the large volume of ice on the Alps. For reasons already indicated, Siberia, one

13 A. P. Coleman, *op.cit.*

(ICE AGE CHART -- Continued at Larger Scale)

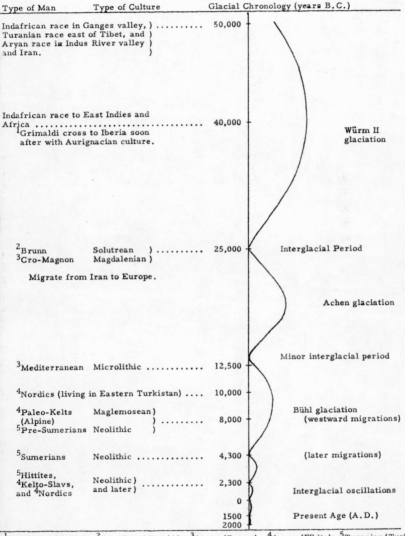

Type of Man	Type of Culture	Glacial Chronology (years B.C.)

Indafrican race in Ganges valley,) 50,000
Turanian race east of Tibet, and)
Aryan race in Indus River valley)
and Iran.   )

Indafrican race to East Indies and
Africa 40,000
  ¹Grimaldi cross to Iberia soon
  after with Aurignacian culture.

²Brunn   Solutrean) 25,000
³Cro-Magnon   Magdalenian)

  Migrate from Iran to Europe.

³Mediterranean Microlithic 12,500

⁴Nordics (living in Eastern Turkistan) 10,000

⁴Paleo-Kelts   Maglemosean)
  (Alpine)   ) 8,000
⁵Pre-Sumerians Neolithic)

⁵Sumerians   Neolithic 4,300

⁵Hittites,
⁴Kelto-Slavs,   Neolithic) 2,300
and ⁴Nordics   and later)
                                          0
                                       1500
                                       2000

Würm II
glaciation

Interglacial Period

Achen glaciation

Minor interglacial period

Bühl glaciation
(westward migrations)

(later migrations)

Interglacial oscillations

Present Age (A.D.)

¹Indafrican (Negro); ²Pre-Dravidian (?); ³Aryan (Brown); ⁴Aryan (White); ⁵Turanian (Turk)

of the coldest regions of the earth, whose ground is perpetually frozen hundreds of feet deep, was not glaciated in any great degree. Southern Europe and southern United States must then have had a climate much like that of northern Siberia today. The cold winds extended even farther south.

In the great change from warm to cold, which may have averaged 10 or 11 degrees Fahrenheit for the area as a whole,[14] vegetation was impoverished, some of it even wholly ruined in the course of time, and the population, insofar as it continued to exist at all, struggled painfully for existence.[15] Living beings were put to the test of natural selection for survival in its most terrible form. The reindeer and many other northern animals migrated as far southward as the Alps and the Pyrenees. Others died from cold and hunger, and in the survival of the fittest new habits and characteristics were evolved. Some passed into higher forms and many new species appeared. Some modifications of the human types doubtless occurred during the climatic revolutions, which changes may have become a part of the biological inheritance of the race.

During the Pleistocene ice age, the Himalaya, Carpathian, Alps, Pyrenees, and Atlas Mountains reached their maximal heights. The duration of the various glacial movements, with other pertinent data, is roughly indicated on the accompanying chart. When the temperature rose in the last glaciation, the ice fronts receded and the marshiness of the land diminished. Man then followed the glacial retreat northward and westward in Europe, which means that the repopulation of Europe by the new races of *Homo sapiens* from the Asiatic highlands occurred slow-

---

14 It has been said that, if the *average annual* temperature of northern North America should drop to this extent, a change less than that ordinarily seen daily on our thermometers, another great ice age would result.

15 W. Maxwell Reed, in an article entitled "Will This Summer Be Hotter?" in *Scribner's Magazine,* June, 1932, discussed the tragic effects of a southward movement of the polar cold during the 14th century A.D. and of the reverse conditions during the years 1920 and 1921, when millions of lives were lost in Europe and Asia because of climatic changes.

ly during subsequent millennia. We are now living in what may be an interglacial epoch that with intermediate oscillations began 27,000 or more years ago.

The retreating ice, in each instance, left behind it various types of soil, such as clay, gravels, and sands. Basins were gouged out to form the existing valleys and lakes. The climate of the ice age was tempered by the proximity of any particular region to the ocean. The average temperature ranged probably from 39 degrees to 43 degrees Fahrenheit, although it may have been somewhat higher in the favored sections of western Europe.

The nature of the land of central and northern Asia and Europe over which man roamed at intervals during and subsequent to the last ice age was of three kinds, as follows:

(1) During the cold moist climate of the glaciation: *Tundra,* which is a moist marshy plains land similar to that now found in northern Canada and in Siberia. The animals in such regions were the reindeer, musk ox, arctic fox, woolly mammoth, woolly rhinoceros, and wolverine.

(2) During the temperate postglacial climate: *Forests and meadow land,* in which the principal animals were the red and fallow deer, wolf, bear, bison, wild boar, forest horse, moose, and cattle.

(3) During the cold, dry post-glacial climate: *Steppe or prairie,* which consisted of level plains covered with grass but without forests. The principal animals were the steppe horse, suslik, saiga, antelope, jerboa, and wild ass.

The great evaporation of water from the ocean and its retention on land in the form of snow and ice during glacial epochs had the effect of lowering the water level in the sea for variable depths, the estimates of which range from 165 feet to as much as 500 feet. A concomitant result was a considerable increase in the surface of land areas. During the early part of the third interglacial epoch, dry land extended from Scandinavia to

France and the British Isles. Then rivers flowed through the broad valleys that have since become submerged beneath the North Sea, the English Channel, and the Irish Sea. To these rivers the Elbe, Rhine, Seine, Thames, and others were tributaries. It was in late Neolithic times, perhaps 5000-4000 B.C., that Ireland became disconnected from Wales and Scotland and that England became detached from France. The subsequent melting of the glaciers over thousands of years gradually restored the sea level by means of the water from the rivers formed by the melting ice. It has been estimated that the melting of the existing ice of Greenland, Antarctica, Alaska, Scandinavia, and elsewhere will raise the water level over the present area of the oceans approximately 165 feet. However, after adjustments of the earth to the shift of weight on its surface, the rise probably will not exceed 125 or 130 feet.[16]

As indicated before, the world now is experiencing a glacial retreat and perhaps the commencement of an interglacial period; but, whether it will be short in duration or extend over thousands of years, only time can tell. The average temperature over the whole world is increasing, glaciers and icebergs are melting, and the waters of the oceans and interior lakes fed by them are rising markedly. It is startling to consider the effects of continual rising of water levels in our Great Lakes and the oceans to 125 or 130 feet higher than now exist. Already some of our coastal cities are being undermined by rising ocean waters. Great damage has been caused by floods and erosion along shores of the North and Baltic seas and along the Asiatic coasts of the Pacific Ocean. Concurrently, interior sources of our water supply are diminishing, the country increasingly is becoming a desert across its southerly two-thirds, and the average temperature is increasing slowly. Analogous changes are occurring in other parts of the world.

---

16 Reginald A. Daly, *The Changing World of the Ice Age* (Yale Univ. Press, 1934), pp. 11-12.

4. *Origin of Man.* The manner and place of origin of the human race are and doubtless will remain the subjects of intensive thought and controversy among scientists. The time also is enshrouded in great uncertainty. These questions are discussed in detail in other works and they will not be treated at length here.

Scientists are agreed that man did not descend from any existing anthropoid stock. There are structural and anatomical differences among the ape species and between them and man that indicate only collateral evolution and at a very remote time. Moreover, there is a fundamental intangible difference between the anthropoids and man that tends to prove that conclusion, namely, the possession by the latter of the faculty of self-consciousness — the awareness of one's own acts or conditions as belonging to himself and of their effects on others — out of which the capability of abstract thought grew. That all human beings and the apes belong to the division of mammals known as *Primates* is conceded by the writers, but the similarities among them do not imply any direct or lineal relationship, since every bone in the body of man is readily distinguishable from the corresponding bone in the body of an anthropoid. However, all probably had a common ancestor not resembling any of them, long since disappeared from the surface of the earth, which we would call neither ape nor man in our accepted definitions of those terms.

In the process of evolution in nature from the lowliest form of existence, causal mutation has resulted in the the establishment of the mineral, vegetable, and animal kingdoms. Later, there arose the orders within each kingdom, the families within each order, the genuses within each family, and the species within each genus. Thus, out of the mammalian order came the family of Primates, from which, after the accrual of definite characteristics, another causal mutation[17] produced the genus *Homo*, Man, from whom various species, represented by the

---

17 Because of this additional mutation, man properly has "dominion over the fish of the sea, the fowl of the air, and every living thing that moveth upon the earth"; otherwise, they would devour him in the course of time. *Genesis* 1:26-28.

different races of mankind, have emanated, apparently in southeastern Asia. The ability of all existing human races to interbreed proves that they had a common origin.

Some men inherit conspicuously great stature or unusually long fingers and thumbs. Other men are short in stature and have short fingers and thumbs, either thin or thick in appearance. The great majority vary between these extremes in those characteristics. Similarly, the particular primates from which man descended must have been a small closely-related family group, the members of which, by biological chance, inherited longer thumbs, among other characteristics, than other contemporaneous primates possessed. Even the evolution of the long thumb by such a small group must have required many thousands of years of existence in tropical forests teeming with many savage animals. The advantages of such thumbs in grasping objects for protection and gain would tend increasingly to develop in their possessors unusual alertness, agility, and other special qualities. These acquired characteristics ultimately would require an outlet by the process of causal mutation[18] in a crowded environment of intense competition among animal life in some tropical region, the process carrying with it a meager faculty of self-consciousness.

Thus, it seems not improbable that man emerged from the most highly-developed of the anthropoid primates in existence on some Indonesian island (probably Java) during the late Pliocene period, 1,500,000 or 2,000,000 years ago, under circumstances of great stress or natural selection in a family group having long thumbs, through a broad causal mutation in which he gained the rudiments of self-consciousness as an inherent and integral element of his nature.[19] At least one male and one female mutant necessarily had to appear and survive in the same family group for the continuation of the newly-created human race. We may call them Adam and Eve. They

18 It was announced by the National Academy of Sciences in 1947 that food which has been exposed to ultra-violet, or sun-tan, rays under controlled conditions has been found to cause genetic (or hereditary) mutations.
19 In this connection, see the deductions of Austin H. Clark in *The New Evolution: Zoogenesis* (Williams & Wilkins Co., Baltimore, 1930), pages 208-233.

were a distinct genus and breeding with the collateral blood anthropoids of the same family group was biologically impossible. In subsequent generations, the segregation of self-concious man from the dumb animals because of greater efficiency followed as a matter of course. Thus, the number of mankind increased despite a high mortality rate, and their gregarious and leadership instincts gradually resulted in the improvement of their status as a separate entity from the animal life about them.

The successive extinct races of mankind may have represented analogous mutations within the same family group at different times or were branches of the original mutation of man in that group, since all seem to have migrated from southeastern Asia. All except *Homo sapiens* were so highly specialized, perhaps because of inbreeding, that they did not possess survival qualities. They constituted what may be called false starts by nature, on the assumption that *Homo sapiens* is here to stay. Of course, it was possible theoretically for more than one race of men to have evolved at different places in the manner just described, but they doubtless would have possessed different physical characteristics and probably could not have interbred.[20] Our interest here is confined to the existing races of mankind, all of which can interbreed and therefore had a common origin.

The development of man's prehensile powers accompanied by his capability of abstract thought accorded him increasingly greater advantages over all other contemporaneous inhabitants of the earth. It is unthinkable that even the simplest culture, represented by such rude

---

20 Some scientists believe that persons living close to the soil are bathed constantly in radon, the gas emanating from radium, both of which give off the same rays. According to geneticists, a few of these rays, striking a living germ cell at the right time, can alter heredity, even to the extent of producing a mutation, which results in a new species. Thus, the earth's natural radium emanations may account for many of the constant, though slight, changes in hereditary characteristics. Is this the fundamental explanation not only of the evolution of man but also of the multifarious racial differentiations that are constantly going on? Such acquired characteristics that are transmitted to successive generations include racial complexions (black, brown, yellow, white) and others. Only further scientific research may determine such questions.

implements as the eoliths, would have appeared among a group of beings which did not possess the creative faculty that grows only out of the quality of self-consciousness. So far as we know, this power is inherent in no other being than man, the only tool-maker on the earth. The phenomenon seems explainable only by the biological principle of causal mutation. It included incipient moral and ethical ideas for the self-preservation of the new beings in successive generations.

It follows that the place of origin of man must have been in some region where such primates lived, but any inferences on this point must rest on the most general and meager circumstances. Central Asia, India, Malaya, Africa, and other regions have their proponents, *but the odds greatly favor the teeming region of both open land and forests in Java,* where the oldest remains of mankind have been found.[21] Primordial man was unstable and the numbers that survived were small. Of the several branches that did survive, one alone, *Homo sapiens,* modern man, was destined to possess the capabilities to outlast and annihilate all of the others. For present purposes, we are most concerned with the question where modern man first evolved and so increased in numbers as to be able to migrate; where he then settled and expanded into tribes, some of which dispersed and became the progenitors of the numerous divisions of the major races of the world today. Here we are on more certain ground, especially as to where he lived before his diversification into separate races and whence his earliest dispersions occurred.

Primordial man apparently moved slowly northward from Java over the Malay peninsula to Indo-China and possibly by water to the Andaman Islands and to Ceylon and southern India, though the principal movement to India must have been to the Ganges Basin and around

---

21 Java embraces 48,504 sq. miles, the same size as Louisiana. In 1880 it had a population of 20,000,000 and today it is nearly 60,000,00, divided into the Javanese proper, the Madurese, and the Sudanese. The first two average nearly 5 ft. 6 in. in stature and the last nearly 5 ft. All are said to resemble or belong to the Malay stock.

the Bay of Bengal to the coastal region and the highlands of the Dekkan (i.e., "the South," meaning the peninsula). Today primitive pre-Dravidian peoples inhabit both the easterly and westerly shores of the Bay of Bengal, subject to repressive environment; but it may be conjectured with confidence that the Turanian (Yellow) race evolved in and east of Burma, that the Indafrican (Black) race evolved in the Ganges River valley, and that the Aryan (Brown) race evolved first on the central plateau of the Dekkan and later in northwestern India. This inference is supported by the fact that the most primitive branches of mankind have been found on and in opposite directions from the shores of the Bay of Bengal and adjacent islands, as in East India Islands and Australia and Tasmania and in central Africa, and by the further fact that the progenitors of the major races of mankind today appear to have dispersed in different directions from the respective regions indicated above. The early density of population in southeastern Asia supports this belief. The earliest-known movements of mankind into Europe came from the southeast. The vast high plateau of Tibet influenced the direction of the early migrations. These observations provided the key by which the emigration of all branches of modern man has been developed in the subsequent pages.[22]

As stated by Guyot, "In the earliest ages of the world, Asia shines alone. It is at once the cradle of civilization and that of the nations which are the only representatives of culture and which are carrying it, in our days, to the extremities of the world. Its gigantic proportions, the almost infinite diversity of its soil, its central location would render it suitable to be the continent of germs and the root of that immense tree [man] which is now bearing such beautiful fruit."[23]

---

[22] The Red and White subraces were not such originally but were derived from the Yellow and Brown races respectively, as explained later.
[23] Arnold Guyot, *The Earth and Man* (Scribner, New York, 1890), page 12.

5. *Geographical Considerations.* No other large area of the earth presents such a varied surface as Asia. Central Asia embraces the largest area of continually dry land known to science. Mongolia has not been submerged since the Age of Reptiles, about 175,000,000 years ago. The plains of northern India, mainly along the Ganges and Indus Rivers, whose present altitude ranges from 300 to 600 feet above sea level, are flanked on the east, north, and west by high mountain ranges, which isolate that country from the rest of Asia. On the south, the plateau of the Dekkan (peninsula) rises to variable heights above the Ganges. The most important mountains are the great Himalayan range on the north, forming the southern escarpment of the high Tibetan plateau. As it extends eastward from junction with the Hindu Kush and Karakoram ranges, it rises precipitately, its greatest peak, Mount Everest, reaching an altitude of over 29,000 feet. On the east, the mountains slope southward into Indo-China. On the west, the Suliman range extends northward from the Arabian Sea to junction with the Hindu Kush where that range connects with the Karakoram Mountains, forming also the eastern escarpment of another great plateau, the Iranian, which comprises Baluchistan, Afghanistan, and Iran.

The southwestern escarpment of the Iranian plateau is formed by the Zagros Mountains, which extend northwestward to junction with the Caucasus Mountains on the north and the Taurus Mountains on the west and the latter in turn continue westward in southern Anatolia (Asia Minor) nearly to the shores of the Aegean Sea. On the north the Caucasus[24] Mountains connect the Black and Caspian Seas, continuing south of the latter as the Elburz Mountains and eastward with the Kuren (or Kopet), Paropamisus, Hindu Kush, Karakoram and Kuen-Lun ranges, constituting a more or less continuous east-and-west mountain chain that forms the northern escarpments of the Iranian and Tibetan plateaus. This long high

---

24 Apparently, the original form of this name in the Indo-European language of Scythia was Graucasus, meaning 'white with snow,' Pliny, *Hist. Nat.* vi. 17.

series of ranges is the boundary between regions of greatly different topography, the territory north of the two plateaus (Western and Eastern Turkistan) being chiefly low steppes (plains) or desert lands. Thus, Tibet (from Töbhöt, meaning High Pod, from the country's name Bod), surrounded by relatively low land, has been called the roof of the world. Low lands lie beyond the mountainous boundaries of Iran, the valley of the Indus on the east, the lowlands of southerly Western Turkistan on the north, and Iraq (ancient Mesopotamia) and the irregular terrain of Turkey on the west.

The Tibetan plateau begins near the junction of the Karakoram and Himalaya Mountains and, broadening, extends eastward between the Kuen-Lun and Himalaya Mountains at elevations ranging from 17,000 feet to 15,000 feet, until it breaks off abruptly near Chengtu, in western China, to elevations of 2,000 feet or less, although the slopes bifurcating toward the northeast and the southeast are more gradual. The northerly slope of the Karakoram Mountains is quite precipitous. Through passes, particularly the noted Karakoram Pass, 18,550 feet high, descent is readily made to the Tarim Basin of Eastern Turkistan. Toward the east, the spreading of the Kuen-Lun Mountains produces a more gradual slope from the highlands over the Altyn Tagh toward the north and east and incloses the Koko Nor lowland and lake region. Both slopes have been the routes of important human migrations.

The Iranian plateau rises to heights of from 4,000 to 8,000 feet between the Indus and Tigris Rivers and intervening mountain ranges. Many peaks between 9,000 and 13,000 feet high adorn it. It is accessible by mountain passes on all sides. The interior valley, plain, and desert lands form depressions that range from 1,500 to 3,000 feet above sea level. In the extreme west, in Turkey, between the Caucasus and Taurus Mountains, lie the irregular highlands of Armenia already mentioned, which are a continuation of the plateau into central and western Turkey.

North of the Hindu Kush and Karakoram Mountains lie Eastern and Western Turkistan, separated by the

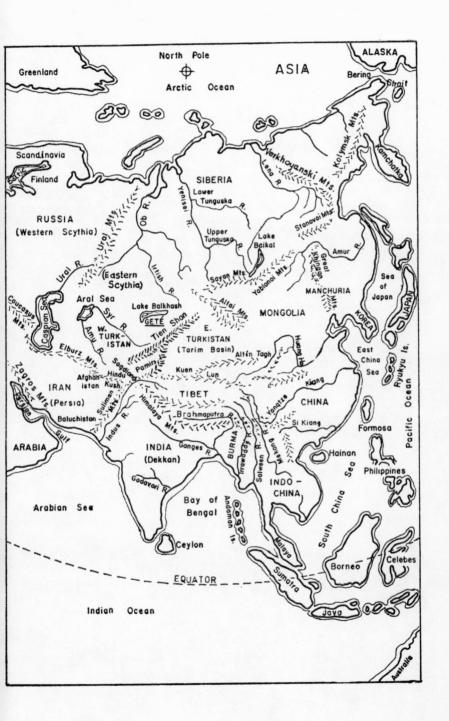

Pamirs and the Tien (Shan) Mountains. The Pamirs are a great, broad, rounded ridge, extending north and south and connecting important mountain chains (the Hindu Kush, Karakoram, Suliman, and northerly ranges). In the Pamirs lie elevated valleys, open and gently sloping toward the east but narrow and confined, with a rapid fall, toward the west. To the ancients it separated Asia *intra* Imaum and Asia *extra* Imaum, i.e., Asia this side and Asia beyond the great mountains. The waters of the numerous valley streams, with the exception of the easterly flow from the Taghdungbash, collect in the Oxus, which flows northwesterly to the Aral Sea; the Aksu, from Little Pamir Lake, receives the easterly drainage, which finds an outlet in the Aktash valley and joins the Murghab, which receives drainage from the Alichor and Siriz Pamirs. As the eastern Taghdungbash stream finds its way into the Sirikol and Yarkand rivers and the Great and Little Karakuls send their waters to the Oxus and the Kashgar rivers respectively, the Neza Tash range and Kizil Art plain must be regarded as forming the watershed between Eastern and Western Turkistan. The Pamirs are important as having been the home of races of people, chiefly Aryan Kelts, from the early times.

The momentous parts that Eastern Turkistan and Western Turkistan have played in the migration of both Aryan and Turanian races is not yet fully realized. They are discussed at length in subsequent chapters. The vast lowland of Western Turkistan was once largely covered by the great Blue (now Aral) Sea, since greatly reduced in area. It is bounded on the west by the Caspian Sea, on the north by Siberia, and on the east by the Tien Shan range and the Pamirs. On the south are the precipitous slopes of the northerly escarpment of Iran. Its elevation ranges from below sea-level to about 400 feet above until the foothills of the Pamirs are reached. As shown later, it was traversed in early migrations of certain branches of the human race. A largely similar contrast prevailed on both sides of the Caucasus Mountains.

Beyond the Karakoram and Kuen-Lun ranges on the north lies the Tarim Basin of Eastern Turkistan, at an elevation of 3,100 feet or less. Formerly, it was not as arid as it is today. It extends to the Gobi Desert of Mongolia on the east and is bounded on the north by the Tien Shan range. It was the homeland of the Nordic Aryans for about 4,000 years, until the Turks arrived. Passes through the mountainous districts of Kashgar and Samarkand on the west afford passage between Eastern and Western Turkistan, and they also have played conspicuous parts in pre-historical human affairs. The city of Kashgar is situated at the junction of trade routes from the Oxus River valley, from Kokand and Samarkand, and from Almati, Aksu, and Khotan, the last two leading from China and India. In consequence, that city has been conspicuous from the earliest times as a political and commercial center. Its altitude is 4,043 feet above sea level. Certain elevated lands on the east, north of the Koko Nor region, roughly mark the division between ancient highland and lowland Mongolian habitations, east of which the rivers flow generally in the easterly direction.

Northeast of the Tien Shan range are other irregular mountain systems of northwest China and Mongolia, the Altai and the Sayan, which are interspersed with valleys and passes from the east to the west. An important passage at low elevation extends westward from the Tarim Basin between the Tien Shan and Altai Mountains to the Lake Balkhash region and the Kirghiz steppe of western Asia. This district and southward, before it became arid, was for a long time the ancient habitation of the Nordic branch of the Aryan race, after its migration from the Tarim Basin. The importance of this fact will appear later. Other important human habitations (of Turanian subraces) were the valleys of the Altai Mountains and those to the north and on both slopes of the Sayan range. At the time that those peoples first settled in these regions, western Siberia and Western Turkistan were largely under water, or marshy, or otherwise forbidding to human habitation because of an intensely cold climate. It was many thousands of years before emigration occurred in the westerly and southwesterly directions, and during this time interracial and cultural intercourse and also conflicts between Turanian and Aryan tribes occurred along the westerly mountain foothills from the headwaters of the Yenisei River on the northeast to the Iranian plateau on the southwest. These activities also will be described later.

We now shall return to Tibet for more detailed consideration. Important streams, chiefly the Hwang, Yangtse, Mekong, Salween, and Irrawaddy Rivers and their tributaries, flow from eastern Tibet down the easterly slopes of that high plateau through southern China, Indo-China, or Burma to the seas. The Brahmaputra and Indus Rivers carry the water in opposite directions from the northerly slopes of the Himalayas, in southern Tibet, down through the plains of northern India. The former actually flows eastward between the Himalaya range and a still more vast mountain range immediately on its north. This high plateau may be divided into two parts, the lake region, in the center, west, and northwest, and the river region, marked by high mountain ranges, in the east, south, and west, which have played important but widely different roles in the evolution of the races of man. The Indus watershed was a primitive habitation of Aryan peoples, while the river region in the east was and still is a series of habitations of Turanian peoples. The Indus is the great arterial water-course in western Tibet and similarly the Brahmaputra is the most important east-and-west arterial water-course in southern Tibet. The lake region of central Tibet apparently is the region of evolution first of the Nordic branch of the Aryan race and afterward of the Turkish branch of the Turanian race and *where the fundamentals of civilization received marked impetus* from the primitive stage more or less common to most peoples. *All the civilizations of both the East and the West originated in regions of high altitude, favored with temperate climates, during the late glacial retreats,* after about 40,000 years ago.

The winds of the tropics, passing over the plains of the Ganges Basin in India, reach the Himalayas, water the southerly slopes, fertilize the inland valleys, and support a wonderful verdure up to the stage of eternal snows at about 13,000 feet elevation. But on the tableland beyond the Himalayas the drought of the regions of the sacred[25] lakes in Tibet, of Eastern Turkistan, and of Mongolia indicates that they are deprived of this beneficial influence. Consequently, human habitations in Tibet have been mainly along the river valleys and around various lakes, especially warm-water lakes. This has resulted from the fact that the snowline on the northerly side of the Himalayas is at an elevation in excess of 16,500 feet. Residence in the vicinity of glaciers is common today in consequence of the higher temperature that melts them. The average temperature of much of this highland region by 35,000 years ago, after the increasing warmth had accelerated the Würm II glacial retreat, probably was not much lower than it is today. The tablelands of Tibet and cold Mongolia touch the temperate or semi-tropical plains of India, southeastern Asia, and central China. The traveler frequently may leave on one side of the mountains the snow and the frost of winter to find on the other side the warm breath of spring, its verdure, and its flowers.

The lake regions of western Tibet and the highland regions of Ladak, Baltistan, Dardistan, and Kohistan, south of the Karakoram and Hindu Kush Mountains, all traversed by the upper Indus River,[26] possess similar climates. The monsoons that move between Africa and the Asiatic highlands modify the temperature of Kashmir and the adjacent regions (which include those just named) and the mountain ranges on the north shelter them from the Siberian coldness. Intense dryness pervades the atmosphere during nine months of the year. The snowfall is light and the western passes are so little subject to snowfall that they are frequently traversable during the entire year. Low temperatures are prevalent throughout these regions, whose habitable altitude varies roughly from

---

25 The term "sacred" as applied to certain lakes in Tibet and to the Ganges River in India should not be lightly regarded. It arose in primitive times because the regions to which it applied represented the habitations where important divisions of the human race evolved from lowly beginnings.

26 The great importance of this geographical relationship in racial migrations is portrayed later.

10,000 feet to 16,000 feet except that the southerly valley of Kashmir proper is at an elevation of 5,000 to 6,000 feet. The intense cold dry air of autumn and winter prevents putrefaction and conduces to rugged health. It is a region well adapted to the European racial type. Kashmir proper has been fabled in song for its beauty and charm (e.g., in Moore's *Lalla Rookh*) and it is the chief health resort of Europeans in India today.

It apparently was during the Laufen interglacial period about 95,000 to 70,000 years ago that the differentiation of the three major races in India and Indo-China largely occurred. At that time Turanians must already have been moving northeastward into southern China and Aryans from northwestern India up the lower Indus River valley. If the racial differentiations had happened earlier, each race would have been greater numerically than it was upon the Würm II glacial retreat and each would not have been confined so sharply to its own separate part of southern Asia, the Aryans on the west, the Indafricans (Negroes) in the center, and the Turanians on the east; there would have been cross-migration and intermingling instead of differentiation.

The fourth and fifth (Würm I and II) glaciations appear to have reached their peaks about 100,000 years and 45,000 years ago respectively. The intervening period of warmth, known as the Laufen retreat, lasted about 25,000 years.[27] During the thousands of years of the Würm I glacial advance snow and ice spread on the high mountains and in the lower regions and the sparse human population in the regions distant from India (chiefly *Neanderthal* and related branches of man) experienced difficulty in adaptation to the increasingly ardous conditions of life. It is doubtful whether *Homo sapiens* had yet reached the higher altitudes of the Indus River or had crossed the passes in the Suliman Mountains to Iran, but on the east he probably had spread over southeastern Asia.[28] Long before that the Neanderthal man had been

---

27 In the Alpine nomenclature, which is used here.
28 Represented perhaps by so-called Peking man.

driven out of India. Even during the Laufen regression, it is doubtful whether the population of each of the three major races was more than a few tribes and they probably formed very little more than distant contact with each other. For reasons of safety, they kept separate.

It has been proved by spear-heads, scrapers, and other artifacts found in lower Kashmir Valley that primitive man had ascended that far north as early as 70,000 to 60,000 years ago.[29] Some even migrated thence across the Suliman Mountains to northern Iran, where skeletal remains of Aryans recently have been found in a cave on the southerly shore of the Caspian Sea.[30] These discoveries are not surprising and more findings in harmony with the conclusions stated herein may be expected in the future.

As the intensity of returning cold weather upon the advance of Würm II glaciation became intolerable about 50,000 years ago, *Homo sapiens* was forced back from the Indus Valley and Kashmir to western India and probably also from Afghanistan to lower lands on the Iranian plateau. When returning to northern India along the Himalayan foothills, these earliest Aryans ultimately turned southward and divided and *drove out of the Ganges valley the progenitors of the Indafrican (or Negro) race*, who emigrated mainly in two directions, eastward down the Malay peninsula toward islands of the Pacific (where they are known as the Melanesians) and westward across southern Iran and Arabia to the continent of Africa. This emigration forced the Turanians eastward and northeastward and left the progenitors of the Aryan brown race in possession of nearly all of India. However, in the hill country of Kumau, along the Himalayas, a small group of the Negroes was left behind and their descendants live there today. The indigenous peoples continued to inhabit the Dekkan and constituted the later Dravidian tribes. Even in the southerly regions, the lowering of the temperature in advance of approaching glaciation was

29 Verified by report early in 1933 by Dr. Hellmut de Terra, of Yale University, who recovered many such artifacts in the Kashmir region.
30 Discovered in 1951 by Dr. Carleton S. Coon, who headed an expedition from the University of Pennsylvania.

felt keenly. In southern Asia the increased density of population stimulated the interplay of human activities, with the result that man there as well as elsewhere gradually was forced to become a social being by his relations with his fellow-beings.

The return of warmth after the retreat of the Würm II glaciation 35,000 to 30,000 years ago stimulated the momentous migration of small tribes of brown Aryan people of northwestern India slowly up the valley of the Indus for the second time. Ultimately, some crossed the passes of the Suliman Mountains to the Iranian plateau and others, perhaps by 27,000 years ago, had reached the valleys of the tributaries of the Indus in Kohistan, Dardistan, Baltistan, Ladak, and western Tibet and the slopes of the Karakoram Mountains. Even earlier, small tribes of yellow Turanian people likewise were moving around the southeasterly and easterly slopes of Tibet and ascending its numerous river valleys, because of the less severe effect of the Würm II glaciation in that region.

Still another glacial advance was destined to descend upon the highlands and disturb the settlements of those people in the west. It was the minor Achen glaciation, whose effects began to be felt seriously about 25,000 years ago. It impelled the descent of the majority of the Aryan inhabitants of the Indus valley from their upper settlements southward to warmer climes; they were the later Indonesians (Polynesians). Those who had reached and settled in the valleys of the high Indus River and its tributaries, such as the Shyok, between the Himalayan and Karakoram mountain ranges in eastern Ladak and the lake region of the northwestern Tibetan provinces of Ngari and Rudok, were permanently separated from those who had retreated down the Indus. The passes over the Suliman Mountains to Afghanistan and Iran also were closed. *These inhabitants who thus were isolated in the broad unglaciated river valleys and around the numerous warm-water lakes of eastern Ladak and western Tibet*[31]

---

31 The lake regions of central and northwestern Tibet are conspicuous for their great number of widely distributed hot springs, which tended to modify the extreme climate of the country during and after the glaciations.

during this glacial period are noteworthy as having been the progenitors of the white Keltic and Nordic branches of the Aryan race, while those who remained west of the Suliman Mountains became the progenitors of the brown Cro-Magnon, Mediterranean, Iranian, and Hamitic branches of the same race. All of these racial divisions will be discussed later.

While this glaciation was not as lengthy as the Würm glaciations had been, it nonetheless made the Tibetan plateau uninhabitable except in the valleys that escaped coverance by ice, chiefly those that contained warm-water lakes.[31] These were inhabited in the west by the above-named Aryan peoples and in the lake region of central Tibet by Turanian (Tungus) tribes that later evolved into the Turkish branch of that race. The latter region had greater expanse, was much more open, and enjoyed immensely more sunshine than the enclosed and bleak habitations of the Aryans did. Other easterly Turanian tribes, progenitors of later divisions of that race, moved eastward and northeastward to lower elevations, where the glacial effects were felt less severely.

After the Achen retreat had made the Tibetan high-lands more widely habitable, approximately 17,000 to 14,000 years ago, the Aryan and Turanian inhabitants there first came into contact in western Tibet. Theretofore, they had been kept apart by the great distances and the different glacial effects and this separation was reflected by marked differences in their physical evolution; but long habitation at the high elevation also resulted in certain similarities of their physical development, to be reviewed later. Eastern Asia, with its peculiar physical nature, always has been the home of the Turanian subraces, with their extremes of culture. Similarly, western Asia has been the home of the Aryan subraces, also with their extremes of culture, but they have expanded since then to embrace all of Europe. The Turks, Bolgarians, Hungarians, Finns, Estonians, Lapps, and certain far northern Ugrians are the only Turanian subraces (other than the Basques and Etruscans) that have been driven by pressure from behind into territory of the Aryans in the west.

Important tribal migrations doubtless occurred in eastern Asia more or less continuously during the warm period between the Würm II and Achen glaciations and also through the latter glacial period because of its minor influence on the lowlands, but such movements were long retarded in the west. The highland valleys and the lowlands of Asia were admirably adapted to receive migrations of early man and, by their highly varied altitude and climate, were conducive to the attainment of diversified racial characteristics. The climate of the Old World during the postglacial era became characteristically dry, extremely hot or cold, and largely arid, and its land area finally consisted of plateaus, deserts, and steppes. Deserts now extend from the Pacific to the Atlantic, across Mongolia, Eastern Turkistan, Iran, Arabia, and Africa. While there was much less aridity and more productiveness thousands of years ago, Asia (except in the extreme south) always has been a region of scarcity of vegetation; but animal life flourished greatly in its dry, hot or cold, exciting climate. It is the domain of the higher animals — the mammalia, wild and domestic, the dog, horse, ox, chimpanzee, gorilla, and orang-utan. Thus, Asia is the primitive seat of high civilization.

Emphasis also must be laid on the existence of a generally temperate climate longitudinally from the Pacific to the Atlantic across central Asia and Europe. This resulted in the same types of vegetation and animals throughout, with the same general forms and the same species. Similarity likewise existed along the great mountain axis through the Himalaya, Hindu Kush, Caucasus, Taurus, Alpine, and Pyrenees ranges, from the far East to the far West. Owing to the peculiar adaptability of southwestern Asia to human activities — its favorable climate, increasing aridity, and the absence of forests — prehistory evolved the most rapidly in that region. History has marked out the temperate climes as the habitation of the progressive and refined branches of the human race; that fact is conspicuous and important, for fundamental reasons. Man's progress is intellectual and moral and it is accomplished by the exercise of his energies and faculties, for which the temperate zones have proved to be the most suitable. Western Asia, from India to the Mediterranean, is the spiritual center of mankind and the cradle of man's social nature. The perfection of Jesus' philosophy and psychology was the result of his supposed 16 years' sojourn in Media and Persia[32] and probably in India. The extremes of the torrid and the frigid zones always have exercised a retarding influence on man's progress, so that stagnation has resulted, as with the Ind-africans (Negroes) of Africa, on the one hand, and the Eskimos, Ugrians, and other peoples of the Arctic zone, on the other hand, causing physical, intellectual, psychological, and other differences with other peoples.

The cold climate of the central Asiatic highlands and northward during the last glacial retreats retarded the progress of the races inhabiting those regions until they had emigrated to more temperate regions, while the people in the gentler climate south of the mountains evolved in a more favorable environment. This is well discussed by Guyot.[33] Along the bicontinental axis the transition is abrupt and the two climates are far apart. The high ridges arrest at once the icy winds of the north and the softened breezes of the south and separate the two domains. The contrast of the two climates could not fail to have great influence on the peoples of the two regions. This has been revealed from earliest times in the most remarkable manner. In the north, the arid tablelands, the steppes, and the forests condemned man to the life of the hunter and the shepherd, and he was nomadic and barbarous. In the south, the fruitful plains and a milder climate invited the people to agriculture, and they created fixed establishments and became civilized. Substantially the same contrast existed on both sides of the irregular chain of mountains extending northeasterly from the

---

32 He apparently was well informed in the philosophy and doctrines of the Magi of ancient Media, and some of his sayings bear noticeable resemblances to those of Gotama (Buddha). He must have been accompanied by two members of the monastic order of Essenes on the trip.
33 Arnold Guyot, *op.cit.*, pp. 261-263.

Pamirs to and beyond Lake Baikal, which separated the cold Siberian region from the warmer Chinese desert and coastal plains. Thus, in the very interior of the historic continent there have existed from early times barbarous and civilized worlds more or less side by side. But two worlds so widely different could not remain in contact without reacting upon each other ultimately. In all ages, waves of barbarous people have issued from the north and overcome the civilized regions by their destructiveness. But, as after the storm nature assumes new strength, so the civilized nations, enervated by too long prosperity, have been restored to youth and vitality by the admixture of these rough but vigorous children of nature from the north. Numerous illustrations will readily occur to the reader and others will be presented in later chapters.

During the last great glaciation (Würm II), the water level in the Pacific, Indian, and Atlantic Oceans was much lower than after the glaciers had melted and their waters had flowed back to the seas. The shores of southern and eastern Asia projected much farther out into the water and formed land bridges to Australasia and Oceanica where thousands of islands now stand. The greater expanses of land in the south Pacific may have reached within relatively close distance of South America and extended in other directions in its waters. Emigration from India in this general direction was then very readily accomplished, and it is probable that Pre-Dravidians and later Indafricans (Negroes) intermittently moved southeastward from very early times, perhaps even during the height of the Würm II glaciation, as the pressure of other peoples behind them became too forceful to resist.

The glacial effects were quite marked on the Himalaya, Caucasus, Taurus, Syrian, Alps, Pyrenees, and Atlas Mountains. This prevented migration northward or westward into the Mediterranean basin, leaving the most feasible courses of migration toward the southeast, the southwest, and the northeast. Even on the plateau of the Dekkan of India the cold was severely felt and the Negroes of the Ganges River basin apparently were not attracted to that region as a new habitation even if they could have gained it from the tribes long settled there and better adapted to withstand the increasing cold. However, the existence of negroid features among some of the existing peoples of the Dekkan indicates that there was some infiltration of Negroes from the Ganges valley in that region.

The climate of Africa gradually became humid and enervating and conduced to human stagnation. The Sahara Desert was drying up rapidly at that time. Northern Africa was connected with Europe across the present straits of Sicily and Gibraltar. The Atlas Mountains and more easterly highlands inclosed the Mediterranean basin. At that time there was no such Mediterranean Sea as now exists. The area then comprised simply a lake in the west and another in the east, each of considerable depth. Professor Suess[34] shows that a large part of the eastern Mediterranean basin was still dry land at the time that the last glaciation (the Achen) reached its peak, so that the present Mediterranean Sea was the result of the action of flood waters from the melting ice during this glacial retreat. Not only was the water level in the two lakes raised, but the glacial floods also raised the water level in the Atlantic Ocean. It is believed that the pressure of water in the ocean burst through at Gibraltar, whereupon progressive erosion during the succeeding thousands of years cut the straits at Sicily and increased the water level in the eastern lake, thereby combining the two lakes into the present sea.

At the end of the Paleoanthropic age of man the British Isles were still joined to the European continent, and an extension of the Rhine River flowed into Norfolk. The Adriatic and Red Seas and the Persian Gulf then were narrower than they are now; in fact, they may have been only small lakes, if they existed at all, and the Near East was much less arid. However, in general, the continents had attained much of their present forms.

Finally, as the Achen glacial retreat was well under way upon the brisk rise of temperature about 16,000

34 Eduard Suess, *The Face of the Earth* (English trans,. Clarendon Press, Oxford, 1904), I, ch.iv.

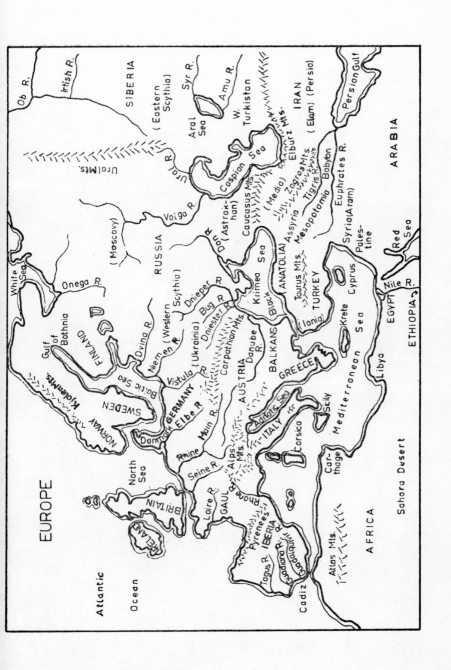

years ago, the glacial effects diminished in the more favorable regions and the masses of snow and ice that had
accumulated in the highlands and mountain passes gradually diminished. This invited migration in various directions, particularly from westerly Iran. Turanian tribes
moved up the Tibetan river valleys on the southeast and
east and the Turks increased in numbers in eastern and
central Tibet. The latter subsequently gained possession
of the lake region of south-central Tibet, whence they
ultimately made contact with the Aryan race in western
Tibet and Ladak and greatly influenced the course of
history, as later portrayed. Even today Tibet is said to
be the loftiest and loneliest country in the world, with
its rare fauna, flora, and birds. It comprises an area of
more than 1,000,000 square miles, about one-third of
that of the United States. Its huge girdle of almost inaccessible mountains has kept the land isolated and
largely unknown. Its present population is only about
4,000,000, wholly Turko-Mongolian of race, for reasons
explained later.

---

6. *Social Emergence of Primordial Man.* The oldest
human remains or prehistoric implements of man that
have been found thus far go back less than a million
years. During the first half-million or more years of man's
existence on earth he must have been so low in intelligence and his acquisition of culture so slight that he
failed to leave any impress of his doings. In appearance
he probably was of medial height, muscular, with prominent shoulders, neck, and mouth and receding forehead
and chin. He was dark-complexioned and also quite
hairy. Since he started from meager beginnings, the great
hazards of life, due to disease, the elements, and the
animals, reptiles and other forms of life, prevented any
rapid increase in population. But his experience in pro-
tecting his life and in gaining sustenance, since he had
to live by his rudimental wits and the use of his hands,
gradually developed his nervous system, imagination, and

mentality. His range of vision expanded and with it came a fuller understanding of the world around him, which continually increased his store of mental impressions.

In the course of time, as a result of this evolution of his higher faculties and of his restless inquisitiveness and growing self-confidence, man's appearance became less animal and more human. His mouth tended to recede and his forehead to grow. As the only being endowed with the faculty of self-consciousness, man was able to wander about the earth with greater skill and rapidity than the primates or other animals and was better able to adapt himself to varying environment and circumvent his enemies and avoid or overcome difficulties and dangers. His continual advancement in human efficiency, sociability, and culture always has been correlated with his erect posture, the increasing use of his thumb, the interaction of his nervous system and brain, and his acquisition of the power of speech. His early struggles with numerous enemies and the forces of nature had the effect of ruthlessly weeding out those unfitted to survive under the new conditions of life in the open. Thus, by natural selection, real men were evolved from the survivors.

As early as the Eocene and Oligocene geologic epochs there is noticeable a sharp and worldwide division between the forest-living and the plateau-living inhabitants of the earth, the former remaining stationary or regressive and the latter becoming the alert, progressive, and forward-looking types. The same division apparently occurred among the primates during the later (Pliocene) epoch.

According to Osborn, the brain of primitive man was far more human in development than the jaw, from which it has been inferred that the evolution of the brain preceded that of the mandible and also preceded the development of pulchritude of facial features and of bodily characters in general.[35] The brain had a bulk

---

35 H. F. Osborn, *Men of the Old Stone Age* (Scribner, New York, 1915), page 141.

of nearly 1,300 cubic centimeters, ranking among the smaller brains of today and surpassing that of the primitive Australians, which rarely exceeded 1,250 cubic centimeters.

Primordial man apparently lived in the open but resorted to trees, rock shelters, and caves as means of self-protection from animal life. Living in a tropical climate, he wore no clothing until forced to do so by the increasing coldness of the glaciations of the Pleistocene age, when he also took to living in shelters and at the entrance of caves. Not only was the population kept down by an appallingly high death rate but the desire for offspring probably was much less intense than it was in later years[36] upon the discovery of agriculture and the domestication of animals, when the labor of children was helpful and the possession of wealth became a factor. Large families were a hindrance to primitive man's movements and the preservation of his life among more powerful enemies. Subnormal offspring died early; deformed children were ruthlessly put to death; adults unable to carry their burdens of life were cruelly punished or executed. Thus, it was a very harsh rule of the survival of the fittest, but out of the welter special types or unusually able individuals evolved.

There was then very little social life and early man probably wandered over the earth in family groups only. He gathered his food, such as insects, lizards, dead animals, shell-fish, eggs, vegetation, etc., from the earth. His only weapon was a stone, without a handle, which he hurled from his hand. His earliest handicraft, simple in the extreme, is represented by the eoliths that have been found at various places. Yet there was a great gulf between man and the animals by his novel possession of the supreme quality of self-consciousness, which in time was to enable him to become the master of the earth.

The flexible and adaptable hand of man, with its devel-

---

36 This is proved by the fact that in 1800, or about 1,500,000 years after the human race had evolved, the population of the globe did not exceed 700,000,000. In 1900, only a century later, it had increased to 1,700,000,000 and in 1950 to 2,500,000,000.

oped thumb, lent itself readily to the use of various natural objects, such as sticks or stones, for weapons or implements. From this stage it was but a step to the
manufacture and the use of tools, which led naturally
to developments in three directions. First, it is unlikely
that any creature possessing the strength of man could
use tools long without striking sparks and discovering
the possibilities of fire. Second, the use of tools led to
the manufacture and use of clothing and ornaments.
Third, the use of tools facilitated the construction of
fixed abodes or domiciles wherein man would be safe
from at least the majority of his four-footed enemies.
Such an abode presumably then became the abiding place
of the female, in which she found protection and to
which food was brought regularly by the male for joint
consumption. Man is the only vertebrate with slowly-
developing young, born one at a time, that live continuously in an enclosed abode or domicile. Such a manner
of life permits the rapid bearing of young, for, with the
mother protected and provided for, she may devote herself entirely to the rearing of the children. The development of a dependent family, including young of many
different ages, doubtless necessitated the interpretation
by the parents of a great number of different sounds,
which may be assumed to have laid the foundation for
the beginnings of articulate human speech. So we find
that all the things that make man human may be traced
back to the potentialities of the flexible hand with its
developed thumb guided by a brain capable of developing those potentialities.[37]
It was the Würm I glaciation that made man a social being, when the clan or tribe, the first social group,
doubtless was formed by the clinging together of related
families. Even in the summertime, the icy winds from
the vast surfaces of snow blew for hundreds of miles
over unglaciated areas. The glaciations increased very
slowly, affording ample time for the adjustment of the
life that was able to survive, but most of the mammals

[37] Austin H. Clark, *op.cit.*, pp. 231-232.

gave up the struggle. Man and his companion, the dog, were the most conspicuous survivors. By being kept in caves and other shelters by the cold weather for long periods of time, social habits were developed by man and progress in the arts was greatly stimulated, such as clothes-making, striking fire from flint, and carving ivory tusks, stone, and bone. Language improved by this social contact, and the exchange of ideas, aims, and ideals gave the impetus to a social revolution. The poorer intellects among the people were then able to profit by the ideas and discoveries of the better, and all who came in contact rapidly progressed in primitive civilization. Thus, this and the later shorter glacial periods hastened and intensified the process of evolution. This increase in general intelligence and the interplay of human relations and activities resulted in the making of better weapons and in the acquisition of better supplies of food. Man, in fact, had evolved from a mere gatherer of readily obtainable vegetable and animal food to the stage of hunting and fishing. He developed formidable weapons, such as shaped stones, sticks, clubs, bolas, flint knives, javelins, darts, and harpoons for hunting and spears, bone-hooks, arrows, nets, and other devices for fishing. As his energy and intelligence improved, he became increasingly skillful as a hunter and fisher and he also became more venturesome in his migrations.

The use of clothing, once adopted for protection during the cold glacial weather, never was discontinued. Skins were used for clothing, also cloth made of grass, leaves, and reeds, woven or plaited. Thread was made of fiber and bone needles were developed and used. Doubtless the increasing use of clothing and the process of artificial selection gradually effected a reduction of the bodily hairiness of man. Both men and women used coloring matter and other modes of decoration on their bodies, mainly to attract the opposite sex. Ultimately, man reached the stage of evolution where his accumulated culture began to exert a greatly accelerated effect and his cultural progress became infinitely more perceptible.

The prevalence of approximately the Chellean type of culture all over the world about 400,000 years ago is not necessarily due to origin in a single place and diffusion therefrom but to the general similarity of human needs and human invention to satisfy those needs. The most practical procedure was first to utilize those natural objects nearest at hand for tools and weapons, such as flint and quartzite for hunting purposes, shaped stones for weapons, etc. The discovery of fire and the development of the hearth by early Acheulean times[38] at the latest is proved by the layers of charred wood and bones found in the industrial deposits of that age. The cold climate of Acheulean times at the close of the third glaciation was the same as that during the preceding late Chellean times. It was followed by the warm Acheulean times of the last major interglacial period, which after thousands of years became cold again as the fourth glaciation began. From that time the home in the cold climes became the social center, which stimulated the growth of human culture and virtues. Man learned to store food for periods of hunger when the frozen streams and pools in winter made shellfish and fish not obtainable and vegetation was scanty. It was necessary for him to depend upon the slaughter of big game for winter's supply of food, and this experience increased his intelligence and skill. An illustration is the many uses to which the man of northern Asia and Europe applied the products of the reindeer. Its hide provided him with clothing, its flesh and bone-marrow were food, and the horns were carved to furnish tools and weapons. Man's gradual cultural improvement from early Chellean times through the warm or cold Chellean and Acheulean periods evidences a corresponding evolution of mental development and manual skill. But the next, or Mousterian, stage shows a turn to retrogression as the Würm I glaciation

---

38 Recent evidence discovered in England indicates that the use of fire was known even earlier, not only in western Europe but as far away as Peiping, China. This demonstrates how widespread were the races that antedated *Homo sapiens,* modern man, on the face of the earth.

began in the West.[39] Neanderthal man was in a state of deterioration because of the blighting hardships of the last great glaciation, when cold and moist climate prevailed all over Europe as far south as northern Spain and northern Italy. Apparently, he was incapable of survival there or on the Russian steppes, where very hot summers were followed by intensely cold winters with high winds.

Our greatest deficiency in information pertains to the cultural status of the ancestors of the *present* races while they inhabited southeastern Asia, mainly Burma and regions eastward, northeastward, and southeastward for the Turanians, the Ganges River basin for the Indafricans, and the Dekkan and western India for the Aryans, during the Pleistocene (Würm I) ice age, 100,000-75,000 years ago. In fact, they are practically undiscovered links in these anthropological lines of descent. While the coolness from the Himalayan glaciers exerted a stimulating effect on them, the absence of extreme glacial effects provided a salutary environment for their cultural advancement, contrary to the forbidding conditions of habitation that prevailed in northern and western Asia and in Europe. Verification is found in the later evolution of the Neolithic culture in central Asia, especially in Turkistan and Iran for Turkish Turanian and Iranian Aryan phases respectively. This culture is characterized by the use of polished stone implements, particularly the stone ax perforated and attached to a wooden handle, the bow and arrow, the use of plants and seeds and the beginning of crude agriculture, the development of pottery and cooking, the domestication of animals, and plaiting and weaving.

The more favorable climatic conditions enabled the ancestors of modern man in southern Asia to develop naturally and more or less uniformly and to attain a high all-around status physically, mentally, and morally while contemporaneous man in Europe was retrogressing.

---

39 H. F. Osborn, *op., cit., Introduction,* pages 1-3. The same opinion was expressed in 1947 by Professor Wilfrid E. L. Clark, of Oxford University, England.

It is inconceivable that they had evolved no higher concurrently than *Homo Neanderthalensis,* a coarse, heavy, brutish type of being. They must then have closely resembled modern man. As stated by Osborn, "No doubt, our ancestors of the early Stone Age were brutal in many respects, but the representations which have been made chiefly by French and German artists of men with strong gorilla or chimpanzee characteristics are, I believe, unwarranted by the anatomical remains and are contrary to the conception which we must form of beings in the scale of rapidly ascending intelligence."[39] The complete extermination of all other branches of the human stock by *Homo sapiens* is acceptable evidence that he had reached a higher stage of evolution physically and mentally than the others long before the Würm I glacial advance. By the time of the second interglacial period, the Mindel-Riss, he probably had progressed far in the Paleolithic (or Old Stone Age) culture, making arrowheads and spearheads and inhabiting caverns where he could find them. But it was still many thousands of years before he had evolved in southern Asia to the status where he could begin his conquest of the surface of the earth, including the extermination of his collaterals wherever he might find them, which he did in Asia and later in Europe. He had yet to reach the density of population in which the formation of clans and tribes became necessary for security and for aggression and migration. This condition perhaps was reached during the last major interglacial period, the Riss-Würm, and the succeeding Würm glaciation.

Osborn shows, by citing from Lucretius' poem *De Rerum Natura,* written before 53 B.C. and based on Greek philosophy and science, that the Greeks had anticipated remarkably well our present knowledge of the prehistory of man,—"his powerful frame, his ignorance of agriculture, his dependence on the fruits and animal products of the earth, his discovery of fire and of clothing, his chase of wild beasts with clubs and missile stones, his repair to caverns, his contest with the lion and the boar, his invention of rude huts and dwellings, the softening of his nature through the sweet influence of family life and of children, all these are veritable stages in our prehistoric development."[40] The evolution of tribal life was a consequence of increasing density of population for the assurance of greater security, and marriage, which doubtless at first was a habit, subsequently became a tribal institution, regulated by custom and law.

It is not our purpose here to enter into any lengthy discussion of man's subsequent social progress other than to say that he ultimately advanced to the pastoral and agricultural stages in Neolithic times and finally to the Copper, Bronze, and Iron stages. But through all the ages the fear of disease, incurable illness, and early death has beclouded man's progress. Ancient man was subject to nearly every ailment known to modern man and there was little or no relief from most sicknesses. Few adults survived beyond 30 years. The "child of nature" of the early ages suffered teeth, bone, and tissue diseases, was crippled by rheumatism and arthritis, and was attacked by germs, vermin, insects, and parasites, so that his short span of life must have been full of distress and trouble aside from the terror caused by wild beasts that beset him on every side. Infant survival must have been appallingly small. But despite his difficulties and periodical retrogressions, an unceasing Divine purpose has pervaded man's existence down through the ages. Human evolution is the unfoldment of life from within or the expanding self-expression of the ego, however crudely it may be done. Since there is nothing in the effect that was not in the cause, the potentiality of man's continued improvement toward moral perfection is implied by his advancement to present standards. His principal requisite is to learn increasingly well how to live in harmony with the laws of nature, which are the laws of God.

The discovery of agriculture was virtually the beginning of civilization, since it produced a settled state of society and the assurance of a food supply. Agricultural

---

40 H. F. Osborn, *ibid.*, *Introduction*, pages 1-3.

implements were then invented. At first probably the hoe appeared, then perhaps the plow, followed by sickles, flails for threshing, stones for grinding into flour, one slightly hollowed and the other a rolling pin, as revealed by objects found at many Neolithic sites and lake dwellings throughout Europe. As the effects of the ice ages passed, desert areas appeared and irrigation became necessary as oases became scarce. As settlements sprang up, population increased rapidly, the domestication of animals followed, dwellings and a fixed mode of life arose, and wealth was accumulated. Trade with neighboring settlements was fostered. Villages grew into intercommunicating towns and cities, and outlying regions were explored. With increased knowledge of distant regions, emigration spread to desirable areas and rivalry for the better sites of habitation increased.

---

7. *Primitive Mankind.* Primordial Man, who originally evolved from the Primates with the endowment of a developed thumb and the peculiar faculty of self-conciousness, however meager it may have been at the time,[41] marked the inception of different species of *Genus Homo*. Among the various outbranchings from this human stem were the precursors of the many past and present races. These branchings, in course of time, assumed diversifications in development, some for the better and others for the worse, considered from the survival standpoint. The fossil remains of members of a number of primal branches have been found among geologic deposits at various places on the earth's surface, by means of which anthropologists have distinguished certain specific races, such as Java Man (*Homo Pithecanthropus Erectus*), Peiping Man (*Homo Sinanthropus*), Rhodesian Man (*Homo Rhodesiensis*), Heidelberg Man (*Homo Heidelbergensis*),

---

[41] Closely approximating this type were the taungs (Australopithecus), apelike men discussed by Dr. R. Broom before the South African Association for the Advancement of Science.

Neanderthal Man (*Homo Neanderthalensis*), *Homo Eoanthropus* (yet to be verified),[42] and Modern Man (*Homo Sapiens*). Thus, for hundreds of thousands of years primitive types of men roamed far and wide over the genial parts of Asia, Africa, and Europe, with the advance and retreat of the glaciations. But modern anatomists[43] generally agree that none of the earlier races was the ancestor of any of the others and that each represented a different branch of the human stem, but the remains of a recognizable ancestor of modern man have yet to be found. The last to appear in this evolutionary process, *Homo sapiens*, attained exceptional skill, a better-balanced nervous system, and a higher intelligence, and was able to supplant all the other races. The acquisition of human qualities doubtless made it possible for man to roam about the earth more rapidly than other mammalia had done, because he was able to adapt his behavior to varying conditions and in the light of his fuller understanding to evade difficulties and circumvent dangers.[44]

Diversification of evolution under varying conditions is a mysterious law of nature. The variety of types and species of plants and animals evolved has kept pace with the diversity of lands, seas, and other physical circumstances that serves as the basis and the condition for plant and animal development.[45] Similarly, the law has operated in causing the emergence of numerous differentiated types of men. The Pleistocene (or last great ice) epoch, which began from 600,000 to 1,000,000 years ago with the advent of the low temperature that resulted in the first known glacial advance, is divided into several periods from the standpoint of improvement of human culture. Their names are derived mainly from the places in Europe where the different types of artifacts were first discovered. The development and diffusion of cultural products were greatly influenced by the glacial advances and retreats. The periods are shown below, correlated according to Ice Age and cultural chronology.

---

42 Earliest skeletal remains in modern man's direct line of descent.
43 H. F. Osborn, R. J. A. Berry, A. W. D. Robertson, M. Boule, and G. Schwalbe.
44 G. Elliot Smith, *op.cit.*, page 48.
45 Arnold Guyot, *op.cit.*, page 112.

Type of Man	Ice Age Epoch	Type of Culture
Paleoanthropic:		
Java Man (Homo Pithecanthropus Erectus)	Pliocene (Pre-Glacial)	Eolithic
Solo (Java) Man (slightly more advanced)[46]	I Interglacial	Eolithic
Peiping Man (Homo Sinanthropus)	I Interglacial	Pre-Chellean
Rhodesian Man (Homo Rhodesiensis)	II Interglacial	Pre-Chellean
Heidelberg Man (Homo Heidelbergensis)	II Interglacial	Chellean
Neanderthal Man (Homo Neanderthalensis)	III Glacial, III Interglacial, and IV Glacial	Acheulean and Mousterian
Neanthropic:		
Earliest in line of descent of Modern Man (Eoanthropic), yet to be discovered, perhaps on Java and in Malaya	?	?
Pre-Dravidian	?	?
Grimaldi Man (Indafrican; Negro)	Würm Glacial Advance	Aurignacian

46 Skulls recently discovered (1931) in the valley of the Solo River, in Java, are thought to be those of human beings one or two stages more advanced than *Homo Pithecanthropus*. But no opinion has been expressed as to whether they were in modern man's direct line of descent.

Earliest Turanian	Same	?
Brünn Man (from Iran or India earlier)	Subsequent Interglacial	Solutrean
Cro-Magnon Man (from Iran via Africa)	Later same Interglacial	Magdalenian
Modern Man:		
Pre-Dravidian, Dravidian and Indonesian, Indafrican (Negro), Turanian (Yellow-Red), and Aryan (Brown-White)	Differentiated evolutions from Eoanthropus man in southeastern Asia	Microlithic Maglomosean Neolithic

All of the Paleoanthropic races are said to stand closer in evolution to the anthropoids than to *Homo sapiens.* Whether or not one or both of the Java men were in the direct line of descent of modern man may never be known; both readily could have been. The other Paleoanthropic races could have branched off at different times before or after Solo man did, but this question likewise may never be determined. Presumably *Homo sapiens* progressed irregularly through all of the earlier stages of cultural evolution in Malaya, Indo-China, and India by 125,000-100,000 years ago, but probably at a faster pace than Paleoanthropic man did, as befitted his greater intelligence; the Mousterian culture of Neanderthal man is still used by certain primitive tribes. Apparently, no descendants of other branches of Paleoanthropic man have existed on the earth during the last 15,000 years. The first Neanthropic man identified in Europe, the Grimaldi, apparently came by the Gibraltar land bridge from Africa and was Indafrican (Negro), later discussed.

Despite their groping toward civilization, as revealed by uncovered products of their industry, Nature ruthlessly cast aside all other species of *Genus Homo* except modern man. As one group exterminated and succeeded another, genetic unsoundness and instability recurred. Man with survival qualities could not be molded from such material. *Homo sapiens* inherited greater survival values, ultimately gained complete possession of the earth, and now has the opportunity to demonstrate whether he can reach greater heights or ultimately will be succeeded by a stronger, wiser, and more deserving race.

Members of all earlier branches of the primordial stem seem successively to have migrated in various directions over the earth from centers of evolution, depending on the geography of the continents at the time. Evidences of them have been found in the East Indies, China, western Asia, Africa, and Europe. It is doubtful whether any reached America prior to the arrival of the earliest Amerinds (Indians) with one possible exception discussed later. As each race in turn became dominant, it drove its predecessors farther toward the habitable remote parts of the earth, where they perished in one way or another. Glaciations and disease were effectual agencies in this extermination. From the severe stages of the Würm II glaciation on the Tibetan highlands about 50,000 years ago until the retreat of that glaciation about 15,000 years later, the crowding of Indonesians in northwestern India from the higher elevations of the Indus valley because of the coldness had the effect of forcing the Black or Indafrican race from that country about 50,000 years ago. Many moved eastward toward the Pacific islands, but the vast majority went westward along the shores of southern Iran and southern Arabia to Africa, where they gradually spread over that land south of the Sahara Desert. As that desert then was drying up, this large migration forced the remainder of Neanderthal man there [47] toward the northwest, whence he crossed to Spain and France and added his cultural achievements to the Achulean culture of his predecessors in Europe, which already had spread northward and eastward in Europe as far as feasible under the rigorous conditions of the Alpine and Baltic glaciers. The result of this impact from Africa was the Mousterian culture shown

---

[47] As the Indafrican (Negro) race gradually spread over central Africa, it is probable that all of Neanderthal man there except those who emigrated to Europe were progressively exterminated.

to have prevailed among Neanderthal man in Europe during the centuries of deterioration of that race, until it was supplanted, at least in the southerly coastal region, by the Auringacian culture of the Grimaldi man of *Homo sapiens* from Africa via Gibraltar during the Würm II glacial retreat of 40,000 years ago.

It was not until approximately 25,000 years ago, apparently at the end of the Würm II glacial retreat and the beginning of the minor Achen advance, that Europe was invaded directly from the East along one shore of the Black Sea and up the Danube Valley by the *Brünn* (*Brux, Pred-most, Combe Capelle,* and *Galley Hill*) race, apparently a branch of the *Veddas*[48] of India or a remnant of earliest Iranians along the southerly shore of the Caspian Sea, who introduced the Solutrean culture. It spread northward to Ukrainia, Moravia, and Poland, and westward to Bavaria and France. It was shortly followed by the Cro-Magnon branch of the Aryans from the Iranian Plateau, which reached western Europe across northern Africa and the Gibraltar land bridge. This race introduced the Magdalenian culture in the west, which soon supplanted the Solutrean and earlier cultures. The thoroughness with which the earlier or all of the Grimaldi, Brünn, and Cro-Magnon branches of *Homo sapiens* exterminated Homo Neanderthalensis in Europe has left the disappearance of the latter a mystery, although essentially it was no different from what already had occurred in Africa. At that time the Neanderthal race apparently was in a state of physical deterioration and hence may easily have been swept out of existence. Pestilences may have taken heavy toll. Its annihilation in Asia probably occurred earlier and even less is known of the movements and customs of its antecessors in that continent. That this race lived there is proved by the fact that Neanderthaloid artifacts have been found recently in the province of Ordos, North China.

The circumstance that no races of men of these earlier

---

48 The Brünn race has not yet been well enough defined for positive identification among the other branches of *Homo sapiens*.

types exist anywhere on the earth today is very significant of two facts: (a) that all who once existed must have been exterminated before, during, or shortly subsequent to the last (Würm II) glaciation and (b) that the extermination was accomplished by people long accustomed to wearing some form of clothes, which afforded protection against the ill-effects of inclement weather and caused a gradual diminution of general body hair to that of the earliest-known modern man.

Several interesting conclusions result from the foregoing discussion. (1) All of the existing races of the world dispersed from northern India and Indo-China. The plateaus of Iran and northwestern Tibet became early secondary regions of dispersion of Aryan subraces. The next continent (other than southeastern Asia and Australasia) to be populated was Africa, where descendants of earlier branches of the human stock were exterminated by the Asiatic invaders or driven across the western Mediterranean land bridges to Europe and the supplanting groups became the ancestors of the present Black or Indafrican race. (2) The latter migrants (Indafricans) moved from India across southern Arabia and into central Africa during the last great glacial (Würm II) advance, the cold winds of which, along with the Sahara Desert barrier, kept them from the inhospitable Mediterranean basin on the north. Southern Arabia was not as dry then as it is now and had a wider shore line on the south. (3) Since the first modern men in Europe, a division of the Grimaldi race, did not arrive in western Europe from Africa until about 40,000 years ago, they had not reached the Near East from India until after the beginning of the last (Würm II) glaciation; otherwise, during the Laufen interglacial period they could readily have advanced into western and northern Europe. That country was too inclement to attract them during the glacial peak. (4) Then came the Brünn race probably directly from Iran during the succeeding warm period but perhaps much earlier from India. (5) Subsequently, Europe was conquered by the Cro-Magnards, Aryans from Iran, who came by way of northern Africa from the east during a cooler period, and they apparently annihilated the Grimaldi and Brünn races. All of these races were black or brown in color. (6) Thousands of years later other branches came from Iran and the Pamirs by both the Mediterranean and the Danubian routes and populated Europe, as further discussed herein.

Curiously enough, most of our studies of the evolution of humanity and human cultures have pertained to the extinct races in Europe, about which anthropologists have gained vast knowledge during the past century. Less research apparently has been undertaken along analogous lines with respect to the ancestors of the living races during the many thousands of years of their evolution in southeastern Asia. Nonetheless, subject to the variable effects of environment and more or less local conditions, we are justified in assuming that the eternal laws governing the ever-increasing efforts of the human ego to broaden its scope of self-expression operated in substantially the same way in southeastern Asia as they did in Europe and with the existing races as with their predecessors. While the Pleistocene ice age affected the surface of Europe to a greater extent than it did that of Asia, it nevertheless exerted a powerful stimulus to the development of human culture on both continents; so that the subsequent discussion pertaining to the development of man and his cultures during this ice age has broad application to the branches of the human stock in both Asia and Europe.

─────────

8. *Racial Beginnings in Asia.* The precise place of origin of the primordial human stock may never be ascertained, but primitive migration must have been northward in Malaya and around the shores of the Bay of Bengal. The inference that the major branches of the present human race developed separately in Malaya and Indo-China and in central and northern India is strongly supported by the available evidence. The primitive movements all point to those regions, from Indo-China on the east to

Pakistan on the west, as the centers of dispersion of the progenitors of the Turanian, the Indafrican, and the Aryan races respectively; the Turanian race in Burma, Indo-China, and southward, the Indafrican race in the Ganges River valley, and the Aryan race in the highlands of the Dekkan and northwestern India.

The tendency toward modification or differentiation into types because of climatic conditions, environment, group isolation, and more intangible factors doubtless has been inherent in man from the beginning and probably will continue forever, since diversification is a law of nature. It has been said that primeval man may have had a greater tendency to diversify into types than modern man shows; but it should not be overlooked that we are considering physical changes in early man over periods of thousands of years and during great climatic extremes, whereas we are inclined to think of the slow differentiations in modern man over much shorter intervals.

Because of an extremely high mortality rate, it may not have been until the Laufen interglacial period, which began about 80,000 years ago and ended about 60,000 years ago, that the population of modern man in southeastern Asia reached the degree of density at which emigration to other regions began to assume marked proportions. In fact, man apparently evolved through many thousands of years in the above-named regions and differentiated into the modern type races there before emigrating or being driven to distant areas, as when the Turanians moved around the easterly slopes of the Tibetan plateau, the Indafricans were driven from northern India, and the Aryans expanded from the Dekkan to Pakistan (the Punjab) and thence up the Indus River valley. At that time, about 70,000 years ago, the Ganges River valley of northern India probably was low, hot, moist and unattractive for habitation and the Tibetan highlands may not have reached their present altitude. The higher plateau of the Indian peninsula (the Dekkan) was approximately the same as it is today. The long habitation of the Indafrican race in the Ganges valley explains why its members became so much darker than the members of the Turanian and Aryan races.[49]

So long as primeval man remained in a single region, racial differentiation was improbable. It occurred only after each division moved into a region with a different climate. It is probable that primeval modern man in southeastern Asia evolved through a negroid physical configuration, but with a dark-brown rather than a black complexion.[50] Variation in stature among the different tribes undoubtedly showed itself early, for we find that every primary race embraces a range in stature from short to tall. It is impracticable to assert with confidence that any one racial type, whether extant or not today, is the nearest to that of the original stock and that all others are greater differentiations therefrom. Apparently certain Pre-Dravidians of southern India represent the oldest type. They must be descendants of primitive migrants along the Bengal shores and continuous residents of those lower lands. Anthropology knows various special groups of people in the Far East who are difficult to relate to larger bodies. Many isolated distinct types that have emerged through the ages have since been absorbed by the larger groups that have become dominant in various regions, and interest in them rests largely on grounds of pure anthropological science.

It is believed that differences in altitude, climate, diet, and environmental conditions account not only for differences of complexion and figure but also for the character of the hair, the width of the nostrils, the cephalic index, and other physical variations of man. Despite the present inability of biological science to explain the phenomena, the fact exists that ulotrichous (curly) hair and platyrhine (wide) nostrils are associated with long continuous life in hot and moist climate and that leiotri-

---

49 It also explains why the subsequent lighter-complexioned invaders from the middle Indus valley and Iran (the Indonesians and Hindus) are becoming increasingly darker.

50 "Mongolian humanity seems to have evolved from a darker prototype." Sir Arthur Keith in *Introduction* to pamphlet *The Races of Mankind*, Field Museum of Natural History, Chicago, 1933, page 11.

chous (straight) hair and leptorhine (narrow) nostrils are associated with long life in a cold and dry climate, which may cause some contraction of the skin. The conditions favoring cymotrichous (wavy) hair and mesorhine (intermediate) nostrils are more variable, such as long habitation in cold and moist or hot and dry climates. The environmental influences seem to become impressed on the germ plasm in some manner, so that definite responses become heritable, such as the persistence of Nordic blondness in an originally brunet race, and when the environmental conditions are markedly altered the racial types undergo modifications. But sufficient time must be allowed for these modifications to become noticeable. [51] During such periods, natural selection or elimination also is effective in causing differentiation in isolated regions.

Once the expansion of the three recognized divisions of early man, the Black, the Yellow, and the Brown, began about 70,000 years ago, during the Laufen interglacial period, it was not long before the Yellow race started to explore the region around the southeastern Tibetan slopes and the Brown race to do the same up the Indus River valley. Spear-heads, scrapers, and other implements of man found in lower Kashmir prove that he had moved that far north about 60,000 years ago. All of the new regions thus explored were at higher altitudes, with cooler and drier climate than northern India, where the Negro remained, and they afforded especial attraction as places of human habitation; but it must have been many thousands of years more before these migrants adventured beyond to the higher, colder, and mysterious regions. The Turanians continued around the Tibetan foothills and the Iranians in the west crossed the passes in the Suliman Mountains to the plateau of Iran and possibly even as far as the Mediterranean shores, where climatic conditions were more favorable. Evidences of human culture in Iraq, east of Kirkuk, in ancient Assyria, fully

---

51 See A. Thomson and L. H. Dudley Boston, *Journal of Royal Anthropological Institute.*

60,000 years ago and in Palestine 50,000 years ago are said recently to have been found.

This early and wide separation of the three grand divisions of mankind resulted in increasing diversification of type among all of them, as we recognize them today.[52] The negroid type in the Ganges valley became accentuated in its Negro characteristics of complexion, hair, and nostrils as it continued to live in that low, moist, and increasingly hot climate, while the members of the other two races tended to diversify more and more toward their present physical characteristics in the higher and cooler environments. The people who remained on the plateaus of the Dekkan continued as the differentiated so-called Dravidian type or types. Their linguistic differences indicate early separation into divisions. Those remaining in the lowlands included the jungle tribes of coastal and southern India, namely, the low-caste Pre-Dravidians and the primitive Australians who emigrated from northeastern India.

A period of approximately 75,000 years embraced the two major glacial peaks (Würm I and Würm II) and the intermediate (Laufen) recession of about 25,000 years. The population of India and nearby regions was not great during Würm I glaciation. During the intermediate period of warmth the population greatly increased and began the migrations stated above, which led to the differentiation among the several races.

The second peak, which was reached about 50,000 years ago, was followed by diminishing oscillations until the supposed final retreat of recent times. Upon the approach of the second (or Würm II) glaciation, with its steadily diminishing temperature at the high altitudes, shortening summers, and lessening food supplies, migration in northwestern India began slowly in the reverse direction, *for it was in that region that the effect was felt the most.* This fact explains why northern India is populated today by the Aryan race rather than by the Indafrican or the Turanian race. As these Aryan Indonesians

---

52 A. H. Keane, *Man, Past and Present* (Cambridge Press, 1920), pp. 165-166.

(including the Polynesians) moved down the valley of the Indus River to and along the Himalayan foothills in northern India, their increasing pressure southward on the Indafrican inhabitants there impelled the emigration of the latter eastward toward the South Pacific and westward along the Iranian shores toward Arabia and Africa about 50,000 years ago.

But not all of the Indonesians who had crossed the lower Suliman passes to Iran were able to return to the Indus valley and descend to northern India before those passes became closed with snow. Inhabitants of the north Iranian plateau apparently moved to the southern shore of the Caspian Sea, where many must have perished from the glacial effects. Those on the south Iranian highlands moved westward to the warmer lowlands of Lower Mesopotamia, where evidences of their habitation recently have been discovered. Their ultimate fate is not known.

The southward pressure by the Indonesians on the Black race in northern India was exerted in the center from the Himalayan foothills, splitting the Negroes into two divisions, as just stated. The existence of distinct types among them in Africa indicates that minority groups joined them en route. Some black pygmies, however, remained in the Himalayan fastnesses, where their descendants live today and where they since have developed a low brachycephalic index. Their existence is further proof of the findings outlined above.

During the progress of the Würm II glaciation, the progenitors of the Yellow-Red race up the Tibetan river valleys merely moved eastward down those streams to more favorable locations in the lower valleys of eastern Tibet and western China and on the coastal plains. Arka Tagh, south of Altyn (or more properly Astin) Tagh, is the actual backbone of the Kuen-Lun range and with the Karakorum range is the northerly border of Tibet. While many of their rounded peaks are crowned with flat glaciers, apparently these mountains never were completely covered with ice. *Therefore, the isolated valleys watered by river tributaries along the slopes of eastern Tibet must have become the habitations of numerous Turanian tribes,* which in course of time gave birth to the diverse Turanian subraces described later. Their cephalic indices are evidence of that fact.

Perhaps 10,000 years of warmth followed the recession of Würm II glaciation until the coldness of the minor Achen glaciation or oscillation began to be felt about 20,000 years ago, especially in the regions of western Tibet and the highlands of Ladak and northern Kashmir. During this warm period, Indonesians of western India again ascended the Indus valley, this time as far as the lake region of the northwestern Tibetan provinces of Ngari and Rudok and also Ladak, where they settled in the valleys of the upper tributaries of the Indus, such as the Shyok. Others crossed the passes in the Suliman Mountains and scattered over the Iranian plateau. These progenitors of the later Brown nations in the valleys of Iran evolved during the subsequent Achen glacial advance separately from their Indonesian cousins in India and under far less rigorous conditions than those experienced by the descendants of the groups in the valleys and lake regions of the upper tributaries of the Indus River in Tibet. In fact, the latter in western Tibet and Ladak became the progenitors of the later White division of the Aryan race. They evolved their light complexion in a region surrounded by glacial snow and ice and with minimal sunshine during the Achen glaciation. More or less simultaneously, a tribe of Turanians (the later Turki) ascended the river valleys of northeastern Tibet to the central lake region. During the same time various other branches of the Turanian race were developing their own physical characteristics and culture under milder conditions in eastern Asia, as indicated earlier.

These were the regions of habitation of these two great racial divisions during the oscillating Achen glacial retreat until the accelerated warmth, like the stealthy approach of spring, enlivened the outlook and stimulated the pioneering spirit of the peoples all of the way from the plateau of Iran to the coastal plains of China. Then followed the remigration of the various Turanians in the upper river valleys of eastern Tibet and toward the north and the beginning of differentiation into a number of derived races. Movements also occurred in central China away from the Tibetan plateau and likewise of Aryans westward from the Iranian plateau, as explained later. Tradition in all branches of the Yellow-Red and the Brown-White races uniformly represents earliest known man as having descended from the high plateaus of Asia, although it was on the fertile lower plains that civilized society first was formed.

As the Indonesian branch of the Brown race slowly expanded eastward in northern India during the Achen glaciation, it gained control of southeastern Asia, from Yunnan southward, and drove the easterly division of the Negro population ahead of it into the Pacific islands, whence it slowly spread to the locations where it is found today. The latter migrants may have been preceded in the South Pacific islands by a sparse population of Pre-Dravidians, but, if so, very little is known of this movement. Perhaps it was a tribe of the latter who established the primitive culture on Easter Island, recognizable from the remains of certain works still extant, which are so remote that the present inhabitants have no knowledge or tradition of when they were constructed. Only recently scientists have discovered various carved symbols, supposed to be writing, and statues on Easter Island that bear close resemblance to inscriptions and figures found at Mohenjaro-Daro, in the Indus valley in India, and in Mesopotamia. These works may represent early phases of Turkic culture in Turkistan brought to Mesopotamia when the Turkic Pre-Sumerians crossed Iran about 8,000 B.C., apparently in consequence of the minor Bühl glaciation, and were transmitted to the Indus valley by refugees from Iran; then, when the glacial effects caused Indonesians from northern India to emigrate to South Pacific Islands, they may have pressed earlier Pre-Dravidian or Vedda people of India ahead of them across the South Pacific to South America. Many island peaks, now

— 60 —

submerged, may have encouraged them onward.[53] Several tribes of Ecuador, Peru, Chile, and the central highlands of Brazil, called *Palaeo-Amerinds* by Haddon, suggest Pre-Dravidian origin.

Indonesians also spread southward to the Dekkan of India, where the impress of their early commingling with the indigenous tribes is clearly recognizable among the present inhabitants. Their descendants constitute the vast Dravidian population of that plateau today. In this migration, they scattered various Pre-Dravidian tribes eastward, southward, and westward to the lower lands. One tribe of Veddas apparently migrated westward in Iran, since it is known that the most primitive human stratum in Persia was Pre-Dravidian or negroid in type. Later these Veddas wandered to central Europe, as subsequently described.

The increasing density of population of the Brown race in northeastern Iran and the coldness of the Achen glacial advance about 25,000 years ago forced a southward movement of inhabitants, which, in turn, pressed upon other Iranian people, called the Cro-Magnards, and caused them to emigrate from that plateau toward the Mediterranean region. Low temperature from the snow and ice on the Caucasus and Alps Mountains deflected them southwesterly to northern Africa, whence they ultimately crossed to Spain at Gibraltar and settled in western Europe. Evidently, the coldness of northern Iran also dislodged certain Pre-Dravidians in western Persia and Armenia, for they migrated shortly afterward across the Bosporus and entered Europe by the Danube valley. They introduced the Solutrean culture in that continent in advance of that of the Cro-Magnards. They are known as the Brünn (Brüx, Pred-most, Combe Cappelle, and Galley Hill) race, mentioned before, and seem to have been of the same stock as the Veddas who inhabit Ceylon today. Their origin in India and migration from Iran is demonstrated by the ana-

---

53 The difference in water level of the oceans between the time of a glacial peak and the end of an interglacial period, after all glaciers have been melted and the water has flowed back to the oceans, is said to be approximately 165 feet.

logy of their artifacts with various others found in India as well as in central and western Asia.

About 14,000 years ago, as the coolness of the minor Bühl glaciation began, important racial movements must have begun along the river courses on the high plateau of Tibet, caused by expansion of Turkic tribes northwestward from the central lake region. This migration brought them in conflict with the Aryan White race in the western Tibetan valleys. The progenitors of the Nordic division moved down the mountain slopes to the Tarim Basin (Eastern Turkistan) [54] and the ancestors of the Keltic division moved westward to the Pamir plateau, as proved by the respective cephalic indices. The great consequences of this event are revealed later.

At this time, the lowest stages of human culture persisted among the Pre-Dravidian and Indafrican races, for it is in the eastern archipelago, in India, and in central Africa that not only the oldest human fossils but also the most primitive cultures of modern man have been found. The Dravidians (Indonesians) and Iranians (Cro-Magnards, Mediterraneans, Hamites, and tribes of northern Iran and Kashmir) had developed higher cultures, substantially those taken to Europe by the Cro-Magnon branch of the Brown race. This was the result of their habitation in temperate and healthful regions. The facts are insufficient to support a definite opinion about the stages of culture of the contemporaneous Turanian peoples of eastern Asia. But it must have been well advanced, since the Neolithic culture of the Pre-Sumerians (represented by the Assyrians) taken westward to Mesopotamia about 8000 B.C. had been developed into the foremost culture of the world at the commencement of recorded history.[55]

The increase of this early population was greatly retarded by an appallingly high death rate among adults as well as among children. The effect of a devastating nor-

54 *Encyclopaedia Britannica*, 13th Ed., vol. 27, page 423d; Aryans in Eastern Turkistan.
55 The beginning of the Christian era will generally be used for time computations henceforth. The estimated dates of remote events include roughly 2000 years as the Christian era.

mal death rate was increased frequently by famine, pestilence, and plague. The casualties of life were taken largely as a matter of course, although the desire to perpetuate life, both in this world and in the next, ever has been one of the major objectives of primitive man. Thousands of years passed before there was any marked density of population in southern Asia. By the end of the Quaternary Period (about 12,000 years ago) the total number probably did not exceed a few millions. For this reason, when the remigrations after the last great glaciations had spent themselves, the various racial groups were more or less separated from each other by natural barriers and each developed its own religion and social state. This isolation, which continued for thousands of years, resulted in stagnation in many instances, especially in the very hot and very cold climes. Upon subsequent increase of population and the occurrence of droughts and pestilences, tribes frequently broke away and moved into territory adjacent to other and different peoples, or even invaded lands of others, which caused conflicts between cultures. If such migrating groups maintained contact with their homelands, the interchange of culture and commerce with foreign peoples stimulated advancement in civilization among the more progressive, so that certain fertile regions, such as Turkistan, Mesopotamia, and Egypt ultimately became the seats of high ancient cultures.

---

9. *Racial Differentiation.* The term "race" connotes a branch of mankind whose members have definite physical characteristics in common that distinguish them from the members of other branches. Reference already has been made to the different types of humanity that arose on the earth prior to the appearance of *Homo sapiens,* but similarly among the latter we find conspicuous differences appearing at an early time, chiefly during the Würm I glaciation and the Laufen interglacial period. These variations in human evolution were accelerated by migra-

tion from northern India and Indo-China to regions of different climate and environment. Scientists largely agree that the earliest modern man ranged from short to tall in stature, probably owing to pituitary differences, was well-built, dolichocephalous, dark-complexioned (but not black), and with dark hair and eyes. His facial features, probably somewhat negroid in configuration, and his carriage have undergone perhaps the greatest improvement of any of his physical characters in the more advanced divisions of mankind.

As the temperature rose toward the north during the early millennia of the post-glacial period, the increased density of population in southern Asia during the Würm II glacial retreat incited the expansion of the races into the higher lands of southeastern Asia and in other directions. Detached groups, families, clans, or tribes, moved to distant valleys and took up their abode, whence, in course of time, because of man's restless nature or of pressure from behind, their descendants emigrated to even more distant climes. This was the beginning of the subracial divisions of mankind. Those units, in turn, were pushed from behind by other expanding groups during successive thousands of years, until *Homo sapiens* had finally conquered all Eurasia and Africa and, in modern times, the rest of the world.

During these thousands of years, various factors operated to change the physical characteristics of the different divisions of mankind, diversification of types under dissimilar conditions being a law of nature. The precise causes of the various modifications are still the subject of study by scientists, but they undoubtedly include such factors as climate, altitude, environment, clothing, economic conditions, alimentation, inbreeding, and artificial selection within the group.[56] In fact, these probably are the major causes unless it be that important variations result from the effect

---

[56] "The question of adaptation to climate and environment, the possibilities of degeneracy, the varying degrees of physiological activity, of successful mutations, the effects of crossing, and all the complicated problems of heredity are involved in the discussion . . ." A. H. Keane, *Man, Past and Present* (Cambridge Press, 1920), p. 2.

on the human organism of the emanation from the
earth of rays from radon, the gas of radium. Different com-
binations, moreover, seem to produce within each division
of mankind marked deviations from a standard,—a variety
of shades of complexion and features,—so that, as stated by
Blumenbach, innumerable varieties of mankind run into
one another by insensible degrees. But racial types, in most
instances, are bound to be generalizations because of the
subsequent commingling of various peoples, often with diverse characteristics, from time immemorial. There are
relatively few wholly pure racial subdivisions of any
of the major races of mankind, although the essential
characteristics of each still are discernible in nearly all
instances.

The characters of man usually accepted as guides in racial classification are the cephalic index, shape of face,
color of eyes, skin, and hair, nature of hair, stature
and physique, shape of nose, skeleton, etc., i.e., mainly
external features. Sometimes emotional tendencies are
given consideration in racial studies. In measuring large
groups of people, average results necessarily are obtained,
particularly where there has been a mixture of subraces.
Under such circumstances, the use of averages may not
present the complete story. Not only will they include composite types but also individuals representing separately
each of the several component types.

Culture and language are of uncertain value in distinguishing races. There is no such thing as a permanent racial culture or language, although each major race for
many thousands of years, prior to contact with divisions of
other races, developed its distinctive language and culture.
The migration and contact of different peoples ultimately
has resulted in blended customs and speech. Culture may
be transferred from one race to another without blood mixture. Language may be imposed upon one race by another,
more highly cultured or more powerful, as the Greek
culture was imposed on other peoples 2500 years ago. As
stated by Smith, "Man can no more avoid accepting and
adapting to his own mental make-up some part of the

rich cultural harvest exposed to him to choose from than he can live without food. Nor can he help adding to the general heritage his own modest contribution."[57]

One of the most useful methods of segregating people is that of determining the cephalic index; i.e., the ratio of maximal width to maximal length of head, ordinarily about the top of the ears. The usual classification is (1) *dolichocephalic,* where the ratio does not exceed 75 percent, (2) *mesocephalic,* from 75 to 80 percent, and (3) *brachycephalic,* where it exceeds 80 percent. Primitive man, having been dolichocephalous,[58] therefore had an average index not over 75 percent. In some instances, in fact, the ratio had been found even less than 70 percent. Thus, the most primitive elements of mankind today, such as the Pre-Dravidians, Fijians, Australians, Zulus, Kaffirs, and even the Eskimos, are all dolichocephalous.

The nose may be concave, convex or aquiline, or straight. It may or may not be depressed at the root and may be wide, intermediate, or narrow at the end. The broad nostrils, as in the Negro race, are described as *platyrhine;* the intermediate type is called *mesorhine;* and the narrow type is known as *leptorhine.* With respect to the hair, the kinky type of the Negro is described as *ulotrichous,* the long straight hair of the Yellow-Red race is called *leiotrichous,* and the intermediate wavy or curly hair of the Brown-White races is called *cymotrichous.*

Variation in color of skin is dependent mainly on climatic conditions, the darkest races having become so by long habitation in low, moist, hot places near the equator and the lightest races having lost skin and eye pigmentation by long habitation in the rigorous dark or hazy climate of the north. Thus, the Black race developed in or near the torrid zone, the Brown race at the lower altitudes of the temperate zone, the Yellow race at the higher altitudes of the temperate zone, and the light-complexioned peoples during and after the glaciations in the cold regions of the high Himalayas or the far North. The Keltic

---

57 G. Elliot Smith, *op. cit.,* page 19.
58 H. F. Osborn, *op.cit.,* page 78.

and Nordic and the Finnic peoples represent blond or near-blond elements of the Aryan and the Turanian races respectively that evolved in cold, bleak regions, the first two in the sheltered vales of Ladak and western Tibet during the Achen glaciation and the other on the high-lands of eastern Tibet and along the headwaters of the Yenisei River in Siberia.

Thousands on thousands of years of continuous habita-tion in extreme climates, whether hot or cold, severely retard the evolution of people's intangible traits, as proved in the cases of the Indafrican Negroes and the Turanian Ugrians (including most of the American Indians); the latter in slightly less degree than the former. But the detrimental effects of the two climates are different, being externally active in the torrid zones and internally re-active in the cold zones; for which reason the Negro is far more inclined toward violent acts than the American Indian.

The characteristic of brachycephaly in human or ani-mal life, of which mesocephaly is merely a sizable degree, is a result of evolution at high altitudes over very long periods. Brachycephaly usually is associated with stocki-ness of physique and for the same reasons, namely, the increasing rarefaction of the air and the diminishing super-ficial atmospheric pressure with rise in elevation from the lowlands. A human being requires a definite quantity of oxygen in his lungs for the functions of life. The higher the altitude and the more rarefied the air, the greater is the volume that he must consume in order to sustain life, especially on the rugged terrain of mountainous regions. The atmospheric pressure on the external surface of the body is diminished from 14.7 pounds per square inch at sea level to 10.1 pounds per square inch at 10,000 feet above sea level. Consequently, we find that branches of the human race which ascended to and evolved on the highlands of Kashmir, Tibet, and the Pamirs developed large air passages through the head, larger necks, and broader and deeper chests than normal and concurrently broader heads in proportion to length[59] and heavy arms and legs. The time necessary for these changes is measured only in thousands of years. Mesocephalic branches are those that either evolved at lower altitudes or did not remain at high altitudes long enough to attain brachycephaly. Thus, it is only coincidental that dolichocephaly and agility are correlated with life on the plains or other open spaces and brachycephaly and slowness are correlated with life spent in the higher mountain valleys, where deliberate and ponderous movement is customary.

The effects of environment, economic conditions, and alimentaton are less readily detectable racially, but they undoubtedly have exercised marked influence. The possible effects of radon in the soil already have been mentioned. Proximity to warlike neighbors for long periods of time may have caused some diminution of the average stature of races, because of the constant killing of the strong and healthy members, leaving the breeding to be done to an ever-increasing extent by the less-favored members of society. The difference in the effects of a predominantly meat diet or a vegetable or grain diet over long periods of time may be noticeable, as also may be that due to the use of heavily mineralized water or otherwise.

An important factor in racial modification is that of artificial selection within the group, dictated by either necessity or fashion. Fat women are highly prized in certain African tribes, where the climate tends to diminish

59 Substantially this same thought seems to be expressed by W. Ridgeway in his discussion of the origin of the Kelts in *Encyclopaedia Britannica,* 13th Ed., vol. 5, page 611.

An interesting study of the effect of altitude in the alteration of the cephalic index of man might be made from the following approximate chronology of the ascent of man to and his descent from the highlands of Kashmir, Tibet, and the Pamirs:

Racial movement	Approximate time	Average index at the time
Indonesians ascend	25,000 B. C.	70-72 per cent.
Nordics descend	12,000 B. C.	75-78 per cent.
Paleo-Kelts descend	8,000 B. C.	80-84 per cent.
Kelto-Slavs descend	2,300 B. C.	85-90 per cent.

intertribal warfare or other great expenditure of energy. In the cold north, where activity enters into nearly every phase of life, a good-sized slender physique obviously is the desideratum. In fact, the activities of life in such a climate probably tend to develop a figure best suited for man's needs. An adipose or an undersized man there suffers a disadvantage. By the same reasoning, long habitation in mountainous regions tends to develop strong stocky physiques, best fitted for slower climbing over rugged terrain for shorter distances. In the more densely populated regions, the effect of competition in human affairs tends to produce different survival types. Each combination of terrain and climate has tended to develop the type best fitted to survive, in the tropics as well as in the cold north. In each environment the less gifted were ruthlessly annihilated and the better endowed were preserved or "selected," so that over the ages the types have progressively changed.

Civilization always arises and advances most rapidly in and proceeds from the more densely populated areas, because of the interplay of human activities, competition of ideas, and struggle for the satisfaction of human wants. This cultural development includes the arts of both peace and war, and it leads to the exploration and conquest of distant regions for both commerce and settlement. Consequently, the dispersion of outermost tribes to more distant regions, where they became isolated and had very little communication with each other, resulted in stagnation of civilization in such areas. Each such advance outward forced the more primitive peoples ahead to even more remote parts of the habitable regions of the earth, because of the greater military effectiveness of the newcomers. Thus, it is not surprising that the most primitive races generally have been found the farthest from the centers of the greatest cultural developments of the ancient racial stock in southern and central Asia, chiefly in Mesopotamia, in Ethiopia and Egypt, and later around the easterly end of the Mediterranean basin. It was in those regions, as we know, that civilization took the lead in succession. There man constantly improved in his development of formidable weapons and of the arts of commerce and it was from those regions that explorations intermittently occurred to the distant habitable parts of the earth. It is the early migrations upon the increase of warmth after the Würm II glaciation, which were attended with the greatest racial differentiation, that shall next receive our attention.

———————

CHAPTER II

RACIAL DIVISIONS AND SUBDIVISIONS

1. *Racial Designations. Terms.* In any discussion that pertains to racial distinctions, it is necessary that the terminology be free from ambiguity and easily be understood and remembered. The names should be reasonably short and apt for the same reasons that make the brevity of family surnames desirable. Insofar as we can utilize suitable terms that already have gained wide acceptance, regardless of the manner of their origin, the education of the people to that extent already has been markedly harmonized and the further exchange of ideas on the subject is facilitated.

Thus, the compound geographical term *Indafrican* for the Black race is indicative of its meaning. Since the Negro race developed in northern India and anciently was dispersed largely to Africa, the term has direct application to these people. Its principal defect is that it does not imply the inclusion of those members of the race who were dispersed in the opposite direction to the islands of the South Pacific, but this deficiency is deemed not to be seriously objectionable. It embraces all of the Negro and negroid branches, wheresoever located.

The fitness of the long-applied term *Turanian* for the Yellow-Red race is readily apparent. It was derived from *Turan* or *Turkistan,* a geographical name, the later homeland of the Turks. Aryan tradition preserved in the *Avesta* and elsewhere depicts frequent conflicts with the Turanians of the north, in a racial sense. In philological usage, the term is applied to all of those peoples whose language basically is agglutinative in construction, namely, the Turks, Finns, Ugrians, Tunguses, Chinese, Japanese, Mongoloids, Malayans, and other members of this race, including the American Indians (or *Amerinds*). The eminent Lewis H. Morgan, in his studies pertaining to the *family*, used the term Turanian in reference to a system in application among miscellaneous peoples of this race.

Three terms are in current use to designate the so-called Brown-White race, namely, *Caucasian, Indo-European,* and *Aryan*. The first is derived from a region where the commingling of diverse subraces probably has attained the maximum of any part of the world. Consequently, it is indefinite and inapplicable in its meaning and in recent years has diminished greatly in use. It is discarded here. The second is both racial and linguistic as well as geographical in its connotation and is more definite and informative, but it has the disadvantages of length and geographical limitation. As the subraces embraced within its scope emigrate to other continents, such as Africa and Latin America, its applicability becomes less suitable. The third term, *Aryan,* is simple in form, ancient in origin in the racial sense, and already has gained wide usage for this purpose. As a proper word, it apparently was first used as a tribal name by the *Arii* of ancient Persia, on the Arius River, which took its name from them, and signifies "of noble stock," but whether of the tribe as a whole or merely of its leaders is not known. Those people probably were a division of the Massagetae, of Bactriana, a powerful branch of the Nordic nation of the *Getae* (the later *Goths*), formerly of Eastern Scythia. They and other related tribes overran and settled in northcentral and northeastern Iran many centuries prior to the beginning of the Christian era. The Sanskrit word *arya,* the root-word of Aryan, thus connotes dignified associations. It was used to distinguish the Nordic conquerors of western India from the darker-skinned Iranians (Hindus). The eminent Persian king, Darius the Great (c. 545-485 B.C.), specially stated in an inscription that he was of Aryan stock. The term gained very early use as a national name in Persia and Bactriana and also in India and now is used by the Brown divisions of the race as well as by the White division. Consequently, its suitability for this purpose is unquestionable. The eminent Max Müller used the term strictly in the philological sense and he was careful to avoid any ethnological signification; but, as shown above, it can be used in either sense with equal facility if due consideration be given to modifications and transfers.

Thus, not only do the two names of *Turanian* and *Aryan* have much in common in simplicity, origin, and form but may be used cautiously in the racial and philological senses with respect to these two major divisions of mankind.[1] A Turanian subrace might adopt Aryan language and customs or an Aryan subrace might adopt Turanian language and customs; in such instances, it would be difficult to find more adaptable, definitive, or expressive terms than these. Strictly speaking, the term "subrace" should be applied to different branches of each, but for ease of expression that procedure may not always be adhered to herein.

In the subsequent discussion of each subrace and its relationships and migrations, the reader may gain the impression that some overlap or repetition appears because of the mention of other subraces in the same chapter. But this mention is unavoidable, as no one subrace may be treated as though it existed in a vacuum. In the search of each tribe for more favorable living conditions in later times, its bands of adventurers while engaged in distant exploration frequently competed with those of other tribes. Thus, there was more or less constant interaction, friendly or hostile, among the inhabitants of adjacent regions, with many of the same causes of friction that arise among nations today. Once a tribe or nation determined to migrate elsewhere, usually it not only had to fight its way through hostile territory but also to defeat and drive the inhabitants from the region that it coveted, although frequently a nation would per-

---

1 The Aryan branches long were without appreciable contact with Indafricans or Turanians and used only their basic Aryan language. The same may be said with respect to the other two major races. Thus the courses of research are clear.

mit migrating tribes to pass through its territory provided they would continue in motion to regions beyond. Consequently, the more quickly and thoroughly the reader makes working tools of the various racial, tribal, and national names as well as the geographical names set out in the chapter on the Classification of Races and elsewhere, the more easily will he be able to visualize these racial or tribal interactions as he proceeds through the text.

———————

2. *Classification of Races.* In very few regions of great magnitude is a single racial type found today because of cross-migration and some commingling of peoples. Thus, in the East Indies, Melanesia, Micronesia, and Polynesia we find branches of the Indafrican, the Indonesian, and the Mongolian races, and some composites of these, such as the Malayans. But this does not mean that dissimilar races have intermarried to any important extent. The primitive Australians may have been descendants of an admixture of the earliest Indonesian (Brown) groups with Indafricans or Pre-Dravidians in the region around Bengal when the former were driving the latter eastward as the Würm II glacial peak was advancing about 50,000 years ago.

In Asia the Turanian and Aryan races mainly abound. In Africa the Indafrican race predominates but various branches of the Brown-White race now are widely represented. It is not improbable that the Bushmen, whose skin is yellowish, while usually classified as Negroes, may actually have originated as a branch of the Turanian race that moved westward from Burma along the Himalayan foothills and later was driven westward with the Negroes. Europe is inhabited almost wholly by branches of the Brown-White race. The western hemisphere is inhabited by Pre-Dravidian (probably), Turanian, Indafrican, and Aryan race, the last-named greatly predominating.

The principal divisions of the primary races are set out below.

(a) PRE-DRAVIDIAN RACES:

1. *Veddas* and other primitive tribes of southern and eastern India and Ceylon; Sakai of southern Malay peninsula, and others of the East Indies.
2. Perhaps also the *Paleo-Amerinds* of South America.
3. The primitive *Australians* may likewise be included.

(b) BLACK (Indafrican) RACE:

1. *Pygmies* (Himalayas, African Congo, Andaman Islands, Malay peninsula, East Sumatra, Philippines, Papua, and Melanesia mainly).
2. *Grimaldi* (who entered western Europe from northwestern Africa).
3. *Bantus* (in Africa).
4. *Papuans* (in the East India Islands).
5. *Bushmen* (Africa,— perhaps originally Turanian).
6. Various crosses, such as the *Hottentots* (who are a cross of the Bantus and Bushmen).
7. Others of various names.

(c) YELLOW-RED (Turanian) RACE:

1. *Eskimos* (Arctic regions of eastern Asia, North America, and Greenland).
2. *Mins* (underlying race of Szechuen, divisions scattered over eastern Asia).
3. *Ugrians* (northern Asia, mainly Siberia, Ural region; also the Finns) and northern Amerinds in America).
4. *Tunguses* (northern Mongolia, Manchuria, Korea, Japan; also Neo-Amerinds of North America).
5. *Turki* (Tibet, Turkistan, Caspian region, Turkey—Mesopotamia, and Palestine (Pre-Sumerians, Sumerians, and Hittites, other-

wise called Semites, Magyars, and Bolgars).

6. *Sinicus* (otherwise called Chinese, mainly eastern China).

7. *Paraoeans* (southern Mongoloids of western and southern China, eastern Tibet, Japan, Burma, Assam, Indo-China and East Indies, also major element in the Malayans).

(d) BROWN-WHITE (Aryan) Race:

1. *Cro-Magnards* (from Iran via northern Africa to western Europe).

2. *Indonesians* (pure Dravidians of Dekkan and northeastern India, certain aborigines of southern Asia, and inhabitants of many Pacific islands, mainly Polynesia).

3. *Mediterraneans* (from Iran, ancient Persians, Pelasgians, peninsular Arabians, Philistines, Akkadians, earliest Egyptians, Kretans, Libyans and other northern Africans, Sicans, Siculians, and Iberians).

4. *Iranians* (eastern Iranians and Hindus of India).

5. *Hamites* (otherwise called Ethiopians, of southern Iran, Baluchistan, and southwestern India; western Arabians centering on Yemen, Chaldeans, Amorites, Phoenicians, African Ethiopians, and later Egyptian conquerors),

6. *Kelts* (Pamirians, Paleo-Kelts or Furfooz-Grenelles, Neo-Kelts or Alpines, and Slavs).

7. *Nordics* (originally the Getae as a nation, embracing later tribes of the Suebi (including Angles, Frisians, Swedes, and Norwegians); the Kimmerii (including the Medians, Kurds, Dorians, Montenegrins, Albanians, Lithuanians, Latvians, Old Prussians, most Europeans westward from the Main and Rhine Rivers except the primitive Mediterraneans and Kelts); the Getae or Goths

(now of southern Sweden, Italy, and Spain,
and the Alani); the Sarmatians (Ukranians
and Poles — a composite of Kimmerii and
Getae); and the Massagetae (of Bactriana)
and the Sakae (of Sogdiana).

Certain similarities in the evolution of the Turanian
and the Aryan races indicate that each, in its own region,
the one in the east and the other in the west of Asia, developed through corresponding stages. For example, it
appears that before the Würm I glaciation an Eskimo
type emerged from primitive dark and coarse Turanian
stock in Indo-China and a Cro-Magnard type emerged
from analogous Aryan stock that had settled in central
India, the Indus River valley, and Iran. They are the
oldest distinctive types of these two races. These types
had marked resemblances, each medium in stature, strong,
intelligent, dolichocephalic but disharmonic, with broad
faces and brunet complexions. Concurrently, an harmonic
dolichocephalic type was evolving in each race, the one in
the Min River valley in Szechuen province, western
China, and the other in the Indus River basin and lower
Iran. That of the Turanian race (the Min branch) is
found very little in its purity anywhere away from
Szechuen. As the Eskimos moved northward along the
westerly slopes of the Khingan Mountains, dolichocephalic Min groups followed behind, settling in the territory
traversed by the Hwang Ho or Yellow River from Kansu
to the coast. The latter since then have been largely submerged in the Ugrian, Amerind, Chinese, and other
branches in northern China, Korea, Japan, and North
America. In the west the corresponding harmonic dolichocephalic element of the Aryan race, comprising the Indonesian, Mediterranean, Iranian, and Hamitic branches,
inhabited western India and the Iranian plateau.
We may carry the analogy further. The next differentiations in each basic race (the Ugrians, Tunguses, Turki,
and Paraoeans, of the one, and the Paleo-Kelts and Neo-
Kelts, of the other) were all brachycephalous. They devel-

oped subsequent to the Würm II glacial peak on the great highlands of Asia, the Turanians in eastern and central Tibet and the river valleys on its slopes and the Aryans chiefly in northwestern Tibet, Ladak, and the Pamirs. These later races from the high and cold regions were invigorated by the more temperate climate in each instance and, when descending to the lowlands, they drove the earlier races before them. Other analogous evolutions in the two major races were the Chinese, of the Turanian race, and the Nordics, of the Aryan race, both mesocephalous. They moved from less high regions to their respective lowland regions more or less contemporaneously and gained the ascendancy over the earlier peoples that they encountered.

The migration of each of the above-named racial branches now will be traced to its present habitation or habitations on the earth. These subracial names are the "working tools" by means of which this subject is developed in the following pages. Because of their numerous divisions and places of migration and their later interrelationships, they will be mentioned repeatedly, sometimes alone and at other times in conjunction with others; therefore, it is urged that the reader have their names well in mind as he begins to travel imaginatively along the routes that they followed. Suitable maps will greatly aid in tracing their ramifications.

---

3. *Pre-Dravidian and Dravidian Races.* This congeries of somewhat diversified groups embraces approximately 60,000,000 people who inhabit the Dekkan and southerly and southeasterly regions of India, parts of northeastern India, southern Malay peninsula, and parts of the East India Islands. Some of them cannot readily be classified with the Black, Yellow, or Brown races. Included are descendants of the aboriginal peoples of India crossed with negroid from the Ganges River valley, with primitive Turanians east of them, or in some instances with early Indo-

nesians and later Iranian Hindu invaders from the north-west. The pure Dravidians probably were the southerly division of the so-called Indonesians of northern India[2] prior to the invasions by Iranians.

The primitive Pre-Dravidian groups may represent collateral branches of the primordial human stock that seem formerly to have inhabited the lower shores of the Bay of Bengal, from which the original stock of the three recognized major divisions of mankind evolved later in Burma and Indo-China, in the Ganges River valley, and on the highlands of the Dekkan and in western India.[2] They appear to have descended from inferior strains left behind when the stronger and more aggressive tribes migrated northward to more favorable climes. They probably have undergone less diversification from the primal stock than have the members of the three major races because of the continuity of their environment. Thus, they may constitute a fourth and low-cultured subdivision of the human race, whose advancement has been meager from the remotest times.

The last advancing (Würm II) glaciation forced Indonesians (the early Brown race) southward from the middle Indus River valley and eastward along the Himalayan foothills, where they sundered the Indafricans of the Ganges valley into two divisions that moved eastward and westward respectively, except for a few groups that were scattered southward and southeastward in India. Thereupon, these Indonesians occupied all of northern India as far eastward as the foothills and mountains of Burma, the present boundary between the Aryan and Turanian races. Then, long afterward, when the foremost Iranians (Hindus) appeared in India across the Suliman Mountains, they pressed western Indonesians eastward in India and beyond and southward to the highlands of the Dekkan. Dravidians of the Dekkan pressed farther south intermingled and in-

---

2 "It is the Pre-Dravidian aborigines, and not the later and more cultivated Dravidians, who must be regarded as the primitive existing race. These Pre-Dravidians . . . are differentiated from the Dravidian classes by their short stature and broad (platyrhine) noses . . . ." E. Thurston, *The Madras Presidency* (Cambridge, 1913), pages 124-125.

terbred with and absorbed some of the Pre-Dravidian tribes there encountered, but this contact did not greatly alter the dialects of the aboriginals, driven to the southeastern slopes. These Indonesians probably were akin to the darker Dravidian race, but were a more advanced division. In later times there was a marked commingling with them of Iranian Hindus from the northwest, with qualitative advantage.

Notwithstanding these migrations, the diversified aboriginals, the Indonesians and Dravidians, and the Hindus are distinguishable today. The first group and some of the second represent the depressed classes of past centuries. The jungle tribes of India, the Veddas of Ceylon, and the Sakai of the southern Malay peninsula represent Pre-Dravidian elements. The tribes of the Brahui, in the mountains of Baluchistan, appear to be Pre-Dravidians who migrated westward from India, perhaps in consequence of the first invasion of that country by Iranian Hindus.

While there are approximately 222 different dialects in India, they may be arranged in three classes, (1) the Dravidic of the numerous Pre-Dravidian and Dravidian tribes of the peninsula, (2) the Hindic of the successive waves of invaders of western India from Iran, and (3) the Sanskrit of the Nordic invaders from Bactriana and Sogdiana. In view of the commingling of diverse groups in the peninsula, it is not surprising that both Aryan and Turanian types are found and that their dialects have both Aryan and Turanian characteristics. The 13 Dravidian languages in 1901 had the following numbers of speakers: Telugu 21,000,000, Tamil 18,000,000, Kanarese 11,000,000, Malayalam 6,500,000, and others about 2,000,000.[2½] The Tamil-Kanarese-Malayalam dialects as a kindred group are related to but were remotely separated from the Telugu, toward which the Kui and Gondi dialects gradually approach. The remainder of the dialects are related to the one or the other of the two principal groups. Most of these people inhabit the oldest geological formation of

---

[2½] Include the dialects named and also Tulu, Kodagu, Toda, Kota, Kurux, and Malto.

India, mainly the central plateau, but the fact that some still persist in northern India proves that they also lived there prior to the invasions by the Iranians (Hindus). Difference of dialect now isolates those in northern India from the other inhabitants of that region.

The primitive Australians appear to have descended from a cross-breed of the earliest Indonesians (Dravidians) in northern India with Indafricans that they pushed eastward and westward from the country as the Würm II glacial peak approached about 50,000 years ago.[3] They differ in many respects from the present inhabitants of the Dekkan. Thus, they must have inherited most of the physical build of the Indonesian and the color, wide nostrils, and mentality of the Indafrican.

Apparently, the Pre-Dravidian Veddas[4] had an important part in transmitting the primitive culture of India to Europe. A division of them, known to anthropology as the Brünn (Brüx, Pred-most, Combe-Cappelle, and Galley Hill) race, seems to have been forced from the lower Indus valley by Dravidians on the east or by the expansion of Indonesians southeastward from the Punjab, more likely the latter. They moved across the Suliman Mountains to Iran and many centuries later, upon southward migrations on that plateau, to its westerly hills as far as the Caucasus region. Ultimately, about 27,000 years ago this pressure in central Iran dislodged both the Brünn and the Cro-Magnon nations and they emigrated to Europe. The former moved along the southerly shore of the Black Sea and across the Bosphorus to the Danube valley and central Europe and the latter moved by way of Syria, northern Africa and the Iberian peninsula to western Europe. The Brünn people must have been brunet and were dolichocephalous (from 68 to 72 per cent), with small skull, short face, and prognathic profile; in all probability, they were of mediocre mental capacity. These people introduced the distinctive and important Solutrean cul-

3 V. Gordon Childe, *More Light on the Most Ancient East* (Appleton-Century, New York, 1934), page 208.
4 Described by A. C. Haddon, *The Races of Man* (MacMillan 1925), p. 115.

ture into Europe, but it is doubtful whether they deserve the credit for its development. It represented the culmination of the flint industry and apparently reflected the contemporaneous level of Aryan civilization in India and more particularly in central Iran and probably was appropriated by them. The great similarity of the Solutrean laurel-leaf spearheads to the Azilian-Tardenoisian flints of the Mediterranean race, which entered Europe from the south much later, proves the early cultural contact of these two races before their emigration from the Iranian plateau. The movement of the Brünn race from Iran to the Caucasus region before emigrating to Europe is revealed by the finding of Solutrean artifacts of the Old Stone Age in that region. None of this race is believed to have survived the later harsh conditions of life in Europe during the minor Achen glaciation, one or two thousand years after their arrival there.

---

4. *Black* (*or Indafrican*) *Race.* The various primitive racial groups in the East Indies, Melanesia, Micronesia, and Polynesia may be classified as Indafrican, Indonesian (Polynesian), southern Mongoloid, and composites of these, such as the Malayans. As already inferred, primitive *Homo sapiens* must have evolved through an approximate negroid configuration of dark complexion in the Malayan peninsula and on both shores of the Bay of Bengal, with the earliest subsequent diversifications of the three major races having occurred in Burma and eastward, in the Ganges River valley, and on the highlands of the Dekkan and Western India. Certain negroid aborigines of Malaya, southern India, the Pacific archipelagos, and central Africa probably represent early branches of this primordial stock, members of which, during the approach of the last great glaciation, emigrated eastward and westward. But the greatest Negro migration from northern India to the east and to the west must have occurred during the Würm II glaciation about 50,000 years ago, when Indonesian tribes in the upper Indus valley were driven

southward by the cold, moved eastward along the Himalayan foothills, turned southward and split the Negroes into two divisions, and dispossessed them of the Ganges valley. Each successive upward step in culture in northern India had the effect of creating as many different strata of society; hence, it is only a natural consequence that the indigenous population of India, the eastern archipelagos and central Africa should be a congeries of subraces speaking many different dialects and representing various stages of culture. To this situation has been added the influence of various Turanian and Iranian invasions of some of those regions at subsequent times.

During the last major (Würm II) glaciation, the Sahara desert was drying up rapidly and forming an extensive barrier between northern Africa and central Africa, so that the latter became the principal abode of the Indafrican or Black race. Its various tribes since have expanded southward. Certainly none of these people entered Africa by way of Egypt, since the population of northern Africa never was negroid but comprised almost wholly major proportions of the Brown race (Mediterranean and Hamitic divisions)[5] until intrusions of Turkic blood during the regime of Hyksos kings in Egypt and Negroes from the south in later centuries.

The Indian source of the primitive Africans[6] is confirmed by the fact that the oldest of the present races in India, the Pre-Dravidian of the south — believed also related to the Australian and island aborigines — possesses more or less negroid features. In the hill country of Kumau, along the Himalayas, are descendants of aboriginal Negroes left behind. They are called *Rawats, Rajis,* or *Doms.* But, while the other races in the higher, drier, and more changeable and stimulating climates of the Tibetan and Iranian slopes and plateaus evolved into the modern

5 Further proof is the fact that the Negro race did not reach the Canary Islands, but both the later Cro-Magnon and Mediterranean races did so from North Africa, as also did the Turkic people of the eastern Mediterranean in sea-going commerce during Neolithic times and the Hamitic Phoenicians during historic times.

6 See J. C. Prichard, *Physical History of Mankind* (Houlston and Stoneman, London). vol. IV, pp. 228-233.

Yellow-Red and Brown-White races, the primitive Negroes who emigrated to the hot and more uniform and enervating climates of the eastern archipelagos and central Africa stagnated and became dormant insofar as marked social advancement is concerned. The living conditions in those regions probably did not differ greatly from the conditions under which these people had lived in northern India before the Würm II glaciation. They subsequently became highly specialized and their Negro tendencies became more accentuated in the torrid zone, but otherwise in general physical configuration they probably have not differentiated markedly from the original common stem in Malaya. The pygmies, who likewise evolved in Malaya, possess negroid features; so that, in spite of other differences in their development, they are properly classifiable as a branch of the Black race.

When the Negroes crossed southern Arabia and entered Africa during the Würm II glacial advance and ultimately spread westward and southward in that continent, they exterminated[7] or drove ahead the earlier branches of humanity that resisted their advance, chiefly *Homo Neanderthalensis,* when many of the latter race escaped across the Gibraltar land bridge to western Europe. Some of these Indafricans, known as the *Grimaldi,* later crossed this land bridge behind Neanderthalers and introduced the Aurignacian culture into Europe. The fact that traces of this culture have been found in southern India, Kurdistan, Syria, Palestine, and regions of eastern Africa[8] is evidence that this was the course of migration of the latest Indafricans to Africa. Unlike their earlier congeners, the Grimaldi must have been a late tribe that crossed Africa north of the Sahara Desert and followed the last Neanderthalers to Europe.

Recently-found evidence of the existence of Neanderthal man in Palestine and Syria subsequent to 35,000 years

7 In 1955 Cambridge University scientists reported the finding of a human jawbone, apparently of Neanderthal man, and other relics with it at least 40,000 years old.

8 V. Gordon Childe, *New Light on the Most Ancient East* (Appleton-Century, New York, 1934), pp. 30-31.

ago indicates that the earlier and principal Indafrican migrants did not go this way but crossed southern Arabia to reach central Africa. The existence of Neanderthal man in Africa is proved by the finding of late Paleoanthropic implements of the Mousterian culture. The Neanderthaler had his last inning in western Europe, where he finally was exterminated by early modern man after the latter entered that continent at intervals beginning about 40,000 years ago.

Thus, the earliest branch of *Homo sapiens* to invade Europe apparently was the Grimaldi of the Indafrican race, with its Aurignacian culture. These people arrived apparently soon after the turn of the last (or Würm II) glacial period, approximately 40,000 years ago. Their skeletons have a negroid aspect, similar to the Oldoway skeleton found in 1914 in German East Africa, and they had a custom of finger mutilation that until recent times has been observed among the Bushmen and the Hottentots of Africa. There was a long interval (15,000 years) before the next race, the Brünn man, with the Solutrean culture, entered Europe by way of the Danube valley. The latter were followed soon afterward by the Cro-Magnards, the first of the Aryans, who invaded Europe by way of northern Africa and the Gibraltar route and introduced the Magdalenian culture there.

Among the most primitive members of the negroid race in the east are the Australians, Tasmanians, and Fijians. The largest center of true Negroes in this region is on the island of Papua, or New Guinea, whence they spread over the Melanesian and nearby islands. While in many respects these peoples differ widely among themselves and from the parental stock, those differences simply are the result of different migrations at long intervals, of the natural law of diversification in new regions, and of some commingling with subsequent races. They have sufficient characters in common with others of this race to justify their classification as descendants of Negroes from northern India or Malaya. All are very dark or black in color, with crisp, curly hair, except that an Indonesian strain produced cymotrichous (wavy) hair on the aboriginal Australians. Their culture is very low, their institutions are simple, their manners are rude, they have no traditions, and cannibalism is customary among them. The differences in their dialects prove not only remoteness of settlement on those islands but also the fact that they migrated thither in different groups and at different times. Their skill and tastes resemble those of the African Negroes, with whom they are most properly classifiable. Their language differs from that of the Indonesians (Polynesians). They are dolichocephalous where no interbreeding with brachycephalic races has occurred. Unlike the Indonesians, they are singularly unskillful mariners.

In addition to Africa, southern India, Australia, and Tasmania, the principal habitations of the Negro race at the present time are the Pacific islands of Papua, Bismarck, Louisiade, Solomon, Santa Cruz, New Hebrides, Loyalty, New Caledonia, Fiji, and small intervening islands. All of these islands except Papua are known as the Melanesian or Black islands.

This race, with the possible exception of presumed Pre-Dravidians who may have reached South America across the South Pacific, was the earliest in the oceanic world. It is strongly represented among the population of the Micronesian Islands of the Pacific, north of Melanesia, which comprise chiefly the Mariana, Pelew, Caroline, Marshall, and Gilbert Islands, where interbreeding also subsequently occurred with intruding Indonesians and southern Mongoloids.

The same succession of types of the Black race as exists in Africa is found in the Pacific region, from the pygmies of Borneo and the Philippines to the Negroes of Papua and Melanesia and the negroids of Micronesia. Included are the lowest peoples of mankind.

The so-called Nilotic Indafricans of the Upper Nile River region are simply the descendants of cross-breeds of Negroes of adjacent regions and Hamites of Ethiopia over a period of many centuries.

In common with their congeners in the East India

islands, the Indafricans of central Africa as a whole are illiterate, have no historical traditions or literary writings, and their meager culture is centered on voodoo and tom-tom practices. Intellectually, they are a retarded race. In the *Digest of South African Affairs* of March 18, 1960, Dr. H. F. Verwoerd, Prime Minister of the South African Union, stated that "The Black man is not capable of maintaining himself in his own state."

In an article by Thomas R. Henry in *The Evening Star* newspaper, of Washington, on February 1, 1957, it is said that, because of blood differences, the serum called "primiquine, sovereign cure for malaria [in white soldiers in Korea], which was developed late in the last war, doesn't work with colored races." It is common knowledge that the two races also developed different intellectual and psychological characteristics in addition to extremes of color through the ages.

Dr. J. C. D. Carothers, in an article entitled *Frontal Lobe Function and the African* in the *Journal of Mental Science* of January, 1951,[9] says that 10 years of experience in an African hospital for mental diseases led him to the belief that the African native of the Negro race in his natural environment is remarkably like a western European who has had the front lobes of his brain disconnected (or like a "constitutional psychopath"). He is unable to see individual acts as a part of a whole situation and is subject to frenzied anxiety, but is free from the more complex types of mental illness. He lives in a world of sound rather than of sight and behaves as if the higher centers of his brain were relatively unused.

The author, John Gunther, in an article entitled *A Visit to Albert Schweitzer*,[10] winner of the Nobel prize after an experience of nearly five decades as a medical missionary among the Negroes of French Equatorial Africa, writes as follows regarding Dr. Schweitzer's observation of those people:

9 Vol. 97, pp. 12-48. See also writing by the same author entitled *African Mind in Health and Disease; A Study in Ethnopsychiatry* (Geneva, Switzerland; World Health Organization, 1953; Monograph Series No. 17, 177 pages).
10 *The Reader's Digest*, Pleasantville, N. Y., August, 1954, pages 43-49.

One can forgive his irritation at Africans who are too stupid or lazy to help him tend his trees. He said, 'I put a mango here, a banana there, a breadfruit here. The Africans do not know enough to tell which tree is which. I explain. They walk away and by the time they reach the river in ten minutes they have forgotten'.

I got the impression that he has little belief in the capability of Africans — at least in his own area — for self-government . . .

In the United States, with its 15,000,000 Negroes, descendants of African slaves imported into the country during colonial times and a period afterward, three distinct classes of them are discernible, viz., (1) the pure Negro, the vast majority, who seldom can graduate from secondary school, (2) the Negro whose ancestors gained Hamitic or Moorish blood in their veins before leaving Africa, relatively few in number, and (3) the Negro whose ancestors gained White blood after their arrival in America. The last two classes, chiefly the third, supply practically all of the Negro students of our colleges.

In the September 21, 1956, issue of *U. S. News & World Report,* of Washington, there appeared a documented article entitled *A Scientist's Report on Racial Differences* by Dr. Frank C. J. McGurk, Associate Professor of Psychology at Villanova University, from which the following paragraphs on the subject of racial integration are excerpted.

As far as psychological differences between Negroes and Whites are concerned, we have wished — and dreamed — that there were no such differences. We have identified this wish with reality, and on it we have established a race-relations policy that was so clearly a failure that we had to appeal to distorting propaganda for its support. When that, too, failed, we appealed to the legal machinery to do what nature was not content to do.

As will be shown in the succeeding sections of this article, there is ample evidence that there are psychological differences between Negroes and Whites. Moreover, those differences are today of about the same magnitude as they were two generations ago. *These differences are not the result of differences in social and economic opportunities,* and they do not disappear as the social and economic opportunities of Negroes and Whites are equalized.

The Educational Testing Service, in a recent report issued at Princeton, New Jersey, shows that in a nationwide educational test of 24 segregated and integrated colleges and universities in the country only 5 percent of the Negroes achieved as well as the *average* White student. From the standpoint of capability of the Negro for self-government and the probable effects of judicial enforcement of social commingling of the two races, the scientific usefulness of this test would have been greater if it had indicated in what degree the results for the Negro had been enhanced by racial interbreeding or what the results might have been if full-blooded Negroes had been the subjects of the test. The same may be said about all data pertaining to the achievements of offspring of members of widely dissimilar races. Mulattos are very susceptible to Communist influence.

Negroes now constitute approximately 55 per cent of the population of the District of Columbia (Washington proper, excluding the Maryland and Virginia suburbs) and the proportion is increasing with migration from the South. Their offspring comprise about 75 per cent of the school children, many of whom are illegitimate of birth, and 85 per cent of the crime is committed by Negroes. The ratio of narcotic addicts among Negroes and Whites is shown by government statistics to be 22 to 1 respectively.

History demonstrates that the social commingling of members of advanced and retarded races results in illicit moral relations, with retrogressive effects on the higher race. The Soviet Union segregates its Aryan and Turanian school pupils in its Asiatic regions, and efforts of India to integrate Hindus and so-called "Untouchables" have met with only meager success.[11]

The retardation of the Indafrican (Negro) race may be attributed chiefly to its evolution and the enervating effect of its habitation in the torrid climate of the Ganges River valley for perhaps hundreds of thousands of years prior to its migration to the East Indies and to Africa, and also to its subsequent habitation in similar climates for the last 40,000 or more years. The nearest analogy to the status of the Negro is that of the American Indian (Amerind), whose ancestral stock in the frigid Arctic region in Siberia seems to have evolved in somewhat higher degree than that of the Negro in the torrid zone of Africa as early as 20,000 years ago. The earliest Indian tribes migrated to the milder climate of the present United States between 10,000 and 20,000 years ago. Their evolution upward during this long period must have been imperceptible. Therefore, hopefulness in this respect for the Negro is scarcely justifiable over the distant future and with it intelligent participation in a democratic electorate, if irresponsibility is to be avoided.

---

5. *Yellow-Red (or Turanian) Race.* This primary race comprises numerous derivatives or subraces. During the Laufen retreat and the last (or Würm II) glaciation it continued to develop, migrate, and expand in a moderate climate over the vast region around the easterly base of the Tibetan plateau, extending from Indo-China, on the south, through Yunnan, Szechuen, and Shensi provinces to Mongolia, on the north. Contemporaneously, several branches of the Brown-White (or Aryan) race, which had spread northward and westward, were experiencing severely cold climatic conditions in and near the higher val-

11 Actually, as shown later in this book, the Hindus are light-brown and the 'Untouchables' are dark-brown branches of the same (Aryan) race; the former evolved on the plateau of Iran and moved into India, whereas the latter remained in the hotter valleys and lowlands of India. Consequently, this is not a case of dissimiliar races but merely a difference in shade of complexion because of ancient climatic differences.

leys of the Indus River and in Iran. The various Turanian subraces range from dolichocephalous to brachycephalous in type, the degree of the latter depending on the duration of their habitation at high elevations. Included are the *Eskimos, Mins, Northern Amerinds, Ugrians* (with *Finns, Bolgarians,* and *Magyars*), *Neo-Amerinds, Tunguses* or *northern Mongolians* (with *Manchu-Koreans*), *Chinese, Japanese, Turki, Paraoeans or southern Mongoloids* (the broadheaded element in the Malayans and Japanese), and others.

The *Bushmen* of South Africa apparently represent an exceedingly early branch of the Turanian race paralleling the Pygmies of the Black race. The former, diminutive in stature, of a dirty yellow color, with slightly slanting eyes and prominent cheekbones, probably evolved on the slopes of southeastern Tibet and were driven to the lowlands of India by the increasing cold of the Würm II glaciation. While there, the return of the Indonesians from the northwest because of the glacial effect on the highlands split the Negroes (Indafricans) as already related, forcing some eastward and the major number westward to Africa, and the progenitors of the Bushmen must have gone along with the latter. Thus, their descendants today ordinarily are classified with the Negroes.

There is evidence in all directions that the underlying stratum in east-central China was a primitive, rather tall and handsome, dolichocephalic people, apparently the original long-headed branch of the Turanian race. They have since been largely absorbed by other races that overran eastern China, Korea, and Japan, but evidence of their commingling with the various groups is unmistakable from data of the cephalic indexes and other physical features. They seemingly represented the earliest expansion of the Turanian race around the Tibetan baselands to western China, centering in the fertile Min River valley in the province of Szechuen, where millions of their descendants live today. To this subrace the name of *Min* is here applied, from the valley in which these people seem to have settled and thrived and from which they expanded very early to populate the Chinese lowlands.

Upon the return of warmth as the Würm II glaciation diminished, many Turanian tribes from the lower lands began to ascend the numerous river courses on the southeasterly and easterly slopes of the Tibetan highlands. Three of the greatest rivers in the world, the Salween, the Makong, and the Yangtze, rise in central Tibet at altitudes of 10,000 to 15,000 feet and sweep down those slopes. The first flows through eastern Burma to the Bay of Bengal, the second flows between Thailand and French Indo-China to the South China Sea, and the third flows generally eastward across China to the Pacific Ocean near Shanghai. The upper reaches of these rivers are as yet imperfectly known. They start southeastward and soon converge and flow southward for many miles parallel with each other through deep gorges within an east-and-west distance of 50 miles before they begin to diverge, forming one of the geographical wonders of the world. Athwart these water passages the ascents and descents must be made over precipitous 8,000-foot slopes. It was in these and other isolated river valleys of this vast region that many Turanian subraces differentiated physically. Their long life at high altitudes is proved by their brachycephalic indices. Much of the life and culture of Asia has centered on these gorgeous water courses. The greatest profusion of flowers, trees, shrubs, and herbs, more or less intermingled, prevails in the mountain fastness of western China. Just above Likiang, in northern Yunnan, the timber-line extends up to 15,500 feet, with forests of spruces, firs, and larches up to 15,000 feet, while the last 500 feet is a vast rhododendron forest, with trees 25 to 30 feet high. This wild border region is now inhabited by various bandit tribes, speaking different languages.

In addition to the absorption of migrant branches of the Min race by subsequent races in eastern Asia, the commingling of Ugrians, Mongolians, and Turks in Siberia has since produced miscellaneous composite peoples now found in northern Asia and European Russia.

A discussion of the various Turanian subraces follows.

(5a) *Eskimo Subrace.* The Eskimos, now living in northeastern Asia, North America, and Greenland, appear to correspond in the Turanian race with the Cro-Magnon people of the Iranian race in having been the earliest type to emerge after the diversification of these primary races on the southerly Himalayan slopes. Like the Cro-Magnards, they are dolichocephalous and disharmonious, with broad face and high cheek-bones. Consequently, they did not evolve on the Tibetan highlands. They seemingly moved northeastward across the base of that plateau and developed largely on the lower lands of western China, probably in the region north of the Wei River in Shensi province. The time of their settlement there was about 35,000 years ago, during the Würm II retreat of the last glaciation. As their numbers increased, various tribes moved up the Hwang River and comprised the Ugrian population of the Altai Mountains and northward.

This similarity between the Eskimos and Cro-Magnards may have more than ordinary significance. It tends to prove that the Turanian and Aryan races diverged very early from a single stem of the primordial stock somewhere along the easterly shore of the Bay of Bengal, one division eventually moving northeastward along the foothills of the Himalayas and the other moving westward to the peninsular plateau of India. With the passage of time, differences of environment and climate caused increasing diversification of those divisions, resulting in the two primary races. Thus, having started with a single culture in the south, it should not be strange if marked similarities be discernible between the primitive culture of the Eskimos in northern China and that of the Cro-Magnards centered at Dordogne, France. In fact, resemblances are reported as having been discovered by Dr. H. A. Ami, Canadian anthropologist.

Some 15,000 years afterward, the Eskimos moved down the Hwang (or Yellow) River to eastern Mongolia, settling perhaps along the slopes of the Khingan Mountains. In that region the main body appears to have remained a long time, since it was not dislodged as subsequent migra-

tions of other Turanians toward the Bering Strait passed
on each side of those mountains. But it is probable that
scattering bands detached themselves or were driven from
the main body and moved away, some perhaps northeastward, whence they crossed to North America. Artifacts
of not later than 27,000 years ago have been found in
Mongolia, which is the oldest large expanse of dry land
on the globe, not having been submerged within the last
20,000,000 or more years. It was not until the Chinese
moved down the Hwang River about 3000 B.C. and forced
Tungus (or northern) Mongolians northward that the
Eskimos were driven into the far north, whence they scattered themselves across northeastern Asia, North America
about 1500 miles north of Winnepeg, Canada, and Greenland. The medial complexion of the Eskimos of today
demonstrates that they have not been in the extremely
cold north as long as the Ugrians and Nordics have
been subjected to such climate. In fact, they may not
have reached their present Arctic habitations in Asia and
North America until after the beginning of the Christian
era.

(5b) *Min Subrace.* While the forerunners of the Eskimos were finding their way to and along the middle upper
courses of the Hwang River, the main Turanian division moved northward and settled in the fertile valley
of the province of Szechuen, along the upper Yangtze
(or Blue) River. This valley is traversed by the Min River
and other tributaries of the Yangtze, and it is only about
1600 feet above sea level. Such ancient settlement of
Szechuen is indicated by the fact that today it is the most
densely populated part of China. With an area of not
over 218,000 square miles, about the combined areas of
Arizona and Colorado, it is reputed to have a population of 60,000,000. These primitive people have remained
a dolichocephalic and harmonic race, and in many respects they bear a close analogy in the Turanian race to
the Mediterraneans or Iranians of the Aryan race. In general physique, they probably more closely resemble the

early Iranians than does any other branch of the Turanian race.

In course of time, as the population increased, some Min tribes moved down the Yangtze River to the coastal regions of China, where they expanded in all directions, mainly northward. After the temperature rise in central Asia had accelerated the Würm II glacial regression on the highlands, it is believed that other tribes from the Szechuen Valley ascended the upper reaches of the Yangtze River to eastern Tibet, where they settled in different valleys. There ultimately they diversified into other important branches of the Turanian race, mainly, the Tunguses (or Northern Mongolians), the Turki, and the Sinicus (or Chinese), as described later.

There is some indication that the *Cheremissions* or *Mari*, who now live about Kazan, on the Volga River, in Russia, and who are mainly dolichocephalous, are a remnant of this Min race; also, certain similar people who reside around Lake Ladoga, south of Finland. They may have migrated from Manchurian territory westward across central Asia and Europe or by a direct route from Szechuen across Turkistan during the last millennium.

The Mins are recognized as a human stratum underlying all the Turanian races that afterward occupied central and northern China successively — the Ugrians, Tungus Mongolians, and Chinese — and also embraced the earliest Amerinds. They are particularly identifiable as a component strain of the Manchus, Koreans, and Japanese. In World War II they were the tall Japanese marines encountered by the American forces, easily distinguished from the Malayan Japanese. Hence, it is not strange that marked similarity between pottery of New Stone Age aborigines of Japan and that of the early Amerinds of Canada and the United States should have been found.

Remnants of this race are rarely found anywhere in Asia in a state of purity except in Szechuen. With the possible exclusion of some detached and scattered bands of primitive Eskimos, they apparently were the earliest branch of *Homo sapiens* to move northeastward along the Asiatic coast toward the Bering Sea; some may have reached North America as early as 22,000 years ago and the north-central American plains a millennium or so later by way of the Mackenzie River. This is indicated by skeletal remains found in various parts of this country, such as those of a young woman of the Mongoloid type recently unearthed in Ottertail County, Minnesota. Among their purest representatives today are probably the earlier of the North Amerinds (Indians) of eastern North America. Their dolichocephalic index proves that they lived at the lower latitudes. They were followed to America by other scattering bands over long intervals, probably between 17,000 and 14,000 years ago, but more is known of those who came much later. At the Bering Sea these Amerinds apparently crossed in rudely equipped skin boats, unless there was then still a land bridge.

The later Mins arrived about 8000 B.C., in consequence of a disturbance of Turks in central Asia at a time of increasing warmth, and most of them finally moved in the wake of melting northern glaciers to the central plains, the Mississippi Valley, and the northern and eastern woodlands. Others turned southward and ultimately reached as far as lower South America. They may not have realized that they were going to a new continent.

Min tribes apparently did not reach Japan from Korea until sometime after a tribe of Paleo-Kelts of the Aryan race, driven from Kashmir or the Pamirs by the Turks about 8000 B.C., had crossed central Asia from the Tarim basin and reached the islands. An influx of Mins in Japan later forced these Whites to the far North, where their descendants, known as the *Ainus,* are found today. Thus, we apparently have the curious circumstance that Japan was first settled by the White branch of *Homo sapiens,* which somewhere incurred a noticeable Turanian strain.

The culture of these later Min tribes may have been in the Neolithic stage, gained by contact with the Turks in Kansu province, in western China. As later shown, the primitive Turks (or Tatars) were the most advanced race in central Asia and evolved or developed the Neolithic culture, which they introduced into western Asia (Mesopotamia) about 8000 B.C. The Northern Amerinds in the northeasterly part of the United States were found to display noteworthy capability for political organization and government.

The earlier and more easterly Amerinds were largely dolichochephalous, but the later arrivals generally were found to tend toward brachycephaly. These facts not only indicate that they arrived at irregular intervals but also distinguish the various subraces in Asia to which they belonged at the time that each tribe emigrated to the American continent. Since those in the west were the later arrivals, their greater cephalic index is of especial significance in this connection; for it is apparent that they were followed or were pressed from behind in Asia by the shorter and brachycephalic Ugrians of Siberia, later described. The foregoing facts tend to demonstrate that the order of emigration from Asia must have been approximately of this pattern: First, tribes of the Min nation, later tribes of the Tunguses or Manchu nation; and, finally, tribes of the Ugrians of interior Siberia, perhaps with tribes of hybrid groups at intervening periods.

The Bureau of American Ethnology is charged with the functions of analyzing and classifying the numerous tribes of Amerinds and their languages or dialects, customs, habits, and so on.

(5c) *Ugrians.* Seemingly, the first brachycephalic division of the Turanian race to move from the northeastern Tibetan highlands to the lower lands of Mongolia was the Ugrians. Their broadheadedness proves that they lived thousands of years at high altitude. Their grayish or olive-colored skin reveals their Turanian origin and the fact that gray or blue eyes prevail among them and other personal characteristics prove their long habitation in cold northern climates. It is probable that they and the Eskimos originated in the same stock, but that the former migrated up the Wei and upper Hwang rivers in Shansi province to the region of Lake Koko Nor during the warm Laufen glacial retreat (about 67,000 years ago) while the Eskimo remained at a lower altitude. Approximately 32,000 years ago, when the Mongolian tribes spread over northeastern Tibet and down its northerly slopes, these Ugrians were driven again to the lower lands and moved across Shansu and Shensi, where they overspread lower Mongolia from the Altai Mountains, on the west, to the Khingan Mountains, on the east.

Today the Ugrians are scattered widely over northern Siberia and European Russia in consequence of the pressure of other tribes behind them. In the west, they embrace the Lapps, Finns, Estonians, and Livonians. They are a squat, sluggish people, suspicious, taciturn, conservative, patient, industrious, and honest. As a race, they are deficient in energy, unprogressive, and, with the exception of the Finnic branch, have little or no ability for political organization. These traits are attributable to stagnation resulting from long life in the harsh climate near the Arctic circle. Because of lack of contact, their progenitors received practically none of the early culture developed by the Turks in central Tibet and in the Turkistans.

A division of Ugrians very early migrated westward by Lake Baikal to the headwaters of the Yenisei River, just north of the Sayan Mountains, where they became the ancestors of the Finns and their offshoots, the Estonians and Livonians. There they were anciently known as the *Tschudes or Chudes*. The name of the modern Finnic nations is *Suomi,* a short form of Suomen Tasavalta, meaning "the land of a thousand lakes." Upper Paleolithic discoveries prove the migration of these people across Shensi to the Yenisei River valley of Siberia.[12] Other Ugrians migrated directly westward from Mongolia and settled at the headwaters of the Irtish River, became subjects of and ultimately interbred with Turkic *Issedones* from Turkistan, and produced the later Bolgarian and Hungarian nations, which subsequently moved to the northerly basin of the Volga River. Later some of them

---

12 George G. MacCurdy, *Human Origins* (Appleton, New York, 1926), p. 201.

settled in central Europe. To these nations the Ugrians contributed lightness of eyes and complexion and the Turks contributed greater brachycephaly and alertness of temperament. The Samoyeds are other Ugrians that moved northwestward in Siberia.

Another Ugrian division moved eastward very early toward the Chinese coast, where it seems to have commingled with some of the ancient dolichocephalic substratum. Groups of these mixed Ugrian-Min people followed bands of Mins across to North America in consequence of increasing pressure of Tunguses behind them. There they are recognizable as the late elements of the Northern Amerinds and the early elements of the Neo-Amerinds of Haddon, reflecting the increasing brachycephaly of the people found from east to west across North America. This implies an increasing proportion of Ugrian blood among the later arrivals of Northern Amerinds, while the Neo-Amerinds that followed them were almost wholly of Ugrian origin.

The culture of the latter was more primitive than that of their predecessors in North America. They moved southward along the plateau of western United States and some settled there; others moved on to the Pacific Coast, to Mexico, and to Central and South America. They pushed eastward the earlier dolichocephalic Min tribes and later in turn found their country invaded by subsequent arrivals of Tunguses or northern Mongolians, who also had come from Asia and followed the American plateau to the south. The Indians of Guiana and the Arawaks of the West India Islands are Ugrian Neo-Amerinds. The Papago, Maya, Toltec, Huaxteca, and Totonac tribes of Mexico and Central America are uniformly brachycephalous and reflect Ugrian origin with a Mongolian strain. Thus, the Ugrian race had a major part in creating the remarkable civilizations of Mexico and Central America, whose influence reached South America and the southern part of the United States.

Not only the variable cephalic index and other physical features of different branches of the Ugrian race in both the Old and the New Worlds prove early interbreeding with the primitive Min race in China, but many Ugrian groups in northern Asia and Europe have in more recent times freely interbred with Tungus Mongolian and Turkic people and even with Slavic Kelts.

The language of all these people was of the agglutinative type, in which the addition of suffixes is the only method of word formation. Since their racial origin was Turanian, the same as that of the Turkic Pre-Sumerians and Sumerians of Mesopotamia, it is not strange that the language of the two peoples should reveal marked similarities. The fact that the more highly-developed agglutinative language of the Finns approaches the inflected European type merely proves the contact in historical times of the Finns with the Slavs and Nordics at and west of the Ural Mountains. The Ugrian races in Asia and Europe were hunters and fishers until relatively late times, probably 1500 B.C.

(5d) *Tunguses or Northern Mongolians.* Roughly about 32,000 years ago, a sizeable division of Turanians, probably Mins, moved up the Yangtze River and its tributaries to their headwaters in the Koko Nor province of northern Tibet, drove Ugrians northward and settled there. In the course of time, a substantial number moved southward to the lake region of central Tibet, to become the progenitors of the Turkic or Tataric race, who are treated later. Those who remained in Koko Nor were the progenitors of the present numerous Tunguses or northern Mongolians. Long habitation at the high altitude produced medial brachycephaly. Increase in numbers, drought, or famine in central Tibet caused the Turkic element to expand northwestward there, while the Mongolians expanded eastward into Kansu province and down the upper reaches of the Hwang River to southern Mongolia. Upon increasing coldness on the highlands about 22,000 years ago, the latter drove ahead of them Ugrians dislodged from Kansu and Eskimos from Shensi, whereupon the Eskimos settled upon the slopes of the Khingan Mountains, as stated before. This disturbance must have caused the emigration of the earliest Asiatics (Mins) to North America.

In central Tibet the Turks developed the rudiments of a relatively high culture, the Neolithic, equal to or more advanced than any then existent. Undoubtedly, it reached the Mongolians and was transmitted by them across Kansu province to Mongolia and northern China. In the south, a small group of Turks spread to the southerly slopes of the Himalaya Mountains in northern India, where their descendants live today.

In Mongolia, in addition to forcing the Ugrians farther northward and causing many of them ultimately to emigrate to North America, the Tunguses also absorbed or drove eastward the remnants of the dolichocephalic Min race that they encountered. Thus, some of the tribes became less brachycephalous than others. In the course of time, the commingled Mins and Tunguses spread over all Mongolia and finally occupied all of Manchuria, Korea, and Japan and they are the principal underlying race of the early Japanese people. They were represented in the blood of the later Neo-Amerinds that went to America. A detachment, known as the Northwest Coast Amerinds, comprised the latest migration to North America. Those in Mongolia became the progenitors of the Huns of history and of most of the Kalmucks of Mongolia, Siberia, and Russia today.

About 3000 B.C. a new Turanian element, the Sinicus, or Chinese, probably an offshoot of this early Min stock, came down the Hwang River from the easterly slopes of the Kuen-Lun Mountains and took possession of central China. This invasion gave marked impetus to movements of Mongolians northeastward along the Chinese coast of Manchuria and Korea. Various branches of the Tungus subrace still inhabit most of northern Asia from the Altai Mountains to the Japan Sea. They also absorbed the remaining Turkish element in Tibet and have settled over that highland. While they are a brachycephalic race, everywhere is evidence of the early blend of underlying dolichocephalic Min blood. It has been said that this Min stem of the Turanian race, which produced the most progressive divisions in the west (the various Turkic divisions), also has generated the largest number of outstanding individuals in China (along with the Sinicus) and in Japan. Perhaps diet and environmental advantages have been the major factors in the different evolution of these peoples.

The present Turko-Mongolian population of Tibet, the loftiest and loneliest country in the world, equals about 4,000,000. The land area is more than 1,000,000 square miles, or fully eight times the size of Great Britain. Its huge girdle of largely inaccessible mountains has kept the land isolated and unknown. Its fauna, birds, and flora are rare. It is a cradle-land of religion, that of Buddhism. The priests are the Lamas. The minds of the people are as simple as those of children. They are in the kindergarten stage of ideas and knowledge; their lives are full of sin and sorrow; they live in fear and they worship and die in doubt. Three days after death, a slit is made in the skull to allow the soul to pass out and the body then is put face downward on a large flat stone, to be cut into strips by the Lamas and fed to the vultures and hyenas. A Tibetan funeral is their feeding time. Concurrently the Lamas, who are cunning and crafty, but ignorant according to our lights, chant their peculiar and doleful songs of idolatry, while the superstitious crowd murmurs and curses the evil omens and ghosts as the animals scramble for the pieces of the body passed to them. Lamaism is a corruption of Indo-Chinese vagaries in the ruder interpretation of Buddhism. Living conditions of the people generally are filthy and dirty.[13]

Red hair is said to be indigenous to certain Finno-Ugrian tribes of western Siberia, such as the Votiaks, and is believed to have been transmitted to the White race by contact of the two races when the Whites inhabited or emigrated westward from the Lake Balkhash region. If, as

---

13 Many great libraries are said to exist in Tibet. Manuscripts and block-prints, for many centuries lost in India, have been discovered in Lhassa, the sacred city of the Lamas. Its artistic literature, bibles, and sacred scrolls are embodied in 16 different languages of nearly all Asiatic countries, from Iran to Japan; also in local and tribal scriptures.

reported, the Great Khan of the Mongol Empire during 1369-1405, Tamerlane, "was tall, strong, fair-skinned, red-haired, broad-shouldered, and muscular," then he must have been a descendant of the cross-breed of a Nordic Aryan and a Finno-Ugrian, whose family gained the ascendancy among the Mongols. As a matter of fact, the Mongols were a congeries of various Turanian subraces of northern Asia. During medieval times, some of their greatest leaders even intermarried with European royal families.

(5e) *American Indian (or Amerind) Subrace.* These peoples, already referred to several times, embraced many different immigrations to America. They represented both unmixed and mixed Turanian subraces, but in non-scientific circles they are usually treated as a single primary or "Red" race, with the following possible exception.

So far as we know now, a division of very early inhabitants of this hemisphere did not belong to the Red branch of the Turanian race. These people may have reached South America via the South Pacific islands when mountain peaks projected above the low water, during the height of a glacial period. If so, they must have been Pre-Dravidians originally from the peninsula of India. They apparently bore no affinity to the Eskimo type. For example, in the region of southern Peru and the Chilean coast there are today certain tribes of primitive origin, including the Aymara and other Quichua-speaking peoples, of whom the Incas were the most prominent nation. They are quite broad-nosed and seemingly represent a type intermediate to the Veddas of Ceylon and the Papuans. In the eastern Brazilian highlands and in Ecuador and Peru there is another very old type, short of stature, very dolichocephalous, with small and very high skull, short and wide face, concave nose of medial width, and prognathic profile, yellowish-brown skin, and long black wavy or curly hair, much like the Veddas. This type formerly existed widely in that continent. Some of these people may even have moved up the Pacific Coast and settled in Mexico and along the southern coast of California, where evidence of dolichocephalic people with broad noses and flat high heads has been found.

The famous Gateway of the Sun and the huge monoliths at Tiahuanaco, on the route from Lake Titicaca to La Paz, capital of Bolivia, denote a high civilization of great antiquity, dating back perhaps 10,000 or more years, according to the estimate of Professor Rudolf Müller, an eminent German scholar. His calculations are based on his own astronomical observations and the history revealed by the Tiahuanacans. The grandeur that was attained by the empire of the Incas is signified by the miraculous architectural feats performed by these people, who lived at an altitude in excess of 12,000 feet above sea level. They built with stones weighing hundreds of tons and are said to have kept them in place with bolts of solid silver. They erected gigantic and grandiose temples, palaces, pyramids, carved statues, monoliths, and a façade of 112 symbolic figures dominated in the center by a figure of the condor god or sun god. This city is characterized as one of the wonders of the world, absolutely unique, without resemblance elsewhere in architecture, sculpture, or culture.

These apparently non-Turanian South American people constitute the *Paleo-Amerinds* of Haddon. They may have migrated via Easter Island, which shows remains of a culture antedating the traditions of the earliest people definitely known to have settled there. The fact that those inhabitants of both places were so adept at handling huge monoliths weighing many tons tends strongly to confirm the hypothesis of a common racial origin, since this use of huge stone is the most conspicuous aspect of the two cultures. They must have moved across the South Pacific during the peak of the Bühl glacial advance,[13] when the islands formed a land bridge far more conspicuous than it is today, owing to the low level of the water in the ocean because of evaporation to form

14 About 10,000 years ago. It has been estimated that the oceanic water level at the peak of a glacial period is approximately 165 feet lower than it is during that part of interglacial periods after all of the glaciers have melted and have become water in the oceans.

the glaciers.[14] The larger island areas that then existed have been reduced by erosion from continual wave action.

If this inference be correct, then these first South Americans were not Turanians, unlike those who came later to the hemisphere. They may be classifiable among the modifications or variants of the Pre-Dravidian or other primitive tribes of the Bay of Bengal and adjacent regions. They do not resemble the Indonesians (Polynesians) of the Aryan race, who are a taller and more handsome people.

All later migrations to South America apparently came by way of Alaska and represented various Turanian subraces, of which the major ones are portrayed below. Despite the appearance of a single racial base to the Amerinds as a whole, the different subracial groups may be distinguished. They all reached North America by way of the Bering Sea, perhaps over the Aleutian Islands from Kamchatka. The time of the earliest arrival, probably 20,000 years ago, before nearly all of northern North America was covered by ice sheets, must have been during an interval of relative warmth. Many of these people are known to have been skilled in water craft. The hides of animals were used to make boats and sails for use in moving from island to island. The boats were large and capable of transporting perhaps 50 persons, with their dogs and supplies. The warmer water of the Japan current made North America more hospitable than northern Asia, with its Siberian ice sheet, and provided plenty of fish for food so long as they sailed along the shore islands.

These migrations from Asia were intermittent and at irregular intervals, dependent on glacial advances and retreats. The Amerinds of the various regions, representing a number of different physical types, revealed the racial divisions from which they came in Asia and their varying degrees of amalgamation, if any, with other groups that preceded or followed them. Different stages of culture also were represented. These differences must be recognized in order to facilitate proper classification. The suggestion that any of them contained a Melanesian strain is untenable for geographic reasons. The earlier arrivals were tall or medium in stature and dolichocephalous and practically all later groups were shorter and increasingly or wholly brachycephalous. Many were still in the hunting and fishing stage when Columbus arrived, although various peoples of the south, such as the Incas, Mayans, Toltecs, and Aztecs, had developed noteworthy civilizations even before the beginning of the Christian era.

Apparently, all of the arrivals from perhaps as early as 20,000 years ago to about 6500 B.C. represented different divisions of the Min subrace, which, with the exception of the Eskimo, seems to have been the chief dolichocephalic branch of the predominantly brachycephalic Turanian race. They are the *Northern Amerinds* of Haddon. They worked their way in the course of centuries from their habitation in the fertile valley of Szechuen, western China, down the course of the Yangtze River to the coastal plains and finally to the northeast. Thence they must have crossed to Alaska by way of the Bering Strait instead of over the Aleutian Islands, for they seem to have moved over the tundra of the Yukon and MacKenzie River valleys and between the Laurentide and Cordilleran ice sheets as they were melting and afforded an open roadway that extended along the westerly border of the great plains. Thus, some of the earliest relics of human habitation have been found in Colorado and New Mexico at the southeasterly edge of the Rocky Mountains. Skulls of these dolichocephalic aborigines have been discovered recently in caves in the Big Bend region of Texas. They lived in the southwest at a time when much of North America was covered by ice sheets and they hunted the bison, musk ox, and other animals. Their stone spearheads have been found in Texan lake bottoms and New Mexican caves associated with the bones of the musk ox. Since this animal thrived at the edge of the northern glaciers but apparently not in a warm climate, it is probable that with the continual diminution of the glaciers these animals moved northward, drawing the ancestors of the northern Indians with them in connection with their hunting. Ultimately, these people moved to the central plains of Canada and the United States, the Mississippi Valley, and the northern and eastern woodlands. They comprised the Indians of New England, the Lenni-Lenape, Iroquois, Chippewa, Blackfoot, Kootenai, and other eastern and central tribes, the Apaches, and perhaps the Pimas and Otomi in the southwest. Some also migrated to Mexico, since remains of a Mexican civilization that existed as far back as 8000 B.C. have been found.

The later arrivals embodied an Ugrian strain in increasing proportions, as disclosed by the variation in physical characteristics from the east to the west across North America. Evidently, the earlier Mins in northeastern Asia were driven ahead and the later members were largely absorbed by the more populous Ugrians behind them. Thus, while the earlier Mins in America represented dolichocephalic or mesocephalic types, the later arrivals revealed increasingly the brachycephalic Ugrian strain, which denoted a close contact of these two subraces as they converged in northeastern Asia. Some of these later migrants moved southward and are represented by early Mexicans and by the Patagonians (Tehuelche), the Pampans, and the Borroro tribes of Matto Grosso, Brazil.

The later Northern Amerinds appear to be related to the present Kamchadale and Karagasi tribes of Kamchatka and eastern Siberia, the Koryak and Tunguses of Kilyma and Anadyr regions, the Yukaghir and Oroch tribes in the east, and the Obi Ostiak and North Vogul tribes in the west. Their culture on arrival, with the possible exception of the latest tribes, was still in the Paleolithic stage. This signifies a lack of contact with the Neolithic culture later diffused by the Turks and Tunguses through Kansu and Shensi provinces in western China.

The next distinctive emigration to North America embraced successive groups of Ugrians, a shorter people, the first wholly brachycephalic division of the Turanian race. Their evolution and movement from the Tibetan highlands to the cold climate of the Lake Baikal region and to eastern

Asia already has been discussed. The fact that in the course of time the northwestern Ugrians tended to become blond while the eastern divisions, including those who came to North America, remained brunet in complexion denotes a long period of separation and early migration of the latter to the milder climate of this continent. These Ugrians are identical with the most typical *Neo-Amerinds* of Haddon. Many of the tribes had a marked Tungus strain and apparently through that blood had the benefit of early contact with the Neolithic culture diffused by the Turks in Kansu and Shensi, since the culture of certain migrants of as early as 6000 B.C. was of that kind. They may have crossed to America over the Aleutian Islands and moved down the Canadian coast, whence they dispersed to the plateau regions and then to Mexico and Central and South America. Among these peoples were such uniformly brachycephalic groups as the Papago, Maya, Toltec, Aztec, Huaxteca, and Totonac tribes of Mexico and Central America and also the Indians of Guiana and the Arawaks of the West Indies.[15] On the foundation of this Neolithic culture, some of these people erected their own noteworthy civilizations several millennia later in central Mexico and Central America.

It is due chiefly to their Ugrian blood that many living Amerinds have attributes in common with their kin in Asia, such as squat physique, scantiness of beard, lack of energy and liveliness, taciturnity, conservativeness, and a suspicious and vindictive nature when aroused.

The third distinctive migration to North America comprised representatives of the Tunguses or northern Mongolians, already described. While generally brachycephalous, some of the tribes had been modified by the doli-

15 Thus, it was reported by James Morris Morgan during 1885-1889 that a French Basque railroad construction foreman then employed on work in Cuba experienced no great difficulty in understanding the native Amerind language of the indigenous workmen. While both races originated in central Asia, the Basque, a descendant of ancient Pre-Sumerians, had gone westward via Mesopotamia and Syria to the western Pyrenees, whereas the Cuban Indian, a descendant of Ugrians of Mongolia, had migrated eastward via Alaska to the American hemisphere as far as the West Indian Islands. Their primitive Turanian dialects were related.

chocephalic Min strain absorbed in northeastern Asia centuries earlier. The Tunguses appear to have moved down from the Tibetan highlands long after the Ugrians, pressing the latter northward to the region between the Khingan Mountains and Lake Baikal. The Tunguses inhabited southern Mongolia and spread over the central Chinese coastal regions. While the Ugrians moved northward west of the Khingan Mountains, the Tungus tribes expanded up the east side of the mountains along the coast. The latter pushed ahead of them the easterly Ugrian and Min tribes that they encountered, some of which they may have subdued and subsequently absorbed by intermarriage. Both routes northeastward converged at the Amur River, whence all who were headed for America followed the coast line to the place of embarkation on the Kamchatka peninsula for the Aleutian Islands and Alaska. In America, the Tunguses probably included the most brachycephalous of Haddon's Neo-Amerinds, who settled on the American plateaus and in Mexico and Central and South America, and the much later arrivals known as the *Northwest Coast Amerinds,* who settled in the region between 60⁰ north latitude and the international boundary and were among the last Asiatics to come to America. There is a striking difference between these Canadian Indians and those of central and southern United States or of the Pacific Coast. The former include mixed types and their racial affinity with their kin in northeastern Asia today is readily discernible. Similarity has been found in the songs of the Indians of northern British Columbia with those sung in Siberia and Mongolia. The lower culture of the latest Alaskan arrivals from Asia is attributable to the fact that thousands of years earlier the contact of Mongolians with Turkic civilization in Eastern Turkistan had been broken by the expansion of the Turks toward the west, when they established their trade routes across Western Turkistan and Iran to Mesopotamia and Anatolia.

The Eskimos, Ugrians, and Mins may have moved to the lowlands of Mongolia and China as early as 30,000

16 Deleted.

to 10,000 years ago, but the greatest impetus to emigration to North America seems to have come from the descent of the Tunguses or northern Mongolians from northeastern Tibet to the lower lands about 8000 B.C.[17] Intermittent migration continued through the ages because of northward expansion of the Tunguses and subsequent pressure on them from behind by the Chinese, who in turn moved from the upper reaches of the Hwang River to the lowlands about 3000 B.C. Normal increase in population in the Chinese coastal plains and conflicts among the various peoples continued this intermittent emigration to North America until comparatively recent times, i.e., since the beginning of the Christian era. This is demonstrated by the verification of 40 or more different types of culture found by scientists among the various Amerind peoples, some of which, such as that of the Aztecs, reveal apparent contact with ancient western Chinese civilization.[18]

Recent archeological discoveries on the plateau of Mexico indicate the existence of a distinctively American culture long antedating the noteworthy civilizations developed in that country and Central and South America by the Mayans, Toltecs, Aztecs, and others. This culture may be attributable to tribes of the latest Northern Amerinds (Mins) to reach this continent, who embodied a marked Ugrian strain through which they had received the rudiments of the Neolithic culture from the Tunguses prior to emigration from Asia. They may have been overrun in later centuries and their culture absorbed and subsequently improved by the later brachycephalic Neo-Amerinds (Ugrians), who created the Mayan, Toltec, Aztec, and other civilizations. On the plateaus of Mexico and Central and South America these people utilized the knowledge of the arts of agriculture brought by them or

---

17 Emigrations about this time from Tibetan and adjacent highlands in nearly all directions may have been caused by glacial oscillations, chiefly the minor Bühl advance.

18 Quoting from *Recollections of a Naval Officer*, by Wm. H. Parker (Scribner, New York, 1883), page 178: "I frequently heard while on the coast [of Peru] that the first Chinese taken to Peru could communicate with the native Indian or *Cholo.*"

their predecessors from central Asia, centering on the propagation of the great American grain, maize. This resulted in settled communities and the gradual creation of higher cultural values, as reflected by the notable civilizations referred to, which date as long ago as 2000 B.C. Urns from 2 to 4 feet high and going back to about 2500 B.C., recently excavated at the site of an ancient Aztec city in the Mexican state of Jalisco, disclose connections between that civilization and early Chinese civilization. The Turkic culture of central Asia was diffused to the Mins and Tunguses of Kansu and the neighboring Chinese along the Wei River, but it did not in any appreciable degree reach the Ugrians farther north in Mongolia. Thus, the only advanced culture brought to America by the Neo-Amerinds was that received by the descendants of the tribes that had intermarried with Tunguses, who had it. When these mixed peoples reached the Mexican plateaus and overran the Northern Amerinds, they had the benefit of the latter's substratum of Turkic culture, thus related to the Chinese and their own, on which to build their later civilizations. Both diffusion and invention are embodied in practically every civilization created by man, however widely separated they may be; hence, on this underlying Asiatic cultural base the later Amerinds created higher civilizations of a distinctively American character but which embraced rudimental resemblances to their Asiatic antecedents.

At its height, the Mayan culture was widespread, touching South America on the one hand and the present southern United States on the other. Nearly a thousand years before Columbus' arrival, the Mayan civilization had reached such heights that a great scientific congress was held in the city of Coba, the center of the old Mayan empire. According to existing records, Coba thrived as a city until about 1613 A.D., when the Spanish *conquistadores* destroyed the remnants of the Mayan empire and scattered its people to the jungles, where they returned to savage life.

Thus, while the primitive central Asiatic (Turkic) culture was being transmitted westward through Mesopotamia to the eastern Mediterranean, Egypt, and Europe, it also was being borne by certain tribes of Amerinds via Alaska to North America, Central America, and South America. For this reason, it is readily understandable why similarity should be found between various fundamental aspects of cultural products in Egypt and in Mexico; for example, paralleling the Biblical story of Noah and the flood is a tradition among the Choctaw Indians of a universal flood from which only one man was saved and so on.

Various mental and psychological differences among the Amerinds (Indians) of the Western Hemisphere and between them and the Aryan population have been noticed. This is due, of course, to the origin of the former in Turanian tribes of different degrees of evolution in northeastern Asia, some more advanced than the others. Despite the habitation of the majority of those in America in the temperate zones, most of them have not yet shown definite capability for mental achievement and self-government in terms of modern civilization. They display little ambition for school education. This is especially reflected in the frequent turmoil, revolutions, and overturnings of governments in Latin American countries. That condition is accentuated in those countries where the Indians and Negroes (originally from Africa) have intermarried and produced a hybrid element in the population.

(5f) *Sinicus (or Chinese) Subrace.* The Sinicus (or Chinese) represent another branch of the Turanian race, which arose in the central and southerly parts of the provinces of Shensi and Shansi, in the valleys and foothills along the Wei River and the great bend in the Hwang River. The indications are that they evolved either from a branch of the primitive Eskimo stock that settled along the Wei River at the time that the main body of the Eskimos migrated down the Hwang River to eastern Mongolia about 25,000 years ago or from an early division of the Min subrace that moved to and settled in the same region. Such origin seems confirmed by the fact that the Chinese are mesocephalous rather than brachycephalous, because of their long habitation at an intermediate elevation. Thus, they never attained the brachycephaly of the Ugrians, Tunguses, Turks, and other Turanians who long had lived on the high Tibetan plateau.

Across the adjacent province of Kansu, at the easterly end of the Turkic caravan route in Turkistan, the Chinese, like the Tunguses, were direct beneficiaries of the Turkic culture through the long period of its evolution from about 8000 B.C. until the Sumerian conquest of lower Mesopotamia about 4300 B.C. Having received first the Neolithic culture and soon thereafter the knowledge of agriculture, they did not become nomads but settled down as planters, depending for food largely upon what they grew. Their fields were cultivated with stone hoes. They used bark to weave clothing and in winter wore skins and furs. Their only domesticated animals were the dog and the pig. This transference of early Turkic culture accounts for the belief of some investigators that the Chinese experienced no old Stone Age.

The later advances in Turkic culture must have occured mainly in Western Turkistan and Mesopotamia, since their centers in Eastern Turkistan were dispersed and commerce with the Chinese had practically vanished. For some unknown reason, perhaps increasing drought in the Tarim Basin, this break must have occurred quite early, since the Chinese were slow in receiving important benefits of the later cultural developments in the west. Their own civilization was about 2000 years behind that of western Asia. It is probable that the Sumerians in Mesopotamia did not continue the same commercial relations with China that their predecessors did, terminating their caravan routes at Kashgar, at the westerly border of the Tarim Basin. Concurrently, the Chinese nation was expanding eastward, away from regular contact with the eastern termini of whatever caravan routes from the west may still have been maintained. When the stimulus from this contact was interrupted or had largely failed or their lands had become less productive because of erosion, the Chinese perceived the advantages to be gained by moving to the lower and coastal lands or at least by encouraging their surplus population to migrate in that direction. In consequence, much of their later cultural evolution was indigenous or was transmitted belatedly to them from the west. Examples are the use of the wheel, which was slow in spreading eastward, and the beginning of their Bronze Age as late as about 1350 B.C. In the west, the wheel was utilized in the Neolithic period.

According to tradition, about 3000 B.C. a large aggregation of Chinese moved down the Hwang River from the foothills of the Kuenlun Mountains and took possession of the central lowlands.[19] There they absorbed or drove northward the earlier Tungues (or northern Mongolians) who then held the country. It was at that time that the latter overran and gained control of the region east of the Khingan Mountains, mainly Manchuria, Korea, and Japan. This movement impelled emigrations of the later Northern Amerinds, Neo-Amerinds, and finally Tungus tribes (North Coast Amerinds) to North America. Thereupon, the Chinese so increased in numbers that they imposed on the older inhabitants the civilization received via Kansu, became the dominant race, and advanced their culture to far higher levels. Their subsequent amalgamation with the underlying peoples and later Mongolian and other invaders has somewhat modified the original type. For example, a tall Tibetan element, the *Khams,* with longer face and lighter skin, has been noted in northern China.

Thus, we can readily perceive the close relationship between the ancient civilization of Turkistan and western Asia and that of China and early America, although each embodied both diffusion and increasing local invention.

(5g) *Turkic Subrace.* As already shown, the progenitors of the Turks (or Tatars) probably branched from the Min[20] subrace in northeastern Tibet and took possession of the lake region of central Tibet about 22,000 years ago. While the kindred Tunguses were expanding toward Mon-

---

19 Sheng Cheng, *A Son of China* (Norton, New York, 1930), pp. 44-45.
20 The ancient kingdom of Tatary comprised the Turks, centered in Tarim Basin, and those of Tibet, and also the Tunguses of Tibet, Manchuria, and intervening regions.

golia, the Chinese coast, and Manchuria during successive centuries, the Turkic element was expanding northwestward from the central lake region and evolving its characteristic physical type. The long habitation of the Turks at this high altitude is proved by their brachycephalic index. Ultimately, about 14,000 years ago in northwestern Tibet they came in violent contact with the White Aryan subrace. One division of the latter, the progenitors of the Nordic Aryans, then moved down the northerly slopes to the Tarim Basin, in Eastern Turkistan,[21] which was much less arid than it is today. The others, the White Kelts, the brachycephalic division of the Aryan race, continued to inhabit that extensive mountain region. When the White Nordics took possession of the Tarim Basin, they displaced an earlier Turkic tribe from the highlands (the later Pre-Sumerians), who then crossed the mountain passes to Western Turkistan. In fact, the latter may have been driven earlier to the lower lands by the Nordics.

Shortly before 8000 B.C., perhaps because of increase of population, coldness, drought, or famine in central Tibet, strife arose and the Kelts were driven westward to the region of the Pamirs, whereupon the Turks gained control of western Tibet. Concurrently, some of the Turks (the later Sumerians) moved through the Karakoram passes to the Tarim Basin and pressed the Nordic Aryans into the Tien Mountains, whence the Tarim Basin became the Turkic (or Tataric) stronghold[20] and soon, in coöperation with the Turks in Western Turkistan, the center of the most advanced civilization (Neolithic)[22] of those times. It slowly radiated in all directions, but mainly eastward and westward. It was a concomitant of the beginnings of urban life there.

This expansion in western Tibet impelled a division of the Keltic Aryans, known as the Paleo-Keltic (or Furfuz-Grenelle) people, to break away soon afterward and undertake a long westward migration, overruning Europe by

---

21 *Ency. Brit.*, 13th Ed., vol. 27, pages 423-424; Aryans in Eastern Turkistan.
22 H. F. Osborn, *Man Rises to Parnassus* (Princeton University Press, 1927), page 106.

way of the Danube River valley in large numbers. Subsequently, the Nordic nation emerged from northern passes of the Tien mountains and settled in the Kirghiz region later known as Geté, south and east of Lake Balkhash, in the present province of Semiryechensk.

Before the lapse of much time, perhaps because of increasing aridity in Tarim Basin, the Turks there (the Sumerians) spread westward through the passes to Western Turkistan, dislodging their predecessors (the Pre-Sumerians),[23] who then migrated with their relatively advanced civilization to Mesopotamia. Cities arose in both Eastern and Western Turkistan and the Neolithic culture spread eastward along the foothills of the Altyn Tagh to the Chinese province of Kansu. There contact was made with remote kin of the Turks, the Mongolians, and also with an isolated group farther up the Hwang River on the slopes of the Kuen-Lun Mountains, the later-known Sinicus or Chinese subrace. Thus, the axis of Neolithic culture extended from Mesopotamia, on the west, to areas beyond Kansu, on the east.

The Aral Sea, now only a lake, must then have covered a vast area and impeded further passage in that direction by the Nordic Aryans when they settled in Geté about 7700 B.C. Their habitation in this region, between Kashgar, Lake Balkhash and the Aral Sea, also prevented Turkic expansion toward the north; hence the movement of the Turkic Sumerians westward through the mountains to Western Turkistan and their displacement there of the Pre-Sumerians, who turned toward Iran, on the southwest. On the Iranian plateau the latter encountered Iranian Aryans, whose resistance had to be overcome before they could reach the rich lands of Mesopotamia. This, the first, Turanian invasion of the west about 8000 B.C. began a series of most important migrations in respect of their influence on later Asiatic and European civilization. Crossing Bukhara and the northerly escarpment of the Iranian plateau, near the present city of

---

23 These people appear identical with the later Elamites, Assyrians, and affiliated tribes.

Herat, the Pre-Sumerians finally gained the ascendancy, drove the Iranians westward, southward, and eastward, crossed the pass of Khowar (Choara of the ancients) in the Zagros Mountains, established a colony and base of operations at Susa, in Elam, and subsequently took possession of lower Mesopotamia, known to later history successively as *Sumer* and *Akkad, Shinar (Genesis* 10:10, *Isaiah* 11:11),[24] and *Babylonia*. It is now a part of the kingdom of Iraq. Their former habitation in Western Turkistan then became the homeland of the Sumerians.

At that time, practically all of southwestern Asia since the age of the Neanderthalers had been populated by the Mediterranean race from Iran. In order that the invaders, the earliest Turanians (Pre-Sumerians)[25] in the west, might secure themselves against future attack, this conquest gradually was extended westward around the Fertile Crescent and northwestward in Mesopotamia and into Asia Minor (Anatolia). Later, the invaders spread into the hills of Palestine. The tribes of the Mediterranean race that were driven toward Egypt ultimately migrated across the north of Africa among their congeners already in the Mediterranean basin and reached western Europe via the Iberian peninsula. They took along a rudimentary knowledge of the Neolithic culture that the Turkish invaders had brought with them. In western Europe it corresponded with the *Capsian (Mesolithic)* culture. Shortly afterward, other Mediterranean tribes that slowly were forced westward in Anatolia carried the Neolithic culture of the invaders to their congeners in the Aegean basin. *Thus was the latter culture transmitted to Europe between* 8000 *and* 7500 *B.C.*[26]

A great mass of literature has been written on the sub-

---

24 *Shinar* is simply a local modification of the earlier name *Sumer.*

25 See E. A. Speiser, *Mesopotamian Origins* (University of Pennsylvania Press, 1930).

26 For evidence that they came from the East, we refer to *Genesis* 11:1-2: "And the whole earth was of one language and of one speech. And it came to pass *as they journeyed from the East* that they found a plain in the land of Shinar and they dwelt there." Conjectures that they came from India fail to allow for distinct racial and linguistic differences.

ject of racial migration to and from the Mesopotamian and other Near East regions, but the problem seems to be solvable. As already shown, the original settlements of modern man were made by tribes of the Aryan Mediterranean race from Iran, perhaps 20,000 to 15,000 years ago. Then followed two successive major invasions by nations of the Turanian Turkic race from Turkistan, which scattered the Mediterranean race wherever encountered, the Pre-Sumerians about 8000 B.C. and the Sumerians about 4300 B.C. Between the two invasions, the Pre-Sumerians, who also included the Elamites in the Zagros Mountains, had spread all over Babylonia, Assyria, Aram (Syria), the Palestine hills, and southern Anatolia. The Sumerians supplanted them in lower Babylonia and pressed their predecessors northwestward. Subsequently, northern Babylonia and areas southward were conquered by Aryan invaders, namely, the Mediterranean Akkadians about 3800 B.C., the Hamitic Chaldeans about 2750 B.C., and the Hamitic Amorites (a branch of the Canaanites) about 2160 B.C., who established themselves there.

These invasions caused many Pre-Sumerians to migrate northwestward in Assyria and to the Mediterranean shores and many Sumerians to Upper Mesopotamia. Two types of long-headed people (apparently Aryan Mediterranean and Hamite) in the Mesopotamian area have been revealed by evidence unearthed at Kish.[27] The third Turanian invaders of the west, the Hittites (Heth, Hitti, Hittim) of about 2300 B.C., later called the Armenians,[28] did not settle in Mesopotamia but crossed the mountains to Cappadocia, in Anatolia. Keltic Aryan invaders from Thrace in later centuries pushed them eastward. After 2000 B.C., Nordic Aryans, expanding southwestward from their old homeland of Geté, south of Lake Balkhash, blocked further Turanian migration southwestward for nearly 30

---

27 V. Gordon Childe, *op. cit.*, pages 178-179. The Aryan Canaanites (including the Phoenicians), who were Hamites, lived in a region from the easterly Mediterranean shore to the Palestine hills.

28 *Ency. Brit.*, 13th Ed., vol. 2, page 564d. The Hittites clearly were an Asiatic people. V. Gordon Childe, *The Aryans* (Knopf, New York, 1926), pages 23, 27.

centuries. The migrations just mentioned are discussed in proper sequence.

When pushing their way across Iran about 8000 B.C. and subsequently maintaining by military strength their long caravan route between the east and the west, the Pre-Sumerian Turks enclosed the remnant of the Aryan Kelts in the valleys of the Pamirs and drove many Iranians into the mountain valleys of Afghanistan and others toward the west and the south. Among those that moved southward, the most notable were the Persians, who took possession of the highlands north of the Persian Gulf. In the southeast of Iran lived tribes that comprised the later *Ethiopians* of Herodotus (vii.69-70), better known as the aforesaid Hamites. Upon pressure from the north centuries afterward, one of the Hamite tribes migrated over the Suliman Mountains to the lower Indus valley and the other crossed the straits of Ormus to southwestern Arabia. Their assimilation of the Neolithic culture of these Turks thus resulted in its diffusion among the Iranian tribes in the region extending from the Indus valley to southwestern Arabia. Later (about 6500 B.C.), it was transmitted by Hamites of Arabia to the African mainland (Ethiopia) and *finally (after 6000 B.C.) down the Nile valley to Upper Egypt,* where it was imposed on the earlier Mediterranean people and *provided the rudiments of the wonderful civilization thereafter developed in that region and subsequently in lower Egypt.*

No definite name has yet been applied in history to these earliest-known Turkish invaders of Mesopotamia.[29] The main body was identical with the subsequently-known Assyrians. That they belonged to that race is demonstrated by the skeletal remains found and by the characteristics of their descendants, which disclose that they were dark-complexioned and brachycephalous in type. The name of Pre-Sumerians will be continued here for the entire nation, including the Elamites, Assyrians, and Palestinians. As their descendants spread northward and westward, they became the dominant race in western Asia and

---

29 V. Gordon Childe, *op. cit.,* pp. 136-137. *Genesis* 11:1-2.

numerous other tribal or national names appeared, some of which have been preserved, such as those of the *Leleges* in Anatolia, the *Kheta* in Syria and Palestine, the *Assyrians*, *Hurrians*, *Gutians*, *Lullubians*, and the *Kassites* and *Elamites*[30] in the mountains north of Mesopotamia. They maintained commercial relations with their congeners still in Turkistan, and in the course of time with additional immigration the so-called Aeneolithic culture (first and second stages)[31] grew out of their Neolithic civilization as copper came into use along with the flint instruments. Much of this metal probably came from the mountains of Armenia. But the lead in cultural development apparently was held by the Turanian race at its centers in Turkistan and not in the west, since each successive migrating group therefrom brought a superior civilization[31] to Mesopotamia. Cultural advancement must have been greatly accelerated between 6000 and 5000 B.C. to approximately the status recently discovered at Tell al'Ubaid, and its benefits were diffused over all western Asia, western India, and Egypt. The culture of ancient Elam and Assyria was identical with that of al'Ubaid.[32] *The spread of Pre-Sumerian (Elamite) culture to the lower Indus valley* (chiefly in the province of Sind) is proved by both the unearthing of brachycephalic skulls there and the similarity of its early culture to that of Susa.[32] It was succeeded in India by Iranian types when the Sumerians invaded the west and drove more Iranians eastward over the Suliman Mountains. Later came the Hamitic conquest of Chaldea, in southern Mesopotamia, and India was left to her own ingenuity in the further development of her culture.

About 4300 B.C. the second recognizable Turanian migration (of Sumerians)[33] from Western Turkistan to

---

30 In this connection, see E. A. Speiser, *op. cit.*, A recent expedition from Liverpool, England, is reported as yielding evidence of civilization in Jericho as early as 6000 B.C.

31 *Ibid.*, pp. 47, 124, 170-171.

32 V. Gordon Childe, *op. cit.*, pp. 204-227, 232-237, 253-254, 274-277. Its descent from the primitive culture of Anau, in Turkistan, as indicated above, seems likely to be established. *Ibid.*, pp. 278-279, 282, 294-296, 298.

33 F. Hommel, *Ethnologia*, 21 ff. and 985, also sponsors the Turkoid theory of Sumerian origin.

Mesopotamia occurred. These invaders had been driven out of Western Turkistan by the Turkic Hittites on their east. The new element, in conquering lower Mesopotamia, made subjects of their predecessors who had not escaped to the north or west and superimposed on them their superior culture in large part. The natives, who then made and used pottery and other objects of the al'Ubaid culture, were required to perform all the arduous labor for their conquerors, but, as is usually the case, a gradual commingling of the two kindred races followed.

The Tigris and Euphrates Rivers rise in the highlands of Armenia and flow southeasterly until they join near the Persian Gulf, into which they flow. At Baghdad (near ancient Babylon), the two rivers swerve toward each other, thereby forming two distinctive areas between them, Upper and Lower Mesopotamia. The original Sumerian settlement in Lower Mesopotamia was made at Eridu in the south and the next was at Nippur in the northwest. Eridu was a seaport at that time, but, because of soil accretion at the lower Tigris since then, it is now 130 miles inland. Babylon, in the northwestern part of Lower Mesopotamia, was a colony of Eridu, while Ur, in the south, was a colony of Nippur. Some of these habitations, instead of having been newly established, may actually have been Pre-Sumerian towns[34] taken over by the Sumerians. "The Babylonians belonged to the Aramaic branch of the Semitic stock, as Sir Henry Rawlinson, by his discoveries among the cuneiform inscriptions, has now made clear."[35] The subsequent Aryan invasions of Babylonia caused many Sumerians to move into Upper Mesopotamia.

About 3800 B.C. the Aryan Akkadians from central Arabia, under the traditional leadership of Nimrod, conquered the northwestern part of Babylonia and established settlements centering on Agadë. Sargon I was their

---

34 The Pre-Sumerians probably had taken over sites established long before by tribes of the Mediterranean race.

35 *Chambers' Encyclopedia* (1881), vol. I, page 598.

greatest king.[36] Thereupon, the southerly part of Babylonia was named *Makan*[37] (later Sumer), with Ur as its
capital, and the northerly part became *Meluchia* (later
Akkad), with Agadë (from which Akkad, a Hamitic ren-
dition of the non-Semitic name Agadë was derived) as its
capital. This conquest separated the Sumerian nation
from the Pre-Sumerians farther northwest in Upper Mesopotamia. A millennium later the Akkadians were conquered by the Aryan Chaldeans, who were Hamites. Despite these conquests and later attacks by the Elamites,
the Sumerians maintained their political entity.

So far as we know, the general domination of Upper
Mesopotamia, Assyria, Aram, Palestine, and most of
Asia Minor by the Pre-Sumerians and of Sumer by the
Sumerians or at times by the Elamites was not seriously
contested by the Akkadians or others during the millennium prior to about 2750 B.C., when the Hamitic Chaldeans appeared from the south. During this time the arts
of civilization made great strides in this region as well as
in Turkistan. The military operations across Iran necessary to keep open the caravan route between Turkistan
and Mesopotamia undoubtedly resulted in the continued
migration of Iranian population across the mountains to
the Punjab of India. The successive accretions to India's
population came from the west, and each new invasion
forced the older inhabitants eastward toward the Ganges
valley or southward to the peninsular plateau. This effect
was repeated by the third important Turanian invasion
of the west, namely, that by the Hittites from Western
Turkistan, who settled in Anatolia (Cappadocia) about
2300 B.C. The *Zend-Avesta*, the sacred book of the Iranians, treats of their many conflicts with the Turanians.
*Thus do we account for the source of the vast Iranian
population of India.* Contemporaneously, commercial in-

---

36 Time set by Nabonidus. *Ency. Brit.*, 13th Ed., vol. 3, p. 103. See *ibid.*, vol.
1, page 457, under Akkad. The name Sargon, more correctly Sarru-Kinu, meaning 'legitimate king,' is a hybrid of the Assyrian word *sar* and the Sumerian
word *gina*.
37 This word appears in the name of the Takla-Makan desert in Eastern Turkistan and it tends to affirm the origin of the Sumerians in that general region.

tercourse was maintained by routes around the foothills of the Altyn Tagh between the Turkic centers in Turkistan and the Mongolian and Chinese peoples chiefly in the provinces of Kansu and Shensi (*Serica*), who appropriated the Turkic culture. *It was on this cultural base that the later Chinese civilization was erected.*

The identity of the ancient Assyrians and Sumerians as members of the yellow-red Turkic race is unmistakable. They were of medial height, stocky in build, and had large noses. They worshipped the elements, particularly the god of the air, as the modern Chinese peasants are inclined to do. They wore a sort of pigtail like that worn by their later congeners, the Hittites[38] of Cappadocia. From this Mesopotamian center other trade routes were developed and maintained in various directions among the Turkic people from Elam to the Mediterranean and along the Taurus Mountains across Anatolia to the Aegean. There as well as along the Mediterranean shores contact was made with European peoples, with whom a large commerce also was developed. Along with it, the progressive culture of the Sumerians was transmitted to Europe.

It is not too much to say that the Pre-Sumerians were the actual creators of the rudiments of western Asiatic civilization. They evolved it, probably in Turkistan, from the food-gathering to the food-producing economy and to the establishment of urban civilization based on industry and commerce. Their culture, developed to a still higher degree by the Sumerians in Turkistan,[39] was diffused by the latter as stated above, through others to central China on the east and through the people in Sumer and others to the various nations of southern Asia, Africa, and Europe in the west. The continuity of the Pre-Sumerian and Sumerian cultures in Mesopotamia has been demonstrated.[40]

---

38 The Hittites were round-headed, with high skull, retreating forehead, and large nose, and are generally believed to have been from central Asia. The high boots used by them are still worn by Mongolians of upper Asia.

39 E. A. Speiser, *op. cit.*, p. 47.

40 V. Gordon Childe, *op. cit.*, pp. 156-157.

The contributions of the Aryan Akkadians, Chaldeans, and Amorites have not been determined. Civilization evolved faster in these areas than in the adjacent mountainous regions. The outgrowths were the marvelous Assyrian and Babylonian cultures that have so engaged the attention of scholars and in addition the foundations of the brilliant Egyptian and the later Indian and Chinese civilizations. To repeat, "man can no more avoid accepting and adapting to his own mental make-up *some part* of the rich cultural harvest exposed to him to choose from than he can live without food. Nor can he help adding to the general heritage his own modest contribution." But, failing to understand the other man's ideas precisely, he picks and chooses only those elements of culture that appeal to him at the time and can readily be adapted to his own status. Thus, no culture is ever diffused without change, but such modifications do not destroy the fact of diffusion.[41]

As already indicated, about 3800 B.C. the earliest invaders of Babylonia from the south, the Akkadians, an Aryan Mediterranean tribe from the Persian Gulf coast of Arabia and not Hamites, established themselves in the northwestern part of Babylonia, with Agadé as its capital. Subsequently, the Elamites conquered Sumer, in the south. Later came the Canaanites, named as 'the sons of Ham', meaning Hamites,[42] who must have originated in far southern Arabia and crossed the land to El Haza, on the Persian Gulf. When advancing northward, they found the Babylonians too strong and swung around the Fertile Crescent to the shores of the Mediterranean Sea, where their country subsequently was known as Canaan. A division inhabited Phoenicia (native name Keft), on the northerly coast, now western Lebanon.

It was not until about 2750 B.C. that the Hamites found the Elamites in Babylonia so weakened, perhaps by the refinements of civilization, that a direct attack was made on them by the Chaldeans, another tribe that apparently had followed the same course as that of the Canaanites and

---

41 G. Elliot Smith, *op. cit.*, pp. 19 and 33.
42 Strabo, *Geography*, xvi. 4.19, 24, 25. The Hamitic invasions are treated at greater length in the chapter headed *Hamites*.

apparently were related to them. They were Sabaeans from the present country of Yemen. They encircled Sumer from the south and overcame it and Agadë, thereby becoming the dominant power in all Babylonia, which afterward was called jointly Sumer and Akkad. This forced some of the Sumerians northwestward toward Padan-Aram (Syria), among the Pre-Sumerians, whose kin inhabited the region from Anatolia and Assyria to the Palestine hills. In the latter area they were known as the *Kheta*.[43] About 2700 B.C. a division apparently of Kheta overran Egypt during the Vth dynasty, when a broadheaded people appeared there in force.

About 2160 B.C. the Amorites, a division of the Canaanites probably from westerly Palestine,[44] invaded and conquered all Babylonia. The greatest king of the Amorites was the eminent Khammurabi (or Hammurabi), c. 2100 B.C.[45] They were overthrown by the Sumerians, aided by the Assyrians and Hittites, about 1926 B.C., as shown later. The subsequent commingling of the Turanian and Aryan races in Lower Mesopotamia resulted in a largely composite race, language, and culture there.[46] Ultimately, all of the Aryan people of the Fertile Crescent became more or less submerged in the numerically superior Turanian inhabitants.

About 2300 B.C. the third division of the Turkic race from Western Turkistan, the Hittites, actuated probably by drought, pressure by Nordics on their north, or other circumstances, crossed Iran toward Mesopotamia. But, upon finding the power of the Chaldeans in Babylonia and of the Pre-Sumerians (Assyrians) in Upper Mesopotamia too strong, they swerved westward over the highlands and took possession of that part of northern central Anatolia later known as Cappadocia.[46½] This invasion drove many Kassites (northwesterly Elamites) south-

---

43 E. A. Speiser, *op. cit.*, page 147 and footnote on page 154. Traditionally, the Chaldean empire attained the zenith of its power in 2234 B.C.

44 *Genesis* 9:18, 10:15-20.

45 *Encyclopaedia Britannica*, 13th Ed., vol. 5, p. 104. His great code of laws and customs has been preserved and translated into modern languages.

46 E. A. Speiser, *op. cit.*, page 155.

46½ See under *Hittites* and *Armenia* in *Ency. Brit.*, 13th Ed.

ward[47] into the mountains of Elam; also inland Mediterranean tribes northward to the shores of the Black Sea, where they were known as the *Caucones*,[48] and westward beyond the Halys River (now the Kizil Irmak) as far as the shores of the Aegean Sea, where they were thereafter known with others as the *Pelasgi*.[49] The descendants of the Pre-Sumerians, known as the Leleges,[50] who had expanded over central Anatolia, were pushed westward beyond the Halys and southward into and beyond the Taurus Mountains. Through the ages some amalgamation of Leleges and Caucones or Pelasgi probably occured in Anatolia, but racial distinction, nonetheless, continued throughout many subsequent centuries.

Recent evidence indicates that, during the long contact (c. 4300 to c. 2300 B.C.) of the Nordic Aryans in Geté, southeast of Lake Balkhash, on the northerly slopes of the Tien Mountains, with the Hittites on their southwest, in Western Turkistan, the influence of the former on the latter, despite the superior culture of these Turks (or in consequence of it), resulted in the modification of their agglutinative Turanian language to approximately the inflectional form employed by the Nordics. The extent of the reverse influence, if discernible, is still an undetermined question. About 1600 B.C. the *Carduchi*. a tribe of the Nordic Aryan Kimmerii then inhabiting western Scythia, moved southward through the Caucasus Mountains and settled in the highlands of eastern Turkey, adjacent to the region of Media, which only a short time before also had been taken over by a division of the Kimmerians, subsequently called the Medians. The Carduchi later became known as the Kurds of Kurdistan. Through the years they have commingled and interbred to some extent with their Turkish neighbors. Both the Medians and the Kurds are discussed further under the heading of the Kimmerii.

Many tribes of Pre-Sumerian Leleges were encountered

---

47 V. Gordon Childe, *op. cit.*, p. 160.
48 Strabo's *Geography* viii. 3.17, xii.3.5.
49 *Ibid.*, xii.8.4, xiii.3.2-3.
50 *Ibid.*, xiii.1.58-60.

centuries afterward along the shores of Anatolia from the Hellespont to the Syrian coast[51] and thence southward. From these shores they had developed a widespread commerce on the Mediterranean long prior to 3000 B.C. that was rivaled only when the Kretan sea-power arose about 2500 B.C.[52] Their chief ports appear to have been on the Carian and Lycian shores,[53] around Alexandretta Bay at the northeasterly corner of the Mediterranean, near important centers in Syria, and along the coast of Palestine, whose ports are described by Strabo.[54] These people[55] conducted extensive maritime operations that reached the northerly Atlantic coast. From their kin who inhabited Palestine came the Hyksos kings, who invaded Egypt about 1775 B.C. in consequence of the conquest of Babylonia from the Amorites by the Kassites of Elam[56] about 1780 B.C. The XIIIth Egyptian dynasty then took refuge in Ethiopia. The Kassite dynasty in Babylonia endured 576 years 9 months. Its kings intermarried with the royal family of the Assyrians, another division of the same race. The Hyksos kings (who comprised the XVth, XVIth. and XVIIth dynasties) introduced the domestic horse and the war chariot into Egypt. But two centuries later, weakened by the Egyptian climate and environment, they were expelled by Thutmose I about 1576 B.C. According to the Egyptian historian Manetho, they then returned to Palestine (east of the Aryan Philistines) and built the city later known as Jerusalem.

Maritime activities of the Kheta along the Palestinian shores declined in consequence of Egyptian invasions

51 Strabo, *Geogr.* xii.8.4, xiii.1.7, 49-51, 56, 58-60, 3.1, xiv.2.27.

52 It was reported in August, 1957, that Archeologist Cyrus H. Gordon, of Brandeis University, has deciphered inscriptions on clay tablets of 3,400 years ago that these Semites then held the island of Krete, which must have been an intermediate base in their water commercial operations. They evidently had taken it from the Aryan Mediterranean inhabitants. Subsequently, it was conquered by the Grecians.

53 *Ibid.*, xiii.1.59, xiv.3.2-4.

54 *Ibid.*, xvi.2.22-30.

55 The Khatti (Kheta) appear on a "prophecy-tablet" referring ostensibly to the time of the Akkadian king Sargon I (c. 3800 B.C.), long before the arrival of the Hittites in Cappadocia. *Ency. Brit.*, 13th Ed., vol. 13, page 535, by David G. Hogarth.

56 *Ency. Brit.*, 13th Ed., vol. 15, page 694.

and other warfare that ravaged the coastal regions about the middle of the 2nd millennium B.C. Sepulchers, remnants of fortifications, and vestiges of settlements of the ancient Leleges long remained throughout Caria.[57] This early Pre-Sumerian civilization was reflected by their descendants prior to the Christian era.[58] In fact, the Leleges occupied practically the whole coastal region of the later Ionia before the beginning of the great Keltic migrations from Thrace across the Bosporus and the Hellespont to Anatolia about 1425 B.C.[59]

The invasion of Cappadocia by the Hittites stimulated the sea adventures and commercial activities of the Leleges in Anatolia because of concentration of the latter on and near the Mediterranean shores. Their perspective of the outside world, the Aegean and the western Mediterranean regions in particular, thus was greatly broadened. Moreover, the Hittites, who had basically the same cultural heritage as the Pre-Sumerians and the Sumerians because of their common racial origin and habitation in Turkistan, afforded profitable commercial intercourse for the Leleges. The Hittites mined and worked iron ores and other minerals in Cappadocia, largely superseding the Leleges in the art. The *Chalybeans,*[60] who were famous iron workers, and the *Moschi, Tibareni, Mares, Alarodians,* and *Macrones* (the modern Armenians, also formerly known as the *Tzani* or *Sanni)* of Herodotus,[61] all of whom lived in Cappadocia and northern Syria, were descendants mainly of the Hittites. The Moschi dealt in slaves with the Tyrians,[62] of Phoenicia.

The Leleges appear from early times to have taken conspicuous advantage of their commercial opportunities

---

57 Strabo, *ibid.,* xiii.1.59.

58 *Ibid.,* xiv.3.2-3, 5.2.

59 *Menecrates* Fr. 1. The *Iliad* of Homer is literally full of valuable references to the people and history of Asia Minor; too numerous for individual citation here.

60 The Chalybeans subsisted by the manufacture of iron (Herod. vii.76, Xenophon, *Anabasis* iv.5.34, 7.15-17, v.5.1, Strabo xii.3. 19-23). They may have been descendants of the earliest iron workers in western Asia, who brought the art from Turkistan or developed it locally.

61 Herodotus, *History* iii.94, vii.78-79; Xenophon, *Anabasis* iv. and v.

62 *Ezekiel* 27:13.

by sea, having introduced agriculture into southern Sweden by way of the British Isles as early as 3000 B.C. By 2700 B.C. Anatolian ships moving out of the Mediterranean and along the coasts of western Europe as far as the British Isles and Scandinavia had on board the Lelegian "prospectors" for metals described in anthropology.[63] As stated by Strabo,[64] every one then admitted "that the ancients appear to have made longer journeys by both sea and land than their successors did." And along such trade routes it was not only logical and convenient, but also safest, for itinerant merchants, religious leaders, magicians, and others to travel in following their vocations, spreading their knowledge and ideas among foreign peoples, and seeking adventure and profit. Alexandretta Bay must have embraced the seaports utilized for water commerce from Syria, the important city of Karkamis (Carchemish), and more easterly centers on and near the Euphrates on the caravan routes from Sumer to Cappadocia and other parts of Anatolia.

The commercial success of the Anatolian Leleges gave rise to another seafaring nation, that of Krete,[65] and from 2500 B.C., or earlier, to 1425 B.C., the Kretans were the chief rivals of the Leleges on the Mediterranean, dominating its northerly shores as far west as Italy, while the Leleges followed its shore via Egypt as far as Malta on route to the Atlantic ports. Both nations began to decline upon the invasion of southwestern Anatolia by the Keltic Carians from Thrace about the end of the 15th century B.C. and the subsequent Achaean advance into Greece. The Carians took over and maintained for several centuries the sea activities of the Leleges in the Mediterranean.[66] After the Trojan War, these operations rapidly deteriorated in consequence of the successive Kelt-

---

63   V. Gordon Childe, *The Aryans* (Knopf, New York, 1926), p. 100.
64   Strabo, i.3.2.
65   *Ibid.*, x.4.17. Actually, this commercial activity may have been conducted by mainland Semites of Syria who took and held the island until it was seized by the Grecians.
66   Strabo, xiii.1.59; Diodorus Siculus, *Bibl. Hist.*, vi.17.

ic invasions of western Anatolia and the rival Kretan and Phoenician sea power during this period.

An early factor in the confusion of races in Babylonia was the resurgence of the Assyrian nation, which under Ninus rose to political prominence prior to 2000 B.C. and made conquests in surrounding regions, even as far as Egypt and Bactria,[67] but probably as a dependency of the ruling Amorites of Babylonia.[68] Its capital, Nineveh, received its name from this leader. This nation as well as Elam was more thoroughly Pre-Sumerian and far less mixed Sumerian and Hamite than Upper and Lower Mesopotamia (or Babylonia). This fact and the influential Akkadian and Chaldean states still dominant in the latter region resulted in marked racial and social differences between its people and those of Assyria and Elam, which were the causes of repeated warfare between the two groups. The ancient racial kinship of the Assyrians, Sumerians, and Hittites is demonstrated by the fact that in warfare the Assyrians utilized the new iron weapons of the Hittites and battering rams of their own invention. In his religion, the Assyrian, like the Sumerian, looked forward to no future state of reward or punishment. His chief god was the war-god Asshur. His written language essentially was analogous to that of the Sumerian of Babylonia.

Flushed with success, the Assyrians broke away from the Amorites of Babylonia and about 1926 B.C., with the aid of the Hittites, they assisted the Babylonian Sumerians to regain the political ascendancy over the Amorites, whereupon eleven Sumerian kings reigned in succession until the last was overthrown by the Kassites[69] of the mountains of Elam in 1780 B.C. Assyria, Syria, and Palestine then became independent.

---

67 Diodorus, *op. cit.*, iii. 1-7.

68 E. A. Speiser, *op. cit.*, pp. 124 and 156. Some writers incline to the belief that the term Amorite merely was an alternative name for the Canaanites, the former being ethnical and the latter geographical. *Ency. Brit.*, 13th Ed., vol. 1, p. 876. But even geographical names often have personal origin, America for example. See *Genesis* 9:18, 10:15-16. What is most probable is that the Amorites and also the Phoenicians were tribes of the Canaanite nation.

69 The Kassites were a division of the Pre-Sumerian Elamites.

Beginning about 1300 B.C., the Assyrians under Shalmaneser I and his successors gradually overcame the Kassites and about 1204 B.C. gained control of Babylonia, which they, as the leading nation, then retained until overwhelmed by the Nordic Aryan Medes under Cyaxares in 606 B.C. Shortly after 1300 B.C., the Assyrians, probably in an attempt to revive the ancient sea-power of the kindred Leleges that centered on Alexandretta Bay, were prevented from reaching the Mediterranean coastal regions by the Phoenicians, and again a century later the Aramaeans (apparently mixed Pre-Sumerians and Sumerians) of Syria obstructed their passage to those Mediterranean ports. By 1200 B.C. the expanding sea-power of the Phoenicians had reached such scope that it became the dominant nation on the Mediterranean and held that status for many centuries.

One of the greatest influences in racial admixture in modern Turkey was the extent of the final conquest of Anatolia by the Aryan Kelts from Thrace, who by about 1150 B.C. had gained all of the region north of the Taurus Mountains as far east as modern Armenia, to which highlands the Hittites had fled from Cappadocia. South of them lived the Nordic Carduchi, the later Kurds. South of the Taurus mountains, it seems clear that the Trojan war of the *Iliad* (c.1300-1250 B.C.) actually represented the determining campaign in which the Kelts from Thrace finally broke the power of the Leleges of southwestern Anatolia.[70] Many tribes of the latter lived in southwestern Anatolia, along the Aegean shores, in the Troad, and eastward along the Mediterranean shore as far as Alexandretta Bay, and there was an affinity between them and the Cilicians there, on the one hand, and the Trojans, on the other.[71] Thus, the Troes and Cilicians were simply tribes of the Leleges, all of whom allied themselves to resist the Keltic invaders. All of the native population, except some scattered tribes[72] who remained as

---

70 Strabo, xiii.1.7-9, quoting from the *Iliad*.
71 *Ibid.*, xiii.3.1.
72 *Ibid.*, xiii.1.7.

subjects, were driven southward[73] and eastward. Thus was the power of the once great Hittite nation finally broken.[74]

The subsequent habitations of these displaced Leleges were the following ancient regions, viz., Caria, Lycia,[75] Pisidia, Pamphlyia,[76] the later Cilicia near Alexandretta Bay[77] and to a minor extent (along with some Hittites) Syria, and even Upper Mesopotamia and Palestine. Their darker color and other physical features distinguished them from the Aryan Kelts (called Leuco-Syrians locally) who had superseded them in Cappadocia[78] and western Anatolia. The present Armenians are descendants of the Hittites, as indicated by their so-called Hebraic (Turkic) features. This dispersion explains why many Hittites spread throughout Syria (Aram) and Palestine in Biblical times[79] and how the original Hebrews acquired an infusion of Hittite blood.

Not only the Pre-Sumerians but also the Sumerians and Hittites, unmistakably branches of the Turkic subrace, developed high civilizations in the west. The chief cities of ancient Shinar were Babel, Erech, Akkad, and Calneh,[80] while other prominent centers arose elsewhere throughout Mesopotamia. The Hittites founded a number of remarkable centers in early Cappadocia, about which we only recently are gaining comprehensive knowledge. A large part of the Babylonian religion and law came from the Sumerians; indeed, the Sumerian continued to be the language of religion, law, and letters long after the Hamites had become the dominant race in that region. The

---

73 *Ibid.*, xii.6.4-5, 7.1-3. xiv.4.3.

74 The king of the victorious Kelts then erected a palace at Troy. Its remains indicate a type similar to those of earlier date erected by Kelts in Thessaly, Transylvania, and Württemberg.

75 Strabo, xii.8.4.

76 *Ibid.*, xiv.1.3, 4.3; Herodotus, vii. 91.

77 Strabo xiii.3.1, 4.6.

78 *Ibid.*, xii.3.9.

79 Palestine (*Joshua* 1:4, 3:10, 9:1, 11:3, 12:8, 24:11; 1 *Kings* 10:29; 2 *Kings* 7: 6; *Judges* 1:21, 26-33, 3:5-6, central uplands (*Numbers* 13:29), Hebron (*Genesis* 23:3, 10). Ezekiel's mother was a Hittite (*Ezekiel* 16:3), and Solomon had a Hittite wife.

80 *Genesis* 10:10.

renowned code of Amoritic King Hammurabi, promulgated about 2100 B.C., was an embodiment of much earlier laws of the Sumerians and their predecessors, although many Hamitic customs doubtless were included.[81] These Babylonians (apparently the Sumerians along with the Hamites) developed the sciences of mathematics (geometry, square and cube roots, and fractions) and astronomy about that time, long antedating the Greeks.

During approximately 22 centuries, through the various political regimes from about 1150 B.C. until A.D. 1071, when the Seljuk Turks appeared in Anatolia from central Asia, the Kelts dominated all of the westerly portion and the region north of the Taurus Mountains as far as the Armenians of Cappadocia and the eastern highlands, but they must have blended markedly with adjacent Mediterraneans and Leleges, as these races were continually in contact[82] on the west, east, and south. However, they were not free from intermittent invasions by Nordic Aryans from Western Scythia, chiefly the Kimmerii and the Getae (later Goths), who left a minor strain in the population. The earliest were the Carduchi of Kurdistan, in the east, and later other Kimmerians invaded the west, chiefly Lydia. Then, in 278-277 B.C., the Gallic tribes of the *Tectosages, Tolistobogii,* and *Trocmi,* after crossing Europe with others of Brennus' ravaging army from Gaul, separated from the main body in Thrace and invaded Anatolia, settling in the region later known as Galatia.[83] They comprised approximately 20,000 men, women, and children, but whether Keltic Gauls or Nordic Kimmerians (whose ancestors earlier had settled in Gaul) is not certain; but the evidence strongly points to the latter.[84] In 1227 the Seljuks were overthrown by the Osman Turks

---

81 In 1948 it was reported from Yale University that an old code of ancient laws of Bilalama, king of Eshnunna, a nation on the east bank of the Tigris River, had been found by Professor Albrecht E. R. Goetze.

82 Herodotus i. 171-173.

83 Strabo xii.5.1-3.

84 The features of the modern leaders of Turkey preponderantly indicate descent from such Nordic people.

from central Asia[85] and under their leader Osman I (who reigned from 1288 to 1326) founded the Turkish empire of the Osmanli, still one of the family of nations, which for a considerable time dominated southeastern Europe.[85] Thus, the present population of Turkey is multi-racial, Aryan Mediterranean, Turanian Turkic, and Aryan Keltic and Nordic — but the different elements have emerged to a marked degree through the ages.

Philologists have ascertained that the ancient Sumerian dialect represented an agglutinative language on a primitive base, one harsher in expression than the other.[86] One was that of the Sumerian conquerors and the other that of the underlying Pre-Sumerians. The former was without gender, had a system of conventionalized pictures, shaped by their type of speech into syllable-signs, exactly like the Chinese, and possessed a vowel harmony strikingly like that in all modern agglutinative languages and a vocalic dissimilation like that in modern Finnic and Estonian. It also is believed that it had a system of voice tones similar to those present in the Chinese. The method of word formation was non-Hamitic. In the complicated Sumerian verbal system, the practice of infixing the verbal object likewise was alien to Hamitic.[87] This phenomenon exists today in the Basque[87] and many North American (Amerind) languages.

The reason for these likenesses is not far to seek. Since all of these races except the Mediterranean and Hamitic were of Turanian origin in central Asia, the language similarities were carried down in different directions by each branch independently. *The Basques are simply descendants of a group of Leleges from Anatolia either planted as a colony near the Pyrenees or shipwrecked on the shores of the Bay of Biscay sometime prior to*

---

85 The western Asiatic steppes are still the home of Turkic peoples, who shade off in the east into the Tunguses or Mongolians. After 1359 the Turks also spread over the Balkan peninsula, imparting a marked Turkic strain to the population of that region. They were driven out in modern times.

86 *Encyclopaedia Britannica*, 13th Ed., vol. 26, pp. 75-77, by John D. Prince.

87 See Rhys and Brynmor-Jones, *The Welsh People* (Unwin, London, 1906), Appendix B by J. Morris Jones, pp. 639-640.

1500 *B.C., probably the latter.* They intermarried with local Aryan people. The North American Indian tribes, or Amerinds, emigrated northeastward to North America while the Finns and Estonians were migrating northwestward in Asia and across northern Europe. The superimposition of the Hamitic language in southwestern Asia merely incorporated a different element into the Turanian dialects originally spoken by the invaders of Elam, Mesopotamia, Syria, Anatolia, and Palestine.

Culturally, the Pre-Sumerians were responsible for the invention of the pictorial hieroglyphs that became the running-hand or cuneiform characters of Sumerian times and also for the foundation of the chief cities of Mesopotamia and the fundamentals of its civilization. The great engineering works by means of which the marshes were drained and the overflow of the rivers regulated by canals date from Pre-Sumerian times. These people also must be credited with the earliest development of architecture, for the oldest known architectural remains go back in the Babylonian region as far as 6000 B.C. The building material used was brick, and these people were the first to construct vaults and arches. Moreover, they appear to have originated the use of metals (copper) before any other people, and their characteristically painted vases and other articles early reached the Aegean and other eastern Mediterranean regions by traders who crossed Anatolia. Gold was known to them in early Neolithic times, when it was used for ornamentation. They developed the technique of painting clay with indelible color that became fixed by firing. The numerous female figurines that they created represented a cult of the Mother Goddess not known in Indo-European religious customs. In primitive man's search for the secret of the preservation of life, the blood was looked upon as the essence of life, the loss of which resulted in death. Since the child received its blood from its mother, the figurine represented the mother as a giver of life and motherhood was revered for that reason. As earlier stated, these people worshipped the elements, particularly the god of the air, as Chinese peasants still do. They also domesticated dogs, cattle, sheep, goats, pigs, and horses.

An important trade center developed by them prior to 8000 B.C. was Anau, in Western Turkistan. Another established by them about 8000 B.C. was the earliest western terminus at Susa, in Elam. Settlements in Mesopotamia and elsewhere followed promptly, as already related. Commerce then followed the Neolithic modes. Since that revolutionary culture, along with other elements of Turkic progress, entered Europe from the southeast shortly after 7500 B.C., we must conclude that the Pre-Sumerians were chiefly responsible for that cultural transition in Europe. In the extension of their primitive civilization, they gradually created trade routes to the eastern and southern Mediterranean shores and across Anatolia, where commercial intercourse was established with the Aegean region and Europe by about 5000 B.C. Sparsely settled in Anatolia, they apparently made no attempt to enter Europe at that time, but freely transmitted their culture and products through the Mediterranean and northern races,[88] in addition to their operation later of extensive maritime trade routes toward the east and the west. During the succeeding centuries, including Sumerian times, this race developed its culture to still higher levels and its wares were dispersed widely, reaching the Indus Valley in India,[89] as far south as Ethiopia and Egypt, and Europe in the west. The introduction by the Turks of the domesticated horse from central Asia to the Near East is demonstrated by its having been depicted in the 5th century B.C. in the frieze of the Parthenon and numerous bas-reliefs of that period. This animal much resembles the wild horse of central Asia in size, the shape of the head and neck, and the peculiar short upstanding mane. The variations in design of many products indicate a migration of culture, resulting perhaps from the labors of itinerant workers along the trade routes. Many Mongolian objects

---

[88] See discussion by V. Gordon Childe in *The Aryans* (Knopf, 1926), pages 103 ff.
[89] V. Gordon Childe, *More Light on the Most Ancient East* (Appleton-Century, New York, 1934), pages 204-277. Mohenjo-Daro, Harappá, and other centers in the Indus Valley have disclosed a high contemporary civilization that embraced features of that of Sumer, in Babylonia. H. Heras, *Studies in Proto-Indo-Mediterranean Culture*, I, pages 201-212.

were taken west and western products were taken far east. By contact with Kelts and Nordics along the transasiatic route, a degree of Pre-Sumerian culture and certain products were gained by those peoples.[90]

Since agriculture was fundamental in the economy of vase-painting, it follows that the Pre-Sumerians also must have developed the cultivation of the soil, for this art entered Europe later from the southeast. It is known that agriculture was practised at Susa long prior to 5000 B.C. The settled community life in both Turkistan and Mesopotamia rested mainly on agriculture. Beer was made in lower Mesopotamia from barley or spelt as early as 6000-5000 B.C. One of the earliest grains grown was emmer, knowledge of which reached Europe from the southeast with the arts of agriculture prior to 4000 B.C. Metal already was in use at Anau by 5000 B.C. and it soon passed westward to Mesopotamia and Egypt. Upon the discovery of tin about 4200 B.C., the Bronze Age was ushered in by the Sumerian conquerors of Lower Mesopotamia. This is proved by the patterns of the urns, which are distinctly oriental. The ores apparently came from Elam, Oman, and the Taurus Mountains. In the Mediterranean the island of Cyprus was one of the chief early sources of copper and timber during the early Bronze Age, prior to 3500-3000 B.C. The Cyprian implements then were of the common Anatolian type, which found markets across the Hellespont and in the Aegean region. Later came the Iron Age, since iron products were known by 3500 B.C. from Kansu, on the east, across Mesopotamia to Egypt, on the west, along the commercial routes of the Sumerians.

During the long period from approximately 8000 B.C. to as late as the overthrow of the Sumerians in the Fertile Crescent by the Hamitic Chaldeans about 2750 B.C., when the Turkic peoples maintained racial connections and trade routes from Kansu to Mesopotamia, Egypt, Europe, and elsewhere, they had the benefit of all cultural advances made by alien peoples along those exten-

90 V. Gordon Childe, *The Aryans* (Knopf, 1926), pages 185-189.

sive routes and maintained a generally improving culture from one end of the central route to the other. Among the outstanding centers at this time were Anau, Seistan, Korassam, Susa, and Eridu as well as Mediterranean coastal points. Upon the rise of the Hamites in the Fertile Crescent, the southern Kheta were pushed southward into Palestine, whence a strong force overran Egypt, as already related. By land and water the Kheta renewed their commercial activity with all surrounding nations, including their kin in Anatolia, and Cyprian objects reached South Palestine as well as Egypt[91] and more distant points, such as Thera (Santorin), Athens, and Troy (Hissarlik). Conversely, foreign objects, such as Egyptian blue-beads and cylindrical Asiatic seals, reached Cyprus.[92]

An important manner in which this Asiatic culture reached the west was by the explorations of the Anatolian "prospectors," who began to follow the Mediterranean and Atlantic shores in commerce about 2700 B.C. Brachycephalous in nature, they undoubtedly were Leleges. They prospected for copper, tin, and gold, which probably were less obtainable in the east because of Hamitic control of Mesopotamia and which in the form of manufactured products had ready markets in the Mediterranean and eastern civilizations. The Hamitic conquest in the Fertile Crescent had forced them to turn toward the west for new sources of raw material and new markets. Eventually, tin was discovered in northern Iberia, France, and Cornwall, England. After the Hittites had gained Cappadocia about 2300 B.C., they may have discovered new sources in Anatolia and Armenia. The ability of these early peoples to find and smelt ores implies a knowledge of geology and metallurgy. Hence, they were the first-known mining engineers. The Hittite invasion, forcing Leleges from northern Anatolia, doubtless is the basis of the Rhodian legend that primitively (before the Dorian invasion) their island had been peopled by skillfull workers in metal,

---

91 V. Gordon Childe, *More Light on the Most Ancient East* (Appleton-Century, New York, 1934), pp. 66, 85, 101-102, 105-106, 120-128.
92 *Encyclopaedia Britannica*, 13th Ed., vol. 7, pp. 697-698, by John L. Myres.

called the Telchines."[93] Their ancestors must have been Anatolian metal workers who had taken refuge on the island. These maritime prospectors were very influential in disseminating eastern culture to the habitations along the shores all the way from Gozo, in the Malta Islands, to the British Isles.

Contemporaneously, apparently others of the same peoples, known as the "Beaker Folk", energetically undertook the opening of trade routes inland to the upper Rhine valley and surrounding country and to the Iberian peninsula as well as the exploring for ores and other precious substances. Their culture differed from that of the indigenous people. A distinctive vase or beaker always was buried in their graves, often along with gold and amber.

The dolmen builders during the late Neolithic period in western Europe (from about 2700 to 1700 B.C.) apparently were Anatolian (Lelegian) journeyman, who plied their craft not only around the Black Sea and in the Caucasus region and south thereof but also at seaports mainly along the southern Mediterranean and northern Atlantic coasts and along the shores of southern India and in adjacent regions. Along with numerous ports in southern Anatolia, the northeasterly corner of the Mediterranean, centering perhaps on the ancient seaport of Iskenderun (Alexandretta), must have been a base of Anatolian navigation from late in the 4th to early in the 2nd millennium B.C. Directly east of Iskenderun lay the important city of Karkamis (Carchemish) on the upper Euphrates, along the route from Sumer through Cappadocia to central and western Anatolia. Still farther east, on a tributary of the Euphrates, was Haran (the present Harran), undoubtedly a city of some note, where the Hebrew leader Terah and his son Abram went from Ur in Chaldea and where the former died.[94] Thus, a combined land and water route for the transmission of culture from Mesopotamia and the east to western Europe by way of the Mediterranean Sea certainly existed. Dol-

---

93 *Ibid.*, vol. 23, p. 258.
94 *Genesis* 11:31, 32.

mens and menhirs have been found along the ancient Turanian trade routes from central Asia across Iran to Anatolia, whence the influence of their craftsmen subsequently reached northward to Circassia, Krimea, and Bulgaria, southward among their racial kin of Syria and Palestine, westward to Cyprus, and along the northern coast of Africa (Tunis, Algiers, and Morocco) to the Atlantic and along its shores (Iberia and Gaul) as far as the British Isles, Belgium, Netherlands, northwestern Germany, Denmark,[95] Norway, and southern Sweden. Dolmens still abound in Palestine. Some of the Moabite dolmens resemble those of western Europe in being surrounded by one or more rings of stone. These craftsmen appear also to have penetrated western India,[96] southern Arabia, and Madagascar, perhaps by water routes from the Persian Gulf. No such dolmens have been found east of Weimar, Germany, in central and eastern Europe. Their absence from the northerly Mediterranean shores indicates that the activities of these craftsmen occurred during the period of about 2500-1700 B.C., partly contemporaneous with the domination of those shores by the Kretan sea-power.

Apparently, the use of dolmens was widely adopted by the Kelts in western Europe,[97] especially in Gaul and Britain, since the earlier types contained remains of brachycephalic Keltic people, with pottery and coarse implements. Later the Mediterranean (dolichocephalic) people also adopted them. Ultimately, they were superseded by stone circles and cisted cairns for burial.[98] The decline in the use of dolmens began at the climax of the Neolithic Age upon the introduction of improved arts of agriculture, sun worship, and megalithic monuments from western Asia about 2000-1700 B.C. That sun-worship and the use of megaliths had an Asiatic ori-

---

95 Spelled according to the Danish form in preference to the less correct English form of Denmark.
96 See H. Heras, *op. cit.*
97 V. Gordon Childe, *The Aryans* (Knopf, New York, 1926), page 181.
98 It is likely that dolmens were erected as late as a few centuries before the Christian era by Goidelic Kimmerians (chiefly Picts) in such distant places as Lewis and Shetland Islands.

gin is demonstrated by their widespread use from Korea across central and western Asia and in western Europe.

The inference is that they were disseminated by the people who developed agriculture, i.e., the Pre-Sumerians or Sumerians. Stonehenge in Wiltshire, England, erected about 1680 B.C.,[99] probably is a creation of these craftsmen. The presence of gold and other distinctive objects in some of the tumuli along this route supports this view. The fact that dissemination to western Europe occurred by water[100] and not by land strengthens this conclusion, since the same people introduced these customs by water along the shores of southern India and in Assam. Furthermore, recently-found evidence in Sind (near Larkana) and in the Punjab (north of the Sutlej River) shows the penetration apparently prior to 3000 B.C. of a civilization analogous to that of Elam and Sumer, including building brick, interment of contracted bodies in cist graves, shell inlays, mace heads and pestles, stamp seals, clay models of rams and female figurines, and painted pottery. That the use of megaliths was imposed by people of superior culture on people of lower culture (the Kelts) is evidenced by the fact that the internal progress of the users was negligible. Their furniture remained rude and barbaric. They continued to use flint or stone, or, at best, copper. when the people of the Near East were using bronze and iron. It was not until toward the end of the 2nd millennium B.C. that the higher culture of the Near East reached western Europe through the Kelts of central Europe.

As indicated before, the Basques along the Pyrenees in France and Spain are descendants of a group of these Anatolian voyagers, who probably became shipwrecked on the shore of France or Spain prior to 1500 B.C. and subsequently intermarried with the natives (Mediterraneans and Kelts), since the present descendants represent a modified type. In consequence of later invasions in the Pyrenean region, they ultimately settled where they are found today. This racial origin is confirmed by the affinity

---

99 Some estimates make this date as early as 2100 B.C.
100 V. Gordon Childe, *op. cit.*, page 172.

between the agglutinative language of the Basques and that of the ancient Pre-Sumerians, notwithstanding that this language may have been modified early by contact with the underlying Aryans in each instance. It is apparent that the Etrurians of early Italy were another colony from Anatolia. While Herodotus[101] asserts, from the information he had, that they were a Lydian people known as Tyrrhenians, who took their name from Tyrrhenus, a son of their former sovereign, who conducted them thither, it is not said that they were Lydians (Kelts) racially. They seem to have been Anatolian subjects (Leleges) expelled by the Lydian nation to diminish internal insecurity. Their culture had an Anatolian aspect. Their word for copper, *urraida,* was derived from the Sumerian *urudu.* The name *Arcles* (from which Hercules was derived) appears orginally to have been the Etruscan name *Hercle* or *Ercle* and perhaps also that of the Babylonian sun. Africanus called one of the Hyksos kings Arcles. Thus, the racial relationship of these various peoples is further verified.

Another racial contribution by the Pre-Sumerians (the Kheta) is the brachycephalic element among the Indafrican races across the continent of Africa from the westerly end of eastern Sudan and in the Canary Islands. It rarely ever appears there in a pure condition. The Anatolian type of skull has been found among the burials in the Gizeh necropolis during the Vth dynasty (c.2750-2625). These skulls represent a larger race than the Egyptians, namely, the Khetan invaders from Syria and Palestine about 2700 B.C. already named. Individual Kheta intermarried with Egyptians while the former were in control in Egypt then and later under the Hyksos kings, but, when control was regained by the Egyptians, most of the Kheta were scattered far and wide, and it is this broad-headed type of people that now is found among the natives across central Africa. During the regime of the Hyksos dynasties in Egypt, they introduced the domesti-

---

101   Herodotus i.94.

cated horse and war chariot from the north.[102] This animal was referred to in Babylonian records as "the ass of the east", which indicates the region of its origination.[102]

Later-known divisions of the Turkic race that played important roles in history prior to and after the beginning of the Christian era were the *Issedones,* the *Oigurs* or *Uigurs* or *Eluthe,* the *Tatars* (Seljuk and Osman conquerors of modern Turkey), and other minor groups. All arose in central Asia and were possessed of relatively superior culture. The progress of the Issedones and the Uigurs will be reviewed subsequently.

Back on the Tibetan plateau, the Turkic tribes who remained there after their congeners had moved down early to the Tarim Basin ultimately commingled with and were largely absorbed by the more numerous Mongolians of inferior culture from northeastern Tibet. This racial amalgamation comprises the present inhabitants of that plateau, the loftiest and loneliest country in the world.

(5h) *Semitic Subrace.* It is difficult to gain a clear understanding of most writers' conceptions of the origin and type of the people who constituted the Semitic race of early history; in fact, the term Semite often has been applied to dissimilar races. Applications of racial and linguistic names seem to have been much confused. The ancient races that settled in western Asia, including Arabia and Ethiopia, were the Aryan Mediterraneans and Hamites and much later branches of the Turki (Pre-Sumerians, the Sumerians, and Hittites), a division of the Turanian race in Western Turkistan, who dispersed the Aryan Mediterraneans that they encountered. The former were dolichocephalous and the latter were brachycephalous; all had dark complexions of different shades and the Aryans usually were the taller and slenderer. Despite the frequent commingling that occurred in certain areas, the two types can be recognized and should be distinguished. We are con-

---

102 See J. L. Myres, *The Dawn of History* (Williams and Norgate, London, 1911), pages 120-122, 151-153, 200-201; also A. H. Keane, *Man, Past and Present* (Cambridge Press, 1920), pages 303, 496-498.

cerned here with the whole Turkic (or Semitic) subrace and only secondarily with its Hebraic branch; for, after all, the Hebrews constituted only a minor portion of the original Semites. Can we say that some Turks were Semites and others were not?[103] Various later tribes and nations, of different names, likewise were Semites, descended from the major Turkic divisions named above as well as from the Hebraic branch.

The Semites took their generic name from Shem and are defined as inhabitants of Elam, Asshur, Arpachshad (or Arphaxad), Aram, and Lud,[104] representing Elam, Assyria, Babylonia, Syria, and southern Palestine or Transjordania,[104] respectively. The inhabitants of Elam, Assyria, and southern Anatolia (except for any Mediterranean subjects) were wholly Pre-Sumerians from Western Turkistan about 8000 B.C. Those of Babylonia were Sumerians from Turkistan about 4300 B.C. in the southeasterly part and Aryans (Akkdians Chaldeans, and Amorites) from southerly Arabia or Canaan about 3800, 2750, and 2160 B.C. respectively in the northwesterly and southerly parts, with a minor substratum of Sumerians.[105] Those of Aram were Pre-Sumerians commingled with Sumerians driven northwestward when the Akkadians and

103 *Genesis* 10:22-24. Except for the Leleges in Anatolia, these regions embraced practically all of these ancient Turkic inhabitants.
104 The location of Lud is not well indicated. Its inhabitants are specifically named as Semites and were not Aryans. Libya, west of Egypt, is excluded by separate mention in *Jeremiah* 46:9 and *Ezekiel* 30:5. Lydia, at the westerly edge of Anatolia, on the Aegean Sea, was inhabited mainly by Aryan Kelts from Thrace who conquered that region after 1425 B.C. and was too far away. The fact that archers from Lud and others served in the Egyptian and Phoenician (Tyrian) armies signifies a homeland in the general region of Palestine. *Ezekiel* 30:5 refers to them as "mingled" people. Named with four other countries as inhabited by Semites, Lud was in Asia and could not have been situated far from them. It follows from the evidence that Lud must have been a hilly region in southern Palestine or Transjordania inhabited by the Pre-Sumerian Kheta, remote kin of the Assyrians, whose ancestors served under the Hyksos kings when they conquered and ruled Egypt for a long time. Semitic features in Hyksos names have been found. Further evidence is the fact that the men of Lud, like the Hyksos followers, are specifically named as skilled in the use of the bow. *Isaiah* 66:19; *Jeremiah* 46:9; also *Hyksos* in Ency. Brit., 13th Ed., vol. 14, pages 175-6.
105 This confusion of Turanian Semitic and Aryan Hamitic dialects was the origin of the term *Babel*, the native name of the city called *Babylon* by the Greeks, the capital of Babylonian province.

Chaldeans conquered northerly Babylonia. Those of the Palestine hills, except for Canaanites (including the Phoenicians, Amorites, Jebusites, and other tribes) and Philistines, were Pre-Sumerians (known as the Khatti or Kheta) before the arrival of the Hebrews.

The third nation of Turkic invaders of western Asia, the Hittites (Heth, Hitti) of about 2300 B.C., likewise may be classified as Semites, although not included in *Genesis* with the others. The dialect of the Hittites had undergone much modification by contact in Western Turkistan with the Nordic nations on their northeast in Geté (the present province of Semiryechensk, Kirghiz) before they emigrated to Anatolia. The Semitic language originally was agglutinative, but that of the Hittites, for the reason just stated, had been changed to the inflectional form. The descendants of the Hittites, now called Armenians, constitute a part of the Turkish nation, whose system of oral and written communication again underwent major improvement during the first half of the present century.

On the other hand, the term Semite did not embrace the Aryan nations of those regions, chiefly the Mediterranean Arabians (largely Bedouins), Akkadians, Philistines (from Krete), and Caucones (of Anatolia) and the Hamites (Chaldeans, Canaanites, Amorites, Phoenicians, Jebusites and others, far southern Arabians, Ethiopians, and Berbers). The original Semites were clean-shaven and these Aryans were bearded. Thus, the Semites clearly were not Arabian in origin but came from Western Turkistan, central Asia; but the two races, mainly in Babylonia and Chaldea, ultimately commingled, probably intermarried, and produced diverse types of descendants, who interchanged the customs of their ancestors to a large extent.

The subsequent wars among the Elamites, Babylonians, Assyrians, and Egyptians apparently did not markedly change the habitations of the main bodies of those peoples, although there were minor shifts of smaller groups. These racial distinctions were recognized in early Biblical times, say about 2300-1600 B.C., for Abram, a Semite (Kassite) from "Ur of the Chaldees" traditionally forbade his son or descendant)[106] Isaac to marry a Hamite woman of Canaan and exacted a promise of his servant (or aide) to take Isaac to Nahor, his brother at Haran, in Aram, the land of his ancestors after they had come from Ur,[107] for a wife, which he did. The southerly Arabian Hamites and the central Arabian Bedouins did not inhabit the Transjordan region but occupied those parts of Arabia in the peninsula. From both geographical and ethnological standpoints, the region immediately east of the Jordan River and the Dead Sea belonged to Palestine and not to Arabia proper. Its inhabitants were (and probably still are) Turkic Semites and not Aryan Arabs except to the extent of later intrusion by the latter. The inhabitants of peninsular Arabia (or Arabia proper) until the 10th century B.C. were wholly Aryan; but about the latter time Hebrews of Canaan were invited to migrate southward to Saba (Yemen) by its King Menelek, for reasons shown later.

The Hebrews[108] are said to have been an offshoot of Aramaeans, and that they largely adopted the language and customs of the Hamitic Jebusites among whom they finally settled in Canaan. This is only partially correct. The Assyrians called Hebrew the language of the west

106 About 200 years passed between the time of Abraham and that of Jacob, so that numerous generations intervened.

107 The land of the Sumerians and later Chaldeans. *Genesis* 24:1-10; 25:19-20; 28; 29; 31; 33:18; 35:26. *Deuteronomy* 26:5. Although these two nations were neighbors, they continued to maintain their separate identities. Chaldea seems to have been situated immediately south or southwest of Sumer. The Habiri lived at Ur long enough for Terah's three or more children to be born there and for the youngest son Haran to attain the age to marry and have a son Lot there before his decease, roughly 30 years. *Genesis* 11:27-32.

108 The early history and movements of the Hebrews may have been associated with the Sumerian cult of Sin, the moon-god, also known as Nannar, the illuminer, which they gained while at Ur, in Chaldea, and carried to Haran (Harran), in Aram (Syria), and later to Canaan, where they finally settled. This god, also called En-zu, "the lord of wisdom," was regarded by the Hebrews at Ur as the head of the pantheon. He was par excellence the god of nomadic peoples, their guide and protector at night during wanderings, just as the sun-god was the chief god of agricultural peoples. "Sin" appears in the root-word of the name Sinai, as in Mount Sinai, where the later Nabataean inscriptions also were in the Aramaic language. *Ency. Brit.*, 13th Ed., vol. 25, pp. 138-139.

country, probably that of Aram.[109] The real Semitic languages were not related to the Aryan languages. Phonetically, the Hebrew language occupies a middle place between blended Turanian Aramaic (Pre-Sumerian and Sumerian), on the one hand, and Aryan Hamitic (Canaanite), on the other,[109] because of the various races among whom they lived. Sir Henry Rawlinson, collaborator in the translation of Herodotus' history, asserts that the Hebraic tribe sprang from ancient Babylonia and spread northward and westward.[110] This statement is acceptable as far as it goes, but it does not go back far enough. The name Hebrew was derived from that of the *Khabira (Habiru, Habiri)*, a tribe of Kassites, who were a division of the Elamite nation of Susa and northwestward, bordering the Medians. These Khabira settled in the Babylonian plain apparently about 1815 B.C. They were Pre-Sumerians and had an agglutinative language in common with the other Turkic Semites. *The word Khabira means "those from the other side" (apparently of the Tigris River).* At Ur, they lived near Sumerians and Chaldeans.

The name Khabira denoted "allies," implying that they were mercenaries who served those nations who rewarded them the most,[111] but in Babylonia they also were known as the *Sa-Gas,* which had the hapless meaning of "robbers";[111] so we may infer that they had been expelled from Elam by their own nation. Their departure from Ur to Aram apparently only about a year before the Kassites conquered Babylonia about 1780 B.C. indicates a desire to avoid another such expulsion by their nation. Their historically arrogant character may have conduced to their difficulties.[111] In Aram the Pre-Sumerian

---

109 *The Jewish Encyclopedia,* vol. 21, page 187. *Genesis* 10:16, 20; *Numbers* 13:29; *Judges* 1:3, 21.

110 George Rawlinson, *The History of Herodotus* (Appleton, New York, 1889), vol. 1, Essay VI, par. 21, pages 356-367, and Essay XI, page 526. *Genesis* 10:11, 21-23; 11:10-32; and 24:10. Also, E. A. Speiser, *Mesopotamian Origins* (Univ. of Pennsylvania Press, 1930; Oxford Press, H. Milford, London, 1930). Speiser presents the names of a number of Pre-Sumerian tribes.

111 *Ency. Brit.,* 13th Ed., vol. 5, p. 141c, vol.10, p. 78b, vol. 15, pp. 372 and 694 (Kassites), and vol. 20, p. 606c. Under Kassites is cited Fr. Delitzsch, *Die Sprache der Kossäer* (1884). Such self-adopted terms as "the master race," "the chosen people," and the like are merely emanations of that attitude of mind.

language could not have differed greatly from that of their kin, the Elamites and their Kassite division.

It is interesting to observe how well Biblical accounts confirm the foregoing outline of racial relationship. *Genesis* 10:1 names the races then known (about 2300 B.C.) as (1) sons of Shem (Turanian Semites), (2) sons of Ham (Aryan Hamites),[112] and (3) sons of Japheth (Aryans of the North).[113] We are concerned here almost wholly with the first two subraces and with the clarification and movements of the Hebrews. Mention in *Genesis* 11:28,31 of the residence of Terah and his son Abram at Ur, in the land of the Chaldees, agrees with what has been said before, namely, that they belonged to the tribe of *Khabira* (Habiru, Habiri) of the Kassite division of the Elamites and had settled in the Babylonian plain about 1815 B.C. The Kassites frequently assailed Babylonia and about 1781 B.C. the Khabira (Hebrews) decided to depart from Ur to Haran, in Aram, and other dissident minorities also fled the country. Finally, about 1780 B.C., the Kassites conquered the country and founded a dynasty that endured 576 years and 9 months.[114] The Hebrews, then under the leadership of Terah, were among kindred people (Pre-Sumerians) at Haran (Harran), in Padan-Aram. Soon Terah died[115] and was succeeded by his son Abram as leader, whereupon the tribe began a further

---

112 *Genesis* 9:18 and 10:6 and 1 *Chron.* 1:8-9. The "sons of Ham" inhabited Cush (southern Arabia), Mizraim (Egypt), Phut (Ethiopia), and Canaan (westerly Palestine).

113 *Genesis* 10:2-5.

114 The dynasty of the Kassites ended about 1204 B.C. In consequence of intermarriage of its members with the royal dynasty of Assyria, Babylonia became nominally subject to Assyria, with some intermittent rule by Elamites and Sumerians, and wholly subject about 680 B.C.

115 *Genesis* 11:31-32; 12:1, 4, 5; 27:43; 28:1-7; *Deuteronomy* 26:5. His children were born while the tribe lived at Ur. *Genesis* 11:28, 31. Since the tribe migrated to Padan-Aram about 1781 B.C., this time affords a basis for the computation of early Hebrew chronology.

migration about 1775 B.C. to its ultimate destination, the land of Canaan, fully 1000 miles away.[116]

In chapter 10:23 of *Genesis* and again in chapter 11:10-26, Arpachshad or Arphaxad is given as the eponymous ancestor of Salah and the latter's son Eber, and Eber is said to have had sons Peleg and Joktan. Arpachshad or Arphaxad, which meant Babylonia, is a compound word of which the derivation of the first part is Turkic and that of the second part is Chaldean. When we recall that the lower part of Babylonia was inhabited by Turanian Sumerians and that the central and upper region was inhabited by Aryan Akkadians, Chaldeans, and Amorites, with a substratum of Sumerians, it is apparent that the word had the connotation of Sumer-Chaldea for the two racial elements of the kingdom then in existence. The genealogy of Peleg in chapter 11:17-26 is that of the Sumerians and the genealogy of Joktan[117] in chapter 10:26-30 is that of the Hamitic nations from and in southern Arabia, "for in his [Eber's] time was the earth divided", i.e., divided between the two dissimilar sub-races, the Pre-Sumerians and Sumerians and the Hamites[118] (Chaldeans). Padan-Aram never was under Chaldean suzerainty and it was not conquered by the Kassites. It extended from central Upper Mesopotamia westward to the mountains near the Mediterranean shores. It was bisected by the Euphrates River, north of which lay Haran. The region of Aram was largely synonymous with that of modern Syria. The settlement of Haran (Harran) is said to have been named for Abram's brother and to

---

116 *Genesis* 11:31. Abram then was 37½ years old. Evidently, the Hebrews again experienced dissension in Aram, for it is said that God told Abram to get out of the country, away from his kin, and to proceed to Canaan and establish a new nation. Thereupon, he took his wife, all of the substance that they had gathered, and all of the people that would follow them and proceeded to the promised land of Canaan. *Genesis* 12:1-9. The estimated dates of about 1781 B.C. for their migration from Ur to Padan-Aram and about 1775 B.C. for their next movement from Padan-Aram have some support in *Genesis* 11:27-32 and 12:4, since Terah's third son Haran is said to have died at Ur, the land of his birth, after having had a son named Lot.

117 For definitions of Biblical names and terms, see Funk & Wagnalls' *New Standard Bible Dictionary* (New York, 1936).

118 *Genesis* 10:25.

be Sumerian in origin, adopted while the Hebrews lived among the Sumerians and Chaldeans at Ur; in fact, they must have intermarried with the kindred Sumerians.

Other evidence demonstrates the accuracy of the foregoing conclusions. Pictorial representations of the ancient Sumerians show substantially the same physical features as those borne by the later Hebrews, including the prominent nose.[119] That the first part of the name Arpachshad or Arphaxad is Sumerian (i.e., Turanian Turkic) in origin is indicated by the fact that it apparently had the same derivation as the word *Arphad* or *Arpad*,[120] the traditional name of the leader of the Magyars (Hungarians), another Turanian nation, when that nation from the Volga River basin moved southward through Vereczka Pass into the region of the upper Theiss River, now in Hungary, in A.D. 895 and completed the conquest of that territory in 906. Moreover, Sir Henry Rawlinson, by his discoveries among the cuneiform inscriptions, has made it clear that Upper Mesopotamians belonged to the Aramaean branch of the Semitic stock (except that the migration was in the westerly direction, as shown above).[121] The dialect of the Sumerians who had moved into Upper Mesopotamia and westward (Aram — Syria) differed appreciably from that of their earlier Pre-Sumerian congeners of Assyria, although both basically were Turanian Turkic. The Sumerian dialect ceased to exist as a spoken language in Babylonia before 1500 B.C., during the reign of the Kassites, but it long continued to be used as a learned language.

Generally, the Pre-Sumerian nation of Assyria was a strong one. Under the leadership of Ninus, its conquests prior to 2000 B.C. extended as far as Bactria, on the

---

119 Since the original Hebrews were Kassites, of typically Turkic build, i. e., with tawny complexion, of medial height and stocky build, with prominent nose, and brachycephalous, all efforts to identify Aryan Nordic people of Europe as descendants of the Lost Tribes of Israel are doomed to failure. A more futile task is inconceivable. For identity of the Habiri as Hebrews, see *Ency. Brit.*, 13th Ed., vol. 2, page 731, under *Asher*, vol. 5, page 141, under *Canaan*, and vol. 15, page 372, under *Jews.*

120 This word is said to mean "strong" or "powerful."

121 *Chambers Encyclopedia* (1881), vol. 1, page 598.

northeast, and Egypt, on the south,[122] though it was probably as a dependency of the Chaldeans of Babylonia, still a strong nation. Babylonia frequently was invaded by the Kassites, Elamites, and Iranians from the mountains on the north. Within a very short time after the Habiri (Hebrews) had moved from the Babylonian plain to Padan-Aram under attacks by the Kassites just prior to 1780 B.C., they undertook their further migration southward to Canaan.[123] As they approached Palestine, they dislodged Pre-Sumerian Kheta (Hyksos or shepherd kings), who then made their memorable invasion and conquest of Egypt, when they established the XVth dynasty, which endured nearly 199 years. Having been a Turkic people,[124] the Hebrews recognized them as a kindred nation.[125]

During the next 180 years, these Hebrews multiplied greatly and their different groups settled at various places in Palestine, as mentioned in the Tell el-Amarna inscriptions (c. 1375-1358 B.C.). Among these tribes of the Habiri mentioned in the Bible, other than the later Israelites in Canaan, were the *Amalekites, Ammonites, Edomites, Ishmaelites, Midianites,* and *Moabites* as well as some others but little known to history. The Ammonites and Ishmaelites settled east of the Jordan River, the Moabites east of the Dead Sea, the Amalekites and Edomites south of the Dead Sea, and the Midianites between the Moabites and Edomites, southeast of the Dead Sea. The Turkic origin of these early Hebrews is demonstrated further by the fact that they called themselves and were referred

---

122 Strabo, *Geography,* xvi.2:34, 4:2, 18, 21-23.

123 These ancient Hebrews, as shown by the ages stated for different personages, counted each year as two years (summers and winters separately), so that all periods given must be divided by two for proper chronology. Since Terah's youngest son Haran already had a son named Lot and Abram's wife was barren before the migration from Ur to Padan-Aram, and Abram was 38 years old (75 divided by 2) when they departed southward from Aram, this tribe must have tarried in Aram only a few years, *Genesis* 11:27-32, 12:1-9, 17:17-21, but its ethnic relationship with inhabitants there is demonstrated.

124 *Ency. Brit.,* 13th Ed., vol. 14, pp. 175-176.

125 *Genesis* 25:4, 16; *Ency. Brit., ibid.,* vol. 5, pp. 140-142, and vol. 14, p. 176.

to by others as *Syrians* of Palestine,[126] who thus had come from that country (Aram). They had taken over territory adjacent on the west to the Hamitic Canaanites, which, with their arrogant character,[127] explains why the Bible represents them as engaged in frequent warfare with the various other inhabitants of those regions. In fact, King David owed his success to the employment of a troop of freebooters.[127]

About 1600 B.C., a serious famine occurred in Canaan and Jacob then led his tribe of Hebrews (later called Israelites) to Goshen, Egypt.[128] Promptly, Jacob had a conference with the pharaoh and assured him of their peaceful intentions. This king belonged to the Hyksos dynasty and was of kindred race. About 1576 B.C., the adherents of the Hyksos were expelled from Egypt, whereupon they returned to Canaan and established the city of Jerusalem (formerly called Urusalim), which forced many of the Canaanites toward the Mediterranean shores. However, the native Jebusite tribe later regained that region. The successive Egyptian kings increasingly tended to persecute the Israelites and in 1446 B.C., during the reign of King Amenhotep II, Moses led the exodus of these people from Egypt.[129] They moved northward toward Damascus, but later returned southward as they began their conquest of westerly Canaan. This southward movement late in the 15th century B.C. disturbed the security of the Canaanites who still lived west of the Jordan River. Under King David, about 990 B.C. the Israelites captured the city of Jerusalem, which became their capital.

The Bible refers frequently to individual Hittites present in Syria and Palestine a century or so afterward. This Turanian nation in Cappadocia had been driven eastward by the conquest of northern Anatolia by Kelts from

---

126 *Deuteronomy* 26:5; Herodotus, *History*, 2:104, 3:5, 7:89.
127 *I Samuel* 22:2. *Ency. Brit.*, 13th Ed., vol. 7, page 856.
128 *Genesis* 46:6-7, 28-29; 47:1-12.
129 *Genesis* 12:5-20, 13:1-18; *Exodus* 6:4. This time of the Exodus represents the latest finding (1957) of Egyptian scholars Doctors Labid Kabachi and Erwin R. Thiele. Their total number is said not to have exceeded 5,730 persons. *Ency. Brit.*, 13th Ed., vol. 25, page 139.

Thrace during the few centuries after 1425 B.C. and are known today as the Armenians; but many of them fled southward into Syria and Palestine. The wife of Solomon and the mother of Ezekiel were Hittites. The latter's father was a Hamitic Amorite. The Canaanites (including the Amorites) were taller than the Semites.[130] The Canaanites were agricultural people and held more of the advantages of early civilization than those retained by the nomadic Hebrews, although the latter had gained much of the culture of the ancient Sumerians and Chaldeans, their neighbors at Ur, which was the most advanced of that age. Apparently, the nomadic life of the Hebrews had caused the loss of many of their traditional advantages and they later relearned the arts and habits of civilized life from the Canaanites. At this time the Hebrews worshipped a multiplicity of gods. An idea of monotheism reflected by the sun-disk God Ra was developed in Egypt by Pharaoh Amenhotep IV, later known as Akhenaton, who reigned during 1383-1365 B.C. He belonged to the XVIIIth dynasty. However, if Moses wrote Deuteronomy in the 40th year after the Exodus,[131] which, according to the above date, would be 1406 B.C., and then urged his people to worship a single God, the principle of monotheism was older than Amenhotep's time; in fact, it may have emerged from higher Canaanite (Amorite) monotheistic tendencies that evolved out of astral religion amidst Babylonian polytheism[131] and apparently was adopted later in Canaan. Thus, it may be that the evolvement of monotheism should be accredited to the Amorites.[132]

Later, the Israelites, in league with the Phoenicians, demolished the superior civilization of the Philistines on the coast, who were Aryan Mediterraneans who had fled from Krete at the time of the conquest of that island by Achaeans from the Grecian mainland. Known as the

---

130 *Deuteronomy* 1:27-28, 44; *Numbers* 13:22, 28-33. The Hamites today are taller than the more stockily built Semites.
131 *Deuteronomy* 1:3. This probability would accord with the high degree of culture that existed in upper Babylonia at the time of their great king Hammurabi.
132 Discussed further in *Ency. Brit.*, 13th Ed., vol. 13, page 178a.

"children of Israel", these Hebrews became more populous and later separated into the two nations of Israel and Judah, which endured for about three centuries.

King Menelek of Saba (Yemen), natural son of Hebraic King Solomon, of Israel, and Hamitic Queen Balkis, of Sheba,[133] in the 10th century B.C., because of his mixed racial heritage, freely invited Israelites to migrate southward to Sheba and many appear to have taken advantage of the invitation. Thereafter, an observable Hebraic strain and Semitic modification of the local language appeared among the inhabitants of that part of the Arabian peninsula. This Hebraic-Hamitic royal dynasty of the Sabaeans intermarried with a branch of or actually became the ancestral stock of the royal line of Ethiopia and the Hebraic strain is conspicuous in the features of members of the latter dynasty today. The migration of these Hebrews to southwestern Arabia and their commingling with the indigenous local Aryan (Hamitic) population is the reason for the frequent erroneous classification of central and southern Arabians as Semites along with the Turanians of the north. It also explains the origin of the Amharic language of Ethiopia, a composite of the Semitic dialect and the local Arabic-Hamitic dialect.

Ultimately, in 722 B.C., the Assyrian King Sargon II captured Jerusalem, when the nations of Israel and Judah were destroyed and the Israelites scattered. The ten tribes of Israel, comprising 27,290 persons, then were exiled to southern Media, now northwestern Iran, southwest of the Caspian Sea, where most of them ultimately became submerged in the local population. Some of their descendants reached Afghanistan[134] and others may be represented by the present Kurdish tribe of *Yezidis*.[134] Another tribe is reported to have migrated as far east as Kaifeng Fu, in the province of Honan, China, where its members long maintained their identity.

---

133 *I Kings,* chapter 10, 11:1-9; *Dictionary of the Holy Bible* (American Tract Society, New York, 1859), *Sabeans II,* p. 380; Pierre van Paassen, *Days of Our Years* (Hillman-Curl, Inc., New York, 1939), page 315.

134 *Ency. Brit.,* 13th Ed., vol. 1, pages 310-315, vol. 18, page 186d, vol. 28, pages 919-920.

The peculiar notion advanced by some writers, chiefly religionists, that these dark-complexioned brachycephalic Turanian people were the ancestors of the blond mesocephalic Aryan Anglo-Saxons is too absurd physiologically to receive further notice.

After the dispersion of the Israelites by King Sargon II in 721 B.C., their part of Palestine was repopulated by alien people from the deserts,[135] officers were put in charge, and the usual tribute was imposed. Thereafter, Hebrew historians saw Judah as the sole survivor of the Israelite tribes.[136] With the tradition of King David as the founder of a royal line, the capital city of Jerusalem as the nucleus, and the cult of Yahweh as a unifying force, another Israelite monarchy arose in Judah, whose prosperity ultimately was its undoing. Assyria was decaying and a Chaldean prince, Nabopolassar, established himself in Babylonia, to whose ambitions Judah displayed a rebellious spirit. The result was that his son and successor Nebuchadrezzar took vengeance and captured and destroyed Jerusalem in 586 B.C. When Cyrus conquered Babylonia in 539 B.C., he found many Judaeans there and the next year transported them back to Jerusalem. There he fostered their rebuilding of the city, although differences long existed between them and the rest of the population.[137] These exiles then introduced into the Hebrew religion the Babylonian traditions of the Garden of Eden, the Creation of the World and of Man, the Flood, and the Babylonian Sabbath.[137] While this religious reform was modeled largely on Babylonian (Turanian) ideas, much of Egyptian, Canaanite, Edomite, and Hittite origin was retained. Such is the source of much of the material of which the Old Testament of our Bible was compiled. Ultimately, all of the mixed population of Palestine was assimilated into the same religion.

While there was much variation in the degree of amal-

---

135 These people must have been Aryan Arabs from distant places, which would explain the origin of certain later Arabian customs among the Hebrews of Palestine, such as the growing of beards by the mixed population.

136 2 *Kings* 17:7-23. The word Jew was derived from the name Judaea.

137 G. W. Wade, *Old Testament History* (Dutton, New York, 1908), pages 37-62.

gamation of the different racial strains that inhabited this region, it is clear that the Kassite along with minor Hittite and Hamite strains continued to dominate the Hebraic stock and to perpetuate the so-called Hebrew physical features, which were characteristic of those Turkic peoples. From the days of Ezra forward, however, there was greatly-diminished intermarriage of Hebrews with surrounding Semitic or Aryan peoples, for this segment of the ancient Hebraic nation was confined within a Judaean church, strictly endogamous and not much inclined to proselyte. The Aramaean dialect (probably composite Pre-Sumerian-Sumerian) of the Semites ultimately became the prevailing language over all of this region, including Assyria, Babylonia, and southwestern (Turanian) Iran. It remained largely so down to the time of the conquests by the Arabs (probably Aryan Bedouins) in the 7th century A.D. It was simpler than the Arabic language, fresh from the desert of central Arabia; but, since there was no outstanding Aramaic nation and no overshadowing Aramaic civilization, there could be no great Aramaic literature. The best-known idiom is the Syriac, but its literature, while voluminous, is disappointing in content.

The southernmost Semitic nations were the Edomites and their successors, the Nabataeans, whose territory was in southern Transjordania, south of the Moabites. It extended southward from the Dead Sea to the Gulf of Aquaba and centered about the city of Petra, the later Nabataean capital.[138] The Edomites, a tribe of the early Habiri (Hebrews), first settled in this region and enjoyed a relatively high culture for about 8 centuries, or until about the 4th century B.C., when their territory was taken over by the Aramaic Nabataeans. The dialect of the latter is known from their inscriptions. They became a rich and populous nation, whose country was traversed by several trade routes between wealthy nations of the Orient and of Palestine. The Nabataean kingdom existed from about 312 B.C. to about A.D. 106, when it became a Roman province. Copper mines near Petra were once worked by the Nabateans or their predecessors.

---

138 Strabo, *Geogr.* xvi.4.18, 21-26.

About the middle of the Ist century B.C. the Roman Empire gained suzerainty over Palestine and about 37 B.C. Herod, of an Edomite dynasty, was appointed king of Judaea. In consequence of the dispersion of many Hebrews from Palestine to European countries during later centuries of the Christian era, they have interbred with the racial stocks of the countries to which they migrated. The Palestinian type,[139] invariably tawny-complexioned, of medial height, inclined to be slender where the Hamitic strain prevails and more stockily and heavily built and generally round-headed where the original Turanian strain predominates, which is the more common,[139] is seldom seen except in modified form in European countries. Thus, the proportion of Hebraic blood in individuals of that race in Europe has greatly diminished generally and today there are Jews of widely different physical types, many largely Aryan in blood. The slender brunet Mediterranean Jew, the stocky medial-complexioned French or south German Jew, or the blond north German, Lowland, or English Jew has not much in common with the original Hebrew except a peculiar type of psychology, some traces of the Kassite or Hittite physiognomy, and their religious and other social customs. The typical short, squat, dark, phlegmatic so-called Jew of eastern Europe descended from Khazar (Turko-Ugrian) and *not Hebraic* ancestry.

Before terminating this section, it may be well to include a brief history of one of the most eminent Hebrew personages, Jesus of Nazareth, in Galilee, later called the Christ. His mission on earth was to teach mankind to live in harmony with the laws of God, physically, mentally, morally, and spiritually. He founded a new religion, that

---

139 In view of the unquestionable racial features of the Hebraic parents of Jesus Christ, we necessarily must infer that this general description also is applicable to him. Writings and paintings that would have him a Nordic blond or Arabian brunet merely reflect a form of intellectual dishonesty. One might well infer that Jesus was about 5 ft. 8 in. tall, tawny in complexion, stockily-built, weighing about 170 lbs., brachycephalous (or largely round-headed), with brown eyes and the typical Hebraic nose, and not a taller, slenderer, and dolichocephalic Arabic Aryan type, as usually depicted. He also should be shown as clean-shaven and with a haircut, as was customary among the Hebrews of his time.

of Christianity, and established a church[140] based on the principle that "God is Spirit and those who worship Him must worship in spirit and truth"[141] and that "You shall know the truth and the truth shall make you free" (of troubles).[142] "The son of man came not to be served but to serve."[143] But, unfortunately, contrary to his intentions, as Durant states in his book *Caesar and Christ,* page 595, Christianity as it expanded did not destroy paganism but adopted it in large degree and practises it in the churches today in ways too numerous to mention here.

Jesus' father was a youth named Joseph (not he who married Mary), son of Heli (Eli, Elijah),[144] a descendant of David and undoubtedly a member of the Sanhedrin, which met at the temple; and his mother was Mary, a handmaid at the temple.[145] Soon after conception, Mary was married to Joseph of different lineage,[146] and had at least seven other children. The time of his birth at Bethlehem, in Judaea, during the reign of King Herod, is fixed by authorities as either 6 B.C. or 7 B.C., with the evidence favoring the latter year,[147] and not at Christmas but at the time of mild weather, probably about September 1, when sheep were at pasture.

When Jesus was 12 years old, he engaged in discussion of religious principles with members of the Sanhedrin, but nothing more is said of him other than that he "grew in stature and wisdom" until he engaged in his ministry when about 30 years of age.[148] During this intervening period of about 16 years, he, apparently at the expense of his grandfather Elijah, must have wandered over

---

140 *Matthew* 16:18, 18:17; *Acts* 2:47, 5:11, 8:1, 11:26 (the disciples were called Christians first at Antioch), 14:23.
141 *John* 4:24.
142 *John* 8:32, 10:10. *Matthew* 18:20.
143 *Matthew* 20:28; *Mark* 10:45.
144 *Luke* 3:23 et seq.
145 *Luke* 1:38, 48.
146 *Matthew* 1:16-23, 13:55-56; *Mark* 6:3-4.
147 If Herod issued his order to slay boys two years and under a year before his death in 4 B.C. (*Matthew* 2:13-16, 19-20) and Jesus was slightly under two years, that would make it 7 B.C.
148 *Luke* 2:42-52 and 3:23. Only close family relationship could have allowed such informality by a child with members of the Sanhedrin (or high court),

Persia and India (probably with two Essenes) to acquire
the wisdom of the Magi and other eastern philosophers,
for some of his teachings show striking similarity with
utterances of Gotama (Buddha). After 40 days spent in
the wilderness to determine his future procedure, he
engaged in teaching religion publicly in opposition to
the Hebraic Pharisees and Sadducees, well knowing that
he might lose his life in his worthy endeavors, which
he did about 3½ years later, apparently in A.D. 27.

When on the cross at the agonizing ninth hour, Jesus
cried out aloud to his grandfather Elijah, of the Sanhedrin, "Eli, Eli, why hast thou forsaken me?" Whereat the
bystanders remarked, "Behold, he is calling Elijah." One
then ran and brought him a drink of vinegar, but the
others said,"Wait, let us see whether Elijah will come to
take him down." He died soon afterward.[149] It is sacri-
legious to say that Jesus, after all of his courageous preach-
ing for the worship of God, actually repudiated God in
the ninth hour, as erroneously translated. Moreover, it
is contrary to the other context of the epistles of Matthew
and Mark.

A puzzling question in this connection is the relationship, if any, of the distinguished Joseph of Arimathea,
counselor at the Sanhedrin, to Jesus' father Joseph, inasmuch as he was a righteous man, was a disciple of Jesus,
had not consented to the crucifixion, and requested Jesus'
body and put it in his own newly-hewn tomb in the
rocks,[150] an act usually only that of a very close relation.
At this time Joseph of Arimathea would have been about
52 years old (and Jesus over 33 years). Could they have
been one and the same person? It appears so.[148]

Jesus' untimely decease greatly stimulated the ministerial efforts of his apostles and disciples and many other followers as did the martyrdom of later Christian heroes, such
as John Huss (1415), Savonarola (1498), and many others,
as well as the wanton burning of Wycliffe's dead body
(1415). Spiritually, we all, like Jesus, are sons and daugh-

149 *Matthew* 27:45-50; *Mark* 15:33-36.
150 *Matthew* 27:57-60; *Luke* 23:50-53; *John* 19:38-42.

ters of God. It is our sacred duty to preserve the right of religious freedom, as there have been religious as well as political dictatorships; in fact, some of varying degrees of severity exist today, based partly on paganistic formalism and inaccurate, unsound, and frozen interpretations of much of the New Testament and its religious principles.

Two other notable Hebrews, influential in the early promotion of Christianity, were Simon, later called Peter, and Saul, later called Paul. The former was one of the original apostles, whereas Paul was converted shortly after Jesus' death. Peter, who was an uneducated fisherman older than Jesus, was the apostle to the Hebrews, and Paul, who was highly educated, was the apostle to the Gentiles. Paul preached and established churches at numerous places, including localities among the Gentiles of western Asia and in Greece and Macedonia during the period of approximately A.D. 36 to 56. Late in year 59 he underwent a stormy voyage in custody to distant Rome. There he found a few Christians who had preceded him and promptly organized a Christian church about May 1, 60. But his religious labors incensed the pagan Romans and he suffered martyrdom about the year 62. He wrote thirteen epistles of the New Testament during his career as missionary. The outgrowth of the Greek churches was the Greek Orthodox organization and that of the Roman church was the Roman Catholic organization, whose first bishop was Linus. Thus, Paul was the actual founder of both divisions, with the teachings of Jesus as the cornerstone. (See *Acts* 27-28).

In A.D. 65, a Roman army assailed Jerusalem. The next year its leader withdrew for awhile, which afforded the Christian inhabitants and doubtless others an opportunity to flee and they did so; but soon the attack was resumed and the city was taken by Titus in 70 and wholly destroyed. Among the regions to which fleeing Christians dispersed were Pontus, Galatia, Cappadocia, and Bithynia, in Asia Minor, and "Asia", meaning Babylon, to which Peter, his son Mark, and his amanuensis Silvanus went for refuge.[151] Peter's first epistle to these dispersed Christians was written from Babylon, as it states, about the

---

151 1 *Peter* 1:1, 5:12-14.

year 66, with the aid of Silvanus, and the second was written about 67 to the same people. He then was approximately 82 years old, for he said in that letter "I know that the putting off of my body will be soon."[152] He undoubtedly died a natural death in Babylon[153] soon afterward.

(5i) *Paraoeans or Southern Mongoloids.* This Turanian subrace, unlike those previously discussed, did not migrate northward around eastern Tibet. Apparently, very early, perhaps about 27,000 years ago, various tribes of Turanians ascended or were driven from Indo-China toward the upper valleys of the Bramaputra, Irrawaddy, Salween, Mekong, and Yangtze Rivers, from the highlands of Burma to those of Yunnan, at a time of favorable climatic conditions. While the main bodies of Turanians were spreading over the country from Yunnan to Szechuen, settling in the fertile valleys, the population of the Southern Mongoloids greatly increased in these upper river valleys. The time, of course, is conjectural and only rough estimates can be made from general considerations; but the fact that these people became markedly brachycephalous proves that they inhabited those high river valleys a very long time.

Ultimately, overpopulation of those valleys and difficulty of gaining adequate supplies of food resulted in migrations down again. The relatively dense population of the Min people along the central Yangtze River prevented movement in that direction, but it left a wide expanse across southeastern China as far as the coast, down to Indo-China, and over Burma. In its wide sweep

152 2 *Peter* 1:13-15, 3:1.
153 Strained attempts to have Peter, the apostle to the Hebrews of the East, among the Gentiles in Paul's territory at Rome and martyred there are unworthy of serious consideration in the light of all contemporary evidence. At his age, that would not have been practicable. In none of Paul's writings from Rome, in the Acts, or in any other contemporary writings is there the slightest intimation that Peter ever had been or was at that city. All statements to the contrary were made centuries later and are fanciful and hearsay. The Papacy was not organized until the second half of the 8th century. It broke away from the eastern church in 1054. *Ency. Brit.*, 13th Ed., vol. 21, page 636, under Pippin III; also *The Papacy,* by Abbe Guetté.

to these lower lands, this race drove out or superimposed itself on the indigenous negroid and Indonesian people encountered in the different areas. The Indonesians have been found to be an underlying stratum in south-eastern Asia, especially in Yunnan, and the commingling of the two racial elements is discernible in the present inhabitants. In some regions, such amalgamation with earlier peoples produced what is known as the Malay sub-race. Medium or short in stature, brachycephalous, and energetic, this subrace forms the principal element of the population of Burma, Indo-China and the Malay peninsula and islands, Southern China, the Philippine Islands and other western Pacific islands, and Japan (by invasion and conquest).

During many past millennia most of central Asia has been increasing in aridity, so that living conditions in those regions have become continually less favorable. This fact together with the expansion of the Mongolian popu-lation in central Tibet had the effect of forcing other peoples eastward and southward from that plateau and the upper river valleys. The evidence indicates a rela-tively late eruption of Southern Mongoloids from the upper river valleys to the lower elevations over an exten-sive period, but especially during the first half of the 7th century B.C. At that time this race spread into the near-by East India Islands and the Philippines, driving the Indonesian (Polynesian) branch of the Brown-White race from southeastern Asia to the distant islands of the Paci-fic, conquering the primitive races on the nearby islands, and overcoming the Mins and Tungus Mongolians of the lower Chinese coastal and insular regions and of Japan. The marked variations in type of the widely-scattered Malay race prove differences of habitation and amalga-mation with the earlier peoples (Pre-Dravidians, Ne-groes, Negroids, and Indonesians) that were encountered in the many regions invaded.

The Southern Mongoloid element is particularly domi-nant in the Canton district of southern China. The racial and linguistic kinship of the people of southern Tibet and of Burma and southeastern Asia is readily admitted by scholars, which tends to prove the directions of migration just described. The period stated above as the approximate time of the latest eruption of the Southern Mongoloids is confirmed not only from Indonesian (Polynesian) sources but also by the fact that the first Japanese emperor of this race, Jimmu, traditionally was enthroned in 660 B.C., at which time that nation's chronology begins. Conquest of the islands probably began on Kiushiu, the most southerly island and progressed northward.

Thus, there is a marked racial distinction between the Chinese of the north and those of the south. The former are chiefly an amalgamation of the underlying Min race, the later Tungus Mongolians, and the Sinicus or Chinese. Those in the south are principally Malayan in type, the substrata being a sparse layer of Aryan Indonesians in the south and Turanian Mins farther north toward the Yangtze River. The history of China is replete with the struggles of the civilized peoples of the eastern plains against the roving tribes of the western highlands.

The physical type and energetic nature of the Southern Mongoloids is indicative of their evolution in a rugged environment, such as that of the upper river valleys named. The conquerors of Japan appear to have moved from the southern Chinese coast northward over the Lu-Chu Islands to Kiushiu Islands. Thus, the Japanese race today is a composition mainly of early Tungus Mongolians (with a Min strain) and later Malayans, with a substantial blend of Chinese that subsequently settled in the country and also the modified White (Keltic) Ainus of the north.

The inhabitants of the Pacific islands vary conspicuously from group to group, depending on the proportions of the different racial components that have amalgamated during the successive migrations thither — primitive Pre-Dravidians, Negroes, and Negroids, and later Indonesians and Mongoloid migrants, as in Micronesia. Thus, the Andamanese are a composition of underlying Negro and later Southern Mongoloid races.

6. *Brown-White (or Aryan) Race.* The Iranian plateau is one of the most isolated of the world's important large areas. It is almost wholly rimmed by lofty mountain ranges, whose crests and many of whose passes lie deep in snow in winter. In consequence of the approximately 100,000 years' duration of the last major glaciation (Würm I and II), the interior of Iran, once fertile and productive, slowly dried up until a desert expanse arose across the country from the northwest to the southeast. Apparently, during the period of warmth between the Würm II and Achen glacial advances, from about 42,000 to about 27,000 years ago, numerous Aryan tribes moved high up the Indus River valley and others crossed the Suliman Mountains and spread over Iran.[154] Scattered bands of adventurers may even have explored the regions as far west as the eastern shores of the Mediterranean Sea, then inhabited by Neanderthal man, since the skeletal remains of certain so-called "Galilee" men seem to represent this primitive Aryan type. Recently, other such remains have been found in Iraq. The growing aridity of Iran resulted in a gradual segregation of the people into isolated divisions, which took possession of the fertile valleys as sources of sustenance. These divisions ultimately evolved into different subraces, with the perceptible diversifications of type and the divergent customs and dialects that seem to arise in consequence of different environments.

The Achen glacial advance (about 27,000 to 22,000

---

[154] Probably as early as 75,000 years ago minor groups of adventurers from the Indus valley crossed to Iran. In the north during Würm II glaciation they seem to have perished along the southerly shore of the Caspian Sea. In the south they probably reached southern Mesopotamia, where they also died out, as no living people can be identified as their descendants. Those in southern Kashmir moved down the Indus valley. Only a few years ago, remains of bodies of migrants to northern Iran were reported as found in a cave at the Caspian shore by a party headed by Dr. Carleton S. Coon, of the University of Pennsylvania.

years ago) impelled the northern divisions of the **Aryans** southward in the Indus valley from the Hindu Kush and Karakoram mountain valleys and subsequently closed the passes in those ranges for thousands of years. Tribes that had penetrated to the valleys and lake regions of Ladak and western Tibet along the northerly tributaries of the Indus were unable to return and must have perished from the cold and snow or starved to death. Those who moved down the Indus to northwestern India and others already there became the progenitors of the Indonesian people. Those who had settled in the central western valley of Iran became the forerunners of the Mediterranean subrace, while those in eastern Iran, including the higher valleys of Afghanistan, were the progenitors of the later Iranian division, a large portion of which later recrossed the Suliman Mountains and spread over Hindustan in several invasions.

Of the other subraces on the Iranian plateau, the *Cro-Magnards* appear to have inhabited the southwest, the Hamites (the later Ethiopians) the south-central region, and certain Pre-Dravidian *Veddas* (the later Brünn race in Europe) the southeast, in Baluchistan, bordering on the shores of the Arabian Sea. Probably just before the approach of the glacial advance, the *Veddas* began their migration northwestward toward the Caucasus Mountains on their long trek to central Europe. The cause of their emigration is not known. As the glaciation advanced, climatic conditions on the Caucasus, Taurus, and Lebanon Mountains discouraged further movement in that direction and tribes comprising some or all of the Cro-Magnard nation migrated southwestward toward the Mediterranean Sea, where others of the race doubtless had preceded them on exploratory adventures.

After this glacial advance had passed its peak and begun to recede, the increasing warmth melted the snow and opened up the higher valleys and mountain passes. Shortly after 17,000 years ago, the expansion of population in southern regions spurred migration again to the higher lands.

Tribes of the Mediterranean race migrated westward to the shores of that sea. Iranians ascended the higher Afghan valleys and Indonesian tribes moved up the Indus River valley, again exploring the regions of Kashmir and the upper river tributaries. One tribe penetrated to the lake regions of Ladak and western Tibet, but when the minor Bühl glaciation appeared, about 14,000 years ago, and other tribes were obliged again to move southward, the tribe around the warm fresh water lakes of western Tibet, not realizing what was occuring until the mountain passes were filled with snow and it was too late, was unable to return. For several thousand years[155] its members were isolated in that region, subjected to a rigorous climate amid snow banks and without sun for a large part of each year, with the result that their brown complexion was bleached and they finally evolved as the great White race. In the *Rig-Veda,* that great literary production of the Nordic invaders of northwestern India at about 1400 B.C., when the Sanskrit language first was introduced in that land, it is related that on their arrival in India they engaged in warfare with the "dark-skinned" natives.

About 14,000 years ago, near the end of the warm Achen-Bühl interglacial period, the Turkish inhabitants of central Tibet had greatly increased and had begun to spread westward, whereupon they encountered the White race. The result was the descent later of the Nordic tribe from western Tibet through the Karakoram-Kuenlun mountain passes to the Tarim Basin of Eastern Turkistan[156] and the movement of the Keltic division westward to the Pamirs, after which the Turks took possession of western Tibet. This descent of the Nordics forced earlier Turks, the Pre-Sumerians, out of the Tarim Basin over the mountain passes to Western Turkistan, as already discussed.

---

155 The Nordic division, as later shown, moved down to the Tarim Basin, in Eastern Turkistan, about 12,000 B.C., but the Keltic division moved to and remained in the higher Pamirs on the west until about 8000 B.C. and later. Some live in that region today.

156 *Ency. Brit.,* 13th Ed., vol. 27, page 423; Aryans in Eastern Turkistan.

By about 8000 B.C. the Bühl glaciation had receded
and sufficient warmth had melted the snows to stimulate
other important movements of these races. Another Turkish tribe (the later Sumerians) descended the Karakoram-
Kuenlun passes from western Tibet to the Tarim Basin
and took possession of Eastern Turkistan, causing a great
Keltic migration westward to Europe and driving the
Nordic tribe northward into and through the passes of
the Tien Shan (or Celestial Mountains) toward Lake
Balkash. This movement of the Kelts and Nordics caused
the Pre-Sumerians of Western Turkistan to invade the
west, when they crossed Iran and settled in Mesopotamia.
Their strife with Iranians on route caused the migration
of large numbers of the latter eastward over the Suliman
Mountains into northwestern India. It was the first of
a number of such movements of Iranians to India, later
described.

The evolution and later movements of the Keltic and
Nordic descendants of the Indonesian people thus long
isolated in Ladak and western Tibet deserve separate
consideration. They are the only distinctively white
branches of the human race, although the Ugrians of the
far north, a branch of the Turanian race, also have undergone noticeable bleaching of their complexion because
of their long habitation in cold and snowy climes, without much sunshine for a large part of the year. The
Kelts long dominated western Europe and the Nordics
became a populous nation in central Asia,[157] when ultimately three tribes emigrated westward to Europe and
two tribes remained in Asia, each division having wholly
different history to be narrated.

(6a) *Indonesian* (*Polynesian*) *Subrace*. The original Indonesian people, who branched from the primary Brown
race from which the Cro-Magnon, Mediterranean, Iranian, Hamitic, and White subraces descended, were dark-
complexioned, tall, slender, and dolichocephalous, with

---

157 Diodorus Siculus, *Bibl. Hist.* iii.1. In Semiryechensk, "the land of the seven
rivers," immediately south of Lake Balkhash, in Western Turkistan.

wavy black hair, mesorhine nose, and straight open eyes. They closely resembled the later Mediterranean type, had fairly regular features, and were well-developed, as is evidenced by their unmixed Polynesian descendants today.

Apparently, when the extreme cold of the Würm II glaciation impelled most of the northerly divisions of the already well-differentiated Brown race down the Indus valley from the foothills of the Hindu Kush, Karakoram, and upper Suliman Mountains about 47,000 years ago and closed the passes of those ranges for several thousand years, these people turned eastward along the Himalayan foothills in northern India to the upper Ganges valley and then swerved southward, sundered the Negro nation into two divisions, and soon expelled them from India. One division moved eastward and the other (the larger) division moved westward, as proved by their habitation in the South Pacific Islands and in central Africa since very remote times. These movements pressed any Turanians encountered in Bengal into the highlands of Burma and the Pre-Dravidians southward to the peninsula. Thereupon, the conquerors took possession of all northern India.

When the glaciation turned a few thousand years later and its retreat was in progress, returning warmth opened the passes between Iran (including Afghanistan) and northwestern India and between the latter and the northern highlands. Migration then recurred up the Indus valley during the warm Würm II-Achen interglacial period. Concurrently, the Indonesians expanded farther eastward throughout Bengal and southward toward the peninsular highlands. This eastward movement caused the final expulsion of the Negroes from Indo-China toward the Pacific Islands, while the southward movement pressed Pre-Dravidian tribes radially outward toward the coastal lowlands, especially southeastward. Intermarriage of Pre-Dravidians with Negroes in the lower Ganges valley and of Indonesians with Pre-Dravidians in the Dekkan resulted from the contacts thus formed; the descendants of the former interbreeding by various negroid peoples (now classed with lower-caste Dravidian tribes) in southeastern India and elsewhere. The Dravidian population of the Indian peninsula now is approximately 60,000,000. Many of the Iranians (Hindus) that came into India from the northwest at intervals from 8000 to 500 B.C. also moved southward to the highlands and interbred with the Dravidians. This southward movement of Iranians occurred after the Laws of Manu had been written. However, the Pre-Dravidian, Dravidian, and Iranian characteristics of the people are still readily discernible among them.

The successive movements of the Iranians (ancestors of the Hindus) to the Indus valley, beginning about 8000 B.C., resulted in such an increase in the population of northwestern India that most of the Indonesians, darker in color, were driven southward to the peninsula. However, many of them in the Ganges valley were driven eastward into Indo-China over a long period. They are found to have been an underlying race in the extensive region from Yunnan on the north to the Indo-Chinese peninsula. This migration finally expelled the Australian and negroid peoples toward Malaya, whereupon the lower Ganges basin was left to the remnant of the Indonesians in northern India. Their descendants, centering in Bengal, have since received strains of Iranian and Mongoloid blood from contiguous regions.[158]

The Australians, thus of Pre-Dravidian-Indafrican (Negroid) origin reveal the traits of both component subraces. They are the most primitive people known. Evidence of the fact that they early had close cultural relations with primitive Pre-Dravidians along the northwestern shores of the Bay of Bengal is their possession of certain customs in common. The Australians use the boomerang and make their canoes in the same manner as the wild

---

[158] Because of this racial commingling and the undernourishment to which these people have been subjected for many millennia, it is doubtful whether any true representatives of the primitive Indonesian division of the Aryan race now exist about the lower Bay of Bengal. Generally they are an inferior type.

tribes of the Dekkan do. They must have made their way in remote times down the Malay peninsula and across various islands to Australia. They reached that country perhaps as early as 7000 B.C., when it was unpopulated save for a sparse settlement of negroid Papuans in the northeasterly region. The latter were sundered by the newcomers; some were driven back to Papua and others went southward to Tasmania. They were the aborigines on Tasmania, but have been extinct since 1876. The Australians not only have been an unprogressive group but their isolation from all other peoples has had a most stagnating effect, so that their culture has continued to be exceedingly low in the human scale until the present day.

The southward migration or expansion of the Paraoeans (Southern Mongoloids) from the southeastern Tibetan slopes expelled most of the Indonesians from southeastern Asia by the 7th century B.C. It is only in isolated Chinese territory in Yunnan and adjacent regions on the north and east, such as the more inaccessible mountains on both sides of the Yangtze River, that their descendants, with marked infusion of Turanian blood, are found today.[159] Those who migrated, once in motion, seem to have continued by slow stages by way of the Malay peninsula and Java until they reached the far islands of Polynesia and the South Pacific Ocean that they occupy today.[160] These final migrations eastward, northward, and southward in the Pacific continued until relatively late times, perhaps as recent as 650 B.C., since the Indonesians were well above savagery when they reached the Pacific islands. They are said to have arrived at the Hawaiian Islands as late as A.D. 500 or thereabouts. Indeed, their elaborate historical legends disclose that

---

[159] This racial substratum is mesocephalous (index 77), medium to tall in stature, with oval face, fairly prominent nose, brownish skin, and wavy hair, but without the Mongolian cast.

[160] This migration may have occurred during one of the late minor glaciations, when the water of the Pacific Ocean was lower than it is today and the peaks of submerged mountains projected above the water to guide them. In 1951 the Secretary of the Navy announced a massive underwater mountain range about 100 miles wide and 1000 miles long between Bikini and Hawaii.

they possessed a considerable knowledge and culture. This fact demonstrates contact through their congeners still in the lower Ganges valley with the earliest Hindus (Iranians) in the central Ganges Valley, whose eastward movement there in consequence of the Pre-Sumerian invasion of Iran about 8000 B.C. is believed to have driven many Indonesians out of India to southeastern Asia. The primitively carved symbols, supposed to be writing, and the statues recently found on Easter Island, now inhabited by Indonesians, which items bear a close resemblance to some found at Mohenjo-Daro and Harappa, in the valley of the Indus, and in Mesopotamia, are too remote to be examples of Indonesian culture at the time that these people arrived in the Pacific Islands. They apparently represent an antecedent Pre-Dravidian culture borne by Vedda immigrants across the South Pacific Ocean to South America, as already discussed. The Indonesians reveal high intellectual capacity, are natural orators, and are aggressive, brave, and self-sacrificing.

The principal habitations of the Indonesian race to-day, aside from those of its mixed descendants in southeastern Asia and the East Indies, are north Sumatra, Borneo, Philippine Islands, and the Hawaiian, Ellice, Phoenix, Union, Manihiki, Marquesas, Samoan, Tongan, Cook, Society, Tubuai, and Tuamotu groups, and many less important islands in the Pacific. The Maori of New Zealand also are a branch of this race. The Indonesians, moreover, are an element of the composite race that inhabits the Micronesian Islands. This emigration of the Indonesians from the continent almost across the South Pacific is indicated by the tradition of that race now on Easter Island that their ancestors had come from the Austral Islands, far to the west.

Although the Indonesian (Polynesian) and Sanskrit languages now are strongly contrasted in structure, some authorities regard them as distantly allied in elemental roots and vocabulary. This deduction should have foundation in fact, since both languages sprang from the Aryan inhabitants of the higher elevations of the Indus River about 22,000 years ago and presumably were analogous at that time. The Indonesians then were separated from their kin and migrated back to the Ganges valley and ultimately as far east as the Pacific Islands, whereas the Nordic division (whose dialect, with Persian, Grecian, and perhaps Turkic modifications many thousands of years later, became the Sanskrit language) ultimately migrated from western Tibet in the opposite direction and settled in Eastern Turkistan and later in Semiryechensk, south and southeast of Lake Balkhash. The origin, evolution, and transmission of the Sanskrit language is developed in a later chapter. Analogous resemblances exist between the Tamulian and the primitive Australian languages and also between those dialects and the Turanian language, for reasons too remote for conjecture here.

In view of the apparent fact that the Aryan Paleo-Kelts, Kelto-Slavs, and Nordics branched from the Indonesian subrace in the higher tributaries of the Indus River, perhaps in the region of Kashmir and Ladak, further research concerning the primitive language and customs of the purest Indonesian people of the Pacific Islands in relation to those of the above-named Aryan divisions should yield interesting results.

(6b) *Cro-Magnon Subrace.* The first division of Aryans that revealed itself in Europe was the Cro-Magnon subrace, but it had been preceded by the apparently Pre-Dravidian Brünn (Brüx, Pred-most Combe Capelle, and Galley Hill) race. The increasing aridity of central Iran tended to divide the plateau into two parts, one in the southwest and the other in the northeast, and to drive the Mediterranean tribes in the center upon the Cro-Magnon and Pre-Dravidian tribes in the west about 27,000 years ago. At that time the summers were temperate, but the Achen glacial period was about to begin and the winters were severe. The movement on Iran pressed these Pre-Dravidians westward across Armenia, whence they invaded central Europe by way of the Danube valley. They moved either along the southern shore of the Black Sea and the Bosporus or crossed the Caucasus passes and followed the northerly shore via Krimea. The Solutrean culture of these people in the Old Stone Age was well represented in the Caucasus region, toward which they may first have migrated from southern Iran. Cro-Magnards also emigrated from Iran shortly afterward, moving across Syria and northern Africa and into western Europe at Gibraltar, which route was less cold and more accessible than the European shores of the Mediterranean basin. Their origin on the plateau of Iran is indicated by the discovery in 1906, in the Niaux cavern in the French Pyrenees, near Tarascon, of silhouettes of horses that closely resemble the Asiatic type now found in the Gobi Desert, but of which they doubtless had knowledge prior to their migration. In the course of the millennia that followed, the Cro-Magnards conquered all of western Europe as far as Poland and western Russia, probably annihilating or absorbing the Brünn race.

When the minor Achen glacial advance interrupted the Würm II glacial retreat approximately 22,000 years ago, Arctic tundra life subsisted in some degree as far south as the Pyrenees range. Banded and obi lemming, the Arctic hare, and the wolverine roamed southward as far as the middle and upper Danube River. The renewal of cold weather forced the Brünn and Cro-Magnon people more and more to shelters and grottoes, during which increased confinement the protrayal of their art and the development of their imagination occurred. The succeeding cold dry climate that accompanied the Achen glacial advance (which reached its peak about 22,000 years ago and which was characterized by the culmination of the Magdalenean culture of the Cro-Magnards) brought the steppe life of western Asia down into Europe.

The Cro-Magnards were a strong and intelligent people, variable in stature but perhaps above the average as a whole.[161] They were dolichocephalous (well under 75 per cent) but disharmonic, with broad faces and brunet complexions. They possessed superior brain power and

---

161 H. F. Osborn, *Men of the Old Stone Age* (Scribner, New York, 1915), page 382.

closely observant and creative minds, with high capability for ideas, reasoning, and imagination, comparable with our own. They also had a strongly marked esthetic and religious sense and a well-developed art of engraving, drawing, and sculpture of human and animal forms.[162] They must have had a tribal organization, with chiefs, priests, medicine-men, hunters, fishers, and makers of useful and ornamental objects. Thus, their talents became widely differentiated in the shelters during this period of cold and dry climate.

These people are more fully discussed in anthropological treatises. Like the earlier Grimaldi and Brünn races in Europe, they were unrelated by any ancestral links to the Neanderthal race that had preceded them there. They introduced the early Magdalenean culture into that continent. It was wholly an Asiatic culture and not African or negroid, but it did not enter through eastern or central Europe. It embodied a profound change from the cultures of preceding peoples in the west. Evidences of it have been found along the course of their migration from Iran, in Syria and Phoenicia, in the grottoes of Lebanon, and across northern Africa to the Iberian peninsula. This art and industry became widely diffused throughout Europe as the population increased and, during the temperate periods, roamed eastward as far as southern and central Russia and the Danube basin, where it supplanted the Solutrean culture of the earlier Brünn race.

Subsequently, for a very long time, the development of Magdalenean art in Europe languished, perhaps because of warfare for the supremacy between the Cro-Magnon and earlier subraces. It was revived during the Bühl glaciation, which lasted from approximately 14,000 years to 10,000 years ago. This period was at first cold and arid; later it was less cold and more moist as the glacial retreat commenced. The country became thickly forested. People lived partly in the open and partly in shelters, and the

---

162 Their skill is demonstrated by the marvelous art work found in the caves at Font de Gaume, in France, and Altamira, in Spain.

fauna changed from steppe to tundra types. The diminution of the flint industry was followed by a high development of bone instruments during the declining period
of the Magdalenean civilization. Trade routes between the
Atlantic coast and interior Europe are indicated by the
wide diffusion of Magdalenean implements, decorations, etc.

During the long prevalence of the Magdalenean culture in Europe, it is probable that at intervals other Aryans migrated from Iran around the Caucasus Mountains
and the northerly shores of the Black Sea as far as western
Europe. They moved up the Danube valley to Austria
and central Germany and elsewhere between the Alpine
and the Scandinavian glaciers. Ultimately, they spread
over southern Russia and Poland. Not only did this new
influx cause some changes in the prevailing skull formation,
which otherwise retained its Cro-Magnon characters, but
the average stature of the people declined.

At approximately 8000 B.C. this civilization appears to
have stagnated and deteriorated, as has happened repeatedly in the history of isolated races of the world. It was
largely supplanted then by that of vigorous newcomers, the
Paleo-Kelts (earliest Alpines) from the Pamirs, along with
that already introduced by the Mediterraneans from the
south and southeast. They are known as the Maglemosean
and the Azilian-Tardenoisian (Mesolithic) cultures respectively. These Kelts brought the Keltic or desert horse
with them. At this time the horse in Europe was used for
food only. The discovery that he might be used for trans-
portation was made in central Asia, apparently by the
Turks.

Certain inhabitants of Dordogne, France, today may
approximately portray the Cro-Magnon race, from which
they seem to have descended, as that race appeared when
it migrated over 25,000 years ago from the Iranian plateau to Europe. A physical characteristic of the Cro-Magnon skull, as viewed from the top, is its pentagonal form,
caused by the prominence of the parietals. Traces of this
head form are found among the living Berbers, due perhaps to the amalgamation of members of the Cro-Magnon
race who remained in northern Africa with later Medi-

terraneans who populated the Mediterranean basin. The former then spoke an agglutinative language, which seems to have been the original form of speech of all primitive races.

(6c) *Mediterranean Subrace.* Upon the emigration of the Vedda (or Brünn) and Cro-Magnon races from the Iranian plateau, various tribes of the Mediterranean race[163] spread over that area, chiefly in the west, since the easterly portion of the plateau was occupied by related Iranian peoples as far as the Suliman Mountains. The Mediterranean race was dolichocephalic and harmonic in type, slender of physique and brunet of complexion, in accordance with Sergi's description. Concurrently with the increasing severity of the Achen glacial advance, with its cold winds from the north and the increasing aridity of Iran approximately 22,000 years ago, there began an intermittent migration of Mediterraneans from Iran across Mesopotamia to the shores of the eastern Mediterranean basin. This movement continued during the subsequent millennia. Ultimately, these people spread over northern Arabia, lower Egypt,[164] and, as the climate moderated, westward along the southerly shore of the Mediterranean Sea.[165] Joppa is said to have been built as a walled city during the Neolithic Age, which began about 12,000 years ago. Apparently, these migrants developed what is known as the Capsian Mesolithic culture, evidences of which have been discovered in Palestine. Graves of 8000 B.C. in lower Egypt have been found to contain vessels for food and drink. Only recently, ancient skeletons of this race have been unearthed in Tunis and Algiers, near the former land bridge across Sicily to southern Italy. All of this region then was more fertile than it is now and

163 This race has been thoroughly studied by the Roman anthropologist, G. Sergi; *The Mediterranean Race* (Walter Scott, London, 1901).
164 The ancient paintings definitely distinguish the complexion of the lower Egyptians from that of the Negroes of Africa and of the dark-colored Ethiopians, both of whom are shown to have been of the same hue as their descendants. See *Did Prehistoric Egyptian Culture Spring from a Marsh-Dwelling People?* by Eric von Rosen (Stockholm, 1929).
165 Herodotus, *Hist.* ii.15, 18, iv.197; Diodorus Siculus, *Bibl. Hist.* vi.14.

northern Europe was tundra or wind-swept steppe. Upon the gradual diminution of the Mediterranean rainfall, the process of desiccation had slowly succeeded.

By 12,000 years ago the Mediterranean race had thinly populated the whole Mediterranean basin and also had explored northern Europe, for by that time it had diffused the Azilian Microlithic culture, in succession to the Capsian culture, along the northerly shores of Africa as far as Iberia and the Canary Islands. This culture (possibly of Veddic origin) has been traced from India through Iran, Syria, lower Egypt, Tunis, Algiers, and the Iberian peninsula and also to the Italian shores. Later, the Azilian culture passed to the Tardenoisian culture. This westward migration was slow and it required 10,000 years for it to populate the Mediterranean basin to the density that impelled much migration to northern Europe, although exploratory expeditions had reached Scandinavia as early as 12,000 years ago. The migration northward was accelerated later by the Turanian invasion of southwestern Asia and much of the region north of the Alps was overrun by 7800 B.C. The Neolithic culture was introduced about this time, probably in the first instance through the Balkan region from Anatolia. A result was the pressing northward and westward of divisions of the Paleo-Keltic race that had arrived about 8000 B.C. The latter people introduced the Maglemosean and related cultures in the Atlantic coastal regions from Spain to Scandinavia and in the British Isles.

Following up its earlier explorations, the Mediterranean race also extended its influence as far north as Scandinavia, chiefly up and down the river valleys. In fact, it appears that in some regions of western Europe these two races alternated in being the first to settle. The Iberians reached the British Isles[166] ahead of the Paleo-Kelts, but the Ligurians, who moved up the Rhone valley, across the Belfort pass, and down the Rhine valley, were antedated (except for exploratory bands) by the Kelts in the

---

166 J. A. Giles, *Six Old English Chronicles, Richard of Cirencester* (Bell, London, 1891), i.3.2. See footnote later regarding this publication.

southerly Scandinavian region.[167] Their burials were made in long barrows. In central Europe the two races met and ultimately commingled in considerable degree. All brown eyes of Aryan people of Europe were inherited from ancestors of the Mediterranean subrace.

Proof that the migrations of the Paleo-Kelts and the Mediterraneans to northern Europe were approximately contemporaneous, that they came from roughly adjacent territory (Pamirs and Iran) in western Asia, and that they were attributable to the same cause is seen in the fact that the Maglemosean culture of the former in the north and the Azilian-Tardenoisian culture of the latter in the south had many similar aspects, despite the different routes by which they reached western Europe.[168] They had types of objects carved from bone and not from flint, which were prophetic of the Neolithic culture, the elementary principles of which they, in fact, did bring with them from the east. Their later microliths, of various geometrical forms, bore marked resemblances.

The long interval prior to 8000 B.C. must have been an era of meager cultural advancement in the eastern Mediterranean region. It doubtless was so found in Mesopotamia when the Pre-Sumerians arrived from Turkistan. By far the greater progress was made after that time, upon the diffusion westward of the Neolithic culture by the latter. After some centuries this culture was taken by the Hamites from Iran across to southern Arabia, whence they transmitted it to Ethiopia after 6000 B.C. The Neolithic culture reached the Mediterranean islands and central and western Europe about 7500 B.C., when, as already stated, hordes of the Mediterraneans moved through the Balkans, up the Rhone valley, and northward in western France. This advanced civilization caused a profound cultural revolution in northern Europe, and its diffusion, following so closely upon the

---

167 Recently it was reported that a wooden idol 12 feet tall and about 10,000 years old, carved from a tree trunk and adorned with rudimentary ornaments, had been found in a peat bog near Bremen; but whether carved by members of the Mediterranean or the Keltic race was not conjectured.

168 H. F. Osborn, *op.cit.*, page 488.

settlement of the Pre-Sumerians in Mesopotamia, further demonstrates that these invaders from central Asia were responsible for the revolution from the Microlithic to the Neolithic culture in the west.

The eastern Mediterranean was ideally adapted by geography and climate to become the center of the most advanced civilizations in ancient times. It was the meeting place of peoples from all directions, with their different ideas. This is particularly true of the Fertile Crescent extending from the Persian Gulf across Mesopotamia, Syria, Phoenicia, and Palestine. Much of the Near East must once have been less arid than it is today. Many sections that once supported vast populations in material wealth and culture are now largely dried up and sustain only meager and backward peoples. For example, the Sinai Desert, which once supported the Children of Israel for a century or more, can now be traversed only with difficulty. The present population of Palestine is only a fraction of that indicated by the census of David,[169] when the food supply must have been far greater.

The Neolithic age in western Europe began with the retreat of the minor Bühl glaciation. Even with the northward penetration by the Mediterraneans, the population of northern Europe then was much sparser than in the Mediterranean basin. Due to isolation, stagnation prevailed generally and the introduction of this culture inculcated a new spirit in the land. Commercial contact with the progressive civilization of the east was accelerated. It was an age of highly finished and polished stone implements in contrast with the rude chipped-stone workmanship of the earlier stone ages. Other customs brought from the eastern Mediterranean were weaving, pottery-making, the burial of the dead in long barrows and later in dolmens,[170] and the rearing of megalithic monuments. The rudiments of agriculture slowly penerated north of the Alps from Susa, Mesopotamia, and Egypt, where such crops as wheat and barley had been grown regularly be-

---

169 2 *Samuel* 24.9. The reliability of these numbers is questionable.
170 V. Gordon Childe, *The Aryans*, page 179.

fore 4000 B.C. Susa was a noted agricultural center. The Pre-Sumerians had learned the use of seeds and plants and of implements for preparing the soil and harvesting the crops. The transmission of this knowledge later to Europe stimulated the domestication of animals useful to man, such as pigs, horses, cattle, sheep, and goats, which long before had been domesticated by them. The resulting civilization in Europe is sometimes known as the Robenshausian type, after the place in Switzerland where it was first discovered, although it apparently was in large measure an importation of the eastern culture.

Contemporaneous with the evolution of the Pre-Sumerian and Sumerian culture in Mesopotamia was the development of that of the Hamites in southern Arabia, Ethiopia, and Egypt. The advance of the Hamites down the Nile soon after 6000 B.C. resulted in their superimposing themselves on the indigenous Mediterranean population, first in Upper Egypt and later in Lower Egypt. Many of the Mediterraneans fled before the invaders to the island of Krete and others later followed them. The latter took along the rudiments of the Hamitic culture impressed upon them by their conquerors, thereby enabling the Kretans to assume the lead in developing the distinctive Mediterranean culture[171] on that island and later in Greece. Investigations have revealed that the indigenous Mediterranean race of Egypt was lighter in color and less rugged than the Hamitic Ethiopians who came down the Nile and subsequently established the dynasties. Thus, the *Keftiu* (who are identified with the Kretans and other representatives of the indigenous Mediterranean race in the Aegean region) are the only people around Egypt who by their elaborate clothing and artistic products reveal themselves on ancient Egyptian monuments as the equals in culture of the Egyptian nation.

The early Mediterranean race in western Asia, northern Africa, and Europe may be segregated for convenience into the following principal divisions, viz., the *Bedouins* (Arabs) in central Arabia and Hedjaz, the *Libyans* and

---

171 Diodorus Siculus, *Bibl. Hist.* vi.14.

other strains across northern Africa,[172] the *Caucones* in Anatolia and Greece,[173] the *Pelasgians*[174] in western Anatolia, the Aegean basin, and Krete (including the Keftiu), the *Sicani* (originally *Iberians*), *Siculi*, and *Ligurians* in Italy, and the *Iberians* on the Spanish peninsula. The Pelasgians, as already stated, spread northward through the Balkan region as far as southern Russia; the Ligurians moved northward in the Rhone valley and through the Belfort pass into southern Germany and eastern France, whence some continued down the Rhine[175] and on to Danmark and even Scandinavia; and the Iberians expanded over western France and into the British Isles.[176]

We thus perceive the beginnings of a composite population in western, central, and northern Europe, with the commingling of Mediterraneans and earlier stocks of Cro-Magnards, Brünn people, and Paleo-Kelts. The first three were brunets and the last were blonds. During the subsequent Neolithic times in Europe, from about 7500 B.C. to about 2300 B.C., only one major type of immigration is discernible there, namely, that of additional hordes of the Mediterranean race from the southeast, but whether by intermittent invasion or by slow infiltration northward is not known. They brought from the Anatolian Leleges improvements in pottery culture, agriculture, and domestication of animals of the Asiatic type, such as oxen of the Urus breed and turbary sheep. This culture, Turanian in origin, thus spread across the Hellespont and the Bosporus to Thessaly, Bulgaria, Transylvania, Ukrainia, and adjacent regions. The Turanian Anatolian mariners, or "prospectors", already referred to, who followed the Mediterranean and Atlantic coasts in commerce, added in a minor degree to the diverse population at and near the ports touched, especially on the Atlantic. It is unlikely that

172 Herodotus, *Hist.* 11.16-18, iv.1917, classified the Libyans separately from the Egyptians. The one was Mediterranean and the other largely Hamitic. See J. C. Prichard, *Physical History of Mankind* (London, 1836), vol. 2, pp. 174, 254-264.
173 Strabo, *Geogr.* viii 3.17, xii.3.9.
174 Herodotus, *Hist.* ii.52, 56, 171. A. H. Keane, *Man, Past and Present* (Cambridge Press, 1920) pp. 462-8.　　　　　　　　　　　　　　　　　　　　L
175 C. Mehlis, *Corresbl. d. d. Ges. f. Anthrop.* (February, 1898), p. 12.
176 Tacitus, *Life of Agricola*, c.11.

many of them reached inland Europe. It was not until approximately 2300 B.C. that the great Kelto-Slavic migration from the Pamirs of central Asia reached Europe, by way of Iran and the Caucasus region, toward the Danube valley, and the Nordics entered eastern Europe (Scythia) soon afterward, pressing the Slavs northward. Geographic and climatic conditions in the north had retarded the migration of races from central Asia to Europe by the route north of the Caspian Sea until relatively late. The use of bronze was introduced into Europe from Anatolia about 2000 B.C. Shortly afterward the use of iron arose at Hallstatt, in central Europe (Austria). Both of these metals long had been used in Mesopotamia, Anatolia, and Egypt. Each greatly modified the European civilization.

Some reference may well be made to the Kretan culture,[177] the highest developed by the Mediterranean race in early times. It seems certain that its development was influenced by the Pre-Sumerian and Sumerian culture diffused over Anatolia (including Cyprus) in greater degree than is generally realized,[178] but this fact does not detract from the credit due the Kretans for creating a civilization largely different from those of other races. The contents of early tombs and dwellings and indications supplied by other objects, such as stone vases and seal-stones, show that they attained a high degree of culture (the Early Minoan) and had opened communication with the Nile Valley at the time of the early Egyptian dynasties. At that time, 2000 years before the Phoenicians introduced letters into Greece, writing by both linear and semi-pictorial signs existed in Krete.[179]

The Nilotic influence visible in the vases, seals, and other fabrics of the Early Minoan age seems to imply a maritime activity on the part of the Kretans going back to

---

177 See *Encyclopaedia Britannica*, 13th Ed., vol. 7, pp. 421ff, by Arthur J. Evans.
178 V. Gordon Childe, *The Most Ancient East* (Appleton-Century, New York, 1934), pp. 288-289.
179 Arthur Evans, in *Journal of Hellenic Studies*, XIV, part II, XVII; "Palace of Knossos," *Reports of Excavations* 1900-1905; *Scripta Minoa*, vol. 1, 1909.

the days of the first dynasties.[180] Minos, a reputed son of Zeus and a king of Knossos, enjoyed the reputation of being the greatest legislator of antiquity. The elaborate methods and bureaucratic control visible in the clay documents of the palace at Knossos point to a highly-developed legal organization. He also is reported as the first monarch who established a powerful fleet and maritime empire that acquired dominion of the sea, although the Anatolian Leleges were far earlier in sailing the Atlantic Ocean. Some 2000 years before the Dorian conquest, Krete was exercising a dominant influence in the Aegean world. These facts confirm what has been said before, namely, that from 2500 B.C. or earlier the Kretans developed a great sea-power[181] and were the chief rivals of the Anatolian Leleges on the Mediterranean until the Keltic invasion of Anatolia about 1425 B.C. and later of Greece (by the Achaeans) caused desolation throughout the Aegean region.

Comparable evidence afforded by Egyptian relics shows that the Great Age of the palaces at Knossos was contemporaneous with the close of the 3rd and the first half of the 2nd millennium B.C., the Middle Minoan period. Extraordinary skill was attained at that time in many branches of art, notably the painting of pottery, often with polychrome decoration, of a class known as "Kamares," the beginnings of wall painting, metal technique, and such arts as gem engraving, the manufacture of faience, etc. The Late Minoan period, best illustrated by the later palace at Knossos and that at Hagia Triada, corresponds chronologically with the Hyksos period in Egypt (1776-1577 B.C.) and some subsequent centuries. In 1908 the Italian mission at Phaestus discovered a clay disk with imprinted characters belonging to a non-Kretan system, which apparently came from western Anatolia. This tends to confirm the early contact of the Kretans and the Anatolians.

A large part of the palace of Knossos was devoted to purposes of cult. The rulers, as was common in ancient

---

180 *Encyclopaedia Britannica*, 13th Ed., vol. 7, pp. 421ff, by Arthur J. Evans.
181 Strabo, *Geogr.* x.4.17.

states, fulfilled priestly as well as royal functions. The evidence from this and other Kretan sites shows that the principal Minoan divinity was a kind of Magna Mater, a Great Mother or Nature Goddess, like that of the early Sumerians, with whom a male satellite was associated. The cult, in fact, corresponds in its main outlines with the early religious conceptions of Syria and a large part of Anatolia, attributable perhaps to a close ethnic affinity between a segment of the primitive Kretan population and that of southwestern Anatolia. Even if we confine this racial affinity to the Mediterranean Pelasgians of Anatolia, it is nonetheless true that the Turanian Leleges of that region, with a basic Pre-Sumerian and Sumerian culture, exercised a profound influence over the Kretans during the Middle Minoan period.

The Minoan culture of Krete, with its characteristic style of polychrome vase decoration, was diffused to Mykenae, Tiryns, and other places on the Grecian peninsula from early in the Middle Minoan period. But it is a noteworthy fact that, whereas in Greece proper Zeus attained a supreme position, the superiority of the Mother Goddess persisted in Krete in the traditions of Rhea and Dictynna and the infant Zeus. This may indicate the ascendancy of Anatolian culture during that age in Krete but not in Greece and a separation of the rule of Krete. The contents of the royal tombs in Greece reveal a wholesale correspondence with the fabrics of the first and in less degree of those of the second Late Minoan age.

The third Late Minoan period, which began about 1400 B.C., was an age of stagnation and decline in consequence of invasions by rude tribes from the north. The Keltic Carians from Thrace had conquered southwestern Anatolia and refugees therefrom had overrun Krete. The Keltic Achaean conquest of the island from Greece came later, at which time widespread desolation fell on the central regions. This tradition of the aboriginal Kretans is preserved by Herodotus.[182] Certain mainland (Achaean) types of swords and safety-pins then made their

182 Herodotus, *Hist.* vii.171.

appearance on the island, which confirms this great invasion that finally overcame the Kretan power. It is further verified by the destruction of the palaces at Knossos and Phaestus during this period, when the early inhabitants were supplanted in control by the Achaeans, whose rule, in turn, was superseded in the 12th century B.C. by other invaders, the Kimmeric Dorians. In the age of Homer (9th century B.C.) the Kretan population included, besides Eteokretans (the original inhabitants), the Pelasgians, Achaeans, and Dorians. Ultimately, by further immigration from the Peloponnese, the last became the dominant race on the island, whose component stocks thus consisted of Mediterraneans, Keltic "Alpines", and Nordics.

The ancient Philistines are believed to have been a tribe of the original Kretans that fled to the mainland of Asia south of Jaffa or Dor at the time of the Achaean invasion in the 13th century B.C. They were pushed into southern Palestine by a migration of Semitic Nabataeans from Syria about 500 B.C., so that their territory extended to the mountains east of the Jordan in Herodotus' time and included Cadytis (Jerusalem), then an important city.[183] The Hebrews were their perpetual enemies.

That the Kretan civilization of the kindred people on the Grecian mainland achieved a high level is evidenced further by the attainments of the various branches of the Pelasgic people prior to the Achaean invasion, such as the Ionians, Argives, Arcadians, and others. Their subsequent contributions to world culture have been prodigious. Upon the overrunning of Krete by refugees from Anatolia at the time of the Keltic invasion of Caria shortly after 1425 B.C., the Pelasgians of Greece lost direct contact with the Kretan nation and thereafter followed an independent course. Later, when the Achaeans invaded Greece, a gradual transition from the Mykenean civilization of the Pelasgian Greeks to one resulting from the combination of that culture and the Keltic culture of the north ensued. The Ionians were descend-

---

183 *Ibid.,* iii.5.

ants of Athenians sent out as colonists to the later Achaea,[184] on the southerly shore of the Corinthian Sea,[185] but this territory they ultimately were compelled to yield to Achaeans expelled from southern Greece by Nordic Dorians who invaded the Peloponnese soon after 1100 B.C.[186] Many of them then returned to the Athenian habitation of their ancestors.

About 1069 B.C., during the reign of Codrus, the last Athenian king, who was a son of Melanthus, former king of Messenia, the Dorians attempted an invasion of Attica, the principal seat of the Pelasgians, but were repulsed.[187] Upon the death of Codrus, the title of king was abolished by Athens and that of archon substituted. About 27 years after this attack, when Medon was archon at Athens, the surplus population of Attica (chiefly Ionians) was sent out under the leadership of Androclus, son of Codrus, to colonize the shores of Anatolia, in Lydia and Caria.[188] There they established 12 cities corresponding with the number that the Ionians had occupied in the former Ionia,[189] and this eastern Aegean region subsequently became known as the Ionia of history.[190] The cities thus established were Phocaea, Erythrae, Clazomenae, Teos, Lebedos, Colophon, Ephesus, Priene, Myus, and Miletus on the mainland and Samos and Chios on neighboring islands.

The descendants of the Mediterranean race, widely scattered around the Mediterranean basin and regions distant therefrom, are a variable racial component of the population of all the nations of the western world. The most positive evidence of Mediterranean blood in Europeans is the possession of brown eyes and black hair.

The Ligurian language was spoken in parts of central Europe as late as 3000 years ago, but its bearers, who

184 Strabo, *Geogr.* viii.7.1.
185 Herodotus vii.94, viii.73.
186 Polybius ii.41, iv.1; Strabo viii.7.1.
187 Strabo ix.1.7.
188 *Ibid.,* xvi.1.3.
189 Herodotus 1.145-146.
190 Pausanias vii.2.1-2; Strabo viii.7.1, xiv.1.3.

inhabited northern Italy, eastern France, Switzerland, and southern Germany, left behind no written language but only the names of a few rivers, lakes, and mountains, such as "Seine," "Rhone" (in somewhat different form), "Leman," and "Alps." The brunet strain in the present inhabitants of these regions is Ligurian. That strain in the inhabitants of western Europe is Iberian and that south of the Carpathian Mountains is Pelasgian.

(6d) *Hamitic Subrace.* When the Pre-Sumerians from Turkistan crossed the Iranian plateau about 8000 B.C. in their invasion of western Asia, which resulted in their settlement in Elam and their conquest of Mesopotamia, they divided the Iranian tribes on that plateau. Some moved westward into the valleys of the Zagros Mountains, others went eastward as far as the Suliman Mountains or crossed into the Indus valley, and the Persians proper were driven southward toward the Persian Gulf and settled principally in Persis, the present province of Fars. This pressure gradually split an old Aryan nation in the extreme south of the plateau — the Ethiopians of Herodotus.[191] Many of them went eastward to southern Baluchistan[192] and to the lower Indus valley[193] and others went in the opposite direction across the strait of Ormus to Arabia. Most of the latter finally established nations converging on the southerly part of that peninsula.[194] Some of the Ethiopians remained in southern Iran until after the time of Herodotus.[195] All of these southern (or Ethiopian) Aryans comprised what are known as the *Hamitic* people.

Conquests by the Hamites in southwestern Arabia extended northwestward half-way up the Arabian shore of

191 Herodotus, *Hist.* vii.70.
192 These Ethiopians (Hamites) descended from the same racial stock as the contemporaneous Hindu population of the Punjab and the Indus Valley regions, who were more civilized than the Indonesian tribes toward the east (Herodotus iii.94., 98-101, vii.70); but the Hamites were darker because of their long habitation in southern Iran, where it is extremely hot much of the year. The Hamitic and Iranian languages have many features in common.
193 Herodotus viii.87-101, J. C. Prichard, *op. cit.*, vol. 2, pages 192-199.
194 Strabo, *Geogr.* xvi.4.20.
195 Herodotus iii.94, 101.

the Red Sea and some centuries later across Bāb el Mandeb to the African highlands, where they established a colony or subordinate kingdom named Ethiopia.[196] The last-named territory was taken from the Indafricans by degrees and the Blacks were driven southward and westward from this pleasant mountain region. The conquered territory extended from the Nubian desert on the north to the lake region on the south and the ocean on the east. "That Abyssinia was peopled from south Arabia is proved by its language and writing, but the difference between the two languages is such as to imply that the settlement was very early and that there were many centuries of separation, during which the Abyssinians were exposed to foreign influences."[197]

That movement is substantiated by the *Odyssey* of Homer,[198] where reference is made to "the distant Ethiopians who are sundered in twain, the uttermost of men, some abiding where Hyperion sinks and some where he rises." Strabo[199] supports Homer in regard to the wide range of habitation of the Ethiopians, saying that "this does not, therefore, refer alone to the land next to Egypt, but rather to the whole southern country extending along the seacoast".[200] That they were Aryan in physical type is attested by repeated passages of Herodotus,[201] who characterized them as the tallest and handsomest of men and very long-lived.

Shortly after 6000 B.C. the Hamitic culture was transmitted down the Nile River to Upper Egypt, as proved by the fact that the grammatical construction of the historical Egyptian language closely resembled the language of Hamitic people in southern Arabia and around the Fertile Crescent farther north. The inflectional languages

196 *Ibid.,* iii.114.
197 *Ency. Brit.,* 13th Ed., vol. 23, page 956. by David Heinrich Müller. J. C. Prichard, *op. cit.,* vol. 2, chapters VI-IX, inclusive.
198 Homer's *Odyssey* i.1-2.
199 Strabo i.2. 27-28.
200 "Caucasian" origin of the Egyptians is asserted by W. M. F. Petrie, *Ancient Egypt,* 1926, pages 41ff. Evidently the Hamites are meant; the term "Caucasian" has no ethnic meaning.
201 Herodotus iii.20, 23, 114.

evolved in the primitive Aryan race, but the agglutinative
form seems to have persisted among the various later
Turanian races, with the apparent exception of the
Hittites, as was said before.

Further evidence of this migration is the fact that the
Hamites took with them to southern Arabia and Africa
the rudiments of the Neolithic civilization that was diffused over Iran during the long operation of the Pre-
Sumerian caravans between Turkistan and Mesopotamia.
This culture was amplified in later centuries by commercial intercourse between the Hamites in Iran and
Arabia and the Pre-Sumerians in lower Mesopotamia;
the course of transmission was predominantly from
Mesopotamia to Africa rather than in the reverse direction. Its influence also reached the Indus valley as is indicated by recent discoveries of primitive Turkic objects
at Mohenjo-Daro and surrounding points. Away from
this river valley, the people of India apparently were
still on an inferior cultural level in Herodotus' time.[202]

On this transmitted Pre-Sumerian foundation the Hamites in southwestern Arabia and Ethiopia evolved a marvelous culture of their own,[203] which by commercial
intercourse and later conquest was borne down the Nile
valley to Upper Egypt, probably in the region of Thebes.[204] The earliest advanced civilization there is said to
have centered on the city of This, near Abydos. Later
it was supplanted by that at Thebes. The district of
Abydos is one of the most ancient in Upper Egypt, antedating 5500 B.C. Its history is said to have begun in the
late pre-historic age, as it was founded by kings that long
preceded Menes.[205] Their towns, temples, and tombs have
been discovered. Kings of the Ist and IInd dynasties
were buried there. Nine or ten temples were built successively on one site from at least as early as the Ist

202 *Ibid.*, iii. 99-101.
203 F. Stuhlmann, *Handwerk und Industries in Ostrafrika* (L. Friederichsen &
Co., Hamburg, 1910); Herodotus ii. 3-4, 18.
204 Herodotus ii.4, 15; Diodorus iii.3; V. Gordon Childe, *The Most Ancient East*
(Appleton-Century, New York, 1934), pages 172-176.
205 W. M. F. Petrie, *Abydos*, ii.64.

dynasty to the time of the XXVIth dynasty. Pharaoh Cheops, of the IVth dynasty, built the Great Pyramid of learning about 4500 B.C.

Four-fifths of the drainage of the upper Ethiopian plateau, which has a temperate and healthful climate, is carried off by rivers that flow northward to the Nile, chiefly the Takazze in the north, the Abai in the center, and the Sobat in the south. Moreover, the general slope of these uplands is in that direction, which was the most feasible course of expansion. The prehistoric population of Upper Egypt, a branch of the Mediterranean race,[206] changed with advent of the dynasties to a stronger type (the conquering Hamitic Ethiopians), better developed in skull and muscle.[207] The former inhabitants had moved down the Nile ahead of the advancing Ethiopians. For twenty-two centuries, apparently until the time of Menes, the conquerors exercised suzerainty over Upper Egypt as a separate domain.

Menes, the reputed first king of combined Upper and Lower Egypt, who arose as a leader of the Hamites in Upper Egypt about 3400 B.C., so changed the simple habits of his subjects, particularly in that region, that it was recorded by a stela at Thebes and a curse was pronounced against him. Upon his conquest of Lower Egypt, thousands of the Mediterranean people fled to Krete and others went westward and settled in Libya.[208] The Egyptian dialect is Mediterranean-Hamitic modified by Pre-Sumerians (Hyksos and others) and the earliest inscriptions in that country are in the Hamitic language. In fact, the very name of Egypt appears to have been brought down the Nile, as it was borne previously by the Thebaid.[209] If, as Herodotus states,[210] Menes changed the course of the Nile, the power and scientific advancement of

---

206 See *Did Prehistoric Egyptian Culture Spring from a Marsh-Dwelling People?* by Eric von Rosen (Stockholm, 1929).

207 *Encyclopaedia Britannica,* 13th Ed., vol. 9, p. 43, by Francis L. Griffith. J. C. Prichard, *op.cit.,* vol 2, Ch. XI.

208 Herodotus ii. 16-18, iv.197, where he classified the Libyans separately from the Egyptians.

209 *Ibid.,* ii.15.

210 *Ibid.,* ii.99.

the Hamitic people must have been wondrous at that time as well as a long time earlier. This is further confirmed by Manetho's account of Venephes, who lived slightly more than a half-century after Menes and who built the pyramids near Kokhome. Diodorus[211] states directly the tradition of descent of the (dominant) Egyptians from the Ethiopians and the transmission of early Ethiopian culture down the Nile. The ancient Egyptians of Thebes always referred to the *Land of Punt* as their homeland. In fact, as Rawlinson remarks, no signs have been found on the earliest Egyptian monuments that indicate a progression from the primitive to the more advanced stages of art or any marked change in the social condition of the dominant people. The ancient Egyptian religion presents indications of heterogeneous and unassimilated concepts, resulting from the imposition of an already developed system (Hamitic) on one of lower order (Mediterranean).[212] The primitive culture included a hieroglyphic alphabet. The pyramids of the earliest dynasties were constructed with a precision not surpassed by any other masonry of ancient or modern times, which proves that the Upper Egyptians already had advanced greatly in the arts of civilization before the age of Menes and before they had migrated down the Nile valley. In fact, the early civilization of Egypt shows a remarkable coincidence with that of Lower Mesopotamia,[212] *which demonstrates not only the common origin of much of both but likewise the remarkably high development of the Pre-Sumerian culture.* In predynastic times commerce flowed freely between Somaliland and Egypt, which tends to verify the above-stated course of migration.

A conspicuous example of the transmission of ideas by the commercial intercourse or migration of peoples is that of the veneration of the cow. It is traceable from Tibet down the Indus valley and on the westerly side of the Suliman Mountains to southern Baluchistan, whence the Hamites took it across to southwestern Arabia and

---

211 Diodorus Siculus, iv.1.
212 *Encyclopaedia Britannica*, 13th Ed., vol. 9, pp. 42-43, by Francis L. Griffith.

Ethiopia. Subsequently, the Phoenicians took it with them from southwestern Arabia via Mesopotamia to the eastern shores of the Mediterranean when they migrated there from El Haza about 2750 B.C.[213] Meanwhile, the Ethiopians already had transmitted it to Egypt. Another idea similarly passed along was that of the inordinately low social status of swineherds. No one would establish any family ties with them and they could not enter a temple without prior purification.[214] An example of the diffusion of ideas northward from Hamitic centers in southwestern Arabia and Ethiopia is the very early casting of horoscopes in Egypt[215] and in Chaldea,[216] by which future events and destiny of persons were predicted at birth by observation of the constellations.[217] Another evidence of primitive migration from Ethiopia to Egypt may be noted. Bineter, a king of the IInd Egyptian dynasty decreed that women might attain royal authority, a mark of respect that probably arose in Upper Ethiopia, where as well as in western Africa women still form the body-guard of the king.[217½]

This Pre-Sumerian culture, extended down the Nile very early and superimposed on the indigenous Mediterranean population[218] in the Delta region, ultimately produced the marvelous historic civilization of Egypt. The Ethiopian influence was felt in the lower Nile valley soon after 6000 B.C., and commercial contact with Iran also was long continued by the Hamites across southern Arabia.[219] An outstanding evolution of Ethiopian culture was the temples of worship and the rites incident thereto.[220] At Meroe, the ancient capital of Ethiopia, situated near the modern Dankalah, in addition to pyramids of remote antiquity, there was a magnificent temple in honor of

---

213 Herodotus ii.44, vii.89.
214 *Ibid.,* ii.47.
215 Iamblichus 8.4.
216 Cicero: *De Divinatione* i.1.
217 Herodotus ii.82.
217½ Arthur Weigall, *History of the Pharaohs,* I, 51, 130-134.
218 Herodotus ii.3-4, 18.
219 Strabo i.2.27.
220 Herodotus ii.29.

Jupiter Ammon, also of remote antiquity. It was a place of great sanctity and devotion and around it there were many sacella or chapels.[221] From Meroe the worship of Jupiter descended to Thebes, from which the rites at Ammon (Libya) and Dodona (Greece) were derived.[222] Thus, the art of divination, as practised in ancient Greece, was procured from Egypt. The Egyptians very early introduced the sacred festivals, processions, and supplications, and from them the Greeks were instructed.[223] Accordingly, Pluto, in his *Timaeus* (page 22B), reports that the Hellenic nation was reminded by the Egyptians that it was in its infancy compared with them. The calendar year of 365 days was introduced in Egypt in 4236 B.C., the earliest fixed date in our history of the world. In this achievement, "the Egyptian of 4241 [4236] B.C. was not unworthy to stand in the direct line of succession which leads to Copernicus and Newton."[224] This fact alone demonstrates the existence of a highly-developed civilization at that early time.

By that time the civilization of Lower Egypt had outstripped that of Ethiopia and the trend of cultural influence had reversed its direction along the Nile, since the evidence demonstrates much subsequent transmission of Egyptian culture across the Ethiopian frontier. The stimulus of Pre-Sumerian culture on the Egyptians was far different from the depressive influence of neighboring Negro tribes on the Ethiopians in the south. It may be that the center of the earliest high Hamitic culture always was in southwestern Arabia and that Ethiopia originally was more in the nature of a frontier colony or outpost and served as the base of operations down the Nile until it was more fully developed.[225] The ascendancy of Egypt over Ethiopia apparently dates from the reign of Sesusri III in the 19th century B.C. A king of the XVIth

---

221 Pliny, *Nat. Hist.*, vi.29.
222 Herodotus ii.42, 54.
223 Herodotus ii.58.
224 James Baikie, *A History of Egypt* (MacMillan, New York, 1929), page 46.
225 The Hamitic race now covers about one-third of Africa and numbers approximately 50,000,000 people.

dynasty, he appears to have defeated the Negroes and the Ethiopians and was the first Egyptian king to rule in the latter country besides having been its benefactor. However, Ethiopia, although still a dependency of the Sabaeans, appears soon afterward to have become politically independent of Egypt, but Egyptian influence in that country continued to be quite marked. Its ruler after 900 B.C. was Menelek, king of both Sheba and Ethiopia, who was a natural son of King Solomon of Israel and Queen Balkis of Sheba. It may soon have become independent of Sheba also, with Menelek's son as its ruler. The trend of culture clearly was southward during the 7th century B.C.[226]

Beginning about 3800 B.C., several bands of Aryans emigrated from southern Arabia over the trade routes from Asir to El Haza on the Persian Gulf,[227] where they surveyed the possibilities of territorial gain in the rich Mesopotamian region. One band seems to have invaded and settled in Upper Babylonia, centering on Agadë, and was referred to later as the Akkadians; but, before long, they were subdued by King Sargon I of Assyria. Another division, known as the Canaanites, who were Hamites from southwestern Arabia, upon finding the Sumerian and Assyrian power in Mesopotamia too strong, swerved by that region on the south and proceeded to central Palestine and the coastal region, where their country was known as Canaan. The coastal area later was called Phoenicia, from one of their subsequent tribes.[228] The Pre-Sumerians, whose territory they crossed, were divided, some joining their kin in Aram and others moving southward to the mountainous regions of Palestine.

The next outstanding appearance of Hamites in the Fertile Crescent was that of the Chaldeans and Phoenicians about 2750 B.C. They were Sabaeans from the present

---

226 Herodotus, *Hist.* ii.30. (Sheba —Saba).
227 Strabo, *Geogr.* xvi.4. 19, 24, 25.
228 The boundaries of ancient Phoenicia changed frequently, but Phoenicia proper may be said to have been the coastal region bounded by Galilee on the south, the Eleutherus River on the north, and the Lebanon Mountains on the east.

Yemen,[229] but were in stronger force than their predecessors. They, too, may have emigrated from southwestern Arabia because of drought. Crossing central Arabia and moving around the Sumerians on the south and west, the Chaldeans succeeded in conquering and settling in the Babylonian region, where they made their headquarters at Ur. They impelled many Sumerians out of central Babylonia into Aram (Syria) and probably Assyria and extended their suzerainty around the Fertile Crescent, reaching the height of their power about 2234 B.C. The other division, the later Phoenicians, continued westward and seized the coastal region of Canaan from their kin,[230] whereupon it became known as Phoenicia, although the earlier inhabitants called it Sidon.[231] Thenceforth, this coastal and adjacent interior region was dominated by the Canaanite nations. The division that expanded northward in the so-called Lebanon region was known as the Amorites. Between 1475 and 1440 B.C., a part of westerly Canaan was conquered by the Israelites from Egypt, as narrated in *Exodus*. Relationship of the Canaanites and the Phoenicians is shown by the similarity of their religious customs, such as the sacrifice of the first-born child to secure the favor of the gods.

About 2160 B.C., the Hamitic Amorites from mainly east of the Jordan River in Lebanon conquered central Babylonia from the Chaldeans and terminated the latter's long reign there, but before long the country was overrun by Elamites, who laid it under tribute for several centuries. The Amorites' most eminent king was Khammurabi (Hammurabi), c. 2100 B.C., who in the 30th year of his reign retrieved his fortunes and drove out the Elamites. Another of his great achievements was the codification of the laws of the country, which have been preserved to the present time. The enforced emigration of

---

229 That the Chaldeans of Babylonia were closely akin to the ruling Egyptians and the Ethiopians is indicated by the fact that they were deemed to be colonists of Egypt (Diodorus Siculus i.28).

230 Herodotus, *Hist.* ii.44, vii.89. They arrived about 2300 years before the time of Herodotus.

231 *Genesis* 10:15. Tyre, in the south, was its most important city.

Sumerians from Babylonia to Aram and Assyria by the Chaldean and Amoritic conquests added strength and ambition to the Assyrian nation and under Ninus it had begun to add surrounding country to its domain by 2000 B.C.,[232] apparently as a dependency of the Amorites. But about 1926 B.C. they broke away from the Amorites and aided the Sumerians in southern Babylonia to regain the ascendancy, whereupon eleven Sumerian kings reigned in succession until about 1780 B.C., when they were overwhelmed by the Kassites of Elam. Under these attacks about a year earlier, the Kassite tribe of Khabira, the later Hebrews, departed from Ur to Padan-Aram (Syria), where racial kin then resided, and soon afterward migrated southward to the promised land of Canaan, as already explained. This southward pressure dislodged Pre-Sumerian Kheta from the hill country of Palestine, who under their Hyksos kings invaded Egypt soon after 1780 B.C., where they ruled the country for approximately 199 years as the XVth, XVIth, and XVIIth dynasties. These two invasions of Egypt by the Kheta caused dispersion of Hamitic Berbers westward across northern Africa.[233] The early contacts of Mesopotamian and Egyptian cultures are revealed by impressions of the former on certain phases of Egyptian civilization as well as on the language of that country. This Turanian dominance of Egypt was terminated about 1577 B.C., when those forces were expelled, as related before.

Beginning about 1300 B.C., the Assyrians under Shalmaneser I and his successors rose again to power and within a century overcame the Kassites and gained control of Babylonia, which they retained until about 1204 B.C. and afterward (except for some intermittent rule by Kassites, Elamites, and Sumerians) until overthrown by Nordic Medes (Kimmerians) under Cyaxares in 606 B.C. However, the Hamitic language remained the national speech of Babylonia, while the old Sumerian language

---

232 Diodorus Siculus ii. 1-7.
233 J. C. Prichard, op.cit., vol. 2, pages 15-42.

continued in use as a sort of "Latin" of religion, law, and letters down almost to the beginning of the Christian era. Concurrently, the Chaldeans persisted as the philosophers and astrologers of that country.[234]

The Tell el-Amarna tablets (c. 1375-1358 B.C.) show that the rule of Egypt over the eastern Mediterranean region during the 14th century B.C. was weak and that, owing to the southward pressure of northern Syrian peoples, a condition of chaos existed. At that time the Keltic Aryan tribes from Thrace were consolidating their conquests of the westerly coast of Anatolia, as later explained, and were pressing eastward on the Turanian nations there and in Cappadocia, which in turn forced many of the inhabitants southward to the Taurus Mountains and eastward into Syria. In addition to Hebraic tribes, hordes of Semitic Aramaeans from Syria and Hittites from Cappadocia overran Palestine (including Canaan).

The favored region between the Euphrates and Nile rivers was a much traveled route for both commercial intercourse and warfare in ancient times, and Egypt at different times alternated with northern nations in exercising suzerainty over the country. The commingling of Hamites with underlying Pre-Sumerian peoples throughout the whole Mesopotamian region ultimately resulted in the later composite Semitic race and language in various areas, although both remained preponderantly Pre-Sumerian and Sumerian, i.e., Turanian.

Eratosthenes (276-194 B.C.) is quoted in Strabo's *Geography*[235] as saying that four great nations controlled that part of southwestern Arabia that lay across Bāb el Mandeb from Ethiopia, namely, the *Minaeans* (on the Red Sea), the *Sabaeans* (on the highlands, with their capital the modern Marib), the *Katabans* (near Bāb el Mandeb), and the *Hadramuteans* (on the Arabian Sea). Judaism was introduced very early, in the 10th century B.C., in southwestern Arabia by King Menelek, natural son

---

234 Diodorus ii.29.
235 Strabo xvi. 4.2.

of King Solomon, of Israel, and Queen Balkis, of Sheba (in Yemen), who ruled both Sheba and Ethiopia. Later it spread into Ethiopia and the Sudan.[236] All of these southern Arabians (Hamites with the new Semitic strain) were settled agricultural people in contrast with the nomadic Mediterranean Bedouins of central Arabia. Marked distinction has persisted since ancient times between these two chiefly Aryan people (Hamites and Mediterraneans) and on the African mainland they seldom have intermarried. [237] The Sabaeans were a great and wealthy nation.[238] They, like other southern Arabian nations, were frequently governed by queens, and it is from the above-named King Menelek that the present dynasty of the Hamitic nation of Ethiopia claims descent.

The ancient intimate relations between the dominant (Hamitic) Egyptians and the Phoenicians affirm their common origin.[239] The fundamental distinctions between the later historic Egyptian culture and the Babylonian culture, despite the common Asiatic origin of many primitive rudiments of each, are attributable to different racial psychology and environment. As already indicated, the former culture was matured by Aryan Mediterraneans and Hamites[240] and the latter by Turanian Pre-Sumerians and Sumerians (prior to the invasion by the Chaldeans), both on the Neolithic base that the Pre-Sumerians had brought from Western Turkistan about 8000 B.C. Some of the common features, those dating from most primitive times, were either basically Mediterranean or a later composite of Pre-Sumerian and Sumerian, or they were embodied in foreign customs that later replaced local customs, such as those of the Ethiopians after 6000 B.C., except for those normal developments independently in society wherever located. As the result of a high civiliza-

---

236 J. C. Prichard, op.cit., vol. 2, pp. 146-148.
237 Ibid., pp. 9, 174-176, 182-183, 260, 262.
238 Diodorus iii. 46-47.
239 Ency. Brit., 13th Ed., vol. 21, page 449, by George A. Cooke.
240 Predominantly by the Hamites on a primitive base developed by the original Mediterraneans in Egypt, since the culture of the latter actually was brought to maturity later on the island of Krete and in Greece.

tion attained as early as 4500 B.C., Egypt is said never to have been surpassed in engineering, architecture, building construction, sculpture, and jewelry manufacture. Its art everywhere reflected a sense of beauty. Our calendar and alphabet came from there, where also were laid the foundations of mathematics, medicine, and surgery. Even a concept of a single God emanated in Egypt. Pharaoh Amenhotep IV, a religious enthusiast of the XVIIIth dynasty, who died during the last half of the 14th century B.C., is recognized under his adopted name of Akhenaton as one of the early monotheists of history.[241] The earliest must have been an Amorite, who apparently developed the idea from monotheistic tendencies that evolved out of astral religion amidst Babylonian polytheism,[242] and was adopted by the Israelites in Canaan before they migrated to Egypt, although in its incipient stages,[243] for Pre-Mosaic polytheism seems to be implied in *Exodus* 20:3, 22:28. Thus, the idea of the Yahweh or Jehovah of Moses represented an advancement of this principle by the Israelites while they were in Egypt. The rite of circumcision was derived from the Egyptians.[244]

It is impossible to say how much of this Egyptian culture was wholly of primitive Mediterranean origin, how much was solely of Hamitic origin via Ethiopia, and how much resulted from the commingling of the two, with due regard to persistent influence from Babylonia. The fact that Egyptian culture differed widely from that indigenous to the Mediterranean race on the island of Krete and the Grecian peninsula suggests that the Hamitic influence had become dominant quite early along the upper Nile. The Phoenicians,[245] who are credited with improving the hieroglyphic alphabet, were of Hamitic origin and their ancestors originally came to southern

---

241 His great hymn to Aton, the Sun, has come down to us in the 104th Psalm.
242 Discussed further in *Ency. Brit.,* 13th Ed., vol. 13, page 178a.
243 *Exodus* 6:2, 3.
244 *Ibid.,* 6:30.
245 As early as 3000 B. C. their congeners in Egypt had invented an alphabet of 24 letters and this appears to have been the source of the later Phoenician alphabet, although the latter could just as readily have been derived from the Assyrian alphabet.

Arabia from Iran, where they gained the rudiments of their civilization chiefly from invading Turkic Pre-Sumerians. The latter also had developed a hieroglyphic system of writing in Shinar, and it is not unreasonable to infer that the basic idea of writing was another creation of the Turanians of Turkistan, for hieroglyphs preceded alphabetic letters, a later invention. The Egyptian hieroglyphs had many points of analogy with the Sumerian system, although the former possessed pure consonants and the latter did not, which probably was a local development. Clearly, the early Greeks had no alphabet.[246] All ancient hieroglyphs, including the linear kind or running hand, were written from right to left, from left to right, or in vertical columns (like the Chinese), according to the space the matter was to occupy, and the mode of reading it was toward the face of the animals or figures used. There were very few exceptions to this general rule. This form of writing was known to the ancient Phoenicians, of course. The extensive commerce of the Phoenicians, which made their simplification of the alphabet necessary,[247] is a notable theme of history, but the earlier Kretan and still earlier Lelegian commerce also deserve greater inquiry.

There is a tendency to attribute too much antiquity to this Phoenician commercial expansion. The widespread Phoenician maritime power in the Aegean region did not begin much earlier than the 13th century B.C., although it arose many centuries before along the eastern Mediterranean shores. The Kretan sea power long antedated it in the region and flourished concurrently with the much older and more extensive commercial operations conducted on the Mediterranean by the Anatolian Leleges. Both were demolished by the Achaean and other Keltic invaders from the north on both sides of the Aegean, whereupon the Carian sea-power became dominant[248]

---

246 Herodotus v.58.
247 Diodorus v. 74.
248 Herodotus i.171; Thucydides, *History* i.4,8.

there for one or two centuries [249] and it was followed
by the Phoenician maritime expansion. Indication that
the latter arose before the 13th century east of the Aegean
are the following circumstances. Phoenicia very early established a colony in the later Cilicia, near the northeastern corner of the Mediterranean Sea.[250] It was engulfed by
Turanian Cilicians driven from western Anatolia after
the Keltic invasion and the Trojan War. No Hittite
monuments have been found in Cilicia and the Syriac intrusion must have occurred later. According to Pliny,[251]
Cadmus, son of Agenor, king of Tyre, about the 15th
century B.C. or earlier,[252] brought the Phoenician alphabet to Greece.[253] Later, the Greeks added other letters. Subsequently, the improved alphabet was brought
into Latium, Italy, by Pelasgi from the Aegean region.[254]
Whether it replaced or was modified by the alphabet of
the neighboring Etruscans (banished from Anatolia) is
an undetermined question. Finally, upon the demolition
of the Kretan sea-power by the conquest of that island
about 1400 B.C., when a period of stagnation set in and
its products attained a greater degree of uniformity, the
Phoenicians promptly took advantage of their opportunity
to become the dominant maritime nation. They diffused
Kretan products, among other commodities, to the Troad,
Sicily, and even the Spanish coast, to southern Anatolia,
Cyprus, and Palestine, and from the Nile valley to the
mouth of the Po River,[255] while maintaining other com-

249 As the first Keltic invaders and conquerors of southwestern Anatolia, the
Carians probably continued in operation the Lelegian sea commerce that they took
over (Strabo xiii, 1.59; Diodorus vi. 17), but this disintegrated after one or two
centuries (subsequent to the Trojan War), due to other Keltic invasions of
western Anatolia and the Kretan and Phoenician sea rivalry.
250 Herodotus vii. 91.
251 Pliny vii. 56.
252 The arrival of Cadmus in Boetica is placed by some writers as early as
1550 B. C. (or earlier; see Herodotus ii. 145 ff.). In any event, it was prior to
the Achaean invasion of Greece (Diodorus v. 1). The citadel of Thebes, in Greece,
which city Cadmus established, was named for him.
253 Strabo ix. 2.3, x. 1.8.
254 Anticlides.
255 *Encyclopaedia Britannica*, 13th Ed., vol. 7, p. 423, by Arthur J. Evans.

mercial routes beyond the Meriterranean to the shores of the Atlantic.

The foregoing circumstances demonstrate that civilization existed very early among the Sabaeans (and other Hamites) in southwestern Arabia and that regular caravan routes or other commercial intercourse prevailed from important points in Iran around southern or across central Arabia to the southwest and to Ethiopia and return. The amber of the Baltic and the tin of Britain,[256] the linen of Egypt, the spices of Arabia, the slaves of the Caucasus, and the horses of Scythia were commodities handled by the Phoenicians.[257]

Perhaps the most remarkable confirmation of the high civilization of the Hamites in southwestern Arabia and later in Canaan and Phoenicia comes not from the eastern Mediterranean but from an ancient Phoenician colony just beyond the Pillars of Hercules in southern Iberia.[258] In the last part of the 13th century B.C. and the forepart of the 12th, subsequent to the Trojan War, when the Phoenicians began to navigate beyond the western end of the Mediterranean, they established colonies, among other places, in the valley of the Baetis (now Guadalquivir) River, in what was much later called Andalusia.[259] Their chief port, Agadir or Gaddir, later Gades and now Cadiz, was founded at that time.[260] This valley, in part at least, is identified as the classical Tartessus, a famous Phoenician mart.[261] Its subsequent name was *Turdetania,* all of whose cities and neighboring places were inhabited by Phoenicians.[262] Strabo remarks how polished and urbane the people were, stating that

---

256 Herodotus iii. 115; Diodorus vi. 7, 8; J. A. Giles, *Six Old English Chronicles, Richard of Cirencester* (Bell, London, 1891), i.6.18-19.

257 *Ezekiel* 27:13-14.

258 It would appear that the Amorites, whether from Canaan, as seems probable, or direct from southwestern Arabia, took a relatively high culture to Babylonia when they conquered and settled there about 2160 B. C. It must have been related to the Chaldean culture that preceded it there and both became integrated in variable degrees with the older Turkic cultures.

259 Strabo i.3.2.

260 *Ibid.,* iii. 5.5.

261 Herodotus i.163.

262 Strabo iii. 2.13.

they had so far adopted the Roman method of life as almost to have forgotten their own language.[263] The same author indicates[264] that these Phoenicians were the dominant people of this region and that they had possessed the richest part of Iberia before the time of Homer. He makes the same remark about their having been long-lived as Herodotus did[265] about that race in Ethiopia. He says, moreover, that the Turdetani were the most intelligent people of all the Iberians and reports their *use of an alphabet* [the Phoenician] *and their possession of historical records, poems, and metrical laws said to be 6000 years old.*[266] The other Iberians had a different alphabet and spoke a different (the Mediterranean) language. Since, unlike the Basques, there is no evidence of any relation of these Turdetani with the ancient Turanian Anatolians, Sumerians or Hittites, it seems certain that this culture was transmitted thither by the Phoenicians and originally had been brought by the latter from the Hamitic center of civilization in southwestern Arabia in the same way that Hamitic culture had been borne down the Nile by the primitive Ethiopians.[267] The Phoenicians also made settlements on the Canary islands[268] and on the British Isles. Carthaginian invaders from the Balearic Islands gained control of Turdetania about 516 B.C., but the Punic wars transferred the supremacy to Rome. Latin civilization was firmly established there in 27 B.C., when Andalusia became the Roman province of Baetica.

But, like other peoples of the west, the Phoenicians apparently had no knowledge of the products of India;[269]

263 *Ibid.*, iii. 2.15.

264 *Ibid.*, iii. 2.14.

265 Herodotus iii. 23,114.

266 Strabo iii. 1.6.

267 According to Diodorus (ii. 2), at the beginning the will of the Egyptian kings was not law, but they followed constitutions of law, both in collecting money and in manner of living, and none of their subjects had the status of slaves. Menes was a noted law-giver (*ibid.*, ii. 5). Thus, written constitutions apparently are not modern inventions! Moreover, their system of legal procedure sounds strikingly modern (*ibid.*, ii. 2). Solon appropriated some of the Egyptian laws for the Greeks (*ibid.* ii. 2).

268 Diodorus vi.6. The Guanches were Hamitic Berbers. J. C. Prichard, *op.cit.*, vol. 2, pages 32-36.

269 Herodotus iii. 139.

consequently, the valley of the Indus was ordered explored by Darius the Great of Persia,[270] and he sent, among others, Scylax of Caryanda (Caria) on that mission. Carthage, African colony of Phoenicia, brought tin from Britain,[271] as the people of Tyre had done long before.

Especial notice may be taken here of the personnel of the ships in the Persian naval force of Xerxes,[272] which roughly corresponds with our naval policy of today. The Persians considered the Phoenicians to be the best mariners and to each crew of approximately 200 men they added 30 soldiers (marines) of the Persians, Medes, and Sakae, who were deemed to be the best troops of the empire. The present-day marine, therefore, may derive much pride from this antiquity of origin of his service (480 B.C.).

East of the Nile in Africa the basic population is Hamitic, from the south or from across the Red Sea. West of that river as far north as 15° north latitude, are the Berbers, who are Hamites of great antiquity, also from the south. North of them are the inhabitants of the Sudan and Libya, Arabs of the Mediterranean race, with a minor strain of Nordic Kimmerians from the Black Sea region, who invaded the eastern Mediterranean region perhaps as early as 1550 B.C. These Arabs came across the isthmus of Suez and settled the Egyptian delta and lands on the west very early, long prior to the earliest descent of Ethiopians on the Nile.

Physically, there is very little difference between the Hamitic and the Mediterranean subraces, the former being darker and of somewhat larger stature. Both originated in the primal Aryan stock that came from the Indus valley to Iran, so that their commingling in Egypt did not greatly alter the basic type. However, there anciently was notable Indafrican (or Negro) racial mixture in Egypt not only among the invaders from Ethiopia but also by sporadic Negro invasions of Lower Egypt, which ac-

---

270 *Ibid.*, iv. 44.
271 Strabo iii. 5.11.
272 Herodotus vi. 12, vii. 96,184.

celerated the decadence of the nation. Some change in type occurred again when the Pre-Sumerian Kheta from Palestine entered Egypt after 1780 B.C. Thus, the present Egyptians are descendants of indigenous Mediterraneans, Hamites, Indafricans, and Turanian Kheta in various degrees.

During the many centuries of Hamitic habitation of Ethiopia, large numbers intermarried with Negroes of various sorts and produced ameliorated Negro strains, whose descendants are scattered far and wide in central Africa today. Such interbreeding finally caused the decadence of this nation also. The so-called Nilotic people of the Upper Nile descended from such a breed. The more energetic and progressive Negro tribes are those that possess an infusion of Hamitic blood.[273] Herodotus[274] makes specific reference to the tall lighter-complexioned, handsome, and longlived men (Hamites) in Ethiopia, opposite the southwestern corner of Arabia, distinguishing them from the Indafricans and discussing their customs briefly. The country produced gold in large quantities, elephants with their large teeth, and trees and shrubs of every kind, including the ebony. It is quite probable that the Colchians who lived on the Phasis River, east of the Black Sea, and who claimed that they were Egyptians[275] were descendants of Hamitic soldiers from Egypt or Ethiopia in the army of Seostris,[276] since they corresponded in physical appearance and had similar customs. That northern territory must then (1321-1300 B.C. or earlier) have been under Egyptian suzerainty and this invasion of Media, the Caucasus, Scythia as far as the Tanais (Don) River, and Thrace was intended to punish and prevent further aggression by Nordic Medians and other Kimmerians of the north.

---

273 A. C. Haddon, *The Races of Men* (MacMillan, New York, 1925), pages 50-53.
274 Herodotus iii. 20-24, 70, 114.
275 *Ibid.*, ii. 104.
276 Diodorus ii.1. ("Sesostris" probably was either a misnomer for Seti or a name representing a compound of Kings Seti I and Rameses II).

Scholars long have been analyzing the various Semitic and Hamitic dialects in the eastern Mediterranean region in an effort to learn more about their evolution. It is unquestionable that they have certain common elements beginning with the original blend of Pre-Sumerian and Hamitic languages in Babylonia. They are segregated into two groups, the southern and the northern. Those in each group are more closely related than they are to the dialects in the other group, the reason for which is apparent. The southern group comprises the Sabaean, Mahri-Sokotri, Egyptian and Ethiopic, and central Arabian dialects, and the northern comprises the Babylonian, Assyrian, Aramaic, Hebraic, and Phoenician. In having the so-called "broken plurals", the southern dialects differ from the northern dialects, which lack them. Those of the south represent mainly the Aryan Hamitic dialects of the 10th century B.C. as modified by that of the Hebrews of Israel invited to the domain of King Menelek, of the Sabaeans, the next century. Hebraic itself was a modified Kassite dialect. The northern group, commonly known as the Semitic, conversely had the Turanian base of the Pre-Sumerian and Sumerian dialects, which underwent marked intrusion of the Aryan dialects of the invaders from the south, chiefly the Akkadians, Chaldeans, and Amorites. The successive wars among themselves and with Egypt caused such commingling of members of the two races in various areas as to result in several composite dialects in that general region. Consequently, since the dialects of the south have an Aryan base and those of the north have a Turanian base, it is not strange that those in each group should be more closely related than they are to the dialects of the other group. The primitive Aryan Mediterraneans of Babylonia, Mesopotamia, Aram, and the hills of Palestine apparently had been driven out or partly absorbed when the Turanian hordes from Turkistan overran those regions. They were represented by the later Bedouins of central Arabia and the earliest Egyptians, with a different language.

Solutions of linguistic problems of these easterly Mediterranean and adjacent regions and of Arabia require consideration of the basic and subsequent racial strains that inhabited them, whether Turanian Pre-Sumerian and Sumerian or Aryan Mediterranean and Hamitic.

(6e) *Iranian Subrace.* The Iranian division of the Aryan race comprises the descendants of the original Persians and all of the present homogeneous population of the approximately Mediterranean type in northern Baluchistan, Afghanistan, Kashmir, Northwest India, and Hindustan (in India), and apparently also in ancient Bactriana and Sogdiana before the Nordic Massagetae and Sakae conquered these countries. Their progenitors were the primitive brunet tribes that migrated from northwestern India to the Iranian plateau about 40,000 years ago, early in the warm period after the Würm II glaciation. The Vedic Brünn, the Cro-Magnon, and the Mediterranean peoples long afterward emigrated from Iran, as already shown. Upon the opening of the snowbound passes over the northerly part of the Suliman Mountains, such as the Khyber Pass, after the Achen glacial peak between 17,000 and 14,000 years ago, the increasing density of population on the partially arid Iranian plateau impelled minor sporadic migrations eastward toward the Hindu Kush range, to Kashmir, and to the Punjab region of the lower Indus basin. But the most important migrations eastward were caused long afterward by invasions of Iran by Turanian and Nordic Aryan tribes from the north.

Probably the earliest such eruption eastward in Iran occurred in consequence of the great invasion of that plateau by the Turanian Pre-Sumerians about 8000 B.C., when they went from Western Turkistan to Mesopotamia. At that time the Hamitic Ethiopians in the south were scattered to regions extending from the lower Indus valley southwestward to southern Arabia, and Iranians in the central regions were driven eastward and westward. Some of the latter settled in the Zagros Mountains of the west, others moved southward, and still others went eastward to or across the Suliman Mountains to India. The Persian division settled in the highlands of the northwest (the later Media) and of the south (in the province then called Persis, now Fars). The latter people apparently were called the *Artaei* originally.[277] The Turkic Sumerian invasion of about 4300 B.C. followed substantially the same route from Western Turkistan to Mesopotamia, and at this time larger numbers of Iranians were driven over the Suliman Mountains to northwestern India and elsewhere in the upper Indus valley. There they forced the earlier invaders farther eastward. Subsequently known as the Hindus, they all pressed the Indonesians ahead of them.

The Pre-Sumerian and Sumerian caravan route or routes across Iran between Turkistan and Mesopotamia and farther west were maintained continuously by those invaders until about 2750 B.C., when the Hamitic Chaldeans from southern Arabia conquered lower Mesopotamia. During the later part of this time, the primitive Iranians of eastern Iran and those of northwestern India were in contact and the former appropriated much of the Pre-Sumerian culture of Mesopotamia and transmitted it to India; in fact, it doubtless is to these Turanian invaders of the west that the Iranians (especially the Hindus) are indebted for their basic Neolithic and much subsequent culture. Their knowledge of copper and their words for it and for ox, steer, star, and ax seem to be of Turanian origin; also their knowledge of metallurgy and stockbreeding and their religion. An advanced civilization thus had arisen in northern India before 3000 B.C., basically derived largely from Turanian invaders of western Iran and Mesopotamia, for pottery writings recently found in Nepal show that the people then were in communication with Elam, a seat of Pre-Sumerians. Much of this transfer of culture occurred in connection with commerce conducted in both directions over developed caravan routes. In fact, there is evidence today of a

---

[277] Herodotus, *Hist.* vii. 61. King Darius, of the ancient Persians, specifically stated in an inscription that he was an Aryan. Proof that the Persians were brunet and thus darker than the Nordic Medians and others in northern Iran at his time is the fact that the complexion of their descendants today in that region (e.g., the *Guebres*) and in India (the *Parsees*) is dark brown.

racial blend of Iranians and Pre-Sumerians or Sumerians in southern Baluchistan, where some brachycephaly prevails. Reference already has been made to the dissemination of Sumerian culture by water along the shores of southern India and to Assam and its penetration up the Indus valley in consequence of the commercial intercourse among these nations.

About 2300 B.C. another Turanian horde from Turkistan, the Hittites, crossed Iran and the western mountains to a settlement in Cappadocia, in northern Anatolia, rather than in Mesopotamia. Evidently, the Hittites (the present non-Aryan Armenians) had been driven from Turkistan by drought and the expansion and unrest of Nordic population (Getae) on their north, whose westerly tribes then began their momentous passage to Europe between the Caspian Sea and the Ural Mountains. The successive Nordic nations settled in southern Russia (Scythia, the Ukraine). It is doubtful whether this Hittite movement caused any Iranian migration to India.

By about 1600 B.C. the first Nordic Aryan nation in western Scythia (the *Suebi*) had been dispossessed of its habitation and driven westward and the country thereupon taken over by the second Nordic nation, the *Kimmerii*. Shortly afterward, an adventurous division of Kimmerians moved southeastward along the easterly shores of the Black Sea and settled in the mountainous region south of Armenia and Lake Van. They were the *Carduchi*, later called Kurds, and their territory now is called Kurdistan.[278] About 1500 B.C. larger Kimmerian armies followed the same route but turned eastward and conquered all of northwestern Iran, where they established the nation later known as Media. They were called the *Manda* in early history.[279] In this conquest, they apparently impelled the resettlement of the Iranian tribe of *Mitanni*[280] southwestward in the Zagros Mountains north of Assyria, whence the latter occasionally raided southern regions.

These invasions of western Iran caused another great

---

278 *Encyclopaedia Britannica,* 13th Ed., vol. 15, pages 949-951.
279 See later chapter entitled *Median Nation Established by Kimmerians.*
280 V. Gordon Childe, *op.cit.,* pp. 18, 19, 23.

emigration of Iranians (Hindus) to western India as the interior tribes in Iran were driven toward the east. About 1450 B.C., India experienced its first great invasion by Nordics[281] from Bactriana. They introduced their Vedic Sanskrit language into the country as they conquered the whole northwestern portion.[282] Perhaps a century earlier a tribe had separated from the parent nation in Geté, the "land of the seven rivers", south and southeast of Lake Balkhash, and had conquered and settled in Bactriana, which apparently then was inhabited by Iranians and perhaps some Pamirians from the highlands of the east. There their original language underwent some modification and they doubtless absorbed whatever Iranian culture appealed to them prior to their subsequent invasion of northwestern India. Within a century afterward the great Vedic literature was in course of compilation under their impetus, but it still is uncertain as to what proportion of the content originated among the Nordics of Geté and how much was gained from the Iranians of Bactriana.[282]

The *Rig-Veda,* the great literary production of these Nordic invaders under the favorable atmosphere of northwestern India about 1400 B.C., refers to their settlement in India and their warfare with the dark-skinned natives, apparently the Iranians, who only shortly before had crossed the Suliman Mountains to the Punjab and adjacent territory, and to the Hamitic Ethiopians on the lower Indus. The writings show that these Nordics were acquainted with most of the metals and had blacksmiths, coppersmiths, goldsmiths, carpenters, barbers, and other artisans. They fought from chariots, as they had learned from the Turanians of the north along with other advanced knowledge. They came to the banks of the Indus and there divided into tribes, pushing Iranians and their dark-skinned predecessors farther east. They were husbandmen, plowed the fields, had cattle, ate beef, and used

---

281 A subsequent chapter describes the Nordic invasions of India.
282 Calvin Kephart, *Sanskrit Language — Its Origin, Composition, and Diffusion* (Strasburg, Va., 1949). This should be a fruitful field for research.

fermented liquor or beer. The women enjoyed high position. Marriage was held to be sacred. Each father of a family was the priest of his own household. Both husband and wife were rulers of the house and drew near to the gods together in prayer. The chieftain, who was elected, was both father and priest to the tribe. Caste, in its later sense, was unknown.

The third great invasion of western India by Iranians occurred in the 6th century B.C., when Nordic armies (*Kushans, Tokhari,* and *Sakae*) from east of the Caspian Sea overran and took possession of northeastern Iran and Bactriana from the native population. They represented the former Massagetae and the Sakae who had moved southward from Geté. The territory of the Kimmeric Medians had been extended from the Elburz Mountains across Khorasan nearly to Herat. When the *Dahae,* a branch of the Massagetae, overran Khorasan, the combined population then formed the Parthian nation, whose resultant dialect was known as the *Pahlavi.* The remainder of the Massagetae, under the name of Tokhari, continued eastward and took possession of the valley of the Oxus River (the *Amu Daria*), north of the Hindu Kush and south of the Hissar Mountains, as far east as the Pamirs. One of their tribes soon became known as the *Ephthalites* (or *White Huns)* and their dynastic tribe took the name of *Kushan.* The dominions of these tribes, which included Bukhara south of the Hissar Mountains, comprised the country known as Bactriana[283] and their capital was at Balkh, now in northern Afghanistan. They must have superimposed their rule on native Iranians and Pamirians. The climate was favorable, water was abundant, and the land was fertile. But before long Cyrus the Great forced Bactriana to become one of the satrapies of the Persian Empire. Meanwhile, probably because of Turanian pressure on the north, the other Nordic nation of the Sakae (and its tribe, the *Wu-Sun*) had taken possession of Sogdiana, north of Bactriana, which comprised the valley of the Jaxartes River (the *Syr Daria*) and the

---

283 *Ency., Brit.,* 13th Ed., vol. 3, pp. 180-181 (Bactria).

valley of the Zarafshan River, including northern Bukhara, Samarkand, and Ferghana. They also must have conquered a native Aryan population. Their capital, formerly called *Maracanda,* later took the form of Samarkand. The descendants today of the Sakae of Sogdiana appear to be the people known as the *Balti.*[284] During the Persian and the later Grecian suzerainties of Bactriana and Sogdiana, the Nordics who served in their armies that invaded India learned much about that country on the south. By 126 B.C., the five Nordic tribes of Bactriana and Sogdiana had thrown off Graeco-Bactrian domination. Half a century later they confederated, soon conquered western India, and promptly thereafter formed the great *Scytho-Indian Empire,* which is discussed at length in the final chapter.

The successive Iranian invasions of and settlements in India through the ages are proved by the differences in the present dialects of the Hindu inhabitants from east to west. The modern language there (other than Sanskrit) is distinguished in three divisions. Each horde of invaders drove eastward into the Ganges valley most of the older inhabitants of the central Indus valley, until the earliest population, the Indonesian, ultimately was forced in large part to the Dekkan and eastward from India into southeastern Asia, as already explained. A portion stayed permanently in the province of Bengal. The Indonesians apparently are either the basic component or a primitive branch of the Dravidian subrace of the Dekkan, which also embodies an Iranian strain that came from the north after the Laws of Manu had been written.

Thus, the present population of Bengal comprises descendants of the Indonesians who did not emigrate and since have commingled with the vanguard of the earliest discernible Iranian invaders of India (about 4300 B.C.) and with infiltrations of Paraoean or southern Mongoloids from Burma. From Benares to Cawnpur, many millons of Hindus speak a dialect (Eastern Hindi) inherited from those Iranians who entered India about 4300 B.C. From

---

284 This name may have had the same origin among the *Getae* as the dynastic name (*Balt*) of the Visigoths, which is perpetuated in the west in the name of the Baltic Sea.

Cawnpur to eastern Punjab are other millions who speak a dialect (Western Hindi) inherited from those Iranians who arrived about 1500 B.C., and in central Punjab are still other millions of descendants of Iranians who arrived in the 6th century B.C. and who speak a dialect (Punjabi) inherited from their progenitors.[285] Thus, each multitude had driven its predecessors ahead, northward, eastward, and southward. When the Nordics seized northeastern Iran in the 6th century B.C. upon pressure by Turkic tribe on the north,[286] they drove certain Turkic or mixed tribes encountered by them into Baluchistan and the Northwest Province of India. These people may have been descendants of ancient Pre-Sumerians or Sumerians who had remained in central and eastern Iran.

These last invaders of India in the 6th century B.C. were the most cultured of all the Iranians because of their long contact in Iran with the leading civilization of Mesopotamia. Like the Hamitic Ethiopians who long resided in southern Iran, they had absorbed a large portion of the Pre-Sumerian and Sumerian culture and when they were driven to the Indus valley they took it with them. In confirmation of this transmission of culture is the fact that the great literary productions of the Hindus have emanated in this and its neighboring division on the east, but in this cultural advancement the impetus imparted by the vigorous Nordic invaders from Bactriana may not be overlooked. Consequently, the present civilization of India is indebted largely to the Turanians of the west for its fundamentals.

Zoroaster, a native of northwestern Media and apparently of noted Kimmerian parentage, was a great teacher and the founder of the national religion of the Medes and also of the Persians in the 6th century B.C. It represented

285 *Ency. Brit.*, 13th Ed., vol. 13, page 479, by George Grierson, and vol. 14, page 382, by William W. Hunter and James S. Cotton.
286 Thus, by the time of Herodotus, Turks had supplanted Nordics in Eastern Scythia (Turkistan), as shown by their dress and customs. The western Asiatic steppes are still the homeland of Turkic peoples, who shade off in the east into the Tunguses (or Mongolians).

mainly a combination of principles and procedure of ancient Kimmerian Magianism and of Iranian Dualism with its worship of the deities of the Iranian tribe of the *Mitanni*. It arose after Magianism had passed under a cloud, as related by Herodotus (iii.61-88).

From what has been said and from what follows, it is evident that, as asserted by Sir William Jones in England about 140 years ago, the Sanskrit, or literary, language of the Hindus was derived from the same primitive source that produced the ancient Persian, Keltic, Greek, Latin, and Gothic languages, to which the Slavic, Suebic, and Kimmeric languages may be added. Similarly, the Aryan vernacular of the Hindus — the Hindic dialects — also had the same primitive origin. In remote antiquity, all of the foregoing peoples spoke the same language as that used by the ancient Mediterranean and Hamitic subraces in Iran and by the parent stock of all of them, the Indonesians primitively of western India; but the early separation of the northerly branches from those in the south, when an agglutinative language probably was used by all, resulted in such subsequent diversification that the original similarity largely has disappeared. The classic work of Friedrich von Schlegel *On the Language and Wisdom of the Indians* in 1808 sustained the conclusions of Jones and is generally regarded as the foundation of the modern science of comparative philology.

As stated by George Rawlinson in his Appendix to Book ii.c.3 of his translation of Herodotus' history, "besides the evidence of a common origin [of religious systems] from the analogies in the Egyptian, Indian, Greek, and other systems, we perceive that mythology had advanced to a certain point before the early migrations took place from central Asia. And if, in aftertimes, each introduced local changes, they often borrowed so largely from their neighbors that a strong resemblance was maintained; and hence the religions resembled each other partly from having a common origin, partly from a direct imitation, and partly from adaptation, which last continued to a late period". In general, the same may be said about linguistic evolution.

(6f) *The Keltic Question.* Most historians unfortunately fail to distinguish the Keltic subrace from the others of Europe, despite the marked differences in physique and culture. The term Kelt often is applied indiscriminately to the *brachycephalic* Pâleo-Keltic and Kelto-Slavic peoples (or Alpines), on the one hand, and to the *mesocephalic* Kimmerian (or Nordic) peoples of western Europe, on the other hand. The former now inhabit eastern Russia and (often modified by Mediterranean or Nordic strain) mainly the slopes and valleys of the great mountain ranges across Europe and the Grecian, Italian, and Iberian peninsulas, whereas the Kimmerians inhabit chiefly the Main and Rhine river valleys, western France, the Lowlands, Danmark, and the British Isles. Obviously, a distinction must be drawn, since they represent two different branches of the White race and possess dissimilar characteristics.[287]

The *Keltoi* of the ancient Greeks were a large-bodied blond people. They inhabited the "woods and wild fastnesses" of the mountainous north; in fact, that is the meaning of the name.[287] But they did not then inhabit the plains still farther north, beyond the Carpathian Mountains and the Black Sea, for those regions had come into the possession of Nordic nations soon after 2300 B.C. The Keltic (or Alpine) subrace, which emigrated from the Pamirs of Asia, is not as tall as the Nordic but is heavily built, with the short but strong and muscular legs characteristic of aboriginally mountainous people, a broad head and face and rather wide nostrils, intermediate or light complexion, and gray, greenish gray, or light-blue eyes.[288] They are inclined to be phlegmatic in temperament and movement. Intermarriage with brunet peoples from southern Europe that they encountered north of the Alps before the arrival of the Nordics resulted

---

287 This distinction was noticed by G. W. Kitchin, *History of France* (Clarendon Press, Oxford, 1892), vol. 1, pages 8-10, as well as by certain other writers. *Ency. Brit.*, 13th Ed., vol. 5, page 611, under *Celt*.
288 The notion that the Keltic Alpine subrace is Mongoloid in origin, as thought by some writers, is unworthy of discussion here.

in a large proportion of hazel and light-brown or brown eyes and darker hair among their descendants. The term "blond" above must be taken in a relative rather than an absolute sense, since the ancient Athenian writers were brunet Pelasgians, of light physique, and they had practically no contact with Nordic peoples above the Black Sea (except the Dorians) until the time of the commercial exploits in the north by Miletus and other cities of Asia Minor. The Kelts very early (about 8000 B.C. and again about 2300 B.C.) had entered Europe by the Danube valley and spread their culture over the whole region from the Black Sea to the Atlantic Ocean. Their burials were in round barrows. They also sparsely inhabited the Baltic plains prior to the westward migration of the Nordic Suebians from southern Russia (western Scythia, the later Ukrainia) about 1600 B.C., when they were pressed westward and southward, chiefly beyond the Rhine. Detached tribes of Kelts, driven from the Caucasus Mountains to the north, remained there and became the progenitors of the Slavs. Indeed, the meaning of the word "Kelt" was inapplicable to the Nordic inhabitants of the plains north of the Caspian and Black Seas and the Caucasus, Carpathian, and Alpine mountain ranges.

The Nordic subrace in Europe, discussed later, comprises only the Suebians, the Kimmerians, and the Getae (later Goths).[289] They are tall, mesocephalous, with long head and oval or long face, narrow aquiline nose, dark, medial, or light hair, and blue or gray-blue eyes, and are active in temperament. They early had a common origin in Asia (Geté) and always were in contact with each other across the northern plains; thus, they used a basically common language in which only dialectal differences arose. The most westerly were the Suebians (of Germany) and the most easterly in Europe were the later Goths. Between them dwelt the Kimmerian nation until it was shattered

---

289 The easternmost Nordic nations, the Massagetae and the Sakae, finally settled in Bactriana and Sogdiana respectively. Nordic tribal off-shoots in Europe embraced the Albanians at the Caucasus Mountains and along the easterly Adriatic shore and the Dorians in Greece, but these people now are largely modified by indigenous brunet and Keltic or Turkic strains of the regions in which they settled.

by the Goths in 634 B.C. In the regions east and south of the Caspian Sea were the other Nordic nations, namely, the Massagetae, the Sakae, and their tribal offshoots, who chose to remain in western Asia apparently because of the disappearance of Turkic nations from Western Turkistan for many centuries.

The approximate similarity of the languages of the three western Nordic nations is proved by comparison of the dialects of the Anglo-Saxons and other recognized Suebians and the Goths with those of the Kimmerian Jutes of Danmark and the so-called "Germans" (Belgae and others) of Julius Caesar who inhabited the central and lower Rhine River valley and became the later Franks. The Jutes and easternmost Belgae and related tribes north and east of the middle and lower Rhine River were the only divisions of Kimmerians in western Europe who were not markedly affected by the Keltic culture of the Danube valley and Gaul. On the other hand, those who in two mass migrations invaded and settled in ancient Gaul were the only divisions that dwelt among Kelts pressed westward and southward from the north. It was detachments of these Gallic Kimmerians who, shortly after their arrival, in continuation of westward migration, took adopted Keltic dialectal changes and customs to Great Britain and Ireland. If they had not lived among the Kelts in Gaul, obviously the language and culture that they would have taken to Britain and Ireland are those then possessed by the kindred Jutes, transrhenish Belgae, Chatti (Hessians), and related Salian and Ripuarian (Kimmeric) Frankish tribes. They were one of the Nordic nations that formerly inhabited the Ukraine, before the non-Keltic Suebi and after the non-Keltic Getae (Goths), and it is incongruous to assume that one-half of the nation possessed Keltic language and culture while the other half did not.

Thus, it follows that the mesocephalic *Goidels and Britons* (*Dananns, Picts, Scots, Caledonians,* and *Britons*) were *not Keltic* of race but were Nordic and that they had largely engrafted the Keltic culture of Gaul on their own culture during the time that they moved up the Danube basin and lived in Gaul before their emigration to the British Isles. The people called Kelts who invaded the Iberian peninsula during various centuries prior to the Christian era and became a component of the subsequent Keltiberian stock there never have been identified as Nordics but rather as of the older brachycephalic Alpine division driven southward from Gaul upon the successive Kimmeric invasions of the north. In the Roman period the Keltic Gauls were described as resembling the "Germans" (the Belgae) but not as tall, as fair, or as savage. This distinction between the Alpine Kelts and the Nordics will be maintained throughout this work,[290] and the descent and migration of the two different Aryan subraces will follow in sequence.

The name of Goidelic Kimmerians for the division that migrated from Scythia to western Europe in 634 B.C. (the Danes in 606 B.C.) and that of Britonic Kimmerians for the division that migrated in 342 B.C. are accepted terms[290½] and the years of their departure are proved by various authorities. If we infer that the movement of their waggons, their families, and all of their possessions and miscellaneous skirmishes on route required two years for these treks, definite bases for the chronology of much subsequent history will have been established. These data will be relied on frequently in subsequent pages here.

(6g) *Keltic Subrace.* The White race descended from those hardy Aryans (Indonesians) of northwestern India who ascended the Indus River and penetrated its valleys in Ladak and the lake region of northwestern Tibet during the warm recession after the Würm II glaciation, roughly about 22,000 years ago, and who remained in one or more of the broad sheltered valleys that escaped glaciation during the rounding of the later Achen peak. Those valleys must then have embraced warm water springs and lakes, such as exist there today. It was not until about 15,000 years ago that returning warmth al-

---

290 This distinction is not observed in the article headed *Celt* in the *Ency. Brit.*, 13th Ed., vol. 5, pages 611-652.
290½ See *Ency. Brit.*, 13th Ed., vol. 28, page 268c, under *Wales.*

lowed them to expand over this lofty region, mainly northward and eastward. This tribe doubtless experienced an appallingly high death rate, but its survival during long habitation at high altitude, with the rarified air, in a very rigorous climate and a modicum of light during most of the year, resulted in the development of hardy physiques, light complexion and eyes, and gradual broadening of the heads.

The Tibetan highlands did not become widely rehabitable until approximately 15,000 years ago, when the glacial effects were diminishing. Then the White race spread over the lake region of western Tibet. Subsequently, by perhaps 14,000 years ago, the passes over the northern mountains were opening for human migration to the lower lands of Eastern Turkistan. Ancient well-known trade routes exist through these passes, by means of which merchandise from the Punjab of India has moved over heights of 16,000 to more than 18,000 feet to reach Tibet and the lower Tarim Basin of Eastern Turkistan as well as the Iranian plateau on the west. The most famous passageways between northwestern India and the Iranian highlands are the Bolan, Gomal, Tochi, Kurram, and Khyber passes, and between India and the Tarim Basin they are the Muztagh, Karakoram, and Changchenmo passes. The Khyber pass is the principal one between northeastern Iran and Tibet. The Karakoram pass, at an elevation of 18,550 feet, leads from Kashmir to Kashgar, in the highlands of central Turkistan, on the great east-and-west caravan route.

A very early migration from Iran over the Suliman Mountains to the land of the five rivers (Punjab) and the Northwest Frontier Province of India is represented today by the pure Sikh race in that region, which preserves a distinct Cro-Magnon cast. However, in large degree these people since have amalgamated with later arrivals of Hindus. Linguistic and mythological connections between the Iranians of Afghanistan and of India readily can be traced across the mountains of Kabulistan. As already shown, it was the several widely-separated migrations from Iran to western India, beginning about 8000 B.C., that forced the Indonesians of western India southward to the peninsular highlands (Dekkan) and eastward down the Ganges River valley, driving the more primitive peoples ahead of them. Along the shores of the mainland and islands of southeastern Asia, the Indonesians developed their skill as seamen before some of them ventured to the far islands of the South Pacific Ocean.

Ladak and western Tibet were peculiarly adapted to the evolution of the White race. This region south of the Hindu Kush and Karakoram Mountains is at high elevations. The altitude of Pangong Lake, for example, is 13,900 feet. The vale of Kashmir is described as the meeting place of the most remarkable fauna and flora of the world. The effects of the glaciers appear to have diminished rapidly because of Ladak's sheltered situation and numerous hot springs there as well as in western Tibet. The surrounding mountains seem to exert an influence of radio-activity. The palm trees slowly extended northward into Kashmir proper and every variety of plant and animal life soon found a favorable environment there. This valley is rich biologically and the fossils of wild animals, such as the rhinoceros, that lived there after the glaciation indicate marked climatic changes since that time.

A common origin of the Cro-Magnon and Iranian sub-races is strongly indicated by a comparison of the susceptibility of differentiation under varying environment. The survivors of the Cro-Magnards in Dordogne, France, are of medial height, but are very susceptible to environment as regards stature, for they are tall in fertile districts and stunted in less productive areas. They are not degenerate but are keen and alert of mind. The face is practically as broad as in the normal Alpine Keltic round-headed type. The head is narrowed at the top, the skull is low-vaulted, the brow ridges are prominent, the nose is well-formed, and the cheek bones are prominent with powerful cheek muscles.[291] The cephalic index averages 76 per cent.

---

291 H. F. Osborn, *Men of the Old Stone Age* (Scribner, New York, 1915), page 451, quoting William Z. Ripley.

With increasing warmth upon the retreat of the Achen glaciation, bands of the Yellow (or Turanian) race reascended the river valleys of eastern Tibet, perhaps even earlier than the Aryans spread from Kashmir through Ladak to western Tibet. They appear to have moved up the Salween, Mekong, and Yangtze River courses, where they continually increased in numbers. One branch, the later Turks, spread from the upper Yangtze River valleys of northeastern Tibet to the central lake region. About 14,000 years ago, these Turks advanced farther westward and later pressed the Aryans of western Tibet into the Pamirs and northward over the mountains to the Tarim Basin. This occurred during an era of mild weather. The tribe of Aryans that made its way through the Karakoram passes to the Tarim Basin, in Eastern Turkistan, was the progenitor of the great Nordic branch of the Aryan race, about whom more is said later.

The main Aryan stock, later known as the Kelts (the Alpines and the Slavs), remained on the highlands of western Kashmir and the Pamirs[292] for thousands of years afterward, until they had attained full brachycephaly, a distinctive feature of both Keltic and Turanian races that inhabited the high Tibetan plateau for many millennia. The country of Shignan and Roshan (in the Pamirs) is sometimes called Zujan (two-lived); its climate and water are so good that when one enters it he is said to have come into the possession of two lives.[293] It also contains an abundant supply of food. The animals of the Pamirs are the ovis poli, ibex, brown bear, leopard, lynx,

---

292 This origin of the Kelts has been determined in a philological study made by James Cowles Prichard, *Eastern Origin of the Keltic Nations* (London, 1831). See William Z. Ripley, *The Races of Europe*, page 473, where he apparently relates them to the Galchas, mountain Tadjiks, Wakhis, and affiliated tribes, which comprise blond, light-eyed, brachycephalic peoples.

293 T. E. Gordon, *The Roof of the World* (Edmonston and Douglas, Edinburgh, 1876), page 140. "We experienced none of the symptoms of great height, viz., headache and difficulty of respiration, on the Pamirs in the exaggerated degree that native travellers have described. None of our camp followers or people suffered in any usual way beyond becoming breathless when exertion was made . . . . . . There was perfect health among our party throughout the journey." *Ibid.*, pages 160-161. This journey was made in the autumn, winter, and spring, from September to June, 1873-1874.

wolf, marmot, and hare, all of which may be hunted throughout the year. Wild fowl swarm on the lakes in summer.[294]

At about 8000 B.C., the Kelts were driven farther westward by another northwestward surge of Turks from central Tibet[295] and scattered over the foothills of the Hindu Kush range, the Pamirs, and the valleys of the upper Oxus River. It is probable that these Turks were impelled by Mongolians following the same course up the northeasterly slopes of Tibet as that originally traveled by the progenitors of the Turks. One Keltic tribe must have moved northward and eastward along the northerly slope and down some river valley to the Tarim Basin of Eastern Turkistan, followed by a division of the Turks, who became the later Sumerians. If so, these Kelts may have commingled with Turanians on their route eastward in central Asia, for the Ainus of northern Japan apparently represent a racially modified remnant of this group; they possess physical characteristics of the Kelts and traces of them have been found across southern Mongolia and Manchuria. A division probably is a component of the hybrid Gilyaks of the Amur River delta, the northern part of Sakhalin, and the Kuril Islands.

At this time of the final glacial oscillations, Europe was thickly forested, marshes were prevalent, and the climate was becoming warmer. The spirit of conquest had revived after the cold weather had begun to wane. In addition to the Turkic tribe that had descended to the Tarim Basin, other bands moved down the mountain slopes of eastern Tibet, where they formed contact with their affinities, the Tungus Mongolians, who inhabited the province of Koko Nor, the province of Kansu, and the upper valleys of the Hwang River. The movement of Turks from western Tibet down to the Tarim Basin about 8000 B.C. expelled the Nordic Aryans northwestward into the mountain passes leading to their new

---

294 *Ibid.,* page 159.
295 This inference is confirmed by the fact that the present inhabitants of the lake regions of Tibet are Turko-Mongolian.

homeland of Geté (south and southeast of Lake Balkhash). These Turks continued westward through the passes of Kashgaria, between the region of Geté on the north and the mountainous habitations of the Kelts in the Pamirs and Bukhara. They were the later Sumerians. This activity dislodged and forced westward from the Pamirs a large division of the Kelts, who, skirting the southerly shores of the Caspian Sea, crossed the Caucasus Mountains and the Ukraine region to central Europe.[296] There they ascended the Danube River basin and ultimately spread over all central and northern Europe, between the diminishing Alpine and Scandinavian glaciers, where they became known as the Furfooz-Grenelle or Paleo-Keltic people. They were the first brachycephalic subrace to enter Europe.[296] The remainder of them continued to abide in the Pamirs and vicinity. In fact, they were enclosed in those highlands by the contemporaneous migration of the earlier Pre-Sumerian Turks from Western Turkistan southwestward across Iran to Elam and Mesopotamia, where they planted the Neolithic civilization. For centuries afterward they maintained caravan routes between those regions and their former homeland in Western Turkistan until overrun by their successors, the Sumerians, who had taken possession of Western Turkistan, as already discussed.

The Pamirs afforded numerous retreats for the Kelts who remained in that region, always noted for its general healthfulness. For example, Sogdiana of the ancients, which lay on the slopes between the Oxus and Jaxartes Rivers, was deemed to be one of the earthly paradises of the Orientals. The Imaus Mountains of antiquity were situated beyond the fountains of those rivers, comprising probably the region where the Hindu Kush, the Karakoram, and other ranges join. Even after the next great migration of Kelts westward about 2300 B.C., a considerable number of them remained behind and their de-

---

296 V. Gordon Childe, *op. cit.*, page 118. The Bavarian historian, J. C. Zeuss, conclusively demonstrated in his *Grammatica Celtica* (1853) the Asiatic origin of the Keltic dialects.

scendants appear to have been the *Dadicae* of Herodotus and the *Tatacene* of Ptolemy.[297] Their progeny today are the Galchas and Tadjiks in the districts of Ferghana, Kohistan, Wakhan,[298] Afghanistan, Baluchistan, eastern Iran, and elsewhere, in some places considerably modified by other strains. In fact, the center of this ancient Keltic habitation apparently is to be found today in the Russian province of Tadjikistan, which includes the Pamirs. The Galchas are said to be the purest of the present Pamiri. They may represent the stock from which the Nordics branched about 14,000 years ago.

Early divisions of this Paleo-Keltic race in central Europe spread westward and northward, and they introduced the Maglemosean and Shell-Mound cultures into northwestern Europe, notably in Danmark,[299] and later the lake-dwelling custom and culture into southern Germany, Austria, Switzerland, eastern central France, and northern Italy. Meanwhile, they changed from hunters to fishers. As fast as the climate along the Baltic became sufficiently hospitable, they spread into that region, just in advance of the Neolithic age in Europe. The Maglemosean culture reached Skäne (Sweden) about 7000 B.C.[299] Its introduction of handsome pigmy flint instruments, such as the double-pointed laurel leaf, much like the Solutrean types, proves the diffusion of this culture from the Danube valley. These people used many bone implements and a stone ax and pick-ax, brought from the east, and they also had the domesticated dog. They acquired their skill in bone-carving in consequence of the plentiful supply of food animals at their former habitation in the Pamirs. Their use of stone implements arose earlier in the rocky river valleys of the Pamirs,

297 Herodotus iii.91; Ptolemy, *Geography* vi.19.

298 "The Wakhis, as a people, are good looking, and many faces of extreme regularity of features are seen. Fair hair and blue eyes are not uncommon. They all speak Persian besides their own peculiar dialect." T. E. Gordon, *ibid.*, page 135. These people are brachycephalous in type, corresponding with the Kelts of central Europe.

299 This estimate of 7200-7000 B.C. agrees well with determination made by Professor Steenstrup. Some of their descendants may reside on islands in the Zuider Zee, the Netherlands, today.

Ladak, and western Tibet. They are said to have originated and practised the rite of cremation, and when found in connection with remains of other races it is said to have been impressed upon or adopted by the latter.

The evidence here apparently is somewhat contradictory, since Anderson, the noted Swedish naturalist, asserts confidently that the Scandinavian peninsula was not inhabited by man prior to the Neolithic age.[300] Probably these primal Keltic migrants actually brought a Mesolithic type of culture, embodying both late Paleolithic and early Neolithic features. However, it is inferable that they were preceded in Scandinavia by an exploratory wave of Ligurians of the Mediterranean race from the Rhine valley, who carried the Neolithic culture that far north. The southernmost province of Sweden, Skäne (the old Scania from which the name of Scandinavia was derived), has a different geological formation from the remainder of the Swedish mainland. It is the most fertile section and is known as the granary of Sweden. At that time it may have been connected by land with Danmark, so that isolated settlements there centuries earlier readily could have been effected by the exploratory bands of Ligurians and the later vanguard of Paleo-Kelts. By the time when Suebic migration occurred farther north, the Neolithic culture, with its sharpened and polished stone implements, may have supplanted the Mesolithic, in substantial agreement with Anderson's conclusions.

Those Kelts, driven in some degree toward the Atlantic coastal regions and the north, particularly into western Spain, France, Belgium, the Netherlands, the British Isles, Danmark, southern Scandinavia, Germany, Poland, and southern Russia, by the Neolithic Mediterranean hordes from the south and southeast,[301] long flourished in those regions where their pigmy flints since have been found. They introduced the Keltic speech into Britain.

---

300 Carl F. G. Anderson, *Svenska växtvärldens historia; i korthet framställd* (Stockholm, 1896).

301 See J. C. Prichard, *op.cit.*, vol. 3, pp. 45-48.

Eventually, they intermarried indiscriminately with the Mediterraneans and subsequent races in those countries, developing the later characteristic Keltic culture. Just what proportion of its fundamentals was brought from the east by them and what proportion by the Mediterranean race is uncertain. One authority[302] says that "we may reasonably conclude that the Alpine [Keltic] man introduced into Europe cultivated grains and fruits, domesticated animals, polished stone implements, painted pottery, weaving, and possibly at a later date the art of metal-working." The migrants were the earliest representatives of the round-barrow people in western Europe. Their racial features are conspicuous in the present population. Some of their remains have been found in caves at Furfooz and Grenelle, Belgium; also in a cave at Ofnet, Bavaria, along with skeletons of the Mediterranean race.

This composite population of the Danubian basin and adjacent regions was not conspicuously warlike in nature. The different races after the Cro-Magnards, chiefly the Paleo-Keltic and Mediterranean peoples, entered that country more as pioneers than as conquerors. The isolation of their settlements and sparseness of population were indicative of peaceful penetration, since there was little incentive to warfare. More attention was paid to agriculture and livestock than to the hunting of wild game. The absence of battle axes, arrowheads, and other weapons deserves especial notice.[303] A condition of general amity seems to have prevailed during the thousands of years until the invasion of central Europe by the more warlike ("Battle-Ax") Kelto-Slavs about 2300 B.C., with the result that the mental characteristics of the people became increasingly like those of the settled peasant. Lack of wandering, narrow conservatism, and intense attachment to the soil during this long period

---

302 H. F. Osborn, op. cit., p. 62. The art of metal-working by the Kelts in Austria should be considered in the light of ancient metal-working by the Leleges in Anatolia, as knowledge of it could have moved across the Balkan region.
303 V. Gordon Childe, op. cit., pp. 139-143.

caused them readily to submit to the overlordship of the later conquerors of the same race from the Pamirs, whose fundamentally similar language and customs readily coalesced with their own. The more warlike invaders preserved the older culture with an infusion of the new as the people gradually amalgamated.[304]

These Kelts are the underlying brachycephalic racial element of central Europe and Russia today, the so-called "Alpines" and the Slavs (Moscovites). They have interbred to a large extent with later arrivals of Mediterraneans from the south and Nordics from the northeast. They are conspicuous and generally predominant in the racial composition of those nations that inhabit the valleys and both slopes of the Carpathians and Alps, the Balkan, Italian, and Iberian peninsulas, central and eastern France, and in minor degree the low countries and the British Isles.[305] They are the people who built the lake and peatbog pile dwellings all up and down the Danube valley and in adjacent regions and in Switzerland and northern Italy. This practice endured several thousand years.

The Maglemosean culture of the Paleo-Kelts was conspicuous by its harpoons made of stag horn and a variety of painted pebbles, also microlithic flakes used for various purposes; but there was an absence of polished stone implements and animal engravings or sculpture such as the Cro-Magnards from southwestern Iran had developed. This cultural intrusion occurred in the closing period of the Old Stone Age in Europe. The thousands of years of lack of contact between these two Aryan races after the westward migration of the Cro-Magnards had resulted in a vast divergence of physical evolution as well as of cultural development.

An affinity of the Maglemosean (and Shell-Mound, Asturian, and Campignian) culture of the Paleo-Kelts with that of their northern or Slavic division and that of the Ugrians has been found. The Finns may have received it from the Aryans. It is probable that the Nordics in Geté had the same primitive culture as the Paleo-Kelts and

304 *Ibid.*, pp. 149, 154.
305 *Ibid*, p. 178.

transmitted it along the foothills of the Altai Mountains to the Finns (Tschudes) in the upper reaches of the Yenesei River or eastward toward Lake Baikal prior to 2300 B.C., as is indicated by the following quotation from Osborn: "The community of style with the painted and engraved figures found in western Siberia and in the central Ural region and north of the Altai Mountains denotes rather an Asiatic and Siberian origin,"[306] In the profuse use of microliths, the connection of those cultures with the Maglemosean culture of the Paleo-Kelts is revealed. Additional evidence of the common origin and early diffusion of all of these types of culture is the fact that remains of the dog, first domesticated in central Asia, have been found in deposits at Maglemosean and Danish shell-mound sites. Moreover, the Mesolithic raft-builders of the Baltic region were largely brachycephalous like the Neolithic pile-dwellers of the Alps. They were hunters and fishers in the forests and marshes of northern Europe. Thus, it is established that the origin of the Maglemosean culture was in central Europe and more remotely in the Far East (centering on the Pamirs) rather than in the west.[307]

The next great Keltic migration from the region of the Pamirs to central Europe, that of the Kelto-Slavs about 2300 B.C., is described in a subsequent chapter.

(6h) *Nordic Subrace.* As already related, about 14,000 years ago the progenitors of the Nordic branch of the Aryan race emigrated from the upper reaches of the Indus River in western Tibet through the Hindu Kush or Karakoram passes to the Tarim Basin, Eastern Turkistan,[308] which they inhabited about 4,000 years. As they descended, they impelled the Pre-Sumerians toward Western Turkistan. About 8000 B.C. they were driven out by the Sumerians from the high plateau and then moved northwestward to the foothills of the Tien Mountains.

---

306 H. F. Osborn, *op.cit.,* page 486.
307 V. Gordon Childe, *op. cit.,* page 170.
308 *Ency. Brit.,* 13th Ed., vol. 27, pages 423d and 424b; Aryans anciently in Eastern Turkistan.

By 7700 B.C. they had crossed those mountains and settled in the northern country subsequently known as Geté.[309] This region remained their homeland for thousands of years. It comprises the foothills and mountainous regions of Western Turkistan beyond Kashgar, from the Tien Mountains to Lake Balkhash. It is the westerly slope of the Imaus range of Ptolemy, in the present Kirghiz province of *Semiryechensk* (from *Semiryechie*, i.e., Seven Rivers), and includes the upper reaches of the Jaxartes River, Lake Issyk, and the Chu and Ili River basins. Its elevation is much lower than that of the Tien Mountains and embraces the northwesterly slopes of that range. It was well-watered, sheltered, healthful, and productive country, containing excellent pasture lands on which numerous animals abounded. At that time, the Aral Sea, now merely a large lake, must have covered the present arid areas west and south of it toward the foothills, blocking human progress westward. North of Lake Balkhash is a high ridge extending from a depression between the Tien and Altai Mountains northwestward toward the Ural Mountains, above which numerous tribes of Ugrian peoples lived. This ridge, which separates the Kirghiz steppe from Arctic Siberia, was an important factor of demarkation in primitive racial movements. It lay between southerly and northerly routes of migration westward. Eastward, beyond the Altai Mountains, lived numerous Tungus Mongolian tribes.

These Getic people thus became the ancestors of the great Nordic branch of the Aryan race.[310] Their descent as a *derived race*[311] from the primal brunet Aryan stock in India is proved by the fact, aside from other physical, cultural, and linguistic evidence, that they are not dolicho-

---

309 This (Geté) name dates in history from very early times. See Sharifu'd-Din's (Sherefeddin's) history of *Timur* (Petis de la Croix's French translation to English by J. Darby in 1722, Vols. 1 and 2).

310 H. F. Osborn, *op.cit.*, page 451, quoting William Z. Ripley.

311 Justin (i.1) recited from the Gothic Scythians the tradition of the great antiquity of their descent from an elevated region adapted at that remote time to the reception of man. This points to the region of Ladak and western Tibet.

cephalous like the Indonesian stock in which they originated but are mesocephalous (intermediate) because of
the long habitation of their forebears at the high elevations of Ladak and western Tibet. But this epoch at
high altitudes was much shorter than that during which
the Kelts lived there and in the Pamirs, for which reason
the latter attained full brachycephaly, while that tendency
among the Nordics was arrested when they moved to the
lower elevation, with its heavier atmosphere. One of the
great principles of human evolution is the fact that racial
types are persistent and differentiation is exceedingly slow.
As late as A.D. 175, a division of fair-haired, blue-eyed
Nordic people, known as the *Usun* or *Wu-Sun* nation, was
encountered on the northerly side of the Tien range in
Zungaria. They have been identified more fully in a subsequent chapter.

It is an Aryan tradition that the early homeland was
situated in the region of Sogdiana and vicinity. But
during the earlier temporary glaciations, northwestern
Asia was not habitable because of the intense cold and
winds and the swampy terrain. Until long after the Bühl
glacial retreat about 7500 B.C., most of the above-named
region, including that around the northerly end of the
Caspian Sea, was more or less one huge lake or morass,
extending to the base of the Ural Mountains. The Caspian
Sea today is much lower than it was once and with this
diminution its northerly shore receded southward. In
those times, the forests were more dense than they are
today and offered serious resistance to tribal intercourse
and locomotion. Siberia also was intensely cold and inhospitable. There were wide variations in climatic conditions and the great Arctic snowstorms on the steppes
were destructive of life. In consequence, migration westward long was impracticable.

While the Nordics in Geté increased in population, continual exposure to the rigorous northern climate and to a
modicum of sunlight accentuated the blondness of their
complexion as it did that of the Kelts centered on the
Pamirs. The Turkish tribes inhabited the more temperate
western Tibetan plateau only about one-third as long as

the two branches of the White race had during the glaciation; consequently, the modification of their complexion was not as marked. In Geté, the Nordics were surrounded on the east and north, beyond the mountains and the great east-and-west ridge, by various Turanian tribes, on the west by marshes, on the southwest successively by the Turanian Sumerian and Hittite nations, and on the south by a high mountain range. Consequently, they developed differences of custom and language from the Kelts of the Pamirs after their separation about 14,000 years ago; but these divergences were far less than those of both divisions from the language and customs of the primitive Indonesian stock during their long habitation in Ladak and western Tibet, when there was very little, if any, contact with their fellow Aryans in India and Iran.

After the antecessors of the Hittites had descended to the Tarim Basin about 8000 B. C., they expanded and scattered their predecessors (the Sumerians) in different directions, but mainly westward through the mountain passes of Kashgaria to Western Turkistan. There they settled after having driven out the Pre-Sumerians, who then went to Mesopotamia. The latter were the first Turanians in western Asia. Small divisions of Sumerians, however, moved eastward into Kansu province of China, where some of their culture was transmitted to the inhabitant of that remote region. It was to these few Sumerians and some Hittites and their descendants, who remained in the Tarim Basin after the main Hittite nation moved over the mountains to Western Turkistan about 4300 B.C. and who took the name of *Issedones,* that the Chinese are indebted for their early culture.

During the era in which the Sumerians inhabited Western Turkistan, from about 8000 B.C. to about 4300 B.C., very little intercourse seems to have occurred between them and the Nordic inhabitants on their northeast. This was due mainly to meagerness of numbers, intervening forests, former strife, and the caution always exercised in dealing with foreign nations. But this situation was markedly different after the Hittites replaced the Sumerians in Western Turkistan about 4300 B.C., for the evidence indicates considerable interaction (at a safe distance) between them and the Nordics and a marked influence of the language and customs of the one people on those of the other, as explained later. It was the result of continual increase of population of the two nations and a growing tendency for each to explore the surrounding country.

After about 4300 B.C., the Nordics in Geté expanded northward toward the east-and-west ridge and overspread the vast Kirghiz steppe toward the Ural Mountains and the Caspian Sea, except where it was unhabitable because of the marshes of the receding Aral Sea. Ultimately, they split into five nations, successively the *Suebi,* the *Kimmerii,* the *Getae* (who retained their place-name), the *Massagetae,* and the *Sakae.* It was not until the terrain and climate had improved, apparently about 2300 B.C., that the westernmost tribe, the Suebi, was able and willing to venture westward into the mysterious region of eastern Europe. By that time, much of the intervening marsh land had dried up and since then vast areas have become arid and unproductive. They were followed by the Kimmerii about 1700 B.C. and by the Getae about 1000 B.C. The historic advance of the Nordics westward in Europe is described in a subsequent chapter.

The original unity of the Kelts and Nordics in the Asiatic highlands is verified not only by racial likeness but also by analogies of culture and language. Each clan had a tribal god and father of its own. As stated by Childe,[312] the primitive Nordic Aryan language appears to have been too nearly a unity to have been formed at different places in such a vast and diversified region as that from the North Sea to the Caspian Sea, in which these people later were found scattered. No words for *sea* and *amber* appeared in their vocabulary, and even in a later maritime region these early people eschewed a fish diet.

As stated by Guyot, "In the drier and more variable climate of the continents, rather than oceanic climate, man is more animated, more active, more intelligent, endowed

---

312 V. Gordon Childe, *op.cit.,* pages 163-164, 167.

with a stronger will; in a word, life is more intense and raised to a higher degree by the variety and the movement impressed upon it by the contrasts that form the very essence of the nature of this climate."[313] The same comparison, but with much greater emphasis, applies to the effects of a frigid or a torrid climate as to an oceanic climate. Each elevation of 350 feet diminishes the mean temperature 1º F., which is equivalent to a latitudinal movement of 60 miles toward the north. Thus, whether living on the westerly Tibetan and adjacent highlands or in the cold lowlands farther north, the Kelts and their related subrace, the Nordics, have evolved from the beginning under more rigorous environment than that experienced by any other race. The nearest approach was that of the Finnic subrace (Tschudes) in the region west of Lake Baikal, but they apparently did not enter that cold territory until long after the Kelts and Nordics had come under the influence of the invigorating partly-glacial climate of Ladak, western Tibet, the Pamirs, and northward. The Turanian divisions encountered less severe climatic conditions during their evolution on the lower lands east of the Tibetan plateau. The ascent of the Tunguses and others to that plateau later brought them under substantially analogous environment to that longer experienced by the Whites, although it was generally milder. Under these circumstances, it is not strange that the lighter-complexioned (the northernmost) branches of the Aryan race have become the most energetic and capable of all races, the darker branches of that race and certain branches of the Turanian the next, and the remaining Turanian subraces and the Indafrican race, in that order, on the whole the most backward.

The subsequent migration of most of the White tribes was in the same direction as but by a different route than that of the two divisions of the Kelts. It was westward in the temperate zone to Europe, which then became their habitation. The two tribes or nations that remained in Western Turkistan, namely, the Massagetae and the

---

313 Arnold Guyot, op.cit., page 113.

Sakae, after a long and notable history,[314] moved southward and gradually merged with the surrounding darker population. Their primitive homeland then was taken over by different branches of the Turanian race in their expansion westward. "From one end to the other of the Old World, over a space of several thousand miles, the migratory tribes are able to pursue their adventurous roaming course by following, according to their custom, the great features of relief of the soil without witnessing any change in the vegetation or the animals that surround them. They change place, but not climate nor ways of life. This similarity of climate over long spaces . . . . must have singularly favored the dispersion of the primitive tribes."[315]

Of the continent on which modern man originated, only India, with its teeming millions, Iran, and small parts of southern Asia as far westward as the Aegean Sea remain in possession of the Aryan race. The remainder of Asia is populated almost wholly by the Turanian branches, since the Indafrican race was almost wholly expelled very early.

---

7. *Confirmation of Migrations.* Remarkable confirmation of the foregoing outline of the migrations of the Turanian and Aryan subraces is seen in the origin and diffusion of the custom of milk-drinking. If a line be drawn from Lhasa, Tibet, northeastward along the Yablonoi Mountains, east of Lake Baikal, in southeastern Siberia, it will separate the peoples who regularly have drunk milk since primitive times from those who have not. Thus, the adoption of the custom was not racial but geographical, proving the separation of those peoples before the custom arose. The milk-drinkers include such subraces as the Turanian Tibetans, Turks, Mongolians, Ugrians, and Finns and the Aryan Nordics, Kelts, Iran-

---

314 Their history included the establishment of the great Scytho-Indian Empire.
315 Arnold Guyot, *op.cit.,* page 189.

ians, and Hamites as well as the composite Semites, Bolgarians, and Hungarians, while the subraces east of the line, all Turanian, in China, Korea, Manchuria, Japan, Indo-China, and Malaya never acquired the custom.[316] The primitive people of India did not drink milk prior to the invasions by Iranians,[316] which began about 4300 B.C.

The domestication of animals was a Neolithic cultural development by the primitive Turks along with the development of agriculture. Cattle originally were reared as draught animals for the plow and for their meat, but not for their milk, the use of which began later. Consequently, the habit of milk-drinking also originated among those Turks. Whether or not this occurred before the Hittites descended from Tibet to Eastern Turkistan about 8000 B.C. is uncertain. It probably did not, but the custom clearly was in vogue sometime afterward in the Tarim Basin of Turkistan. It was taken to Sumer during the operation of the caravan route between Turkistan and Mesopotamia from about 8000 B.C. to about 2750 B.C. From the Tarim Basin it spread back to the Tibetan highlands, if not already in existence there, northward to the Mongolians, and northwestward to the Nordics in Geté. It also was taken northward around the easterly end of the Tien Mountains by the minor tribe of Sumerians who moved to the steppes of central Siberia, west of the Altai Mountains, and there commingled with the Ugrians. This mingling produced the composite Bolgarian and Hungarian nations. From these northern migrants, the custom reached the Finns and other Ugrians of Siberia around the west of Lake Baikal.

Long before the Chaldeans of southern Arabia conquered central Mesopotamia about 2750 B.C., the Turks then in the Tarim Basin were moving westward through the mountains of Kashgaria, due to pressure from behind or increasing aridity in Eastern Turkistan. Accordingly, the easterly course of the long caravan route to Elam and Mesopotamia ultimately was shortened to Western Tur-

---

316 Berthold Laufer, *Fundamentals of Chinese Culture,* in *The Journal of Race Development,* vol. 5, No. 2, October, 1914.

kistan, centering perhaps on the town of Anau or nearby territory. At the same time, the Chinese were moving eastward down the Hwang River, further widening the intervening space. These circumstances and the emigration of the Hittites from Western Turkistan about 2300 B.C., whether because of drought or of pressure by Nordics from Geté, severed the contact of the cultured Turks with the Chinese nation at the Kansu border. Inevitably, the Tungus Mongolians farther north were separated into western and eastern divisions by the increasing aridity in central Mongolia, with the result that the Manchus east of the Gobi Desert did not acquire the milk-drinking custom. The sporadic contact of the westerly Mongolians with the races in northern China lacked the power to impress this habit on the latter and thus it never reached the more easterly peoples of Korea and Japan. The geographical barriers between the Turks remaining in the lake region of Tibet and the races in central China prevented the transference of the custom in that direction and this was even more true with respect to the Malayans in the isolated river valleys of eastern Tibet and southern China and in adjacent territory on the south.

Thus, before 2750 B.C., the region west of the aforesaid line of demarkation had become a separate world from that east of it. The same fundamental cultures in both regions thence followed different channels of progress. The peoples that inhabited the former, regardless of race, adopted not only milk-drinking but also other customs in course of time that were not assumed by the peoples east of the line, and the latter developed customs different in many respects from those found in the west. The migration of the Chinese from the upper reaches of the Hwang River to the coastal plains about 3000 B.C. finally assured the separation of the cultural evolution of eastern Asia from that of the western world. Linguistic and basic cultural similarities are the chief evidences of the primitive contacts that the eastern people formerly had with the western peoples in central Asia.

CHAPTER III.

MAN'S PROGRESS AND DISPERSION

1. *Progress of Man from 20,000 to 2300 B.C.* This epoch comprehended such remarkable advancement in the civilization of mankind that it deserves brief summarization embodying a certain amount of repetition.[1] Since Neanderthal man was widely dispersed over the habitable parts of Eurasia and Africa at the time of his progressive annihilation by *Homo sapiens,* we may infer that practically every branch of *Homo sapiens* had attained at least the Neanderthal man's Mousterian culture when his migrations began upon the advance and retreat of the Würm II glaciation. Some subraces, such as the Cro-Magnon, had risen higher, and it may be said that their culture before migration westward represented the maximal civilization among the Aryan population of the Iranian plateau at the time that the dispersions began there. Whether it equaled or exceeded that of the most advanced Turanian subrace of the same period is not known. The greatest progress among Turanians was made by their Turkic branch, which had moved westward in the Tibetan river valleys, whence it ultimately took the cultural lead of all the races. Certainly, the culture of the Indafrican race was quite low.

After the Indafrican race anciently had been dispersed eastward to the Oceanic islands and westward to Africa, Asia remained in the possession of the Turanian and the Aryan races. In the course of time, the Turanians split into various tribes or nations and increased in population on the arc of a circle around the eastern slopes, with their river valleys, of that part of the Tibetan plateau. There and on the lower lands beyond they generated the various Turanian subraces already described. The early advantages of more favorable climate in those regions than that en-

---

1 This repetition should not be allowed to confuse anything that has been said earlier.

dured by the evolving Aryan race in regions northwest and west of India resulted in a more rapid increase of population and the ultimate preponderance of the Turanian race in eastern and central Asia, from the extreme southeast to the extreme north. Excepting India, in which the Aryans gained early preponderance because of favorable climate, glacial effects from the northwest, early return migration of Indonesians from the Indus highlands, and protection by mountain barriers on three sides, the rising Turanian tide in the north made the habitation of the Aryan subraces on both the highlands and the lowlands of central Asia increasingly untenable and they finally moved westward to Europe or remained to be submerged among the Turanians in Asia.

At the beginning of the Aryan migrations westward, the rising waters in the Mediterranean basin that flowed down river courses from the melting glaciers slowly submerged a large part of what had been low grasslands surrounding two lakes. At the same time, the cold winds from the Alpine glaciers tended to divert migration southward to the shores of northern Africa. As the northern winds abated, the Cro-Magnards from Iran followed those shores and crossed at Gibraltar to the Iberian peninsula and moved northward into Europe. The cause of departure of those migrants from Iran created a conflict with the Veddic Brünn tribes in southwestern Iran, dislodged them, and impelled their migration over the Caucasus Mountains and perhaps Krimea to the Danube basin and central Europe. They reached this region before the Cro-Magnards reached western Europe and some time elapsed before the two groups encountered each other again. Subsequently, the Mediterranean race began slowly to move westward from Iran, settling Mesopotamia and the regions about the eastern end of the Mediterranean Sea, including Lower Egypt. They ultimately spread westward on both shorelands of that sea as far as the Atlantic Ocean before 10,000 B.C. The gradual formation of straits by rising waters at Gibraltar and Sicily and other erosion finally separated the various southerly nations already named. The Mediterranean people in Mesopotamia, Syria, Assyria, Palestine, and southerly Anatolia seem almost wholly to have been driven westward and southward by the successive Turkic invasions from Asia.

During the retrogression of the Würm II glaciation and the subsequent climatic oscillations, the successive waves of Turanian subraces radiated from the western Chinese highlands eastward, northward, and westward over Asia. Meanwhile, the Turkic tribes in Eastern and Western Turkistan increased in population; some comprised those divisions that later overran southwestern Asia. North of the Sayan Mountains the Ugrians already were pointing toward the west, while the Nordic Aryans were growing in numbers in Geté and Asiatic Scythia. Through the many centuries that the cold northern Siberian steppes were a vast morass and inhospitable to man, the wide lower lands of Western Turkistan also were largely submerged as far as the foothills. It was thousands of years before the peoples in the mountain fastnesses and the foothills between the Pamirs and Lake Baikal were able to move down to the lowlands of western Asia. During this long period, various nations formed contact with each other along the foothills and some interchange of culture resulted; especially was this true of the Hittites and the Nordics.

The first Turanian break across the Aryan lines in the west occurred prior to 8000 B.C., when a tribe of Turks (the aforesaid Pre-Sumerians) moved through the mountain passes of Kashgaria from Eastern Turkistan to Western Turkistan, where they became a great nation. This Turkic intrusion permanently separated the Nordics of Geté from the Kelts centered on the Pamirs and from the Iranians of Iran and India. About 8000 B.C., these Turks were driven out of Western Turkistan by other Turks (the Sumerians) from Eastern Turkistan. The impassable barrier of marshes on the north and west left movement toward the southwest their only recourse. After conflicts with the Iranians, they shortly reached Elam and lower

Mesopotamia and established the Neolithic civilization on the primitive cultural base of the sparsely settled Mediterranean people found there. Before long, they developed caravan routes between Mesopotamia, on the west, and Kansu province of western China, on the east, across the mountains of Turkistan. These were continued by the Sumerians until about 2750 B.C., when the Chaldeans conquered a part of Babylonia.

This strife in Turkistan about 8000 B.C. also dislodged the Paleo-Kelts from the slopes of the Pamirs and they undertook their long migration westward, finally reaching and spreading over central Europe by way of the Danube valley. There they implanted the fundamentals of the Maglemosean and related cultures.

In Elam and Mesopotamia the Pre-Sumerian culture reached a relatively high state of development. It was appropriated to a large extent by Aryan Hamites in southern Iran, but increasing pressure on these people by the Turks resulted in the emigration of a large division of them about 7000 B.C. across the straits to southern Arabia, where they established a progressive nation. Within a millennium later they conquered Ethiopia, on the African mainland, from the black Indafricans and planted an important colony there.[2] Other Hamites crossed the Suliman Mountains to western India.

In the course of time, apparently after 6000 B.C., the Hamitic culture of Ethiopia was transmitted down the Nile valley, was impressed on the indigenous Mediterranean population that remained there, and later was reflected by the wonderful civilization found in all Egypt at the dawn of history. This achievement closely followed the evolution of the same rudiments of culture by the Turks in lower Mesopotamia after their conquest of that region about 8000 B.C. The subsequent civilization in all Mesopotamia was that jointly of Assyria and Babylon (commingled Turkic and Hamitic), whose full splendor

---

[2] Due allowance must be made for the time factor, because we are dealing with relatively small nations moving to vast territories to settle, develop, and increase in numbers.

is yet only partly known. The third great culture in the Near East was that developed about 2000 years after the early Egyptian by the Mediterranean race in areas south of the Aegean Sea, centering on Krete. It was transmitted later to Greece, where the same race was then dominant.

After 8000 B.C., the next known migration of peoples westward from central Asia was that of the Turkic Sumerians from Turkistan to Babylonia about 4300 B.C. Another interval of two millennia followed, when about 2300 B.C. some climatic condition in central Asia caused the simultaneous emigration of (1) the Turkic Hittites from Western Turkistan to Cappadocia, in Anatolia, (2) the Kelto-Slavs from the western Pamirs through the Caucasus mountains to southern Russia and central Europe, and (3) the foremost tribe of the Nordic nation (the Suebi) around the north of the Caspian Sea into European Scythia. These migrations of about 2300 B.C. were the beginnings of a new series of great racial exploits in the west, which are recounted later.

In the north, first the Nordics in Geté and later the Finnic Ugrians at Lake Baikal lived in such cold climates that they affected both peoples physically and psychically, but far less the former because their environment was more favorable. An increasingly blond complexion was acquired by both. Around the protective camp fires the people developed sociability. The man was a hunter and brought home game and animals for food during the winter and made and decorated his weapons. His womenfolks made the clothing, did the housework, and cared for the children. His early, rough stone, weapons were replaced by those of the Neolithic stage and arrowheads and spearheads were developed to hunt animals. Most of the Turanian Amerinds were probably in the hunting and fishing stage when they reached this continent from northern Asia via Alaska, since they early had lost contact with the growing Turkic civilization in Eastern Turkistan. Many still were living on that cultural level when Columbus arrived, although various nations in the south, such as the Incas, Aztecs, and Mayans, had developed high cultures from as early as the beginning of the Christian era.

In the course of time, man in central Asia had advanced to the pastoral stage. Numerous improved articles were made and the dog, pig, horse, ox, cow, sheep, and goat were domesticated by the Turks in Turkistan. The arts were acquired in varying degrees by the Aryans on the south and to a less extent by the Paleo-Kelts on the Pamirs by the time that they migrated to central Europe. Since neither the Nordics of Geté nor the Finns farther north possessed a highly advanced culture when they entered Europe, it is apparent that they had only minor contact with the Turks, chiefly the Hittites, and that cultural leadership belonged to the Turanians and was the basis of their advanced Mesopotamian civilization.[3] The Mediterranean Bedouins in central Arabia and other parts of the Near East remained in the pastoral state until recent times.

Undoubtedly, some conflict occurred in primitive times among the different races in central Asia, as when the Turks drove the Nordics and Kelts from the Tibetan highlands, took possession of Eastern Turkistan and later Western Turkistan, and finally forced their way across Iran to Elam and Mesopotamia, scattering the Kelts and Iranians encountered on their route, but it is probable that in the earlier stages of civilization warfare was not general[4] among mankind and mainly punishment and blood revenge prevailed. Nonetheless, the exigencies of life caused a very high mortality rate, especially among the children. Early man had increasingly to use his mind for his sustenance, his protection from the elements, and his defense, and only by such use was it so developed that he improved in alertness and judgment. In this way, the constant improvement of tools and weapons resulted and the usefulness of domesticated animals appeared.

---

3 The early habitations of these first Turks in central Tibet and later in sheltered Tarim Basin of Eastern Turkistan apparently were somewhat milder in climate and more stimulating to cultural advancement than those of the Nordics in northwestern Tibet and later in Geté, exposed to winds from the north.

4 J. A. Thomson, *What is Man* (Putnam, New York, 1924), page 214.

In due time the planting of seed to reproduce nutritive vegetation had been discovered by the Turks in the lake region of southern Tibet and agriculture began, whereupon this form of culture succeeded the pastoral stage. This progress was epoch-making for civilization, for it caused man to settle down and control property to till. These Turks then developed the plow to prepare the earth for cultivation and with it the use of cattle for draught animals as well as for meat, but not yet for milk. Whether or not all of this advancement had been made before the descent of the Sumerians to the Tarim Basin of Eastern Turkistan about 8000 B.C. is not known. Subsequently, they invented the wheeled vehicle, probably in Western Turkistan, as wheels were not used in China until 2,000 years later. First came carts for agricultural use, which revolutionized production, and ultimately for war chariots. Thus, their civilization was founded on agriculture and cattle-breeding, the same basis as that on which our modern system of economy rests. The wheel principle was taken by these people to lower Mesopotamia and later was diffused to the Iranian Aryans, but it was absent from all other early civilizations.

Settled economy, however, had a tendency to bring on more general warfare, since it was materially advantageous for a people to possess fertile territory, and less-favored groups coveted the lands of those who had been more successful. This circumstance and the increasing density of population led to formation of related groups into tribes or nations, each headed by a chieftain. Thus, out of the turmoil and struggle for the fertile valleys and plains emerged constantly higher civilization in central Asia and elsewhere as the art of agriculture spread. With improvement in speech because of more intensive human intercourse, there arose a pictorial written language in either Western Turkistan or Mesopotamia early in the Neolithic Age, probably by 6500 B.C. Clay pottery came into common use in certain regions, especially along the trade route from central Asia to Mesopotamia as commerce expanded, weaving was improved, and houses of stone, mud, sod, and timber later were built.

The cultures of the Turks and the Hamites ultimately reached their climax in Mesopotamia and Egypt respectively. They were imparted to other peoples and became the heritage of the west during the succeeding thousands of years. This diffusion of culture occurred mainly along the numerous trade routes that were established in different directions, particularly from Mesopotamia across Anatolia to the Aegean region, whence passage to Europe was easy. It is probable that some commercial intercourse was maintained between the early Hamites of southern Arabia and Ethiopia, on the one hand, and those of Iran and India, on the other, and between the Turks of Mesopotamia and the Iranians of Iran and India; but apparently the Turkic nation was the first to maintain by force a continuous trade route from central Asia (Kansu) across Turkistan and the plateau of Iran, then peopled largely by hostile races, and across Mesopotamia and Anatolia to the Mediterranean. It must have continued in more or less uninterrupted use from about 8000 B.C. to about 2750 B.C. What an effective channel for the transmission of knowledge and artifacts it must have been!

Each new invention was a powerful stimulus to cultural advancement. The Stone Age, Copper Age, Bronze Age, and Iron Age followed in succession. Especially epochal was the initiation and dissemination of the use of metals and of the arts of agriculture by the Pre-Sumerians, who transmitted these advances westward to Anatolia, where many of them went. The earliest grain raised by central European farmers was emmer, a species of wheat, indigenous to western Asia and introduced into Europe by way of Anatolia. Beer was made from barley or from barley and spelt in Mesopotamia as early as 7000 B.C. Picture-writing evolved into an alphabet successively in Mesopotamia, Egypt, and Phoenicia, whence it subsequently was improved by the Greeks. Thus, the means of communication were raised to a more expeditious and efficient plane.

The high state of civilization attained by the Sumerians in Mesopotamia, centering on Babylon, in science, art, virility of character, and moral and social idealism is evidenced by the vast array of folklore, romances, temple prayers, psalms, marriage contracts, commercial documents, deeds, and business and social correspondence found on the hundreds of baked clay tablets since unearthed in that region. The ancient laws of the Pre-Sumerians and Sumerians were integrated with those of the Hamitic Chaldeans and Amorites and culminated in the illustrious code of Hammurabi, the Amoritic king of Babylonia, which was promulgated about 2100 B.C.

After 5500 B.C., Hamites from Ethiopia implanted a well-organized political system in upper Egypt under the jurisdiction of a number of their own kings. By 3500 B.C., the country was being merged into only two kingdoms, Upper and Lower Egypt, and about 3400 B.C. the first ruling dynasty of all Egypt was founded, with Memphis as its capital. Great engineering works were consummated throughout the country. A calendar had been created (4236 B.C.) and definite weights and measures were adopted, which greatly aided commerce. Thus, Egyptian civilization had passed directly from the Neolithic state to a more complex type, but this evolution was greatly influenced by invasions of Turanian armies from the north and the diffusion of their culture through Syria, Palestine, and Lower Egypt. Egypt already had created a high moral and ethical system, at least as an ideal to be kept in mind by those in authority, however imperfectly it may have been practised.

Mesopotamia and Egypt, the earliest centers of western civilization, were for ages the battleground of contending races, the Turanian and the Aryan, as proved by the number of gods and goddesses and racial intermixtures. The degree of interrelation of the ancient Mesopotamian and Egyptian cultures has not yet been clearly established. It is certain that the former exerted great influence on the Iranians as far as India. In fact, the stimulus to culture in India and China came by way of trade routes from the peoples who had made the most progress in the areas nearer the cold regions of central and western Asia.

The Kretan civilization, representative of the Mediterranean race, emerged from the Neolithic age to the age of metal in the wake of Egypt and was progressing while the conquering Hamites in Mesopotamia were assuming and adapting to their own uses the combined Pre-Sumerian and Sumerian culture found there. The Kretans had chiefly a simple nature religion, with one great Mother Goddess (the Earth). The evidences of Kretan civilization unearthed at Knossos and Phaestos disclose a high order of culture, which had been extended to the Grecian peninsula. But it was largely dissipated in consequence of the invasions of Anatolia by the barbaric Achaeans and other Kelts from the north about 1425 B.C. and afterward by their invasion of Krete itself. Its influences, however, were largely impressed on the northern invaders. The Philistines are believed to have been a division of the ancient Kretans who were driven from that island to the Asiatic mainland by Achaean conquerors from Greece.

---

2. *Situation about* 2300 *B.C.* In résumé, we have found that during the first half of the 3rd millennium B.C. the Indafricans were in possession of Africa south of the Sahara Desert excepting the Hamitic kingdom of Ethiopia. The Mediterranean race inhabited the shores of the Mediterranean basin, with the Anatolian Leleges and the Kretans masters of the sea. The civilization of Egypt, a culmination of the early underlying Mediterranean and dominant Hamitic cultures (the latter with Pre-Sumerian impress) modified by later western Asiatic influences through invasions and commercial contact, was casting luster in all directions. On Krete and the Grecian mainland the Mediterranean race was developing its own partially independent culture. Hamitic tribes from southwestern Arabia had conquered the Sumerians in Lower Mesopotamia, where the latter long had been dominant[5] in consequence of widespread commercial activities. Thence, Babylonia was known as Sumer-Chaldea.

The domination of Mediterranean commerce and culture by the Anatolians and by the Kretans lasted until

---

5 Menecrates (Fr. 1).

about 1400 B.C. The occasion for their disintegration by Kelts from Thrace appears later. The culture of the Anatolians, a heritage from the Pre-Sumerians, Sumerians, and Hittites, is demonstrated by that possessed by their later congeners, the Tyrrhenians (Etruscans), who migrated from Lydia to Italy[6] early in the 13th century B.C.

The commercial route of the Turanians across Iran had been abandoned owing to their loss of Sumer and an increasing hostility of Aryan peoples on their north. It is probable that prior to this time the principal Turkic habitation in central Asia centered on Anau in Western Turkistan. But that region was subject to disastrous raids by adjacent Nordic tribes on the north and by Keltic tribes on the southeast. The latter inhabited the highland valleys and retreats on the upper reaches of the Oxus River in the Pamirs and the Hindu Kush Mountains. They may long have captured goods from Turkic caravans moving to and from the west, carrying the booty to their mountain strongholds for distribution among the tribes.

The Mongolian pressure on the Turks in Eastern Turkistan appears to have been transmitted also to the rearguard of the Nordics north of the Tien Shan at Lake Balkhash and to the Ugrians west of the Altai and Sayan Mountains. It caused these people gradually to move westward from the mountain valleys to the lower foothills and steppes, the widespread marshes of which then were rapidly drying up toward the north, the south, and the west. The Finns (Tschudes) and other Ugrian tribes north and northwest of the Sayan Mountains had not yet felt Mongolian pressure from the east, perhaps because of the unattractiveness of the extremely cold climate that prevailed in that part of Asia. A more inviting outlet for the numerous Min, Ugrian, and Tungus tribes of Manchuria and adjacent territory was northeastward toward the Bering Sea and North America and to Korea and Japan.

At this time all of central Europe, from the Caspian Sea to the British Isles and from the Alps to the Baltic

---

6 Strabo v.2.2-3.

Sea, was inhabited by the brunet Mediterranean and blond Keltic races, which except in isolated regions were coalescing more or less. The Kelts were much the superior numerically. All of the brown eyes and other brunet traits of modern Aryans in Europe were inherited from these Mediterranean people.

The chief centers of culture in the west at that time were Mesopotamia and adjacent regions, southern Arabia, and the shores of the eastern Mediterranean Sea from Egypt to Greece, and Krete.

---

3. *Great Dispersions of* 2300 *B.C.* About 2300 B.C. an intense and disastrous drought must have overspread central Asia, creating great disturbance and causing a dispersion of Mongolians from the present central desert region into areas of other peoples on the east, north, and west. A large migration of Amerinds to North America must have followed. Northern Ugrian tribes that moved to Semipalatinsk, northwest of the Altai Mountains, pressed southward above Lake Balkhash upon the Nordic tribes in Geté, their homeland, which lay in the foothills and lower mountains of Western Turkistan between Kashgaria and Lake Balkhash, partly in the Bolor range. Thereupon, the Nordic tribes encroached on the territory of the Turanian Hittites on their southwest. During the 2000 years in which the Nordics and the Hittites had been neighbors, a considerable interchange of customs and ideas occurred, as said in the last chapter.

The southerly edge of vast oak and beech forests extended across Siberia and Russia north of a line from the Altai Mountains to the middle course of the Obi River in central Siberia, thence southwestward to the southerly end of the Ural Mountains, and beyond to the upper reaches of the Dnieper River. South of this course, below the great east-and-west ridge, the lands were still largely marshy from the waters of melting glaciers in the mountains. This was particularly true around the northerly shores of the Caspian Sea, and Lake Aral still

covered an immense area, much of which now is arid.
In the extreme north, in both Siberia and Russia, vast
tundras extended to the Arctic Ocean.

The nomadic Nordic tribes, moving westward around
Lake Aral and southward toward the Oxus River, soon
attacked and displaced the Hittites in Western Turkistan.
The latter followed approximately the old Sumerian caravan route across Iran, but, encountering strong Hamitic
control in lower Mesopotamia,[7] they turned northwestward across the mountains and took possession of Cappadocia, in Anatolia. That region then was sparsely settled
by and in control of their Pre-Sumerian kinsmen of earlier times along with scattered Mediterranean tribes, the
Caucones, the Pelasgi, and others. While the northerly
rim of Iran is mountainous, it is narrow and readily
passable from the steppe of Turkistan to the intermoun-
tain plains of Media, with passage thence along the
Aras River to the fertile heart of Anatolia, despite the
apparent obstacle of the Ararat Mountains. The central
desert of Persia, drier than it was 2000 years earlier, when
the previous westward Turkic (Sumerian) invasion occurred, was readily avoided. This movement of the Hittites across Iran forced the westernmost Iranians southward. The southwestern part of Iran, bordering the Persian Gulf, known as Persis or Fars, ultimately became the
seat of the Persian power. The Hittites had long experience in the use of horses in Turkistan and this migration
presented but little difficulty. Mares gave rich and copious
milk; colt's flesh was a delicate viand; and the horse, wary
as a watchdog, offered defense with his heels, ate leisurely
at night, and lost little of his owner's time. Moreover,
he was a great aid in warfare. As the possessors of the
most advanced arts of civilization, the Turks found migration a more facile procedure than it was with the nomadic
tribes of the north.

After their expulsion of the Hittites, the Nordic peoples
expanded both westward and southward into the regions
north, east, and southeast of Lake Aral, including the

---

7 The Chaldean nation reached the height of its power about 2234 B.C.

lower courses of the Jaxartes and Oxus Rivers. Ultimately, they separated into five tribes, which became
different nations themselves because of their fecundity. The
first Nordic tribe to move farther west, as far as the Ural
River, was the Suebian. This migration must have been
accelerated by the movements of others on their east, and
about 2300 B.C. the vanguard of the Suebians entered
Europe around the north of Caspian Sea. By 2200 B.C.
they had conquered the rich lands of the Ukraine (western ancient Scythia), for it was soon after this time that
their bands of adventurers poured over the Carpathian
Mountains into Transylvania, Moravia, and Bohemia,
and even across Hungary, Bosnia, Croatia, and Dalmatia
as they explored the regions on the south and the west.
They brought a complete civilization, far less advanced
than that of the Turks but representative of the status
of the Nordic nations at that time.[8] They were largely
hunters and herdsmen, whose leaders, upon the conquest
of Danubian peasant lands, established themselves on
hilltops. They brought new types of vases, corded ware,
strange implements, and splendid stone and copper battle
axes. They heaped a barrow over their dead. All over the
region from the Caspian Sea to the Dnieper River, graves
containing skeletons covered with red ochre and surmount-
ed by a mound or kurgan have been found; also the
bones of sheep, cattle, and horses, the last-named being
the desert species used by the Turks in Turkistan, the
steppe horse. They possessed wheeled vehicles, which they,
like the Iranians, used as habitations. Grain found in
kurgans shows that they practised some agriculture, and
that later they settled in villages. Their armory corresponded closely with that of the Iranians and their industry showed the imprint of Sumerian and Hittite culture,
gained by long contact with Turkish tribes from Turkistan to Iran, but not that of the Minoan, Egyptian, or western European civilizations, as proved by the existence in
the graves of female figurines like those of Mesopotamia.
  Ultimately, the Nordic adventurers abandoned the lands

---

8 V. Gordon Childe, *op. cit.*, pp. 151, 157, 177, 185-186, 196, 199-203.

overrun by them south of the Carpathian Mountains and rejoined the nation in the north. About 1600 B.C., they were assailed by the next Nordic nation behind them, the Kimmerians (the *Kimmerii* of the Greeks), and migrated westward to the region south of the Baltic Sea, their chief habitation today. Their old homeland was taken over by the Kimmerians. In 635-634 B.C., the latter likewise were attacked and scattered in part by the Getae (the later Goths, the principal Scythians[9] of Herodotus), who took over the country and made subjects of a part of the Kimmerian nation. The Massagetae and Sakae, the easternmost Nordic nations, who remained in Asia, moved down from the river valleys and foothills of Geté toward the lowlands as the whole former Nordic nation was separating into five tribes.[10] This successive emigration of the three Nordic tribes from Western Turkistan to Ukrainia is verified by Diodorus.[11] According to Herodotus, the first patriarch and king of the Scythians (the Getae or Goths) was Targitaus some 1000 years before the invasion by Darius Hystaspes, or about 1600 B.C.[12] This was about the time of the migration of the Suebians from Western Scythia to the Baltic Sea and of the Kimmerian conquest of the former region, and also that when the foremost Getae moved from Turkistan across the Kirghiz steppe and the Ural River to the bor-

---

9 Herodotus relates that the Persians distinguished "all the Scythians" above them i.e., all the northern nomads, as Sakae; and this statement is confirmed by the inscriptions of Darius. The Babylonians employed the name *Gimiri* (i. e., Kimmerians) in the same sense. *Ency. Brit.*, 13th Ed., vol. 21, page 203. Early laborious attempts to prove that these Scythians were Turanians are no longer accepted. As long as 1848 the noted German philologist, Jacob Grimm, in his *Geschichte der Deutschen Sprache*, showed by an elaborate examination of Scythic word roots that the strongest reasons existed for believing that the Scythians of Herodotus were Indo-European (i.e., Aryan) people.

10 Strabo xi. ch. 7-8.

11 Diodorus ii.43.

12 This Scythian tradition noticed by Herodotus (iv.5-7) may have implied that the descendants of the three princes named represented the dynasties of later divisions of the Getic (or Gothic) nation, viz., the so-called Royal Scythians, the Ostrogoths, and the Visigoths. The name *Skoloti* included by him did not apply to the Getic Scythians but to their Kimmerian subjects; it is the name from which the modern term *Scotti* or *Scot* was derived.

ders of Europe. The Massagetae and the Sakae remained east of Lake Aral, near the ancient homeland. They subsequently played a very important part in the history of the Middle East, which will be presented in a later chapter. If the name Targitaus had in its root an affinity to the name Turk, the connection of the Getae with the country of Turkistan is evident.[13] Apparently, under that leader the western Getae (the later Goths) had become an independent nation by separation from the Massagetae, who remained east of the Caspian Sea.

About the time that the second Nordic nation, the Kimmerians, gained possession of Ukrainia from the Suebians (c.1600 B.C.), adventurous bands of them passed southward along the westerly shores of the Caspian Sea and invaded the territory of civilized nations of western Asia. In fact, practically all of the numerous raids of the southland committed between 1600 and 635 B.C. by Nordic bands may be charged to the Kimmerian nation. The first invaders were the *Carduchi* (or *Kurds*), who settled in Kurdistan. The next invasion was the conquest and settlement of Media, in northwestern Iran. Shortly after 1500 B.C. another band moved across the Fertile Crescent, collided with the Hamitic Amorites, and must have been scattered by them. A portion moved on to Libya, west of Egypt, where they were absorbed by the native population, and the remainder coalesced with the Amorites. This Nordic strain in these natives was noticed by the ancients and still is recognizable by the greater stature, mesocephalic index, and blondish complexion of certain Mediterranean groups of the Palestinian region, such as the Rualá tribe, and of a small part of the population of Libya.

Kelts from the Pamirs and the Hindu Kush, who earlier had spread to the middle courses of the Jaxartes and Oxus rivers, were uprooted and driven westward by this huge irruption of Asiatic population about 2300 B.C. and made their way around the southerly shores of the Caspian Sea. As pursuing Hittites turned into Iran, these Kelto-Slavs

13 See article on *Turk* by d'Herbelot.

continued through the passes of the Caucasus Mountains. The division later known as the Moscovites (Slavs) then detached themselves and moved northward. The remainder continued westward along the northerly shores of the Black Sea and across Krimea to the Danube River, whose vast basin they ascended as far as western Europe, causing devastation all along the way. They are known in history as the "Battle-Ax Folks". Their force gradually was spent as they progressed westward, but most of the tribes kept moving until they reached the upper tributaries of the Elbe, Rhine, and other rivers, which they descended, and central Gaul. On the route across Europe, they took possession of what territory they could hold and imposed their rule on the less warlike natives, but the fact that various tribes reached the west indicates that they had been repelled at places on route. This was the second great Keltic invasion of Europe. There is much evidence of their habitation in central and western Europe and of their having reached the Baltic Sea in due time. This invasion and the resultant strife caused the older inhabitants to construct lake dwellings[14] wherever practicable, not only in the Alps but as far north as East Prussia, as far south as Italy, and as far west as Ireland.

Since these Neo-Kelts (Alpines) had invaded territory in central and western Europe inhabited for thousands of years by their own kin, who had continued many of the old customs of the invaders and spoke mainly the same language,[15] not much time was required for their amalgamation with the existent population. The invaders either originated or aided in carrying to higher stages of development the remarkable system of Druidic religion and philosophy and the rites and ceremonies incident thereto[16]

14 Herodotus v.16.
15 Strabo iv.1.1.
16 The Druidic doctrines made a deep impression on ancient writers; even Aristotle referred to them and their place among the Galatae and others. This peculiar religious system is without parallel anywhere among Aryan peoples. A strongly organized priestly class, students of nature and custodians and teachers of apparent esoteric doctrines, interpreted the moral code, administered justice, practised magic and divination, and participated in the sacrifices (Strabo iv.4.4-5).

that prevailed subsequently among the Kelts of western Europe. The later indigenous population thus represented the descendants of both Paleolithic inhabitants (commingled Mediterraneans and earlier Kelts) and their Neolithic conquerors, all of whom finally lived in comparative peace because of the sparseness of the population. However, the Neo-Keltic invaders must have exercised influence in some regions, such as the Balkans, until their warlike spirit had abated.

These Keltic peoples later developed the noted Hallstatt culture in Noricum (Austria)[17] and they were widely known to the primitive Pelasgic Greeks. About 1500 B.C. they began to move southward and overrun Grecian territory, where they became known as the *Hellenes* (Achaeans, Aeolians, and Aetolians). These incursions were provoked by invasions of the lower Danube valley by Kimmerians of the Ukraine. For many centuries, the affinities of the Keltic language were the subject of much dispute, but a Bavarian historian, J. C. Zeuss (1806-1856), demonstrated conclusively the Asiatic origin of the Keltic dialects. His *Grammatica Celtica* was first published in 1853.

While the more advanced Nordic nations slowly spread across Western Scythia (southern Russia), forcing the Slavs northward, the easterly Nordic tribes or nations remained in contact through the mountains of Kashgaria with Turks (Issedones) in the Tarim Basin of Eastern Turkistan. But the resistance of the Nordics in and south of Geté to westward migration of the Issedones must long have been effective, for the former retained the territory between the Syr and Amu Rivers and around Lake Aral until about 700 B.C. and the Issedones reached the Siberian steppes only by skirting the easterly end of

---

Nevertheless, the ancient Aryan gods were known. The cult is presumed to have had some connection with the Neolithic stone monuments. Druidism may have been a natural development of primitive Keltic beliefs and practices. Its vast diffusion by the Kelts is indicated by the fact that some of its principles were embodied in the Pythagorean philosophy.

17 Greater part of modern Steiermark, Kärnten, and Upper Austria, Salzburg, and southeastern Bavaria.

the Tien Mountains and emerging through Zungaria and across the ridge north of Lake Balkhash.

By the time that the westerly Nordics had spread over the vast grassland expanse north of the Black Sea as far as the Carpathian Mountains,[18] about 2200 B.C., the number of tribes in each division or nation had increased. Diminishing contact among them over the vast marshy river bottom lands nonetheless required effective coöperation for defense against attacks of the Slavs, whom they had separated from the rest of the Kelts on the south. Ultimately, for better defense, the closely related tribes coalesced more firmly into independent nations, which took respectively the aforementioned names of *Suebi, Kimmerii,* and *Getae.* This grouping occurred even before some of them left Asia.[19] A branch of the Getae, known as the Thyssagetae (the later *Alani*), broke away and subsequently followed an independent course. They held the region at the southern end of the Ural Mountains about Ufa and Orenburg until about the 1st century A.D. The easternmost nations, the *Massagetae* and the *Sakae,* took over the vast area south of the Siberian ridge between the Caspian Sea and the foothills of Kashgaria. In some instances, different names subsequently were used for some of these people by Herodotus and other Greek historians, as explained later.

The gradual exsiccation of the lower grasslands from Lake Aral to the Carpathian Mountains provided a rich and productive habitation for the nomadic Nordics, which they possessed for many centuries afterward. But they were constantly subject to strife with the Slavs and Ugrians on the north and to sporadic but increasing pressure from Turanian nations on the east, the most vigorous of which were the Issedones and the Huns (Mongolians). With constant increase of population, this pressure had the effect of driving intermediate Nordic nations against those

---

18 V. Gordon Childe, *op.cit.,* p. 183.

19 The Getae (the later Goths) appear to have been the nuclear division of the entire original Nordic nation, with which the ruling family or dynasty remained as different tribes detached themselves, such as the Massagetae and the Thyssagetae. Whether or not scions of that dynasty led the divergent tribes is not apparent.

ahead, who resisted dispossession of their rich Scythian lands. Herodotus[20] commented on the attractiveness of Western Scythia, where the soil was rich and abundantly watered, saying that it "is, of all that we know, the fullest of moisture, which evidently appears from the dissection of their cattle." About 1600 B.C. this pressure became so great on the Kimmerians in the center that detached bands of this nation ventured over the Caucasus Mountains to the south in search of new highlands, as mentioned before and as explained later.

There is no evidence that any Suebian groups invaded southwestern Asia, and the earliest Nordic contact with the advanced civilization of those regions thus was made by these bands of Kimmerian adventurers. The Suebian nation must have been unaware, except perhaps by hearsay, of the existence of the ancient Babylonian and Assyrian culture anterior to their migration to the Baltic plains. The peoples of the south had not yet penetrated the unsheltered and mysterious regions north of the Caucasus range and the Black Sea, as the Greek Milesians and the Persians later did. Even in the 8th and 7th centuries B.C., when the Milesians established their commerical outposts around the Black Sea and received amber from the Baltic shores, the information gained by the Greeks regarding the Scythian nations was largely second-hand. Hence, the Suebians were the least civilized of the ancient Nordic peoples. They had scarcely passed beyond the nomadic stage at the beginning of the Christian era[21] and their native customs had been subjected to the minimum of foreign influence at the time that Tacitus wrote his *Germania,* about A.D. 98.

By about 1600 B.C., the Suebian nation had been expelled from Scythia by the Kimmerians and had taken possession of the vast territory between the Baltic Sea and the Carpathian and Erz Mountains, north and south, and between the Vistula and Elbe Rivers, east and west, pushing the Kelts westward and southward. The migration of these Nordic nations from Asia is proved by the fact that, not-

---

20 Herodotus iv.58.
21 Strabo vii.1.3.

withstanding the presence of amber on the Baltic shores, they had no name for this precious gum. The Riesen Gebirge, the Thüringer Wald, and the Teutoberger Wald formed the ethnic frontier between the Suebians and the Keltic tribes on their west and south. The victorious Kimmerians[22] then possessed themselves of the rich Ukrainian lands[23] and the Getae later followed them to Europe and appeared in the lower Volga River basin. The time stated above is confirmed by Herodotus.[24] It also is verified directly by Gothic tradition that the Getic kingdom had its inception (in Europe) about 1490 B.C.[25] Farther east, the pressure on rearmost Nordic nations by Turkish tribes moving westward in Asia to the steppes west of the Altai Mountains tended to impel those nations, the Massagetae and the Sakae, southward in Western Turkistan. Actually after 1000 B.C. they settled mainly in Bactriana and Sogdiana (Bukhara and Ferghana) respectively.

In their westward migration, the Suebians had split asunder the Keltic tribes of central Europe; those impelled farther north were the progenitors of the later Moscovites or Slavs, while those on the south were driven into the great mountain valleys and the foothills of the Alps,[26] where their descendants (the so-called Alpines),

---

22 The ethnic name of the Kimmerians (the *Gimiri*) appeared in the Assyrian cuneiform records of the time of Darius Hystaspes. It probably referred to the Kimmeric Carduchi or Kurds, invaders from north of the Caucasus about 1600 B.C. who had settled on their northeastern border in present Kurdistan, as also appears from the writings of the prophet Ezekiel (xxxviii.6), who wrote about 600 B.C. The Kurds are discussed later. The earlier allusions by Homer in the *Odyssey* (xi.13-22) to the habitation of the Kimmerians as a land "immersed in darkness and beyond the ken of the light-giving sun" had application to the region north of the Black Sea. Aeschylus placed Kimmeria in the same region (*Prom. Vinct.* 748-750). The Greek poet Callinus (Fr. 2) had witnessed the incursions of Kimmerians from the north through Thrace into Anatolia, where their name spread terror throughout the whole of that region. See also Herodotus iv.11-12.

23 Herodotus iv.11-13; Diodorus vi.8.

24 Herodotus iv.7.

25 C. C. Mierow, *The Gothic History of Jordanes* (Princeton, N. J., 1915), p. 38.

26 The following item discloses the close contact of the Kelts and the Nordics and their interchange of culture at this time. " . . . these [Nordics] differ but little from the Keltic race, except in their being more fierce, of larger stature, and more ruddy in countenance; but in every other respect their figure, their customs, and manners of life are such as we have related of the Kelts . . ." (Strabo vii.1.2). H. C. Hamilton and W. Falconer, *Geography of Strabo* (Bell, London, 1892).

commingled with Nordics, are found today. Thus, Empress Catherine II of Russia discovered in her linguistic studies that the Keltic language was like that of the Ostiaks,[27] a mixed tribe of people inhabiting the Ural region, in whom traits of the White race predominate. The rich Ukrainian lands long have been known as the granary of Europe. With its great natural advantages of soil and climate,[28] this basin was the habitation desired at one time or another by all of the European Scythian nations.[29] The Kimmerians inhabited it uninterruptedly from about 1600 B.C. to 634 B.C.,[30] when they were supplanted in part by the Getae, the later Goths, who then made the remainder their subjects for 292 years or until 342 B.C.

When the Kimmerians first gained Western Scythia, they drove the Kelts[31] farther into the valleys of the Balkan region. The outstanding result of this disturbance of the Keltic nations in the valley of the Danube was the emergence afterward of some of them in the south as the aforementioned barbaric *Hellenes,* who through the subsequent centuries spread themselves over the territory of the Pelasgic Greeks and ultimately created with them the highest civilization in some respects in the history of the world. Similiar movements of Kelts[32] in Austrian and south Suebian territory ultimately caused certain tribes to overrun and conquer the greater part of Italy, where with the indigenous Ligurians and the Etruscans they created another great civilization, the Roman, which in many respects complemented that of the Greeks.

The migration of the Suebians to the Elbe River and Thuringian territory forced the Kelts of the north to the

---

27 W. K. Sullivan, *Introduction* to Eugene O'Curry's *Manners and Customs of the Ancient Irish* (Williams and Norgate, London, 1873), vol. 1, p. xlix.

28 Herodotus iv.58-63.

29 Strabo vii.4.3; xi.2.5.

30 *Ibid.,* vii.4.3.

31 This was their own name for themselves (Caesar's Commentaries 1.1) and it also was used by the Greeks (Strabo vii.1.2). The Latins called them Galli or Gauls, whence the Greeks also used the name Galatae. The word "Kelt" means simply "one who inhabits woods and fastnesses." It has no application to Nordics, who were not mountain dwellers but inhabited mainly the plains regions.

32 The personal characteristics of the Gallic Kelts are described by Strabo iv.4.2.

Rhine valley and across to northern Gaul, which resulted in Keltic expansion southward toward the Pyrenees and in their invasion of the British Isles by 1450 B.C. In Britain they encountered and ultimately amalgamated with the earlier round-barrow and bronze-using Kelts and the still earlier brunet Iberians who had not yet been driven to the westerly shores of those isles.

The Kelts long held the Rhine valley against the Suebians, for during the next 1000 years apparently the only Suebian tribe to get well beyond the lower Elbe was the Frisian, which seems to have settled in the basin of the lower Weser. On the east of the Elbe, the Suebian tribes of the *Sitones* and *Suiones*[33] had spread slowly up the Danish peninsula by about 1000 B.C., pushing ahead of them into Skäne whatever earlier Keltic and Ligurian or mixed peoples they encountered. Ultimately, these primitive inhabitants were driven to the westerly shores of Norway, where their descendants are found today.

At this point an interesting observation may be made. As has been shown, the ancient underlying races of Greece, Italy, and the Iberian peninsula comprised two racial types, first the primitive Pelasgians, the Ligurians, Sicians, and Sicels, and the Iberians of the Mediterranean race[34] and later their conquerors, the two principal waves of Kelts from the Pamirs via the Danube basin, who, coming from the north about 1500 B.C., superimposed themselves on the natives. This fact is demonstrated by the increasing brachycephaly of the early population in each country from the south to the north. The broad-headed Kelts had poured over the mountains in consequence of the movement of the Nordic Suebians into western Europe about 1600 B.C. and of other Nordic movements in the Danube Basin later.[35] Strabo quotes Polybius' reference[36] as late as the 2nd century B.C. to the fact that

---

33 The later Norwegians and Swedes.
34 Strabo, *Geogr.*, i.3.21 and ii.5.28-30.
35 The brachycephaly of these inhabitants has been modified in more recent times by invasions of Nordic Dorians in southern Greece and Krete, Ostrogoths in northern Italy, Visigoths in Spain, and Normans in Sicily.
36 Strabo, *ibid.*, ii.4.4.

Kelts possessed western Europe and the Iberian peninsula as far west as Gades (Cadiz).

In the Near East, there were only a few subsequent racial movements, other than the invasions by Kurds and Medes, that are worthy of notice. The Hyksos dynasties of Egypt weakened under the influence of a warm climate and other environmental factors, and about 1577 B.C. they were overthrown by the Theban kings and expelled from the country. This is only one of numerous instances in history in which the prowess of vigorous northern people waned and ultimately disappeared among peoples of southern climes, better adapted to the more enervating conditions. The subsequent periodic warfare between Assyria and Egypt is treated at length in general histories. For thousands of years, along the Palestine hills there passed to and fro individuals, commodities, and ideas, and over this route also went armies when a power of either the north or the south was strong enough to strike at the other.

A fact that must not be overlooked in connection with the study of diverse racial types in isolated regions is the tyrannical practice of kings through all ancient and some medieval times of removing rebellious tribes, usually of subject peoples, from their homeland to a far distant part of the kingdom. Ordinarily executed as an act of punishment, it also afforded more effective control of their subjects. Herodotus gives repeated examples of this practice and Tamerlane and Nadir Shah carried it out with much rigor. An analogous principle was followed by the Merovingian and Carolingian dynasties of the Franks when they transferred the heirs of vanquished rivals or rulers, mainly Frankish, Frisian, Danish, and Saxon,[37] to distant frontier regions of the empire, where after suitable marriages they were appointed markgrafs under oaths of fealty.

---

37 Scions of Merovingian families were sent to southern Swabia and eastern Bavaria, Poppo from Frisia to Thüringia, Skiöldung Duke Godfred's son Wermund's son Godfred from Frisia to Upper Franconia, and Wittekind from Saxony to Touraine. Each, after marriage with a lady related to the current royal family, was appointed a frontier count. These are only a few known examples of many such instances.

4. *Lifting of the Scythian Veil.* The ethnology of the inhabitants of ancient Scythia has been largely an unsolved problem from the earliest times. From age to age, the nations in possession of the various sections were not always the same, as already shown; one supplanted another as circumstances changed. This vast expanse, described by the ancients as Eastern and Western Scythia, extended from the foothills of the Altai, Tien Shan, and Hindu Kush ranges, on the east, to the Carpathian Mountains, on the west, with the Ural Mountains and the Ural River as the lines of division. The authority of Herodotus, the Father of History, and the writings of other historians, enable one to clarify the ethnic question in the light of what already has been set out in these pages. The designation of "Scythian" was used in the geographical sense on some occasions and in the racial sense on others; so that one must exercise caution in distinguishing the different peoples reported. Ethnically, there was no Scythian race.

Homer was aware that in his time the Kimmerian nation dwelt on the Krimean Bosporus.[38] In fact, Krimea derived its name from that of the nation in possession. Homer and other Greeks utilized the expression "Kimmerian darkness"[39] to describe the long and severe winters of Scythia. It agreed with the description of the winters left by Herodotus, in which he says that the snow fell so densely as to obstruct the view. Similarly, it was his description of the various barbaric customs of the western Scythians (our Nordic ancestors) that led to the expression that in our cultural progress "we are getting rid of our Scythian habits."

The great Kirghiz steppe of western Asia, lying between the Ural River and Kashgaria, east and west, and between Lake Aral and the Jaxartes (or Syr) River, on the south, and the great east-and-west ridge above Lake Balkhash, on the north, is the region over which the rising Nordic people expanded westward from the foothills. There they lived in contact with the waters of several rivers and of

---

38 Strabo i.2.9.
39 Homer's *Odyssey* xi.1.

Lake Aral and the Caspian Sea and their language gained many words relating to bodies of water and the use of boats. The easterly area was their ancient homeland of Geté,[40] which accounts for the use of the root-word "Getae" by Greek historians and others in the names applied to different Nordic nations as they expanded westward and southward. On their north were numerous Ugrian tribes. Across the mountains on their east and south, the Turks held sway until the Aryans largely replaced them in Iran after about 2750 B.C.

After the Nordics had driven the Hittites from Western Turkistan about 2300 B.C., the Turkish *Issedones* from the Tarim Basin pressed westward through the mountain passes of Kashgaria, in the upper reaches of the Oxus and Jaxartes Rivers (now the Amu and the Syr), and formed contact north of Bukhara with the easterly Nordic tribes on the foothills and plains of Geté, east of Lake Aral. This contact continued relatively unchanged for more than 1500 years.

By about 2200 B.C., the Nordic nations had increased in population and under their five national names, mentioned before, were in possession of the vast grassland region of Eastern and Western Scythia extending from Geté, on the east, to the base of the Carpathian Mountains, on the west, through which their bands of adventurers soon explored. With Turks on their east, Ugrians and Slavic Kelts on their north, and other Kelts on their west and south in Europe, self-preservation required them to develop military skill for defense and offense. By about 1600 B.C., their foremost nation, the Suebians, had been pressed from behind and had moved westward to the Elbe River, whereupon the nation behind them, the Kimmerians, took over the Ukraine[41] and held it until 634 B.C. This region was a vast level prairie, with deep soil.[42] Following them from the east was the third Nordic

---

40 Sherefeddin's history of *Timur* i. and ii. (Petis de la Croix's French translation to English by J. Darby in 1722). The name 'Geté' may have the connotation of a "newly-found homeland," one newly gained or acquired, in the ancient Gothic.
41 Strabo, *Geogr.*, vii.4.3.
42 Herodotus, *Hist.*, iv.23.

nation, the Getae (later Goths) and its branch, the Thyssagetae (the later Alani).[43] In 634 B.C. the Getae shattered the Kimmerian nation.

The westward advance of the Huns (Mongolians) through the passes of the Altai Mountains forever sundered the above Nordic nations from their kin, the Massagetae and the Sakae, who remained in Asia, south and east of Lake Aral,[44] and represented the easternmost division of the Nordics.[45] After about 1000 B.C., because of pressure from Turks on the north, the Massagetae (later called the Tokhari, at least in part) moved southward and eastward and finally settled in Bactriana, as far as the Pamirs and southeast of the Hissar Mountains, and the Sakae settled in Sogdiana (Bukhara and Ferghana).[46] Apparently, it was the Tokhari who originally introduced the Sanskrit language into western India,[47] and the two nations later jointly established the great Scytho-Indian Empire, when the Sanskrit dialect was reintroduced into India. This nation long endured.

Eastern Turkistan, at the time of Herodotus, was known as *Issedon*. It was the easterly terminus of a commercial route that extended into western Scythia, among the Nordic nations.[48] It still was a seat of high culture. Ptolemy also located Issedon in the Tarim Basin, relating how a Syrian merchant had penetrated far into central Asia. Aeschylus says that the Sakae were noted for their good laws and were preëminently a righteous people. They must have gained much culture from their more anciently civilized Turkic neighbors, as shown by the possession of such laws by the Issedones of the Tarim Basin.

---

43 The Goths originally were known to the Greeks as the Getae, but often were referred to as Scythians, a geographical term. Thus, such compound tribal names as Massagetae, Thyssagetae, Tyrigetae, etc. show a striking analogy to the later names of Ostrogoths and Visigoths used by the same people. The later Roman name was Gothi or Gothones.

44 Herodotus, *ibid.*, i.201, 204-206, 208-211, vii.64; Pliny vi.17; Strabo xi.8.2.

45 Diodorus Siculus ii.43.

46 Arrian, *Anab. Alex.*, iii.8, iv.1.4.

47 Calvin Kephart, *Sanskrit Language — Its Origin, Composition, and Diffusion* (Strasburg, Va., 1949).

48 Herodotus, *Hist.*, iv.24.

Before Strabo's time, a number of small tribes had split from the Massagetae, such as the *Dahae,* the *Chorasmii,* and others.[49] The Kimmerians of Media ultimately extended their sway eastward across Khorasan, in northerly Iran, the later Parthia,[50] where they formed contact with the Massagetae (the Tokhari) in Bactria. Dahae from around the Caspian Sea, who also had invaded Parthia, joined with Medians and soon formed the Parthian nation of northerly Iran. Because of the movements of both old and new tribes and variations in knowledge of geography among ancient writers, some confusion exists in the reports of tribal names, river names, and locations. For example, the Jaxartes occasionally was referred to as the Araxes and Lake Aral as the Caspian Sea.

Diodorus[51] regarded as Scythians all of those peoples situated east of the European Kelts. Pliny did the same, considering the Scythians and the Suebians and Kimmerians as one and the same people.[52] Procopius, who wrote later than either, says that the Goths anciently were named Scythians.[53] Herodotus[54] asserts that the Sarmatians, of the province of Astrakhan, were distant kin of the Scythians (the Getae or Goths), of whose language theirs was a dialect. Apparently, the Sarmatians were descendants of Scythian Getae who about 550 B.C. intermarried with certain surviving young women of an early colony of Kimmerians who inhabited the southerly shore of the Black Sea above Cappadocia, between Sinope and the Thermodon River.[55,56] Having become troublesome to their neighbors, probably the tribe of the *Mossynoeci,* the men of this colony (named the *Amazons*) were massacred and many of their women were transported back

---

49 Strabo, *Geogr.,* xi.8.1-8.

50 *Ibid.,* xi.8.1-8. and 9.2; Pliny vi.17; Justin, *Hist. Phil.* ii.1,3,

51 Diodorus Siculus vi.8.

52 Pliny iv.12.

53 Procopius, *Gothic War,* iv.

54 Herodotus, *Hist.,* iv.110-120.

55 Strabo, *Geogr.,* xii.3.14; Diodorus iii.12.

56 C. C. Mierow, *The Gothic History of Jordanes* (Princeton, 1915), pages 62, 66. The Amazon tribe was well known and was sizeable in numbers. See Plutarch, *Pompey* (Oxford Edition, Little, Brown & Co., Boston, 1919), page 95.

to the northerly shore. Their Getic husbands then took them all beyond the Don River, north of the Caucasus Mountains, and established homes in what later became known as Sarmatian territory.[57] Thus, they became a mixed nation. It is remotely possible that the women had acquired a minor strain of Anatolian White Syrian or Keltic blood[58] before arrival and introduced some dialectal differences and new customs north of the Black Sea. These variances distinguished them from the other Nordics there and made a separate place of abode desirable.

It is believed that this colony of Kimmerians near Sinope represented those whom the Getae pursued through the Caucasus range in 634 B.C., after shattering the Kimmerian nation, but who escaped when they turned sharply westward along the shore of the Black Sea and settled near Sinope, whereupon their pursuers overran Asia Minor for 28 years. The former assumed the tribal name of Amazon. Men of this tribe served as auxiliaries of the *Albani,* who lived farther east, near the Caspian Sea,[58] and who also were Kimmerians, which tends strongly to confirm the above inference.

Herodotus reports that these Sarmatians spoke an impure dialect and allowed their women to engage in warfare and to enjoy much freedom. They were the ancestors of the original Poles and Ukrainians, who since the beginning of the Christian era have acquired a marked strain of Slavic blood, because of their proximity to tribes of the Slavic nation and the westward and southward intrusions by members of such tribes.

The Thyssagetae appear in history as the later *Alani,* a minor group. They may have acquired a minor strain of Slavic or Finnic blood during their long habitation near those peoples in the region of Orenburg, west of the Ural Mountains. According to Herodotus, the Massagetae were

---

57 Justin ii.4. The present Astrakhan.
58 Syrians dwelt along the Thermodon River. Herodotus, *Hist.*, ii.104. They apparently were Leuco-Syrians, i.e., White Syrians or Kelts, with whom the Amazons may have intermarried and from whom they may have acquired a foreign strain. Possibly these Kelts were the Mossynoeci, already mentioned.

a great and powerful nation, who in their clothing and food, method of travel (in waggons), manner of fighting (on horseback), and other customs[59] resembled the western Scythians. Its eastern branches had some customs like those of the Turkic Issedones, with whom they had cultural relations to some extent, which caused Herodotus to doubt whether this nation should be classified as Scythian (Nordics).[60] In the same manner, by contact with these Turks along the northern mountain slopes, the Sakae also appropriated considerable culture from them, as intimated by Aeschylus. This commercial and cultural intercourse between these two nations and the Issedones may have been one of the reasons why the former made no sustained effort to follow their fellow-Scythians to the country west of the Caspian Sea. According to the craniologist, De Ujfalvy, the Sakae essentially were of the Nordic type and the Massagetae obviously were likewise.[61] Other events of history prove conclusively that they were White nations. Their later activities will be discussed at length hereafter, for they played important parts in history that have not yet been adequately clarified.

Thus, we readily account among the ancient Scythians for the Suebians, Kimmerians, Getae (Goth), Alans, and Sarmatians as the western representatives of the Nordic race.[62] The Medians, Parthians, Dahae, Massagetae, Tokhari, Sakae, and other tribal or national groups, as its eastern representatives, ultimately acquired all of the territory from the Caucasus Mountains to and around the southerly shores of the Caspian Sea,[63] all of northern Iran, Bactriana, Sogdiana (including Bukhara), and northern Afghanistan and western India. Their descendants live there

---

59 Herodotus, *Hist.*, i. 215, 216, iv. 46, 61, 121, 136.

60 *Ibid.*, i. 201, 215, 216.

61 A. H. Keane, *op.cit.*, pp. 167-168.

62 The Scythians made certain assertions regarding the time and manner of their origin. Herodotus, *ibid.*, iv. 5-7. The legend of three divisions of their people may imply three divisions of the Getic nation (Getae, Thyssagetae, and Massagetae), but it could mean the Suebic, Kimmeric, and Getic divisions of the Nordic peoples, which as separate nations migrated from Asia to Europe. The former conjecture is the more probable.

63 Strabo, *Geogr.*, xi. chapters 6-11.

today, but they have so commingled with brunet Iranian blood as to be almost unrecognizable. Various detached groups took tribal names not included above, as an outgrowth of the necessity for localization of authority for defensive purposes, because of difference in aims, etc. In all that follows, it should be borne in mind that, with the rising density of population on the earth's surface and the increasing indulgence in warfare as the chief manly pursuit, sharp distinction must be made between the migration of whole or parts of nations to new habitations for one reason or another and the mere invasion of foreign territory by armies of established nations led by ambitious warriors (princepes) for plunder or training for tribal leadership. History is replete with instances of each.

----

5. *Kimmeric Invasions of the South.* The Nordic Kimmerian nation of the east was the ancestral stock (1) of the earlier central and western French, Goidelic Irish, Manx, Highland Scots, Netherlanders (except Frisians), lower Rhinelanders, Rüstringers, and Danes, and (2) of their later kinsmen, the northerly French, Franconians and Hessians, middle Rhinelanders, Belgians, Britons, Cornish, Bretons, Kymric Welsh and Scots, and northern Irish. The present language of the Flemings of Belgium does not differ fundamentally from that of the Dutch spoken in the Netherlands. Gomer, the Biblical name of a race in the list of nations,[64] is identified as the Kimmerians of "the uttermost parts of the north" and an ally of Gog[65] and its hordes. After gaining Ukrainia from the Suebians about 1600 B.C. and before their warlike propensities had subsided, the Kimmerians, a venturesome nation or one made restless by aggressive neighbors on all sides, undertook various incursions during subsequent centuries into territory south of the Caucasus Mountains and the Black Sea. They dislodged tribes of Iranians and others, who then overran

----

64 *Genesis* 10:2,3.
65 *Ezekiel* 28:1-6.

Syria and Mesopotamia.[66] Once in motion among hostile peoples, these bands of Kimmerians kept going until they had reached regions that they could hold or until they were dispersed or captured. We thus account for the tall, blue-eyed mesocephalic strain found among the Amorites of Palestine, including the present Rualá tribe of Transjordania, and among the Libyans of northeastern Africa. There is no indication that the Amorites basically were other than a Hamitic race,[67] but it is equally certain that they included a noticeable Nordic strain, as reflected in Egyptian paintings of them.[68]

Another more conspicuous group of these invaders was the Carduchi[69] (*Gordyaeans* or *Kurds*), who settled soon afterward in northern Kurdistan, in the highlands south of Lake Van and north of the Tigris River, in eastern Turkey, as mentioned before. This invasion occurred by way of the westerly end of the Caucasus range and thence southward, as proved by the fact that over one-half of the western Kurds have a cephalic index of approximately 75 per cent, whereas the eastern Kurds, long in contact with the Turanian race in northern Iraq (formerly a part of Assyria), reveal a substantial strain of Turkish blood. Light gray or blue eyes are common among the upper-caste Kurds.[70] Moreover, their tribal system unmistakably resembles in some respects that of their kin of the highland clans of Scotland[71] and it is believed that the bagpipe originated in the Kimmerian nation. There is an underlying peasant or laboring caste, different from the warrior Kurds, which apparently represents the conquered

---

66 E. A. Speiser, *Mesopotamian Origins* (University of Pennsylvania Press, 1930), p. 101, citing J. Friedrich, *Reallexikon der Assyriologie* (Berlin and Leipzig), I, pp. 144-148.

67 *Genesis* 10:16.

68 A. H. Sayce, *Expositor*, July, 1888.

69 Xenophon, *Anabasis* iv. 1.2ff; Strabo, *Geogr.*, xi.14.8, xvi.1.24.

70 *Encyclopaedia Britannica*, 13th Edition, vol. 15, p. 949, by Charles W. Wilson and H. C. Rawlinson; also V. Gordon Childe, *The Aryans* (Knopf, New York, 1926), pages 41, 160.

71 *Encyclopaedia Britannica*, 13th Edition, vol. 15, p. 949, by Charles W. Wilson and H. C. Rawlinson: also V. Gordon Childe, *The Aryans* (Knopf, New York, 1926), pages 41, 160.

aboriginal population. About 1500 B.C., the Kimmerians conquered the region and established the strong colony of Media, in northwestern Iran.[72] These Kurds and the Medes were some of the Scythians asserted to have been subdued by King Sesostris (probably a misnomer for Seti or a name representing a compound of Kings Seti I and Rameses II), of Egypt, about 1321-1300 B.C.,[73] when his forces reached the Caucasus region.[74] This army may even have passed into Scythia as far as the Tanais (Don) River, either through the Caucasus Mountains or around the easterly end of the Black Sea.[75] An outstanding character of the Kurdish race, a world hero, was the knightly Saladin (A.D. 1138-1193), a warrior leader of the Muhammadans against the Christians during the Crusades, of whom even his opponents conceded the highest virtues. The Kurds number about 1,500,000 today.

In view of the transmission of the tribal name *Albania* by the Kimmerians to the Adriatic shores (Albania) and to the British Isles (Scottish Highlands), it is certain that the *Albani*, a people that inhabited the modern districts of Shirvan and southern Daghestan, at the easterly end of the Caucasus range,[76] comprised another band of Kimmerians who very early had settled in that region via the Albanian Gates, a defile at Derbend, on the Caspian Sea. Further proof is the physical description of these people.[77] They were scattered long afterward by the army of Genghis Khan.

The earliest-known Kimmerian raid southward on the west of the Black Sea occurred about 1450-1425 B.C., when their pressure on the Kelts of the lower Danube and Thrace forced Keltic tribes to migrate across the Bos-

---

72 *Ency. Brit.*, 13th and 14th Editions, under the name Media.

73 This date may have been as early as 1375 B.C. (See Diodorus i.53-58).

74 Herodotus ii.103, 110.

75 Diodorus ii.1. The Egyptian invasion of Media, the Caucasus, Scythia, and Thrace was actuated by increasing forays by Medes and other Kimmerians of the north into regions to the south, then under Egyptian suzerainty. The Kimmerians of Kurdistan were referred to as the sons of Gomer and in the Assyrian writings of the time of Darius Hystaspes as the *Gimmira.*

76 Strabo, *Geogr.*, xi.1.5.

77 *Ibid.*, xi.4.1-8.

porus and the Hellespont to Anatolia and through Macedonia to northern Greece. The first Kelts of Thrace to enter Asia were the *Bryges* (or Phrygians), who established the interior kingdom of Phrygia.[78] They were followed by the *Carians, Lydians,* and *Mysians,* who settled along the Aegean shores. Those who first entered Greece were the *Achaeans,* who slowly penetrated southward until they had conquered most of the Peloponnese by 1350 B.C. All of the foregoing tribes were related. Homer was an Achaean. About 1200 B.C., a band of Kimmerians (the later *Dorians*) reached as far south as Doris, in Phocis, northern Greece. Their earliest invasion of southern Greece occurred about 1190 B.C. They ultimately became the dominant race in the Peloponnese, in consequence of which many Pelasgian and Achaean Greeks fled across the Aegean to the Asiatic coast.[79] The facts that the Doric dialect differed fundamentally from the other Grecian dialects, that these people embodied a conspicuous pride of race, and that there was a survival of a tall, mesocephalic, blond, and light-eyed type among the people of Thebes and various other localities in Greece is convincing evidence that the Dorians were a different subrace from the Keltic Achaeans, Aeolians, and Aetolians. They occupied a single continuous territory and all their chief cities were inland rather than on the seacoasts, notably Sparta, Stenyclerus, Argos, Troezen, Corinth, Megara, and Sicyon.

The Dorians are known to have come into Greece from the northeast,[80] probably from the territory north of the Danube inhabited by the Kimmeric *Treres;*[81] in fact, they must have been a division of the Treres. Clearly, they were a branch of the Kimmeric nation in the Ukraine, which, more than any other Nordic group, produced successive invaders of the civilized south.[82] Confirmation is found in Homer's statement[83] that the in-

---

78   Strabo vii.3.2, vli.Fr.25.
79   Herodotus ii.171.
80   *Ibid.,* i.56.
81   Strabo i.3.21.
82   *Ibid.,* xi.2.5.
83   *Odyssey* iv.

habitants of the Peloponnese were Achaeans (Kelts), Argives (Pelasgians), and Danaans (Dorians). The name Danaan was derived from that of the goddess Danaë,[84] a descendant of the ancient god Danaus, a native mythical hero of Argos. This also is the source of the names of other Kimmerians, notably the Danes and the Tuatha Dé Danann. The latter, from north of the Black Sea, invaded the British Isles from Gaul and their vanguard reached Ireland as early as 585 B.C. The outstanding descendants of the Doric invaders of Greece were the Spartans of Lacedemonia.[85] Pouqueville remarked about the long flaxen hair of the women of Sparta, their majestic air and carriage, their elegant forms, and the regularity of their features, animated by large blue eyes bordered with long eyelashes. The men, fair of complexion, had noble features and were tall of stature.

This taste of the climate, culture, and products of Anatolia and Greece only whetted the appetite of the Kimmerians for further adventure in those regions. The marked influence of their acquisition of the arts of the southern civilizations on the later culture of western Europe, to which they migrated, apparently has escaped the notice of earlier historians. The greatest notice has been achieved by the historians of Ireland.[86] Repeated hordes of these people swept southward over that much-traveled pathway west of the Black Sea to the mainland on both sides of the Aegean, but chiefly on the Asiatic

---

84 The Dorians reckoned the goddess Danaë as ancestress of their chiefs. Herodotus vi.53, vii.94. She was esteemed as the goddess of dry earth, which under rains of the golden spring-time bursts into verdure and bloom; sometimes also as goddess of the dawn, through whose golden rays of heaven the youthful sun is born. She is said to have married Jupiter. The statement that her ancestor, the god Danaüs, came from Egypt is believed to be an attempt to explain the influence of Egyptian civilization on Greek culture. The Kimmerians must have become followers of the god Danaüs about this time. They gave the name to the Danube River. The *Danaoi*, always in the plural form and referring to warriors and lovers of war, are mentioned 147 times in the Iliad and 13 times in the Odyssey of Homer.

85 However, the Spartans appear to have had a general reputation in Greece for susceptibility to corruption. See footnote 5 to c.57 of book iii of George Rawlinson's translation of Herodotus' history.

86 The idea of the primitive origin of poetry in a White Goddess must have been brought from the Aegean region by the Kimmerians.

side. They also invaded the Caucasus region. Only recently Russian archaeologists report the finding of skeletons of 6-foot men and relics of their culture of about 1000 B.C. in Azerbaijan.

Eusebius states that Sardis, later the capital of the kingdom of Lydia, in Anatolia, was first captured by Kimmerians (the Treres) in 1078 B.C.[87] In fact, Grecian territory, particularly Aeolia and Ionia, was invaded repeatedly by these northern barbarians.[88] The ancient city of Cardia, at the head of the Gulf of Saros,[89] probably was established by them, since its name was derived from their word *Caer*. The power of the Phrygian nation, in Anatolia west of the Halys River, was broken by an invasion of Kimmerians about 685-680 B.C. by way of the Caucasus Mountains and Armenia.[90] At the zenith of the later Assyrian empire under Esarhaddon (680-668 B.C.), Kimmerian soldiers served in the forces of that king in his widespread conquests. They were known as the *Gimmira* or *Gimiri,* which name in the Babylonian transcripts of the Achaemenian inscriptions and in later reports was applied chiefly to the Kimmerii of Kurdistan, Media, and Parthia, in and west of northern Iran.[91]

The Lydian kingdom, successor of the Phrygian nation, was nearly destroyed by still another Kimmerian invasion under Dugdammé about 670 B.C., during the reign of Gyges, founder of the Mermnad dynasty, when they took the lower town of Sardis, and again in 652 B.C., when Gyges was slain.[92] In a subsequent raid about 640 B.C. during the reign of Ardys, his successor, the Kimmerians destroyed the original temple of Artemis at Ephesus.[93] Remains of the verses of Callinus, a Grecian poet who flourished in the 7th century B.C., urge his fellow-citizens

---

87 *Encyclopaedia Britannica*, 13th Edition, vol. 17, p. 158, by A. H. Sayce.
88 Strabo *Geogr.* i.1.10, 2.9, iii.2.12, xiii.4.8.
89 Herodotus, *Hist.* vi.33.
90 *Encyclopaedia Britannica*, 13th Ed., vol. 2, page 760, by C. W. Wilson and D. G. Hogarth.
91 *Ibid.*, vols. 3, pages 105-106; 7, page 806; and 21, page 206.
92 *Ency. Brit.*, 13th Ed., vol. 17, page 158, by A. H. Sayce.
93 Herodotus, i.15; Callimachus, *Hymn to Artemis.*

to resist the attacks of the Kimmerians.[94] The descendants of these last invaders, who belonged to the Treres tribe from the lower Danube, after the shattering of their parent nation in Ukrainia by the Getae in 634 B.C. withdrew from Lydia during the reign of Alyattes, 609-560 B.C.[95] He was the grandson of Ardys and son of Sadyattes and the father of the famous king Croesus, who succeeded him. This withdrawal, which occurred in 606 B.C.,[96] was motivated by the approach of a victorious Getic army from the east after it had ravaged western Asia for 28 years. The departing host comprised the followers of the renowned Odin (the ancestors of the Danes, Salian Franks, and related tribes), who evaded the Ukraine, where the conquerors of their nation, the Getae, were in control, and moved up the Danube basin to the Elbe and down that river. Their kin, the Goidelic Kimmerians, after their defeat by the Getae in 634 B.C., also had migrated up the Danube valley, but, instead of going down the Elbe River, had continued westward into central and western Gaul. With all of their possessions, it must have required about two years to cross Europe and become settled.

When raiding Lydia, then one of the richest nations, the Kimmerians were less interested in subjecting the cities than in robbing them of their wealth.[97] Thus, they carried back to Scythia the treasure and other spoils taken during these incursions and also all of the southern culture that appealed to them. The latter fact is proved by their development of agriculture in the northern river valleys and in Krimea, which with the Kimmerian Bosporus took its name from them, and by such engineering works as ferries and earthworks constructed by them in those regions.[98] One of the chief contributions of the Lydians to civilization was the art of coining gold and silver. It was through these returned Kimmerians that west-

---

94 *New International Encyclopedia,* vol. 4, page 352, by Robert N. Bain; **Strabo** xiv.1.40.
95 Herodotus i.16.
96. *Ibid.,* i.26.
97 *Ibid.,* i.6.
98 *Ibid.,* iv.3,20.

ern Asiatic coins later reached western Europe as far as Ireland; especially when the remnant of the Kimmerian nation, the *Skoloti*, broke away from the Getae (the Goths) in Ukrainia[99] and migrated to western Europe in 342 B.C. On that occasion they diffused to western Europe a far greater measure of the culture of the Near East than is portrayed in history.

---

6. *Median Nation Established by Kimmerians.* After the Kimmerians had conquered the rich Ukrainian region and the Getae had moved behind them north of the Caspian Sea and the Caucasus range, eruptions of the former, flushed by their success, occurred down the easterly shores of the Black Sea to western Asia, as stated before. Apparently, the first was that of the *Carduchi* (the Kurds), but the second and most important, about 1500 B.C., was the conquest of the highlands of northwestern Iran, the later Media, which was gained from Iranians and Assyrians (in the mountains).[100] Their settlement[101] there dislodged many Iranian tribes, which subsequently caused the migration of Iranians over the Suliman Mountains to India, as revealed by the *Rig-Veda* of the Hindus and by other evidence. They made Ecbatana their capital. They were uniformly called the *Manda*, a name applied to the Kimmerian nation of Scythia. Iranians, Turks, and mixed inhabitants who remained were made their subjects.[102] Many Iranians, such as the *Mitanni*, who did not move eastward were dispersed to the mountains of western Iran or southward to the province of the Persians (the ancient Persis, now called Fars). Thus, the treaty between the Hittite king and the king of the Mitanni, in the west, at the beginning of the 14th century B.C., contains the name of Aryan gods. The Iranians who had moved into Persia greatly strengthened and aided in

---

99 The term 'the Ukraine' or 'Ukrainia' is used here as a later name for Western Scythia.
100 Diodorus iii.2.
101 V. Gordon Childe, *The Aryans*, pages 37, 41, 160.
102 Herodotus i.120, 129.

the development of the later powerful Persian nation, whose people, having been brunets, considered themselves to be a different subrace from the Medes[103] and the Greeks.[104] The Medians extended their sovereignty as far south as the territory of the Persians and completely sundered what may have remained of the ancient route of communication between the Turanians of Western Turkistan and those of Mesopotamia.

This conquest and settlement by the Kimmerian Medes is verified by a series of circumstances. The existence at the easterly end of the Black Sea, in modern Georgia, of the ancient colony of Colchians, said to have been founded by transplanted Egyptians[105] who had served in the army of Sesostris, harmonizes with the Egyptian tradition of an invasion of the Caucasus region and Scythia about 1321-1300 B.C. or earlier.[106] There is a corresponding tradition in Gothic history[107] that Tanausis, king of the Getae about 1323-1290, after defeating the Egyptians who had attacked them on the Dnieper (?) (probably the Don or Volga) River, returned and conquered much of western Asia "and made it subject and tributary to Sornus, king of the Medes, who then was his dear friend." Thus, the Medes already had settled in that country.

In 838 B.C. the Assyrian nation, in renewal of its claim on the territory, overcame the Medes and imposed its sovereignty over them. By the middle of the 8th century B.C., the Medes had gained sufficient strength to initiate an unsuccessful revolt against the Assyrian power. The Median dynasty, founded by Deiokes (c.740-656), thus represented an uprising of the Nordic element of the population. Deiokes apparently succeeded in uniting the indigenous population[108] by about 709 B.C., but the open revolt against the Assyrians actually was undertaken by

---

103 *Ibid.*, i.131-140.
104 *Ibid.*, i.4.
105 *Ibid.*, ii.103-105; Diodorus i.55.
106 *Ibid.*, ii.103, 110; Diodorus i.27-28.
107 C. C. Mierow, *op.cit.*, page 63.
108 Herodotus i.101.

his son and successor, Phraortes, who had brought the Persians in the south under his sway.[109] Upon the death of Phraortes in an attack on the Assyrians[110] about 635 B.C., he was succeeded by his famous son Cyaxares, who reigned 40 years until 594 B.C. This period embraced the *epochal 28 years* from 634 to 606 B.C., during which an expeditionary force of Scythians (Getae), after defeating the Kimmerians in Ukrainia and the Medians, overran and dominated western Asia and caused the departure of Odin's host of Kimmerians (Treres), the later Danes, from Lydia in 606 B.C. The fact that the Median dynasts, who rebelled against the Assyrians between 680 and 634 B.C., were allied with Kimmerian chieftains[111] who had come from the northern shore of the Black Sea is evidence of Nordic racial affinity. When the Getic forces overran Media in 634 B.C., they transferred a rebellious tribe of Medes (the later Lithuanians, Latvians, and Borussians) from that country to their newly-gained Ukrainian territory on the north shore of the Danube River as colonial subjects.

The ancient Kimmerian language of all these people was best preserved by the Magi,[112] the priestly caste of the Medians.[113] Magianism was an old Scythic religion, professed everywhere that the Kimmerians settled. A tradition among the Medes at the time that the Magian books (the *Zend-Avesta*) were composed indicated that the race originally had migrated from a country (undoubtedly Geté) surmised to have been near Sogdiana, since the latter region is mentioned as near to it.[114] Mention is made in the *Avesta* of the Albordj (Elburz) mountain range south of the Caspian Sea. Through the millennia a certain degree of culture transference occurred between

---

109 *Ibid.*, i.102.
110 *Ibid.*, i.102.
111 *Ency. Brit.*, 13th Ed., vol. 18, page 21, by Eduard Meyer; see also A. H. Keane, *op.cit.*, footnote on page 267.
112 See J. C. Prichard, *Physical History of Mankind* (Houlston and Stoneman, London) IV, 28-44.
113 Herodotus iii.65,67,73,79,126.
114 J. C. Prichard, *op.cit.*, page 50.

the white Nordic people of Western Turkistan and the brunet Iranians by way of the Turanian route of communication, but the tribes were not always the same. In the *Rig-Veda* of the Hindus the gods Indra and Agni predominate, whereas in the *Zend-Avesta* of the Nordic Medians the gods Indra and Agni and other Hindu deities can scarcely be traced or were wholly unknown, although the lower religious ideas and the ritual agree closely.

Returning now to conditions in Media after the Getic expedition of 634-606 B.C. had become weakened by climatic conditions and by defections and was dispersed by Cyaxares, the Medians succeeded in overthrowing the Assyrian empire and destroying its capital, Nineveh, in 606 B.C. The dominion of the Medes then was extended westward to a recognized boundary at the Halys River, bordering the kingdom of Lydia. But the leadership of the Median kings was of short duration, for Cyrus, king of Anshan, east of Elam, in western Persia, overcame them and assumed leadership of both Medes and Persians about 558 B.C.[115]

Magianism made notable progress among the Persians. The popular dialect of the Medians was greatly modified by the Assyrian during the sovereignty of that nation and it was carried into Persia by the diffusion of Magianism. The religion and mythology of both Medes and Persians appropriated many ideas from Babylonia and Assyria. In the 6th century B.C., the Magus Gaumata (Gomates), the pseudo-Smerdis of Herodotus,[116] led a revolt in Persia in an attempt to put the religious caste in control of the civil government of the empire. But, after eight months of his rule, it was overthrown by Darius the Great who became the king. With Magianism under a cloud, he restored the Arian Dualism of the great mass of his subjects. Zoroasterism, of the northwest, which subsequently emerged among the Medes and Persians, comprised an intermixture of the two religious systems and paid marked respect to Darius, the great religious reformer.

---

115 Herodotus, *Hist.*, i.125-129.
116 *Ibid.*, iii.61-68.

During these centuries the Persian nation proper consisted of nine tribes in the southwest, apparently in three stages of eminence, viz., first, the *Pasargadae,* the most noble, from which the royal family came; second, the *Maraphians* and *Maspians;* and third, the *Panthialaeans, Derusiaeans,* and *Carmanians,* who were husbandmen, and the *Daians, Mardians, Dropicians,* and *Sagartians,* who were pastoral tribes.[117] The dynasty established by Cyrus of Anshan endured for more than two centuries and extended its power widely, but in the 4th century it weakened and in 330 B.C. came under the sway of the Macedonian kingdom of Alexander the Great.

Media's splendid capital city of Ecbatana was well situated where the present city of Hamadan lies. Its foundation and description have been treated by several ancient writers.[118] Rages, another noted city of antiquity, lay about 150 miles to the east. This region is historic as the place of captivity of the ten tribes of Israel carried away by the Assyrians of Nineveh. These Israelites were dispersed among the native population, whence they ultimately lost their identity, mainly by absorption, but at least three tribes seem to have emigrated elsewhere, one to western China, one to Afghanistan, and one to Kurdistan (the *Yezides*). Some of the customs of each are Semitic in character. Other tribes of Turkish origin, known as the *Illiyahs,* roam over Iran today as nomads. It is not known whether they also represent some of the tribes of ancient Israel.

Before Herodotus' time, the Medians were known also as the Arii,[119] which name later was used by one of the tribes of the Massagetae in north-central Iran. According to Strabo, the ancient Greeks applied the name Ariana to the whole Iranian plateau between Assyria and India, with its conglomeration of brunet and Nordic blond tribes. The name Aryan, derived from inhabitants of that plateau, now is applied to the Brown-White race

---

117 *Ibid.,* i.125. Various writers have reported still other names.
118 *Ibid.,* i.98; Polybius, *Hist.* x. Ex. 4; Diodorus ii.13; also *Judith* 1:2.
119 Herodotus vii.62.

as a whole. The word Iran had the same origin. Originally, the root word meant those of the upper ruling class. The Medes were noted for the breeding of fine horses, by the use of which they developed the best cavalry in Asia. Their military dress was adopted by the Persians.[120] Their horses were recognized by nearly all ancient geographers and historians for their size, beauty, and swiftness. They were reared on the Nisaean pastures in the beautiful country above the Zagros Mountains, between Ghilanee and Kermanshah.[121] The widespread use of horses also was a custom of the Getae in western Scythia, who utilized them to good advantage when their country was invaded in 521 B.C. by Darius the Great, king of Persia, about which more will be said in a later chapter.

In the course of time, the Kimmerians of Media expanded eastward and conquered and settled in Khorasan, a large region along the northerly escarpment of Iran toward Herat. On the north, just east of the Caspian Sea, lived the *Dahae,* who had broken away from the Massagetae.[122] They also were known as the *Aparni* or *Parni.* A tribe of the Dahae named the *Caspi,* mentioned by Herodotus, Pliny, and Strabo, settled in eastern Transcaucasia (Azerbaijan) and gave their name to the Caspian Sea. Their descendants came in contact with the later *Sarmatians,* other Nordics to be described subsequently, who originally lived north of the Caucasus Mountains in Astrakhan.

In 255 B.C. the Bactrian tribe of the Tokhari (Massagetae) attacked their kin, the Dahae. The latter then fled into Khorasan and merged with the local population, where they aided in the foundation of the before-mentioned Parthian nation,[123] which won its independence of Media in 248 B.C. The composite language of the people (mod-

---

120 *Ibid.,* vii.61,62.
121 *Ibid.,* vii.41; Diodorus xvii.11; Arrian vii.
122 The Dahae are referred to by Strabo, *Geogr.* xi.7.1. The name "Dahae" meant "the enemy" to the Iranian peasants assailed by them.
123 The Parthians are mentioned by Justin, xli.1, and the latter also by C. C. Mierow in *The Gothic History of Jordanes* (Princeton, 1915), page 63.

ified by Median and Getic) became known as the *Pahlavi* (meaning Parthian).

The religion of Zoroaster, a native of Media, was adopted by the populace, as set out in the writings of the *Avesta,* translated and interpreted in the *Zend* of the Pahlavi.

We now shall suspend consideration of the Nordic nations for a while in order to devote some space to a review of the ancient Keltic culture, migrations, and conquests throughout central and southern Europe. These people later were overrun by Nordic nations from central Europe and since then have amalgamated largely with them; so that they and ancient Mediterranean divisions of the Aryan race, blond and brunet of complexion respectively, now are underlying strains of all such regions overrun by the invaders from the north.

———————————

CHAPTER IV.

EUROPEAN CONQUESTS BY KELTS AND TURANIANS

1. *Keltic Culture in Central Europe.* When the second horde[1] of Kelts (Kelto-Slavs), the Battle-Ax Folks, migrated from the Pamirs around the south of the Caspian Sea, crossed the Caucasus region,[2] and invaded the Danube basin, spreading over western Europe about 2300 B.C., they brought with them the knowledge of bronze metalwork and were armed with bronze weapons. They also domesticated a sheep descended from stock that was indigenous to the Pamirs. They were a large-bodied people short legged, of medial stature and blond complexion, and brachycephalous. They are generally phlegmatic in temperament. The center of their highest cultural development in Europe was in ancient Noricum, which comprised chiefly present Austria (except Lower Austria) and southeastern Bavaria. On their southwest was Italy, populated by Ligurians, Sicans, Siculians, and others of the Mediterranean race. On the southeast was Illyria, corresponding roughly with the present Yugoslavia and Albania, populated in the south by Pelasgians and in the north by Paleo-Kelts. Westward these Kelts spread down the Rhine and across northern Switzerland and central France as far as the Atlantic Ocean. By 2200 B.C. they had reached southern Sweden and by 1800 B.C. the British Isles.

Over the Balkan region as far south as Thessaly a cultural modification at about 2300 B.C. has been noticed.

---

1 As already shown, the first invasion of central Europe by Kelts from the Pamirs up the Danube River basin occurred about 8000 B.C., whence they ultimately spread both northward and southward.

2 V. Gordon Childe, *op.cit.*, p. 118.

It was the product of these brachycephalic, round-barrow, bronze-using people. After several centuries, they discovered at Noreia (now Neumarkt), in Noricum, the most famous iron ore deposit of antiquity, which was opened for mining. The ore was practically smelted by nature and the metal produced required no tempering. There they developed iron implements, which superseded bronze, first for ornamentation, next for edge-cutting instruments, and finally for practically all purposes and in all forms. Elsewhere in Europe, as these implements passed from tribe to tribe, a sudden transition from bronze to iron occurred; but such had not been the case in Noricum, where this transition from the Bronze Age through to the fully-developed Iron Age was the result of the creative genius of these people before others were extended the benefit. Subsequently, they developed iron ore deposits in the region of the Erzgebirge, which separate Saxony from Bohemia. Gold and salt also were mined in Noricum, but silver was unknown. Strabo alludes to the iron and gold mines.[3]

At Hallstatt, a short distance from Noreia, a marvelous collection of Keltic products has been unearthed from numerous graves. The custom followed in disposing of the dead was partly inhumation and partly cremation. In the graves were discovered objects of form and decoration like those since found throughout Illyria, Epirus, northern Italy, France, Spain, and Britain. They include swords, daggers, spears, javelins, axes, helmets, bosses and plates of shields and hauberks, brooches, various forms of jewelry, and amber and glass beads. Many of the objects are decorated with animal and geometric designs. A few of the weapons are of bronze but most of them are of iron. The swords are leaf-shaped, with blunt points for cutting and not for thrusting. The hilts differ essentially from those of the Bronze Age, being shaped like a crescent for grasping the blade and having large pommels.

---

3 Strabo iv.6.12, v.1.8. See *Ency. Brit.*, 13th Ed., vol. 19, page 748, under Noricum.

Noric iron and Noric swords were highly prized and dreaded by the Romans.[4]

Brooches of various types have been found in great numbers at Hallstatt. They are of the same types that have been found down the Balkan region and in Greece. These objects, of date as early as 1350 B.C., have been found in the lower town of Mykenae; consequently, they were invented in Noricum long before that time.

Cattle-breeding was practised by the inhabitants of Noricum to a greater extent than general agriculture. Their culture was at the same stage as that of the kindred Achaeans who invaded Greece. In fact, Keltic products passed from tribe to tribe up and down the Danube valley, down the Elbe and Rhine valleys, and to France and elsewhere in Europe.[5] Thus, the Kelts exercised supremacy over the ruder Suebians on their north. Very early, these Kelts spread over Illyria and the rest of the Balkan area, prior to the times that some of the tribes, known later as the Hellenes, of Macedonia and Thessaly, penetrated Greece. During succeeding centuries, a constant struggle persisted between the Pelasgians and the Kelts in Macedonia, until amalgamation occurred, and subsequently between the latter and Kelts from Illyria. Kelts from Illyrian territory once attacked the Temple of Delphi.[6] Around the northerly head of the Adriatic Sea, the Kelts of Noricum began early to overrun Italy.

When the Suebians invaded and settled in western Europe, south of the Baltic Sea, about 1600 B.C., and victorious Kimmerians reached the lower Danube River, the Keltic tribes in their pathway north of the Carpathian Mountains were driven westward toward the Rhine valley, southward into the highlands, and into the valleys of the Danubian basin inhabited by other Keltic tribes. This displacement stirred the inhabitants of the invaded regions and subsequently caused an exodus of population to the countries south of the Balkan and Alpine mountain

---

4 Pliny, *Hist. Nat.* xxxiv.145; Horace, *Epod.*, 17.71.
5 V. Gordon Childe, *op.cit.*, p. 178.
6 Herodotus ix.43.

ranges. With certain exceptions, the Keltic strain predominates in those regions today.

In addition to the Keltic invaders of Anatolia about 1450-1425 B.C. and the Hellenes, who from about 1425 B.C. began their conquest of northern Greece, other tribes, such as the *Umbri,* began about the same time to overrun Italy along with the Kelts from Noricum. In Italy they found kindred Paleo-Kelts who had arrived there from the north and northeast many centuries earlier.

A later phase of the Keltic Iron Age is that represented by the La Tené cultural period of from c. 500 B.C. to A.D. 100. Typical objects were found at La Tené, the site of a lake dwelling at the northerly end of Lake Neuchâtel, Switzerland. They consist mostly of iron, such as swords, spear-heads, axes, scythes, and knives, and agree with the description of the weapons of the southern Kelts (in Italy) given by Diodorus Siculus (who flourished c. 60-21 B.C.). There also are brooches, bronze kettles, torques, small bronze ear-rings with little glass pearls of various colors, belt-hooks and pins for fastening articles of clothing, etc. This culture made its way across France to Britain, where it is called the Late Keltic. Thus, while the earlier Kelts invaded Italy from Noricum and Illyria, the later Kelts did so from eastern Gaul via northwestern Italy, because of disturbances in Gaul.

The Keltic Greeks, originally mountain people, were not inherently seafaring and it required several centuries before they spread far from the shores of their country. However, the nature of the Grecian region and the commercial intercourse that prevailed between the islands of the Aegean Sea and the mainland were conducive to their development as seafarers. The Phocaeans were the earliest Greeks to take long sea voyages.[7] They discovered (for the Greeks) the Adriatic and Tyrrhenian Seas and Iberia, although the Anatolian Leleges, the Kretans, and the Phoenicians, for centuries or millennia before, had carried on regular commercial relations through the Mediterranean Sea and up the Atlantic Ocean as far as the

7 *Ibid.,* i.163.

British Isles and Scandinavia. From the 9th century B.C., skilled Ionian Greek artists and workmen migrated in large numbers to Etruria.[8] In 600 B.C. the Phocaeans defeated the Carthaginians and established Marseille, in southern France.[9]

The Keltic language and customs were so long dominant all over Europe, particularly in the uplands and mountainous regions of central Europe and over all France as far as the Atlantic, that barbaric nations coming among the Kelts could not escape the imposition of this civilization, including the Gaulic language. This culture extended from the Dniester River and the Dobrudja at the Black Sea westward along the uplands to the Atlantic coast of Gaul and northwestward to Westphalia.[10] When conquering Italy, the Keltic invaders largely adopted the language and customs of the Mediterranean peoples whose territory they had overrun, which is what also happened later to Nordic invaders of Keltic territory in northern Gaul. These Nordic invaders were chiefly the later so-called *Goidelic* and *Skolotic* (*Britonic*) Kimmerians from the Ukraine, who reached western Europe during the 7th and 4th centuries B.C. respectively and absorbed and transmitted the Keltic language and customs of Gaul to the British Isles. It is not strange, therefore, that the barbaric part of the Latin dialect should coincide so closely with the Goidelic dialect of the Irish, even though the two peoples are different subracially. Few dialectal differences are observable in what little is known of the ancient continental Gaulic or Keltic. This primitive Keltic culture deserves further research.

The Goidelic dialect is that appropriated from the Kelts of Gaul by the earlier Kimmerians (Irish, Manx, and highland Scots) in modification of their own language when they invaded Gaul about 632 B.C., which was the same speech as that used originally by the Cimbric (Kimmeric) Danes. The Britonic dialect of the Skolotic

---

8 Pliny, *Hist. Nat.* xxxv.12,43.
9 Thucydides i.13.
10 While it must be designated as Keltic culture because the Kelts wholly domin-

Kimmerians is that of the later *Scotti* or Milesians of Ireland, the northern Welsh and Cumbrians, the southern Scots, and the Britons of southeastern Scotland, southern Wales, Cornwall, Devon, and other parts of England, and of Brittany. It represents an analogous appropriation by the second horde of these Nordics who invaded northern Gaul c. 340 B.C. The *Skoloti* there found descendants of their predecessors of the same nation, those who had not retired south of the Seine after their arrival nearly three centuries earlier. Thus, the Keltic influence on them was not as strong as it had been on the Goidels and they retained more of their original speech than the earlier division did, which explains the difference between the Goidelic and Britonic dialects. The Gaulic language of the continental Kelts is particularly notable in having preserved the final vowels much longer than the Goidelic and Britonic dialects did.

The continuation of the Keltic culture of central Europe is evidenced by Julius Caesar's references to it. An outstanding Kelt himself, he said that there was little difference beween the speech and customs of the Gauls and of the Britons in his day.[11] Despite the relatively advanced status of the Belgae, Caesar described them as the bravest people of all Gaul because they were the farthest from the *civilization and refinement* of Roman Gaul.[12] Again, Divitiacus, the Aeduan king and Druidic high-priest, a Kelt, complained to Caesar[13] that a large force of wild and savage Germans (Belgae or Franks) had invaded the territory of his nation after Ariovistus and his earlier German army (mainly Suebic Allemanni) "had become enamored of the lands and the *refinement and abundance* of the Gauls" and that the *habits of living* of the

---

ated that portion of Europe, it must be borne in mind that in their absorption of the Mediterranean peoples who ventured north of the Balkan and Alps ranges they may have appropriated whatever elements of the Mediterranean culture attracted them.

11 *Encyclopaedia Britannica*, 13th Ed., vol. 5, pp. 612-613, by Edmund C. Quiggin; Julius Caesar, *Gallic War*, v.14.

12 Caesar, *Gallic War*, i.1.

13 *Ibid.*, i.31.

"Germans" were not comparable with those of the Gauls. The cultural leaders of the Kelts were the Bards, the Vates, and the Druids.[14] In fact, the great order of Druids seems to have originated among the Keltic people[15] and was developed by them in the lower Danube valley, whence it spread early to western Europe. There it was adopted from the Keltic Gauls by the Goidelic and Skolotic Kimmerians and transmitted to Britain and Ireland, where it flourished.

An evidence of a more or less common Keltic culture throughout the entire length of Europe is the similarity of customs that prevailed before the Christian era between the Kelts of Lacedemonia and those of Lusitania (northern Portugal) in Iberia.[16] This widespread prevalence of ancient Keltic culture no longer is seriously questioned.[17] The Keltic and Mediterranean subraces are the chief underlying strains of most of the European nations today, the major exceptions being northwestern Germany, Danmark, Scandinavia, Netherlands, parts of France, and Britain, where their proportion is small.

---

2. *Keltic Conquest of Anatolia and Greece.* Prior to the appearance of the Thracian Achaeans, Aeolians, and other Kelts from the eastern Balkan mountains, the territory comprising Macedonia,[18] Epirus,[19] and the rest of Greece[20] and the Aegean Islands was populated by Pelasgians of the Mediterranean race.[21] Among the outstanding nations were the Argives, Athenians, Arcadians, Crestonians, Samathracians, Lesbians, Lemnians, Ionians, and

---

14 Strabo iv.4.4-5. The bards were the poets and singers (like the later minnesingers), the vates were the prophets (who foretold the future), and the druids were the priests (who performed their religious rites and sacrifices).
15 Caesar, *ibid.*, vi.13-21.
16 Strabo iii.3.3,6.
17 Thomas Nicholas, *Pedigree of the English People* (Longmans, Green, Reader & Co., London, 1874), pp. 403-423.
18 Aeschylus, *Suppl.* 261; Justin vii.1.
19 Strabo vii.7.10.
20 Herodotus viii.44.
21 Strabo v.2.4, xiii.3.3.

the inhabitants of the Cyclades generally.[22] In fact, the Athenians regarded themselves as the most ancient nation in Greece and the only Greeks who never had changed their abode.[23] The region later known as Hellas formerly was called Pelasgia.[24] Moreover, southern and central Greece for thousands of years was the objective of expeditions from Krete and other eastern Mediterranean nations.[25] It was the earlier civilization of the Kretans[26] that prevailed there at the time of the foremost Phrygian and Achaean incursions about 1500 B.C., after the Kimmerians had reached the Ukraine and began to press southward. In fact, the Minoan civilization in Greece reached its zenith about 1600 B.C., shortly before the Keltic invasions began.

In Anatolia, the Turanian Anatolians (or Leleges) had occupied its southerly half from the time that their Pre-Sumerian ancestors had expanded westward from Mesopotamia after about 7600 B.C. and after the Turanian Hittites had spread over Cappadocia about 2300 B.C. These Turkish invaders successively imposed their civilization on the indigenous Mediterranean population that they encountered in western Asia, so that the Anatolians were a partly mixed race,[27] although the Turanian influence dominated the entire region.

The Keltic overrunning of western Anatolia and Greece was caused by Kimmerian raids west of the Black Sea, as far south as the lower Danube valley, about 1425 B.C. Keltic tribes of that region were driven southward upon others in Thrace, forcing many to migrate across the Bosporus and the Hellespont and into Macedonia. While numerous tribes also were driven westward toward Illyria, there is very little indication that Keltic invasions of Greece proceeded from that region, although there were

---

22 Homer, *Iliad* ii.681,840, xvi.223; Herodotus i.57,146, ii.51, v.26, vi.137; vii. 94,95,161; Ephorus, Fr. 54; Strabo v.2.4.
23 Herodotus vii.161; Thucydides i.2.
24 Herodotus ii.56; Thucydides i.3.
25 Strabo vii.7.1-2.
26 Homer, *Odyssey* xix.
27 Strabo vii.7.2.

minor incursions into Epirus and nearby territory that had influence on Grecian history.[28] Ancient Illyria, which was west of Thrace, included roughly the present country of Yugoslavia, from the mountains to the Dalmatian coast of the Adriatic Sea. Thrace included Romania east of the Transylvanian Alps, Bulgaria, and eastern Greece, embracing the fertile grassland region on the lower Danube.[29] Thus, there was a great increase in the density of the Keltic population of both Thrace and Illyria, as proved by the large number of tribes in those regions named by ancient historians[30] and other writers. From early times, the encroachments of Kelts in the Balkan region had gradually forced the Pelasgians toward the south; so that subsequently, when the Kelts of Thrace repeatedly were pressed upon by Nordics from above the Dniester River, racial amalgamation greatly increased in the former region,[31] despite the emigration of various tribes or nations.

By about 1425 B.C., the great Keltic outpouring from Thrace into the northern parts of Greece and across the Bosporus and the Hellespont into Anatolia had begun.[32] In the latter region the Kelts drove the Pelasgi and Leleges eastward and southward.[33] The foremost Keltic tribe, known as the Phrygians, who branched from the Thracian tribe of the Bryges,[34] moved up the Sangarius River to the central plateau of Anatolia[35] as far as the Halys (Kizil) River, where they established the kingdom of Phrygia.[36] According to unvarying Greek tradition, the Phrygians were closely akin to tribes of Thrace and Macedonia, and their near relationship to the Hellenic stock is proved by all that is known of their language and art. This

---

28 Thucydides i.24; Strabo Fr. 11.
29 Strabo vii.7.1.
30 Herodotus v.3 and elsewhere; Strabo vii. Fr. 46; Thucydides ii.96; Pliny *Hist. Nat.* iv.11.
31 Strabo vii.3.2.
32 *Ibid.*, xii.4.4-7 and Fr. 11.
33 *Ibid.*, xiii.3.1-3, xiv. 1.6.
34 Herodotus vi.45, vii.73; Strabo vii.3.2.
35 *Ibid.*, Fr. 24.
36 J. L. Myres, *op.cit.*, pp. 208-9.

fact is recognized by almost every modern authority.[37] They were followed by the Carians, Maeonians (later called Lydians),[38] and Mysians,[39] who had a common origin among the Balkan Kelts[40] and who, upon crossing the Hellespont, spread in that sequence from south to north along the Aegean shores during the 14th century B.C.[41] As already stated,[42] the Trojan War (c. 1260 B.C.) actually represented the determining campaign in which the Keltic invaders broke the control of the Leleges over western Anatolia.[43]

The Aeolians came across next, about three generations before the Ionian emigration across the Aegean Sea[44] and about 60 years after the Trojan War. They established a numbers of centers.[45] Subsequently, other Keltic tribes from Thrace,[46] crossing the Bosporus, dispersed eastward along the southerly shores of the Black Sea, scattering the Mediterranean *Caucones*[47] and settling Bithynia,[48] Paphlagonia,[49] and Pontus as far east as modern Armenia.[50] During the succeeding century, the Phrygians on their south spread eastward across northern Cappadocia along the central Halys River as far as western Armenia,[51] where they broke the Hittite power and established colo-

---

37 See *Encyclopaedia Britannica*, 13th Ed., vol. 21, page 541, by Sir William Mitchell Ramsay.

38 Herodotus i.7.

39 According to Homer (*Odyssey* xi, quoted by Strabo i.1.10), the Mysians formerly dwelt on the banks of the Ister (Danube) River. They may have branched from the Maeones (Strabo xii.3.20, 8.13).

40 Herodotus i.171; Strabo xiv.2.23.

41 Strabo xiii.4.12.

42 *Ante;* see index.

43 Ruins of the palace erected at Troy by the victorious Keltic king have been discovered. As symbols of their power, these kings wielded heavy battle-axes of noble stone, richly carved and superbly polished, similar to those found across central Europe.

44 Strabo xiii.1.3-4.

45 Herodotus i.149.

46 Strabo vii.3.2.

47 *Ibid.*, viii.3.17, xii.3.5.

48 Herodotus i.28, vii.75; Xenophon, *Anabasis* vi.4.2, Strabo xii.3.3, 4-8.

49 Strabo xii.3.8.

50 *Ibid.*, xii.3.12.

51 Herodotus i.72.

nies.[52] This expansion pushed the Turanian Hittites eastward into Armenian highlands and the Leleges[53] southward into and beyond the Taurus Mountains[54] as far
as the coast and to some extent into Syria, Mesopotamia,
and Assyria.[55] Armenia then became the principal habitation of the Hittites, whereupon that nation for a long
time allied itself with the Assyrians, whose capital was
Nineveh, on the opposite side of the Tigris River from
the present city of Mosul. Many Hittites wandered as far
south as Canaan (Palestine), for certain of them are named
in the Bible, Uriah for example.

Thus, from the time of the first Kimmeric pressure
southward in Thrace about 1425 B.C. until their (Dorian)
invasion of the Peloponnesus about 1180 B.C., the Thracian Kelts conquered from the Mediterraneans, the Pre-
Sumerian Leleges, and the Hittites all of western Anatolia and that part north of the Taurus Mountains as far
east as the boundary of modern Armenia. Later they were
known as the *Leuco-Syrians* (or White Syrians), to distinguish them from the dark-complexioned Turanians on
their south and east.[56] Except for the Aegean shore that
was settled during this interval by the Pelasgic Ionians
from Greece and other areas occupied by scattered tribes
of subject Pelasgians, Caucones, and Leleges,[57] this part
of Anatolia remained in the possession of the Kelts down
through the Median, Persian, Macedonian, and Roman
reigns until all of Anatolia was conquered by the Seljuk
Turks from Turkistan in A.D. 1071. The latter and their
successors, the Osman Turks, have held it as a unit since
that time and the present Turkish nation is a product of
these heterogeneous races plus the Galatian Kimmerians.

In consequence of this early Keltic population of northern and western Anatolia, the Turanian racial prepon-

---

52 *Ibid.*, vii.73.
53 Strabo xiii.1.58-60.
54 Strabo xii.6.4-5, vii.1-3.
55 Herodotus vii.63; Scylax 80; Dionysus Periegetes, i.772; Arrian, Fr. 48;
Strabo and others.
56 Strabo xii.3.9, xvi. 1.2.
57 *Ibid.*, xii.8.4.

derance was confined chiefly to the region in and south of the Taurus Mountains and to Armenia, Syria, Mesopotamia, and Assyria south of Kurdistan (Kimmerian territory) and into the Zagros Mountains. The continuous intermingling in Palestine of the Hittites and various other people from Cappadocia, in consequence of the Keltic invasions, accelerated the merging of the Turanians with the Aryan Hamites in Syria and Palestine, chiefly the Phoenicians, Canaanites, Amorites, and others, thereby enlarging the scope of the *increasingly composite* Semitic race. The geographic name Cappadocia no longer was associated with the Hittites but with the Kelts who had taken that region, while the name Syrian became confined chiefly to the Turanians of Syria and the south and sometimes to their affinities, the Semites of Palestine.[58]

The Keltic conquest of most of Anatolia and the earlier Hamitic conquest of the Syrian and Palestinian coasts severed all direct contact of the Turanian and other peoples of Mesopotamia, Armenia, and Assyria with the Mediterranean region, in which their kin formerly had played a mighty part in commerce. This interposition of other peoples also had singular effect in the west. It effaced from the minds of the inhabitants of the Mediterranean basin nearly all knowledge concerning the shores of western Europe that the Anatolians and other Turanians had gained much earlier as mariners. This is shown by the confessions of Herodotus, Eratosthenes, Polybius, Diodorus, Strabo, and other writers of later times expressing their ignorance of the geography of that region. From Mediterranean mariners they had meager traditions about the Cassiterides (or Tin Islands, i.e., Britain), but, as stated by Polybius,[59] the part of Europe beyond Iberia bordering the exterior sea (the Atlantic) "had been but lately discovered and possessed by a race of barbarous

---

58 Linguistic research devoted to the inhabitants of the Mesopotamian and Anatolian regions necessarily must take into consideration this commingling of dialects of various Turanian nations and Aryan Hamites, Kelts, and Nordics.

59 Polybius iii.4.

people . . . . the reports concerning them ought to pass
for fable or invention." Diodorus,[60] speaking of the
Kelts of Gaul and their neighbors, the Kimmerians of
northern France, Belgium, and the Rhine valley, said
that they were so fierce and cruel that it was reported
that they ate men, as the people of Ireland (also Kimmerians) did. At the same time he regarded as Scythians
all those situated on lands east of the Kelts, i.e., the
Franks and Suebians, which proves that the ancient
Scythian people were simply the different branches of
the Nordic race, as already stated. Consequently in the
Aegean region, the great cultural influence of the Anatolians, which emanated from ancient Mesopotamia, had
terminated abruptly upon their subjection by the Kelts
by 1250 B.C.

The Keltic origin of the people of ancient Illyria is
proved by their numerous tribal names, and Keltic place-
names are quite common today in Dalmatia.[61] Because
of distance, the Kimmerians of the Ukraine had not
assailed them as they had the Keltic tribes in the lower
Danube basin, causing the latter to migrate southward,[62]
perhaps more in the nature of a slow infiltration than
of an organized invasion. All of these Kelts had passed
through the same stages of culture as the lake-dwellers
of Switzerland and other parts of the Alpine range had
from the Neolithic age onward. Having come from the
north, they had no knowledge of copper, the earliest
known metal, which long had been in use in Mesopotamia. It was their kin who had developed the outstanding Hallstatt culture and the primary La Tène culture.[63]

As early as 1400 B.C., Thracian Kelts under Eumolpus
had taken possession of Eleusis, in Attica, where they instituted the mysteries of Ceres,[64] but the first formidable
movement of Achaeans[65] into southern Greece occurred

---

60 Diodorus v.32.
61 *Encyclopaedia Britannica*, 13th Ed., vol. 14, p. 326, and authorities there named.
62 Strabo ix.5.6.
63 See footnote 61.
64 Strabo vii.7.1.
65 *Encyclopaedia Britannica*, 13th Ed., vol. 5, pp. 611-612, by W. Ridgeway.

about 1360 B.C.,[66] when under Pelops they overcame the Pelasgian tribes there[67] and appropriated the existing Mykenian civilization in large measure. They are said to have been Phrygians, but whether from Phrygia in Anatolia or from the parent stock of Bryges in Thrace is not certain; probably the latter. The Thracian element in Greek topographical nomenclature has been recognized. Pelops' name was then given to southern Greece. They were followed sometime later by others of the same race, such as the Aeolians, who settled principally in northern Greece.[68] Other Aeolian tribes crossed the Hellespont to Anatolia[69] and there inhabited the Troad after the Trojan war.[70] The Achaean conquest finally was extended as far south as the island of Krete.[71] Quoting other historians:

In the Homeric poems [1000 B.C.] the Achaeans are the master race in Greece; they are represented both in Homer and in all later traditions as having come into Greece about three generations before the Trojan war * * *. They found the land occupied by a people known by the ancients as Pelasgians, who continued down to classical times the main element in the population, even in the states under Achaean and later under Dorian rule. * * *

The Achaeans, on the other hand, were tall, fairhaired, and gray-eyed, * * *. They brought with them iron, which they used for their long swords and for their cutting instruments; * * *. The Achaeans, or Hellenes, as they were later termed, were on this hypothesis one of the fair-haired tribes of upper Europe known to the ancients as *Keltoi,* who from time to

---

66 About three generations before the Trojan War. The author of the life of Homer and also Herodotus and Thucydides placed the Trojan War at about 1260 B.C., 80 years earlier than given by Eratosthenes. Herodotus (ii.145) has it about 800 years prior to his time.

67 Thucydides i.9; Strabo vii.7.1, viii.5.5.

68 Strabo x.1.8, xiii.3.2-6.

69 Herodotus v.122.

70 Strabo xiii.3.2-4.

71 Herodotus vii.171.

time have pressed down over the Alps into the southern lands, * * *. The culture of the Homeric Achaeans corresponds to a large extent with that of the early Iron Age of the upper Danube (*Hallstatt*) and to the early Iron Age of upper Italy (*Villanova*).[72]

The Homeric heroes are Achaeans, a fair-haired Keltic race, whose home was in the Danube valley, where they had learned the use of iron. In Greece they are newcomers, * * * they have acquired the language of their subjects in the course of a few generations. The Homeric civilization is thus Achaean, i.e., it is Pelasgian (Mykenian) civilization appropriated by a ruder race; but the Homeric culture is far inferior to the Mykenean.[73]

When the Thessalians, a Keltic tribe from Illyria that had settled in Epirus, migrated southeastward in Greece about 60 years after the Trojan War and took possession of the region that bears their name, they drove out the Keltic Boeotians and other Aeolic tribes, which then moved farther south.[74]

The fact that this ascendancy of the Kelts in Greece was gained gradually by the intrusion of successive tribes from the northeast,[75] and not by a sudden military conquest, is attributable to the derangement of the Kelts

---

72 *Encyclopaedia Britannica,* 13th Ed., vol. 1, pp. 141-142, by W. Ridgeway. In this connection an important fact appears, namely, that the Kelts of western Europe and the British Isles knew the use of bronze at this time but apparently not the use of iron, whereas their congeners at Hallstatt (Austria) were replacing bronze with iron. This seems to confirm Ridgeway's belief that the Kelts first developed the use of iron in the Hallstatt area, where there were rich ores, and caused its diffusion to Switzerland, France, Spain, Italy, Greece, and the Aegean area. It did not reach northwestern Europe until taken there by the Kimmeric invaders after 634 B.C., as later discussed. But it is probable that the Kelts learned the art of making and using iron implements and weapons from the Turanians of Anatolia, through whose influence its use extended to Egypt and the Aegean Sea.

73 *Ibid.,* vol. 12, p. 442, by James B. Bourchier, citing W. Ridgeway's *The Early Age of Greece.*

74 Herodotus vii.176.

75 Thucydides i.12.

south of the Danube by the invasion of that region by Kimmerians from the Ukraine, mainly the Treres on the lower Danube. As each tribe entered the country, there was no sharp conflict of race, or between a conquered and a conquering class, or the imposition of one type of culture on another and different type by military force. The Achaean age is an integral part of Grecian history. There seems to have been a regular transition from the Mykenean civilization to one resulting from the combination of that and the Keltic culture.

This conclusion is verified by the prominent status maintained throughout early history by the Pelasgic people of Attica and of Ionia. The Ionians, who are said to have been descendants of Athenians, were sent out as colonists to the southerly shore of the Corinthian Sea,[76] but this territory (Old Ionia, later Achaea[77]) they were compelled to yield to Achaeans expelled from southern Greece by the Dorians who invaded the Peloponnese about 1180 B.C.[78] In old Ionia the Achaeans developed a powerful democracy. While many Ionians remained behind as subjects,[79] the greater number sought an asylum among their kin in Attica, to which place other refugees had fled.[80] Many of these Ionians thus settled temporarily at Eleusis. Apparently, other displaced Ionians settled in Cynuria,[81] which comprised a single valley (that of *Luku*) and the adjoining hills between Sparta and Argos, on the easterly coast of the Peloponnese.

The Grecian Kelts, later known as the Hellenes,[82] were fair-haired in comparison with the brunet Pelasgians. They were of medial height, stockily built, and had gray or blue eyes. Anthropological research, particularly by such craniologists as De Ujfalvy, has demonstrated that they were brachycephalous in type. The Aegean islanders were

---

76 Herodotus vii.94, viii.73.
77 Strabo viii.7.1.
78 Polybius ii.41, iv.1; Strabo viii.7.1.
79 Herodotus viii.73.
80 Strabo ix.1.7.
81 Herodotus viii.73.
82 Strabo ix.5.6.

more brachycephalolus than the inhabitants of the main land, being of purer Achaean descent.[83] According to Stephanos, the ideal heads of the classic statuary are brachycephalous in proportions and not dolichocephalous, as the native Pelasgians were. The dolichocephalic skulls found represent mainly the latter race. The Achaean Greeks recognized a racial affinity between themselves and the Kelts of Illyria, Thrace, and Anatolia.

An abrupt change in Greek civilization occurred, however, upon the Doric invasion of Greece under the Heracleidae about 1180 B.C.[84] The Dorians were Nordic Aryans, a division of the Treres tribe of the Kimmerian nation of the Ukraine, who inhabited the northerly shore of the lower Danube. As they entered Greece, they settled first at Doris in the north,[85] but subsequently resumed their invasions southward. The effect of this superimposition of the less-advanced barbarian culture on Grecian civilization was quite marked. It is discussed in other works. Known also as the Lacedemonians, the Dorians gained the dominance of most of the Peloponnese, then inhabited by Pelasgians and Achaeans, and established their capital at Sparta. Later they founded numerous colonies throughout Greece and elsewhere.[86] As the Achaeans had done earlier, they extended their conquests to various islands in the Aegean Sea and to Krete. Thus, Krete acquired a decidedly mixed racial and cultural aspect.[87] It is due to the Doric influence that the Grecian language is said to have more in common with Pahlavi and Sanskrit than it has with Latin.

About 1078 B.C. another division of Kimmeric Treres from the lower Danube crossed the Hellespont and overran western Anatolia, but they returned later.[88] During all of this time there was intermittent infiltration of other

---

83 *Ency. Brit.*, 13th Ed., vol. 12, page 442, by James B. Bourchier, citing W. Ridgeway's *The Early Age of Greece*.
84 Strabo viii.6.10, ix.4.10. 80th year after the Trojan War. Thucydides i.12.
85 Thucydides iii.92.
86 *Ibid.*, vi.80, vii.57,58; also Strabo viii.8.5, citing Ephorus.
87 Strabo x.4.6-18.
88 Strabo xiv.1.40.

Kelts from Illyria and Thrace to north Grecian territory and to Aeolian territory on both sides of the Hellespont,[89] since the Aeolians had supplanted the Dorians in the region formerly occupied by them in northern Greece.

About 1069 B.C., during the reign of Codrus, the last Athenian king, who was a son of Melanthus, former king of Messenia, the Dorians attempted an invasion of Attica, but were repulsed.[90] Attica lost only Megara, where Dorians subsequently settled. Approximately 27 years after this attack, when Medon was archon at Athens, the surplus population of Attica was assembled and sent out under the leadership of Androclus, a son of Codrus, to colonize the Aegean shores of Anatolia, in Lydia and Caria.[91] There they established 12 cities, corresponding with the number that the Ionians had occupied in old Ionia,[92] and this region subsequently became known as the Ionia of history.[93] The names of the cities thus established were Phocaea, Erythrae, Clazomenae, Teos, Lebedos, Colophen, Ephesus, Priene, Myus, and Miletus on the mainland and Samos and Chios on neighboring islands.

The Kimmerian nation in the Ukraine was subjected to increasing pressure by the next Nordic nation behind them, the Getae (later Goths), and a number of other armies of the Treres moved southward during the next four centuries and overran and ravaged parts of western Anatolia, chiefly Lydia. The last such invasion occurred about 640 B.C. The absence of this army from the north must have been detected by the Getae, who suddenly attacked the Kimmerians in 635 and defeated and scattered them the next year, making many (the *Skoloti*) their subjects and driving many westward and others over the Caucasus Mountains and southwestward across Transylvania. The last-stated band dislodged the Keltic

89 *Ibid.*, vii.3.2.
90 *Ibid.*, ix.1.7.
91 *Ibid.*, xiv.1.3.
92 Herodotus i.145-146.
93 Pausanias, *Desc. of Greece*, vii.2.1-2; Strabo viii.7.1, xiv.1.3.

Trausi (probably a tribe of the *Agathyrsi* of Transylvania),[94] *Edoni, Dolonci, Odrysae,* and other tribes, which then moved eastward and occupied central Thrace as far as the Black Sea.[95]

The Getae thereupon supplanted the Kimmerian nation north of the Black Sea in Ukrainia. This contact of the Kelts of east-central Thrace with the Getae is referred to by Herodotus[96] when he speaks of the people north of the lower Danube as inhabiting a vast and almost endless space. He also refers to the *Sigynae* (of coastal Illyria — the northerly Dalmation coast), *who in dress resembled the Medes and called themselves a colony of Medes* (and who, in turn, were a branch of the Kimmerian nation 900 years earlier, when it lived north of the Black Sea). The Sigynae thus were Kimmerians and formerly had been subjects of the Getae.[97] A portion of them earlier on the lower Danube were the progenitors of the Lithuanians, Latvians, and Old Prussians.[97] Herodotus says[98] that the Keltic Thracians *had different manners* from the Getae and others. It is to these Getae of northern Thrace that he refers as "the bravest and the most upright" people, who pretended to immortality, believing that when anyone of them died he was removed to the presence of their god Zamolxis.[99]

The primitive Mykenean culture of the Pelasgian Greeks was not destroyed but was utilized by the Achaeans when they came down from Macedonia and Thrace upon the conquest of Ukrainia by the Kimmerians from the Suebians about 1600 B.C. It follows that the later glorious Grecian civilization was an outgrowth chiefly of the blending of the culture of the civilized Pelasgians and that of the barbarous Kelts with the basic Mykenean culture. It was leavened further by the energetic Nordic Dorians

---

94 Herodotus iv.125.
95 *Ibid.*, iv.74,93,100, v.3,4,124, vi.34; Xenophon, *Anabasis* vii.2,32, 3.16; Strabo vii.3.11-14.
96 Herodotus v.3,9.
97 Treated later in a separate section.
98 Herodotus v.3.
99 *Ibid.*, iv.93,94, v.3. How like modern formal Christianity!

prior to Homer's time.[100] But these Kimmerians were not well assimilated during the dark period of Grecian history and the subsequent flowering of Grecian civilization in the 8th and 7th centuries B.C. and they ultimately humbled Athens in war. This left Greece weakened and a prey in part to Macedonia and later wholly to Rome in 146 B.C.

During the great Slavic migration westward and southward at the close of the 8th century A.D., the ancient population of Greece suffered a widespread racial blending and the Keltic-type Greeks of modern times are said to be largely Byzantinized Slavs.[101] However, some writers contend that the Slavic infusion was not as great as sometimes stated, which probably is correct. The Slavs were similar in physique and originally were a division of the Kelts when they came down from the Pamirs and overran Europe; hence, they were remote kin of the Keltic Greeks.

In reviewing the monumental contributions of the Greeks to world culture, a degree of caution is necessary. Herodotus,[102] with marked candor and fairness and on better information than that possessed by many other ancient writers, asserts that the Greeks borrowed their early lessons of philosophy and science from the Egyptians. Clemens says repeatedly[103] that "the Greeks stole their philosophy from the barbarian" (or foreigner), and he observes that Plato did not deny its origin.[104] The same is said by Diodorus, Plutarch,[105] Philo, and other ancient writers, some of whom censured the Greeks for their vanity and disregard of truth; for it was not agreeable to the Greeks to admit their obligations to foreigners and their vanity led them to attribute everything, even the words of foreign languages, to a Grecian origin. Even the Iliad is said to have originated in an epic poem of

---

100 *Ibid.*, i.58.
101 *Ency. Brit.*, 13th Ed., vol. 12, p. 429, by James D. Bourchier.
102 Herodotus ii.123 and elsewhere.
103 Clemens, *Strom.* i.303, ii.358, vi.612, and elsewhere.
104 *Ibid.*, i.355.
105 Plutarch, *De Is.* s.10.

India written centuries before Homer was born. It was similar with respect to religion, much of the ancient Grecian mythology having come from Babylonia or Egypt along with other culture transmitted by Anatolians or Phoenicians. Iamblichus[106] says that "the search after the truth is too troublesome for the Greeks." Even Pythagoras is supposed to have been among the later writers who had utilized foreign ideas.[107] But this subject is beyond the scope of the present work.

———————

3. *Keltic Conquest of Italy.* As already shown, Italy originally was populated by the Mediterranean race. The principal tribes, from north to south, were the *Ligurians, Sicans,*[108] *Siculians,*[108] *Oenotrians, Morgetes,* and others. The Siculi formerly lived in central Italy, east and north of the present city of Rome.[109]

On the occasion of the Neo-Keltic (Kelto-Slavic) invasion of central Europe about 2300 B.C., at the beginning of the Early Bronze Age, Alpine (or Paleo-Keltic) lake-dwellers from Switzerland moved into Lombardy. During the later Bronze Age, about 1600 B.C., numerous other Alpine invaders (Neo-Kelts) arrived. They were driven southward by the contemporaneous Nordic Suebian invasion of Europe south of the Baltic Sea and east of the Elbe and upper Weser Rivers, which forced the Keltic peoples of that area southwestward into the Ardennes and Gaul and to the Danube, the upper Rhine, and other river courses near their cultural center at Hallstatt, Nori-

———————

106 Iamblichus, *De Myst.* vii.5.
107 In this connection, see George Rawlinson's appendix to Book ii.c.7 of his translation of Herodotus' history, relating to the intellectual contacts of the ancient Greeks with the higher civilization of the Egyptians and Babylonians. See also his footnote 5 to iii.148.
108 Virgil, *Aeneid* vii.795, viii.328, xi.317 and Servius' note. The Sicani are said to have been Iberians who were driven from the coastal region east of the Rhone River by the Ligurians.
109 Servius' ad. *Aeneid* viii.795; Dionysus Halicarnassus, *Roman Antiq.* 1.9.22; Thucydides vi.2.

cum. They were largely free in the mountain valleys from attacks from the north, but the subsequent congestion of population and resultant strife in those regions had the effect of stimulating Keltic invasions farther south.

In the 15th century B.C. still other Keltic intruders, the *Umbri* from Illyria, entered the Po River valley and pushed earlier arrivals ahead of them down the eastern coast[110] and the Apennines. In consequence, the Siculians overran the southerly half of the peninsula during the early part of the 14th century B.C. During the first half of the 13th century B.C., further southward pressure was exerted on the people in central Italy as well as on the Latins and Siculians by the invasion of northern Italy by Turanian Leleges from Lydia, in Anatolia,[111] — the *Etruscans* under the leadership of Tyrrhenus — who settled in the valley of the Po River, driving the Umbri to central Italy.[112] These intruders were descendants of the Pre-Sumerian inhabitants of western Anatolia, who had been vanquished by Keltic invaders (Lydians) from Thrace after 1425 B.C. They either emigrated to escape oppression or were expelled by the Lydians. Their language and customs were not Aryan but bore definite relation to those of Turanian Anatolia. In fact, the name "Etruscan" or "Tusci" seems to be an abbreviation of Tursci or Turski (Turki?). Later, other bands of Etruscans came from Lydia to those settlements.[113] They brought the highest-known civilization with them.

They were acquainted with letters, cultivated literature and physical science, had orders of priests, haruspices, and diviners, and preserved memorials of the periods of their history, connected with the revolutions of cycles, at the beginnings or ends of which the world was fated to undergo successive changes in its moral and physical state. They had a system of religious discipline and mythology

---

110 The skulls of the Latins and the Helvetians bear a very marked resemblance.
111 Tacitus, *Ann.* iv.55; Herodotus i.7,94; Strabo v.2.2.
112 Dion. Hal. 1.26; Plutarch, *Sulla,* 7; Plautus, *Cistellaria* 2.3.19; Varra, quoted by Censorinus c.17.6.
113 Thucydides iv.109; Herodotus i.57.

not less complicated and elaborate than the systems of the Indian Brahmans and the Egyptian priests. The remains of architecture, of sculpture, and of ornamental fabrics discovered in Etruria prove that there existed among its people a cultivated taste, a refinement of manners, and much of the splendor and luxury considered to be characteristic of a high state of civilization.

Only recently, archaeologists have discovered near Venice a few stone tablets left by the Etruscans, on which appear inscriptions in the style of modified pictures — a mode of writing used by the Leleges of Anatolia, which was closely related to the Assyrian. The alphabetical characters are said to be almost identical with Runic inscriptions used in Scandinavia, Germany, and Britain as late as the Roman conquest. Apparently, all the alphabets of the western world had their origin in the symbols developed by the descendants of the early Turanian conquerors of western Asia. A corresponding relation probably exists with respect to the alphabets of the eastern world.

Early in the 11th century B.C., in consequence of Kimmerian raids in the lower Danube valley, a disturbance was created among the Kelts along the central Danube and other Keltic invasions of Italy from northern Illyria and Noricum began. The *Safini* (the later Sabines), who were of the same cultural level as the Keltic Achaeans who earlier invaded Greece from the north,[114] moved down into the valley of the Po, driving the Etruscans southwestward over the Apennines to the region north of the Tiber River.[115] Etruria (the present Tuscany) took its name from the last-named people. South of the Etruscans, across the lower Tiber, were the *Latini* (who apparently were an amalgamation of primitive Siculi and Paleo-Kelts), while many of the Sicans, thus dislodged, emigrated to the present island of Sicily,[116] which they called

114 Strabo v.4.12.
115 *Ibid.*, v.1.10.
116 According to Thucydides (vi.2), the Sicanians were Iberians from the Sicanus River in Iberia, from which they had been driven by Ligurians. But, since the Ligurians inhabited northwestern Italy and southeastern France, he must have been in error in naming them as the impellers.

Sicania. The *Oscans* may have been Paleo-Kelts, the *Volsci* were a branch of the Umbri in central Italy, and the *Samnites* were later tribes of the Safini. They may have included many earlier peoples amalgamated with them. The province of Umbria east of Tuscany perpetuates the name of the Umbri. About 606 B.C., the *Messapians* were driven from the Dalmatian coast of Illyria by the Kimmeric *Sigynae* and invaded and conquered eastern central Italy. This conquest forced the Samnites southward along the Apennines with the most southerly Safini between them and the Umbri.[117] It also impelled many of the Siculi, who were akin to the Oenotri, to emigrate to the easterly part of Sicily. They drove the Sicans to the westerly and southerly parts of that island, to which they then gave their own name in lieu of Sicania.[118] A certain king of Oenotria was named Italus and the Oenotri adopted it as their national name, from which their country subsequently was called Italia; whence Italy derived her name. Ultimately, by about 400 B.C., the Samnites had gained all of Campania, Lucania, and Bruttium,[119] although in the meantime the Etruscans had extended their power into Campania, where a Tuscan League was formed.

The extent of this Keltic conquest is demonstrated by the cephalic index of the ancient people of the peninsula, which shows a preponderance of the Mediterranean race in the extreme south and of the broadheaded Kelts in the central and northern sections, with the influence of the later mesocephalic Ostrogoths (including the Lombards) reflected in Lombardy and adjacent sections.

The province of Liguria, in northwestern Italy, and the Ligurian Sea, which includes the Gulf of Genoa, took their names from the primitive Ligurians,[120] while the more southerly Tyrrhenian Sea perpetuates the name of the leader of the Etruscans. Ligurian tribes also inhabited the Maritime Alps on the present Franco-Italian border.[121]

---

117   See Strabo v.2.1.
118   Thucydides vi.2.
119   Strabo v.3.1, vi.1.2-4.
120   Diodorus iv.20-21, v.39, vi.8.
121   Strabo iv.6.1-6.

The manufacture by the Neo-Kelts at Hallstatt of effective iron weapons and other useful articles enabled them to overcome their southern opponents without great difficulty. These weapons and other objects passed from tribe to tribe up and down the river valleys, so that all of the Kelts had the benefit of their use. The Keltic invasion of Italy occurred between two and three centuries after their Achaean kinsmen had penetrated southern Greece and resulted from an analogous cause. The original territory of the Latini was confined to narrow areas on both sides of the Tiber River. They had a settlement on Palatine Hill. The Sabini subsequently invaded Latium and occupied Capitoline and Quirinal Hills. After considerable indecisive warfare, the uselessness of their strife appeared and they formed a perpetual alliance, thereby laying the foundation for the future greatness of Rome. The neighboring Etruscans on the north afterward overran the city and gained control, supplying the Tarquinian line of kings. But this merely strengthened the unity of the founding elements and the Tarquin kings were overthrown in 510 B.C. Nevertheless, the Etruscans long exercised influence on the development of the city, though the Etruscan culture was conspicuously modified by inroads of Ionian Greek culture. Subsequently, the Latini annexed and assimilated the rest of Italy, after which the glory of the vast achievements of the later Roman kingdom, republic, and empire followed.

Beginning only shortly after the Trojan War,[122] various Greek colonies were established in southern Italy. Insofar as they consisted of descendants of Achaeans or other Kelts, they tended to increase the brachycephalic Keltic strain in southern Italy, while Pelasgic colonists from the Aegean merely added to the indigenous population of the Mediterranean subrace there.

Following the Messapians, other Keltic tribes moved around the north of the Adriatic Sea into Italy in consequence of displacements along the Dalmatian coast by the arrival of the Sigynae from the lower Danube. They had been preceded farther south on that coast by the

---

122 Strabo vi.1.2.

Albanians only a short time earlier (about 633 B.C.). The most notable of these Keltic tribes was the *Veneti*[123] from northern Illyria. They took possession of the lower Po River valley, driving Sabines to the high region of central Italy.[124] The Veneti are said to have been Thracian Kelts from Paphlagonia, south of the Black Sea, who emigrated after the Trojan War toward the head of the Adriatic.[125] Their descendants founded and gave their name to the city of Venice. Their language was related to that of the Messapian and Sabellic dialects of eastern Italy, which had come from Illyria.[126] Hence, they must have had a common origin.

Later, early in the 6th century B.C., there was a distinctly different Keltic invasion, namely, that of the Gauls from eastern France and Switzerland, in consequence of the first Kimmerian invasion of northern Gaul in the previous century.[127] Chief among the tribes or parts of tribes thus passing to Italy were the *Aedui, Ambarri, Arverni, Aulerci, Bituriges,* and *Carnuti,* all under the leadership of the Bituriges. They came from that part of central Gaul extending from the lower Loire River to the Jura Mountains. They were joined by Ligurians (brunets) from southeastern Gaul, whose influence on the racial composition of northern Italy is plainly evident today. These invaders used the national name of *Insubri* and made Milan their metropolis. Again, perhaps due to other disturbances in northern Gaul, there was a later Keltic invasion of northern Italy, including *Boii* (originally from Bohemia) as well as others *(Cenomani, Salluvii,* and *Senones)* from Gaul, which resulted in the burning of the city of Rome in 390 B.C. In consequence of the Nordic invasions in the early Chris-

---

123 Herodotus, *Hist.* i.196.

124 *Ibid.,* v.9; see index.

125 Strabo xii.3.8,25.

126 The word *Sabelli* is said to denote "Little Sabines," which indicates an affinity with the Safini (Strabo v.4.12).

127 The so-called "Keltic unrest" of the 6th century B.C. was caused by congestion of Keltic tribes in eastern and southeastern Gaul and Switzerland in consequence of the first Kimmerian invasion of northern Gaul about 632 B.C., as more fully discussed later. *Ency. Brit.,* 13th Ed., vol. 5, page 612, by W. Ridgeway.

tian era, chiefly by the Gothic Lombards and Ostrogoths, the Roman empire disintegrated about A.D. 476 and the Italian peninsula never was reunited nationally thereafter until the overthrow of the papal states as late as 1870. The Latin language was supplanted in Italy under Gothic influence.

---

4. *Keltic Invasions of Iberia (Spain and Portugal).* The time of the earliest invasion of the Iberian peninsula from north of the Pyrenees range is not known, but it must have been long prior to 1500 B.C. The so-called "Keltic unrest" in western Europe about the beginning of the 6th century B.C. resulted from the dislodgment of many tribes of the upper Rhine basin and central Gaul by the great invasion of that region by the earliest wave of Kimmerians about 632 B.C. The movement of these Keltic tribes southward in Gaul created widespread disturbance among the Kelts of Switzerland and central Gaul, and some of the former and perhaps also of the latter soon crossed the Pyrenees.[128] The principal Keltic nation that thus invaded Iberia was the Biturges, who overran most of the central and western parts of the country. A part of this nation invaded Italy at the same time. The great confusion caused then is indicated by this sundering of the great Biturges nation. In the course of time, these Keltic invaders, like their predecessors, merged in large degree with the indigenous Mediterranean Iberians and increased the number of the composite people subsequently known in history as the Keltiberians,[129] especially in central Iberia. Later various other Keltic tribal names appeared in Iberian history.

The congestion of Keltic tribes in central Gaul also was the ultimate cause of the Gallic invasion of northern Italy in 390 B.C.[130] At that time there may have been other Keltic invasions of Iberia, for Xenophon, in speaking of

---

128 Strabo iii.4.5.
129 *Ibid.,* iii.4,5,12,13; Diodorus v.33-34.
130 Strabo v.2.3.

mercenaries who served with Dionysius of Syracuse in 368 B.C., says that "the ships brought Keltoi and Iberes", apparently from the Iberian peninsula. Again, about 340 B.C., when the second great wave of Kimmerians settled in the middle Rhine valley and northern Gaul, pushing the Goidelic Kimmerians across the Seine as far as the Loire River, there must have been further dislodgment of Keltic tribes in central Gaul. Some of these also may have reached Iberia.

Like the Kimmerians who invaded central and northern Gaul and the Kelts who invaded Greece and Italy, the Keltic hosts that overran Iberia largely adopted the langauge and customs of the indigenous inhabitants. The degree to which the native language and customs are modified by newcomers in such instances depends upon the relative numbers of the portions of the population, the cultural level of the native people, and various intangible elements.

———————

5. *Westward Advance of the Turanian Finns, Bolgarians, Hungarians, Huns, and Issedones.* The ancient habitation of the *Finns,* a peaceful Ugrian people, was the territory in central Asia north of the Sayan Mountains, between Lake Baikal and the headwaters of the Yenisei, Obi, and Irtish Rivers.[131] This territory, which Herodotus seems to have included in Europe, was rich in gold,[132] silver, and copper, as since has been proved. The Finns were producers of these metals, chiefly in the present provinces of Sayan and Kolyvan. They, too, were responsible for the numerous tumuli, with their gold and silver objects and copper utensils,[133] discovered in that region and westward across Siberia to their later habitation on the slopes of the Ural Mountains as far as the upper Volga River. None of these tumuli has been found in the

131 Herodotus iv.13,22-27.
132 *Ibid.,* iii.116.
133 William Tooke, *Archaeologia,* vol. 7, pages 223 *et seq.*

Ukraine, where the Nordic nations lived. Repeated reference to the metal-working culture of the *Tschudes* (Finns) in the Altai Mountains is found in their songs of the *Kalewala*. They used paintings or effigies of griffins[134] in an endeavor to scare raiders away from their mining operations, as the figures of griffins were common in the ornamentation of objects in Scythia.[135] But, whatever effect they may have had on superstitious Ugrians, they evidently failed to keep away the Mongolian Arimaspians (Huns), for, as related by Herodotus,[136] the latter took the gold by violence in disregard of the griffins.[137]

On their north were other unwarlike Ugrian tribes, the *Hyperboreans* of Herodotus,[138] whose territory extended northward to the (Arctic) sea and who, of all the nations of this region, were not continually engaged in war with their neighbors. They were the ancestors of the present Lapps, Samoyeds, and related peoples along the Arctic Circle.[139]

On their south, in the valleys lying in and between the Sayan and Altai Mountains, lived the Mongolian tribe later known as the *Huns,* who then were emerging upon the foothills of Semipalatinsk. They were the aforesaid *Arimaspians* of Herodotus,[140] a hardy and warlike people who took the gold of the Finns. Regarding these and other peoples of this region, Herodotus[141] relied chiefly on the facts in the poem *Arimaspeia* written by Aristeas, an eminent Grecian born about 600 B.C.[142] of a noble family

---

134 Herodotus iii.116; iv.27.

135 *Ibid.,* iv.79. See also Dubois, 4e Série, pls. 11,20,22,24,25.

136 Herodotus iii.116; iv.27.

137 It was these attacks of the Huns on the Finns that resulted in the migration of the latter to the central Ural region several decades prior to the time of Aristeas, and reports thereof were "received by the Scythians from the Issedonians and by them passed to us Greeks." Herodotus iv.27.

138 Herodotus iv.13; Pliny iv.12.

139 V. Gordon Childe, *The Aryans,* page 178.

140 Herodotus iv.13-17,27.

141 *Ibid.,* iv.13-16. Callimachus refers to the "yellow Arimaspians" in *The Hymn to Delos.*

142 Herodotus (iv.15) names an earlier date for Aristeas, while dates as late as 580 B.C. have been assigned to him. Since the last part of the 8th and the early part of the 7th centuries B.C. was a period of great activity in the establishment of Greek colonies along the Black Sea, it must have been during this time that Aristeas wrote.

of Proconnesus (now Marmora Island), a colony of Miletus in the Propontis (present Sea of Marmora). He lived at the time of King Cyrus of Persia and King Croesus of Lydia. His poem also was known to Pliny and Aulus Gellius. Upon separation of the facts and the fables of this poem, the statements of fact used here are found to agree with similar writings of others and with later historical data.

Apparently as early as 1500 B.C. or before, certain Turkic tribes from Issedon (Eastern Turkistan) had moved around the easterly end of the Tien Shan and then northwestward through Zungaria to the plains of Semipalatinsk above the ridge north of Lake Balkhash. This course enabled them to avoid conflict with the Nordic tribes in Geté,[143] but it took them into territory inhabited by less warlike Ugrian peoples. They ultimately amalgamated with those inhabitants, producing the composite peoples known to later history as the Bolgarians and the Magyars (or Hungarians).[144] These two nations were the *Iyrcae* and the *Argippei* of Herodotus.[145].[146] They lived then east of the foot of the Ural Mountains and west of the Altai Mountains in Semipalatinsk respectively.[147] The Argippei were reported to be a mixed nation that used seven languages,[148] doubtless because of alliances with

143 The foothill and mountain country between Lake Balkhash and the Kashgarian passes, between Western and Eastern Turkistan, as already described.

144 A. H. Keane, *op.cit.*, page 319, quoting J. R. Aspelin; J. C. Prichard, *op.cit.*, vol. 3, pages 324-339. The above stated racial amalgamation receives confirmation in the recently found manuscript of the Szeklers, Magyar mountaineers of Transylvania, who are supposed to be the purest representatives of that race. This mysterious writing, in old Runic characters, is related both to Turkish writing and to Ugrian writing found in Siberian caves. It has been studied by the Hungarian National Museum at Budapest. It reads from right to left, like the Hebrew, which had Kassite (Turkic) origin in central Asia. Further confirmation appears in a recent tendency of some Hungarians to turn from Christianity to a revival from legend of the recognition of the Turanian war god Hadur, worshipped by the ancient Magyars,—a stern god whose temple is the whole outdoors and who demands sacrifices and righteous living but is scornful of dogma and formalism. The meetings are usually held in a forest and grain and flowers are tossed into the flames to honor him.

145 Herodotus *Hist.*, iv.22.

146 *Ibid.*, iv.23.

147 *Ibid.*, iv.24,25.

148 *Ibid.*, iv.24.

various Ugrian tribes over which they held sway, since
we are told by Herodotus that their neighbors applied
to them in matters of private controversy and whoso-
ever sought an asylum among them was secure from
injury.[149]

Concerning the Issedones, the Greeks seem to have known
but few particulars. While retaining many of the crude
and harsh customs of other ancient peoples, they had
descended from the cultural leaders of primitive times
in the Tarim basin of Eastern Turkistan and had the
advantage of a remnant of the cumulative Turkic culture
developed successively by their earlier kin, the Pre-Sumerians, Sumerians, and Hittites. Their chief habitation
was still in Eastern Turkistan, at the end of trade routes
from Mesopotamia and western Scythia,[150] whence some
of the tribes had moved westward through the mountains
of Kashgaria to the foothills of Western Turkistan, as
noted by Herodotus, Pliny, and Ptolemy. Silk and other
articles from China were transported over the ancient
caravan routes through Kashgaria to the southwest and
the west.

All of the Nordic nations except the Massagetae and
the Sakae by this time had emigrated westward around
the northerly end of the Caspian Sea to Europe. These
two nations, still in Geté,[151] thus were bounded on the
north by the aforesaid Turanian nations above the Siberian
ridge and on the south by other Turanian Issedones inhabiting chiefly the mountains of Kashgaria.[152] The Issedones who still remained in the Tarim basin[153] were
known later as *Yugures* or *Oigurs* and their high cultural level was recognized by the Chinese many centuries
afterward.

Herodotus[154] took special notice of available informa-

---

149 *Ibid.*, iv.23.
150 *Ibid.*, iv.24.
151 Or slightly toward the south, between the Jaxartes and the Oxus Rivers.
152 Herodotus, *Hist.* i.201,204. A millennium later these Turanians overran and
vanquished the Scytho-Indian Empire established by the Massagetae (Tokhari) and
the Sakae — the last Nordic sovereignty in Asia.
153 *Ibid.*, i.201, iv. 13,25.
154 *Ibid.*, iv.26.

tion regarding national social customs of the Issedones, particularly their recognition of equitable principles, saying that they venerated the principles of justice and *allowed their women to enjoy equal authority with the men*. Obviously, well-developed legal principles could not have existed in a minor social environment, which demonstrates that the Issedones were the inheritors of an antecedent superior culture. Some of the practices attributed to the Issedones by Herodotus[155] may be treated as fabulous along with other fantastic items that appear from time to time in his history. Nonetheless, in this atmosphere of notable culture and refinement, we have convincing evidence of the origin of the legal principle of the Conjugal Community among the Pre-Sumerians or Sumerians, who were racial antecessors of the Issedones in the Tarim Basin. With other ideas and customs, it was taken by the Sumerians from the Tarim basin to Mesopotamia, whence it subsequently became incorporated in the Amorite code of King Hammurabi of Babylonia about 2100 B.C. In modified form, it ultimately reached western Europe and finally America chiefly through the Visigoths of Spain.[156]

That the Issedones believed the earth to be spherical is clear from statements by Herodotus, who disdained such beliefs. He asserts that[157] "The ocean, they say, commencing at the east flows all around the earth; this, however, they affirm without proving it." Again,[158] "They pretend, without the smallest reason or probability, that the ocean encompasses the earth". This is additional evidence of their advanced culture. The concept of the earth as a globe thus arose in central Asia long prior to the time of Pythagoras and was adopted by him. Herodotus' knowledge of the northern (Arctic) sea also was obtained from the Issedones through Aristeas' poem.[159] The extensive knowledge of the Issedones is further evidenced by

---

155 *Ibid.*, iv.26.
156 See Calvin Kephart, *Origin of the Conjugal Community (or Community Property Law) and Other Ancient Laws* (1938).
157 Herodotus iv.8.
158 *Ibid.*, iv.36.
159 *Ibid.*, iv.16.

Herodotus' reluctant report of their information regarding the Hyperboreans, who bordered on the Arctic,[160] when he says[161] that 'Neither the Scythians nor any of the neighboring people, *the Issedones alone expected,* have any knowledge of those Siberian Ugrian tribes, and indeed what they [the Issedones] say merits but little attention." The antecedent culture of the Oigurs, descendants of the Issedones, was known to the Chinese, to whom the Oigurs were known as the Eluths. They provided the Moguls with their learning and science, and their alphabet was so much better than that of the Chinese that it was used instead. They were the most learned people of the time, and Genghis Khan and his successors regularly employed them as secretaries.[162] This additional array of facts leaves no reasonable doubt that the origin of Neolithic civilization was among the Turkic tribes of antiquity, first in Tibet and later in Eastern and Western Turkistan.

The civilization of the Oigurs, or Eluths, continued on a relatively high level down to modern times. During a period of oppression early in the 13th century, they appealed to Genghis Khan for protection, which led to his invasion of Turkistan. The Chinese defeat of the Eluths in the 18th century is a prominent feature of the former's military history. All of Eastern Turkistan ultimately was subjugated and became a part of the Chinese empire in the 19th century. Since the civilization of the Turks in Eastern Turkistan antedated that of the Chinese, it is clear that the *Chinese as well as the people of the west trace their Neolithic cultural origin to a single fountainhead in this region.* Carrying this thought still further, since the earliest Turks migrated or were driven by the Nordics from the highlands of western Tibet down to the Tarim basin about 14,000 years ago, it is not unreasonable to infer that the rudiments of their culture evolved on that plateau and that its flowering

160 *Ibid.,* iv.13,36.
161 *Ibid.,* iv.32.
162 Petis de la Croix, *History of Jinghis Kan,* vol. 2, ch. 7.

occurred in the Tarim basin, which became the center of diffusion to the peoples of the west and of the east. M. Souciet, in his *Observations Mathematical, Astronomical, etc.*, page 146, quoted in Astley's *Collection* (iv. 416), says that the writing characters used by the Eluths were the same as those used in Tibet, where they were denominated Tangusian. While the Turks apparently descended from a tribe of the Min race that moved up the Yangtse River to eastern Tibet, the Mongolians, who now dominate the highland, originated in the Tungus division of that race who ascended the Hwang River in the northeast.

Incessant pressure by the Huns (Arimaspians) on the east forced the Finns by 650 B.C.[163] to migrate westward to the central Ural Mountains (as far as the Yama River), on both slopes of which range most of them lived for over 1350 years. However, one band, the later *Aestii* (Estonians), broke away and finally settled on the Baltic shore prior to the Christian era. This was the first intrusion of Turanians in European Russia. There along the Urals occurred the transition in Finnic culture from the Bronze Age through the so-called Tschudish Iron Age to and through the unbroken Finno-Ugrian Iron Age. The community of style of the painted and engraved figures found in the territory north of the Altai Mountains, in western Siberia, and in the central Ural region verifies this migration from a distinctly Asiatic and Siberian source.[164] The habitation of the Finns along the lower Irtish River from (Omsk to Tobolsk) and the central Ural Mountains[165] was the center of the ancient country of Jagog and Magog, according to the geographies of Edrisi, Ibn al Wardi, and other ancient writers, who placed it north of the Turkic peoples around the southern end of the Urals. The region is said to contain the remains of numerous cities and towns, ditches, ramparts, sepulchers, etc., which are sug-

163 Thus, the Finns actually had migrated from the slopes of the Sayan Mountains to the central Ural region long prior to the time of Herodotus (iv.14), as reported by Aristeas, on whom he relied.

164 H. F. Osborn, *op.cit.*, page 463.

165 Later that of the *Iyrcae* and of the *Argippei*.

gestive of the early culture that the Finns brought from the northern slopes of the Sayan Mountains. The many analogies in the primitive Aryan and Ural-Altaic (Finnic) languages arose from personal contact, since tribes of both races for many centuries inhabited the cold and bleak north from the upper reaches of the Irtish River to the Volga River, within short distances of each other through the forests.

During the same period (650-635 B.C.), the Huns gradually pressed the *Argippei* (Hungarians), known to Pliny[166] and Pomponius Mela[167] as the *Armiphaei*, upon the Iyrcae (Bolgarians), known to Pliny[168] and Mela[169] as the *Turcae*. This pressure also pushed the Getic nation westward upon the Kimmerians, who in part were driven from the Ukraine[170] while the remainder became subjects of the Getae when they took possession of that territory, as later recounted. Several centuries afterward, the Iyrcae were driven by the Argippei across the base of the Ural Mountains, when they expelled the Thyssagetae from and took possession of the western slope between the present towns of Orenburg and Ufa. There they established the kingdom of Great Bolgary. The Urals were known to Pliny and Mela as the Riphaean Mountains. The Thyssagetae (Alani) then moved southward along the Volga and Don Rivers, where they are known to have lived when the Huns approached the Ural River on their later invasion of the west about A.D. 372-375. The historic effect of the latter event is discussed in another place. The present Kalmucks of Mongolia, Siberia, and Russia undoubtedly descended from those Mongolians to which the ancient Huns belonged. Although of small stature, the Huns were noted as fearless horsemen and fierce warriors and precisely the same can be said of the Kalmucks. Another name for the Argippei, who moved to the territory vacated by the

---

166 Pliny vi.13.
167 Pomponius Mela, *De Situ Orbis* i.21.
168 Pliny vi.7.
169 Pomponius Mela, *ibid.*
170 Herodotus iv.13-16.

Iyrcae, may have been that of the *Ablai,* whose name was given to that part of the steppe southwest of the Irtish. Finally, as these people were pushed across the Ural range, the Iyrcae took possession of the region between the lower Volga and Don north of the Thyssagetae, where they reëstablished their Great Bolgarian kingdom, and the Argippei took the region between Orenburg and Ufa and established the Hungarian nation there. The latter people (the later *Magyars*) migrated to central Europe late in the 9th century of the Christian era, while the kingdom of Great Bolgary, even after a tribe broke away late in the 7th century and settled in central Europe, endured until the 13th century. Descendants of the latter Bolgars today are known as Tatars (dark-complexioned Khazars, who adopted Judaism about 730).

In addition to Herodotus' remarks regarding the Argippei or Hungarians, Pliny[171] and Mela[172] made certain interesting comments. They (called the Arimphaei) lived in the forests and used berries largely for food. They were scanty of beard. They were courteous in manner and were held inviolable by their neighbors, who left them and the people who took refuge with them undisturbed. Some of the historians of Alexander[173] highly commended the Abii (Ablai),[174] believed to have been another name for the Argippei, for their justice and forbearance, for which they seem to have been celebrated far and wide. They did not engage in warfare except when compelled to do so. They had commercial relations with the Greeks on the Black Sea.[175] This notice of both the prowess and the fairness of rule of this Turkic-Ugrian nation should be considered in the light of what has been said here several times regarding the evident high culture of the primitive people of Issedon, from whom the Magyars in part descended.

---

171 Pliny vi.13.
172 Pomponius Mela i.21.
173 Arrian iv; Curtius vii.61.
174 Homer *(Iliad,* xiii.v.6) names certain *Abian* Scythians as the best and justest people on the earth. Either he had wholly different people in mind or the fame of the Abii had reached Grecian circles as early as the 9th century B.C.
175 Herodotus iv.24.

Shortly after A.D. 700, because of the irruption of Turanian hordes (the Tatars and others) in western Siberia and eastern Russia, the Finns were dislodged from their above-described abode. The main body of the Finns (the Suomi) moved westward to their present territory of Karelia, Finland, and nearby regions. The Finnic nation originally included the Estonians and the Karelians. The Syryenians, Votiaks, Obi Ostiaks, Bashkirs, and Permiaks of Russia also are branches of the Finnic race. Generally, they all are rather blond because of their long life in the far north, but in some instances are conspicuous by their red hair, notably the Votiaks.[176] The Mordvinians and Cheremisses on the Volga River are related to the Bolgarians, and apparently the Voguls and the Ostiaks east of the Volga are related to the Hungarians.

In the 12th century, Finland was conquered by the Swedish King Eric IX, better known as Saint Eric. Christianity was brought to the Finns by Henry, Bishop of Uppsala, Sweden, now their special patron. Their country long was the scene of conflict between Sweden and Russia, and in 1809 the whole territory was absorbed in the Russian empire. During all of this long subjection, a code of "fundamental laws", sacred to the masses, survived and because of it Finland was accorded a Constitution when other parts of the Czar's realm were denied even the merest shadow of self-government. Throughout these centuries the Finns received a marked strain of Swedish blood and the Karelians and Estonians received a Slavic strain. The Estonians also have absorbed considerable Letto-Lithuanian (Kimmeric) blood. These differences of blood mixture among the various Finnic divisions as well as lack of contiguity have resulted in differences of national feeling and aspiration. In consequence of World War I and the Russian revolution, the Finnic republic was established

---

176 If, as reported, the Great Khan Tamerlane of the Mongol Empire during 1369-1405, was "tall, strong, fair-skinned, red-haired, broad-shouldered, and muscular," he must have been a descendant of the cross-breed of a Nordic Aryan and a Turanian Finno-Ugrian, whose family gained the ascendancey among the Mongols.

on June 17, 1919. In modern times the Finns have received consistent recognition for their hardiness, persistency, and good government. They possess an honored position in the family of modern nations. Unfortunately, they suffered a reduction of territory by the aggressive attitude of the Soviet Union toward the end of World War II.

In A.D. 679, a tribe of the Bolgars, fierce and barbarous horsemen, appeared on the banks of the Pruth, crossed the Danube, and, after subjugating the Slavic inhabitants of Moesia, advanced to the gates of Constantinople. They were ceded the province of Moesia and during the next two centuries gradually became submerged in the Slavic population. Like the Franks in Gaul, the Bolgars gave their name and political organization to the more civilized race that they conquered, but adopted its language, customs, and local institutions, so that now scarcely a trace of the Turkic-Ugrian element is to be found in the Bulgarian speech. This complete assimilation of a conquering race has many parallels in history.[177] The Hungarian nation invaded and settled in southern Europe in 895, likewise superimposing itself on a mixed population caused by the overrunning of that area by Slavs several centuries earlier. The name of Magyar used by them at that time may have been that of an ancient deified leader.

Concurrently with the above migrations, various Ugrian tribes moved westward across northern Siberia and Russia, as the condition of the tundra afforded them passage. Among them were the Lapps, Samoyeds, and others. The Ugrians appear to have shunned the open steppes and to have spread widely through the wooded country, especially on the banks of lakes and rivers. Physically, they vary considerably. Generally, they are of short or medial stature, somewhat squat and stockily built, mesocephalous or brachycephalous, with grayish or olive-colored skin, gray or blue eyes, light or red hair, and scanty beard. They are deficient in energy, slow, lethargic, taciturn, and melancholy,

---

177 *Encyclopaedia Britannica*, 13th Ed., vol. 4, p. 779, by James D. Bourchier.

but industrious, patient, and faithful. Conservative and
unprogressive, they are distrustful of strangers, but, when
this suspicion is allayed, they are kindly and hospitable.[178]
They thus reflect primitive evolution in the northeastern
Tibetan highlands and long subsequent life in the cold
and bleak north. As a rule, they reveal slow progress in
civilization, largely because of their harsh environment.
Some divisions have remained stationary or even have
retrogressed. The marked progress of the Estonians, Finns,
Bolgarians, and Hungarians is attributable to better climatic environment or the infusion of more aggressive
racial strains. Despite outside influences, the Estonians and
Finns have retained the agglutinative language of their
Turanian ancestors in the Lake Baikal region.

Now, we shall resume consideration of the activities
and migrations of the Nordic Aryans of western Scythia
(Ukrainia and eastward), beginning with the Kimmerian
nation because of its invasions of the south and finally its
overthrow and widespread dispersion to various other
regions of Europe.

---

178 *Ibid.*, vol. 10, p. 388, by Charles N. E. Eliot.

CHAPTER V

DISPERSION OF KIMMERIANS AND OTHERS

1. *Commercial Expansion of Miletus.* In consequence
of the invasion of southern Greece by the Dorians about
1180 B.C. and of later Doric incursions in the Aegean
Islands, thousands of Achaeans and Ionians emigrated
across the Aegean Sea to the coastal region of Anatolia,
where the fires of a brilliant culture were relighted on a
new altar. The 12 cities there established by the Ionian
immigrants ultimately were confederated into the Ionian
nation of historic times. By the subsequent Kimmeric invasions of the Anatolian mainland, these Greeks gained
knowledge of the character of the people residing north
of the Black Sea and of the possibilities of commercial
relations with them. Many of the Kimmerians settled in
various Ionian cities and established commercial houses
themselves or encouraged Greeks to do so. But, whatever
the contributing causes, it is certain that Miletus, in Ionia,
a colony of Athens,[1] took the lead in developing commerce across the Black Sea, exchanging manufactured commodities for agricultural products. Thus, at the time of
the Persian conquest she was far ahead of any other
Grecian city in wealth and population. The last part of
the 8th and first half of the 7th centuries B.C. was a
period of great activity in the establishment of Greek
colonies in the north. By 650 B.C. upwards of 80 such
colonies in the Black Sea region acknowledged Miletus
as their mother city.

While her trade extended from Gibraltar on the west
to the interior of Anatolia on the east, more especially did
she seek and win a large share of the Black Sea trade
with the Kimmerians, whose country was agricultural in
nature. In fact, the Black Sea commerce was the greatest
source of wealth of all the Ionian cities, and, in thus

---

1 Herodotus v.97.

aggressively turning her attention chiefly to the north, Miletus succeeded in monopolizing it through her colonies. These outposts, which were mostly on the Hellespont, Propontis, and Black Sea coasts, included Sinope,[2] on the southerly shore of the Black Sea (the terminus of a great caravan route from the Euphrates River through Pteria), Odessus (now Varna) on the west coast, ports at the mouth of the Ister (Danube) and Tyres (Dniester) Rivers, Olbia at the confluence of the Hypanis (Bug) and Borysthenes (Dnieper) Rivers, Pantikopion (now Kertch) in the Krimea, and others at the mouth of the Tanais (Don) River. Many of these colonists, such as the Istrians, Tyritae, and Olbiopolitae, are alluded to by Herodotus.[3] The port of Olbia was the center of all Milesian commercial activities in Scythia. Far to the northeast, between the Tanais and Oarus (Volga) Rivers, in the territory of the *Budini,* there were husbandmen or cattlemen of Greek origin, named the *Geloni.* They had been expelled from the towns on the Black Sea coasts and took refuge among the Budini, where they erected temples in the Grecian manner to Grecian deities.[4] The Budini themselves were a Votiak tribe [5] and probably had branched from the Finnic stock. They had red hair and blue eyes.

These facts are borne out by the discovery at Olbia of Milesian pottery of the 7th century B.C. That city stood at the head of trade routes leading far to the northeast[6] and for a long time enjoyed friendly relations with her Kimmeric neighbors in Scythia, through whom her wares penetrated far inland.[7] After 634 B. C., when a part of the Kimmerian nation was driven out of the Ukraine by the Getae (Goths) and the others made subjects, there was a change in the dominant population, which interrupted

---

2 Xenophon, *Anabasis* vi.1.15.

3 Herodotus iv.17,18,51,78.

4 *Ibid.,* iv.108. The Greeks appear also to have established colonies of Achaeans and Lacedemonians on the shores of the Black Sea at the foot of the Caucasus Mountains (Strabo xi.2.12-14).

5 Herodotus iv.108-109.

6 *Ibid.,* iv.24.

7 Strabo vii.3.17.

this commerce, and the north coast cities were hard pressed to defend themselves against the new barbarians. But, by establishing Greek agricultural colonies or by encouraging local peoples in the production of grain products,[8] Olbia regained her influence[9] and continued her active existence until about 50 B.C., when she was entirely destroyed by the Getae and lay waste for many years.[10]

Miletus reared sheep and made fine clothing and carpets from their wool. She exported wine and manufactured cloth into southern Russia (Scythia), and her colonies on the northerly shore of the Black Sea drew from that region grain, skins, hides, wool, and slaves in exchange.[11] The most important commodity was grain, as it is today. The north supplied food to Athens, Corinth, and many other Grecian towns,[12] whose territory failed to yield sufficient sustenance for their numerous inhabitants.[13] Another important article of commerce was amber. This commodity was then and still is mined on the Baltic Coast in East Prussia. It moved over the trade route by the Vistula River and across the Ukraine to the Milesian ports on the Black Sea, whence it was transported southward to the Mediterranean consuming points.[14]

Commercial relations of this magnitude inevitably resulted in the simultaneous transmission of Grecian and western Asiatic culture to the inhabitants of the Ukraine. The cultural influence of Miletus on the Kimmerians had untold effect in developing the later civilization of northern Gaul and the British Isles. Their young men were sent to Miletus for education and training at the behest of Kimmerians residing in that city. Miletus constantly had to defend herself and her dependent settlements from the Lydians[15] and other peoples, and young Kimmerians gained efficient military training and other advantages in

---

8 Herodotus iv.17,51,52.
9 Ibid., vi.5.26.
10 *Encyclopaedia Britannica*, 13th Ed., vol. 20, pp. 63-64, by Ellis H. Minns.
11 Herodotus iv.17-18.
12 Strabo vii.4.6.
13 H. de B. Gibbins, *History of Commerce in Europe* (1897), pages 12-13.
14 Herodotus iii.115.
15 Ibid., i.6-29.

the service of the Milesians. This was the channel by which the use of iron passed from the Aegean basin to the Kimmeric nation which transmitted it to northern and northwestern Europe upon the dispersion westward of a part of that nation by the Getae in 634 B.C. We shall review later the manner of diffusion of this southern culture over northwestern Europe by these Nordic nations.

------

2. *Defeat and Dispersion of the Kimmerians.* About 640 B.C., a powerful tribe of Mongolians, the aforementioned Arimaspians of Herodotus, a vigorous people, later known to history as the Huns, emerged from the foothills of the Altai Mountains. On the plains of Semipalatinsk they encountered and pressed westward the Turko-Ugrian nations of the Argippei (Bolgarians) and Iyrcae (Hungarians)[16] and various other Ugrians, including the Finns. This pressure on the Argeppei and Iyrcae forced the Massagetae southward toward Dahestan and Bactria and the Thyssagetae northwestward to the westerly side of the Ural Mountains. The last-named tribe centered on the Orenburg district and the Iyrcae lay opposite them on the easterly side of the mountains. Subsequently, when the Iyrcae passed to the westerly base of the mountains, the Thyssagetae moved to the Volga River,[17] pushing the central Scythians (the Getae or later-known Goths) westward across the Ural, Volga, and Don (or Tanais) Rivers[18] upon the Kimmerians, who for more than a millennium had possessed the Ukrainian basin.[19] Meanwhile, the Kimmerian nation had been weakened by the departure of its southernmost tribe (the Treres), which overran Lydia, in Asia Minor. Knowledge of its absence doubtless had reached the Getae.

In an epochal war, culminating in 634 B.C., the Getic Scythians gained an overwhelming victory and took the

------

16 C. C. Mierow, *The Gothic History of Jordanes* (Princeton, 1915), page 60.
17 Herodotus, *Hist.* iv.22.
18 C. C. Mierow, *ibid.*, page 62.
19 Herodotus, iv.11-13.

Ukraine. The major portion of the Kimmerians was dispersed in various directions,[20] as told later, which created an untold influence on the civilization of western Europe. The widespread effects of this great dispersion have scarcely been considered by historians. It meant the annihilation (for the time being) of an important nation and the rise of another, the Getae, in its place — the third Nordic nation successively to occupy the Ukraine (the bread basket of Europe).

The Kimmerians were scattered in the major part only. One large division, known as the *Skoloti,* thus named for its leader and comprising the more elderly and property-owning and ruling caste,[21] was made a subject-group of the conquerors and was confined to an area on the easterly side of the lower Borysthenes (Dnieper) River, as is described by Herodotus.[22] Along with the Getae, they were known to the Greeks generally as Scythians and were the husbandmen or plowing Scythians.[23] The Getae thus imposed their name and their yoke on all the populace that remained on the Euxine steppes, but their arrival did not change the basic type of the population as a whole, which continued to be Nordic Aryan.[24]

One tribe of Kimmerians, the *Tauri,* either fled to or remained among the mountains of the Krimean peninsula, where they were surrounded by the Milesian colonies of the Greeks and apparently were not molested further by the conquerors.[25] They seem to have continued an approximately independent status.[26] In consequence of their isolation, they practised the peculiar and barbaric customs described by Herodotus.[27] When the Skoloti ultimately broke away from the dominance of the Getae in 342 B.C., the Tauri on this peninsula were not organized or pre-

---

20   *Ibid.,* iv.11-13, vii.20; Strabo xi.2.5.
21   Herodotus iv.6,11.
22   *Ibid.,* iv.18,54.
23   Herodotus iv.11,18,53,54.
24   *Ency. Brit.,* 13th Ed., vol. 24, page 529, by Ellis Hovell Minns.
25   Herodotus iv.99.
26   *Ibid,* iv.119,120.
27   *Ibid.,* iv.103; Edward Gibbon, *History of the Roman Republic,* vol. 1, p. 421.

pared to do likewise, for about the end of the 2nd century B.C. they were dependent allies of the Getic King Scilurus. That the Tauri were a Kimmeric people is indicated by the fact that an ancient Krimean city named Carcinitis [28] had the Kymric *Caer* as its first syllable.

The larger division of dispersed Kimmerians separated and were pursued by the victors in four different directions. Some went eastward along the shores of the Black Sea and by-passed the Caucasus range into Asia,[29] where they were known to the Assyrians as the Gimirrai;[30] the remnant of the southerly tribe of the Treres went southward along the westerly shore of the Black Sea and through Thrace into Anatolia,[31] where they rejoined their congeners in Lydia; and some fled southwestward to the Dalmatian coast.[32] The largest aggregation hastened directly westward, followed by a large army of the Getae as far as the Vistula basin,[33] where the latter stopped for two reasons; (1) they had driven their foe into the territory of the Suebians, there leaving them to their fate, and (2) they were enamored of the rich Ukrainian region as a new habitation, which they desired to retain. Thereupon, they reëstablished their entire nation on this land, settling on both sides of the Dnieper River,[34] north of the Black Sea. Enclosed between them and that body of water were the Kimmerian Skoloti, who had failed to escape and remained subjects of the Getae for three centuries. Thereafter, the Getae were represented in ancient writings as the "Scythians," as the Suebians and the Kimmerians had been called before them and as the Sarmations were designated subsequently.[35]

We shall follow separately these dispersed divisions of defeated Kimmerians to their respective havens, where each

---

28 Herodotus iv.55,99.
29 *Ibid.,* i.103-104, iv.12.
30 *Ency. Brit.,* vol. 24, page 526, by Minns.
31 *Ibid.,* vol. 6, page 368, vol. 24, page 526.
32 Strabo v.4.5, citing Ephorus.
33 Herodotus iv.11.
34 *Ibid.,* iv.53,71.
35 Procopius, *Gothic War,* iv.

later exercised important cultural influence.[36] All of them (including the subsequent Goidels of the west[37]) comprised mainly the younger and more vigorous members of the nation, having been chiefly the defeated soldiery and their families but the less advanced portion of the population. They were among the tallest people of the world, as is indicated by the effect of this strain in increasing the average stature of the populace with which they later commingled on the Dalmatian coast and in Ireland and Scotland.

The sizeable division (the *Skoloti*) that remained behind as subjects of the Getae [38] apparently represented the older and more settled members of the Kimmerian nation, who preferred to continue their life on their rich lands and take their chances with the conquerors.[39] The "enslavement" of defeated peoples by northern nations seems to have been far less severe than it was among southern nations. "Subjection" to the conquerors, with the privilege largely of following their own laws and customs, more frequently was the rule in the north.[40] This clearly was the situation with respect to these Skolotic Kimmerians, as is attested by their later influence on the civilization of western Europe.

The aforementioned southwesterly movement of the Huns on the Kirghiz steppe also pressed the Turkic Issedones down upon the Nordic Sakae, in Western Turkistan, impelling them toward the south and the east, where they settled in Sogdiana and Ferghana. The very important part played by the Massagetae and the Sakae in later Asiatic history will be narrated in a subsequent chapter.

The approximate 6-year period of strife in the Ukraine

36 The names Kimmerii, Kymry, Cymry, Cymru, Cimbri, Cumbria, Cambria, et al. are merely different forms of the same appellation of this ancient nation or a place of habitation of a division of it.

37 Bede, *Ecclesiastical History* (J. A. Giles' tr., Bohn's Library, London, 1871), i.1.

38 *Ency. Brit.*, 13th Ed., vol. 24, page 526d, where the Skoloti are named as subjects of the Royal Scyths (the Getae).

39 Herodotus iv.11,53.

40 *Ibid.*, vii.108.

(Scythia) from 640 to 634 B. C., before the Getae finally
overcame the Kimmerians, is indicated by the prophecies
of Zephaniah, which were uttered about the year 639
B.C., according to a prominent Jewish rabbi of Washington. Widespread warfare in the barbaric north usually
was followed by destructive raids in the civilized regions
of the south by bands of one or both participants. Information of this strife had spread to the south and the prophet
apprehended that desolation in the Biblical region would
follow decisive action in the north. History discloses that
his fears were realized (see *Ezekiel* 38 *et seq.*), as reviewed in the next section, but the subsequent 28-year
domination of western Asia by the Getic invaders (634-
606 B.C.) bore immeasurable fruit later in the enhance-
ment of culture in western Europe.

---

3. *Getic Pursuit of Kimmerians through the Caucasus.*
We now approach an historical event of stupendous but
still untold influence on the advancement of civilization in
western Europe; namely, the manner of acquisition by the
victorious Getae of Babylonian, Assyrian, and other western Asiatic culture in consequence of the pursuit by one
of their armies (under Idanthrysus [41]) of the dispersed
Kimmerians who entered western Asia around the westerly end of the Caucasus Mountains. Through their subjects, the Kimmeric Skoloti, this culture subsequently was
transmitted to western Europe by the method explained
later.

According to Herodotus,[42] these Kimmerians in 634
B.C, fled southward to Asia along the northerly and
easterly shores of the Black Sea and thence turned westward along its southerly shores as far as the lands of the
Milesian colony of the *Mossynoeci* at Sinope,[43] east of
which they took refuge. Their tribal name became that
of *Amazon* and their capital was called Themiscyra, on

---

41 Strabo xv.1.6.
42 Herodotus i.103-104.
43 Xenophon, *Anabasis* v.4.2 ff.

the Thermodon River.[44] Their settlement at this location is additional evidence of the close relations that long had existed between the Greeks of Miletus and the Kimmerian nation of the Ukraine.

By turning westward toward Sinope, this band of Kimmerians was missed by its pursuers, who had taken a longer route toward the east, through either the defiles of Derbend or the Dariel Pass in the Caucasus Mountains, to northern Media. There they encountered not only primitive peoples but also the 1000-year old Kimmeric nation of Medians,[45] whom they defeated and some of whom they took as prisoners. The subsequent exploits of these Getae in western Asia are portrayed by the following excerpts from other writings:

> Further developments [by the Medians] were arrested by the Scythian invasion described by Herodotus. We know from Zephaniah and Jeremiah that these northern barbarians in 626 B.C. overran and harried Syria and Palestine . . .[46]

> Cyaxares, king of Media, reigned, according to Herodotus, forty years, . . . he renewed the war against the Assyrians, . . . but was . . . attacked by a great Scythian army under Madyes, son of Protothyes, which had come from the northern shores of the Black Sea in pursuit of the Kimmerians. After their victory over Cyaxares, the Scythians conquered and wasted the whole of western Asia and ruled twenty-eight years, . . . it is probable that this invasion was the principal cause of the downfall of the Assyrian empire. After the destruction of the Scythians, Cyaxares regained the supremacy, renewed his attack on Assyria. . . .[47]

---

44 Herodotus iv.110-117.

45 *Ibid.*, iv.1,12. These Median prisoners (the Sigynae) played an important part in history, as shown later.

46 *Ency. Brit.*, 13th Ed., vol. 21, page 206, by Karl H. Ethe: also vol. 6, page 368, by Ellis Hovell Minns.

47 *Ency. Brit.*, 13th Ed., vol. 7, page 680, by Eduard Meyer. The translation of Herodotus (i.103-107) by A. D. Godley makes Cyaxares' reign approximately 634-594 B.C., but it began at least a year earlier. The Getic domination of western Asia was from 634 to 606 B.C. See *Ezekiel* 38:9,15,16.

. . . In 606 B.C. Cyaxares captured and destroyed Nineveh and the other Assyrian cities . . . To the east the Median empire extended far over Iran, even the Persian owning its sway. . . .[48]

With these inroads of the Kimmerians and Scythians [Getae] we must doubtless connect the great ethnographical revolution in the north of anterior Asia . . . .[48]

During the period of 28 years (634 to 606 B.C.) in which these Getae dominated western Asia, they, as well as the Kimmeric Treres (the Danes) who withdrew[49] from Lydia upon the approach of the victorious Getic army in 606 B.C., as related by Alyattes, appropriated and carried back to the Ukraine and to western Europe respectively a vast knowledge of Babylonian, Assyrian, and Grecian culture. It included the code of Hammurabi, the great Amoritic king of Babylonia, which had been promulgated about 2100 B.C. Numerous Getic expeditionary bands traveled back and forth between the south and their northern homeland during this period, as the Kimmerii frequently had done before them. By this means, the spoils of war, coins of Lydia, and other treasures of the conquered peoples were transported northward, while the learned Getae interested themselves in the habits, customs, laws, arts, and science of the ancient civilizations of the south. Ample proof of these acquisitions exist, primarily the fact that the Getae of Scythia are recognized by historians as having been far more civilized than the Suebian tribes on their west or the peoples on their east.[50] More of these circumstances appear later.

But these conquerors could not withstand indefinitely the effects of their contact with and lack of restraint in a wholly different and in many respects a superior environ-

---

48 *Ency. Brit.*, vol. 21, page 206, by Karl H. Ethe; also vol. 6, page 368, by Ellis H. Minns.

49 They were far from being extirpated, as Alyattes boasted.

50 J.C.L.S. de Sismondi, *Fall of the Roman Empire*, vol. 1, pages 101-102.

ment, far from their homes and families, under lower moral conditions,[51] and in a warmer climate than that to which they had been accustomed. The older and abler men gradually returned to their families in the north and their places in the southern army were taken by younger and less-disciplined men, who gave way to licentiousness and pillage.[52] In consequence, their military efficiency diminished, they weakened as an armed force, and finally they were repelled and dispersed by Cyaxares,[53] whereupon they retreated homeward.

This story is only one of many similar pages in the military history of the world, more particularly of northern armies detained long in warmer climes. When the remnants of this Getic army returned to the Ukraine,[54] where that nation had supplanted the rule of the Kimmerians, they were a sadder but wiser people for their wonderful adventure in the south. But, on their return, they found it necessary first to overcome a revolt of their subjects, the Skolotic Kimmerians, which is described by Herodotus.[55]

Altogether, this expedition had provided the Getae with an abundance of political, theological, philosophical, legal, and economic knowledge from the older civilizations of the south. Centuries later, it was to exert marvelous effect, through themselves and their Kimmerian subjects, on the relatively crude society of western Europe and to diffuse to that region of the world the culture of western Asia.

This route of the transmission of culture from east to west, apparently not notably considered hitherto, is deserving of more comprehensive and intensive investigation by scholars. It is discussed further here in connection with later movements of the Skolotic Kimmerians, who broke away from the Getae in 342 B.C., and of the Getae (or Goths, a name that arose later).

---

51 Herodotus i.105.
52 *Ibid.*, i.106.
53 *Ibid.*, i.106.
54 *Ibid.*, iv.1-4.
55 *Ibid.*, iv.3-4.

4. *Kimmeric Dispersion Through Thrace.* (a) *The Later Goidels and Danes.* The Kimmerians (later Goidels) who escaped southwestward then continued westward across Europe through Thrace and the Danubian basin, as recounted subsequently. The members of the southernmost tribe, the Treres,[56] who had remained behind north of the lower Danube, then hastened across the Hellespont and rejoined their congeners who had invaded Lydia a few years earlier.[57] The southern Getic army, which crossed the Caucasus in pursuit of a division of the foe, missed the latter and ravaged the Near East for 28 years, as stated. The later epical migration of the whole tribe of Treres (the later Danes) from Lydia to the mouth of the Elbe River, in northwesern Europe, under their renowned leader Odin, is also narrated in a later section.

(b) *Albanians and Montenegrins.* A portion of the shattered Albanian tribe of the Kimmerian nation turned southwestward from Scythia along the age-old caravan route that led across the Balkan region, through territory inhabited by Kelts,[58] to the Adriatic Sea.[59] This group, later known as the *Dardanii,*[60] settled near the Dalmatian coast,[61] long maintained its identity, and ultimately founded the present Albanian nation,[62] which, because of many years of Turkish rule, since has incurred a marked degree of Turkish blood and also local strains. A wholly different group that settled just north of the Albanians on the Dalmatian coast shortly afterward was a division of the aforementioned Sigynae,[63] later known as the Montenegrins and perhaps by other local names. They were a minor portion of a rebellious division of Kimmerians of

---

56 *Ency. Brit.,* 13th Ed., vol. 24, page 526, by E. H. Minus; also Strabo xiv.1.40.
57 Herodotus, *Hist.,* i.16.
58 *Ency. Brit., ibid.,* vol. 14, page 326.
59 Herodotus iv.33.
60 Ancient *Dardanica* was the mountainous country of southern Serbia (Strabo vii.5.1,7). It was reached up the Drin River from the Adriatic Sea.
61 Strabo vii.3.8; 5.2; 6.7.
62 *Racial History of the Albanians,* by Calvin Kephart, in *Unconquerable Albania* (Albanian Liberation Committee, Chicago, 1944).
63 *Ency. Brit.,* 13th Ed., vol. 25, page 84.

Media, who had been captured by the victorious Getae and transferred as subjects to the northerly shores of the lower Danube. They had broken away from their captors in 6o6 B.C. and escaped to the Dalmatian highlands, where they ultimately commingled with the indigenous Illyrian Kelts and more recently with the Slavic Croats.[64]

The Kimmerians were the tallest of the Nordic Aryans and we must attribute to the blood of these two groups the great stature of the present inhabitants of the Dalmatian coast, sometimes erroneously called the *Dinaric* race. They rank with their kin, the highland Scots, as the tallest people in the world because of this racial influence. Their kinship with the highland Scots is confirmed by their division into clans with hereditary chieftains, by their interminable blood-feuds, and by their conspicuous fondness for music and playing upon pipes as well as stringed instruments.[65] Further confirmation is the fact that the name used by the more southerly division, the Albanians, also was the early name of the Scottish highlands.[66] Moreover, their savage condition in Strabo's time points to their having been an immigrant people. Even today, "retaining their original language and preserving the customs and institutions of remote antiquity, they present a distinct type and differ in many essential particulars from the other nations of the [Balkan] peninsula . . . . The tribal organization in northern Albania is an interesting survival of the earliest form of social combination; it may be compared in many respects with that which existed in the *Scottish highlands* in the time of the Stuart kings."[67] Another evidential fact showing the kinship of these people with Kimmerians is the existence at Pollina, the ancient Apollina, of the remnants of a Doric temple, of which a single column is still standing. In Montenegro the

---

64 *Ency. Brit.*, 13th Ed. vol. 25, page 84.
65 Strabo vii.5.7.
66 J. A. Giles, *Six Old English Chronicles* (Geoffrey of Monmouth's British History) (Bell, London, 1891), Book iv. ch. 17. This is the origin of the name *Albany*.
67 *Ency. Brit.*, 13th Ed., vol. 1, page 484.

evidences of this racial amalgamation other than stature long since have disappeared, although funerals are still celebrated by an orgy very like an Irish wake.[68] This country was overrun during the Slavic Serbo-Croat invasion of the 6th and 7th centuries of the Christian era, and its tribal system, while still extant and divided into clans, possesses less significance than that in Albania, owing in part to the long centralization of authority at Cettigne. A more important reason is the fact that, as transplanted Medians, they represented an olden break from the parent nation in ancient Scythia, whereas the Albanians represented a break that occurred nearly a millennium later.

The marked increase in physical stature by introduction of the Kimmeric strain is analogous with that which occurred in the region of Lombardy, Italy, in the old Burgundian district around Dijon, France, in western Switzerland, and in Alsace, where the effect of the northern Gothic, Burgundian, and Allemannian peoples in causing increased stature of the indigenous population is apparent today, even though the people in general have reverted largely to the primitive type.[69]

A band of the Kimmerians in Dalmatia soon crossed the Adriatic to central Italy, where they seem to have been scattered. They may have been driven from Dalmatia by some feud. One group reached Campania, where it settled in a valley between Barae and Cumae, near Naples, in the vicinity of the present lake of Fusaro. Its members are reported as having lived in caves for secluded refuge. The habits and customs of these people were described by Ephorus, a highly credited Greek historian, who wrote about the middle of the 4th century B.C.[70] Later, this colony either was exterminated by local rulers or was absorbed by the surrounding population. Another group found refuge in a secluded spot in Latium, southeast of Rome, where a temple was consecrated to *Diana Taurica*

68 *Ibid.*, vol. 18, page 769.
69 W. Z. Ripley, *The Races of Europe* (Paul, Trench, Trübner & Co., London, 1913), pages 143-144, 234-236.
70 Strabo v.4.5.

(recalling the *Taurici* of Krimea) and the rites performed therein were "barbarous and Scythic." [71] The temple was situated in a grove on the shore of a lake and all was surrounded by abrupt and lofty precipices. Migration from Illyria to southern Italy and commercial intercourse between the two regions was quite common in antiquity.[72] Other tribes are known later to have crossed the Adriatic.[73]

(c) *Lithuanians, Latvians, and Borussians.* At the time of the epochal defeat of the Kimmerian nation by the Getae in 634 B.C., of the dispersion of the larger part of it, and of the possession of Ukrainia by the victors, armies away from home on distant ventures always took their families along with them, so that they might settle on new land and reëstablish themselves. The nonmilitary, better educated, and ruling classes of the defeated Kimmerians, under the generic name of the *Skoloti*, remained behind as subjects of their conquerors. Their habitation was southern Scythia, extending as far south as the Bug or Dniester River. The southernmost division of the subject Kimmerians composed the captive Nordic Medians mentioned before under the tribal name of Sigynae,[74] transplanted thither by the Getae after their defeat of the Median nation in 634 B.C. when in pursuit of Albanians across the Caucasus Mountains. All of these subjects were guarded by bands of Getae posted at intervals as far south as Thrace, on the southerly side of the Danube River. But when the Skoloti revolted in 606 B. C. a minor division of the Sigynae stole away from their Getic guards and moved to and settled in the Dalmatian highlands, north of the Albanians. This area included Montenegro and northward toward the head of the Adriatic Sea. The long separation of the Medic Kimmerians from the parent nation in Scythia and the consequent dimming of traditions resulted in a cleavage between these two kindred

---

71 *Ibid.*, v.3.12; vii.4.5.
72 *Ibid.*, vi.3.8.
73 Pliny iii.11.
74 Herodotus, *Hist.* iv.11,18,53,54,94; v.9; vii.108. Other sections of Book iv. also are informative in this connection. *Ency. Brit.*, 13th Ed., vol. 25, page 84.

peoples on the Dalmatian coast that continues today. While the Albanians have preserved their identity, the Sigynae have become merged with the Kelts that lived there before them and with the Slavs that invaded that region since then.

But of the greatest importance here is the fact that the larger body of the Sigynae did not or could not thus break away from their subjection to the Getae. They had been settled near the northerly shores [75] of the Black Sea, between the Dniester and Danube Rivers, and those who remained behind *were the ancestors of the present Lithuanians, Latvians, and Borussians (Old Prussians)*. Lithuanian songs and folklore indicate this site of habitation, for in one song the maiden sings that "my mother sent me to the Danube River to fetch some water." Their application of the name Danzig to a Baltic seaport demonstrates ancient relationship with Kimmerians in this southerly region. The contact of ancient Lithuanians with inhabitants of northern Thrace is indicated further by the fact that the god of some of the latter, called Gebeleizis,[76] seems to correspond with the Lithuanian expression *Gyva leyis,* meaning the "giver of rest.[76] Habitation in this region also affords a ready explanation of the recognized influence of the Greek and Latin languages in the evolution of dialects of these Baltic peoples.[75]

Grain and other agricultural products of Scythia constantly passed southward through Thrace in exchange for products of the Aegean region and southwestward over the age-old caravan route across the Balkan region and the Adriatic Sea to Italy in exchange for products of that region. Consequently the dealings of the Scythian tribes with agents of Greek and Latin merchants for more than a century resulted in the engrafting of expressions of the latter peoples on the dialect of the former. Finally, the fact that the Sigynae formerly had lived in Media accounts for the discernible Iranic influences on their lan-

---

75 Alfred Senn, *Standard Lithuanian in the Making,* in *The Slavonic and East European Review,* vol. XXII, 1944.
76 Herodotus, *ibid.,* iv.94; Gottlieb S. Beyer, *Sinieus Origins,* p. 283.

guage, customs, and traditions.[77] Thus, the statement by Herodotus that the Sigynae were a colony of Medians possesses great significance in this connection. Prior to 635 B.C., the Medians were struggling vigorously under Phraortes, father of Cyaxares, to regain their own independence in northwestern Iran, and obviously they were unable to establish a colony voluntarily in the faraway Balkan region; so that there is no reason whatever to question the accuracy of Herodotus' assertion that the Sigynae were Medians transferred in the manner indicated.

The principal value of captives to ancient nations was the service that might be obtained from them in clearing the forests, preparing the land for whatever purpose it was intended to be used, tilling the crops, attending the droves or flocks of livestock, and otherwise saving the tribesmen from such labor, so that they would be free for hunting, military service, and the social life of the nation. Anciently, the subjection of conquered peoples by northern nations was far less severe than that among southern nations and they usually were allowed to retain their own laws and customs.[78] This is proved by the willingness of the Skoloti to remain on their ancestral lands as subjects of the Getae and by the later influence of these subjects on civilization in western Europe after they escaped in 342 B.C. and migrated westward. They were the later Franconians, Hessians, Ripuarian Franks, Belgae, Britons, Scots, and others. We have no reason to believe that the subjection of the Median Kimmerians (Sigynae) was markedly severer than that accorded to the Skoloti by the Getae other than the fact that a minor number of the former escaped to Dalmatia.

In consequence of the historic invasion of western Asia by the Getic army during 634-606 B.C. after that nation's defeat of the Kimmerians, the Getae became the most cultured of all the Nordic nations. They brought iron weapons from Anatolia and introduced the Iron Age in

---

77 See Calvin Kephart, *Origin of the Conjugal Community* (*or Community Property Law*) and *Other Ancient Laws*, third section, entitled *Politics and Jurisprudence in Ancient Media*, page 24.
78 Herodotus, *ibid.*, vii.108.

Western Scythia (Europe). Their subject Kimmerians profited but also were controlled thereby. In 512 B.C., King
Darius the Great, of Persia, made a historic but fruitless invasion of the vast territory of the Scythians (Getae)
in Ukrainia by way of the west of the Black Sea. He sought
to avenge the death of his predecessor, Cyrus the Great,
in a disastrous campaign against the Massagetae (a Nordic nation) in Western Turkistan in 529 B.C. The Getae
and their subjects avoided him by moving up the basin
of the Dnieper River. Soon afterward the Getae besought
King Cleomenes of Sparta for a combined attack on the
Persian kingdom, but the negotiations came to naught.[79]
In consequence, the former most southerly Kimmerian
subjects, the main body of the Medians (Sigynae) on
the lower Danube, who had failed to escape to the Dalmatian coast — the ancestors of the Lithuanians, Latvians,
and Borussians, *then were resettled farther northward in
the basins of the Dnieper, Pripyat, and upper Niemen
Rivers.* There they resumed their former status of tree-
fellers and agriculturists under the Getae. This final
transfer must have occurred about 510 B.C. Hereafter,
the Getae will be called the Goths, by which name they
are better known in history.

It is said in the books that from the time of Darius'
invasion the Scythic Goths appear as a declining power.
Such is far from the fact, however; they were too populous
and virile a nation thus to be eclipsed.[80] By about 500
B.C. the seat of that nation had been firmly established
on the central Dnieper River, approximately at the site of
the present city of Kiev. On several occasions its leaders
proceeded to inflict punishment on Slavic neighbors on
the north, chiefly the *Neuri,* later called *Wends,* for their
failure or refusal to come to its aid against Darius. They
pushed these Slavs farther northward and gained much of
their territory, particularly that between the Vistula and
Dvina Rivers. Those Goths and their Kimmerian subjects
still in the south were the Scythians of Herodotus, the

---

79 Calvin Kephart, *The Swedes and Swedish Goths* (1938).
80 Herodotus, *Hist.* iv.46,71,81; also C. C. Mierow, *The Gothic History of Jordanes* (Princeton, 1915).

Skolotic Kimmerians along the Dniester River having been the aforesaid husbandmen or plowing Scythians.[81]

The invasion of Western Scythia in 342 B.C. by King Philip II of Macedonia, which "was comparable to nothing in antiquity since Darius' famous march to Scythia,"[82] resulted in the historic breaking-away of the Skoloti from the Goths and their migration to western Europe. Already, at the time of Philip's invasion, the military forces of the Goths were operating mainly in the north.[83] Consequently, the seat of the Gothic nation again was moved farther north on the Dnieper River, probably to a region cleared by the Sigynae (Lithuanians) earlier transferred from the lower Danube. Shorn of its subjects in the south, the nation increased the intensity of its exploration of the Baltic littoral region and the territory northeasterly along those shores was gained for expansion in that direction. These activities of the nation were noticed by the writers of antiquity. One of them, Pytheas, of the Greek colony of Marseille, in southern Gaul, who lived at the time of Alexander the Great (356-323 B. C.), wrote a book of his travels, some fragments of which have been preserved in the works of other writers. In one of these accounts, quoted by Pliny the Elder (A.D. 23-79),[84] mention is made of a tribe of *Guttones* (Getae) bordering on the Suebians and living around the gulf later known as Frisches Haff, on the East Prussian shore at the mouth of the Vistula River. No mention whatever of the northerly Kimmerians (Sigynae) at this early time has been found, from which fact we may infer that they still lived inland, between the upper Niemen and Dvina Rivers.

Before the Gothic nation could undertake extensive explorations on the waters of the Baltic Sea, it was necessary for it to develop port facilities and fleets of sailing ships, all constructed from timber cut from the inland forests.

---

81 Herodotus, *Hist.*, iv.11,18,53,54,94, v.9, vii.108.
82 Discussed in detail in a later chapter. See *Ency. Brit.*, 13th Ed., vol. 21, page 377c, under *Philip II* (382-336 B.C.).
83 Strabo, *Geogr.* vii.3,17.
84 Pliny, *Nat. Hist.* xxxvii. 1, 11, and 12.

Their achievements in this respect are confirmed by Tacitus [85] in his description of the customs of the people on the easterly shores of the Baltic whom he inaccurately referred to as "the tribes of the *Aestii* (Estonians)," who lived still farther north. The people he thus described actually were the Kimmerians (Sigynae) employed as seaport workmen by the Gothic nation, for he commended their industry (in preparing for Gothic expeditions on the Baltic Sea) and remarked that "they even explore the sea and are the only people who gather amber, which by them is called *glese* and is collected among the shallows and upon the shore." As stated by Pliny, it was the Guttones (Goths) who formerly inhabited this lower coast and gathered amber for fuel and for sale to neighboring Suebians. This meagerness of comment implies that the Goths had not yet (A.D. 90-92) made any conspicuous conquests on the Baltic but were actively preparing to do so.

It is not known precisely how many ports the Goths developed and maintained, but they must have included the most favorable sites from the Bay of Danzig to the Gulf of Riga, apparently those of the present ports of Danzig, Königsberg, Memel, Libau, Windau, and Riga. As rapidly as developed, they became bases of military operations on the Baltic, especially toward the west, as is revealed by other sources. The interior regions were heavily forested and much timber was required for the construction of port facilities and ships. Even after construction of those facilities, a numerous population of civilian employees was necessary at the ports to maintain the ships and the supply and embarkation service. In consequence, there was a concentration of workers where these activities were in progress, namely, inland in felling and shaping the timber and growing food supplies and at the ports in building wharves and ships and maintaining and repairing that equipment. These workmen were recruited from the Kimmerian subjects in the interior, groups being assigned and transferred to the different port sites for their develop-

---

85 Tacitus, *Germania* ch. 45.

ment and subsequent operation and maintenance. All of this service was performed under Gothic military control and supervision, probably with a member of the royal Amal family in command. He must have directed a staff of subordinates from headquarters somewhere up the Niemen River, whence both inland and shore activities could be supervised conveniently.[86] Any doubt whether these port workmen were the Kimmerian subjects of the Goths is resolved by Tacitus' remark that their "rites and fashions and style of dress are those of the Suebi, while *their language is more like the British.*" As we already know, the British were a division of the Skolotic Kimmerians who were northerly neighbors of the Sigynae while both were subjects of the Goths in southern Ukrainia.

The fortunes of the Gothic nation in this region are discussed at length later, but in A.D. 374 the nation was attacked from the east with great violence by the Huns under Balamber and its development halted. After a heroic resistance of two years, the nation was defeated and shattered. The Visigoths escaped southward, but the Ostrogoths became subjects of the Huns for 77 years afterward. The Kimmeric subjects (Sigynae or Lithuanians) of the former great Gothic nation in this region, *both inland and at the ports,* were out of the path of the Huns, which was farther south. The prosperous trade routes were suddenly terminated by this disaster and the Kimmerian Lithuanians and their Gothic overseers were left without a dominant nation. Thereafter, it was necessary for each group to fend for itself; but, with the Huns rampant and intrusive Slavs left unhindered as unfriendly neighbors, the Gothic leadership continued to maintain for 4½ centuries afterward a form of military organization of all these abandoned Kimmerians and Goths, mainly for self-defense. This Kimmeric territory extended as far as the present easterly boundaries of the Lithuanian habitations. Each district had its own clan and villages and was partly dependent on the marshes for defense against

---

86 Calvin Kephart, *The Swedes and Swedish Goths* (1938).

the Slavs on the east. Apparently these people were not disturbed by the Sarmatians (the later Poles) on the south. That this general course was followed is proved by passages in Jordanes' history of the Goths preserved in the writings of the Roman statesman and historian Cassiodorus (c. 490-585). Thus, in the 6th century all of these people were reported under the national name of the *Vidivarii*, "a people gathered out of various tribes" that became one nation, while beyond them on the Baltic shores dwelt the Aestii (Estonians).[87] That it was a loosely knit association formed mainly for self-protection is seen in the fact that these people separated into three divisions about the year 800 and that the name Vidivarii then disappeared. By this time the Huns had ceased to be a menace and the intrusive Slavic Wends had emigrated to central and southern Europe. In splitting asunder, each of the three divisions of Kimmerians remained linked to a pair of the Baltic Sea ports. *Those in the north later became known as the Latvians, those in the center, the larger division, extending far inland, became known as the Lithuanians, and those in the south took the name of Borussians (or Prussians).* It was a natural division, both an outgrowth and an explanation of the manner in which the former Gothic nation had assigned, organized, and supervised these Kimmerian subjects for the development and operation of the six Baltic ports.[88]

The Lithuanians extended as far eastward as the headwaters of the Niemen and Berezina Rivers and constituted the main body of the Sigynae or Medic Kimmerians transferred from the lower Danube to the basin of the Dnieper, Pripyat, and upper Niemen Rivers about 510 B.C. The dynastic tradition of the former Gothic nation, for reasons already indicated, continued with the Lithuanians alone, and they were the only division of

---

87 C. C. Mierow, *op.cit.*, pages 60 and 78.

88 If the Vidivarii had not been assigned to port development in separate and loosely connected divisions from the 1st century, Jordanes would not have reported them as a nation gathered out of various tribes. It cannot be said that they inhabited this Baltic littoral region prior to their assignment to port development by their superiors, the Goths.

the Vidivarii later to create and perpetuate a royal dynasty, which reigned at the time that they first appeared in medieval history. Along with this tradition, they retained many of their primitive and heathen customs.[89]

Other evidence in support of the foregoing findings is at hand. All of the Lithuanians, Latvians, and Prussians are Nordic in build and appearance. Having been largely isolated from the main body of the Gothic nation and resentful at their subjection,[90] they tenaciously retained their original language and customs to a major extent, with only minor Gothic, Greek, Latin, and Slavic influences. Their language does not belong to the *kentum*-division of the Aryan languages, to which the Gothic belongs, but rather to the *satem*-division, which includes the language of the ancient Medians[91] of northwestern Iran and of the Albanians,[92] both of whom originally were Kimmeric nations. The Medians were called "the Manda" in ancient writings, which is a term that was applied to the Kimmeric chieftains of ancient Scythia, and, finally, the resemblance of their language with that of their fellow-Kimmerians, the ancient British, has been verified by Tacitus.

In harmony with these facts is the knowledge that the ancestors of the present Lithuanians, Latvians, and Borussians have lived in the same region since the Bronze Age. It was the Kimmerians who introduced the Iron Age in western Europe; in fact, iron was not in common use in Danmark until as late as about A.D. 100, while in northern Russia and Siberia it was not introduced until about A.D. 800.[93] Any iron implements used by the ancestors of the Lithuanians, Latvians, and Borussians in the basins

---

89 Their chief priest, the judge of the judges, under whom were numerous classes of priests and elders, worshipped in the forests. The waidelots brought their offerings to the divinities at the foot of oaks. Even now the veneration of great oaks is a widespread custom in the villages of the Lithuanians and Latvians.

90 This relationship is indicated by an ancient Lithuanan saying as follows: "Oh God of Thunder, strike not a Zemaitis (Samogitian of Lithuania) but strike a Gudas (Goth) as you would a brown dog."

91 *Ency. Brit.*, 13th and 14th editions, under heading *Media*.

92 Calvin Kephart, *Racial History of the Albanians, supra.*

93 *Ency. Brit.*, 13th Ed., vol. 14, page 800, under *Iron Age.*

of the Dnieper, Pripyat, and upper Niemen Rivers either were brought by them originally from Media or were passed to them by their superiors, the Goths, and, in any event, were taken to that far northern region when they were transferred there by the Gothic nation about 510 B.C. The scarcity of such implements made necessary the long continuance of use of the bronze tools.

All three divisions of the ancient Vidivarii, the later Lithuanians, Latvians, and Borussians, except the overhead military and civil governmental organization of the Ostrogoths associated with the central (or later Lithuanian) division, had descended from enforced agricultural or labor elements (captive Medians) of the former Gothic nation, without the stimulus of a glorious past or of an encouraging future; so, they have tended until recently to be unprogressive and without the normal aims of a cohesive nation.

Beginning in 1229, the Borussians (Prussians) gradually fell under the dominion of the Teutonic Knights, who with the aid of the sword succeeded in introducing Christianity in some degree as far north as the Gulf of Riga. The knights then settled on vast areas of land taken from the indigenous population, who were subjected to the status of peasants or serfs under conditions of great misery. The Borussians then ceased to exist as a separate nationality and left only their name to the state later called Prussia, although most of the knights and the Rhinelanders brought in to replace them originally also were of Kimmeric stock, so that the basic population was not markedly changed. Old Prussian ceased to exist as a spoken language in the 17th century.

The Gothic leadership left among the Lithuanians after the destruction of the Gothic nation by the Huns in A.D. 374-376 provided both personnel and traditions of the royal Amal family. By these they erected a central government for Lithuania and her kin on the north and south under the aforementioned generic name of the Vidivarii, which endured until the 9th century. The Latvians and Prussians, unfortunately, then detached themselves and went independent ways and the dynastic tradition was continued in Lithuania alone, for this nation had been the dominant division of the Vidivarii. Its overlordship may have become oppressive to the other divisions. After a Lithuanian prince, Jagiello, had married Yadviga, the queen of Poland, on February 14, 1386, and also was crowned king of Poland, a nominal union of those two countries existed under this dynasty until 1569, when Sigismund II was king, at which time the union was greatly strengthened. Between 1362 and 1494 the Lithuanian Empire was at the peak of its territorial expansion. Its frontiers then extended from the Baltic to the Black Sea, and it protected western Europe from the powerful Tatar Empire in the east; but this joint history of Lithuania and Poland was a turbulent one. In 1795 both nations lost their independence, having been seized by and apportioned among Austro-Hungary, Germany, and Russia. Nearly all of Lithuanian territory went to Russia. On four occasions (1812, 1831, 1863, and 1904-5) Lithuania paid with her blood in attempts to regain her freedom, but none of these revolutions was successful. In recent times, chiefly between World Wars I and II, the Lithuanians and Latvians were accorded another opportunity to work out their own destinies as democratic nations, but subjection again by the Soviet Union since World II unfortunately terminated that opportunity. The cold fact is that they were far too successful internally for their independence to be condoned by the Soviet Union. It was in sharp contrast with the arbitrary and less successful economic system of that domineering neighbor.

----

5. *Other Racial Movements in Western Asia.* Concurrent with the major activities of the Nordic nations of Scythia were important racial movements in western Asia, nearly all of which already have been discussed under the headings of the Turks, Semites, Hamites, and others. Consequently, they will only be alluded to here. In the north, the Massagetae had moved eastward to Bactriana and

the Sakae had moved to Sogdiana, to diminish the pressure by Huns on their north.[94] As each nation expanded, it lost members who became independent under other tribal names.[95] Owing to their fair hair and blue or gray eyes, these Nordics were recognized in ancient Chinese histories, as found by Abel Remusat.[96] By the 6th century B.C. they had sundered all routes of communication between the Turkish Issedones of Eastern Turkistan and their kin in western Asia. Thus, down to the time of Alexander the Great, the people of western Asia knew nothing whatever about China. India was new country to the Persians who formed the original empire of Cyrus the Great, and much more so were the countries farther east. The intermediate mountains tended to keep the people of India and China at home. The Hindus, excluded from the north by the Himalayan ranges, knew nothing about the country beyond. Herodotus had heard only about a "vast desert [the Gobi], unknown and unexplored, in eastern Asia."[97] Strabo, who wrote nearly five centuries after Herodotus, believed that there was no country beyond India; so that knowledge of China apparently never reached the Grecians and the Romans until late.[98] China was not definitely known in Europe until as late as the 13th century A.D.

About 722 B.C., the ten tribes of Israel had been deported by the Assyrian King Sargon to Media, southwest of the Caspian Sea. North of Mesopotamia several Arabic tribes had settled among the Iranians. They were not recognized as Semites by Sennacherib, king of Assyria and Babylonia during 708-681 B.C.

---

94 V. Gordon Childe, op.cit., page 160. The *Aegli*, an independent tribe of the Sakae, are mentioned by Herodotus, iii.92.

95 The name of the Massagetae was supplanted by the tribal names of *Tokhari*, *Kushan*, and *Ephthalites*. The last may have been a designation by others rather than an actual name. The tribe called the Wu-Sun by the Chinese was a branch of the Sakae. Herodotus i.201-204. See E. A. Speiser, op.cit., page 101, citing J. Friedrich, op.cit., pages 144-148.

96 He names two of these tribes as the *Usun* and the *Khouti*.

97 Herodotus, *Hist.* iv. 40.

98 Prior to the time of Strabo and Pliny, an extensive channel of commerce had been opened between the Roman Empire and Serica (China) across Turkistan. Pliny vi.17.

The repeated raids into western Asia by the Kimmerians from about 1600 to about 640 B. C., while disastrous politically to the Phrygian and Lydian nations, did not markedly introduce a new ethnic element in that region except the Kurds south of Lake Van, since those armies later returned north. However, they did cause intermingling of the native population — Mediterranean, Lelegian, Hittite, and Keltic — and tended to press many of these inhabitants eastward into the mountains of Armenia. Thus, there came to be an incredible number of different groups of people and languages in the region of the Caucasus Mountains, as remarked by both ancient and modern writers.[99] Those mountains long separated the Nordic nations from the older nations of the south, but ultimately they were overrun by all. The region south of those mountains seems to have retained a specimen of each passing tribe from the time of the earliest migrations, — Pre-Dravidian, Iranian, Turkic, Keltic, and Nordic.[99]

By 1500 B.C. the Hittites had expanded westward as far as the Halys River, and they may long have allied themselves with the Assyrians for defensive purposes, for the ancient kingdom of *Nairi* extended from Cappadocia to the frontiers of Media. But this nation's domain in the west was shattered by the Keltic invasions from Thrace, which began about 1425 B. C., and the Assyrians thereupon overran and took Babylonia from the Kassites of Elam about 1270 B. C. These Keltic invasions continued until they had established new nations in Pontus, Paphlagonia, and Bithynia along the southerly shores of the Black Sea, in addition to the nations of Mysia, Lydia, and Caria along the Aegean coast. Occasionally, the former people were referred to by writers as Leuco-Syrians (white Syrians). Turanian Leleges were pressed southward into the Taurus Mountains[100] and Hittites southward to Syria

---

99 These facts and others noted herein demonstrate the utter inapplicability of the term "Caucasian" to designate the White Aryan race or any branch of it. See census of Caucasia by races taken by Russian authorities in 1798 in *Ency. Brit.*, 13th Ed., vol. 5, page 548.
100 Strabo, *Geogr.* vii.7.2.

and the main body eastward into the mountains of Armenia,[101] where their descendants live today and are known as Armenians, although Kelts and others have commingled with them to some extent.

Upon the conquest of Babylonia about 1270 B.C. by Shalmaneser I, the Assyrians continued with varying fortune to retain dominance over all Mesopotamia until the overthrow of that nation by Cyaxares, king of the Medes, in 606 B.C., which ended Turanian suzerainty over western Asia for nearly 17 centuries. This warfare caused the spread southward from upper Mesopotamia and Syria of the *Aramaeans,* who racially were Pre-Sumerian and Sumerians commingled (i.e., Semites).

The *Colchians,* who lived at the easterly end of the Black Sea, in the westerly part of the present Georgia, were characterized as descendants of transplanted Egyptians[102] in the army of Sesostris that invaded the Caucasus region about 1321-1300 B.C. About a century later, a band of recalcitrant *Iberians* was transferred by the Phoenicians from the Iberian peninsula to an adjacent region east of the Colchians, immediately south of the Caucasus Mountains,[103] where their descendants today are known as the *Georgians.* Still farther eastward, bordering on the Caspian Sea, lived the *Albani,* who were Nordic Kimmerians from Scythia. Since then many of these peoples have commingled and interbred more or less with surrounding brachycephalic Turanian peoples of the region.

Under Darius the Great, who succeeded Cyrus of Anshan as king of Persia and reigned during 520 to 485 B.C., the Persian empire was divided into 20 satrapies, as outlined by Herodotus,[104] and his description of them affords a comprehensive knowledge of western Asiatic geography and population at his time. In the 4th century B.C. this empire weakened and in 330 B.C. it came under the sway of the Macedonian kingdom of Alexander the

101 Herodotus, *Hist.* i.72.
102 *Ibid.,* ii.103-105; Strabo, *Geogr.* xi.2. 14-18.
103 Strabo, *ibid.,* ii.5.12, xi.1.5, 2.15-19, 3.1-6.
104 Herodotus, iii. 89-94.

Great (356-323 B.C.), son of the famous King Philip II.

The great Iranian plateau has been a crossroads of migration throughout the ages. Iranians, Turanians, and Nordics have lived there and many of their descendants still do so. The Nordics conquered the entire northerly half, the Medians in the west and tribes of the Massagetae in the east, as already shown. The Pahlavi dialect of the Nordics of Parthia was unintelligible to the Persians. In the mountains of the west were the Iranian tribes of the *Saspeirans* and *Matienni* (perhaps Mitanni), named by Herodotus,[105] in the south were the Persians, and in eastern Iran and middle Indus valley (aside from the Ethiopians or Hamites of Baluchistan)[106] were the *Pactyans, Sattagydians,* and *Gandarians* of Herodotus.[107] The *Parsi* dialect of the Persians ultimately became modified by the Pahlavi of the Nordics of Parthia.

It is worthy of note here that the arts of magic and necromancy attained their highest development under the auspices of the Magi, the powerful religious caste of the Kimmerians of Media.[108] These practices spread all over Anatolia and were adopted by the Persian and Babylonian kings.[109] They became known to the Greeks of Ionia through their long contact with the Dorians and other Kimmerians, especially by commercial intercourse of the merchants of Miletus with the Kimmerians at their Black Sea ports until the defeat of the latter by the Getae in 634 B.C. When the Tuatha Dé Danann, a large division of the vanquished Kimmerians, reached Ireland about 585 B.C. the art of necromancy was carried along with them.[110]

No subsequent important ethnic changes in Iran are

---

105 *Ibid.*, iii.94. The *Matieni* may have been the Mitanni, probably Iranians from the Zagros Mountains north of Assyria; *Ency. Brit.*, 13th Ed. vol. 13, page 539a, under *Hittites*, and vol. 18, page 182d, under *Mesopotamia*.

106 Herodotus, vii.70.

107 *Ibid.*, iii.91, 102.

108 Herodotus, *Hist.* i.101, iii. 73, 126.

109 *Ibid.*, i. 107-111, ii. 141-159, vii. 19; *Daniel* 4.7; 2 *Kings* 19; 2 *Chron.* 25, 33.

110 *Ency. Brit.*, 13th Ed., vol. 14, page 757, by Edmund C. Quiggin.

known. However, probably a millennium later, about the middle of the 6th century A.D., the Turks of central Asia spread over the Oxus region and it came under their dominance. This event was an imminent threat to the great Scytho-Indian empire developed by the Nordic Tokhari and Sakae and their related tribes of Bactriana and Sogdiana about the beginning of the Christian era as the last outburst of Nordic energy in Asia. Its dominion embraced eastern Iran and western India. Already weakened because of the vast territory covered, it collapsed and fell to the Turks in A.D. 570 and these Nordic people of Iran soon became engulfed in an ocean of darker peoples that surrounded them.[111] It was a tragic event of history that has been inadequately treated thus far.

In Anatolia the situation was different. There an important ethnic change occurred when that country was conquered by the Seljuk Turks from Turkistan in A.D. 1071 and later by the Osman Turks; but these conquests merely increased the Turanian strain in the population, especially in the northern portion of the country, and restored to that race a dominion gained by it after 8000 B.C. and lost in 606 B.C. Nonetheless, the influence of the Aryan strain in Turkish affairs is conspicuous today. Many present Turkish leaders are of Nordic (Kimmerian) descent, at least in part. The recent emergence of Turkish nationality from blighting influences affords promise of her recovery of much of the ancient cultural glory of her kindred predecessors in collaboration with large Keltic and Nordic elements.

---

111 See Calvin Kephart, *Sanskrit — Its Origin Composition, and Diffusion* (Shenandoah Publishing House, Strasburg, Va., 1949). This subject also is treated later herein.

CHAPTER VI.

KIMMERIC INVASIONS OF WESTERN EUROPE

1. *Sundering of the Kimmerians.* At the time of the epochal shattering of the Kimmerian nation in Ukrainia by the Getae in 634 B.C., one large division, the later *Goidelic* Kimmerians,[1] fled to western Gaul, another large division, the later *Skolotic* (or *Britonic*) Kimmerians, remained behind as subjects of the victors, and the southernmost tribe, the Treres, the later Danes, rejoined its army that had invaded Lydia about 640 B.C., while other smaller divisions fled elsewhere, as has already been stated. The absence of the Danish Treres from the homeland may have been the major cause of the downfall of their nation in Scythia. They also migrated to western Europe in 606 B.C. This early partition of the Kimmerian nation resulted in the arising of linguistic differences later,[2] the Goidels having appropriated the dialect of the Gaulish Kelts (Alpines), with whom they were long in contact in the upper Danube and more westerly regions, in far greater degree than the next Kimmeric arrivals, the *Skoloti* (Belgae, Britons, Scots, and others), did three centuries later. The latter moved into the basins of the middle Main and lower Rhine, from which the Kelts already had been pressed westward and southward. The Keltic influence on the dialect of the Danes was negligible because they moved down the Elbe River.

The victorious Getic armies overran western Asia during the 28 years from 634 to 606 B.C. As one army approached Lydia in 606 B.C., the Danish Treres, upon learning of the defeat of their nation and not knowing the size of that army, withdrew under the leadership of

---

1 For their Scythic origin, see Bede, *Hist. eccl. gentis Anglorum*, vol. 1, c.1; also J. A. Giles, *op. cit.,* Geoffrey's *History*, book iv. ch. 17.

2 J. C. Prichard, *op.cit.,* vol. 3, page 141.

the renowned Odin and followed the Goidels up the Danube valley. They then crossed to the Elbe River and went down this river to its outlet.[3] King Alyattes, of Lydia, took advantage of the opportunity to announce to his subjects that he had driven the invaders out of his country. The Danes took possession of the region on both sides of the lower Elbe, as far west as the Ems River, where settlements were made, and the major division under Odin then continued into Jutland and established the nation of Danmark. This peninsula took the national name of the conquerors, the Cimbric (Kimmerian) Chersonese. The Salian Franks descended from the Danish units (the *Salii*) that settled west of the Elbe along the shores of the North Sea. These people are discussed in a later chapter.

In 342 B.C., the Getae of lower Scythia moved northward to evade the punitive expedition of King Philip II of Macedonia, in consequence of which the Skoloti, who had greatly increased in numbers, took advantage of the opportunity to regain their freedom and to escape Philip's army by fleeing to western Europe, as their kinsmen had done earlier. They took possession of the lower Main River and central Rhine River regions and ultimately extended their possessions west of and down the Rhine and across the Seine River toward the Loire in Gaul. They finally overspread Franconia, Hessen, Rheinpfalz, northern France, Belgium, the lower Rhine valley, and southern Netherlands. They formed contact and at times fought with Danes about the lower Elbe and north of the lower Rhine and also with those Goidels and Kelts in northern France who had not yet moved south of the Seine River.

Anciently, confusion sometimes arose among historians regarding the names of the different nations and of their various tribal offshoots. The former, in the majority of instances, were geographical in origin, but the tribes

---

3 Thus, instead of continuing westward as far as Gaul, they turned northwestward, down the course of the Elbe River, apparently in their search for unconquered lands and to avoid conflict with their earlier congeners in Gaul.

customarily took their names from patriarchs or heroes,[4] their military leaders in most instances, and this custom was followed when a tribe branched from a large division or nation. Minns[5] has found that the name *Skoloti,* derived perhaps from an earlier tribal leader, applied to the Kimmerian subjects in Scythia and not to the Getae. This unquestionable fact provides the logical name by which to designate this branch of the Kimmerian nation, since it was carried westward and is perpetuated in the modern name of Scotland.

Each of the westward migrations of Kimmerians exerted untold influence on the subsequent history of western Europe[6] and they will be discussed in sequence. Each left the Kimmeric name in western Europe in such forms as Cimbri, Kymry, Cymry, Cumbria, and Cambria in Danmark, France, England, Wales, and Scotland. They also imparted tribal or national names as groups separated from the main body, such as those of the nations of Belgium and Britain and of numerous places in France.

The British *Triads* of Wales not only confirm the emigration of the Kimmerii *(Kymry)* from the Ukraine but also indicate the Goidelic and the Britonic divisions and subdivisions.[7] Identification of the Kimmerii who anciently inhabited Scythia as the Danes *(Cimbri* and *Teutones)* and the Kimmerii of France (and of Britain and Ireland as well) appears in Plutarch, *Caius Marius,* where they are reported as of large stature and with gray eyes and as having been driven out of Scythia in consequence of a quarrel, some going to Asia Minor and others to northwestern Europe. It is to the great credit of the Welsh people that they should continue today their historic national name of Kimmerii (Cymry) and the name of their country as Cymru. The name of Wales, applied by the English, means merely 'foreigner.'

4 Strabo, *Geogr.* x. 3.6.

5 *Ency. Brit.,* 13th Ed. vol. 24, page 526, by Ellis H. Minns.

6 Each took to Britain the custom of painting the body, a practice common among Scythian nations. See citations by Joseph Ritson, *Annals of the Caledonians, Picts, and Scots (Edinburgh,* 1828), pages 92-96.

7 J. A. Giles, *op. cit.,* footnote on pages 422-423.

2. *Westward Flight of the Goidelic Kimmerians.* The later-known Goidelic Kimmerians, having been driven past the Carpathian Mountains into southerly Suebian territory by the Getae and with the possibility of return closed to them, pressed westward along the valley of the Danube River to its source and then across the Rhine valley to central Gaul, where they arrived about 632 B.C. There the country was populated mainly by Kelts, whom the Kimmerians pushed westward and southward. The latter then seized the region of the lower Seine and Loire Rivers. Quoting from Guizot and De Witt:

> From the 7th to the 4th century B. C., a new population spread over Gaul, not at once but by a series of invasions, of which the two principal took place at the two extremes of that period. They called themselves *Kymrians* or *Kimmerians,* . . . which recalls Kimmerii or Kimmerians, the name of a people whom the Greeks placed on the western bank of the Black Sea and in the Cimmerian peninsula, called to this day Crimea.[8]

The Goidels represented the first division of those Kimmeric invaders and they expanded promptly in Gaul southward beyond the Loire River.[8] They spread the Keltic La Tène culture in western Europe, including the British Isles.

The Danish division of the Kimmerians (the Treres) arrived from Lydia about 30 years later, approximately 604 B. C., and moved down the Elbe River, driving the last of the *Suiones* and *Sitones* from the Danish peninsula to southern Sweden and Norway. The chief tribe under Odin then took possession of the peninsula about 603 B. C.; hence the application of the name Cimbric Chersonese to Jutland. They were adherents of the cult of the Egypto-

---

8 Guizot and De Witt, *History of France* (London, 1872-1881), vol. 1, page 16. Tacitus, *Life of Agricola*, ch. 24.

Grecian god Danäus,[9] derived from the Aegean region, and the root-word *Dan* later was used in naming the country; in fact, this root-word appears in geographical names all the way across Europe from the Aegean basin to Danmark and Ireland.[9] The Danes conquered the *Angli,* a sister tribe of the *Warni,* east of the lower Elbe, and Odin's eldest son Balder was imposed on them as their king. These were Suebic tribes. Danish units also settled west of the lower Elbe, along the North Sea as far as the Ems River, and they were the ancestors of the inhabitants of Rüstingen and of the later Salian Franks. They pressed the Suebic Frisians to the lowlands and islands where they now live. Tradition affirms that the Danes were related to the Tuatha Dé Danann, the earliest Kimmerians in Ireland.[10] The differences between the languages and customs of the Cimbri of Jutland and those of the Tuatha Dé Danann at the time of these settlements thus represented substantially the extent to which the latter had adopted the language and customs of the Kelts with whom they had mingled in Gaul.

West of the Rhine and throughout all of the mountainous regions of central Europe the Keltic language and customs were deeply-rooted and widespread; so that, instead of the Kimmerians contributing appreciably to them, their own Nordic language and customs were largely modified by those of the people whose country they had invaded. It is a common occurrence in history for the customs of the conquerors thus to become lost in those of the conquered, especially when they are fewer in numbers and when the conquered are the more highly-civilized, more conservative, and more tenacious of their customs, as was the case here. This invasion had the effect of driving Kelts farther into the Carpathian and Alpine ranges, whence some of them invaded Italy[11] and others crossed the Pyrenees to Iberia. In the latter peninsula, they

9 See Herodotus, *Hist.,* vi. 53, vii. 94. In primitive history and mythology, the name of Danaan applied to his adherents. The name Dan later was applied to persons in the Danish royal line. These Kimmerians on the lower Danube gave that river its name.

10 *Ency. Brit.,* 13th Ed., vol. 14, pages 757-758, by Edmund C. Quiggin.

11 Livy, *Historiae and Annales,* v.34.

intermarried with the native Iberians and augmented the numbers of the later-known Keltiberian subrace, as mentioned earlier.

After about two generations, about 587 B.C., numerous bands of these Goidels, under the national names of the Dananns and the Picts, undertook an invasion of the British Isles from the south of England. They drove the earlier Iberians and Kelts ahead of them westward and northward and soon reached Ireland and Scotland respectively. In the conquest of England by other Kimmerians (the Skoloti), beginning about 290 B.C., their predecessors were pushed toward the north and we ultimately find all of the Dananns in Ireland[12] and the Picts in Scotland.

The customs of the Dananns, as described by Strabo,[13] had a distinctly Scythian aspect and, along with the persistent tradition in Irish history,[14] tend to confirm that origin of the race. The traditions of migration via Greece, while questionable in detail, are readily explainable in the numerous raids that the Kimmerians of the Ukraine made in southwestern Asia. The leading families possessed many relics that they had taken in their plundering expeditions among the civilized nations of western Asia, many of which they took with them when they invaded western Europe and finally settled in Ireland and Scotland. This fact likewise harmonizes with primitive Irish traditions.

The Goidels had received some taste of the Grecian and Lydian cultures during their contact with the colonies of

---

12 Not only does the array of historical facts but also the repeated allusion in Irish history to Scythia as the place of origin of both the Tuatha Dé Danann (Goidels) and the later Scotti confirm the migration here recounted. Particularly is this emphasized when we consider the great part played in Irish history by its historians and genealogists. Cennfaeldh the Learned (c. A.D. 610-678), head of an institute of learning and noted writer, wrote a well-known poem of 14 stanzas on the migration from Scythia of Golamh (Milesius), traditional dynastic head of the Scotti and whose descendants conquered northern Ireland. Eugene O'Curry, *Manners and Customs of the Ancient Irish* (Norgate and Williams, London, 1873), vol. 2, pages 94 and 231-233.

13 Strabo, *Geogr.*, iv. 5.4.

14 *Encyclopaedia Britannica*, 13th Ed., vol. 14, pp. 757-758, by E. C. Quiggin. Bede, *Eccl. Hist.*, 1.1.

Miletus on the Black Sea and their invasions of the civilized south, but it will be shown later that, owing to the superior civilizing influence to which the Skolotic Kimmerians had been subjected for three centuries by the Getae north of the Black Sea, they (the Skoloti) exerted the far greater influence on western civilization. However, the Goidels were less mixed in strain than the Skoloti and they used Iranian proper names (obtained through their fellow colonists, the Medians on the lower Danube), and represented the Nordic element in greater purity.[15] Known in Irish history as the Tuatha Dé Danann or Danann people, they reached Ireland from Gaul via England and Scotland about 585 B.C., and, according to acceptable tradition, they introduced the use of iron there. While driving the Iberian and Keltic population of Britain westward and northward, the Dananns found their ascendancy contested by Viking sea-pirates (Fomorians), but they soon gained control of the island. Belgic tribes (Firbolgs) from northern Gaul long afterward entered Ireland from the south and in the 2nd century B.C. conquered large areas throughout the island, establishing their capital at Tara, but they were subjugated later by the Dananns. The latter held this dominance, despite sporadic uprising of the earlier inhabitants, until inroads in the north began to be made after 100 B.C. by their kinsmen, the Skoloti (Scotti), of northwestern England, who gained increasing control during the subsequent centuries, as shown later.[16]

Certain Gauls made a historic invasion of eastern Europe during the last quarter of the 3rd century B.C. The division that settled in and gave its name to Galatia, in ancient Phrygia, in Anatolia, apparently were southerly Kimmerians who came from the south of the Cevennes Mountains. They were the *Tectosages,* whose capital became Ancyra (Ankara), the present capital of Turkey, the *Trocmi,* who settled around Tavium, and the *Tolisto-*

---

15 *Ency. Brit.,* 13th Ed. vol. 24, page 526, by Ellis Hovell Minns.
16 Strabo (iv. 5.2) distinguished the taller and slenderer Nordic Kimmerians from the stocky and large-bodied Kelts of Gaul.

bogii, who settled around Pessinus. A descendant was the late eminent Turkish soldier and statesman, Kemal Attaturk. The other division split off under Brennus and invaded Greece in 279 B.C. The Goidelic Kimmerians constituted a numerous people in western France in Julius Caesar's time, living mainly south of the Loire River. Their descendants inhabit that region today.

When the Skolotic Kimmerians reached the west about 340 B.C., they settled first on the easterly side of the Rhine,[17] north of the Main River and west of the Weser, chiefly in modern Hessen. The Frisians, who were the westernmost tribe of the Suebic nation and inhabited territory along the North Sea west of the Weser, were separated from the rest of their nation east of the Elbe River by the arrival of the Danish Kimmerians about 604 BC. and afterward were driven westward toward the Zuyder Zee. Some Keltic tribes that remained in the region between the Weser and Rhine Rivers, where they warred with the Danes, were driven southwestward by the latter. From their habitation on the Middle Rhine, the Skolotic tribes made large-scale incursions down that river and across and up the Mosel River valley into northeastern Gaul. The Kelts enclosed in the lower lands made their last stand along the present Belgic coast, where they were overcome as the Skoloti took over all of that lowland region.[18] The *Tungri,* a formidable tribe, are said to have been the first Skoloti to cross the lower Rhine[19] and the town of Tongres, in Belgium, was named for them.[19] Having come into regions north of those overrun by the earlier (or Goidelic) Kimmerians, the Skoloti received less positive cultural influence from the Kelts, most of whom they pushed southward, than the Goidels had acquired. This circumstance explains the noticeable difference between the language of the Goidels

17 Tacitus, *Germania,* ch. 2.
18 Those Kelts subsequently merged with their conquerors. The Keltic strain is quite noticeable among the present inhabitants of Belgium and other parts of the lowlands.
19 Tacitus, *Germania,* ch. 2.

in the British Isles and that of the Belgae, Scotti, and Britons, in which the latter had advanced further in relinquishing inflectional endings.[20] East of the Skoloti in Hessen, the Suebic *Thuringi* had reached and settled the upper course of the Werra River. Even today the Elbe and the Werra represent the boundary between the former Suebian nations on the east and the Kimmerian nations on the west, except for the Frisians. The Danes and the Skoloti are treated at length in other chapters.

In the light of what has just been said, it becomes practicable now to separate "the wheat from the chaff" in the early history of Britain and Ireland, particularly of the latter, which *prima facie* presents a confused picture to the historian. The traditions concerning Iberian, Grecian, and Scythian origins of Irish peoples already have been explained. The traditional emigrations from the Near East via Spain apparently relate only to early voyages of small numbers of seafaring Anatolians, Kretans, and Phoenicians, all brunet peoples, and not to the blond Irish people. Those seafaring nations explored most of the coasts of western Europe in very remote times and some of their colonists settled in villages and towns in the British Isles as well as at continental ports, perhaps largely for commercial reasons. Tradition dating from antiquity usually is valuable as a clue or general guide, but it must be relied upon very cautiously and then only after verification in so far as detail is concerned.

---

3. *Migration of Danish Kimmerians Verified.* The westward migration of the Danish Kimmerians from Lydia is verified by traditional facts presented in the Danish saga, *The Prose Edda*, written in the 13th century by Snorri Sturlason.[21] As Thomas Nicholas well says, "tradition, the memory of a nation, is wonderfully retentive and upon

20 *Ency. Brit.*, 13th Ed., vol. 5, page 613, by E. C. Quiggin.
21 Snorri Sturlason, *The Prose Edda*, translated by Arthur G. Brodeur (The American-Scandinavian Foundation, New York, 1916).

the whole singularly accurate."[22] In the *Prologue* it is said that under the leadership of Odin a great multitude of people, young and old, men and women, departed from the vicinity of Troy, in Turkland [Asia Minor], *with much goods of great value.*[23] They made no end to their journey, which took them through Thrace and across central Europe, until they arrived in the territory of the Saxons, which then was on the easterly side of the lower Elbe River. There they tarried for a time, while Odin made conquests far and wide on both sides of the Elbe, after which he and his followers moved northward and settled in what now is Jutland, in Danmark, to which country these followers of the god Danäus later gave their name. The year is not stated, but the above facts and the apparent year are provable from other history and constitute important contributions to the history of western Europe. The subsequent deification of Odin because of his exploits and great wisdom was in accord with the prevailing custom of the Nordic and other early peoples.

Upon examination of pertinent history, we find that the Kimmerians of the Ukraine (southern Scythia) repeatedly invaded western Asia Minor, especially Lydia, from as early as about 1600 B.C. to as late as about 640 B.C. While many continued in the south with their families, others returned to their homeland with booty from the countries overrun and were replaced by younger men interested in adventure. The last large army of the Danish Treres was in Lydia when their nation in Scythia was assailed by the Getae about 635 B.C., and their absence undoubtedly contributed to the nation's defeat the next year, as already related. The rest of the Treres north of the Danube then joined their army in Lydia. Traditionally, all of them were expelled from Lydia by its king, Alyattes, in 606 B.C.,[24] but they

---

22 Thomas Nicholas, *The Pedigree of the English People* (Longmans, Green, Reader & Co., London, 1874), page 30.
23 Traditionally, Odin was a son of god Borr and goddess Bestla, deified human personages. Wednesday was named for him. Ancient coins and other objects of Troy have been unearthed in the caves of Ireland, where they must have been deposited by the Tuatha Dé Danann.
24 See *ante,* by Index.

already knew that their nation had been overwhelmed in 634 B.C. and partly dispersed and partly made subjects of the Getae and that a victorious Getic army was over-running Asia farther east. When this army approached Lydia in 606 B.C., these Danish Treres, probably not knowing its size, decided to withdraw from the country and to follow those of the nation who 28 years earlier had emigrated to western Europe. They must have reached Jutland in 603 B.C., allowing two years for their migration westward from Lydia and one year for warfare on the lower Elbe.

When this horde of Danish Kimmerians (*Cimbri*) tarried awhile in Westphalia, on the western margin of Saxonland, they found some Keltic tribes blocking their way farther westward and hostile Saxons on their east. Under Odin's leadership, they then conquered widely and settled some of their tribes on lands west of the lower Elbe and imposed their rule on the nearby *Engili* (*Angli*) on the east, a sister nation of the *Warni* (*Werni* or *Varini*) who lived around Lubeck Bay.[25] Traditionally Odin's eldest son Baldeg *(Balder)* was imposed on the Angles as their king, and this tribe evidently remained allies of the Cimbri. The Keltic tribes thus dislodged moved south-westward toward the lower Rhine, whereupon the central division of the Danes under Odin moved northward, driving the rest of the *Suiones* and *Sitones* into the Scandinavian peninsula, and settled in Jutland (called (*Cimbric Chersonese* for them). The Angles then moved into and occupied all of Holstein behind the Danes, with the Saxons on their southeast. Only recently, representatives of Oslo University found a large collection of weapons and jewelry of about 600 B.C. on a rocky slope near Droeback, south of Oslo, in Norway. Upon the decease of Odin, he was succeeded by his younger son Skjöldr of Denmark as king.

These Cimbri were known for their large stature — a characteristic of all Kimmerians, the tallest of all Aryans.

---

25 *Ency. Brit.*, 13th Ed., vol. 11, page 776, under *Lex Angliorum et Werinorum.*

One of their earliest tribal names was that of *Teutoni*, whom Pytheas (339 B.C.) seems to indicate as inhabitants of the extreme north of Jutland, west of the main body of the Cimbri in what is now Alborg.[26] The word Teutoni, as commonly written, is Keltic in form. It apparently was preserved in the name of the district called Thyland or Thythsyssel until recently. Soon these Cimbri added the islands of Funen, Langland, Laaland, Falster, and Zealand to their dominions.[27]

At least two of Odin's tribes settled along the North Sea between the Elbe and the Ems Rivers. Traditionally, they were headed by his sons Vegdeg and Sigge. Apparently, the line of the former soon terminated and the two tribes coalesced, whereupon the aggregation took the name *Sigambri* (for Sigge) and became the nuclear tribe of the *Salii*. The later *Ambrones* also came out of Jutland. The division east of the Elbe ultimately split into a number of smaller tribes, with different names.[28] Only a small number seem to have crossed the Ems River into central Netherlands prior to the Christian era, but some of the eastern tribes moved up the Weser River. About 300 B.C. the Danes introduced the Iron Age into Sweden.

Jutland in ancient times, while well-wooded, largely was barren drift sand in the interior and was inadequate to support a large population. In consequence, a Cimbric expedition made its way out of the peninsula about 120 B.C. and wandered over Europe, defeating a Roman army in Carinthia in 113 and again in southern Gaul in 105. After a repulse by the Keltiberi in Spain, they returned north as far as the Seine River, where they were repelled by the Belgae. In 103, under a well-defined plan, they were joined by a force of the Teutoni and by the Am-

---

26 Shown without qualification to have been Jutes. J. C. Prichard, *op. cit.*, vol. 3, page 360.

27 Snorri Sturlason, *The Prose Edda*, transl. by Arthur B. Brodeur (The American-Scandinavian Foundation, New York, 1916), *The Beguiling of Gylfi*, Sec. I-II.

28 *Chauci, Fosi, Cherusci, Chamavi, Angrivarii, Attuarii, Ansibarii, Dulgibini, Tubantes.* Tacitus, *Germania*, ch. 34.

brones for an expedition on Rome, but they were defeated
by the Romans in 102-101 B. C. The remnant returned
to Belgic Gaul, where their descendants became known
as the *Aduatuci*.[29] The main body of the Cimbri remained
in Jutland, for it is recorded in *Monumentum Ancyranum*
that about A.D. 5 a Roman fleet reached Jutland and
received the nominal submission of a people of this name
and several other tribes, and Jutland appears on Ptolemy's
map as the Cimbric Cheronese.

Early in the Christian era, Saxons advancing westward
pressed the Sigambri and their allies, constituting the subsequent Salian nation, into the basin of the Yssel River,
which took its name from them; from there they later
spread into Rüstringen and over Gelderland along the
lower Rhine. In 8 B.C. Tiberius already had moved some
of them into this region on condition of military service
for the Romans.

Thus, it will be seen that, while the Frisians, Swedes, and
Norwegians descended from the Suebian nation, the Danes
and Salian Franks descended from a branch of the Kimmerian nation. Unlike their congeners in Gaul, Britain,
and Ireland, the Danes were substantially unaffected by
contact with the Keltic language and customs of western
Europe. According to Bede, their Jutish dialect differed
somewhat from that of the Angles and Saxons in England. This difference represented the variance between
the contemporaneous Kimmeric and Suebic dialects.

In the light of the foregoing, we readily can understand
why the Elbe and the Werra Rivers separated the Suebian
and the Danish and Skolotic Kimmerian nations and why
Odin's sons Balder, Vegdeg, and Sigge are said to have
ruled on the lower Elbe and Weser Rivers and the younger
son Skjöldr later in Danmark. We also see the basis for the
assertion that Sigge and his descendants ruled over Frank-
land.[30] In the *Chronicon* of Fredegarius it is said that the
Franks descended from Trojans, meaning the Danes who

---

29 Julius Caesar, *op.cit.*, ii. 29.
30 Snorri Sturlason, *Prologue to The Prose Edda, op. cit.*

had hastened from Troy, in Turkland (Lydia), as recited in the Edda. Balder and his descendants traditionally were the ruling dynasty of the Angles, who went from Holstein to England and for whom the latter country was named.

When the Skolotic Kimmerians appeared on the central and lower Rhine about 340 B.C., they fought some of the earlier tribes north of the Rhine that had branched from the Sigambri, causing them all later to form the confederation of Salian Franks. The Sigambri were the central tribe of this federation headed by the royal dynasty. The Skolotic tribes, later known as the Ripuarian Franks, settled on both sides of the middle Rhine, where they subsequently were called "Germans" by Julius Caesar.[31] The inapplicability of the terms "Germans" and "Teutons" to the Suebic people of present Germany (Deutschland), east of the Weser and Werra Rivers, is discussed later. The *Suebi* and the *Kimmerii,* although Nordic peoples, politically were separate nations as early as 4500 years ago.[32] The confusion of these two nations by historians is due simply to inadequate interpretation of the available ethnographical evidence.

Other interesting developments followed this migration and settlement of the different divisions of the Danish Kimmerians. Upon conquering Jutland from the Suiones (Swedes), the Danes instituted a government modeled on that about which they had learned in Asia Minor (chiefly Lydia), appointing chieftains in the manner that prevailed at Troy, ordaining the laws and customs of the Trojans, and naming 12 doomsmen to administer the criminal and civil laws thus prescribed.[33] The Danish language is indicated as having been somewhat different from that

---

31 Julius Caesar, *Commentaries on the Gallic War,* book II, ch. 3-4, 15, book IV, ch. 3-4, 6-8, 14-19. "German" from wehrman (soldier) through the forms werre and guerre to German.

32 Tacitus, *Germania,* ch. 38-39.

33 Sturlason, *The Prologue.* These laws and customs must have been a composite evolution of those of the primitive Pelasgans, their conquerors, the Pre-Sumerian Leleges, and the next conquerors, the Kelts from Thrace.

of the Swedes and other Suebic peoples.[34] The increase of Danish territory, particularly on Zealand (Selund) and other islands, was made later at the expense of the Swedes, whose earliest-named king was Gylfi and who were much troubled at the success of the Danes (the Aesir-people *from Asia*).[35] That this period antedated the Gothic conquest of southern Sweden is proved by the fact that the Danes[36] made no mention of crossing Gothic territory when passing between Jutland and the Swedish capital, Uppsala. Moreover, the warfare of the Danes was with the Swedes or Saxons and not as yet with the Goths.[36]

Tacitus says that "in the same quarter of Germany [Frankland], adjacent to the ocean, dwell the Cimbri [Kimmerii], a small state at present but great in renown. Of their past grandeur extensive vestiges still remain in encampments and lines on either shore, from the compass of which the strength and numbers of the nation may still be computed and credit derived to the account of so prodigious an army. It was in the 640th year of Rome [113 B. C.] that the arms of the Cimbri were first heard of . . . ".[37] At the time of Tacitus, the population of the Cimbric Chersonese, later called Danmark, was greatly reduced by the emigration of the Cimbri, Teutons, and Ambrones, who ravaged Gaul and undertook to invade Italy, where they were defeated by Caius Marius in 102-101 B.C.

Eventually, early in the 2nd century A.D. (by about 120), the Goths appeared and conquered southern Sweden, including Skäne, and the Danish islands of Zealand, Falster, and Laaland. Skäne then became known as *Riedgotland* and the islands as *Eygotland*,[38] although in the *Prologue* the former name, apparently in error, is applied to Jutland. Traditions of this kind are apt to be incon-

---

34 *Ibid.*, and *The Poesy of Skalds*, Sec. XLII.
35 *The Edda, The Beguiling of Gylfi*, Secs. I-II.
36 *The Edda, The Poesy of Skalds*, Sec. XLIII; Calvin Kephart, *The Swedes and Swedish Goths* (1938).
37 Tacitus, *Germania*, c. 37, where the term "Germany" was applied to territory of the Franks.
38 *The Edda, The Poesy of Skalds*, Sec. LXV.

sistent at times and it is hazardous to rely unreservedly on all details, especially without support from independent historical sources. About A.D. 150, the Danes reorganized their forces, attacked the Goths, and regained Zealand, Falster, and Laaland and also took Skäne from them.[39] Skäne was restored to the Swedish nation only as late as the 17th century. This early reversal of the Gothic fortunes was the cause of the return[39] of the *Heruli, Langobardi,* and *Gepidae* to the Vistula River basin on the mainland, as later explained.

In the light of the foregoing, *The Prose Edda* apparently is a production of the Kimmerians rather than of the Scandinavians. Danmark primarily is a Kimmerian nation, although it has acquired a Scandinavian strain from its neighbors since early times. This origin is confirmed by the fact that the Danes practiced necromancy[40] as the Goidelic Kimmerians in Ireland did.[41] The modern term "Scandinavia", therefore, properly is applicable in its original sense to only the peninsula of Sweden and Norway and not to that of Danmark. The Danes, while essentially Nordic, are somewhat darker in complexion than the Scandinavians, which is a Kimmerian attribute. Minor darkness may also have arisen from their commingling with brunet people during their invasions of Lydia before and in the 7th century B.C. Thus, the Kimmerians of Great Britain were darker than the Anglo-Saxon invaders[42] and the Danish invaders of Ireland were known as Black Heathens (*Dubhgaill*) while the Norwegians were known as White Heathens (*Finngaill*) because of difference of complexion.

---

4. *Salian Franks.* We have just shown that the later Salian Franks were descendants of Danish Kimmmerians who had settled between the lower Elbe and Weser Rivers about 604 B.C., under Odin's sons Vegdeg and Sigge.

39 C. C. Mierow, *The Gothic History of Jordanes* (Princeton, 1915), pages 57 and 78.
40 *The Edda, The Beguiling of Gylfi,* Sec. XXXIII.
41 See *ante,* by Index.
42 See *post,* by Index.

Their name of *Salii* and their legends indicate that their ancestors inhabited this region along the North Sea. During the next few centuries, they expanded into a number of tribes and moved westward toward the Ems River and the lower Rhine. Since the dynasty of Vegdeg had become extinct among these people, it apparently left the descendants of Sigge, original leader of the *Sigambri,* without rivals in the Danish royal line among these westerly tribes. In 8 B.C. the Roman General Tiberius moved the Sigambri from the right bank of the Rhine northward to the Veluwe, between Nykerk and the Yssel River, in Gelderland. After inflicting defeats on them, the Romans held them as allies along with the *Batavi* (a branch of the *Chatti*) on condition that they should provide the empire with men and arms.

In the 2nd century of the Christian era, the Suebic tribes east of the Elbe, for reasons later shown, accelerated their widespread migrations southward. Their pressure on the Danish and Skolotic Kimmerians on the right bank of the Rhine from the North Sea to the Main River soon made itself felt. It resulted in the formation of defensive alliances among the latter about the beginning of the 3rd century, first by the Danish tribes on the lower Rhine and then by the Ripuarian tribes on the middle Rhine. These federations subsequently matured plans for offensive operations to take from the Romans the lands south and west of the Rhine that their congeners (Goidelic Kimmerians) centuries earlier had gained from the Kelts. In doing so, they pressed the Goidels southward toward the Loire River.

The Salian Franks had not been heard of by that name prior to A.D. 358, when they inhabited the Yssel River basin and were driven by the Saxons to the Betuwe (Batavia), between the Waal and the Rhine, in the Netherlands. Various writers deemed them to have been descendants of the Sigambri and associated tribes. This inference appears to be entitled to full credence. This nation, along with the Batavi and segments of other Danish Kimmerian tribes, mainly the *Chamavi,* the *Chauci,* the *Attuarii* (or *Chasauri*), the *Angrivarii,* the *Ansibarii,* the *Cherusci,* and the

Tubantes, from the region between the lower Elbe and the Ems united under the name of the *Salii,* or Salian Franks, preparatory to assault by their armies on the Roman Empire south of the Rhine.[43] The royal line of the Sigambri appears to have been recognized as the preëminent dynasty, later called the Merovingian, after a king named Merwich, Merovech, or Meroving. In 431, the Salic King Chlodio, the earliest-known member of Merovingian lineage, crossed the Rhine, defeated the Roman General Aetius, took Cambrai and extended his dominion to the Somme River, west of the Maas (or Meuse) River. His 20-year reign ended in 447 and was followed by that of Merowech for a decade. Childerich then reigned from 457 to 481. He resided at Tournai, in modern Hainault, Belgium, where his grave was discovered in 1653. His son Clovis, born in 466, succeeded him in 481. Portions of the Salic dominion were governed at this time by other chieftains than Clovis, probably representing the other tribes that had entered the confederation. The subsequent fortunes of these Salian Franks will be narrated later.

---

5. *Getae and Skolotic Kimmerians Civilized in Scythia.* We already have related how the Getae took the Ukraine from the Kimmerians in 634 B.C., pursued escaping divisions of them in various directions, and made the remainder their subjects. The most important pursuit was that through the Caucasus Mountains, when, missing their quarry, the Getae ravaged all of western Asia, which they dominated for 28 years — from 634 to 606 B. C. In maintaining the line of communication with their homeland during this period, they established the first segment of the most influential early course of diffusion of western Asiatic civilization to western Europe. It apparently has been unknown heretofore to historians. The culture of

---

43 The names of all of the tribes allied with the Salians in the operations southward in Gaul are not believed to have been ascertained. Others than those named may have been included.

the Assyrian Empire was appropriated to the extent that
the Getae were able to absorb it. Learned men, taken as
prisoners, were impressed into their service and also were
assigned to train their youths for leadership in military
and civil pursuits. Commercial intercourse between western Asia and Scythia was greatly stimulated.

This civilizing influence was shared with the Skolotic
Kimmerians that were held in subjection by the Getae.
These subjects represented mainly the settled, non-military,
commercial, and property-owning classes of their shattered
nation. They at first resisted subjection, as is proved by their
uprising during the long absence of the Getic army in
the western Asiatic campaign described by Herodotus,[44]
when they usurped the places of their masters. Upon
the return of this army across the narrow strait at Kertch,
it met the resistance of the rebellious Kimmerians at the
fortifications erected by them across the neck of the Krimean peninsula leading to the mainland of the Ukraine.
The revolters were then subdued.[45] But this subjection
of the Skoloti was not slavish.[46] It endured approximately
300 years, during which time their numbers increased
greatly. Their habitation, confined between the Dnieper
River and the Sea of Azov, just east of Olbia, the noted
Milesian colony, afforded contact with the culture of
this prominent Grecian outpost on the one hand and with
Babylonian and Assyrian cultures gained by the Getae
on the other hand. The Skoloti were the husbandmen and
cordial relations apparently arose between the two peoples.
No other serious uprising by the Skoloti is recorded until
their emigration westward in 342 B.C.

This long period of political subjection of the Skoloti
was one of great cultural advancement and the subsequent
transmission of this culture to western Europe by both
nations produced a new superior civilization there. One

---

44 Herodotus, *Hist.* iv, 3-4.
45 This must have been the occasion (606 B. C.) when some of the captive
Medians, the later *Sigynae*, broke away and settled on the Dalmatian coast north
of the Albanians. See *ante*, by Index.
46 See Tacitus, *Germania*, c. 25.

of the most important acquisitions by the Getae and the Skoloti alike was the remarkable legal system of the ancient Sumerians and other nations of Mesopotamia as revised and codified by King Hammurabi of Babylonia about 2100 B.C. and as modified through the subsequent centuries. No system of cultural filtration can be devised by which theological, philosophical, political, and economic ideas can be appropriated by one nation from another and legal ideas be kept out.[47] Laws are easily transplanted from one nation to another by conquest, by simple borrowing, and by the intercourse of commercial life.

When the expedition of King Philip II of Macedonia against the Getae in Scythia in 342 dislodged the Skoloti, these Kimmerians, like their kinsmen three centuries earlier, fought their way to freedom westward between the Suebic tribes and the Alpine Kelts until they reached the territory west of the Weser and Werra Rivers (south of the Danish Kimmerians) and in the Main and middle Rhine valleys. The division that finally settled on both sides of the lower Rhine took the name of Belgae, from their leader, but other tribal names soon arose, as shown later. Two divisions that subsequently conquered England from Gaul were known as the Scotti and the Britae (or Britons), the former bearing the shortened national name of the Skoloti and the latter the name of a leader called Prid or Brit (or Prydain).[48] The Scotti settled in northern England and southern Scotland and the Britons in southern England. Upon conquering northern Ireland when the Romans invaded Britain, the Scotti named it *Scotia Major,* and southern Scotland they subsequently called *Scotia Minor.* Thus, the origin of the names of Belgium, Britain, and Scotland is found in the personal names of leaders of the Skolotic Kimmerians,

---

47 *The Legacy of Israel,* Essay on *The Influence of Judaism on Western Law* by Nathan Isaacs (Oxford University Press, 1927), page 378.

48 In the British *Triads* the father of Prydain is given as Aedd, a name used by the Scotti of Irish Dalriada who colonized Argyllshire, Scotland. This tends to confirm that the Britons were a division of the Skoloti.

which, as then was customary, had been adopted by their tribal followers. Quoting Guizot and De Witt:

> The Kymrians, who crossed the Rhine and flung themselves into northern Gaul toward the middle of the 4th century B.C., called themselves Bolg or Belg, or Belgians, a name which is indeed given to them by Roman writers and which has remained that of the country they first invaded. They descended southward to the banks of the Seine and the Marne. *There they encountered the Kymrians of former invasions,* who not only had spread over the country between the Seine and the Loire, to the very heart of the peninsula bordered by the latter river, but had crossed the sea and occupied a portion of the large island opposite Gaul, crowding back the Gauls who had preceded them upon Ireland and the highlands of Scotland.[49]

The Asiatic culture thus transmitted to western Europe by the Skoloti was best preserved in Wales and Ireland. That which had been planted in Belgica, England, and southern Scotland was largely annihilated by the Romans. Undoubtedly, the Skoloti had absorbed minor Getic and Grecian blood strains as well as culture in addition to whatever Asiatic culture the former Kimmeric nation as a whole had gained in consequence of its earlier raids of southern countries. This division, like the Danish, is recognized as not having been as pure Kimmerian racially as the Goidelic division that preceded it to western central Gaul.

An outstanding principle contained in the Babylonian code that was adopted by the Getae and Skoloti and ultimately transmitted to western Europe is that of the Conjugal Community, more commonly known in the United States as the *Community Property Law*.[50] It had

---

49 Guizot and De Witt, *History of France*, pp. 16-17.
50 Calvin Kephart, *Origin of the Conjugal Community (or Community Property Law) and Other Ancient Laws* (1938).

been improved in practice during the 1400 years after Hammurabi's time. The Skoloti took it to Britain and Ireland and the Visigoths took it to Sweden and Spain, in which countries it was enacted into law. Through the influence of King Dagobert I of the Franks (A.D. 620-639), who intervened in the political affairs of the Visigoths of Spain, it was brought to France and incorporated in the *Lex Ripuaria* (ch. 37, 2), whose influence extended throughout the lower central Rhine region, including Westphalia. From Spain and France it ultimately reached the United States by way of the Gulf states and Mexico.

We now can readily understand why such cognate names as Kimmerii, Kymrian, or Kimrian, Cimbri, and Kymry or Cymry as well as Danaan, Danube, Danzig, Danmark, and Danann have been found at various places across Europe from the Ukraine and Aegean regions to Danmark, Wales, and Ireland besides having belonged to ancient invaders of southwestern Asia.

The Frankish name actually originated among the eastern or Ripuaric Franks, the Skoloti or Belgic Kimmerians east of the Rhine, whose territory lay between that river and the Werra and between the Ruhr and Main Rivers. Their units consisted mainly of the *Chatti,* the *Mattiaci,* and the *Bructeri* and possibly several smaller tribes. Many of their kin, known generically as the Belgae, crossed the Rhine very early, where they fought the Romans. Thus, their territory comprised not only a part of present Belgium but also the region east of the Rhine comprising the present Hessen and Rhineland south of the Ruhr. However, before long they crossed the Main River and settled Franconia along with earlier settlers, expanding later up that river valley.

The Ripuarians began their first combined attack on the Roman empire when they settled in a compact mass on the left bank of the Rhine in the 5th century. They seized Köln (Cologne) in 463 and subsequently occupied all of the country from that city to Treves (Trier), including Aachen, Bonn, and Zülpich. Cologne was their chief city. Thus, the territory taken by them lay east of the Maas (Meuse) River. Although allies of the Salian (or

Danish) Franks against the Romans, as yet they were operating independently. In their southward march they were halted by the Suebic *Allemanni (Alemanni, Alamanni)*, who already had gained northern Switzerland, Baden, and Alsace and were extending their conquests in various directions. The Ripuarians under Sigebert called on the Salians for aid, and under Clovis,[51] king of the Sigambri, of the Salian royal line, all of the Franks were united on the left bank of the Rhine. In the memorable battle of Zülpich in 506, when Clovis turned Christian and for the first time called on the Christian God for aid when his forces were facing defeat, the Allemannians finally were worsted and returned southward into Alsace. Thenceforth they recognized the Frankish dominion. The Franks also imposed their suzerainty on their kin still on the right bank of the middle and lower Rhine (excluding Frisian territory) and those up the Main River.

Clovis was also ambitious to gain the Gothic territory in southern Gaul, with whose inhabitants he had been more or less in contact. Alaric II, king of the Visigoths, was peacefully inclined, but Clovis found a pretext for war in the Arian Christianity of the Gothic ruler, most of whose followers lived in Spain. When the two armies met near Poitiers in 507, the Franks emerged victorious and the Frankish domain ultimately was extended to the Pyrenees as the remainder of the Visigoths crossed into Spain.

————————

6. *Kimmeric Influence in Western Europe.* From even the scant evidence available, it is certain that the immigration of the Skolotic Kimmerians, with their advanced culture, to western Europe exerted a wonderfully quickening effect on the unattractive social conditions that then prevailed in that region, as thus described:

————————

51 He must have been a descendant of Odin's son Sigge, chief of the Sigambri and allied tribes.

. . . Three or four centuries before the Christian era, on that vast territory comprised between the ocean, the Pyrenees, the Mediterranean, the Alps, and the Rhine six or seven millions of men lived a bestial life, enclosed in dwellings dark and low, the best of them built of wood and clay, covered with branches or straw, made in a single round piece, open to daylight by the door alone, and confusedly heaped together behind a rampart not inartistically composed of timber, earth, and stone, which surrounded and protected what they were pleased to call a town.[52]

Considered as a whole prior to 340 B.C., those inhabitants were the composite descendants of all of the races that had entered western Europe from the earliest times. Those races were the Cro-Magnards in southern France, the Mediterraneans and Paleo-Kelts of about 8000 B.C., the Kelto-Slavs (or Alpines) of about 2300 B.C., minor groups of Anatolians along the coasts, and the Goidelic Kimmerians of 632 B.C. The Danish Kimmerians of 604 B.C. still lived northeast of the Rhine. In Scandinavia, on the Frisian lowlands, and on and east of the lower Elbe and the Werra rivers lived the principal tribes of the Suebic nation, on land that they possessed from about 1600 B.C. Their culture had been affected very little by contact with other nations that had appropriated ideas from the western Asiatic and Aegean civilizations.

Real knowledge of these later peoples begins with the three Kimmeric invasions,[53] that of the Goidels in the later part of the Bronze Age (632 B.C.), that of the Danish Kimmerians 28 years afterward, and that of the Skoloti of 340 B.C., in the Iron Age. It was the epochal overrunning of western Europe by the first two divisions and their conquest of central Gaul and the lower Elbe and Weser watersheds that caused "the great unrest and movements in the Keltic world in the 6th and 5th cen-

---

52 Guizot and De Witt, *op.cit.*, page 10.
53 In western Europe, as stated before, this name frequently took the form of Cimbri, from which Cumbria and Cambria were derived. Diodorus Siculus, *Bibl. Hist.*, vol. 2.

turies B.C." Since these newcomers were not of Keltic race but Nordic,[54] it follows that the Goidelic and Britonic Kimmerians markedly adopted the dialects and customs of the Keltic people whose territory they invaded, for by the time of Julius Caesar all of the inhabitants of Europe west and south of the Rhine and of the British Isles had become conspicuously Keltic in speech and customs.[55] The Danish Kimmerians, however, had appropriated very little Keltic culture.

The Kimmerians had not arrived in Gaul as an organized nation but as divisions of a shattered one. They apparently did not assume any general or rigid rulership over the Keltic Gauls among whom they had settled but soon tended to coöperate with them. In adopting the Keltic language and customs in various degrees, the Kimmerians differed from the Dacians, Hispanians, and Gauls of Caesar's time, who, upon subjection, abandoned their own speech and adopted the Roman. On the other hand, the Kimmerians of England retained the Keltic culture during the Roman rule there but largely abandoned it upon the consummation of Anglo-Saxon rule. The Romans exercised more rigid control over their other provinces than they did over Britain, but in England the Anglo-Saxons later enforced the substitution of their own speech by a strong and unified rule.

After all, these were cognate languages. The Goidelic speech is held by Grimm and Pictet to embody much of the true Keltic, and the Britonic is said to be Keltic modified by "Germanic," whatever that may mean.[56] It is more

---

54 Thomas Nicholas, in his otherwise excellent treatment of *The Pedigree of the English People* (Longmans, Green, Reader & Co., London, 1874), failed to distinguish the brachycephalic, stocky, phlegmatic, and light-complexioned Kelt of central Gaul from the taller, mesocephalic, and light-complexioned Kimmerian Nordics of Gaul, who had conquered the British Isles. See Prichard, *op. cit.*, vol. 3, pages 53-55.

55 *Ency. Brit.*, 13th Ed., vol. 4, page 583, by Hector Munro Chadwick. Also see W. K. Sullivan, *op.cit.*, pages lix-lx and lxxv-lxxvi.

56 This is an example of the confusion of national dialects. Is the uncertain term "Germanic" intended to mean the Suebian or the Kimmerian, the Hochdeutsch or the Plattdeutsch?

correct to reverse this statement and say that both represent the ancient Kimmeric speech (as used by the Danes) modified in different degrees by the Keltic speech with which they came in contact. The difference may be explained by the fact that the Goidelic Kimmerians, as the earlier invaders of Gaul, settled among native Kelts and more completely adopted their language, whereas the Skolotic (or Britonic) Kimmerians, who arrived about 292 years later, settled farther north, near, in, and west of the middle and lower Rhine valley, from which the Kelts had been driven westward and southward, and therefore adopted the Keltic speech to a much less extent. St. Jerome, a noted linguistic scholar, who had lived among the Belgic *Treveri* at Treves (Trier) and later among the Galatians who had emigrated from Gaul to Asia Minor, commented on the slight variation in their dialects. The Keltic (Alpine) strain is conspicuous today in the Luxembourg and Ardennes regions, including Treves.

Clearly, the richest part of the pre-Christian civilization of northern Gaul, Britain, and Ireland was contributed mainly by the Skolotic Kimmerians[57] from the Ukraine, in consequence of the contacts they and the Getae had with the western Asiatic and Grecian civilizations. Many singular points of coincidence have been discovered in the religious systems of the ancient Britons and the Hindus, as shown by the British Triads; also many striking similarities in the proverbs and forms of expression derived from their national customs and religious ceremonies.[58]

---

57 Thomas Nicholas, *ibid.*, pp. 59-80; J. A. Giles, *op.cit.*, *Gildas, Richard of Cirencester*, chapters iii-iv; Eugene O'Curry, *Manners and Customs of the Ancient Irish* (Norgate and Williams, London, 1873) vol. 2, pp. 169-175, vol. 3, pp. 83-86.

58 J. A. Giles, *ibid., Richard of Cirencester*, i.4.1-15 and footnotes. In view of the reliance herein on the work entitled "Richard of Cirencester," a brief explanation of its history is desirable. It had been described as a "literary forgery" first produced in the 18th century by Charles Bertram (1723-1765), an Englishman who as a child went with his parents to Copenhagen, Danmark, where later he became an instructor in English in a school for naval cadets. The details of its inception, composition, presentation, and exposure are described in the series of articles by B. B. Woodward, F.S.A., librarian of Windsor Castle, entitled "A Literary Forgery; Richard of Cirencester's Tractate on Britain," that appeared in *The Gentleman's Magazine* for March, May, and October, 1866, and October, 1867. See also the

The British patriarchal system resembled that of the east.[59]

In conquering northern Gaul, the Skoloti drove the Goidels south from the Seine River as far as the Loire, between the Kelts of central Gaul and of Armorica. Some of these Goidelic tribes, such as the Pictones, subsequently crossed the Loire toward the ocean.[60] About 590 B. C. some of the Goidels, chiefly the Dananns (later of Ireland)

---

sketch by Henry Bradley on Charles Bertram in *Dictionary of National Biography*, vol. II, p. 412, and another sketch in *Encyclopaedia Britannica*, 13th Ed., vol. 3, pp. 813-14. In spite of the exposure, a translation of this work with no expression of doubt as to its genuineness was published in 1872 by Dr. J. A. Giles as one of the *Six Old English Chronicles* in Bohn's Antiquarian Library.

Under those circumstances, it may be asked why reliance should now be placed on such a writing. The fact, as demonstrated by Mr. Woodward, is that the presentation and *not the basic contents thereof*, in the main, constituted the forgery. It actually was a plagiarism from the publications of an eminent and reliable writer, the 16th and 17th century antiquary and historian, William Camden (1551-1623), whose biography appears in *Encyclopaedia Britannica*, 13th Ed. vol. 5, p. 101. He traveled over all England collecting materials, and the resulting work, called the *Britannia*, was first published by him in 1586. About 1597, while Camden occupied the position of Clarenceux king-at-arms, the York herald, Ralph Brooke, led an attack on his genealogical accuracy. Camden replied to Brooke in an appendix to the 5th edition of the *Britannia*, published in 1600, and his reputation came through the ordeal untarnished. After bringing out an enlarged and improved edition of this work in 1607, Camden published other notable histories. He was offered and declined knighthood. His reputation as a historian subsequently became so well recognized that in 1838 the Camden Society was founded in his honor and much valuable work has been done under its auspices.

Without necessarily accepting everything in this publication called "Richard of Cirencester," it can be said that the parts accepted as facts herein constitute so clearly a continuation of the tribal history of the same peoples on the Continent and are supported by contemporaneous reports from other sources that they must have been taken by Camden from reliable reports transmitted from ancient times. Consequently, no apparent reason exists as to why they should not be relied upon here.

Various cultural similarities must have been the common property of the primitive Nordic tribes while they resided in Geté. They were taken to western Europe by the Kimmerian nation and to western India by the Nordic founders of the great Scytho-Indian Empire (c. 50 B.C.-A.D. 570), as shown in the last chapter herein.

59 Seumas MacManus, *The Story of the Irish Race* (Irish Pub. Co., New York, 1921). p. 294, and authorities cited.

60 The summary of temper and personal character of the Gauls by J. C. Prichard, *op. cit.*, vol. 3, page 178, quoting chiefly from Dio Cassius and Strabo, pertains essentially to the Kimmerians and not to the Kelts proper. Compare the Gaels of Britain. By about 335 B.C. the tribe of the Parisii must have made a settlement on the island of Lutéce, around which the city of Paris ultimately grew.

and a division of the Pictones — the Picts of Scotland — crossed the channel to England. Further proof that these Goidels originated in Asia is found in the fact that "stone querns, the hand-mills for grinding corn still used in eastern countries, (and also Samian ware and Greek coins) have been recovered from hut-circles, lake-dwellings, brochs, and even from the earth-houses and caves" of Scotland.[61] The swords of the Dananns in Ireland corresponded with those found in lower Bavaria, the central Rhine valley, and northern France, demonstrating the presence of their ancestors in those regions[62] in the course of their migration to western Europe.

The Skolotic settlements (by the Scotti and the Britons) in Britain occurred from the mainland beginning about 290 B.C.[63] and they increased in numbers in connection with commercial and military ventures there during the subsequent two centuries,[64] until these nations had gained dominance over most of Britain except Pictland in the far north.

That the Scotti and Britons consisted of divisions of various tribes in all parts of Gaul is demonstrated by the names found in both places, such as *Aedui, Attrebates, Belgae, Britanni, Catalauni, Chauci, Menapii, Morini,*

---

61 Archibald B. Scott, *The Pictish Nation* (Foulis, Edinburgh, 1918), pp. 63-64, 67.

62 W. K. Sullivan, op. cit., pp. ccclv-cccclvi.

63 Caesar, *Gallic War* v. 12. The fact that the ancient Britons had a tradition that they descended from the Trojans (J. A. Giles, *op. cit., Nennius,* Sec. 10) must be considered in the light of the numerous incursions that their ancestors had made from the Ukraine to western Asia Minor and of the return of some from that region just before their migration to western Europe, as the Trojans were a Turanian (Turkic) race. Their tradition of crossing from Gaul to Britain is correct, of course.

Danish Kimmerian and Skolotic or Britonic Kimmerian tribal names of the lower Main and central and lower Rhine river valleys included these, among others, named by the writers: Chatti, Mattiaci, Dulgibini, Chausauri, Ansibarii, Tubantes, Chauci, Cherusci, Fosi, Cimbri, Batavi, Nervii, Treveri, Bructeri, Chamavi, Angrivarii, Sigambri, Menapii, Tencteri, Usipii. These locations tend to prove that the Britonic Kimmerians came from the east via the Main River valley, whereas the Goidelic Kimmerians crossed from the upper Danube River to central Gaul. See Strabo, *Geogr.,* iv. 196, for names of tribes of the Belgae.

64 Caesar, *ibid.,* iii.8, 12-14, iv.20.

Parisii, Remi, Senones, and others.[65] The Skoloti that remained in northern Gaul and the Rhine valley (besides
the Hessians) were chiefly Belgae, whose high praise by
Julius Caesar proves that they were a people who possessed
pride of race and uncommon ability.[66] Among them was
a remnant of the *Britanni* (Britons) in the valley of the
Somme.[67] While absorbing the Keltic language and customs, they also exerted a stimulating effect on the less
advanced civilization of the Goidels and the Kelts, for
by Caesar's time the culture of the Gauls had attained
marked improvement. The population of northern Gaul
at this time was not comprised within a few nations but
consisted of a congeries of nations or tribes. They followed
a feudal system, with power in the hands of the Druids
and the knights respectively.[68] But the civilizing influence
of the Belgae in northern Gaul was arrested before its
maturity and largely obliterated before the opening of
the Christian era by Julius Caesar and his successors, with
the aid of the Roman army and civilians, and the Roman
culture was substituted in large measure therefor. How
it was done is thus stated by Guizot and De Witt:

> But, side by side with this work in the cause of
> civilization and organization, Augustus and his Roman
> agents were pursuing a work of quite a contrary ten-
> dency. They labored to extirpate from Gaul the
> spirit of nationality, independence, and freedom;
> they took every pains to efface everywhere Gallic
> memories and sentiments . . . . Everywhere, whether
> it was a question of the terrestial fatherland or of
> religious faiths the old moral machinery of the Gauls

---

65 The Aedui were Kelts and the Pictones (Picts) were Goidelic Kimmerians.
The Chauci were Danish Kimmerians. The fact that so many tribes were represented proves that emissaries must have gone from central Gaul to the lower Weser
River to assemble volunteers for this mighty army bent on the conquest of Britain.
66 Strabo's classification of the Belgae west of the Rhine in 15 nations (iv.4.3)
may also have included some of the Goidelic Kimmerians in central Gaul, since the
described territory extended as far south as the Loire River.
67 See Detlefsen's Pliny's *Historia Naturalis,* iv. 106.
68 Caesar, *ibid.,* i.21, 31, 43, vi. 13-20.

was broken up or condemned to rust and no new moral machinery was allowed to replace it; it was everywhere Roman and imperial authority that was substituted for the free national action of the Gauls.[69]

It is not strange, therefore, that the Gauls in Caesar's time, including the Kimmerians, because of inferior training and equipment,[70] became incensed as their pristine glory in warfare was being extinguished[71] by so many defeats by the Romans and that they should have concluded that it was better to be slain in battle than not to recover their ancient glory and that freedom which they had received from their forefathers.[72]

But not all of the Belgic culture was lost forever. It partially escaped the devastating hand of the Roman when large numbers of these Kimmerians scattered northward and eastward to havens among their kinsmen across the Rhine, to reappear centuries later when the Salian and Ripuarian Franks vigorously forced themselves upon the arena of history. This transrhenish escape of numerous Belgic tribes is proved by facts relating to two of them, the *Menapii* and the *Chauci,* the latter a southerly branch of the Danish tribe of that name. So-called "Germans" (Franks), they yet spoke the Keltic language acquired earlier in Gaul, for it was the Keltic and not the Kimmeric language that their later colonists to southern Ireland took with them.

The Frankish tribes on the easterly side of the middle Rhine, contingents of which later confederated as the Ripuarian Franks, actually were descendants mainly of Skolotic Kimmerians, such as the *Chatti* (the later Hessians), who had settled there[73] about 340 B.C. On their

---

69   Guizot and De Witt, *op.cit.,* p. 69.

70   Caesar, *ibid.,* v. 42, vii. 29.

71   *Ibid.,* v. 29.

72   *Ibid.,* vii. 1.

73   This is confirmed by Strabo (iv.4.2) in his description of the Kimmeric Gauls (Goidels and Belgae) in comparison with the so-called "Germans" (Skoloti) east of the Rhine, thus: "These two nations, both by nature and in the form of their government, are similar and related to each other. Their countries border on each other, being separated by the river Rhine, and are for the most part similar." This belief of relationship is not seriously questioned by ethnologists. See *Ency. Brit.,* 13th Ed., vol. 11, page 830, by F. G. M. Beck.

north, west of the Weser River and along the seacoast, lived the descendants of the Danish Kimmerians who had settled in that region about 604 B. C., one of the westerly tribes of which was the *Sigambri* the later *Salii*.[74] Never having lived in Gaul, these Kimmerians retained most of their Ukrainian language and customs, while their kin in northern Gaul, the Scotti, Britons, and Belgae, acquired Keltic language and customs. The language of these Danes and of the Skoloti east of the Rhine was the so-called "German," otherwise called "Plattdeutsch." This dialect and their customs did not differ greatly from the language and customs of their fellow Nordics, the Suebi and the Getae, as proved by a comparison of the traits of the Cimbric Jutes who conquered Kent, England, with those of the Anglo-Saxons who gained other parts of England. The dialect of the Suebi on the continent is called "Hochdeutsch." In the course of a century after the arrival of the Skoloti in the west, the discernibly growing differences in language and customs across the Rhine raised a distinction between the divisions on the east and those on the west. Those on the right bank appeared to later writers to be different racially from their kinsmen in Gaul, even though these differences had been lessened by the presence among the former of Skolotic tribes that had escaped from Caesar's legions in Gaul.

A widespread misconception persists today among both writers and laymen regarding the application of the terms "German," "Teuton," and "Frank," none of which may properly be applied to the inhabitants of modern Germany east of the Weser, Werra, and upper Rhine Rivers except the Main River valley. The name "German" was derived from *wehrmann,* meaning "warrior," and evolved through the Frankish forms *werre, gerre,* and *guerre* in the same way that Welf and Waiblingen were transformed in history to Guelf and Ghibelline and Warin to Guérin. It was

---

74 They were mentioned for the first time by Ammianus Marcellinus (xvii.8.3) in 358. Their legends are connected with the (North) sea and their dynastic name Meroveus signifies "sea-born." The name Sigambri also was retained by these Franks at least to the time of Clovis.

applied first by Julius Caesar to Frankish tribes of the former Kimmeric (Cimbric) nation in the middle and lower Rhine valley.[75] It never was used by the Suebi farther east. It required a nine days' march for the Roman army to proceed from the Rhine River across a sort of no-man's land (often maintained by ancient nations at enmity) to reach the territory of the separate Suebic nation,[75] which lay east of the Werra River chiefly along and east of the Elbe. The existence of the Suebian as a wholly separate nation is well known.[76] "Some kind of political union seems to have existed among all of these [Suebic] tribes."[76]

The Suebic and Kimmeric nations had been politically separate as far back as 4500 years ago, during which long cycle of time they evolved somewhat differently in language and customs, although both still were clearly cognizable as Nordic nations. Tacitus wrote about these nations nearly a century after Caesar's time. Not realizing that the latter had applied the term "German" primarily to the Franks, he applied it indiscriminately to all of these Nordics, although he noted a distinction between the Franks of the Rhine valley and the Suebi on the Elbe (ch. 38), for by turning their hair sideways and tieing it beneath the poll in a knot the Suebi differed from "the rest of the Germans."

The largest Frankish (Kimmeric) tribe was the Chatti or later Hessians.[77] The *Remi,* unquestionably a Belgic tribe, who declined to participate in revolution against the Romans, declared that the Belgae (excluding the Kelts) were descendants of the so-called "Germans" and that their ancestors had crossed the Rhine at an early period and settled there because of the fertility of the country.[78] The *Treveri, Nervii,*[79] and *Ubii,* likewise Bel-

---

75 Julius Caesar, *Gallic War,* book ii, ch. 3-4, 15, book iv, ch. 3-4, 6-8, 14-19.

76 *Ency. Brit.,* 13th Ed., vol. 26, page 20, by F. G. Meeson Beck. Tacitus, *Germania,* ch. 38-39.

77 *Ency. Brit.,* 13th Ed., vol. 13, page 410.

78 Julius Caesar, *op. cit.,* ii. 3-4; iii. 11.

79 Appian, *De Reb. Gall.,* iv.1.4, says the *Nervii* were descendants of Cimbri and Teutons (Danes), and they apparently were cognate with the Belgae.

gic tribes, admitted their descent from the so-called "Germans" (most certainly the Skoloti) along the banks of the Rhine, the Ubii having crossed into Gaul because of strife with the Chatti.[80] The *Batavi,* formerly a tribe of the Chatti, for the same reason emigrated to the lower Rhine, where they remained in alliance with the Romans.[81]

A similar error persists regarding the meaning and use of the term "Teuton", which was derived from the Cimbric (Kimmeric) tribe of *Teutoni,* of Jutland, in Danmark.[82] They first appeared in Roman history by warfare in central Europe in 113 B.C. and became better known to the Romans in 103 B.C., when, according to the *Epitome* of Livy, together with the *Ambrones* (other Kimmerians) they reinforced the *Cimbri* of Danmark after the repulse of the latter from Spain by the *Keltiberi,* and all then moved to invade Italy.[83] In 102-101 B. C. they were defeated by the Romans and the remnant returned to Gaul, where they were known subsequently as the *Aduatuci.*[83] All of these Cimbric tribes were cognate with the Franks and Belgae as members of the former Kimmeric nation of Scythia and not with the Suebi; hence it follows that the name "Teuton" along with those of "German" and "Frank," has no application whatever to the Suebi or their descendants in modern Germany. The Suebi are discussed separately in a later section.

The Sigambri, the westernmost division of the Danish Kimmerians, who formerly inhabited the shores of the North Sea, were the principal Kimmeric tribe around which the Salian Franks later confederated, apparently because its dynasty had descended from Odin's son Sigge. They are mentioned in history separately from the Suebi.[84] The name Sigambri seems to have been retained

---

80 Tacitus, *Germania,* ch. 28.

81 The Belgae ("Germans") along the Rhine asserted to Caesar "that they were inferior to the Suebi alone, to whom not even the immortal gods can show themselves equal; that there was none at all besides on earth whom they could not conquer." *Ibid.,* iv. 7.

82 This is another instance of the misspelling of a national name by English-speaking people. The preferable form is Danmark, as used officially by that nation.

83 *Ency. Brit.,* 13th Ed., vol. 4, pp. 939-40, vol. 11, p. 533, vol. 26, p. 673:

84 Julius Caesar, *ibid.,* iv. 16, 18, 19.

along with that of *Salii,* which became fixed while they inhabited the Yssel basin and Gelderland and denoted their former habitation at the North Sea. This dynasty of the Salian Franks is that later known in history as the *Merovingian,* which founded the nation of France; in fact, the name Meroveus signifies "sea-born." After the federation of Frankish tribes early in the 5th century for their later advance to assail the Roman Empire, a number of their tribal names disappeared. The possession of the central Rhine valley by the Skoloti and of the territory thence to the North Sea by the Danish Kimmerians restricted the Suebian nation, except the Frisians and Scandinavians, mainly to the basin of the Elbe and Werra Rivers and the country eastward. The Frisians had been pushed to the lowland and islands at the Zuyder Zee, in northern Netherlands, by the Danish Sigambri, and the Scandinavians had been forced very early out of the Danish islands. The Weser River ran through the territory of the Danish *Chauci,* according to Tacitus, who reported their boundaries as the North Sea on the north and the land of the Chatti on the south. It is probable that other Danish tribes lived in this region. The chief Suebic tribe on their east was the Saxons. The region between the Weser and the lower Elbe long was disputed ground and much annihilative warfare occurred between Danish and Suebic tribes on the opposite sides of it.

Meitzen's map of ancient settlements of the lower Rhine valley and adjacent territory shows that many Keltic and Belgic refugees were forced across to the easterly and northerly sides of the Rhine in Julius Caesar's time. Keltic types of habitation have been found in the Netherlands and northwestern Germany as far east as the basin of the Weser River and Upper Hessen, including the territory of the Chatti. Kelts who did not migrate elsewhere were merged into the Nordic population. On the east of those regions, only purely Nordic (Suebian) types were found.

The presence of the Skolotic Franks, especially the Chatti, on the east bank of the middle Rhine deflected the Suebian tribes through Middle Franconia toward the upper Rhine when they began to migrate southward.

Their first incursion across that river into Gaul was made by mercenaries under Ariovistus in 71 B.C., at the invitation of the Keltic *Sequani* and *Arverni,* to aid them in their struggle with the *Aedui.*[85] Ariovistus was a member of the senior Suebic tribe, the *Semnones.* His force of 15,000 warriors comprised marauders who had been expelled from their habitations by various tribes; they had not slept beneath a roof for 14 years.[86] Their detachments bore the names of the *Harudes, Marcomanni, Sedusii,* and *Semnones.*[87] They were joined by other Suebians and by three Frankish tribes named the *Vangiones,*[88] *Nemetae,*[88] and *Tribocci,*[88] which increased the whole aggregation to about 120,000 men, women, and children, all of whom planned to settle at different places on the westerly bank of the Rhine, in Roman territory. The warriors under Ariovistus suffered defeat by the Romans in 58 B.C. as also did an attempted invasion across the lower Rhine in 55 B. C. by the Skolotic *Usipetes* and *Tencteri.*[89] These were the only expeditions across the Rhine reported during Julius Caesar's time. The Frankish followers of Ariovistus remained west of the Rhine as subjects of the Romans, centering as follows: The Vangiones at the present city of Worms, the Nemetes at the present city of Speyer, and the Tribocci near the present city of Strasbourg.[90] The Suebians who had not been slain escaped back across the Rhine.

Additional evidence supporting this distinction between Kimmerians and Suebians is the fact that the Treveri, a Belgic tribe, reported to Caesar, much to his alarm, that

---

85 *Ibid.,* i.31.

86 *Ibid.,* i.36.

87 *Ibid.,* 1.51. The Semnones, apparently the nuclear tribe of the Suebi, ultimately settled in the present southeastern Württemberg and southwestern Bavaria and perpetuated the national name of the Suebi in the present form of Schwaben, of which there was an important stem-duchy in medieval times.

88 According to Tacitus, *Germania,* ch. 28, these three tribes, without doubt, are 'German' [Skolotic Kimmerian] tribes" and therefore not Suebic. Thus, Ariovistus' aggregation of invaders comprised both marauders from the Suebian nation and a large number of Franks who aimed to settle west of the Rhine in Roman territory after the invasion.

89 Caesar, *Gallic War,* i.55.

90 Tacitus, *Germania,* ch.28.

a hundred cantons of Suebi had approached the easterly bank of the Rhine (near the Main) and were attempting to cross it.[91] They returned home after Caesar had defeated Ariovistus and the latter had been pursued by the Ubii, another Kimmerian tribe on the Rhine,[92] with great slaughter. It was 4½ centuries before the Suebi invaded Gaul again, when the *Allemanni* took possession of Alsace.

When Caesar was told that the *Eburones* had enlisted other "Germans" (Skoloti) through the Treveri to aid them against the Romans,[93] he began an investigation. The Ubii assured him that such auxiliaries had not come from their state and that they should be spared punishment, "lest in his common hatred of the 'Germans' the innocent should suffer the penalty of the guilty". Caesar found that the auxiliaries had come from the Suebi and he accepted the plea of the Ubii. He then made inquiries concerning the routes and approaches to the territory of the Suebi,[94] apparently east of the Thüringerwald. They (unlike the tribes along the Rhine and in Gaul) were said to be "barbarous and ignorant people."[95] Thus, Caesar drew a distinction between the culture and habits of the Suebi and of the Skoloti along the Rhine.[96] The former contrived to maintain large areas between them and their nearest neighbors,[97] — on their west, the Skoloti. To cause fear among the Suebi, Caesar and his army spent 18 days beyond the Rhine without encountering the enemy.[98] This time indicates a long march, probably as far as the basin of the upper Werra River. He subsequently made another incursion against the southernmost Suebi, the Semnones, who already had approached the central Main River valley in their southward migration. They retired

---

91 Caesar, *ibid.*, i.37, also i.43 and 44. The noted city of Treves (Trier) took its name from the Treveri.
92 *Ibid.*, i.54.
93 *Ibid.*, vi.5.
94 *Ibid.*, vi.9.
95 *Ibid.*, vi.10.
96 *Ibid.*, iv.1-4, vi.21-22.
97 *Ibid.*, vi.23.
98 *Ibid.*, iv.19.

to the Hercynian Forest (Thuringia) upon the approach of the Roman force.[99]

Tacitus also drew a sharp distinction between the variously-named tribes that inhabited eastern Germania under the common national appellation of the Suebi and the wholly separate nations that lived along the central and lower Rhine.[100] Other facts confirm the accuracy of that conclusion. The Suebic Saxons repeatedly fought the Danish Kimmerians along the shores of the North Sea west of the Elbe and also on the Weser River when they extended their dominions westward. The tribes thus assailed included mainly the *Chauci,* the *Fosi,* and the *Cherusci,* but other Danish tribes (so-called "Germans") were grievously oppressed by them. Moreover, the *Frisians* in northern Netherlands, a Suebic tribe cut off from the others on the lower Elbe by the Danish Kimmerian invasion about 604 B.C., contended with Danish tribes north of the lower Rhine and showed no inclination to ally themselves with the Salian Frankish[101] confederation organized in a later century by these Danish tribes. Consequently, it is clear that the Salian Franks who later overran Gaul consisted mainly of the Danish Kimmerian tribes from north of the lower Rhine, and that the Ripuarian Franks who coöperated with them comprised mainly Skolotic Kimmerians from both sides of the middle Rhine.[102]

99 *Ibid.,* vi.21-29.

100 Tacitus, *Germania,* ch. 38-39.

101 A tradition that seemingly corresponds with the Kimmeric and Gothic invasions of Asia Minor prior to and during the 7th century B.C., as heretofore discussed, appears in the treatment of the origin of the Salic Franks by Sir Samuel Dill in *Roman Society in Gaul in the Merovingian Age* (MacMillan, New York, 1926), p. 5-6.

102 The *Treviri, Nervii, Attrebates, Bellovaci, Ambiani, Suessiones, Remi, Menapii, Morini, Caleti, Veloscasses, Veromandu,* and *Aduatuci* are asserted by Julius Caesar to have been Belgic tribes, although the last-named originally was Danish in origin (*Gallic War,* i.37, ii.4). Thus, they were related to the Belgae (Skoloti) who remained on the easterly bank of the middle Rhine and whose presence with that of the Danish Kimmerians farther north deflected the Suebians toward the south across the central Main River. These Belgic tribes east of the Rhine (so-called Germans) supplied sizeable contingents to the confederation of Ripuarian Franks whose armies crossed into Gaul, chiefly the *Chatti, Batavi, Mattiaci, Usipii, Tencteri, Amsivarii,* and *Bructeri.* There they joined other Ripurian Franks for the conquest

The *Condrusi, Eburones, Caeraesi,* and *Paemani,* "called by the common name of Germans," appear to have been Skolotic Kimmerians, since they allied themselves with the Belgae against Julius Caesar as a matter of course[103] and the Eburones were friendly with the Belgic *Menapii.*[104] Furthermore, we find settlements of the Chauci and the Menapii with other Kimmerians in southeastern Ireland subsequent to Caesar's time (c. A.D. 135)[105] and that they were allied with the Scots. The fact that the Menapii and Chauci were so-called "Germans" but took the Keltic and not the Suebic language to Ireland is of itself confirmation of the foregoing deductions. And, finally, we must take notice of the marked similarity between the Welsh and Irish law codes and the Carolingian code of the Franks as indicative of common racial origin (Kimmerian). Since the former people had adopted a large measure of the Keltic culture of Gaul and the latter, because of their habitation on the Rhine, had not, this similarity must have resulted from traditions derived from an earlier common culture.

Every reason exists for believing that the ancient language and customs of the Kimmerians, before they became subject to Keltic influence in Gaul, did not differ greatly from those of their Nordic kinsmen, the Danes, the Suebi, and the Getae, since all had a common origin in Asia.[106] Thus, when the Danish Cimbri, said to have been "Germanized" Kimmerians,[107] moved into Jutland in 603 B.C., this peninsula became known to the ancients as the Cimbric Cheronese. When, as the later Jutes, some of their descendants entered England in the 5th century of the Christian era, their dialect could not have differed

---

of Gaul. Danish tribes that contributed dominantly to the Salian Franks included the *Sigambri, Chauci, Fosi, Cherusci, Chamavi, Angrivarii, Dulgibini, Attuarii, Ansibarii, Tubantes,* and *Ambrones.*

103 Julius Caesar, *Gallic War,* ii.4.
104 *Ibid.,* vi.5.
105 John Rhys and David Brynmor-Jones, *The Welsh People* (Unwin, London, 1926) pp. 84-85.
106 W. K. Sullivan, *op. cit.,* p. lxxvi, and as already shown herein.
107 Strabo vii.2.2.

greatly from that of their allies, the Angles from Holstein and the Saxons from the lower Elbe, but the difference was sufficient to be noticeable to Bede and other early writers.

O'Curry reports:

"That some system of law — and by this I mean not merely some body of separate enactments but really a *system* — existed among the Milesian [Scotic] race from a period contemporary with, if not anterior to, their original landing in the island [of Ireland] is perfectly plain from all their traditions and records." [108] The analogy between its penalties for wilful murder and contract violation and those of the ancient Hebrews is quite marked.[108] Only in the ways already outlined here can we account for the striking similarities in the construction of the Salic law of the Franks and of the ancient Babylonian code of Hammurabi.[109] Knowledge of the latter had been gained by the Kimmerian nation of Scythia in its numerous invasions of western Asia prior to 635 B.C. and by its successor, the Getae, and their subjects, the Skolotic Kimmerians, when the Getae ravaged western Asia from 634 to 606 B.C. Thus, in the same way as the Skoloti transmitted western Asiatic culture and legal and other principles to the British Isles,[110] their Danish kinsmen north of the lower Rhine exerted major influence in the formation of the Salic code by their knowledge of the Babylonian legal system gained by them while in Lydia and passed down from generation to generation after their migration to western Europe, as indicated in the Danish saga, *The Prose Edda*, by Snorri Sturlason. Such transmission of knowledge also was common among ancient peoples of the Iberian peninsula.[111]

Furthermore, the Skoloti on the right bank of the Rhine appear to have passed down the tradition of separate nationality from the Suebi living on and east of the Elbe, and

---

108 Eugene O'Curry, *op. cit.*, vol. 2, pages 24, 29.
109 *The Legacy of Israel*, Essay on *The Influence of Judaism on Western Law* by Nathan Isaacs (Oxford University Press, 1927), page 381.
110 Rhys and Brynmor-Jones, *op.cit.*, pages 186-188.
111 Strabo, *Geogr.* iii. 1.6.

the relations of the two nations were not amicable. When the martial band of the Cimbri moved out of Jutland about 120 B. C. on an invasion of southern Europe, it proceeded southward on the west of the Rhine to avoid the Suebi, of whom its members had less knowledge and probably deemed less friendly than their kinsmen in Gaul. They also had more knowledge of the Romans through those kinsmen. Another tribe, the *Teutoni*,[112] known to have been a branch of the Danish Cimbri, likewise emigrated from Jutland soon thereafter. Both tribes are held to have been identical with the *Jutes*.[113] They settled for a time among their kinsmen on the lower Rhine, where a Roman fleet came in contact with some of their descendants about A.D. 2.[114] These facts tend further to distinguish the Kimmeric and the Suebic peoples in the region between the Weser and the Elbe, which distinction was not clearly recognized by most of the contemporary writers.

Reference already has been made to the successful assault on the Roman Empire in the 5th century by the federated Danish (or Salian) Franks and the federated Ripuarian (or Skolotic) Franks, the former from west of the Maas (or Meuse) and the later from east of that river. In the formation of the Frankish nation, the historic codes of Salic Law and Ripuarian Law were preserved separately. The hopeful city of Paris, center of the tribe of the *Parisii* on the isle of Lutèce in the Seine River, in Neustria, was the capital of the Merovingian dynasty of the Salian Franks. Metz, in Austrasia, was the capital of the Ripuarian Franks. In 843, Metz became the capital of Lotharingia (Lorraine).

The assertion by Belloguet a half-century ago that the Kimmeric people in western Europe never formed more

---

112 These people are referred to further in a discussion on the settlement of Scandinavia.

113 This is proved by the fact that the *Aduatuci,* named by Julius Caesar as a tribe of the Belgae (ii. 4), are stated by him to have been descendants of the Cimbri and Teutoni whose forces had been defeated earlier in an attempt to invade Italy (ii. 29); also by the fact that the remnants settled among the Kimmerians of Gaul.

114 *Ency. Brit.*, 13th Ed., vol. 6, page 368, by F. G. Meeson Beck.

than a ruling class is not defensible, in the light of what already has been presented here. The number that settled in central, western, and northern Gaul and Britain is known to have been quite large.[115] As stated by Julius Caesar, "the Belgae rise from the extreme frontier of Gaul, extend to the lower part of the River Rhine, and look toward the north and the rising sun."[116] Yet they did not dominate any other Keltic Gauls than those in the territory conquered and permanently held by them [117] until the Frankish conquests. Divitiacus, of the Keltic Aedui, "the most powerful man of all Gaul," also had been king of Britain.[118] In fact, the Gauls said that they formerly excelled the "Germans" (Skoloti) in prowess, waged war on them offensively, and, because of the large number of Gauls and the insufficiency of their land, sent colonists eastward across the Rhine.[119] Among the latter were the *Helvetii,* the most powerful Gallic nation, who later moved southward to Switzerland under pressure from the north.[120]

———————

7. *Kimmeric Influence in the British Isles.* An historic aftermath of the settlement of the Goidelic Kimmerians in western Gaul shortly after 634 B.C. deserves consideration now. It must have required about two generations for the transition from their own dialect and culture to those of the local Keltic people,[121] for it was the third generation that shortly before 585 B.C. crossed the channel to the British Isles. There they drove westward and northward

---

115 Caesar, *Gallic War,* ii. 4; see also F. P. G. Guizot, *History of France* (London, 1872-1881), pp. 11-12. This is proved by the numerical superiority of their descendants today.
116 Caesar, *ibid.,* i. 1.
117 *Ibid.,* i. 3, 17, 21, 40, 43.
118 *Ibid.,* ii. 4; also J. A. Giles, *op. cit., Richard of Cirencester,* ii. 1.9.
119 Tacitus, *Germania,* ch. 28.
120 Caesar, *ibid.,* i. 2, 3.
121 Without this transfer of culture, the Goidels would have taken to Britain the dialect and culture of their kin, the Danes of Jutland, rather than that of the Kelts of Gaul.

the Iberians and Kelts that they encountered.[122] Soon the Goidels spread to southern Scotland and a division crossed to northern Ireland,[123] continuing to press the primitive inhabitants[124] ahead of them. Thus, the brunet Iberian and the brachycephalic Keltic strains are found today in the westerly parts of England, Wale Scotland, and Ireland.[125] Descendants of Iberians also persist in Glamorgan and Monmouth shires, Wales. Keltic types found in Perthshire and the northern highlands of Scotland may be attributable to intermarriage with Kelts of Gaul (such as the Aedui) during the period that those Nordics sojourned there and to the fact that some Aedui are known to have been among the Kimmerians who emigrated from Gaul to the British Isles.

The size of this invading Kimmeric horde was not great, since a part of each tribe remained in Gaul, but it received reinforcements from those divisions and other tribes in Gaul from time to time. The chief *national* names that they preserved in history are those of Dananns in Ireland and Picts (Pictones) in Scotland, although they long retained other tribal names as well. For example, the Albanians and Caledonians were Pictish tribes of Scotland. According to Irish history, the Dananns were related to the Danes of Jutland, the Cimbri who gave their name to Danmark. They are said traditionally to have gone across the North Sea to Scotland, whence they subsequently passed to Ireland. While the racial relationship

---

122 Tacitus, *Life of Agricola*, ch. 11. Rhys and Brynmor-Jones, *op.cit.*, pp. 10-12.
123 Thomas Nicholas, *op.cit.*, pp. 45-46. This date agrees with the statement in the preface to the ancient poem of Carman (and in stanza 21) that it was 580 years from the date of the first Fair of Carman held by the Tuatha Dé Danann to the beginning of the Christian era. Eugene O'Curry, *Manners and Customs of the Ancient Irish* (Williams and Norgate, London, 1873), vol. 3, Appendix pp. 527 *et seq.* Carman was situated in the present Wexford, a non-Scottic part of Ireland. Down to modern times, the Scottish highlanders have called their dialect *Gaidhlig Albannaich* while the Irish have called theirs *Goidheilg Erinnich.*
124 Rhys and Brynmor-Jones, *ibid.*, pp. 11-13. The aborigines preceded the Goidelic Dananns and Picts.
125 It is no longer seriously questioned that, except for primitive brunet immigrants by boat from Anatolia, Phoenicia, or Iberia and Nordics from Danmark and Scandinavia, Great Britain and Ireland anciently were peopled from Gaul. Thomas Nicholas, *ibid.*, pp. 36-37.

seems clear, the supposed movement across the North Sea is not acceptable, since they would have brought to Ireland the language of their kin in Jutland, which did not differ greatly from that of the Anglo-Saxons, instead of transmitting mostly the Keltic culture of Gaul. This tradition of passage across the North Sea doubtless refers to later Danish raids on Scotland and Ireland. Moreover, the Ogam inscriptions[126] of the oldest Goidelic speech have been recovered in southern England (chiefly Devon and Cornwall) and Wales as well as in Scotland, the Isle of Man, and southwestern Ireland. These facts indicate original settlement in southern Britain by the strait of Dover.[127] The Dananns may have been joined by some of Odin's Danes from the lower Rhine valley before the former migrated from Gaul to Britain, but this is merely conjecture. The Picts, who included or were associated with the Albani,[128] Caledonians, and other highland tribes, were immediately behind the Dananns as the latter crossed to Ireland, but they remained in England and southern Scotland until driven northward on the invasion of England by the Skolotic Kimmerians (Scots and Britons) about three centuries later. They represented parts of various tribes associated with the Kimmeric Pictones of Gaul, who in Julius Caesar's time lived between the Seine and Loire Rivers, toward the sea.[129] They had been driven southward beyond the Seine upon the invasion of northern Gaul by their kinsmen, the Skoloti. In fact, this inter-river region and the south is recognized as the ultimate

---

126 These represent simply an adoption in major part of the Latin alphabet, imparted to the Goidels perhaps while in Gaul by some learned Latin captives, emissaries, or wanderers, or were brought back to them in Gaul by some Goidelic explorers in the south. It may be supported by the finding of coins of the Roman Republic (c. 500 B.C. and later) near Rathfarnham, in County Dublin, as reported by Petrie in *Proceedings of Royal Irish Academy*, vii. 441ff. (1856).

127 Caesar, *Gallic War*, v. 12.

128 The name Damnii Albani, used by Richard of Cirencester, may mean either that these Albani were a remnant of the Scottic Damnii cut off from the rest of the tribe in Strathclyde when the wall was erected across the isthmus or that they were a division that had been captured by or joined the Albani in consequence of the Roman invasions. In any event, they became merged with the Pictish tribes in the highlands. J. A. Giles, *op. cit.*, *Richard of Cirencester*, i. 6. 41, 48.

129 Caesar, *Gallic War*, vii. 4.

habitation of most of the Goidelic Kimmerians of Gaul.[130]

Ireland apparently was uninhabited by human beings during the Ice Ages. To the earliest, or brunet, inhabitants the country was known as *Iberiu,* which is Keltic in form. This name was applied by Iberian colonists of the Mediterranean race, who moved northward from the Iberian peninsula through Gaul and finally crossed to Britain perhaps as early as 6500 B.C. Within a few centuries they must have been followed by the vanguard of the first Keltic invaders of Europe, the so-called Furfooz-Grenelle Paleo-Kelts, blond, brachycephalic people who reached the coast of the North Sea about 7700 B.C. They had extended their Maglemosean culture as far north as Skäne, in southern Sweden, by about that time. Down through the ages the Iberian element probably dominated western Ireland while Keltic invaders controlled the easterly half. During the 3rd millennium B.C., Anatolian mariners brought products of the eastern Mediterranean region to Britain and Ireland in exchange for tin and other commodities. A long time was still to intervene before the first Nordics should reach Ireland.

This sparse primitive population of Great Britain was augmented by new arrivals from the continent about 1700-1600 B.C., who represented the second (or Neo-) Keltic invasion of continental Europe of about 2300 B.C., already described. About 1450 B.C. the vanguard of the Neo-Keltic invaders, who had introduced bronze into Britain,[131] crossed the water from southern Scotland to Ireland and conquered the easterly half of that island from the earlier inhabitants, the Iberians and Paleo-Kelts,[132] while the rest of the Neo-Kelts remained in Britain. The earlier inhabitants continued in possession of western Ireland.

These broad-headed Kelts of the Bronze Age cremated

---

130 F. P. G. Guizot, *History of France* (London, 1872-1881), pp. 11-12.

131 The Neo-Keltic invasion of Britain probably occurred about 1700-1600 B.C., in consequence of the migration of the Suebi westward to the Elbe River, dispersing Kelts who formerly lived in that region.

132 Neolithic objects of these people (of about 1450 B. C.) have been found recently in a prehistoric tomb near Dunloy, in County Antrim, Ireland.

their dead as the Kelts of southern Germany did centuries earlier. Their bronze weapons resembled the types used in northern France but differed from those in Scandinavia and Hungary. Like their kin in the Alps, they frequently erected their dwellings on piles in shallow bays and lakes. Such dwellings are known as crannogs. An example is that recently discovered at Ballindery, County Westmeath, which is believed to have been constructed about 1400 years B.C. Among the findings was a heart-shaped lamp of bronze, probably used to guide the dwellers back to their settlement from the mainland after darkness had fallen. Other objects included bits of pottery, implements of stone, and daggers of bronze used to fight beasts and men, wooden tubs, barrels, knives, axes, and pins made of bronze; also dug-out canoes, paddles for propelling them, and stones for grinding grain. These people probably first brought the system of Druidic rites from Gaul to Britain and Ireland.

Late in the 2nd millennium B.C. the Phoenician colonies in southern Iberia were established and maritime routes subsequently opened between that base and the British Isles. In order to broaden their markets, the Phoenicians encouraged the settlement of immigrants at western seaports where their ships touched,[133] for the establishment of commercial relations with the local population. This was only following a practice of the earlier Pre-Sumerian Leleges of Anatolia. In the course of time, the descendants of these colonists from Anatolia and Phoenicia merged with the native population. Moreover, British and Irish Kelts may have enlisted or been impressed into the Anatolian and the Phoenician sea service and thus brought back tales of adventure in the Mediterranean region; so that the traditions of voyages back and forth over the Mediterranean, of sea raids along its shores, etc. were woven into Irish history. Some of the present brunet people of southern Wales, mainly Pembrokeshire, clearly are decendants of inhabitants of Phoenician colonies in the

---

133 1100-1000 B. C. (from both Phoenicia and her Iberian colonies). J. A. Giles, *op. cit., Richard of Cirencester*, ii. i.6.

valley of the Guadalquivir River in Iberia or of earlier seaports of the Leleges in western Anatolia. The latter is indicated by their physique and Hebraic-type of countenance.[134] Thus, the traditional invaders of Ireland around 1000 B. C. were mainly Phoenicians or their Iberian subjects, and not Kimmeric Milesians, as is asserted by some historians. To them are due the Hamitic aspects of the colloquial dialects and the personal name system of the ancient pre-Goidelic Irish and Welsh.[135] They also introduced various eastern Mediterranean religious and other customs.

From as early perhaps as 1000-750 B.C., the coasts of Scotland and Ireland were raided sporadically by Scandinavians, probably Vikings from southern Norway. The historic Fomorian invaders of Ireland apparently came from that region, since the name was applied to large or giant pirates.[136] Confirmation is seen in the finding in a lake-dwelling at Ballindery, County Westmeath, of a Viking sword and an ancient gaming board much like similar objects on view in Scandinavian museums. But it is doubtful whether these early raiders made any permanent settlements worthy of note.

The next invaders of Ireland, who ultimately succeeded in conquering the island, were the Goidelic Kimmerians, the first Nordic settlers. They came from southern Scotland in groups at close intervals shortly after 590 B.C. The earliest arrivals were the followers of Parthalon, small in number, who traditionally were wiped out by a plague.[137] They were followed by the Nemedians,[138] who suffered severely in combat with Fomorians. By 585 B. C.

---

134 Thomas Nicholas, *op.cit.*, page 441. Thus, they would be a Pre-Sumerian strain.

135 Rhys and Brynmor-Jones, *op. cit.*, pp. 36-74; Appendix B, pp. 617-641. It is possible, of course, that the tradition of ancient bonds between Spain and Ireland arose from these commercial relations of the Phoenicians. Such relations could conceivably have kept alive and strengthened a tradition of a far earlier migration from Iberia.

136 *Encyclopaedia Britannica*, 13th Ed., vol. 14, pages 757-758, by Edmund Crosby Quiggin.

137 Eugene O'Curry, *op. cit.*, vol. 2, p. 184; *Ency. Brit.*, *op. cit.*

138 W. K Sullivan, *op cit.*, pp. cclxiii-cclxiv; also Eugene O'Curry, *op. cit.*, vol. 2, pp. 110, 184-185, 232-233.

the main body, the Tuatha Dé Danann (traditionally a branch of the Nemedians from Scythia), had arrived and begun a systematic conquest of the island, particularly the northerly and easterly parts. Most of the native population avoided early subjection by moving to western Ireland, where it remained independent for a long time. There is no evidence that the Goidels exterminated the brunet and Keltic natives in any large degree; they made them subject people as their conquests progressed.[139] The possession of the arts of necromancy by these Goidels[140] clearly relates them to the hordes who often invaded western Asia while their (Kimmeric) nation lived north of the Black Sea. In fact, as in the case of the related Danes of Danmark, the traditions of these adventures in the Aegean region were perpetuated in Irish history. Their tribal system was quite analogous to the patriarchal system of the east.[141] They used long bronze leaf-shaped swords. Himilco, a Carthaginian, who passed the Pillars of Hercules and surveyed the northwesterly coasts of Europe at the height of his nation's prosperity (c. 362-350 B.C.), is reported by Festus Avienus as saying that the people of Albion (from the *Albani*), later called Britain, were a "numerous race, endowed with spirit, very dexterous, all busy with the cares of trade."[142] His remarks certainly pertained to the Goidels and others then living at the coastal ports, who were in constant contact with Gallic civilization.

Early in the 3rd century B.C., while the Skolotic Kimmerians (Scotti and Britons) were progressively conquering England from northern Gaul, their Belgic congeners in Gaul conducted expeditions of conquest to southern Britain and Ireland. They planted one colony in and around the present Somersetshire and others in Munster, Leinster,

---

139 This explains, of course, why the Goidelic population became mixed and its dialect embodied more primitive elements than the Britonic dialect by the time that the Skolotic Kimmerians reached Britain. Rhys and Brynmor-Jones, *op. cit.*, pages 13-24.

140 W. K. Sullivan, *op. cit.*, pp. ccclvii-ccclviii (footnote).

141 Seumas MacManus, *op. cit.*, pp. 293-295, with the authorities there relied upon.

142 Thomas Nicholas, *op. cit.*, pp. 59-60.

and the Boyne River valley of the present County Meath, whereupon their seat of government was established at Tara by a chief named Liath.[143] In Ireland they were known as the *Firbolg* element (the men of *Bolg* or *Belg*, i.e., the Belgae),[144] and they were successful in gaining large areas. "That the tribes included under the general name of Firbolgs were identical with many tribes in Great Britain and along the Belgic and Frisian [Hollandic] coast there seems no reason any longer to doubt."[145] They were the first to introduce the use of iron to the Irish in the form of weapons.[146] But gradually the Goidels (Damanns) gained the ascendancy, concluded by the great battle of *Magh Tuireadh* near Cong, County Mayo, and some of the Firbolgs scattered to the Hebrides and other Scottish Islands. Those who remained behind became subjects of their conquerors, whose king, Breas MacElathan, imposed burdensome rents on them[147] and their other subjects and who dominated Ireland until the appearance of strong forces of Scotti from Strathclyde[148] about the middle of the 1st century B.C. These Dananns divided the island into five kingdoms,[149] which in the main corresponded with the later kingdoms of Ulster, Connaught, Laigin (Leinster), East Munster, and West Munster. Under the provincial kings were tribal kings whose territory roughly corresponded with the present baronies, which in many instances preserve the tribal names.

From Iberiu the name of Ériu, Érin, or Eire for Ire-

---

143 Eugene O'Curry, *op. cit.*, vol. 2, pp. 187, 189 (Footnote), 235; vol. 3, pp. 5-6.
144 The tradition in Irish history of the Firbolgs having been in Grecian territory before migrating to western Europe identifies them as members of the earlier Kimmeric nation north of the Black Sea, from which many marauding expeditions invaded the regions around the Aegean Sea, as already discussed.
145 W. K. Sullivan, *op. cit.*, page lxxvi; Eugene O'Curry, *op. cit.*, vol. 2, page 243.
146 Eugene O'Curry, *op. cit.*, vol. 2, pp. 235-237, 274-275, 299-301.
147 W. K. Sullivan, *op.cit.*, page xxiii.
148 Traditionally, for a period represented by five generations of kings.
149 Eugene O'Curry, *op. cit.*, vol. 2, page 13, without citing his source, asserts that the ancient provincial divisions were made by the Firbolgs. If so, they must have been in large numbers and gained temporary control of more of the island than is generally supposed to have been the case.

land was derived. The original name continued in use down through the ages and was accepted by the Goidelic Kimmerians (the Dananns), who were called by the Iberians the Féini (waggon-men),[149] from which the modern term of Fenians originated. The name of Iberiu to the Greeks was *Ivernia* and to the Latins *Iberio* (as in the *Confession of Saint Patrick*), from which the form Hibernia evolved. The subsequent Nordic (Kimmeric) conquerors of the island called it the land of the Eires, or Ireland.

When we come to the conquest of the British Isles by the Skolotic Kimmerians we are on even more certain ground. The evidence is not clear as to just how soon after the Skoloti reached the region of the central Rhine from the Ukraine their expeditions began to invade the British Isles. It certainly was several decades, since they had first before them the task of conquering northern Gaul from the Kelts. These Skolotic tribes, therefore, originally settled east of the Rhine, as far as the Weser and Fulda River basins in modern Hessen, whence they began their conquest of northern Gaul. The Tungri, the tribe from which the Belgian district of Tongres was named, were the first to effect a crossing of the Rhine,[150] after which the progressive conquest of that region by the Skoloti (Scotti, Britons, and Belgae) followed and the Goidelic Kimmerians finally were pressed south of the Seine. But many of the Skolotic tribes or divisions of them remained east of the Rhine and were the later "Germans" of Julius Caesar as distinguished from the Suebic nation. After pressing the Kelts westward to the Belgian coast, where they later were absorbed by the conquerors, and southward into the Ardennes and Gaul, most of the Scotti and the Britons crossed to Britain while the Belgae remained in control of northern Gaul.

Upon crossing the channel to Britain, the Scotti and the Britons began the conquest of that island from the

---

150 Tacitus, *Germania*, ch. 2.

south.[151] Their culture was far superior to that of the Goidels and was under a patriarchal form of government.[152] They were a highly commercial people in consequence of their former habitation adjacent to the Greek colonies on the Black Sea. Their expeditions were strongly and efficiently organized, after the manner of the ancient Greeks of Miletus when the latter established their commercial outposts on the Black Sea, with which the Skoloti were so familiar. About 290 B.C. the Scotti gained a foothold in southeastern England, where they established trading posts.[153] Upon their successful advance in the island, they were followed by the Britons,[153] who ultimately forced the Scotti northward. This had the effect of driving the Goidelic Picts and their associated tribes wholly into Scotland. In Scotland the greatest concentration of Picts was in the midlands between the Firth of Forth and the Grampian Hills, which came to be known as *Pictavia,* both locally and to the Scandinavians who occasionally made incursions into the country. Thus, the Firth of Forth anciently was called the *Mare Picticum.* The importance of these names will appear later. Subsequently (c. 200-175 B.C.), the Belgae likewise established colonies on the southerly shores of England, mainly in Somerset.[154] The influence of the Skolotic tribes in the British Isles continually increased and, with military support, they gained substantially all of England and

---

151 Caesar, *Gallic War,* v.12; Bede, *Ecclesiastical History,* i.1; J. A. Giles, *op. cit., Richard of Circencester* i. 6. 32, ii. 1.9. Archibald B. Scott, in *The Pictish Nation* (Foulis, Edinburgh, 1918), page 7, errs in naming the *Brigantes* (Scots) as Picts. The latter spoke a Goidelic dialect along with the Manx and the Irish. Britonic was spoken in southern Scotland by Scots and Britons driven northward from England.
152 J. A. Giles, *op.cit., Richard of Cirencester* i. 3.19 and footnote.
153 *Ibid.,* ii. 1.6, 9.
154 Many of the tribal names were carried from Gaul to Britain, such as those of the Britanni, Attrebates, Albani, Catalauni (from whom the name of Chalons was derived), Bibroci (Remi), Chauci, Parisii, Senones, Durotriges (Morini), Cimbri, Belgae, and others, but probably in some instances the invading bands represented coalitions of parts of various tribes that ventured forth under more general names.

Wales by the middle of the 2nd century B.C.[155] The *Scotti* ultimately settled in northern England, where the *Brigantes* were their dominant tribe, and the Britons over most of central England.[156] The dark-complexioned Iberian *Silures*[157] continued dominant in southern Wales. Among the invaders of England from Gaul was a division of the *Parisii* from along the Seine River, where their capital was on the isle of Lutetia (Lutèce). In Caesar's time, these people inhabited the East Riding of Yorkshire. They apparently came over as allies of the Britons, for their habitation in Gaul was near the southerly Belgae. Those who remained on the island in the Seine River gave the city of Paris its name; they were insignificant in numbers in Julius Caesar's time and were dependent on neighboring Senones on their southeast for protection.[158] The Senones are reported to have been Kelts, who were defeated by the Romans about 51 B.C., but some evidence indicates that they were Kimmerians.

The Belgae of southwestern England long were politically subject to the continental Belgae, for Julius Caesar[159] mentioned a certain Divitiacus, king of the Keltic Aedui and of the Belgic Suessiones (whose name is perpetuated in that of the city of Soissons), as the most powerful prince in Gaul and as also ruling over Britain.[160] This fact was late enough to be within the memory of men in Caesar's time. The British *Triads* carry the tradition of the Skolotic Kimmerian conquest of England, Wales, and (southern) Scotland.

As immigration from Gaul to southern England increased, pressure by the Britons gradually forced the Scotti toward the north and many finally passed over the Cheviot Hills into southwestern Scotland.[161] The latter, in turn

---

155 Rhys and Brynmor-Jones, *op.cit.*, pp. 10-11.

156 See note 151.

157 *Ency. Brit.*, 13th Ed., vol. 5, page 578b, under *Cave*.

158 Caesar, *Gallic War*, vi. 3. Lutetia must have been settled by the Parisii as early as 335 B.C., soon after their arrival in Gaul.

159 *Ibid.*, ii. 4; J. A. Giles, *op.cit.*, *Richard of Cirencester*, ii. 1.9.

160 It is probable that this rule in Britain pertained only to the colonies of the Belgae there and not to the Britons or Scots.

161 Bede, i. 12, 34; *Anglo-Saxon Chronicle*; Thomas Nicholas, *op. cit.*, pp. 237, 423.

pressed the southernmost Picts northward in Strathclyde and eastward in Lothian,[161] whence they soon were driven north of the Scottish isthmus. Caesar's invasions of England (55-54 B.C.), were confined mainly to the south and in contact with the Britons, many of whom moved into Wales; but the pressure also was felt by the Scotti in the north,[162] for the Brigantes sent troops south to aid in resisting the Romans.[163] The Picts, then largely north of the Firths of Forth and Clyde (in Pictavia),[164] were beyond the reach of explorers or historians from southern Europe, which explains why they were not mentioned in the writings of Julius Caesar, Tacitus, Ptolemy, or Dio Cassius.[165] By the time of Caesar's invasions of Britain, the population of the British Isles had become largely Keltic in language and customs but not in race, in which respect it was mainly Nordic. The close kinship of the Kimmerians of Britain and of Gaul was noted by Caesar (*Gallic War*, v. 14), whose

---

162 At the time of Caesar's invasions, the Scotti appear to have comprised the *Selgovae, Gadeni, Novantes, Damnonii, Attacotti,* and perhaps other tribes of Strathclyde, and the *Brigantes, Voluntii,* and *Sistuntii* of northwestern England. The *Ordovices* and *Cangiani* (or *Deceangi*) of central England and northern Wales and also the *Cornabii* on the northeastern Welsh border were British. The last three tribes may have merged during the Roman conquest. In addition, the Britons comprised the *Ottadini* and *Parisii* in northeastern England, and the *Coritani, Iceni, Trinobantes, Dobuni, Cantii, Catalauni* (*Casii*), and *Dumnonii* in central and southern England. Some of these tribes also probably consolidated during the Roman conquest. The *Silures* held southern Wales and the *Dimetae* were in the southwest, while some Cimbri and Belgae inhabited Devon, Somerset, and eastward. Ultimately, north Britain was divided into three Roman provinces, viz., *Valentiana,* from Hadrian's Wall (mouth of Tyne River to Solway Firth) north to the Wall of Antoninus Pius (between Firths of Forth and Clyde); *Vespasiana,* from this wall to a line from Moray Firth to Loch Linnhe; and *Caledonia,* north and northwest of the preceding province. On the south were *Britannia Prima, Secunda* (Wales), *Flavia,* and *Maxima* (to Adrian's Wall).

163 Despite Caesar's reports, it is probable that he did not fare well in these expeditions. J. A. Giles, *Six Old English Chronicles* (*Geoffrey of Monmouth's British History*) (Bell, London, 1891), Book iv., chs. 1-14.

164 *Bede* 1.1. Rhys and Brynmor-Jones, *op.cit.,* p. 7.

165 Perhaps the earliest mention of the Picts was by Eumenius, a professor of rhetoric at Augustodunum (now Autun) in Gaul, delivered at Treves, in Germania, in 296, when he referred to the Britons as a rude nation, contending (doubtless even prior to the time of Julius Caesar) with such adversaries as the Picts and Irish, half-naked enemies. Joseph Ritson, *Annals of the Caledonians, Picts, and Scots* (Edinburgh, 1828), vol. 1, pp. 71-72, 91.

reason for invading Britain was that "in all his wars with the Gauls" the Britons had extended assistance to them. The deepest national sympathy existed, communication across the channel was easy, and Caesar's military plans soon were known to the islanders.[166] The speech and customs of the two peoples differed little because of several centuries of commercial and cultural relations. The Goidels of Scotland and Ireland were farther away and were much less influenced.

In warfare, notably in resisting Caesar, the ancient Britons and Scots used a special 2-horse type of chariot, whose wheels were mounted with sharp sickle-shaped blades that cut to pieces whatever they encountered.[167] This was an invention of the Persians and was used in large numbers in the armies of Cyrus the Younger, who was a satrap in Asia Minor (408-401 B.C.).[168] Through the Greeks under Clearchus, who engaged in warfare with Cyrus, the Skoloti became acquainted with this form of chariot and adopted it when they emigrated to Britain. This fact conduces to the identification of the Scots and Britons as descendants of the Skoloti who lived along the northerly shores of the Black Sea.

Julius Caesar's invasions of Britain prompted the Scots to begin their historic conquest of Ireland from northern England.[169] They invaded northeastern Ireland in the third quarter of the 1st century B.C. Their headquarters then were in Cumbria (derived from Kimmeriu), the habitation of the Brigantes, whose chief city, Carlisle, received its name from the Kimmeric *Caerluel* (Caer-Luel or City-Luel). The name Cumbria is perpetuated by the English shire of Cumberland. Strathclyde, Scot-

---

166 Caesar, *Gallic War* v. 15, 19.
167 See also Tacitus, *Life of Agricola*, ch. 12, ch, 15; Eugene O'Curry, *op.cit.*, vol. 2, p. 300; J. A. Giles, *op. cit., Richard of Cirencester* i. 3.14; C. C, Mierow, *The Gothic History of Jordanes* (Princeton 1915), p 55.
168 *Encyclopaedia Britannica*, 13th Ed., vol. 5, p. 860, vol. 7, p. 708; Xenophon, *Anabasis* (Boston, 1893), i. 7.10-12; 8.10.
169 The tribes contributing to these invading forces were the *Brigantes, Voluntii* (and perhaps *Sistuntii, Cangiani (Concangii)*, and *Damnonii*, J. A. Giles, *op. cit., Richard of Cirencester*, i. 6.34-36, 8.9, 12-17, ii.1.17.

land, seems originally to have been called Cambria,[170] but, when the Kymric rulers changed their seat from Strathclyde to northern Wales, the name became applied to the latter region. The Scottish tribe of *Voluntii* made the first conquest of Irish territory by their establishment of the colony of Uladh (Ulidia),[171] from which the name of Ulster was derived. The leader of this expedition traditionally was Ir, a scion or *princeps* of the royal Milesian line of the Scotti, which may have been the senior tribe or division of the earlier Skoloti.

The northern Firbolgs who, when defeated by the Dananns (c.150 B. C.), had fled to the Hebrides and other Scottish islands, were driven out by the Caledonian Picts late in the 1st century B.C. and (as the Umorians)[172] returned to Ireland. This incident confirms the habitation of the Pictish tribes in northern Scotland at this time and the partial conquest of southern Scotland by the Scots. The return of the Umorians was induced by the success of the Ulidian colonists against the former's old enemies, the Dananns; in fact, they may have been allies of the invaders.

The Scots, a seafaring commercial people, established numerous trading posts on both sides of the Irish Sea, in Ireland, Wales, England, and Scotland, and also conducted commercial activities with the continent, particularly with the Belgae. Scholars only recently have begun to realize how close were the relations among the peoples of eastern Ireland, Wales, Cumbria, and the continent in ancient times.[173] The ability and commercial advantages of the Scots enabled them to gain from the Goidels desirable coastal districts in northeastern Ireland in addition to their Ulidian colony, over all of which they installed their own rulers. Their traditional ruler of these Irish colonies at the beginning of the Christian era was

---

170 *Vita Kentegerni*, ch. 11; quoted by Ritson, vol. II, pp. 146-149. This was true as late as the last half of the 6th century.

171 Their early presence in Ireland is shown by Bede (i. 1); J. A. Giles, *op. cit.*, *Richard of Cirencester* i. 8.15-17.

172 Eugene O'Curry, *op. cit.*, vol. 2, p. 122.

173 *Encyclopaedia Britannica*, 13th Ed., vol. 14, pp. 756-759, by Edmund Crosby Quiggin.

Concobar MacNessa. They maintained close commercial relations across the Irish Sea with the Britons of southern Wales and southern England as well as with their own people in northern Wales, Cumbria, and southern Scotland;[174] also with the coastal points on the continent as far as Iberia and perhaps even in the Mediterranean.[175]

In their conquest of northern Ireland from the Goidels, the Cumbrian Scots had as their allies, among others, a strong force of the Scottish tribe of Damnonii[176] of Strathclyde, and the later Connaught (Connacht) was allotted to them[176] by the Milesian leaders. The book of Leinster names Tinne MacConrath (20 B. C.) as the first of this line of kings of all Connaught. The great Irish epic, the *Táin Bó Cuailgne*, depicts strife growing out of early rivalry between the Scottish rulers of Connaught and of Ulster.[177] The Damnonian dynasty held its own until the 4th century A. D., when, perhaps because of dissension with the *ard-righ* or over-king of all Ireland (Muireadhach Tireach, who reigned at Tara from 331 to 357), that dynasty was ousted by him and thereafter the throne was occupied by Milesian rulers.[178] The renowned Patrick performed highly successful Christian missionary work among these Scots as he did among those of northeastern Ireland.[179]

---

174 Tacitus, *Germania*, ch. 24.

175 Julius Caesar, in his *Gallic War*, v. 13, refers to this commercial sea-route between Cumbria and Ireland, with the Isle of Mona (Man) in the middle of the voyage. In further proof of this early sea commerce between Spain and Ireland is the reference by Tacitus, in his *Life of Agricola*, c. 24 (as of A. D. 82), to Ireland as lying between Spain and Britain, commodiously situated as to the Gallic Sea (Bay of Biscay), whose inhabitants differed little from those of Britain and *whose ports and harbors were better known* (than those of eastern Britain) *from the concourse of merchants for the purposes of commerce.*

176 W. K. Sullivan's *Introduction* to Eugene O'Curry's *Manners and Customs of the Ancient Irish* (Williams and Norgate, London, 1873), pp. xx, xxi.

177 Their two great traditional dueling champions, Ferdiad and Cuchullian respectively, learned the art of war among their kin in Scotland. W. K. Sullivan, *op. cit.*, pp. xx, cccclxx-cccclxxi, and O'Curry, vol. 2, pp. 302, 329, 367-371. Neither was a Firbolg or a Danann. There the Scots of northern Ireland used the scythed chariot as their congeners in Britain did. W. K. Sullivan, *ibid.*, p. cccclxxix, note 873.

178 *Encyclopaedia Britannica*, 13th Ed., vol. 6, page 951.

179 J. A. Giles, *op. cit., Nennius*, Sec. 54.

The dominant tribe of the Scots, the Brigantes, inhabited Yorkshire, Durham, and, with the Voluntii and the Sistuntii, also Cumberland, Westmoreland, and Lancashire, extending "from sea to sea." Besides their Irish colonies, one of their possessions was the isle of Anglesey, the *Mona* of Tacitus,[180] in northwestern Wales. Like northwestern Wales, it was inhabited largely by Goidels.[181] On that isle was the port through which supplies were furnished to the revolting Britons at the the time that Claudius and his successors were conquering Britain (beginning in A.D. 43).[182] During these three or four years of warfare, Claudius and his generals conquered all of England east of the Severn and south of the Humber Rivers, but not the Silures of southern Wales. Many Britons were driven into central Wales and the Ordovices took refuge in northern Wales.[183] But the hills and tribes of Wales and Yorkshire offered far greater resistance and 30 years of intermittent warfare followed (A. D. 47-78). During Nero's reign, Suetonius Paulinus directed an expedition (c. A.D. 60) against the isle of Mona,[184] slaying the Druidic bands, cutting down their sacred groves, and otherwise ravaging the countryside.

Taking advantage of these circumstances, the Picts of Scotland assailed the Scots on their south, in resistance to the further advance of the latter in Scotland. The Picts were turned back at the Cheviot Hills and finally returned north of the Firth of Clyde. With enemies thus on the north and south, the Scots undertook further and extensive emigration to northern Ireland about this time.[185]

During these 30 years of strife (A. D. 47-78), the Britons in eastern England north of the Humber (chiefly the Ottadini) crossed the Tweed River and, driving the Scots westward to Cumbria and Strathclyde, took possession of

---

180   Tacitus, *Life of Agricola*, ch. 14.
181   Rhys and Brynmor-Jones, *op.cit.*, pp. 7, 9, 112.
182   Tacitus, *ibid.*, ch. 13, 14.
183   Rhys and Brynmor-Jones, *ibid.*, pp. 7-10; J. A. Giles, *op. cit., Geoffrey, Gildas, Nennius, Richard of Cirencester.*
184   Tacitus, *ibid.*, ch. 14.
185   J. A. Giles, *ibid., Richard of Circencester* ii. 1, 17, 19.

ancient Lothian (comprising the counties of Roxburgh, Berwick, Selkirk, Peebles, Edinburgh, Haddington, and Linlithgow).[186] The Scots thus displaced in the east (chiefly Brigantes) then crowded over into Cumbria and Strathclyde[186] (the latter comprising the Scottish counties of Dumfries, Kirkcudbright, Wigton, Ayr, Lanark, and Renfrew). These Scots then called themselves by their ancient national name of *Kymry* (Kimmerii) rather than by any of the subordinate or tribal names.

Vettius Bolanus, the Roman governor sent to Britain by Vespasian in A. D. 69, was unable to maintain discipline in his army during this civil war[187] and Petillius Cerealis was sent over to replace him as commander. The latter promptly attacked the Brigantes, who composed the most populous state in the whole province, striking terror among them, and a war of annihilation followed.[188] Many more of these Scots crossed to Strathclyde and numerous others crossed to Ireland,[189] where they re-established themselves. Those who remained in Cumbria were brought into subjection to the Roman power. Julius Frontinus, another Roman commander, subsequently conquered the Silures of southern Wales, then a strong and warlike nation.[190]

In the summer of A.D. 78, Agricola came from Rome to become governor of Britain. He first conquered the British Ordovices, who had settled in northern Wales[191] exclusive of the isle of Anglesey, and then he assailed this island.[192] Among his auxiliary troops were *Batavi* and *Tungri,* Belgae from northern Gaul.[193] The fact that the people of Anglesey expected the arrival of a Roman fleet and an invasion by sea instead of the land attack actually made[194] is evidence of their seafaring activities as an outpost of the Scots.

---

186   *Bede* i. 1, 12 and iv. 26.
187   Tacitus, *op.cit.,* ch. 16.
188   *Ibid.,* ch. 17.
189   J. A. Giles, *op. cit., Richard of Cirencester* i. 6, 36, 8.9, 17; ii. 1.7, 19.
190   Tacitus, *ibid.,* ch. 17.
191   Rhys and Brynmor-Jones, *op. cit.,* pp. 8-9, 95-96, 501-502.
192   Tactius, *ibid.,* ch. 18.
193   *Ibid.,* ch. 36.
194   *Ibid.,* ch. 18.

Subsequently (A.D. 79), Agricola began his campaign against northern Britain.[195] He overcame the Britons in northeastern England and Lothian and the Scots in Cumbria and Strathclyde, so that by the year 80 the conquered territory extended as far north as the Firth of Tay.[196] The recalcitrant Scots (chiefly Brigantes) intermingled with Britons who resisted subjection were driven north of the isthmus between the firths of Forth and Clyde (where Agricola erected a line of forts)[197] and westward into Argyllshire. The territory north of Agricola's forts thus taken over by the commingled Scots and Britons (and its people known as the *Maeatae* or *Miathi* of Dio Cassius and the *Verturiones* of Ammianus Marcellinus) comprised the midland counties of Dumbarton, Stirling, Fife, Kinross, Clackmannan, southern Perth, and finally Argyll, known collectively as Pictavia. The Picts, in turn, were driven northward over the Grampian Hills and Loch Leven, and the highlands thenceforth became their habitation.[198] They were succeeded in Pictavia by Skolotic (Britonic-speaking) Kimmerians, i.e., Scots and Britons.[199] Thus, the inhabitants of Pictavia no longer were Goidelic Picts. Their successors, therefore, should be referred to as Pictavians, as once reported,[200] and not confused with the highland Picts. They were also known as the people of Fortrenn (Earn), with their centers at Dun Earn, Fortevoit, and Scone.

---

195 *Ibid.*, ch. 20.

196 *Ibid.*, ch. 22; J. A. Giles, *op.cit.*, *Richard of Cirencester*, i. 6.36.

197 Tacitus, *ibid.*, ch. 22, 23. See footnote 201.

198 J. A. Giles, *ibid.*, *Gildas* Sec. 14, 21; *Nennius* iii. 8, 12, 38. This change of population is the cause of the difficulty experienced by historians in determining who the Picts were. The fundamental error of treating the Pictavians as Picts occurs in such books as *The Pictish Nation* by Archibald B. Scott, which refers only meagerly to the real Picts of the highlands and treats chiefly of the culture of the Scots and Britons from the south, generically known as the Kymry. *Ibid.*, pp. 7-8, 11-18, and 415.

199 The Scots included *Brigantes* from Cumbria, the *Selgovae, Gadeni, Novantes,* and *Damnonii* (who had not already gone to Ireland), and the Britons were chiefly the *Ottadini*. J. A. Giles, *ibid.*, *Richard of Cirencester* i. 6.37-41; J. C. Prichard, *op. cit.*, vol. 3, p. 165.

200 See footnote 197, also ch. 23, 24.

The year 81 was spent by Agricola in securing the country thus overrun, including the islands of Bute and Arran in Argyllshire.[200½] Although he contemplated the conquest of Ireland, he made no attempt to do so, since the Scots and Britons on the north, in alliance with the Picts of Caledonia, were laying plans for a united attack on the Roman forces.[201] The Picts were thoroughly aroused about their own safety[202] and enlisted the aid of the disorganized Scots and Britons north of the isthmus in the common defense.[203] Their forces were assembled for action at the foot of the Grampian Hills[204] under the leadership of Galgacus (Gilgidh or Gilgig), a renowned Pictavian chieftain,[205] and the Roman forces moved to the attack. This battle (in 83) was disastrous to the allied army and the triumph of the Romans was complete.[206] In one of his most impressive passages, Tacitus describes the deep despair to which the vanquished peoples were reduced by this overwhelming defeat,[207] which terminated hostilities. While leading his army southward to winter quarters, Agricola directed the Roman fleet to circumnavigate Britain. After completion, the fleet returned to its station in the Firth of Forth.[208] The location of the winter quarters of the Roman army is not known, but it must have been in northeastern England. Agricola then returned to Rome.

The strife over, the Britons[209] (chiefly the Ottadini) resumed possession of southeastern Scotland (Lothian) and the Scots[209] (chiefly the more southerly Brigantes) regained the territory on the west (Strathclyde, i.e., Dumfries, Kirkcudbright, Wigton, Ayr, Lanark, and Renfrew).

200½ Tacitus, *op. cit.*, 23, 24.
201 *Ibid.*, 25, 26, 27, 29-33; Rhys and Brynmor-Jones, *op.cit.*, pp. 97-98, 113.
202 Tacitus, *ibid.*, 25.
203 *Ibid.*, 27.
204 *Ibid.*, 29.
205 *Ibid.*, 30-32.
206 *Ibid.*, 35-38.
207 *Ibid.*, 38.
208 *Ibid.*, 38.
209 Due to intermingling, the generic name of Kymry replaced those of Britons and Scots among themselves.

The capital of the latter was Alcluyth (or Dumbarton). By this time the Britons of central England had largely intermingled with the remnants of the Scots in Cumbria and those in Strathclyde[210] and their enemies frequently referred to them all generically as "Britons." The Roman frontier apparently was the Cheviot Hills and the Tweed River. The Silures, Dimetae, Ordovices, and Cangini remained in possession of Wales west of the Severn and Dee rivers.[211] The history of this whole region during the period from A.D. 85 to 120 is a void, but this was a period of historic events in Scandinavia, narrated later, whose repercussions extended throughout Yorkshire and northward.

Ptolemy reports at about this time the presence of the following-named tribes in Scotland, viz., (1) *Kerones* along the whole west coast from Loch Linnhe to Cape Wrath; (2) *Kornavioi*[212] in Sutherland and Caithness; (3) *Lougoi* along the coast of Sutherland from Caithness to Dornoch Firth; (4) *Smertai* in the interior of Sutherland and north Ross; (5) *Dekantai*[212] between Dornoch and Moray firths; (6) *Taixaloi* along the coasts of Banff and Aberdeen; (7) *Vernikones* in Kincardine, Forfar, and Fife; (8) *Vakomagi* in the highlands between the Moray and Tay firths; and (9) *Keledonioi* (Caledonians) in the western upper midlands, with their capital at Dumkeld on the Tay River. He also mentions the inhabitants of the Skye, Hebrides, and Orkney Islands. In addition, the *Albani* were somewhere in the highlands. All of these people (except the Kornavioi and the Dekantai) and the other highlanders were Goidelic speakers and may be referred to generically as the real Picts of history. South of them in Pictavia (the midlands) were the mingled Scots and Brit-

---

210 J. A. Giles, *op. cit., Richard of Cirencester* i. 6.23, 36.

211 *Ibid.,* i. 6.21-24. The Cangiani had a small territory along the northern shores. *Ibid.,* i. 6.25.

212 The *Kornavioi* and *Dekantai* were divisions of the Britonic tribes of Cornabii (of Cornwall) and Cantii (of Kent) who, upon the conquest of southern England by the Roman General Ostorius about A.D. 50, migrated by sea to the northerly end of Pictland. J. A. Giles, *ibid., Richard of Cirencester* i. 6.54; ii. 1.16. Another division of the Cornabii previously had migrated to Cheshire, *ibid.,* i. 6.27.

ons, bordering on the Kymry of Lothian and Strathclyde who earlier had spread over the Cheviot Hills and the Liddell River.[213] The *Epidici* of Kintyre and other parts of southern Argyll were Brigantes or other Scots, for they comprised Britonic-speaking people.

About 115-120 the Britons in Yorkshire revolted and destroyed the 9th Roman Legion at York. A clue to the circumstances of this revolt may be obtained from what was transpiring in Scandinavia at this time. During this quarter century (100-125) the Goths completed their subsequently-described conquests in southern Sweden. In all probability, numerous refugee bands of Scandinavians, driven westward by the Goths, crossed the water and raided the Orkney Islands and northern Scotland, temporarily pressing the Picts toward the south, as the Norsemen had done many times before and as they did afterward. In 122 Hadrian established his frontier across Britain from the Tyne River to Solway and constructed a rampart over 75 miles long, to protect England from incursions from the north. The Picts (of the north) and the Scots (of Pictavia) received a considerable strain of Scandinavian blood from the earliest times even as the Irish did that of the ancient Viking *Fomorians*[214] and of more recent Vikings.

The Norse invasions resulted in numerous incursions of Britons, Scots, and Picts into Roman territory in northern England, and the revolt of the Britons at York undoubtedly occurred in this connection. They apparently also prompted the invasion of the Scottish colony of Ulidia in northeastern Ireland by the Pictavians, who drove many of the Ulidians southward and westward and some of whom reached as far as County Roscommon. These Pictavians were Britonic-speaking people, as the Ulidians originally had been, and in Ireland they were known as

---

213 They fought with chariots as the Britons did. Rhys and Brynmor-Jones, *op. cit.*, pp. 97-98, 113. Their name *Maeatae* or *Miathi* had the same origin as Meath (in Ireland) from the Britonic "medd", central region. It means midlanders and was used by Britonic-speaking people and not by Picts or other Goidelic-speaking people. Archibald B. Scott, *op. cit.*, p. 11.
214 Thomas Nicholas, *op.cit.*, pp. 492-3.

Cruithné.[215] Ultimately, these Pictavians consolidated chiefly in the modern County Antrim and adjacent areas under the national name of *Dalriada*. They remained independent until the 8th century, first under Pictavian rulers and later under Milesian rulers. When the latter gained the ascendancy, many of the Pictavians moved southward into the modern County Down, which became known as *Dalaraida* (*Dal-Araidhe*).

During the reign of Hadrian's successor, Antoninus Pius, about 142, after conditions in the north of Britain had subsided, the Roman governor Lollius Urbicus advanced to the old frontier between the Clyde and Forth rivers and connected the forts of Agricola with a deep fosse, 40 feet wide and 20 feet deep, and a huge earthen rampart. In 209 Severus constructed on this frontier line a solid masonry wall 74 miles long, with lofty battlements facing the north. In Scotland, south of this wall, were the Britons of Lothian and the Scots of Strathclyde, who recognized the Roman rule, while immediately north throughout Pictavia (including Argyllshire) were the irreconcilable Scots and Britons (Pictavians), who disdained the Romans.[216] The Picts controlled the highland territory thence to the northern islands, which was known as Albania.[217]

All of Britain south of this fortified frontier, which required the Romans 166 years to conquer, thereafter was a part of the Roman Empire, with its composite Keltic and Roman culture from very early times. On the north were the "barbarians," with their largely Keltic culture. When the empire adopted Christianity, through the influ-

---

215 Thus, Scott in *The Pictish Nation* errs in classing the Ulidians and Cruithné as Picts, since each originated in the Scottish Brigantes and affiliated tribes. Tradtionally, they had as allies descendants of Firbolgs earlier driven from Ireland to Scotland (*ante*, footnotes 144 and 172), who finally settled on the Aran Islands in Galway Bay. Seumas MacManus, *op. cit.*, pp. 302-303.

216 Archibald B. Scott, *op.cit.*, pp. 171-172.

217 J. A. Giles, *op.cit.*, *Gildas*, Sec. 14, 21; *Nennius* iii. 8, 12, 38. This name, from the tribe of the *Albani*, had a common origin with that of Albania, on the Adriatic Sea, and of ancient Albania, at the eastern end of the Caucasus Mountains, including the Albanian Gates, a defile at Derbend. See *ante*, where its antiquity is indicated. When the Goidelic Kimmerians migrated from Gaul to Britain, all of the tribe of Albani did not go along, for Suidas (p. 100) reports a nation of that name still in Gaul.

ence of missionaries from Gaul that part of Britain south of the frontier became a Christian country. Subsequent invasions from the north into the Roman territory became more formidable as the Roman Empire grew weaker in her struggle with the continental barbarians. About 300 "the Caledonians and other Picts[218] were making incursions into northern England, harrying the Romans down to the wall of Hadrian." Soon thereafter disastrous raids also were made by the "Picts [Pictavians] and Scots."[219] The latter came from Ireland, but whether the Pictavians came from Ireland or Scotland or from both countries is veiled in doubt. The indications are that they came from Ireland. In fact, the Irish king, Niall Noigiallach, was undertaking an invasion of the continent in 405 with a large force of Irish Scots and Pictavians when he met his death.[220] Finally, in 410, during the reign of Honorius, the Romans abandoned Britain. The chaos and strife that followed was the occasion for the coming of the Jutes, Saxons, and Angles.

Only shortly before, in 397, the great Christian missionary, Saint Ninian, a Briton, established a famous religious community known as *Candida Casa*,[221] now Whithorn, Galloway, in territory of the Scottish Novantes, from which many trained leaders went forth to Christianize the Scots and Britons of southern Scotland. He had been trained at the great ecclesiastical community of Saint Martin's at Tours, Gaul, and his work made Candida Casa the mother-church of Britain. Prior to his death in 432, Saint Ninian also conducted a great missionary tour along the eastern coast of Pictland and established the church among the inhabitants there.

Coming now to the situation in Ireland, we find that the leaders of the Scots who migrated from Cumbria to

---

218 The highlanders.
219 This union of forces of the Pictavians and the Scots of Ireland, both descendants of the early Scotti (Brigantes), is significant when we later consider the union of the same people of Dalriada and Pictavia, which ultimately resulted in a united Scotland. Eugene O'Curry, *op. cit.*, vol. 2, p. 287.
220 See footnote 219.
221 J. A. Giles, *op.cit.*, *Richard of Cirencester* i. 6.40.

the basin of the Boyne River in A.D. 50-70, during the Roman invasion of Britain, were the sons of a chieftain named Miled, and their followers were called Milesians. Traditionally, as in the case of the Dananns, their habitation had been Scythia, which already has been verified.[222] Perpetuating the name of the Skoloti, they gave the name of *Scotia Major* to Ireland, while *southern* Scotland, where most of their congeners lived,[223] was known to them as *Scotia Minor*.

The Milesians defeated the Dananns at the battle of Taillte,[224] in County Meath, and established their capital at Tara, an earlier Belgic capital and seat of learning in the same county, where, by their superior ability and resources rather than by large numbers, they began the reëstablishment of their prestige west of the Irish Sea and the slow acquisition of control of Ireland.[225] On their north, in what is now Ulster, were most of the Ulidians, descendants of their earlier kindred colony of Ulidia, while on their west was the other Scottic kingdom of the Damnonians (in Connaught); all of these were well disposed toward the newcomers.

The magnitude of the task of revival and reconstruction that confronted these Scots in Ireland is indicated by the fact that by the end of the 3rd century their acknowledged rule was still confined largely to the valley of the Boyne and the district around Tara. The additional migrations from Cumbria probably were not yet numerous.[226] These Scots did not have any authority

---

222 According to all Irish annalists, the successive colonies of Nemedians, Tuatha Dé Danann, Firbolgs, and Milesians all spoke the Gaelic language (acquired in Gaul).

223 Irish history makes frequent reference to the relationship of the Irish Scots with their kin in Alba (Scotland).

224 Eugene O'Curry, *op. cit.*, vol. 2, p. 240.

225 The outline of Irish history by Edmund Crosby Quiggin in *Encyclopaedia Britannica*, 13th Ed. vol. 14, pp. 757 *et seq.*, is largely relied upon here.

226 But they did include representation from a number of tribes of Scots and Britons. Their names, as given by Richard of Cirencester and quoted by Joseph Ritson in vol. II, page 9, plus some names ascribed to Ptolemy, were the *Brigantes, Damnonii, Gadeni,* and *Voluntii,* the *Menapii* and *Chauci* (Belgae and Danes from the Rhine Valley), and the *Coriondi, Eblanae,* and a few others of uncertain spelling. Archibald B. Scott, *op. cit.*, pp. 1, 11, 16, 17, is in error in designating the Brigantes and Menapii as Picts.

over their kindred Ulidians and Damnonians on the north and west, and it required a long time for them to regain sufficient strength to aspire to bring Ulidia and Connaught under their sway and to undertake the subjection of the Goidelic people of central and southern Ireland,[227] since the Scottish overkingship under the Milesian rulers was not finally acknowledged in southern Ireland before the 4th century.[228] Widespread commercial activities with Britain and Gaul enabled these Scots eventually to become a rich and powerful nation again.

This rebuilding of the Scottish nations on both sides of the Irish Sea, first in northern Ireland and later in Cumbria and southward to and including northern Wales, during the early centuries of the Christian era, is an achievement of these Scots worthy of especial notice. It was due mainly to their development of sea commerce.[229] The established water routes of the Scots between Cumbria and Anglesey, in Britain, and northeastern Ireland were widely known at the time of Caesar. He wrote that the passage from Ireland to Britain (Cumbria) was equal in distance to that which he first sailed from Gaul[230] to Britain, and that in the middle of the voyage there was an

---

227 In Ulidia and Connaught the early Scottish conquerors were the ruling element and the Goidels and others (*aithech tuatha*) were the subject or common people. These two nations were rivals and engaged in frequent strife with each other. To the Giodels of the south, the ruling Scots of the north were known as the *Earnaan*, which may have been derived from the name *Earn* used by the Scottish Pictavians who had driven the Picts from that region in central Scotland. Seumas MacManus, *op.cit.*, p. 41.

228 W. K. Sullivan, *op. cit.*, pp. xxiii-iv. This early conquest of southern Scotland and northern Ireland by the Scots, led by descendants of the ancient king Miled or Milesius, is affirmed by the first stanza of an ancient poem in the Book of Conquests, quoted from the Saltair of Cashel, as follows: "The two renowned sons of Milesius, Who conquered both Erinn and Albain: With them hither there came a comely poet and a gifted harper." Eugene O'Curry, *op. cit.*, vol. 2, p. 4.

229 Caesar, *Gallic War*, iii. 8, 12-16, iv. 20. This intercourse is further proved by the finding of coins of Roman provinces from the time of Emperor Tiberius (A.D. 14-27) through the reign of Constantine (323-337) in the Scottish counties of Antrim, Down, and Meath. *Proceedings of Royal Irish Academy*, ii. 184-188 (1843), vi. 525 (1856); *Proceedings of Royal Society of Antiquaries of Ireland*, xxx. 176 (1900).

230 From the mouth of the Seine River (Strabo, iv.3.3) or of the Somme (*ibid.*, iv. 5.2).

island called Mona (Manna), now the Isle of Man.[231]
This Irish Sea commerce also was recognized by Tacitus.[232]

Apparently, the royal name of Miled had been carried
down from the ancient Ionian city of Miletus, a colony of
Athens.[233] At Miletus this Scottish king's ancestors must
have obtained cultural and military training[234] in the service of the Greeks while the Skoloti inhabited the northern
shores of the Black Sea adjacent to the Greek colonies of
that city. The generic name of the Kimmerians (Kymry),
formerly used by the Britons and Scots of northern Wales
and southern Scotland,[235] persists in Wales, where the people still call themselves the Kymry and their country Kymru, to their great credit. The Saxons called them Welsh
or foreigners, whence the name of Wales came to be used
in English history. When the Scots transferred their capital to Ireland, they used a shortening (Scotti) of their primary national name, the Skoloti, under which the Britons
and the Belgae originally were tribal divisions. With increase in numbers, numerous tribal names subsequently
were adopted by subdivisions of all of them, but these
three appellations ultimately became national names (Scotland, Britain, and Belgium).

The Scots in County Meath, Ireland, originally a relatively small division,[236] soon were augmented by bands of
others from Cumbria and Strathclyde, some of whom may
have been Firbolgs driven earlier from Ireland to Scotland.
The descendants of their traditional King Miled subsequently intermarried with Goidelic regal families[237] in
southern Ireland, to enable them to increase and retain
their leadership in the whole country. Among their de-

---

231 Caesar, *ibid.*, v. 13.
232 Tactius, *Life of Agricola*, chs. 14, 18, 24.
233 Herodotus v. 97.
234 This background is indicated by the antiquity of learning among the Scots of
Ireland. Seumas MacManus, *op.cit.*, pp. 213-214.
235 It was used also by the Kimmerians (Cimbri) in Denmark and in western
Gaul as well as in Britain.
236 As stated by Saint Patrick in his *Confession*, they were a ruling minority,
which comprised the nobility or gentry. The native Irish (Goidels and others) were
the common people.
237 Seumas MacManus, *ibid.*, p. 43.

scendants were the monarchs of Ireland down to Roderick O'Connor, the last native king, whose reign ended in 1202. In the course of time, because of this minority of numbers, the Britonic dialect of the Scots in Ireland was modified and ultimately became nearly as Goidelic[238] as that of their subjects.

Heber Find, of Munster, appears to have been the most powerful contemporaneous Goidelic king, while Heremon was the chief leader of the Milesians. The former was slain in warfare between them and Heremon gained nominal control of Munster as well as of Leinster, thereupon declaring himself the first overking of the distinguished Milesian line. Members of the reigning family then were assigned to rule those districts, and base-rents were imposed on the subject peoples, the Firbolgs, Dananns, and primitive inhabitants. This ascendancy was bitterly contested and uprisings were frequent during the reigns of several successive kings. One uprising during the 1st century of the Christian era[239] resulted in heavy slaughter of Milesian nobles and the temporary ascendancy of Connaught and Ulster and Goidelic chieftains, but Heremon's dynasty was restored on the accession of Tuathal Techtmar, whose reign began about A.D. 130. In order to strengthen his rule in southeastern Ireland, he (c. A.D. 135) planted a colony of Brigantes from Cumbria in that region and also induced distressed Chauci and Menapii to emigrate from the lower Rhine basin and settle there.[240] All were Britonic Kimmerians (Skoloti). Tuathal is conspicuous as the ruler who carved out the central kingdom of Meath, comprising Meath, Westmeath, Longford, and portions of Monaghan, Cavan, King's, and Kildare, to be his mensal land. The capital

---

238 For this reason, Archibald B. Scott, in *The Pictish Nation,* errs in naming as Picts rather than as Pictavians or Scots the numerous eminent Christian missionaries who went out from the religious community at Bangor, in Scottish Ulster, to Christianize Ireland, Britain, and the continent. He concedes that Bangor changed from Britonic to Goidelic after the Scottish power was transferred from Ireland to Scotland. *Ibid.,* p. 51. It was a famous cultural center.

239 W. K. Sullivan, *op.cit.,* pp. xxvii-xxx.

240 Rhys and Brynmor-Jones, *op. cit.,* pp. 85-86; J. A. Giles, *op. cit., Richard of Cirencester* i, 8.14.

remained at Tara. He then proceeded to consolidate the rule of Scotia Major under the king at Tara as the *ard-righ* or supreme ruler or overking of all Ireland (as well as being the local king of Meath), to whom the provincial kings were to be subject. He also levied a tribute, the *boroma*, which was the cause of much oppression and strife. It was remitted only in the 7th century.

Tuathal was succeeded by his son Feidlimid Rechtmar, the Law Giver, but, in consequence of an uprising, the latter was followed as overking by the noted Goidelic king of Leinster, Cathair Mor, whose claim to that throne must have been based on the intermarriage of an ancestor with a feminine member of the Milesian dynasty. Cathair ultimately was defeated and overthrown in a great battle in Meath by Feidlimid's son, Conn of the Hundred Battles, grandson of Tuathal.

Constant warfare between the new king, Conn Cetchathach (who reigned during the period A.D. 157-177), and a descendant of Heber Find in Munster named Eogan Mor, also called Mog Nuadat, resulted in a draw. Eogan's claim, too, must have been based on Milesian descent through a female line. Both shared the island, the northern part being called Leth Cuinn (Conn's half) and the southern part Leth Moga (Mog's half), but Leinster soon regained independence of Munster. The rulers of Leinster and Munster seem most of the time to have been but little more than nominally subject to the overking at Tara. Evidence that scions of early Goidelic Leinster and Munster kings intermarried with the Milesian family and thereby retained the local thrones of their ancestors is the fact that practically all Milesian pedigrees converge on three antecessors in the 2nd century, one Milesian and two Goidelic in origin in the male line, viz., Conn Cetchathach, king at Tara, Cathair Mor, king of Leinster, and Ailill Aulom,[241] king of Munster, son of Eogan Mor. The annals and tales as well as the history of other countries are replete with instances of such alliances.

---

241 This king himself, in fact, married Sadhbh, a daugher of Conn Cetchathach. Eugene O'Curry, *op. cit.*, vol. 2, pp. 139 and 206; vol. 3, pp. 177 and 259.

Conn's grandson, Cormac,[242] son of Art, reigned in great splendor (227-266). He was a distinguished patron of learning, which indicated the culture that the Scots had brought from Scythia and which flourished in their intercourse with their kinsmen on the continent. The three Collas, cousins of the Ard-Righ Muredach, invaded Ulidia early in the 4th century (331) in order to subordinate and reunite its people with the Scottish nation. They drove many of the Ulidians back across the Newry River into Dalaraida (Down and southern Antrim), then dominated by Pictavians. The apparent object was to force an integration with and neutralization of influence of the latter, over whose region and Dalriada (Antrim), constituting the true Ulidia, a member of the Milesian ruling family thereupon was installed. They also founded the kingdom of Oriel (Armagh, Monaghan, North Louth, and southern Fermanagh) out of former Ulidian territory in order to consolidate Scottish territory in the northeast and to form a buffer state between Ulidia and Connaught.

With the advent of Niall Noigiallach, who reigned during 379-405, the supremacy of the overking at Tara became firmly established. He engaged in many sea-raiding expeditions and directed incursions of mixed bands of Scots and Pictavians (Cruithné) from Ireland into Britain.[243] He also established Scottish colonies in south Wales, Cornwall, Devon, and Somerset and in Argyllshire.[244] These colonists included some Goidelic subjects from Ireland. He died while on a sea raid in the English Channel in 405. All the rest of Ireland (Scotia Major) came under succeeding Milesian overkings during the 5th century. The kingdom of Ailech was created in the north-

---

242 During his reign, the sept of the *Desi* was expelled from the district of Deece, county Meath, and settled in Munster, where their name still survives in the barony of Decies, in county Waterford. Their descendants were the "Scots who dwelt in the south of Ireland" and whose religious customs were referred to by Bede (iii. 3) as of A.D. 635. Long afterward some of these people migrated to Pembrokeshire, in Wales. Rhys and Brynmor-Jones, *op. cit.*, pp. 30-31.

243 Gildas Albanius, *De excidio Britonum* (ca. 560), chs. 11-12, as quoted by Ritson, vol. 1, pp. 151-157.

244 Gildas, chs. 13, 14, and 15, as quoted by Ritson, vol. 1, pp. 157-168; also footnote, p. 164.

west,[245] but Dalriada remained independent of the others as the historical kingdom of Ulidia[246] and a heritage of the Milesian regal dynasty.

During all of these centuries close commercial relations existed between the Belgae on the continent and their Skolotic kinsmen in the British Isles. The latter provided the Gauls with military aid in their wars with the Roman Empire.[247] The importance of this contact has been emphasized by Heinrich Zimmer.[248] In fact, these people were the principal commercial intermediaries between the populations of the two countries. Because the Belgae possessed the commerce of Britain, they resisted the passage of Julius Caesar to that island.[249]

Caesar said that Britain was well-peopled, full of houses built after the manner of the Gauls, and that brass and gold money and iron rings of a certain weight were used in barter.[250] The people of Kent were the most civilized, differing but little from the Gauls. This condition was attributable to their close contact across the channel with the progressive Belgae. The most of the population in the interior was little given to tilling land but lived on flesh and milk and was clad in skins, which was the mode of life of the more civilized Gauls.[250] The following quota-

---

245 As shown by Archibald B. Scott, *op.cit.*, footnote on page 2, at the beginning of the 6th century the Scots (in name) dominated practically all of northern Ireland. But they had become largely merged with the local Goidelic element.

246 Seumas MacManus, in *The Story of the Irish Race* (Irish Pub. Co., New York, 1921), p. 1, makes the following statement: "The races that occupied the land when the so-called Milesians came, chiefly the Firbolg and the Tuatha Dé Danann, were certainly not exterminated by the conquering Milesians. Those two peoples formed the basis of the future population, which was dominated and guided and had its characteristics moulded by the far less numerous but more powerful Milesian aristocracy and soldiery." With this we are in agreement so far as it goes but it fails to mention the earlier Iberians, Kelts, and Phoenicians chiefly in western Ireland. In the light of what we have presented here, the legendary account of the origin of the Irish people, as set out by MacManus in Chapter III, is an interweaving into a single story of disconnected legends of different races from widely separated places, who migrated to Ireland at vastly different times. This work has aimed to disentangle and construe those traditions.

247 Caesar, *Gallic War*, iv. 20.

248 In papers in the *Abh. d. Berl. Akad. d. Wissenschaften* (1909).

249 Strabo iv. 4.1.

250 Thomas Nicholas, *The Pedigree of the English People*, pp. 61-62.

tion from Chadwick portrays the relatively high state of civilization of these people before the beginning of the Christian era:

> But, at least in the south, market centers had sprung up, town life was beginning, houses of a better type were perhaps coming into use, and the southern tribes employed a gold coinage and also a currency of iron bars or ingots. . . . . . . In religion the chief feature was the priesthood of Druids, who here as in Gaul, practised magical arts and barbarous rites of human sacrifice, taught a secret lore, wielded great influence, but, at least as Druids, took ordinarily no part in politics. In art, these tribes possessed a native Late Keltic fashion descended from far-off Mediterranean [?] antecedents and more directly connected with the La Téne culture of the continental Kelts. . . . The Late Keltic age was one which genuinely delighted in beauty of form and detail. In this it resembled the Middle Ages rather than the Roman Empire. . . . . . .
> The Roman conquest of northern Gaul (57-50 B.C.) brought Britain into definite relation with the Mediterranean. It was already closely connected with Gaul, and, when Roman civilization and its products invaded Gallica Belgica, they passed on easily to Britain.[251]

Thus, there was in Britain, as in northern Gaul, a curious intermingling of Keltic and Nordic tribal rites with elements of the higher civilization of western Asia appropriated by the Getae and impressed on the Skoloti while they lived along the northerly shores of the Black Sea. The impress of the western Asiatic culture was more thorough than is generally realized. It provided the groundwork on which, with the stimulating influence of Christianity, was erected the brilliant civilization that attained its fruition in Ireland during the first eight centuries of the Christian

---

251 *Encyclopaedia Britannica*, 13th Ed., vol. 4, p. 583, by Hector Munro Chadwick. As already stated, the Roman conquest of England occurred between A.D. 43 and 85 under Claudius and Agricola.

era, while the Scottish traditions dominated the island and before the recurrence of the Viking invasions. This fact is proved by the singularly advanced stage of organization of the administration of justice by these Scots for so early a period.[252] It was the Scots who developed the fundamentals of the Brehon Laws in Ireland. Poetry also is said to have been invented by them in Ireland,[253] but the poem *Carman* may have been composed there by Goidels before the arrival of the Scots.

When the Romans withdrew from Britain in 410, the Britons gradually regained control of all eastern England, and the Pictavians, who established their capital first at Abernethy and later at Forteviot, in Perthshire, overran the Kymric territory of southern Scotland.[254] Under the stress of these circumstances, a Kymric prince named Cunedda,[255] of Lothian and Strathclyde, assumed the recognized powers of the *Dux Britanniarum*,[256] the Roman officer who governed the upper province of Britain. He shortly afterward transferred his court and residence to Deganwy, in ancient Gwynedd, near modern Llandudno, on the northern coast of Wales, among the kindred tribe of the Ordovices. He took the title of Gwledig (supreme) and was the ancestor of a line of Kymric kings.[257]

However, the Pictavians were more interested in ravaging the former Roman territory farther to the south than in disturbing the Kymry in Strathclyde and Lothian. It was a traditional obsession among them to avenge their past defeats by the Roman armies, and perhaps also to annoy the intermediate Britons who had accepted the Roman rule. Thus, they speedily began their invasions of

---

252 W. K. Sullivan, *op.cit.*, pp. cclxii-ccxcv.

253 Seumas MacManus, *op. cit.*, pp. 176-180.

254 Bede i. 12, 14.

255 He was of the British tribe of *Ottadini*, south of the Firth of Forth. Rhys and Brynmor-Jones, *op.cit.*, pp. 21, 98, 112-3, 120.

256 *Ibid.*, pp. 106-7, 118-9.

257 *Ibid.*, pp. 8-10. It is not improbable that he was succeeded in Strathclyde by a son named Ceretic (or Coroticus), whose forces raided Ulidia, in Ireland (Scotia Major), and who was the subject of Patrick's letter *The Denunciation of Coroticus*. See Rees, *Welsh Saints*, p. 135.

England across the Tweed River that resulted in the invitation from the British King Vortigern to the seafaring Jutes (Danes), who were fellow-Kimmerians, to come to his aid.[258]

Upon the landing in England of the Jutes under Hengist and Horsa in 449 and their subsequent quarrel with the Britons, the conquest of that country began. They were followed by Frisians in 477, Saxons in and after 495, and Angles less than a century later.[259] Saxons came from the left shore of the lower Elbe and the Angles from Holstein. The Angles ultimately gained all of northeastern England as far as the Tweed River and the Cheviot Hills, which forced the Pictavians back to central Scotland. Southern Scotland (mainly south of the Tay River) then became a battleground of the Pictavians on the north, the Scots of Dalriada (Ireland), the local Kymry whose greatest strength was in Strathclyde, and the Angles of Northumbria. It also suffered raids by Danes.[260] Its subsequent fortunes are considered later.

The Irish Scots were Christianized chiefly through the efforts of a famous missionary, a Briton named Succat, later known as Patricius and ultimately as Saint Patrick (c. 389-461). While most of his work was in northern Ireland, his sphere of activity also included southern Ireland. He was a son of Calpurnius, a decurion under Roman rule. He is believed by Bury to have been born in Glamorganshire and by others in Monmouthshire, south Wales, and was taken to Ireland as a youthful prisoner on one of the vessels of the Scots engaged in raids of Britain. His preparation at Auxerre, in Gaul, for his subsequent religious work and his activities are matters of record. Beginning his ministerial work in Ireland in 432 under the friendly auspices of a Gallican bishop named Germanus, he was highly reverenced and was more respected as the head of the free Irish church than a Gallic missionary named

---

258 Gildas, ch. 17-23, as quoted by Ritson, vol. 1, pp. 170-174; Bede i. 14, 15.
259 Bede i. 15.
260 *Chronica Pictorum,* as quoted by Ritson, vol. II, pp. 73, 78, 82-83, 92.

Palladius (373-463) sent by that bishop in 431, who tried unsuccessfully[261] to revise the form of the Irish Christian Church and was expelled. This independent church in an independent country, logically denied that the Roman bishopric had jurisdiction beyond the limits of the Roman Empire,[262] and nowhere in Patrick's writings does he refer to Rome. The assertion that he visited or represented Rome is mere fiction and not supported by any extant facts; his mother church was in Gaul.

The brilliant outburst of culture in Ireland during the 3rd and subsequent centuries, especially in the 6th and 7th, is attributable to a growing spirit of civil and religious independence and a zealous and widely-expanding monasticism under the Milesian kings in the northerly half of Ireland,[263] dominated by the Scottish element. The culture of the Goidels in southern Ireland was far inferior,[264] since they had not, while in the Ukraine, enjoyed the contacts with western Asiatic civilization that their Skolotic kinsmen later had. This circumstance is the reason for the occasional historical references to a barbaric state of culture in Ireland. It already has been stated that Cormac MacArt, who reigned from 254-266, was a noted patron of learning. He codified (c. 265) the criminal laws of his

---

261 Archibald B. Scott, *op.cit.*, pp. 113-114. The simplicity of Christianity in early Ireland did not lend itself well to the development of such ecclesiastical shrines as arose after the Roman Catholic influence gained substantial headway on the island in and after the hapless year of 1173.

262 Letter of an Irish saint, Columbanus (who led 12 Irish monks into Gaul and Burgundy), to Boniface IV, Roman Bishop (608-615). *Encyclopaedia Britannica*, 13th Ed., vol. 24, pp. 430-431, by Andrew Lang; Seumas MacManus, *op. cit.*, pp. 239-240.

263 The teachers, chiefly monks, were Scots. Bede ii. 2, 4, 19, iii. 1, 3, 4, 5, 6, 17, 19, 21, 25. The most outstanding center of religious and other culture in Ireland was at Bangor, in the Scottish colony of Ulster, where Saint Comgall the Great ruled as abbot in the 6th century. The Christian church of Gaul was the mother church of the people of Britain and Ireland.

264 Strabo, *Geogr.* ii. 5.8; iv. 5.5. Similarly in Britain, where the culture of the highland Picts was inferior to that of the Scots and Britons in the south. J. A. Giles, *op.cit.*, *Richard of Cirencester* i. 3.6, 4.1-15. In fact, in Britain and Ireland, as in other learned countries of the early ages, education was for the few and the mass of the people was not educated. Only the exceptionally bright and ambitious of the latter, freeing themselves from the fetters of tradition, rose above the level of their kin.

people, which later were revised by Ceannfalad. Loigaire (son of Niall Noigiallach), who reigned from 428 to 463, likewise was more interested in internal cultural development than in raiding Britain, as his predecessors had done. An outstanding achievement of his reign was the codification (c.438) by Patrick, Dubthach, Ros, and Fergus of the system of ancient unwritten Brehon civil laws, based variously on ancient Kimmerian tribal laws, on Keltic and Scriptural customs and precepts, and conspicuously on such systems as the Babylonian code of Hammurabi, in the forms in which they had evolved in western Asia or in western Europe. Their knowledge of Hammurabi's code is proved by the inclusion *inter alia* of the principle of the Conjugal Community in both ancient Irish and Welsh laws.[265] It is clearly a concomitant of an early settled and relatively stable economic condition of society and of a markedly superior standard of culture, wherein private property rights and rights of women were recognized. Confirming the transmission of knowledge of the later Babylonian code from western Asia to western Europe is the finding of numerous coins and other objects of pre-Christian western Asiatic art in the caves of Ireland. The foregoing laws are preserved in the code of the Book of Aicill (chiefly criminal) and of Seanchas Mor (civil). They were abrogated during the reign of the English King James I (1603-1625).

The Scottish missionaries of Ireland were not only the pioneers of Christianity at home and on the continent, in both of which regions their labors were highly successful, but they also were pioneers in the other culture of the age. As stated by Zimmer:

> They were instructed in every known branch of science and learning of the time, possessors and bearers of a higher culture than was at that period to be

---

265 Lawrence Ginnell, *The Brehon Laws* (1894), p. 212; Sophie Bryant, *Liberty, Order, and Law under Native Irish Rule* (1923), pp. 78-82, 87-88; Hubert Lewis, *The Ancient Laws of Wales* (Stock, London, 1889), pp. 8-9; Seumas MacManus, *op. cit.*, pp. 154-155.

found anywhere on the continent, and can surely claim to have been the pioneers, — to have laid the cornerstone of western culture on the continent, the rich results of which Germany shares and enjoys today, in comon with all other civilized nations.[266]

At that time, the Suebic tribes east of the Elbe and the Werra were just emerging from their tribal customs and beginning to feel the stimulating influence of primitive Christianity. So notable was the educational advancement of these northern Irish scholars that youths were sent from the continent to Ireland to gain the benefit of this high culture. Thus, the great civilizing influence of the Skoloti in transmitting the civilization of western Asia to western Europe by the way of the Ukraine and Ireland is apparent.

During the later part of the 5th century, the Scottish kingdom of Dalriada, in northeastern Ireland, augmented its colonial settlements in Argyllshire, Scotia Minor. A band of 150 colonists is recorded as having arrived in 498. In support of them against the Pictavians, Fergus son of Erc, a descendant of Conor II, *ard-righ* or high-king of Ireland, made additional settlements on Kintyre, Islay, Jura, Bute, and other islands. They also drove the Caledonian Picts northward beyond Loch Leven. Shortly after this time, in fear of repeated Scandinavian raids on the east and north and the growing conquests of the Irish Scots in Argyllshire, the Picts of the highlands, poorly organized, effected an agreement with the Pictavians whereby they recognized the overlordship of the latter's king in return for his military support against the invaders. Thus we find that Brudé MacMaelchon was the undisputed sovereign of both Pictavia and the highlands from 554 to 584 and was seated at his capital in Inverness in 563 when the Scottish Saint Columba of Dalriada, in Ireland, was introduced to him by Saints Comgall and Cainnech of Ban-

---

266 H. Zimmer, *The Irish Element in Medieval Culture* (Putnam, New York, 1891), pp. 130-131.

gor, in Ulster.[267] *Actually, this alliance rather than the ascension of Kenneth MacAlpin to the throne in 843 marks the union of the kindred Scottish people (the Brigantes and their congeners of Pictavia) and the highland Picts of Scotland into a single nation.*

For a time the Scottish colonists in Argyllshire were dependent on Dalriada, but by the second half of the 6th century the primary interests of the Scots of Dalriada had been transferred from Ireland to Kintyre, the seat of government of Scottish Dalriada, and in 575 King Aedhan declared its independence of Ireland.[268] By repeated intermarriage with Goidelic families, the reigning Milesian line and its adherents in Ireland gradually had been transformed from Scot to Goidel in blood[269] as well as in dialect, and the ancient traditions and prowess of the Scots had greatly diminished on the island. Their prestige had been upheld mainly by the branch that ruled Dalriada, among whose subjects were descendants of the Ulidian colonists and the Dalriadian Pictavians, doubtless then well amalgamated into a single Scottish state. Thus, the authority of the ancient Scotti, violently driven from Cumbria to Ireland by the Romans early in the

---

267 Archibald B. Scott, *op. cit.*, pp. 8, 219. The ancient Britonic dialect of the Irish Scots when they migrated from Cumbria had been Goidelicized in Ireland; hence, Saint Columba required an interpreter when interviewing Britonic-speaking Pictavians. The so-called Q-using people were the Irish Scots and Irish, the C-using people the Cruithné (Goidelicized Pictavians in Ireland), and the P-using people the Britonic-speaking Scots and Britons south of the Grampian Mountains.
268 Bede i. 1. The people of the Irish and Scottish Dalriadas belonged to the same kingdom and Aedhan claimed rulership over both. But Aed, *ard-righ* or overking of Ireland, held in 574 that the tributes and military service of the Irish Dalriada belonged to Tara; hence Aedhan's declaration of independence. Seumas MacManus, *op.cit.*, page 169. The petty rulers of Dalriada in Argyllshire from the time the land was seized until its independence of Irish Dalriada, as well established (according to Tigernach's chronology), were:

(1) Loarn Mor	(? -499)	(5) Gabhran MacDomangart	(538-560)
(2) Fergus Mor	(499-501)	(6) Conaill MacComghall	(560-563)
(3) Domangart McFergus	(501-505)	(7) Aedhan MacGabhran	(563-606)
(4) Comghall MacDomangart	(505-538)		

269 Saint Patrick, in his *Confession*, refers to the Scotti — the conquerors, masters, military men — as the nobility or gentry, but he nowhere calls the native Irish other than *Hiberionae*, the common people. He names their place of origin as Scythia, which confirms the conclusions presented herein.

Christian era, was transferred to southern Scotland (Scotia Minor) five centuries later. The name Scotia Major thereupon vanished from history and Scotia Minor subsequently became the Scotland of today.

By winning the battle of Deorham in 577, the Anglo-Saxons in England conquered that country as far west as the Severn River. The Britons who resisted were pressed westward and northward and thereafter were confined to Devon and Cornwall, Wales,[270] northwestern England (Cumbria) commingled with Scots (former Brigantes),[271] southwestern Scotland among the Kymric Scots of Strathclyde,[271] and Lothian. The domain of the Kymry in Cumbria, chiefly in Cumberland and Westmoreland and parts of Yorkshire and Lancashire as far south as the Derwent River, began to be assailed by the Angles prior to the year 600.[272]

In 603, the Scots of Dalriada, concerned about the westward expansion of the Angles under Ethelfrid, appeared in Cumbria with a large army under their King Aedhan, but were repulsed by the Angles.[272] At the battle of Chester in 613, the Angles drove a wedge between the Britons of Cumbria and those of Wales through Lancashire to the Irish Sea. This act isolated King Cunedda in northern Wales and prevented his assertion of further sovereignty over his kindred people in Strathclyde and Lothian. Thereafter, rule under the Kymric name was confined to Wales. The greatest concentration of these Scots and Britons remained in western Yorkshire, Cheshire, and Lancashire, where they frequently conflicted with the Angles. In general, the conquest of England by the Jutes and Anglo-Saxons resulted in considerable displacement of the older inhabitants[273] of the easterly half of the country and their concentration in the westerly half, including the above

---

270 Many were driven there from central England and subsequently the Welsh were known as western Britons, although they called themselves Kymry (from their former national name Kimmerii). Rhys and Brynmor-Jones, *op.cit.*, pages 8-9; J. A. Giles, *op. cit., Gildas*, Sec. 27-36.

271 Thomas Nicholas, *op.cit.*, pages 191-192; J. A. Giles, *op.cit., Richard of Cirencester* ii.2.23.

272 *Anglo-Saxon Chronicle*, J. A. Giles translation; *Bede* i. 34.

273 *Anglo-Saxon Chronicle*.

areas, Wales, and the southwest, with a thinning out toward the eastern coast.

All of these Scots and Britons generally were called Britons by such writers as Bede,[274] since at his time the Scottish name had been continued chiefly by the division in Ireland. The Scots remaining in Cumbria and Strathclyde had merged with the Britons under the Kymric name,[275] and those just north of the Firth of Forth were known as Pictavians. Thus did Bede (673-735) write that the languages of Britain were those of the Picts, Scots, Britons, and English.[276] It was during the Saxon conquest of southern England in the 5th, 6th, and 7th centuries that thousands of Britons emigrated from Devon and from Cornwall to Armorica,[277] the present peninsula of Brittany (Bretagne), in France, to which they gave their name. There their descendants have since amalgamated largely with the Kelts and any Goidelic or Britonic Kimmerians who still inhabited that region. The later Cornish dialect thus was nearer to that of the Britons who had emigrated to Brittany than it was to the dialect of the commingled Britons and Scots of northern Wales.

During the 7th century, the Kymry of northern Wales often fought beside their kinsmen of Strathclyde against the Angles, but in 635 the English King Oswald finally conquered the Britons of Cumbria as far as the Irish Sea.[278] In 638, Gureit, the sovereign of the Kymry in Strathclyde and Lothian died. By 682, the English had extended their dominion over the Britons of Lothian and the Pictavians immediately on their north[279] as they had done over the Cumbrians.[280] King Egfrid even sent an army into Ireland in 684, but an ill-advised invasion of

---

274 Bede i. 24, 34, ii. 2, 4, 5, 20, iii. 6.

275 Thomas Nicholas, *op.cit.*, pages 368-370.

276 Bede iii. 6.

277 Thomas Nicholas, *op. cit.*, pages 271-303; J. A. Giles, *op. cit., Gildas*, Sec. 25; J. C. Prichard, *op.cit*, vol. 3, page 168.

278 Bede iii. 6. Cumbria was then made a part of the Northumbrian kingdom of Deira.

279 *Ibid.*, iii. 24, iv. 12. Lothian thereupon was included in the kingdom of Bernicia.

280 *Anglo-Saxon Chronicle.*

Strathclyde and Lothian the next year resulted in his disastrous defeat by Brudé MacBilé (of Strathclyde)[281] and his subsequent death in the mountains of Forfar. In consequence of this defeat, the English influence north of the Cheviot Hills and the Tweed River waned, and the Scots (Brigantes and others), Britons, and Pictavians there regained their lands and liberties.[282] Generally speaking, the original Picts remained north of Loch Leven on the west and the Firth of Tay on the east. The construction by the Mercian King Offa about 780 of the huge earth-work known as Offa's Dyke marked the boundary between England and Kymru (Wales).[283]

Meanwhile, in 563, the noted Scottish Christian missionary Saint Columba (521-597) was exiled from Ireland and established a mission and monastery on the island of Iona (Hy), off the coast of Argyllshire, then a part of Dalriada. In 565 he proceeded to convert the Pictavian king Brudé MacMaelchon, in Inverness, and his followers of western Pictland.[284] This was about one and one-half centuries after Saint Ninian and his co-workers and successors had Christianized the eastern inhabitants of Pictland. During the first part of the 7th century the Christian Church of Ireland and north Britain was still independent of the churches on the continent that were subject to the bishoprics within the Roman Empire, for in 634 the Scots and the Britons asserted that "all the world errs; Rome and Jerusalem err; only the Scotti and the Britons are in the right."[285] The Roman Catholic papacy began to assume definite form only in the later part of the 8th century, after it had gained certain temporal

---

281 The fact that the ruling family of MacBilé of Strathclyde was related to the royal stock of the Pictavian Brigantes, represented in the 8th century by Angus I. MacFergus, tends to substantiate the earlier statement that the Scottish Brigantes were still a strong element in Strathclyde (although doubtless much commingled with Britons driven northward from central England) as well as being the dominant element of Pictavia. Archibald B. Scott, *op. cit.*, page 417.

282 *Anglo-Saxon Chronicle*; Bede iv. 26, v. 23.

283 Rhys and Brynmor-Jones, *op. cit.*, pp. 140-141; J. A. Giles, *op. cit., Nennius* Sec. 57.

284 Bede iii. 3, 4; *Anglo-Saxon Chronicle*.

285 *Encyclopaedia Britannica*, 13th Ed., vol. 24, p. 431, by Andrew Lang.

power,[286] and it reached its greatest sway in the Middle Ages. "The Irish Church also remained independent and yielded no obedience to Rome until Henry II of England (1154-89) conquered part of Ireland and brought its church into subjection to Rome in 1173." [287] Thereupon, the Irish people were compelled to become Roman Catholics.

Late in the 8th century, the Scots in Argyllshire successfully assailed the unruly highland Picts,[288] who still were governed by the high-king of Pictavia, under whom petty kings or chiefs ruled the various provinces.[289] At the same time, what remained of Irish Dalriada was overrun by the neighboring Pictavians, and the name there fell into disuse as this region came under the rule of the overking of Ireland. In 787 the Danish raids on Northumbria (England) began.[290] Subsequent conquests of the Orkney Islands and adjacent parts of northern Scotland by Scandinavian (Norwegian) sea-raiders (802-839) weakened those Picts further[291] and the Pictavian ruling dynasty finally was overcome in 843 by Kenneth MacAlpin, king of the Scots of Argyllshire, a descendant of Dalriadic king Aedhan. He then became sovereign of the Scots, Pictavians, and highland Picts (Rex Pictorum), with his capital at Scone, in eastern Perthshire, thereby insuring an ultimately united Scotland by the inclusion of the Irish Scots from Dalriada. He died in 860, after a reign of over 16 years. In 870, after the battle of Lochmabar, certain recalcitrant Britons of Cumbria migrated to Wales and joined their kindred, the Kymry. In 900 the new northern kingdom (under Donald II MacConstantine) assumed the Pictish name of Albania[292] from the highlanders in lieu of a Scottish or Pictavian name, in the interest of harmony.

---

286 Abbe Guetté, The Papacy; Ency. Brit., 13th Ed., vol. 21. p. 636, under Pippin III.
287 Thatcher and Schwill, Europe in the Middle Age (Scribner, 1896), p. 239.
288 Ulster Annals, also Asserius, p. 27; quoted by Ritson, vol. I, p. 248.
289 Archibald B. Scott, op.cit., pp. 12-13.
290 Anglo-Saxon Chronicle.
291 Archibald B. Scott, ibid., pp. 50-54.
292 Ibid., pp. 2 (footnote) and 486.

Thus, practically all the strife between the "Picts" (Pictavians) and the Scots reported in history was not between people of different origins but was merely dynastic in nature. It arose between rival claimants of the two branches of the ancient Scotti, the Pictavians and the Irish Scots, for the throne of the united Pictavians and Picts, whose territory then comprised all of Scotland north of the firths of Forth and Clyde except Argyllshire (held by the Scots). There appears to have been very little strife between the real Picts of the highlands and the Pictavians; their relations probably had been amicable from the time of common defense against the Roman army in the year 83. Moreover, in times of dynastic peace the Pictavians and the Dalriadic Scots of Argyllshire increasingly fused by commingling and intermarrying. These conclusions are affirmed by the early joint raids[293] of the Scots and the Pictavians of Ireland against the Romans in Britain, the ease with which a Dalriadic Scot (Alpin)[294] gained the Pictavian throne in 726 through the intermarriage of a Scot and a Pictavian, and the bearing of the Scottish name of Fergus by the noted Pictavian king Angus I. MacFergus (died in 761), indicating Scottish ancestry at least in part. These circumstances make it readily understandable why the dialect of southern Scotland is an intermingling of Britonic and Goidelic (from Ireland) and why the Goidelic dialect of the highland Picts is less pronounced than that of Ireland.

It probably was in consequence of the Danish sea-raids in the 9th and subsequent centuries[295] that the Jutish name *Fibh,* pronounced Fife and meaning "forest", became applied to the present Fifeshire, a part of ancient Pictavia. In the 9th and 10th centuries the Scots also suffered reverses at the hands of the English.[296] But, by subsequent alliances with the Kymry of Strathclyde, one of whose princes had married a daughter of Kenneth Mac-

---

293 J. A. Giles, *op.cit., Gildas* Sec. 14, 15, 19, 23; *Nennius* Sec. 15, 23, 30; *Geoffrey,* Book ix. ch. 5; Eugene O'Curry, *op. cit.,* vol. 2, pp. 60, 287.

294 Was he an ancestor of Kenneth MacAlpin? Perhaps in a younger line. Did Kenneth's dynastic claims rest on such a relationship?

295 *Ulster Annals* and Asserius, cited above.

296 *Anglo-Saxon Chronicle.*

Alpin, the Scottish dominions gradually were extended by 1018[297] over that section and over Lothian and the remainder of southern Scotland long dominated by the English. This consolidation of territory was facilitated by the increasing Danish invasions of Northumberland.[298] Thus, the descendants of the ancient Scotti through the centuries had erected a new nation by uniting two divisions of the Kimmeran race in northern Britain, the Goidelic and the Skolotic. In their country alone the name of Scotia (Scotland) became fittingly established in the 12th century, and its freedom from English rule was assured by Robert Bruce at Bannockburn in 1314. The later political union of Scotland with England occurred in 1707. As a result of numerous early invasions by Scandinavians, the northerly and easterly parts of Scotland and the islands to-day embrace a large proportion of descendants of those people.

In Ireland the situation evolved differently. There the Scots, except those in the north (including the Pictavians), always were a minority, although the Scots of Meath had instituted the Milesian line of monarchs under whose patronage the country achieved its brilliant culture. Ultimately, the Scottish blood of Ulster, Connaught, and Meath became almost wholly submerged in the underlying Goidelic stream and the provincial and territorial kings asserted increasing independence of a central authority or over-king. Consequently, when, in the 6th century, the Scottish traditions were transferred from Irish Dalriada to Scottish Dalriada, that distinct national strain had practically lost its identity in Ireland. With tradition thus weakened, in 558, after the curse of Saint Ruadan and the death of the king, Tara was abandoned as the seat of the supreme

---

297 When James VI of Scotland became King James I of England, he stated at his coronation on April 21, 1603, that a cause for careful consideration of the welfare of Ireland was the fact that the early kings of Scotland were descended from the ancient kings of Ireland. See *Chronica Pictorum*, quoted by Ritson, vol. II, pp. 96-97. The rule that a king could not be succeeded by a son of his own but usually by a sister's son, thus making succession through the mother, appears to have prevailed among the Skolotic Kimmerians, for it was followed by the Scots of Ireland and the Pictavians of Scotland. Rhys and Brynmor-Jones, *op.cit.*, pp. 14-15; Archibald B. Scott, *op.cit.*, p. 12.

298 *Anglo-Saxon Chronicle.*

government there,[299] although the Milesian lines of monarchs continued down to the end of the reign of Roderick O'Connor in 1202. The fact that the Milesians thus represented an aristocratic minority explains why the Irish are proud to be considered of that element.

The Goidelic kings of Munster never forwent their rivalry for the overkingship against the male Milesian line, although none of them gained the office by warfare during the latter's existence. As territorial kings, they sought very early to strengthen their position in another way, namely, by intermarriage with the Milesians. They probably considered the throne heritable through the female line, as was the case among the Picts of Scotland, and the claims of the various aspirants were posited on the prestige and rights thus derived from the Milesian dynasty. Irish history abounds with intermarriages of this kind.[300]

Prior to 795, Ireland had escaped the stress of the political vicissitudes of Europe. In that year disastrous Norse invasions began. Practically all of the seaports of Ireland were established by the Vikings. These conquests and settlements within her borders and the numerous internal quarrels kept the country in more or less turbulence until the beginning of the Anglo-Norman invasion in 1159. This later conquest and the imposition of the formalism of the politico-ecclesiastical Roman Catholic papacy, in substitution for the simple Christianity recognized by Roman Emperor Constantine and introduced in Ireland by Patrick, wrought a conspicuous change in the course of Irish history. After 1172, the people no longer

---

299 J. B. Bury, *Life of St. Patrick* (MacMillan, London, 1905), p. 263. The last Feast of Tara was held in the year 554 by the Irish King Dermot MacCerbail. The underkings were invited to these periodic festivals, when opportunity was afforded for a discussion of the common affairs of the realm, its laws, etc. During this king's reign, the hill and palace of Tara were cursed by Saint Ruadan of Lothra (Ormond), and after his death in 558 the overking, from whatever family he came, fixed his residence wherever he chose, but generally within his immediate provincial territory. Eugene O'Curry, *op.cit.*, Vol. 2, pp. 17-18, 115 (footnote), 337. 300 An outstanding example is the noted Saint Columba (Colm Cille), of the royal Milesian stock, whose mother, Eithne, was a daughter of a Leinster chief of the line of Cathair Mor. Seumas MacManus, *op.cit.*, p. 160.

were independent politically or religiously; they had become subjects of monarchies centered in London and Rome respectively, which was to bring them much woe in subsequent centuries.[301] The appellation of Scotia Major had long before fallen into disuse, to be replaced by that used by the Norsemen, namely, Ireland, the land of the Eires, from the original Iberiu. The recent south Irish republic adopted the name of Eire.

In England, the Scots and Britons who had not joined the Kymry became subjects of the dominant Suebic Anglo-Saxon peoples, particularly in the easterly half of the country. The Roman occupation had resulted in the annihilation of most of the literary productions of the Britons. Their other learning almost perished with the destruction of the Druidic order, for it was in England that an influential school of Druidism was revealed in Caesar's time.[302] Ireland had been more fortunate at that time, in consequence of which she became the most learned northern country of the early centuries of the Christian era under the reign of the Milesian rulers, although much of her literature was lost during the Viking invasions after 795 and the Norman conquest of 1169-1172.

---

301 *Ibid.*, pp. 319-331. "The Norman kings used the [Roman Catholic] church for all purposes of statecraft; its higher officers were checks and spies upon popular movements; . . . The Irish [Independent] Church was treated with great cruelty and the direst oppression . . . From the pulpits they thundered: 'It is no offense against God to kill any Irish human being' . . . . . They extended the long arm of excommunication against our race; rarely did they uplift the hand of benediction . . ." *Ibid.*, p. 131. The elimination of ecclesiastical favoritism in the Irish constitution and the restoration of the original independent Irish church would be a sound foundation for the union of all Ireland; but do the Irish have the initiative to promote such steps?

302 Caesar, *Gallic War* vi. 13. It has been suggested that Caesar was misinformed and that the most influential school of Druids was in Ireland; also that it was developed to its greatest height by the Goidels rather than by the Skoloti. Rhys and Brynmor-Jones, *op. cit.*, p. 83. The account of the first battle of Magh Tuired between the Firbolgs and the Tuatha Dé Danann in Ireland shows the presence of Druids, whose order must have come to that island with the Kelts. They also are referred to in the ancient poem of Carman, presented in the Book of Ballymote. The fact that this order is not known to have existed among their congeners, the Cimbri of Danmark, or among the Suebic tribes is evidence that the order was of Keltic and not Nordic origin. W. K. Sullivan, *op. cit.*, pp. cccclvii-cccclviii (footnote); Julius Caesar, *Gallic War* vi. 13-21.

It is in Kymru (Wales), recognized as a single nation first under provincial kings and later an overking, similar to the Scottish rule in Ireland,[303] that the ancient traditions, dialects, and customs of the Scottish and Britonic Kimmerians were best preserved in the enduring name of the Kymry [Kimmerii]. Upon Cunedda's conquest of Wales, one of his subordinate kings, a noted legislator named Dyfnwal Moelmud, so skillfully established land laws and divided the land of the country that when King Howel Dda the Good enacted a new system of laws he did not change the applicable land laws "because Dyfnwal was the best measurer."[304] From as early as the 7th century, the Britons and Scots of Wales had been cut off from their kinsmen in northern and southern England by Saxon conquests to the Irish Sea and the Severn River, but their substantially uniform traditions, language, and customs was more conducive to political coherence and stability than those that prevailed in Ireland or Scotland. This concentration in Wales of the culture of the British-Scottish Kymry of Strathclyde (or Cambria) and of Cumbria with that of the same race already in Wales was accelerated by the frequent incursions of the Danes, English, and northern Scots into Cambria and Cumbria late in the 9th and early in the 10th century, when those who refused to submit to the invaders migrated to Wales.[305] A famous ancient literary production of the Welsh Kymry is the *British Triads,* a compilation of precepts, rules, and Druidic teachings of philosophical ideas.[306]

The harp was a distinctive musical instrument of these people in both Britain and Ireland. They (especially in Ireland) also were extraordinarily proficient in gold, silver, and other work, as exemplified by their illuminated manuscripts, personal ornaments, etc.[307] The French romantic

---

303 Rhys and Brynmor-Jones, *op.cit.,* pp. 119, 134, 135, 189.

304 *Ibid.,* pp. 129-134.

305 *Caradoc,* by Wynne, 1697, p. 37; quoted by Ritson, vol. II, pp. 180-181.

306 J. A. Giles, *op.cit., Richard of Cirencester* i. 4.1-15. Wales, as a member of the British commonwealth, might well adopt the name of Kimmeria and become one of the most promising centers of research in ancient Kimmeric (Skolotic) culture.

307 Seumas MacManus, *op.cit.,* pp. 307-318, and the authorities there cited.

epics were colored greatly by the Arthurian legend carried by oral transmission and Druidic writings from Britain to Gaul, and the influence of the early mythology and folklore of these Kimmerians on the later Anglo-Saxon literature is incalculable. King Howel Dda the Good (c. 885-950) is ever celebrated in Welsh history as the codifier of the ancient laws of his countrymen. They were assembled in three codes, the Venedotian of the north, the Gwentian of the southeast, and the Dimetian of the southwest. The fact that they, like the ancient laws compiled by the Scottish Milesians, contain the principle of the Conjugal Community and that it was preserved by these two divisions of the ancient Skoloti demonstrates a common earlier union and habitation. This habitation already has been shown to have been in the Ukraine, where they had gained their knowledge of the ancient modified code of Hammurabi of Babylonia through the Getae. Conquered by the English in 1282, Wales since then has been united with that country, with its own representation in Parliament.

Summarizing, we reach an interesting conclusion regarding the ethnographical composition of the population of the British Isles. Except for the primitive Iberians, Paleo-Kelts, Neo-Kelts, and Phoenicians, substantially all of the immigrants to Britain and Ireland prior to the Anglo-Saxon invasions were of the Kimmerian nation of the Nordic race from north of the Black Sea, referred to by Herodotus. The Anglo-Saxons, who belonged to the Suebic nation of that race, represented a substantial minority that settled chiefly in the easterly half of England. While perhaps a large portion of the Britons who lived in that section moved to western Britain upon the arrival of the Anglo-Saxons, many remained as subjects of the conquerors. Relatively few Anglo-Saxons settled in western England; they merely imposed their rule on the Kimmerians.[308] The Jutes and the Danes of the 8th to 11th centuries, including the Vikings, greatly increased the proportion of Kimmerian population in eastern England, and the vast

308 See Thomas Nicholas, *op.cit.*, pp. 227 ff., and elsewhere.

majority of the army of William the Conqueror — Normans (originally Danes), Bretons, and others, mainly descendants of the early Kimmerian invaders of northwestern France — were of that stock. The persecution of the French Protestants (Huguenots) between 1530 and 1787 brought many other Kimmerians from France to England.

It is doubtful, therefore, whether the Anglo-Saxon blood equals one-fifth of that of all England, and it is meager, if not negligible, in Wales, Scotland, and Ireland. The Kimmerian was tall,[309] light-eyed, and dark-haired, with a long straight or oval face, whereas the Anglo-Saxon was slightly shorter in stature and had lighter hair and a shorter oval face. Both were mesocephalous. The eventual amalgamation of the two elements, of course, was inevitable.[310] This subject has been well treated by Dr. Thomas Nicholas in his *Pedigree of the English People,* although allowance must be made, among other things, for his failure to distinguish the stocky and phlegmatic Kelts (Alpines) of central France[311] from the tall and active Kimmerian Nordics of northern and western France and of Britain.

Consequently, the once powerful Kimmerian nation of antiquity, shattered in the Ukraine by the Getae (Goths) in 634 B.C., ultimately achieved a brilliant resurrection in the west, in Danmark, northwestern Germany (chiefly Hessen, Franconia, and the Rhine valley). the Low Countries, northwestern, western, and southern France, and in the British Isles, without reference to the United States. Undoubtedly, many of what are reported in the books as Anglo-Saxon customs, laws, and traditions had their inception among the antecedent Kimmerian peoples, whose civilization was superior to that of their conquerors.[312] Their distinctive cultures have been only

---

309 J. A. Giles, *op.cit., Richard of Cirencester* i. 3.20.
310 Thomas Nicholas, *op.cit.,* pp. 230-266.
311 See W. Z. Ripley, *op. cit.,* Seumas MacManus, *op. cit.,* pp, 7-8, also confused the two subraces.
312 Francis Palgrave, *Rise and Progress of the English Commonwealth* (Murray, London, 1832), vol. 1, pp 37-38; *Ancient Laws and Institutions of Wales,* Public Records Ed., vol. 3, ch 1; Thomas Nicholas, *ibid.,* pp 442-550.

scantly reported thus far.[313] However, much of the achievement credited to the present British nation is doubtless due to the leavening effect of the Anglo-Saxon blood on the earlier population of England. A comprehensive survey and appraisal of the history and culture of the Goidelic, Danish, and Skolotic Kimmerians in western Europe prior to the Anglo-Saxon invasions should be an attractive task for some future historian; but due allowance would have to be made for the Keltic culture appropriated by the Goidelic and Skolotic Kimmerians after they reached the upper Danube and Gaulic territory and which their emigrants took to the British Isles.

Approximately 87 per cent of the British immigration to the United States (in colonial times and later) consisted of persons whose antecedents reach back to *western* England and to Scotland, Wales, and Ireland.[314] Large contributions of people of Kimmerian origin also have been made by Danmark, the Netherlands, Belgium, France, and Frankish Germany. Thus, it follows that the American people today embody a major proportion of Kimmerian blood and that the influence of that primitive nation of the Ukraine is still very much to the fore on both sides of the north Atlantic Ocean.

———————

313 It also is unfortunate that the ancient national names of both the Kimmerii (except in Wales) and the Suebi (except in diminished degree in medieval Swabia) have not been perpetuated as such.

314 Based on the statistics of the U. S. Department of Labor and the assumption that two-thirds of the immigrants from England had such antecedents. Thus, the aptness of the term "Anglo-Saxon" to the whole British nation or its culture is questionable.

CHAPTER VII.

SUEBIC NATION AND ITS TRIBAL MOVEMENTS

1. *Habitation in Europe.* Already it has been shown how the Suebic nation anciently migrated by stages westward from its homeland of Geté, situated between the central and western Tian Mountains and Lake Balkhash, in western Turkistan, and how it crossed the Khirgiz steppe and Scythia to the extensive region south of the Baltic Sea, now known as *Deutschland*.[1] It was the first Nordic nation to enter Europe (c. 2300 B.C.). Its habitation in Western Scythia endured from about 2200 to about 1600 B.C. Judging by subsequent events, it must have been dislodged by the next Nordic nation that possessed Western Scythia, the Kimmerii, who already have been discussed at length.

The Suebians reached the Elbe River about 1600 B.C., after they had driven displaced Kelts southward among other Keltic tribes in the Carpathian and Alpine mountains and westward to the Rhine valley[2] and northern Gaul. Except for the Swedes, Norwegians, and Frisians, Saxon intruders in central Netherlands, and later Anglo-Saxon invaders of England, the westerly boundary of the Suebians south of the Baltic has been mainly the Weser and Werra Rivers and the easterly boundary generally has been the Vistula River in the north. This nation remained more intact than the other Nordic nations did. A century or so prior to the Christian era, some of the tribes

---

1 Since Julius Caesar applied the name "Germans" to the Franks in the Rhine valley, it was a mistake of English-speaking historians to apply the name *Germany* to the non-Frankish part of Deutschland, i.e., the portions east of the Weser and Werra Rivers and south of Franconia. The term "Deutschland" possesses no historic significance, and the name of that nation today might more suitably be Suebia (Swabia, Schwaben).

2 V. Gordon Childe, *The Aryans,* pp. 176-177.

began a southward movement into territory inhabited by Keltic nations, then nominally subjects of the Roman Empire.

While the Suebians inhabited the Ukraine, on their north were various Keltic tribes, commonly called the Slavs (Moscovites), long before separated at the Caucasus range from those Kelts who continued westward up the Danube basin to invade central and western Europe. These eastern Kelts had been forced northward by the westward migration of the Suebians. They comprised the *Melanchleni* and *Androphagi* of Herodotus. When Darius the Great invaded Western Scythia in 512 B.C., they were joined on the west by the *Neuri,* another Keltic (Slavic) nation that formerly inhabited the slopes of the Carpathian Mountains between the Suebians, on the west, and the Getae and their Skolotic subjects in Scythia, on the east. These three Keltic nations were the progenitors of the later Moscovite or Slavic people, the Neuri ultimately being known as the *Wends.*

When the progenitors of the Goidelic Kimmerians, dislodged from Scythia by the Getae in 634 B.C., migrated westward, they followed a course south of the Suebians, along the upper Danube valley and across the Rhine to west central Gaul, driving many of the Kelts in those regions southward, where most of their descendants still reside. In 606 B.C., the Danish Kimmerians (of the tribe of the Treres), who had invaded Lydia and learned about the destruction in 634 B.C. of their parent nation in Scythia, abandoned their Lydian settlement upon the approach of a victorious Getic army from the east and followed their congeners across western Europe. They apparently moved south of the Suebians (probably along the Danube valley) and across to and down the Elbe River, as already narrated. According to tradition, their leader was Odin, who later was deified. Upon reaching the lower Elbe, they conquered far and wide. East of the Elbe they subdued a small tribe called the *Engili (Angli,* a sister nation of the *Warni, Werni* or *Varini),*[3] on which Odin imposed his

3 *Ency. Brit.,* 13th Ed., vol. 11, p. 776, under *Lex Anglicorum et Werinorum.*

eldest son Balder as king, according to Anglian tradition and other evidence.

Certain Danish tribes took possession of the region west of the Elbe, bordering on the North Sea. They drove the indigenous Kelts westward and southward toward Gaul and forced the detached Suebic tribe of the Frisians into the lowlands and marshes of northern Netherlands. These Danish tribes were headed by Odin's other sons, Vegdeg and Sigge. The division under Vegdeg soon was lost to history, probably by tribal merger. That under Sigge became known as the *Sigambri,* the later Salii, who subsequently were the nucleus of the Salian Franks and, with the Ripuarian Franks of the central Rhine valley, were the conquerors of Gaul and the founders of the French nation. But all these Danes did not move southward as Salian Franks. Many remained behind as inhabitants of the region later known as Rüstringen, between the lower Weser and Ems rivers.

The main division of the Danish Kimmerians *(Cimbri)* advanced northward into and occupied all Jutland and Schleswig, afterward called *Cimbric Chersonese,* and the Angli followed them and took possession of Holstein. It is evident that the Angli long remained allies of the Cimbric Jutes. Later tribes of these Cimbri were known as the Teutons and the Ambrones.

When the Kimmerians advanced into Jutland, they pressed into Scandinavia those members of the Suebic tribes of *Sitones* and *Suiones* (Norwegians and Swedes) who had remained behind. Aside from these two tribes and the Frisians, the other Suebic tribes continued to inhabit the region south of the Baltic Sea and east of the Weser river during the many centuries prior to the Christian era, and they greatly increased in population, with a corresponding increase in number of tribal names. Their easterly boundary remained the Vistula River. The power and prestige of the Roman Empire on the south and west discouraged their exploration and migration in those directions until a century or so before the beginning of the Christian era. Their external warfare was confined chiefly to conflicts with the Kelts in the south and west and to the defense of their eastern frontier against the Wends. Diodorus[4] and Pliny[5] correctly regarded them as (former) Scythians. All of the Kimmerian migrations westward were made hastily up the basin of the Danube River, through territory populated wholly by Kelts, rather than directly across the domain of the Suebians, which indicates the respect in which they held the prowess of the Suebian nation. Similar respect for them was shown later by the Getae while that strong nation was centered on the upper Dnieper River and made its numerous conquests in Russia and on the Baltic Sea.

The Suebians' knowledge of the outside world, especially that of the western Asiatic and Grecian civilizations, was vastly more restricted than that possessed by the Kimmerian and Getic nations, because of their lack of contact with those southern cultures. Consequently, they continued to follow their own inferior tribal customs and usages. These are described by Tacitus in his *Germania,* but he failed to distinguish adequately between the Kimmerians who lived east and north of the Rhine and the Suebians who lived east of the Weser and Werra and their different cultures. His treatise, with a few other works, presents a comprehensive description of the early cultures and habits of these two Nordic nations, *which had been separate politically for at least* 2500 *years.* According to him, metals were used but little by the Suebians, but were better known to the Kimmerians. He names the different tribes into which the Suebians had divided as the nation's population expanded during its approximately 1700 years' habitation of northern "Germany" prior to his time. The tribal names mentioned hereinafter represent chiefly those that wandered away from their home-sites.

As in the case of the Kimmerians and the Getae while they inhabited Scythia, the knowledge of the Mediterranean civilization that the Suebians gained by their contact with the various Roman armies sent to the north and by the use of Suebian mercenaries by the Romans only whetted their appetites for adventure toward the south. Conse-

4 Diodorus Siculus, vi. 8.
5 Pliny the Elder, iv. 12.

quently, during the few centuries before the Christian era they began sporadic incursions into the regions of the Alpine foothills in Keltic territory claimed by the Romans. This activity was greatly accelerated by the Gothic raids on the southern Baltic littoral and their settlements there and conquests elsewhere on the Baltic Sea during the last quarter of the 2nd century B.C., as later related.

---

2. *Settlement of Scandinavia.* About 2000 B. C., the Kelts introduced bronze into Skäne, in southern Sweden. By 1500 B.C., two westernmost Suebic tribes must have advanced up the Danish peninsula and begun to explore the islands leading to Skäne, which were less eroded by wave action than they are now. Among these islands were Funen, Langland, Laaland, Falster and Zealand. The sparsely-settled inhabitants of far earlier times, the Ligurians and Kelts, probably more or less commingled, moved ahead to Skäne and ultimately northwestward along the coast toward Norway as the Suebians took possession of Skäne. In the sagas these aborigines are called *Iotuns* and their migration northward already has been discussed. Their existence is proved by the fact that the present population of southwestern Sweden and Norway comprises roughly 10 per cent of pure brunet complexion and a sizeable proportion of mixed types.[6]

Several centuries later, the Suebic tribes advanced across the islands and gained the Scandinavian peninsula. The dominant tribe or nation in Sweden was known as the *Suiones* and that in Norway as the *Sitones,* according to Tacitus.[7] No other tribal names are given by him as of the 1st century A.D., although Pliny later refers to certain inhabitants of western Skäne as the *Hillevions,*[8] whose name is perpetuated in the modern name of Halland province. About 603 B. C., the leading tribe of the Danish Kimmerians moved from the lower Elbe River and took

---

6 W. Z. Ripley, *op.cit.,* page 68, citing Hultkrantz for Sweden and Topinard for Norway.

7 Tacitus, *Germania,* chs. 44, 45.

8 Pliny, *Nat. Hist.,* iv. 13.

possession of Jutland,[9] driving the rest of the Suebians thence to Scandinavia. They gave their national name to the Jutish peninsula, which thereafter was known as the Cimbric Chersonese.[10] Tribal names appeared in later centuries for other peoples in Scandinavia, such as the Turanian *Lapps* (Finnae) in northern Sweden, the Nordic Ostrogoths and Visigoths (*Gauti*) in southern Sweden about A.D. 115-120, and the Danes in Skäne, which they held after having driven out some of the Gothic invaders, the *Heruli, Lombards,* and *Gepidae* (with some *Rugii*), about A.D. 150.

---

3. *Migration of Suebic Tribes.* The southward migration of the Suebians was accelerated ultimately by the progressive decline of the Roman power north of the Alps along with their own increase in numbers during their long habitation south of the Baltic Sea. They also gained knowledge of the manner in which the Romans conducted war by their contact with them. The Slavic Wends constantly pressed upon them from the east, between the Sarmations (the Poles) and the Lithuanians after the former reached their present habitation about A.D. 90;[11] so that the weakening of Roman resistance afforded the Suebians an opportunity to move into the upper Rhine valley and toward the milder climate and advanced civilization south of the Alps.

As stated before, the first attempt of the Suebians to enter Gaul occurred in 71 B. C., when an allied army of 15,000 warriors recruited from both Suebic and Kimmeric tribes bearing the names of the *Harudes, Marcomanni, Sedusii,*

---

9 Traditionally, under the leadership of Odin, whose son Skjöldr succeeded him as king of the Danish Kimmerians. Thereafter, the Skjöldungar family was the ruling dynasty of Danmark. It appears in the form *Scyld* in the ancient poem *Beowulf*.
10 See *Kimmeric Influence in Western Europe, ante.* Only recently representatives of Oslo University, Norway, found a large collection of weapons and jewelry of about 600 B.C. on a rocky slope near Droebak, about 32 kilometers south of Oslo. Their deposit there must have resulted from pressure northward of Sitones by the Kimmerians of Jutland.
11 See subsequent chapter on the Sarmatians.

Semnones, Vangiones,[12] *Nemetes,*[12] *and 'Tribocci,*[12] led by the Suebian Ariovistus[13], crossed the Main and then the upper Rhine rivers. They had come at the invitation of the Keltic *Sequani and Arverni in* Gaul to aid them in warfare with the Keltic *Aedui,*[13] a powerful nation. Soon afterward, they were followed by 105,000 more members of the Frankish *Vangiones, Nemetes,* and *Tribocci,* apparently their total populace, who settled and remained on the western bank of the Rhine after the army of Ariovistus had been annihilated and driven out of Gaul. Soon afterward, the Roman Empire conquered Gaul and dominated the region between the Rhine and the Weser and Werra, occupied by Kimmerian "Germans," until the first century of the Christian era. They also established an east-and-west frontier between the Suebi and the Alps. After the defeat of the Roman General Quintilius Varus by Hermann, chief of the *Cherusci,* a Danish Kimmerian tribe, in A.D. 9, the territory northeast of the lower Rhine was lost to them.

The primitive capital of the Suebic nation — a political union or confederation of various tribes[14] — was the seat of the *Semnones,* the senior tribe.[15] It was situated between the Elbe and the Oder Rivers, in the modern province of Brandenburg, approximately at the site of the present city of Berlin. For reasons already stated, the tribes of the Suiones (Swedes), Sitones (Norwegians), and Frisians had been sundered and lost to the nation. The others, besides the *Angli* and *Warni* and the dominant *Semnones,* comprised the *Saxons, Rugii, Lygii* (the later *Vandals*), *Hermunduri* (the later *Thuringi*), *Narisci* and *Marcomanni* (the later Nordic Bavarians), *Skyrii, Turcilingi, Elysii, Quadi,* and *Allemanni,* and perhaps others less known.[14] The Semnones, as the most ancient and honorable tribe,[15] were the nucleus from which the other tribes had branched earlier. In primi-

12 These three tribes were Skolotic Kimmerians (Tacitus, *Germania,* ch. 28); the rest were Suebi.
13 Julius Caesar, *Gallic War,* i. 31, 37, 51. Ariovistus was a member of the Semnones.
14 *Ency. Brit.,* 13th Ed., vol. 26, page 20, F. G. M. Beck; Tacitus, *ibid.,* ch. 38-39, 43.
15 Tacitus, *ibid.,* ch. 39.

tive times, when tribes became so large as to be unwieldy, groups successively detached themselves under new names, either that of its chieftain or of an earlier hero, so that there was a variation in the antiquity of the different tribes as separate entities.

Julius Caesar wrote that "the nation of the Suebi is by far the greatest and the most warlike nation of the Germans [Nordics]."[16] This is indicated by the fact that the dominion of the Semnones alone embraced a hundred cantons at the time of Tacitus, extending as far south as Lausitz (Lusatia). The widespread conquests of the Goths on the Baltic Sea during the 1st century B.C., and especially in the 1st and 2nd centuries A.D., included destructive raids along its southerly shores. These incursions disturbed the Suebians and impelled them to action. The easternmost tribes, those between the Vistula and Oder Rivers and nearest the Goths, were the first to feel the urge to move southward; from north to south these were the *Lygii* (or *Lügii*), who were allies of several smaller tribes,[17] the *Elysii*, and the *Quadi*. The last-named, a powerful tribe, moved southward before the inception of the Christian era from the basin of the upper Oder to Moravia, where their territory extended as far as the Danube in Austria. They participated in what is known as the Marcomannian War. Their allies were the Marcomanni, probably not a definite tribe but an aggregation of warriors from other tribes organized especially for frontier service. Under their leader Maroboduus, a Semnon, the Marcomanni had moved from the basin of the Saale River early in the reign of Augustus, before the opening of the Christian era, and in 12 B.C. they subdued the Keltic *Boii,* the later Czechs,[18] in Bohemia, of which country they took possession while the Quadi retained Moravia. The Romans deemed them to be the fiercest of the Nordic tribes that inhabited the country between Illyria and the source of the Danube. They frequently fought these tribes in frontier warfare.

16 Julius Caesar, *op. cit.,* iv. 1.
17 Tacitus, *Germania,* ch. 43.
18 Since the ancient Kelts and Slavs had a common origin, it does not seem tenable to identify the Keltic Boii as members of the Slavic nation of the far north.

The former homeland of the Quadi on the upper Oder was taken over by the Elysii, from their north. These people became the later Silesians, whose name is perpetuated in that of the modern province of Silesia. They were followed by the Lygii, who resettled in Posen and Lower Silesia, along the Warthe River.

The former abode of the Marcommanni on the Saale River was promptly taken by the Hermunduri (the later Thuringi), one of the most powerful Suebic tribes, which stood in prestige in the nation next to the Semnones. They had moved from the central Elbe to that region. Thereupon, the Semnones moved southwestward from the basin of the Havel River to the junction of the Elbe and Saale Rivers. Subsequently, they continued southward across the central and upper Main River, in present Franconia, avoiding the strong Skolotic Kimmerian tribe of the Chatti in Hessen and the basin of the lower Main.

The power of the Gothic nation in Ukrainia in the 2nd and subsequent centuries was feared far and wide, and the Suebic confederation, in its own interest, resolved upon the general conquest of southern territory from the Kelts and the Romans, for it was about the middle of the 2nd century that most of their tribes began their migrations in that direction. In A.D. 167-168, Marcus Aurelius went to the Danube basin to ward off their attacks. In 168 the Marcomanni sued for peace, but in 169 they, together with the Hermunduri, the Quadi, some of the Lygii and their allies, the Sarmatian *Iazyges* and certain other Sarmatians of central Hungary, renewed hostilities, resulting in the Marcomannian war, which lasted approximately three years. In the end, the Marcomanni were driven out of Pannonia by the Romans and suffered severely in their retreat across the Danube River. In 174 Aurelius gained a decisive victory over the Quadi. The Marcomanni finally took possession of territory south of the Danube, in Upper Austria and Bavaria, where, after extending their territory to the Alps, most of them gradually merged with the indigenous Kelts under the name of the *Baiouarii,* the later Bavarinas,[19] and their name disappeared from history in the 4th century.[19]

By the 3rd century the Semnones had reached and settled in the region between the Lech River and the Black Forest, in modern western Bavaria and Württemberg. There they applied their ancient national name of Suebia (the modern Schwaben[20]) to their domain, whereupon their tribal name disappeared from history. Their western-most division must have received accretions from various other Suebic tribes and detachments of tribes on route, including those who had served under Ariovistus (such as the Harudes and the Sedusii), for about this time the Romans commenced to call this aggregation the *Alle-manni*,[21] meaning "all-men". In the 4th century the latter conquered western Württemberg and southern Baden from the Keltic *Helvetii*. Thenceforth, the Allemanni were in continual conflict with the Romans and caused that empire a vast amount of trouble along the upper Rhine. In 406 they broke through the Roman frontiers (*limes*) and conquered Liechtenstein, northern Switzerland, and Alsace, driving the Burgundians from the last region and sealing the doom of the Roman Empire in the north.[22] This territory then was abandoned to them by the Roman Emperor Honorius. Their kingdom endured until 495, when they were overcome in Alsace by the combined forces of the Salian and Ripuarian Franks under Clovis in the famous battle of Zülpich. Thereafter, they became part of the Frankish dominions under the name of the duchy of Allemannia. It is from these people that the present French name for Germany (*Allemagne*) was derived.

The *Narisci* also moved southward and took possession of Bavaria north of the Danube River and adjacent to Bohemia, in the present Oberpfalz, which remained their

---

19 *Ency. Brit.,* 13th Ed., vol. 3, pages 5b and 545a; vol. 13, pages 215d and 897c; vol. 17, page 693c.

20 Historically, this name might more properly be the national name of Deutschland.

21 This name was understood by the Romans to apply to a conglomeration of small tribes and detachments of tribes.

22 Thereafter, for more than a century a torrent of barbarian armies swept through the Empire, which retreated behind the Alps, there to breathe its last.

habitation.[23] On their northwest was the main body of the Hermunduri, later known as the *Thuringi,* who earlier had migrated southward from the lower Elbe and had taken possession of the territory that now bears their name: Thüringen. The Quadi and Iazyges later moved from Moravia and settled in lower Austria and western Hungary,[23] and their names also disappeared from history in the 4th century.[19]

A large proportion of the Keltic population of the foothills and mountain regions of the south thus invaded by the Suebians had some knowledge of them, did not evince a rigid choice of rulers as between Romans and Suebians, and did not offer resistance to the point of annihilation. These inferences are proved by the fact that the descendants of the Suebians of southern Germany have amalgamated freely with the Keltic population as also have those of Alsace, northern Switzerland, and Austria, since brachycephaly is preponderant throughout those regions. Thus, while the language now is mainly Suebic (Hochdeutsch),[24] the local names and persistent ethnic type bear witness to the primitive Keltic occupation.

In the north, by the middle of the 2nd century, the *Saxons* had moved northwestward from the lower Saale basin and had expanded the Suebic frontiers in that direction. They took possession of the region directly south of the *Angles,* the Suebic tribe that was conquered by the Danish Kimmerians about 604 B.C. and had settled in Holstein. The Saxon territory then extended westward to the Weser River, in the modern Hanover; it is Saxon tradition that this land formerly had been occupied by the Hermunduri, ancestors of the Thuringi. Their neighbors west of the Weser were Danish Kimmerians, and those west of the Werra were the Chatti (later Hessians), who were Skolotic Kimmerians. By about A.D. 286 the Saxons and Angles were using Elbe River bases for piratical opera-

23 Tacitus, *Germania,* ch. 42.
24 As distinguished from the language of the Kimmerians of the lower Main and Rhine River valleys, which is known as Plattdeutsch; the one High "German" and the other Low "German".

tions on the North Sea,[25] including ravaging the coasts of Britain. By the middle of the 4th century, the Saxons had advanced wedgewise to the basin of the Yssel River, from which they pressed the westerly division of the Danish Kimmerians (the *Sigambri* or *Salii*) into Batavia (Betuwe). In the following centuries they advanced up the Weser River as far south as the Diemel, where they bordered on the Chatti (Hessians).

About the middle of the 5th century, traditionally in 449, on an invitation of the British King Vortigern, seafaring Jutes under Hengist and Horsa landed in England to aid him in his contests with "Picts" (actually Scots and Britons of Pictavia, south of the Grampian Hills), who had penetrated far south in consequence of the departure of the Romans from Britain in 410. The Jutes spread over Kent and subsequently the Isle of Wight and adjacent parts of Hampshire. Upon the repulse of the Pictavians, the Jutes saw the advantage of settling in Britain themselves. In 455 they became involved in conflict with the Britons, in which Horsa was killed, whereupon they called to their aid other Jutes, Frisians, Saxons,[26] and Angles from Jutland and Schleswig, Frisia, the left bank of the lower Elbe, and Holstein, respectively, to begin a general conquest of this island.

Aella landed with Frisians in 477, and Cerdic and his son Cynric brought over Saxons in 495. Other Saxons followed around 530. The Angles came later (in 540, 547, and 585), settling in northern and central England and ultimately giving their name to the country. The invaders won their way only by slow and painful efforts, for the Anglo-Saxon power was not triumphant in England until the reign of Egbert in 827. Britons who did not submit were gradually forced westward into Devonshire, Cornwall, Wales, Cumbria, and northward into Scotland. That the Jutes were Kimmerians and not Suebians, as already stated, is proved by Bede's reference

---

25 Ammianus Marcellinus, *Rerum Gest.*, 26.4.

26 In the Welsh *Triads* these invaders are referred to as the *Gwyddyl Ffichti* (Danes from Jutland), the *Coroniaid* (Angles), and the *Saeson* (Saxons). Myvyrian *Archaeology of Wales*, ii. 57-58.

to their different dialect and social organization and customs; for example, the custom of gavelkind in ancient Kent was analogous to that in Ireland.[27] The outgrowth of all these settlements was the Suebic mastery of England, after the older inhabitants of the easterly half of the country had been largely driven out and replaced by the invaders.

Before the end of the 7th century, the dominions of the Saxons on the continent covered Westphalia as far as the Ruhr River. Toward the end of the 8th century, this whole territory, including Holstein, was conquered and annexed to the Frankish dominions by Charlemagne, which greatly perturbed the Danes in Schleswig and Jutland.

Among the smaller tribes of the north were the Rugii, who perpetuated their name in Rugenwald, Rugen Island, and Rugen Bay, on the Baltic. Divisions of the Rugii and other small Baltic tribes had joined the Goths in their conquests in southern Sweden early in the 2nd century A.D. and had settled there, as shown by Jordanes, while the main body of the Rugii, known as the *Ulmerugii*, remained on the southerly shores of the Baltic Sea. The latter were driven westward when the Gothic *Heruli* returned to the mainland upon their expulsion from Sweden by the Danes[28] a generation or so later, c. A.D. 150. During the 4th century, as the Slavs forced their way into eastern Germany, the Rugii, with other small Suebic tribes, chiefly the Skyrii and Turcilingi, moved southward to the north of the middle Danube.[28] Early in the 5th century they overran and took from the Roman Empire the territory of Noricum and Pannonia, across the Danube, from Passau to Pest, near the dominions of the Gothic Heruli in central Hungary. Odovacar, of the Skyrii (or the Turcilingi),[29] entered the Roman service and gained the

---

27 W. K. Sullivan, *op.cit.*, p. clxxxiv.

28 C. C. Mierow, *The Gothic History of Jordanes* (Princeton, 1915), pages 56-57 and 177 (quoting Hodgkin, II, 510). According to Procopius, however, the Rugii were a Gothic tribe. *Bell .Goth.* ii. 2. He may have drawn this inference because a contingent served with the Goths when they entered Sweden.

29 C. C. Mierow, *ibid.*, page 119. Some historians infer that he belonged to the Skyrii and not to the Turcilingi.

Roman throne in 476. He achieved the ascendancy over all of these tribes of the middle Danube basin in 487. He was assassinated in 493.

The *Lygian* and *Silingian* tribes reunited under the name of the Vandals when they moved to the regions in the basin of the Warthe River known as Posen and lower Silesia. About 270 one of their armies invaded Pannonia and about 280 they were fighting in Dacia. Defeated by the Goths under Geberich, when their King Visimar was slain, the nation was allowed by the Romans to settle in Pannonia, where they remained Roman subjects for about 60 years. In 406 they moved westward and, crossing the Rhine at Mainz, proceeded to Gaul, where they were defeated by the Franks and their king Godegisel was slain. He was succeeded by his son Gunderic. Following the great Suebic conquests on the upper Rhine in 406, a mixed force of Suebi, Vandals, and Alani (a division of the Getae, from the northeast)[30] defeated the Franks, ravaged Gaul,[31] and in 409 invaded the Iberian peninsula in conjunction with the Visigoths, who earlier had invaded Italy from the Ukraine via Thrace. In the partition that followed in 411, Gallaecia[32] fell to the Suebi and their allies received other districts. The Vandals settled in two detachments, one in Gallaecia, where they quarreled with the Suebi, and the other in Andalusia. The Alani, who earlier had been defeated by the Goths and later by the Huns and driven from the Ural region, settled in eastern Spain (Catalonia). In consequence of 15 years of strife with the Visigoths, the Andalusian detachment of the Vandals was nearly exterminated. The remnant was joined by the Galician[33]

---

30 *Ency. Brit.*, 13th Ed., vol. 1, page 469c, where it is said that they were Sarmatians; but, since they inhabited the region bordering the southern end of the Ural Mountains, in Getic territory, and were reported by Herodotus in the 5th century B.C., before the Sarmatian nation made its appearance in history in Astrakhan, they must have been a division that broke away from the main body of the Getae.

31 Bede i. 11.

32 C. C. Mierow, *ibid.*, pp. 115-117. This was the northwestern corner of Spain as far south as the Douro River, now called Galicia.

33 After an independence of nearly 175 years, Galicia was annexed by the Visigoths in 585.

division and by the Alani, and they all took possession
of Andalusia. In 428-429 they abandoned Iberia and sailed
to Africa under Gaiseric. By May, 430, they had gained
six African provinces from the Romans. In 439 they took
Carthage, in the present Tunisia, which they held for 94
years, becoming a maritime power in the Mediterranean.
In 455 Gaiseric captured and sacked Rome. He died in
477. The African climate and environment slowly demoral-
ized and disintegrated this Nordic nation and finally it
was defeated by the Byzantines and its population scattered
among the indigenous population. Thus, the nation disappeared from history, although the blood of its people
still flows in the veins of their descendants of mixed types
that live in Morocco and Tunisia today. They are represented chiefly by the so-called "blond Berbers", among
whom blue or gray eyes may still be found. One notable
example apparently is Habib Bourguiba, now president
of Tunisia.

The *Burgundians* appear to have been dislodged from
their habitation between the Oder and Vistula Rivers, in
the present Pomerania, by the Slavic advance westward
about the beginning of the 4th century. After engaging in
various warfare and being repulsed in Alsace by the Allemanni in 406, they finally settled (by 411) in Gaul on the
west of the Jura Mountains. Their kingdom was shattered
by the Franks in the 6th century and its lands were re-
distributed in the 7th century, but the Burgundian duchy
continued long afterward to participate in Frankish history.

The *Warni* (or *Varini*), sister nation of the Engeli
(later Angles) in Holstein, continued to inhabit the
region later called Mecklenburg. The Warnow River and
the town of Warnemunde preserve their tribal name.

Tacitus and other writers mention a number of other
Suebic tribes near the Baltic shores and in other parts of
Germany. They seemingly remained in those regions and
did not migrate far.[34] Consequently, no discussion of them
is necessary here.

In consequence of the extensive Slavic movement from

---

34 Tacitus, *op.cit.*, ch. 40, 43.

the east into Germany as late as the late 9th century and the subsequent transfer of Kimmerians from the lower Rhine to the northeast, a vast blending of ancient Kelts, Nordic Suebians and Kimmerians, and Slavs has been in progress in that country since the early Middle Ages. The ultimate result will be a composite race variously different from each component in personal characteristics, physical and mental, from the Nordic Suebians described by Tacitus.

Many descendants of these early Suebians have emigrated to America along with others of western Europe, both during and subsequent to colonial times. They have experienced no difficulty in merging into the general American populace and becoming solid and substantial citizens, accepting established rules and customs and making their own contributions.

---

4. *Observations on Suebian History.* The history of the Suebic nation, whose enlarged domain now is called *Deutschland* (or *Deutsches Reich*), meaning simply "the land (or nation) of the people", has been unfortunate in many ways — apparently the result of excessive internal disagreement and national leadership lacking in political acumen and farsightedness. The extensive northwestern part of the country is inhabited by Skolotic Kimmerians, called "Germans" by Julius Caesar, whose nation was separated 4500 years ago from their fellow Nordic nation, the Suebians, who comprise the greatest proportion of the population of the whole country. It was the Kimmerian nation that produced the Merovingian, Carolingian, Franconian, Luxembourg, Hohenstaufen, and Wittelsbach dynasties, with their notable histories. All of them, at least by intermarriages, apparently may claim descent from Odin along with the ancient Skjöldung dynasty of Danmark and Scandinavia.

When the Suebians, after inhabiting the region immediately south of the Baltic Sea for 1600 years, began to move southward early in the Christian era because of

Gothic incursions along those shores, they readily coalesced with the broad-headed indigenous Keltic population of the Alpine foothills. A century or so afterward
the westward-moving Slavs (Wends) took possession of the
abandoned littoral region as far west as Holstein, bringing
another brachycephalic element into the population. Several other Slavic tribes in later centuries settled in upper
Saxony. When the northeast was reconquered in the Middle
Ages, it was not done well or with adequate regard to
racial or historic boundaries, such as the Vistula River,
so as to distinguish the nation from the habitations of
Old Prussians, Lithuanians, and Latvians, and the Kimmero-
Getic Sarmatians (now remissly called the Poles); consequently national confusion has prevailed in that region
since then. In the central east, after the Marcomanni and
Quadi had abandoned Bohemia and Moravia, the western
monarchs throughout subsequent centuries permitted Slavic
tribes to gain possession of those countries, with all of
their resources, to the perpetual disadvantage of the
Suebic nation. A marked Slavic entity arose in those
regions while great time and effort were being wasted
in continual interference by the northern monarchs in the
affairs of nations south of the Alps. This policy was contrary to that applied with respect to Austria, which was
recovered from the Slavs and Hungarians in 955 mainly
by the sons of Bavarians, Württembergers, and Franconians under Otto I the Great. In 976, Otto II appointed
Leopold of Babenberg graf of this so-called East Mark, and
he ruled it successfully. In the Holy Roman Empire it continued as a separate political entity from the time of Henry
of Babenberg, its first duke[35] in 1156, and never was
united with the other Suebic provinces in a spirit of common nationality[35] until the attempt in the *anschluss* of
World War II, which failed in the subsequent peace plans.
Even if Hitler had displayed some knowledge of early
history and the sense to stop after he had seized Austria and
Bohemia, is the German temperament such that the expanded nation could have lived in amity with its neigh-

---

35 The subsequent expansion of this duchy is a matter of history. *Ency. Brit.*,
13th Ed., vol. 3, pages 5-6.

bors afterward, or would there have been a repetition of the improper seizure of the province of Schleswig from the Danes in 1866?

In the south, after the Allemannians had conquered northern Switzerland and Alsace in 406 and settled in those regions, they promptly began to amalgamate with the indigenous Kelts among whom they had taken their new abodes. In a more tranquil and conservative environment than the turbulent and increasingly feudal society on the other side of the Rhine, they developed a sense of freedom and a difference of political outlook that tended to separate them permanently from the other Suebians. In northern Switzerland, they and the Kelts have been leaders in the development of a form of republican government unexcelled elsewhere in the world. One advantage is their unwillingness to undermine the stability of the home by permitting their women to enter the maelstrom of politics. They would disdain any thought of diminishing their complete independence of their remote kin in other lands.

During the past century Germany has been unable to avoid creating suspicion in the minds of leaders of western nations about her territorial motives. It would seem that the time has ripened for a reorientation of her position. First, the perpetual "Kilkenny cat" relation between her and France is without solid foundation. It has been perplexing to others of the West and ruinous to both nations. It reflects a vainglorious attitude of mind. The rest of the world has not more than a casual interest in ancient quarrels between the two peoples. Repeated modern wars cause a tremendous waste of natural resources, which should be preserved for the benefit of future generations. Another unnecessary war in western Europe might be adequate basis for the permanent detachment of the Kimmerian Rhineland and its allotment fairly among the predominantly Kimmerian nations of the Netherlands, Belgium, and France, in the interest of greater peace in western Europe.

Far more intelligent plans for her interest would have been those briefly discussed at the end of Chapter VIII,

Section 7, and Chapter IX, Section 4, herein, in relation to the Lithuanians, Latvians, and Prussians and to the Sarmatian nations on her east, the Poles and Ukrainians. These are Nordic and not Slavic nations inherently, although they have procured some Slavic strains in the lower strata of their population because of their proximity to the Moscovite nation. They are entitled to their own "places in the sun."

5. *Viking Operations.* Armed sea expeditions of one nation have raided coastal regions of other nations from primitive times. But the term "Viking" has been confined to those from the *viks* or bays at the mouth of rivers and creeks in Norway, Sweden, and Danmark against the British Isles or the continent, mainly for plunder but sometimes for conquest of territory in which to settle their excess population, as in the case of Normandy, in France. The earliest known to western history were the pre-Christian Fomorians, apparently Norwegians, who invaded Ireland and doubtless Scotland on numerous occasions. In those far northern countries, nearly every young man of prestige and means and with a sufficient number of followers made one or more Viking expeditions as a recognized part of his education and training for leadership.

Such raids in the lower North Sea from the 3rd to the 7th century are reported, but the so-called Viking Age ordinarily is reckoned from the date of the first historic attack of the Danes on England in 787 to the final settlement of the Normans in Normandy in 912. Generally, the Swedes confined their efforts to Russia and Finland, on their east, the Norwegians to Scotland and Ireland, and the Danes to the Lowlands, France, England, and Ireland. During the first half of the 9th century, numerous Swedish settlements were made on the easterly shores of the Baltic Sea via the Aland Islands, mainly in Russia and Finland. About the same time, band of Vikings established permanent camps at the mouths of French rivers, often operating from bases established earlier in the Lowlands. France was an especial target for them because of apprehensions created in the north by the vast expansion of her empire. Nearly all of the sea-ports of Ireland were established by Norwegian Vikings. Danish Viking armies settled in East Anglia and Northumbria, in England, and a large aggregation of Danish and Norwegian Vikings settled in Normandy. Other raiders entered the Mediterranean Sea and founded kingdoms in lower Italy and Sicily as early as the second half of the 9th century.

Intermingled with the Danish Viking operations and perhaps stimulating them to some extent were the dynastic difficulties of the Skjöldung regime in Danmark. From A.D. 150, when some of the Gothic invaders were driven out of southern Sweden, the Danes possessed Skäne, the southernmost province, and it was returned to Sweden only in the 17th century. Prior to the individual unifications of Danmark, Sweden, and Norway, those countries were divided into various provinces, each with its own king. He either represented a local family or he was the scion of the dominant family of the country, and was seated in one province and constantly increased its domain by arms, marriage, or other means. After the Danes seized Skäne, a younger member of the Danish Skjöldung family was appointed to be its ruler; and he established the line of the later rival Yngling claimants for the throne of Danmark. In fact, the tradition grew that only descendants of Odin held the privilege of ruling nations.

Subsequently, upon defeating the Goths in Gotland, the Danes of Skäne also took over that Swedish province and, with a member of the Yngling family granted the rulership, held it for two centuries. About 485, Godfred the Bountiful, king of Gotland, married a daughter of Olaf, king of upland Sweden, for which act he was slain some years afterward, leaving descendants.

Those two branches of the Yngling line later were rivals in Scandinavia for the rule of Sweden and Norway, from which lines the claimants for the Danish throne subsequently arose. One scion was the ancestor of the unifier of Norway, the eminent Harald Haarfager (850-933.) Other descendants established seats about the chief *vik* (or bay) of Norway, where they extended their sway.

From a seat on that bay, one aspirant of the family acquired Wendil Island, at the northerly end of Jutland, as a foothold in Danmark proper. Later he gained the southerly province of Schleswig. The contemporaneous king of these areas, named Siegfred, gave refuge in 777 to the Saxon chief Wittekind; in fact, the latter is said to have married one of the king's daughters. Other leaders in Westfold, Norway, were given permission to settle followers in Schleswig. Siegfred left no adult son and another of his daughters, named Alfhild, married Godfred, leader of a closely related branch, who was appointed by Siegfred to be underking of Schleswig. Then, when Siegfred died in 798, Godfred, while holding Westfold, gained control of both Wendil and Schleswig and by 803 had seized all of Danmark, over which he ruled successfully until assassinated in 810. He was known as the Generous Usurper. He was an able monarch and left a number of ambitious sons and daughters. Saxo Grammaticus devotes a whole volume to his exploits.

Harald Hildetand (c.660-735), representing the senior Skjöldung line, had succeeded his brother Roerek as king of Jutland. He married a daughter of King Eystein, of Hademark, in Norway, of a junior line of King Siegfred's family. He was the great unifier of Danmark. His youngest son Halfdane was appointed king of Zealand. Halfdane's son, Harald Halfdanesson, ruled Danmark from about 750 to about 770, when he was succeeded by his nephew, the eminent king Wermund, who ruled from about 770 to 794. The latter was followed by Harald's son Halfdane, "the first Christian of the North." This Halfdane's eldest son Harald (Klak), born c. 784, married Ragnhild, eldest daughter of King Godfred the Generous Usurper, so that the royal rights of all three rival lines then merged in him, the eldest of the senior Skjöldung line, but he was soon disturbed by regal aims of his uncles, his mother's brothers. Godfred's son Hemming succeeded him as king during 810-813 and in 813 he gained the historic agreement of the Frankish empire to the Eider River as the boundary between the two nations. It represented the boundary between Danish Schleswig and Suebian Holstein. Hemming was poisoned in that year.

Godfred's other sons, however, disputed Harald's claim to the Danish throne at Hemming's death, and Harald gained it later in 813 only after strife. He ruled 14 turbulent years (813-827) and was given the appellation of 'Klak' because of his complaints about interference with his regime by his brothers-in-law and their followers. Finally, in 827 he was dethroned by the forces of his mother's youngest brother Eric (sometimes called Horic), who then ruled as King Eric I from 827 to 854. He was succeeded by another Eric, son of Hordknut and grandson of Sigurd Snogeje, who had been king from 794 to 803. Thereupon, Harald Klak and his brothers Roerek and Hemming were exiled and were granted countships in Frisia by the Frankish Emperor Louis I (the Pious) to defend his northern borders against Viking raiders.[36]

---

36 In 826 the Danish king, Harald Klak, being hard pressed to retain his throne against the claims of the party of his maternal uncle Eric, appealed to Emperor Louis I (the Pious) for aid. While visiting the latter at Ingelheim, on the Rhine near Mainz, that year, Harald, his family, and about 400 of his followers were baptized as Christians in an elaborate ceremony presided over by the emperor himself, as described in extant records. When King Harald finally lost his throne in 827, being a Christian and the son of a Christian, the Frankish emperor granted to him the county of Rüstringen, comprising East Frisia and northern Oldenburg, between the Ems and Weser Rivers, fronting on the North Sea and extending southward to Meppen, the Hase River, and Bremen. His younger brothers Hemming and Roerek were granted the counties of Walcheren and the Betuwe respectively. They were expected to defend the Frankish frontiers against the raids of the new King Eric of Danmark. Upon the partition of Charlemagne's domains in 843, Harald exchanged countships with Roerek and proclaimed himself Duke of Frisia. In some records he is referred to as king of Frisia. But dissatisfaction arose and Harald was assassinated by Franks in 850, whereupon Roerek succeeded him as Duke of Frisia until Roerek's departure to Russia in 859. He was then succeeded by Harald's son Godfred, who appointed his elder son Wermund as Count of the Betuwe at Herispich, now Herwen, also the ducal seat, and his younger son Harald as Count of Rüstringen. But the father and both sons were assassinated by Franks in 885, whereupon children of the sons, including Wermund's son Godfred (born c. 870), heir to the duchy, fled for refuge to the second cousin of these sons, Count Godfred of Walcheren (descendant of Count Hemming), who in 881 had married Gisela, daughter of King Lothar II (825-869) of Lotharingia (Lorraine), and they were settled on his manor named Raet (now Reet or Reeth), 14 kilometers south of the present city of Antwerp. The duchy of Frisia then passed to Frankish

They were related by marriage to the former Frisian royal dynasty, and this fact was a basis for the grants. This situation incensed King Eric, of Danmark, and many of the so-called Viking raids actually were directed by him against his rivals, his nephews thus well-placed within the Frankish domain. His aim was to ruin them. Harald, who had proclaimed himelf duke of Frisia in 843, was assassinated by certain discontented Franks in 850.

Harald was succeeded by his younger brother Roerek (otherwise Rurik), count of Rüstringen, in eastern Frisia, and duke of Frisia from 850 to 859, when Harald's son Godfred claimed the duchy. Rurik then accepted the traditional invitation from quarreling Slavs of the region of Lake Ilmen to bring an army and pacify them after they had driven Swedish raiders southward, which he did. Thereupon, Harald's eldest son Godfred became duke of Frisia.[37]

Rurik then decided to remain in the North and in 862 he seized the city of Novgorod for his capital and

counts. *Chronicon* of Regino of Prüm, *Annals of Fulda,* and others. When King (later Emperor) Arnulf, of East Francia, defeated the Danes on the Dyle River, in Belgium, in 891, he seized young Godfred, heir to the Frisian duchy, and put him in the custody of Count Conrad I of Oberlahngau, in Hessen, whose wife was Glismuda, Arnulf's natural daughter. He soon married their eldest daughter, whereupon in an elaborate ceremony in 897 Arnulf installed the young man as imperial markgraf at a place 3 or 4 kilometers east of Forcheim, in Upper Franconia, which he named Raet (for his former residence), now called Reuth-bei-Forchheim, then in Nordgau, for the defense of the frontiers against the Slavs and Hungarians. *Monumenta Boica,* vol. XXXI(1), pages 178-179 (year 908) and *Monumenta Germ. Historiae,* vol. 1 *(Die Urk. d. d. Koenige und Kaiser),* page 67 (year 932, executed at Reot — Raeut). Godfred's son Graf Warmund I moved his seat eastward to Raeut (Reuth-bei-Erbendorf), in Oberpfalz, now northern Bavaria. After Grafs Warmund II and III came Graf Godfred von Raeut (c. 980-1043), who was duke of Bavaria from July, 1039, to Lent, 1043, with a southern seat at Vogtei-Raeut (now Vogtareuth). He left only two children, a daughter Reginlind, who was the first wife of Graf Arnold II von Wels and Lambach, and another daughter, who married Dietrich von Hall, first *Hall* Graf von Wasserburg. Duke Godfred had at least two younger brothers named Warmund and Harald, who left descendants, those of Harald at Oehringen, in Kochergau, where Count-Bishop Gebhard III of Regensburg had appointed him dominus over many church properties. *Wirt. Urkundenbuch,* I, pp. 254, 266, years 1037 and 1042. His son Godfred, serving the count-bishop at Würzburg, was father of Hugibert, first dominus von Erlach. Also see *Origin of Heraldry in Europe* (1953), by this author.

37 This duchy was officially recognized by Frankish Emperor Charles III (the Fat) in 882, but Godfred was slain in 885.

established himself as the first prince of the new nation. The name of Rüs from the first syllable of Rüstringen, the home of himself and his followers, was given to the country, whence the later form Russia.[38] The Swedish Vikings continued southward and established themselves in the Ukraine, only to be taken over by Rurik in 883, when a strong local government, with its seat at Kiev, was installed. A considerable Swedish population subsequently was added, and active military, commercial, and social intercourse with the great city of Constantinople, glittering capital of the Grecian empire, promptly arose. In consequence, the Christianity of the East rather than that of the Latin division in the West became the accepted faith of the conglomeration of barbaric peoples of the Russian state. Rurik's dynasty long continued in Russia.

In 911 Frankish King Charles III (the Simple) ceded to Rolf (Rollo), one of the Viking chiefs, the region later known as the duchy of Normandy, France. The climax of the Danish invasions of England was reached under the reign of their King Knut (Canute) the Great in the first half of the 11th century (1017-1018).[39] Subsequently, the English regained possession of this territory, only to be reconquered a half century later in 1066 by another branch of the same people, the Normans of France, under William the Bastard (later called the Conqueror), whose descendants long continued on the British throne. There was no actual extermination of the conquered peoples of England but rather a gradual amalgamation of the ancient Mediterraneans, Kelts, Britons, Scots, Frisians, Danes, and Normans into a single nation. All belonged to the Aryan race and the far greater proportion to the Nordic branch of that race.

---

38 Calvin Kephart, *Origin of the Name Russia*, magazine *Morskiya Zapiski* (New York), vol. II, No. 4, November, 1944.
39 *The Anglo-Saxon Chronicle.*

CHAPTER VIII.

GETIC (GOTHIC) NATION AND ITS FORTUNES

1. *Scythia in 5th and 4th Centuries B.C.* Herodotus informs us fully regarding the population of Western Scythia during the first half of the 5th century B.C. We know how in the previous century (529 B.C.) Cyrus the Great of Persia was killed in a disastrous campaign against the Dahae, a division of the Massagetae, in southwestern Turkistan, under their Queen Tomyris, and how in 512 his successor, Darius the Great, in revenge,[1] conducted an expedition around the west of the Black Sea against the Getae in Western Scythia, whose king was Idanthyrsus. Before the Persians had begun their circuitous and fruitless pursuit of the Getae and their allies, these people temporarily had sent their waggons with their familes and their cattle far to the north, out of reach of the invaders. All returned to their former abodes upon the disappearance of the Persian army from Scythia.[2]

At the time that Herodotus wrote (c. 450 B.C.), the *Sauromatae* (Sarmatians) still inhabited the region (Astrakhan) between the lower Tanais (Don) and the lower Oarus (Volga) rivers and the Caspian Sea,[3] the *Thyssagetae* (Alani) and the *Iyrcae* (Bolgarians) that between the middle Volga and the southerly end of the Ural Mountains,[4] and the Finns the central Ural region, while north of the Getae in Russia were the Slavic tribes of the *Neuri*,[5] the *Melanchleni,* and the *Androphagi,* ancestors of the Moscovites. The first-named Slavs, harassed by

---

1 Herodotus, *Hist.* iv. 1.
2 *Ibid.,* iv. 120-142.
3 *Ibid.,* iv. 21, 57, 115-117, 122-123.
4 *Ibid.,* iv. 21-22, 123-124. Thyssagetae will hereafter be known by their later name of the Alani.
5 *Ibid.,* iv. 100, 125.

both the Getic Scythians and the pursuing Persians under Darius, "fled in alarm to the deserts of the north." Thus, the Neuri (the later Wends) had deserted their Galician homeland for the region along the east of the upper Borysthenes (Dnieper) River. They subsequently were unable to return because of the operations of the Getae northwestward to the Baltic Sea, where the Getae were reported by Pliny as located at his time.[6]

The Keltic *Agathyrsi* still lived in northeastern Hungary, which, by the use of the Carpathian Mountains as a strong frontier, they had been able to hold against the Scythians pursued by the Persians when they completed the western part of this circuit.[7] But subsequently, for reasons later stated, some of their minor tribes began to cross the mountains to the Danube valley in Thrace. West of the Vistula River were the Suebian tribes, which were increasing in population. We already have shown how these tribes had been confined toward the shores of the Baltic by the Kelts and the three westward flights of the Kimmerians, the Goidels in 633 B.C., the Danes in 605 B.C., and the Skoloti in 341 B.C. (one year after each had started westward). The Carpathian, Alpine, and other mountain regions and southern Europe thus were left mainly to the Keltic and Mediterranean races, which had lived there for thousands of years previously, more or less commingled. Very few, if any, Nordics had penetrated or settled in those regions at this time.

About the middle of the 3rd century B. C., the pressure of the Huns (*Arimaspians*) between the Ural and Altai Mountains forced the Hungarians (*Argepp*ei) to the southerly end of the Ural Mountains. There they ultimately displaced the *Iyrcae* in the region between Orenburg and Ufa, whereupon this region came to be known as the seat of the Hungarian nation. The Iyrcae, as already said, moved to the district between the lower Volga and Don Rivers after they had divided the Alani and certain Getic secessionists and pressed the Alani southward. There they established the kingdom of Great Bolgary. Not only did this Hunnish pressure from the

---

6 Pliny iv. 12.
7 Herodotus iv. 100, 125.

east occur intermittently before the time of Herodotus,[8] but the later invasion of Europe by the Huns proves that it continued after his time. The region at the head of the Caspian Sea, west of the Ural River, was still the seat of the Alani at the beginning of the Christian era.

As prolific tribes so increased in numbers that central control was ineffective, groups often broke away and took other tribal names. But ordinarily such groups long remained nominally subject to or allied with the dominant tribe, until in time they might become sufficiently strong to assume an independent status. This was particularly true of the Getae,[9] and such a secession (mentioned before) was noted by Herodotus,[10] who refers to certain secessionists from the Royal Scythians (the later Ostrogoths) at the Palus Maeotis (Sea of Azov) who had moved east of the Volga River to the head of the Caspian Sea, just south of the Alani. Subsequently, they became allies of the Alani.[11] But these two groups were sundered by the Huns in the third quarter of the 4th century A.D. and the Alani joined the Vandals, a Suebic tribe, in an invasion of southwestern Europe. Both finally crossed Iberia to and ultimately disappeared from history in northern Africa (from Morocco to Tunisia). The secessionists fled toward the Caucaus Mountains, where their descendants live today as the *Ossetes* or otherwise as the White "Khazars."

The Turanian Issedones referred to by Aristeas[12] actually were the Iyrcae and the Argeppei, all of whom were descendants of amalgamated Issedones and Ugrians in Semipalatinsk. The homeland of the Issedones was in the Tarim basin of Eastern Turkistan, whence from the earliest times (after the Nordics moved northward to Geté about 7700 B.C.) Turkic groups have spread over the mountains to Western Turkistan, a "springboard" for migrations to distant regions north, west and south of the Caspian Sea.

Between the time at which the Getic Scythians (the later Goths) conquered the Ukraine and the time of Herodotus,

---

8 *Ibid.,* iv. 13.
9 *Ibid.,* iv. 93-96.
10 *Ibid.,* iv. 22. The Sea of Azov anciently was kown as the *Bosporus Cimmerius.*
11 C. C. Mierow, *The Gothic History of Jordanes* (Princeton, 1915), pp. 2-3.
12 Herodotus, *ibid.,* iv. 13.

they had greatly increased in numbers.[13] The ruling division was the Royal Scythians (the later Ostrogoths)[14] and its headquarters were a considerable distance up the Borysthenes (Dnieper) River. Its territory embraced the region between the Tanais (Don) and the Borysthenes (Dnieper) Rivers, from the Sea of Azov on the south to the territory of the Slavic Melanchleni at about 51° latitude. As the most numerous and the most noble division of the nation, it comprised the great body of freemen and all other tribes of the nation were looked upon as subjects.[15] Among the latter were not only the conquered Skolotic Kimmerians, whose territory extended apparently from the Bug River to as far south as the Dniester River, but also the captive Medians (also Kimmerians), who lived between the Dniester and the Danube Rivers. Both groups were kept in subjection by certain detachments of Getae posted west of the Royal Scythians,[16] on the upper Tyres (Dniester) River, and southward along the Prut River as far as the Danube, since these outlying commands clearly were allied with the Royal Scythians in warfare.[17] This habitation of bands of Getae on the Prut and lower Danube Rivers to the Black Sea[18] and the fact of their determined resistance to the passage of Darius[19] tend to confirm the inference that they originally were posted at those locations to guard and confine the two groups of subject Kimmerians to their assigned territory. The force of guards must have been strengthened after the revolt of the Skoloti in 606 B.C.[20] and the escape of some of the captive Medians to the Dalmatian coast, where they subsequently were known as the *Sigynae,* discussed before.[21]

13 *Ibid.,* iv. 71.

14 *Ibid.,* iv. 20.

15 *Ibid.,* iv. 20, 93-96.

16 *Ibid.,* iv. 56.

17 C. C. Mierow, *op.cit.,* pages 66-69.

18 *Ibid.,* pages 60-61.

19 Herodotus, *Hist.,* iv. 93.

20 *Ibid.,* iv. 3-4.

21 Cassidorus was correct in identifying the Getae of northern Thrace and the chief western Scythians (other than the Skolotic Kimmerians) after 634 B. C. as the Gothic nation, and it was erroneous for both Hodgkin and Mierow to

GETIC (GOTHIC) NATION AND ITS FORTUNES

After the transfer by the Getic (Gothic) nation of the
rest of the captive Medians to the basin of the Dnieper,
Pripyat, and upper Niemen Rivers about 510 B. C., where
they became the ancestors of the Lithuanians, Latvians, and
Borussians, and after the escape of the Skoloti to western
Europe in 342 B. C., these southerly Getae continued to
occupy the lands relinquished by their former subjects
between the Dnieper or Bug River and the Danube River.
Only recently the Russians reported the finding of a massive
stone mausoleum north of Yalta used as a burial place for
Getic chiefs for six centuries. It contained gold and precious stones.

The southern Getae expanded across the lower Danube
in Thrace, but these groups were defeated and scattered
in 279 B.C. by those Gauls who, after crossing Europe
and detaching themselves from Brennus' army, finally
settled in Galatia, in Asia Minor, which took its name
from them. The defeated Getae fled westward over the
mountains to what is now Transylvania, where they joined
their kin, the *Dacians*,[22] whose territory extended along
the central Danube toward Bohemia. In recognition of
their kinship, other Scythian Getae in 256 B.C. crossed
the Carpathians to reinforce those people and they all
drove the Romans from Dacia. The Getae in Moesia, on
the lower Danube, as late as the reign of Emperor Constantine, frequently served as auxiliaries in Roman armies.[23] From that time, the Dacians and these Getae,
along with another detached Getic tribe, the *Bastarnae,*
commingled with the Kelts in the Danubian basin.[24] Most
of the present blond or partly blond Romanians are descended from this commingled Daci-Getic and Keltic stock,
while the brunet people, mainly the Wallachs, are descended from the primitive Pelasgic stock. A Pelasgic
strain also is discernible in the Kelts.

In view of the claim made by the Royal Scythians re-

---

reject chapters V-XIII of the *Getica* as a source of Gothic history. These chapters
merely require interpretation in the light of other available sources and are valuable
for developing the racial history of the regions dealt with.
22 Strabo, *Geogr.* vii. 3.12.
23 C. C. Mierow, *op.cit.,* pages 82-83.
24 *Ibid.,* pages 74-82.

garding the origin of their nation,[25] it is not improbable
that they represented the original nucleus of the Nordic
nation in Geté,[26] east of Lake Aral, from which all of
the other Nordic tribes successively branched as their
numbers increased and became too unwieldy to be controlled by central authority. While the original national
name of the Goths was the Getae,[27] derived from their
homeland of Geté, the later name of Goth was derived
from the personal name of *Gaut,* the founder of the royal
Amal family of the Ostrogoths.

---

2. *Expansion of the Getae and other Nations.* Constantly-
increasing pressure on the Getae in Ukrainia by the various
nations on their east, including the fierce Huns east of the
Ural River, began to be felt as time passed. The strong
Suebic nation lay on their west and the Roman power grew
on the south. The expedition of the Persians under Darius
in 512 B.C. had convinced the Getae of the superior
military strength of that nation as well as of the Romans.
Despite the fruitlessness of Darius' attack, which was
one of vengeance, the Getae were impressed with the
necessity of finding a way out in case the attacks were repeated. Solicitation of their neighbors on the north, west,
and south for joint action for the common defense of
the country had demonstrated that the Keltic and Slavic
nations were unwilling to participate. These nations included the *Agathyrsi* south of the Carpathians, the *Neuri*
on the northwest, and the *Melanchleni* and the *Androphagi*
on the north.[28] Therefore, the Getae led Darius' army
around a circuit that took it successively through the country of the three Slavic nations, all of whom fled to the
far north.[29] The Getae thereby not only saved their own

25 Herodotus, *Hist.,* iv. 5-7.
26 This name dated from very early times. See Sharifu'd-Din's (Sherefeddin)
history of *Timur* (Petis de la Croix's French translation to English by J. Darby
in 1722), books i. and ii.
27 C. C. Mierow, *ibid.,* pages 67-68, 76-77, 87-88.
28 Herodotus, *Hist.,* iv. 119-120.
29 *Ibid.,* iv. 124-125.

lands but also effectually punished their unwilling neighbors.

It is stated in the books that from the time of Darius' invasion the Scythian Getae appeared to be a declining power. But such is far from the fact; they were too large and virile a nation thus to be eclipsed.[30] Upon the retreat of Darius, they proceeded not only to inflict further punishment on their neighbors but also to take some of their lands. First, they drove the Keltic Agathyrsi across the Carpathian Mountains to Thrace, where Herodotus reported them.[31] Next, they took possession of all the land on the northwest, between the Vistula and Dvina (Daugava) Rivers and bordering on the Baltic Sea, which had been abandoned by the Neuri and the other Slavs. It lay to the west of the captive Medians[32] who had been transferred by them about 510 B.C. to the basin of the upper Niemen River. This action permanently separated the Slavic tribes of the far north from the Keltic tribes of the Carpathians and the Alps and left each Keltic division to its own evolution.

After punishing the Slavic nations, the Getae raided the Thracian Chersonese about 495 B. C.,[33] again to impress their power on the Agathyrsi. A few years later they besought King Cleomenes I of Sparta for a joint return attack on the Persian kingdom, the Getae to proceed along the northerly shores of the Black Sea and up the Phasis River and the Spartans (Kimmerians) to advance from Ephesus.[34] But the negotiations came to naught. It was from these Scythian emissaries that Cleomenes contracted the habit of drinking strong liquor, which resulted in his death in 488 B.C. The Getae then promptly established their seat on the upper Dnieper River,[35] at or near the site of Kiev, and directed their efforts toward conquests in northerly directions. This decision must have been due

---

30 *Ibid.*, iv. 46, 81; C. C. Mierow, *ibid.*, page 76.
31 Herodotus, *ibid.*, iv. 100.
32 Ancestors of the later Lithuanians, Latvians, and Borussians (Prussians), but then still subjects of the Getae.
33 Herodotus, *Hist.*, vi. 40.
34 *Ibid.*, vi. 40, 84.
35 *Ibid.*, iv. 53, 56, 71.

partly to the diminution of their trade through the Black Sea ports because of the disaster to Miletus about that time.[36] They sought development mainly toward the northwest[37] and gained control of the trade route between the Gulf of Danzig, on the Baltic Sea, and the Milesian colonies, on the Black Sea. This route gave them a monopoly in the exportation of amber from the East Prussian shores of the Baltic and of agricultural products from the interior to Asia Minor and Grecian territory.[38] The Scythian rulers exercised a sort of qualified sovereignty over the Greek towns within their territory,[39] evidently under a treaty of some form, but the routine public acts of the town officials were performed in the name of a number of archons, who ordinarily were Greeks. The Getae long refrained from incurring attacks from the Romans and others and were conspicuously successful in their aims in the north. Concurrently, their influence was less felt in the south than formerly.

Thus, the 5th century and the first half of the 4th century B.C. must have been a period in which the Getic nation chiefly settled its troubles with its Slavic neighbors on the north, strengthened its alliance with its remote kinsmen, the *Sauromatae* (or Sarmatians), on the southeast, improved and strengthened its internal conditions, and explored the adjacent Baltic shores and consolidated its possessions there. After the middle of the 4th century, it conducted exploratory voyages from the easterly Baltic shores to foreign lands in the west. About this time, notice of their activities on the Baltic Sea was taken by writers of antiquity. One of them, Pytheas, of the Greek colony of Marseille, in southern Gaul, who lived at the

36 *Ibid.*, vi. 18-22.

37 Strabo, *Geogr.*, vii. 3.17.

38 Herodotus, *ibid.*, iii. 115. Scions of the Balt family of the Visigoths must have led exploring parties on the Baltic Sea, for it received its name from that family. In 330 B.C. Pytheas of Marseille personally went to this amberland to purchase amber for his clients and after his return referred to it by the name of Baltia convinced that it was an island. Pliny the Elder, *Historiae Naturalis Libri XXXVII*, Book IV, ch. 27.

39 Herodotus, iv. 78; C. C. Mierow, *op.cit.*, page 59.

time of Alexander the Great (356-323 B.C.), wrote a book of his travels, some fragments of which have been preserved in the works of other writers. In one of these accounts, quoted by Pliny the Elder (A.D. 23-79),[40] mention is made of a tribe of *Guttones* bordering on the Suebians and living around a gulf called Mentonomon, a day's sailing from the island of Abalus, where they used to gather amber. Some of the amber they sold to the neighboring Suebians for fuel, and the remainder they exported through the Milesian colonies on the Black Sea.[41] The gulf referred to, it seems certain, was Frisches Haff, situated on the East Prussian shore of the Baltic near the mouth of the Vistula River.

Thus, when in 342 B. C. King Philip II of Macedonia made his invasion of the Ukraine, which was "comparable with nothing in antiquity since Darius' famous march to Scythia", the Getic military forces were engaged largely in operations in the north.[42] The result was a serious disorganization of the Getic power in the south, for the Skolotic Kimmerians then broke away from their subjugation and fled westward across Europe to the central Rhine valley and northern Gaul. It was the epochal migration already described. Upon reorganizing his forces, the Getic King Ateas attacked the Macedonian army under Philip at the Danube and was killed in 339 B. C.[43] Thereupon, the Getae retired within their own territory and concentrated their efforts on internal economic and cultural improvement on the one hand and territorial exploration in the Baltic region on the other.

Early in the 3rd century B.C. the Huns arose in the east, moved across the Ural Mountains, and gained possession of the central Ural River basin, the eastern frontier of Europe. As the seat of the Getic government was moved farther up the Dnieper River toward the headwaters of that

---

40 Pliny iv. 27, xxxvii. 1, 11.
41 The finding of coins of the time of Alexander the Great on the island of Ezel, at the entrance to the Gulf of Riga, proves that the Baltic shores were in commercial relation with the civilized world at an early period.
42 Strabo vii. 3. 17.
43 *Ibid.*, vii. 3. 18.

stream, the *Roxolani*, the westernmost division of the Sarmatians, supplanted the Getae in the lower Ukraine. The main body of the Sarmatians crossed the lower Don River to the region north of the Sea of Azov,[44] and the Alani crossed the Volga and took possession of the area between that river and the Don above their great bends. The allies of the Alani, the seceded Getae, remained on the easterly side of the lower Volga. With certain exceptions in the Baltic region, the following 625 years (c. 250 B.C. — A.D. 374) must have been a period of relative peace throughout most of European Scythia, for each of these nations inhabited substantially the same territory during all of that time. Nonetheless, the Huns had gradually spread to the westerly side of the Ural River, which caused the Getic allies of the Alani (the later *Ossetes*) to move to the westerly side of the lower Volga. This, in turn, brought the latter into conflict with the Sarmatians on the lower Don River,[45] who moved westward and adjoined the Roxolani, their cognate tribe that had settled in the Ukraine.[46] About 100 B. C. the Roxolani, apparently in a short westward movement, were defeated at the Krimea by Diophantus, a general of Mithradates VI,[47] king of Pontus. Strife in this region then continued intermittently during the next century, in connection with which the Roxolani and the Getae raided Black Sea towns. These and other later depredations aroused the Roman government and the Roxolani were defeated by the Romans on the lower Danube about A.D. 60 and again under Marcus Aurelius, whereupon they returned to their prior Ukrainian home. The repeated successes of the Roman armies threat-

---

44 *Ibid.,* ii. 5.7.

45 Some of these conflicts forced groups of Sarmatians into and across the Caucasus Mountains, where they were living at the beginning of the Christian era (Strabo xi. 2.16, 3.3).

46 Strabo ii. 5.7.

47 Pontus lay north of Cappadocia along the southern shores of the Black Sea. Its suzerainty was recognized by the Greek colonists of the Kimmerian Bosporus and the Tauric Chersonese when Mithradates aided them in strife with the neighboring Scythians (probably the Roxolani).

ened the freedom of the north, and the Getae then began their extensive Baltic Sea conquests.

The increase in population of the Getae during this long period resulted in the inevitable disintegration of parts of the nation, because of the difficulty of maintaining central control. After the Baltic conquests by the Getae early in the 2nd century A.D., including that of southern Sweden, the *Heruli, Vinili* (Langobards), and *Gepidae,* three Getic tribes driven from southern Sweden by the Danes about the year 150, returned to the mainland;[48] but they soon forsook the parent nation, as other tribes had done before, and started independent migrations. Even long before this time the main body of the Getae had divided into two closely allied units, the *Greutingi* inhabiting the region east of the Dnieper River and the *Thervingi* the western side. They were distinguished later in history as the *Ostrogoths* and the *Visigoths* respectively. The kingship of the whole Getic nation apparently had become hereditary in the renowned Amal[49] family of the Ostrogoths (the Royal Scythians), while the Visigoths looked for leadership to a rival family, the Balt, in their own division. However, the latter division, like the other tribes named above, who had their own chieftains, long continued nominal recognition of the supremacy of the Ostrogothic kings.[50] The Ostrogoths represented the conservative division[51] and the Visigoths the restless divi-

48 C. C. Mierow, *op.cit.,* pp. 56-58, 78.
49 C. C. Mierow, *ibid.,* pp. 72-74. The first reported hero in this family was Gaut, in the time of the Roman Emperor Domitian (A.D. 81-96). He was followed in successive generations by Hulmul, Augis, and Amal, the last-named of whom gave his name to the family. It is of interest that the name "America" originated in the appellation of this royal family. "Amal-ric" symbolically means all-conquering work, service, or leadership. When the Ostrogoths overran Italy, it became Amalrico, which was softened in the Italian patois to Amerigo, as it appeared in the forename of the Italian navigator, Amerigo Vespucci, for whom this great hemisphere was named. It is truly an inspiring name, transmitted by two ancient performers of worthy deeds. See Calvin Kephart, *Origin of the Name America, The Quartermaster Review,* March-April, 1938.
50 *Encyclopaedia Britannica,* 13th Ed., vol. 12, p. 273, by Edward Augustus Freeman.
51 Herodotus, *Hist.,* iv. 17-20.

sion,[52] since the latter had more intimate contact with the Greek colonies on the Black Sea, with the Skolotic Kimmerians while they were Getic subjects, and with other peoples southwest of the Ukraine. Moreover, the captives taken in the southwest were more intelligent persons than those taken on the east,[53] and the territory of the Visigoths undoubtedly received more frequent visits from inquisitive Greek and Roman writers and soldiers of fortune. In the course of time, the Visigoths chafed under Ostrogothic leadership and forced recognition of their own leaders, so that the kings for the allied nation came to be chosen from the Balt family as well as from the Amal family.[54]

The primary duty of the Ostrogoths, as the governing element of the nation, appears to have been the defense of the eastern frontiers, while the active leadership of the forces engaged in exploring and taking Baltic Sea territory devolved upon the Visigoths. Hence that body of water received its name from the latter's ruling family.[54] The outstanding exploit of the Getae during this long period of 625 years, aside from their conspicuous cultural progress, was their conquest of certain Scandinavian territory, as narrated later.

---

3. *Dacians, Bastarnae, and Peucini*. Ancient Dacia comprised the region between the Theiss and Dniester Rivers, on the west and east, and between the Carpathian Mountains and the Danube River, on the north and south, mainly the modern Romania and Transylvania. Its population in the highlands was mostly Keltic, of numerous tribal names, of which the *Agathyrsi* were the most notable. Its eastern lowlands, known as northern Thrace, frequently

---

52 C. S. Walton, *Civil Law in Spain and Spanish-America* (Tandy, New York, 1909), pp. 34-35.
53 Herodotus, *ibid.*, iv. 1, 3.
54 This was a recognition about the end of the 2nd century A. D. of successful Visigothic leadership in the earlier conquest of Scandinavian territory and the prestige that thereby accrued to the Balt family. It was a page from Roman history.

were overrun by Kelts from the west and by invaders from the north; the earliest of history were the various Thracian Kelts whose divisions emigrated to Asia Minor and established important nations there.[55] It was the route by which the Kimmerians (mainly the Treres) frequently invaded the southerly regions. Their successors in Scythia, the Getae, extended their territory to the Danube, where they confined the "captive Medians" discussed earlier.[56] Some of these Medians escaped to the Dalmatian coast, where they were known as the *Sigynae,* and the remainder were transferred by the Getae (Goths) to the basin of the upper Niemen and upper Dnieper Rivers and became the ancestors of the Lithuanians, Latvians, and Borussians.[57]

One of the early groups to break away from the Getae in Scythia was that which took the tribal name of the *Daci,* crossed the Carpathian Mountains, and gave its name to this region. In 279 B.C., another division of Getae, defeated in Thrace by Gauls detached from Brennus' army, fled over the mountains and joined their kin, the Dacians.[58] Again, in 256 B.C. other Getae crossed the mountains from Scythia to aid these colonists and they all drove the Romans from Dacia. As late as the reign of Emperor Constantine, Getae of Moesia frequently served as auxiliaries in the Roman armies.[59] The descendants of these Getae (Goths) of Dacia constitute the major part of the Nordic element in the population of Romania and eastern Hungary today.

Another Gothic tribe, the *Bastarnae,* first noticed in Galicia and Bukovina, appeared on the lower Danube about 200 B.C. They had acquired a strain of Sarmatian blood. While in the service of King Philip V of Macedonia, they were defeated by adjacent Thracians, whereupon they left a portion of their number on the land at the mouths of the Danube, principally the island of Peuce,

---

55 See *ante.*
56 See *ante.*
57 See *ante.*
58 Strabo, *Geogr.,* vii. 3.12.
59 C. C. Mierow, *op.cit.,* pages 83-84.

from which they took the name of *Peucini*.[60] The main body moved westward to the territory between the eastern Carpathians and the Danube, adjacent to the Daci, with whom they subsequently merged and added to the Nordic element in the Romanian population.

Thus, the original basic racial elements in the Romanian population were the Pelasgi from the Aegean region, the Kelts of the highland regions, and the Nordics, chiefly those named above together with other groups unnoticed in history who came from Scythia. In modern times there has been a considerable foreign accretion comprising Khazars, Armenians, Gypsies, Greeks, Suebians, Turks, Tatars, Magyars, Russians, Serbians, and Bulgarians.

———————

4. *Getic (Gothic) Conquests on the Baltic Sea.* By a series of circumstances we can determine closely when the Gothic nation made its territorial conquests on the Baltic Sea. The chief areas gained were the modern countries of Latvia, Lithuania, East Prussia, the isle of Gotland, southern Sweden, and certain Danish islands. The Gothic population around the mouth of the Vistula River at the time of Pytheas in the 4th century B. C. had been diverted about three centuries later to territorial expansion in the direction of the Gulf of Riga, for Tacitus found the nearest Gothic tribe far up the basin of the Vistula.[61]

Vital reasons motivated that diversion and the achievements that followed. Mithradates VI, King of Pontus (121-63 B.C.), in return for assistance that he had extended to the Greeks of the Kimmerian Bosporus and the Tauric Chersonese against the Scythians, was accorded suzerainty over those Milesian colonies. He subsequently incurred the wrath of the Roman Empire by his conquests south of the Black Sea, and several campaigns were conducted against

———————

60 *Ency. Brit.,* 13th Ed., vol. 3, page 500; Tacitus, *Germania,* ch. 46.
61 See also Pliny the Elder (xxxvii. 1, 11), where he refers to the Guttones as having formerly inhabited this seacoast. There they used amber as fuel and sold it to the neighboring Suebians for the same purpose.

him. In 66 B.C. the Roman triumvir, Pompey (Gnaeus Pompeius), cowed the Albanians and Iberians south of the Caucasus Mountains in his pursuit of the army of Mithradates, but the latter fled around the east of the Black Sea in 64 B.C. and established himself at Panticapaeum, the modern Kertch.[62] There he was among tribes that, along with the neighboring Greek colonists, recognized his suzerainty. Having a strong army, he then made plans for marching through Scythia and Pannonia into Italy. But, when his army revolted under the leadership of his son, he committed suicide in 63 B. C.

Subsequently, about 50 B.C., after the withdrawal of Mithradates' army, the Goths farther north[63] and the Roxolani, who had been defeated by Mithradates, raided the shores of the Black Sea and destroyed the important Greek city of Olbia. This and other similar acts in defiance of Rome in the middle of the 1st century A.D. together with the ambitions of Roman leaders menaced the northern nations with conquest and servitude. With the strong Suebic nations on their west, the obvious direction of escape of the Goths with the least resistance was toward the easterly shores of the Baltic Sea, whose broad waters offered them vast opportunity for exploration and martial activity. This program accordingly was undertaken without delay under joint Ostrogothic-Visigothic leadership. The increasing pressure of nations on their east, chiefly the Huns, also created a stimulus to such a plan, since the sea would provide a means of escape from dangers that might come from that direction as well as from the south.

In consequence, the Goths then directed their military efforts against the weaker Finnic and Slavic nations of the north. The major part of this armed force was recruited from the Visigoths. It included a considerable number of the Kimmerian subjects (descendants of the former captive Medians, the Sigynae or later Lithuanians), who continued to inhabit the basin of the upper Niemen River and ad-

---

62 Plutarch, *Pompey* (Oxford Ed., Little, Brown & Co., Boston, 1910), pp. 86-103.
63 Horace, in Liber III, Ode 24, refers to "The Frozen Getae" (Goths) of the north.

jacent areas. The Aestii (Estonians) were driven northward to the district they now occupy and the Slavs were
forced back to the interior of Russia. The seacoast to the
middle of the Gulf of Riga was taken and several sites
became the bases of operations on the Baltic. This region
was heavily forested and timber was necessary for the
construction of ships. Lines of water communication
had to be maintained in connection with exploratory
undertakings. Traffic routes, then established under naval
protection, could be actively continued thereafter. Not
only was the water route from the Latvian coast[64] the
most direct and shortest course westward via the isle
of Gotland, but the Gulf of Riga afforded a haven in case
of attack by enemies on the sea. Other ports as far south as
Danzig also were developed. In addition to strong military
and naval forces necessary to establish and protect the
lines of communication and make conquests, a numerous
military and civilian population was required for ship
construction and for supply and embarkation service at the
bases of operation. This resulted in a concentration of
population, chiefly Kimmerian under Gothic supervision,
at six ports to support and maintain the fleets, for which
purposes vast quantities of timber regularly had to be cut
and shaped and food had to be provided. Much of this labor
was performed inland by the Kimmerians (later Lithuanians) and perhaps by some captive Slavs, each element living apart but all working under Gothic supervision.[65] Since
the Ostrogoths were busy defending the eastern frontiers,
most of the sea operations were conducted by the Visigoths,
although the leaders were recruited from both divisions of
the nation. Long and widespread preparatory activity along
the nearby Baltic shores preceded any attack on distant
lands. The conquest of the isle of Gotland and subsequently of the isle of Oland was necessary before any conquest of the Swedish mainland could be undertaken.

---

64 Windau, with a good harbor, ice-free throughout the winter, must have been
the chief port of operations. Libau, largely ice-free, may also have been so used.
The Gulf of Riga is frozen over for about four months of the year.
65 See *Lithuanians, Latvians, and Prussians, ante.*

In discussing the various tribes in Scandinavia, Tacitus describes the Sitones of Norway and the Suiones of Sweden, but he makes no mention whatever of Goths in southern Sweden.[66] The only logical inference is that at the time when he visited the far north (c. A.D. 90-92) the Goths had not yet reached Sweden; but Ptolemy, who wrote his geographical treatise about forty years later, specifically shows the Goths (*Gautoi*) in control of southern Sweden and the Danish islands of Zealand, Falster, and Laaland. The threat to the Sitones of the modern Norway by this invasion caused many to flee to the isles and the mainland of northern Scotland. Most of the Swedes were driven to the uplands. Jordanes refers to the Suiones on the north and the Finns (Lapps) beyond them and to the Danes on the south. A generation later, the Danes, for their own protection, attacked the Goths, regained their islands, and also took Skäne from them. This forced the three Gothic tribes, the Heruli, Vinili (Langobards),[67] and Gepidae, back to the southern shores of the Baltic. The Heruli are reported to have come from Ostergotland and the Venili (Langobards) and the Gepidae from Skäne. Skäne was returned to the Swedish nation by the Danes only in the 17th century. The foregoing circumstances and certain events that occurred in north England enable us to fix the date of completion of the Gothic conquest of southern Sweden as about the year A.D. 120.[68]

These achievements of the Goths are confirmed by Tacitus[69] in describing the inhabitants on the easterly side of the Baltic Sea, to whom he inaccurately referred as "the tribes of the Aestii, whose dress and customs are the same as those of the Suebi *but whose language more resembles that of the British*". The people he actually meant comprised the Gothic port colonists, for he commended their industry (in preparing for the Swedish adventures) and remarked: "*They even explore the sea and are the only*

---

66 See chapter entitled *Verification of Migration of Goidels, ante.*
67 The *Vinili* or *Winnli* (Langobards), like the Heruli and the Gepidae, preserved ancient sagas regarding their migration from Scandinavia.
68 See Calvin Kephart, *The Swedes and Swedish Goths* (1938).
69 Tacitus, *Germania*, ch. 45.

people[70] who gather amber, which by them is called *glese*
and is collected among the shallows and upon the shore."
The likeness of their language to that of the British Kimmerians unequivocally proves them to have been Kimmerians. The Aestii proper (Estonians) were farther north.
Tacitus' brevity of comment indicates that the Goths had
not yet conquered southern Sweden but were actively preparing to do so. Since this was to be an invasion of the
territory of a people about whom the Goths must have had
meager information, clearly the expedition required much
time and preparation. The undertaking also was interrupted by recurrent military operations against the Roman
armies on the lower Danube River.

It was necessary for the Goths first to control all the
region around the Gulf of Riga, then to drive the Suebians
from the lower Baltic shores, and finally to gain the isles
of Gotland and Oland as intermediate bases of operations
for the conquest of the mainland. Some of these preliminary
aims must have been achieved during the last half of the
first century, as indicated by Tacitus. Visby, the capital of
Gotland, has been from antiquity one of the most important trading towns in the Baltic Sea and the chief distri-
buting center of Oriental commerce. Its wares moved
by regular routes from central Asia across Europe north
of the Caspian Sea and along the rivers of Russia[71] to the
Black Sea ports and, upon this Gothic conquest, to Scandinavia.

This achievement of the Goths bears a striking resemblance to the later Anglo-Saxon and Danish conquests of
England and the subsequent Norman conquest of northwestern France. It redounded immensely to the credit of the
Visigothic Balt dynasty, and this family's name is deservedly
perpetuated in the name of the huge sea on which these
exploits occurred. When the Gothic forces settled down to
maintain the conquered territory in Sweden, the western
part, since known as Vestergotland, was allocated to the

---

70 Pliny the Elder (xxxvii, 1, 11) said it was the Guttones (Getae) who formerly
inhabited this coast and gathered amber for fuel and sale.
71 *Encyclopaedia Britannica,* 13th Ed., vol. 12, page 276.

Visigothic division of the nation and the eastern part, since known as Ostergotland, was allocated to the Ostrogothic division. A member of the Ostrogothic royal family then was appointed governor (or king) of this new Gothic domain across the Baltic Sea.

These conquests are confirmed by other historical facts. During the reign of Emperor Domitian (A.D. 81-96), of the Roman Empire, the Goths (Getae) on the lower Danube River, in fear of his treachery, attacked and routed his forces. Oppius Sabinus then was Roman governor there and Dorpaneus (Dekebalus) was the Gothic king. A larger Roman army was then sent forward, but it also was defeated. The leader of the Gothic forces was a brilliant soldier named *Gaut,* the founder of the renowned *Amal* family. He and his descendants in successive generations, *Hulmul, Augis,* and *Amal,* owing to their feats, were deified by the people. This family became the hereditary dynasty of the nation.[72] Since the Gothic conquests in Sweden promptly followed Gaut's exploits on the lower Danube and doubtless were inspired by his success, the Goths in Sweden were known as his followers, or the *Gautoi,* as reported by Ptolemy. It was common for the names of ancient heroes to be used later as tribal names. History is replete with instances of this kind. The name Goth thus was derived from Gaut.

These Baltic exploits, chiefly of Visigothic forces and the installation of an Ostrogothic ruler over the conquered territory, increased the rivalry between the two factions of the nation on the mainland; so that early in the 3rd century A.D. the Visigothic division, as a semi-independent unit, gained for its ruling family a status of substantial parity with the ruling family of the Ostrogoths. The reign of King Ostrogotha endured approximately from A.D. 218 to 250. Then the Balt family of the Visigoths formally was admitted alternately with the Amal family to the kingship of the whole nation, for the first time in the person of Ovida or Cniva.[73]

---

72 C. C. Mierow, *The Gothic History of Jordanes* (Princeton, 1915), pp. 72-73.
73 These two names apparently for the same individual occur in Jordanes' history.

When the Heruli (under their King Berig or Berich), the Vinili (Langobards), and the Gepidae had been expelled from southern Sweden after the Danes assailed the Goths and took Skäne from them about A.D. 150,[74] they seceded from the Gothic nation and moved to territory near the southerly shores of the Baltic, bordering on the Suebians. There they attempted to maintain independent status, but, crestfallen and discontented at their fate, they were restless and did not remain settled long, as soon shown by their migrations.

Few historians rely upon the vague tradition advanced by Jordanes of the origin of the whole Gothic race in the Scandinavian peninsula. As stated by Beck:

> The credibility of the story of the migration from Sweden has been much discussed by modern authors * * *. It has been observed with truth that so many populous nations could hardly have sprung from the Scandinavian peninsula * * *.
>
> In the case of the Goths, a connexion with Gotland is not unlikely, since it is clear from archaeological evidence that this island had an extensive trade with the coast about the mouth of the Vistula in early times. *If, however, there was any migration at all, one would rather have expected it to have taken place in the reverse direction * * *.*[75]

If the reported migration from Sweden simply be treated as the return to the mainland of Gothic tribes engaged in the conquest of southern Sweden and driven out by the Danes a generation later, it is readily understandable. It also clarifies Jordanes' assertion that the Heruli originally were driven from southern Sweden by the Danes and explains why the Vinili (Langobards) and

---

74 C. C. Mierow, *ibid.*, pp. 57, 78, 84. This expulsion occurred probably the next generation after Gothic conquests in Scandinavia. Again the Danes had upheld their military renown, as reported by Tacitus, *Germania*, ch. 37.

75 *Encyclopaedia Britannica*, 13th Ed., vol. 12, page 272, by F. G. Meeson Beck.

the Gepidae had a part in such migration.[76] A large force of Goths was required to conquer southern Sweden, and a generation later their territory "abounded in men." [77] This was conducive to disorder and strife, which was relieved by the migration back to the mainland about A.D. 150.

But the Langobardi did not stay long beside the lower Vistula, owing to exactions regarding pasturage made by their neighbors on the southwest, the Lygii *(Vandals)* in Posen and lower Silesia. Some of the Suebic tribes at this time were moving southward from the shores of the Baltic, and for that reason the Langobardi migrated southwestward (avoiding the Burgundians in modern Pomerania) to the basin of the lower Elbe, probably to the west side of the great bend north of Magdeburg. But before long they decided to continue toward the south. In 165, when in alliance with the Marcomanni, they were defeated on the Danube by the Romans. They long remained in the Danubian basin. The Heruli (under their King Filimer), after repelling the Vandals, migrated to the shores of the Black Sea about A.D. 238.[78]

Extensive commerce between Swedish territory and the Gothic nation in the Vistula basin at this early time is proved to have existed by the finding of numerous Roman objects, coins, glass and bronze vessels, etc., in Skäne and on the islands of Oland, Gotland, and Bornholm. Gotland alone has yielded nearly 4000 coins and Bornholm about 500, while only an insignificant number has been found in Norway.

Flushed with the tradition of their conquests in the

---

76 C. C. Mierow, *op.cit.*, page 78. The "three ships" bringing these Goths back from Skäne are inferred to be synonymous with the return of the three tribes.

77 Of the numerous tribes named by Jordanes (pages 56-57), the *Scerefennae* were probably the Lapps; the *Suchans* were the Suiones (Swedes); the *Halkins* (of modern Halland) and the *Rugii* and others were Suebic mercenaries of the Goths; the *Vagoths, Gauthigoths, Ostrogoths*, and others were Gothic tribes; and the *Dani*, of course, were the Danes.

78 C. C. Mierow, *ibid.*, pp. 57,59, 78, 84. This date at about the beginning of the Scythian war, fixed by Muellenhoff, is acceptable, since Filimer was the fifth king of the Heruli after Berig, who ruled at the time that they were expelled from Scandinavia by the Danes (approximately A.D. 150).

north, a later division of Ostrogoths and Visigoths, following warfare as one of their manly pursuits under a succession of great warrior kings, turned toward the south early in the 3rd century, in the reign of Ostrogotha, and began a series of successful incursions against the Romans in Dacia and along the Black Sea. They raided Dacia as early as 222, and about 260 they were joined in these attacks by the Heruli. The Roman Emperor Aurelian finally permitted them to settle there about 270. The Visigothic army was posted along the northerly shore of the Danube, while the Ostrogothic force was camped on the shores of the Black Sea. The assaults on the Romans in Dacia then ceased and Ostrogotha turned his attention to the unruly Gepidae in the north. The Heruli joined them in this attack, which is thus related by Bradley:

> Jordanes records several traditions of their conflicts with other Teutonic [?] tribes, in particular a victory won by Ostrogotha over Fastida, king of the Gepidae, and another by Geberich over Visimar, king of the Vandals, about the end of Constantine's reign, in consequence of which the Vandals sought and obtained permission to settle in Pannonia. Geberich was succeeded by the most famous of the Gothic kings, Hermanaric, whose deeds are recorded in the traditions of all Teutonic nations * * *. From Anglo-Saxon sources it seems probable that his supremacy reached westward as far as Holstein * * *.[79]

The defeat of the Gepidae and the Vandals on the lower Vistula River by the predecessors[80] of Hermanaric (reigned during 351-376) left the latter free to turn his attention to the expansion of his kingdom. The Gepidae then moved southward to Pannonia (western Hungary).

---

79 H. Bradley, *Story of the Goths* (Putnam, New York, 1883), ch. 5. C. C. Mierow, *op.cit.*, pp. 78-79, 83-85.

80 After Ovida (or Cniva) (251-283), the kings of the united nation were the Ostrogothic Athal (284-317) and the Visigothic Geberich (318-350), followed by the Ostrogothic Hermanaric.

According to Tacitus, it was from the nobles that the kings were chosen by those tribes having the feudal form of government. Descent was so highly regarded that youths of noble birth were chosen as *princepes* to lead select bands of devoted warriors. Without such service, they would soon sink out of sight among their fellows and lose their natural advantages of birth, as they had no legal claim to official rank under the Gothic monarchy. Their chief advantage over other candidates due to descent was a privilege rather than a right.[81] Thus the most laudable outlet for their activities, not only by tradition but also because of the opportunity for greater leadership and position, was in military service. If we accept the traditional accounts in the Anglo-Saxon Chronicle, Hengist and Horsa and Cerdic and Cynric were among those *princepes* who were wont to lead select bands of warriors upon adventurous expeditions in foreign lands when their own land was at peace.[81] The young Gothic nobles had ample opportunity for such service under Hermanaric, as said by Bradley:

> Hermanaric * * * * was a great warrior, like many of his predecessors, but his policy and the objects for which he fought were markedly different from their * * *. Hermanaric made no attempt to invade the provinces of the Roman empire, but resolved to make his own Ostrogothic kingdom the center of a great empire of his own. The seat of his kingdom, as tradition tells us, was on the banks of the Dnieper *(and it extended to the Baltic * * *)*. A Roman historian compares Hermanaric to Alexander the Great, and many ages afterwards his fame survived in poetic traditions of Germans, Norsemen, and Anglo-Saxons.[82]

His feats embraced the defeat of the contentious Heruli and the conquest of the domain of thirteen or more war-

---

81 Edgar Holmes McNeal, *Minores and Mediocres in the Germanic Tribal Laws* (Columbus, Ohio, 1905), p. 8-9.

82 H. Bradley, *op. cit.*, ch. 5. The meaning of the term "Germans" here is obscure. It apparently means the Suebi and the Kimmerii jointly, although Suebic Norsemen and the Anglo-Saxons are mentioned separately.

like tribes of the north, including the Aestii and numerous Slavic peoples, among whom were the Neuri (Venedi, Wends).[83] After their defeat, the Heruli were engaged in various military operations on the lower Rhine and elsewhere.

But the unanticipated attack by hordes of savage Huns (Mongolian Arimaspians) from Asia under Balamber, who crossed the central Volga basin in 374, was disastrous to Hermanaric's plans and suddenly terminated his achievements, as narrated in a subsequent section.

After the hapless fate of the Gothic nation and subsequent to service with the Roman armies on the lower Rhine and some piratical forays in that region, the Heruli in the 5th century moved southward to central Europe, probably to the basin of the upper Elbe or the Moldau. From this base, they and certain allies invaded southern Europe and in 476 captured the capital city of Rome, completing the fall of the western empire. Odovacar, of the Skyrii (or the Turcilingi), then became the first barbarian king of Italy. In 487 the allies gained the ascendancy over the Rugii and other Suebic tribes in Noricum[84] that had moved there early in the 5th century. Odovacar was assassinated in 493. Shortly before 500, the Langobardi conquered Noricum from their allies, subjects of the Heruli, and then defeated the latter. After thus losing to their former subjects and without a friend on the Roman throne, some of the Heruli returned to Sweden through the lands of the Slavs (in southern Holstein) and the Danes and settled among their kin, the *Gotar*.[85] This event occasioned the first reported use of the national name of the Danes. The remainder of the Heruli entered the Roman service and settled in Pannonia.

Early in the 6th century, incited by Emperor Justin-

---

83 C. C. Mierow, *op.cit.*, pages 84-85.
84 Anciently bounded on the north by the Danube River, on the west by Raetia and Vindelicia, on the east by Pannonia, and on the south by Pannonia and Italy, embracing the greater parts of modern Steiermark and Kärnten and parts of Austria, Salzburg, and Bavaria.
85 Procopius, *Bellum Gothicum*, ii. 15.

ian I,[86] of the Eastern Empire, the Langobardi became involved in strife with their kin, the Gepidae, in Pannonia. It continued intermittently until the arrival there about 565 of the Ugrian (Turanian) *Avars* from northern Asia, who had been enlisted in their cause. While the Avars did not participate in the final battle, the Langobardi nonetheless were victorious, thereby gaining the ascendancy over the various other Nordic tribes in Noricum and Pannonia.[87] Their king thereupon married a daughter of the deceased king of the Gepidae. In 568, under an agreement, all of these Nordic tribes abandoned Pannonia to the Avars. The Langobardi, in coalition with their subjects and allies, the Gepidae, the remnant of the Heruli, and the Rugii, Skyrii, and Turcilingi, then passed over the mountains to Italy, where they founded the mighty kingdom of Lombardy in the north. This kingdom remained independent until overthrown by Emperor Charlemagne in 774. Since then it has merged in the Italian nation.

———————————

5. *Cultural Advancement of the Getae.* During the long interval from 606 B.C., when the Getic army returned home from its domination of southwestern Asia after defeating the Kimmerian nation, to A.D. 374, when the Huns appeared on the eastern horizon, the Getic nation progressed from a nomadic state to a more or less settled condition. This was accompanied by outstanding advancement in the arts of civilization.[88] It was the direct result

———————————

86 Surnamed the Great, he was the most famous of all the emperors of the Eastern Roman Empire. He was born in 483 and his original name was Uprauda. His place of birth was Küstendil or Usküb, in the district of Dardania, Illyricum. His parents were barbarians, probably Albanians, of the branch of the shattered Kimmerian tribe of this name that fled to that region in 634 B. C. Their original tribal name there was *Dardanii.*

87 Names of Keltic tribes are not mentioned in these historical connections. They probably lived quietly on their lands, as of old, and waited for the invaders to depart or settle down.

88 Strabo, *Geogr.* vii. 3.5-9, where they are referred to as the most just, noble, and undeceitful of all people; C. C. Mierow, *op.cit.,* p. 61.

of the stimulus that they had received in their contacts with the ancient civilizations of western Asia and of the increased military[89] and commercial intercourse with the southern peoples. Moreover, they long maintained contact with the Medes and Persians, in Iran. Such relations always afforded knowledge of the social customs, learning, and habits of others. We have no reason to believe that the great trade routes between the Black Sea ports and the Aegean region, opened by the Greek Milesians centuries before, had been abandoned.[90]

In the main, however, the Getae were not tradesmen but land-owners and slave-holders. This is indicated by the various tribal names of their subjects. In consequence of their taste of southern civilization and their possession of the richest part of Europe, they increasingly appropriated the arts of that civilization and adapted them to their own uses. The wandering life of the herder, with its simple needs, gave way to a settled state of society. The attachment to the soil of the formerly roving clans and tribes meant the individual accumulation of property and the beginning of political life. Rules had to be formulated for the government of a more complicated society. This situation afforded a favorable ground for the infiltration of more advanced theological, philosophical, political, economic, and legal ideas already developed and applied by people far beyond this social stage. As observed by de Sismondi:

> The Goths * * * had fertilized by their labor the rich plains which lie to the north of the Danube and of the Black Sea. *More civilized than any of the kindred Germanic tribes, they began to make rapid progress in the social sciences. * * *.*[91]

To such an extent is this true that the Getae were

89 Herodotus, *Hist.*, vi. 40, 84.
90 Strabo, *ibid.*, vii. 3.7.
91 J. C. L. de Sismondi, *Fall of the Roman Empire*, vol. 1, pp. 101-102. The term "German" here apparently has application to all "Nordic" Aryans. It has no ethnic significance, meaning merely "warrior."

recognized as the most cultured of all the northern so-called barbaric nations.[92] No others except the Kimmeri-ans had similarly tasted the fruits of the highly-developed civilizations of southwestern Asia and the Aegean region. In the field of political science the Getic people made outstanding progress. The famous code of laws of the Baby-lonian King Hammurabi, revised and brought down to their time, was known far and wide. The idea of a hered-itary monarchy, with strong powers lodged in the king, as found in western Asia, had made a deep impression on the Getic leaders. Slaves were a useful commodity and every plundering raid had as an object the gaining of as many captives as possible. The prowess of a leader often was demonstrated by the number of enemies he captured. Such captives were not confined to the lower classes; in fact, the greater the individual seized the greater the prize. An enemy law-maker, who ordinarily was of noble birth, was more to be desired and was far more useful to his captors than a lowly sheep-herder. Such worthy captives did not remain long in complete slavery. Those from the southern nations, imbued with the culture of their people, found important niches among their captors, depending upon their attainments. This was one of the most common ways in which culture was transmitted from one nation to another. The extent of such influence never has been adequately appraised. A conspicuous example is that of the eminent Arian Bishop Ulfilas (A.D. 311-383),[93] who sprang from a captive family of one of the Christian na-tions of Cappadocia, in Asia Minor, and who translated the Bible into old Gothic and converted the Visigoths of Dacia to Christianity about the middle of the 4th cen-tury. Another instance is the conversion of the Iberian (or Iranian) nation of Georgia, just south of the Cau-casus Mountains by a nun named Nino (or Nuno) at about the same time. These wholesale conversions were

92 S. Baring-Gould, *Story of Germany* (Putnam, New York, 1887), p. 31.
93 C. A. A. Scott, *Ulfilas, Apostle of the Goths* (MacMillan & Bowes, Cambridge, 1885); *De Vocatione Gentium*, ii. 32, quoted by J. B. Bury, *Life of St. Patrick*, p. 5. The replacement of Arianism by Trinitarianism has had a baleful effect on Christianity.

facilitated by the earlier influence of many Christian captives similarly swept from their homes in Moesia, Greece, and Asia Minor and carried away to spend the remainder of their lives in the service of the barbarians;[93] also by the effects of the expanding missionary enterprise of the early Christian church.

Anciently, under the democratic system of government of the Getae, their kings, other officials, and *princepes* were elected by the freemen. No single noble family had hereditary claim to the major offices. The members of such families had to earn their right to them. But, as the ideas of hereditary leadership assumed definite form among the dominant members of society, in imitation of the more civilized nations of the south, those offices fell to outstanding individuals in the families then in the ascendancy in the Ostrogothic and Visigothic divisions of the nation. Since long-standing customs and usages ordinarily can be changed more effectively under a strong centralized monarchial government than under a loose democratic regime, the improvement in the Getic legal system undoubtedly coincided with the nation's adoption of monarchial rule. This development, long before the evolution of such rule among the Suebic and Kimmeric nations of the west, is striking evidence of the utilization of an idea gained by a barbaric nation in contact with more advanced peoples. According to Tacitus,[94] the Goths that he found east of the Lygii (who inhabited lower Silesia, Posen, and adjacent territory) in the same direction as that pointed out by Pytheas, though not on the seacoast, then (c. A.D. 90-92) lived under a monarchial form of government "somewhat more strict than that of the other German [Nordic] tribes, yet not to a degree incompatible with liberty."

Law is the expression of the will of a people rather than that of a ruler and is closely connected with all the elements of culture that a people possesses.[95] Thus, as a

94 Tacitus, *Germania*, ch. 43-44. The Lygii were the later Vandals. The term "German" here evidently is synonymous with the term "Nordic."
95 Guy Carleton Lee, *Historical Jurisprudence* (MacMillan, New York, 1900), p. 360.

concomitant of the improvement in the economic and political condition of the Goths, the rights of women in the family circle were granted increasing recognition. This is proved by the adaptation to their usages of the age-old principle of the Conjugal Community,[96] first revealed in the ancient code of Hammurabi[97] and which was also adopted by their subjects, the Skolotic Kimmerians. According to Ephorus, the Getae were just toward one another and the families possessed everything in common,[98] which must have followed the adaptation to their society of this matrimonial principle prior to the 4th century B.C. and most likely in the 7th century B.C., after their armies had overrun western Asia.[99] While Herodotus[100] commented on the uprightness of a western division of this nation (the Getae in northern Thrace), he said[101] that when the nation formed alliances it consummated them with certain solemn ceremonies. It may safely be inferred, therefore, that the Getae had developed a coordinated and unified system of national laws long before the opening of the Christian era;[102] so that the codification of the Visigothic customary laws by Euric in western Europe in the 5th century A.D. rested upon a broad knowledge of intermingled barbaric customary laws and Babylonian and Grecian written laws. The early zeal of the Getae for learning is indicated by the avidity with which they welcomed instruction from learned men, both before and after the beginning of the Christian era.[103]

The relatively high standards of culture of the Getic nation in Western Scythia, transmitted by its Skolotic Kimmerian subjects to Gaul and the British Isles before

96 R. F. Harper, *Code of Hammurabi* (Univ. of Chicago Press, 1904), secs. 151, 152, 176, 176a.
97 C. C. Mierow, *op.cit.*, pp. 69-71.
98 Strabo, *Geogr.* vii. 3.9.
99 Calvin Kephart, *Origin of the Conjugal Community (or Community Property Law) and other Ancient Laws* (1938).
100 Herodotus, *Hist.*, iv. 93, 94.
101 *Ibid.*, iv. 70.
102 Strabo, *Geogr.*, vii. 3.11; C. C. Mierow, *op.cit.*, page 70.
103 C. C Mierow, *ibid.*, pp. 69-71.

the opening of the Christian era, afford a striking contrast with the condition of the peoples who lived east of the Getae and of the Suebic tribes on the west. This course of diffusion westward of the civilization of the Near East and the Aegean basin arose (1) many centuries after the transmission by the Kelts of rudiments of the same civilization along the central European mountain ranges as far as the British Isles and Scandinavia, as exemplified by the so-called Hallstatt and Villanova cultures, and (2) three centuries after the transmission of the so-called Keltic La Téne culture to western Europe by the Goidelic Kimmerians (about 632 B.C.). This subject provides a fruitful field for future research.

Henceforth, we shall refer to the Getae by the name by which they are best known to history, the Goths.

---

6. *Dispersion of Alani and Getae (Goths) by the Huns.* The invasion of Europe by the Mongolian Huns (Arimaspians) in the later part of the 4th century A.D. is one of the epochal events of history. It terminated a thousand years of relative tribal stability between the Ural and Elbe Rivers, interrupted by periods of strife along the shores of the Black Sea, by the Gothic conquests on the Baltic, and by the southward advance of Suebic tribes. The seats of the various tribes had not shifted much, but the population of each had vastly increased; so that about 372, when the Huns deserted their habitation on the central Ural River for their calamitous invasion of central and western Europe, no longer were they able to meander across sparsely settled territory and avoid conflict with other peoples determined to retain their habitations. It was necessary for them to fight their way westward, and the Huns proved themselves equal to the occasion. Their original momentum was gained by use of the military element of surprise. So far as history records, they were the first Turanian nation after the Finns, Bolgarians, and Hungarians to cross the European boundary.

First, the Huns attacked the Alani west of the Volga

River, sundering the two divisions of that nation (the Alani and secessionist Getae). The main body (the Alani) fled to the southerly Baltic shore, where they joined the Vandals. About the beginning of the next century this latter aggregation of people itself went on the war path, ravaged Gaul,[104] and in 428-429 overran Spain and northern Africa. In 455, operating from Africa, they pillaged the city of Rome, despoiling it of its treasures of art, literature, and civilization. They established themselves in northern Africa, but their kingdom was overthrown in 533 by Belisarius and soon thereafter they disappeared from history. However, their strain is still visible in the inhabitants of Morocco and Tunisia. The eastern division of the nation, the secessionist Getae, who earlier had allied themselves with the Alani, were dispersed about the Russian steppes until medieval times, when they were forced to the Caucasus Mountains by other hordes. There their descendants are known today as the *Ossetes*.[105]

Next, the Hunnic invaders proceeded directly toward the very center of the Gothic nation.[106] From the moment that, under Balamber, they unexpectedly reached the territory of the Goths on the Dnieper in 374, they began to burn the villages, destroy the crops, and indiscriminately massacre men, women, and children, ravaging and devastating everything within the reach of their horsemen.[107] The great Hermanaric, whose kingdom then extended from the Black Sea to the Baltic and across to the Scandinavian peninsula, was suddenly diverted from his achievements, but he did not abandon his position without intense resistance. A fierce two-year war ensued. However, this invasion, combined with the circumstance that his subjugated people on every side had prepared for rebellion, proved to be too great a handicap and his support fell away. The alliance between the Ostrogoths and the Visi-

104 Bede i. 11.
105 Josef Stalin (parental surname Dzugashvili), a native of Georgia (south of the Caucasus), the former Soviet leader, was of Ossete ancestry on one side. He also had a strong Turkish strain.
106 Strabo, *op.cit.*, ii. 5.7.
107 J. C. L. de Sismondi, *op.cit.*, vol. 1, ch. 3 and 5.

goths also was broken. The Ostrogothic division of the nation, after a ferocious defense, was subdued and impressed into the military service of the Huns, but it was allowed to maintain its separate identity under an Amal king and engage in some independent forays. Hermanaric either was murdered or in his distress committed suicide while the critical attack was in progress.

For 77 years the Ostrogoths remained vassals of the Huns, until the annihilation of the latter under Attila at Châlons (France) in 451. During this interval (in 405), one of the Ostrogothic leaders in central Europe, Radagais, assembled a vast aggregation of Ostrogoths, Vandals, Suebians, Burgundians, and others, said to have comprised 200,000 warriors[108] and their families, and raided Italy. Since that country was unprepared, they were able to reach Florence, but the Roman leader Stilicho there surrounded them and caused their surrender. They were then reduced to subjection.

Upon the success of the Hunnic attack, the Visigoths fled southward from all parts of their territory and joined their more southerly kinsmen, the division of the Getae that inhabited the banks of the lower Danube River.[109] The entire aggregation of some 200,000 warriors, with their families and subjects from Scythia, crossed the Danube into Moesia and Thrace in 376. There exactions of the Roman governors soon led to a quarrel, which ended in the complete defeat of the Romans in 378 at the great battle of Adrianople, in Thrace. After a temporary alliance with the Roman nation, the Visigoths chose Alaric, of the Balt family, to be their king, declared their independence, and departed from Thrace. They raided Greece and then made their way to Italy, which they also raided throughout its length. There, Athaulf succeeded Alaric upon the latter's death. He gave consideration to the establishment of a Gothic nation in place of the Roman, but was induced by Emperor Honorius to attempt to seize the distant provinces of Gaul and Spain, already nearly lost to the Romans, for a habitation for his people. After

---

108 This number is believed to have been overstated.
109 Strabo, *Geogr.*, vii. 3.2.

sacking Rome, he undertook this adventure.[110] By 411 the Visigoths under Athaulf had settled in southwestern Gaul. About 412 their forces crossed the Pyrenees into Spain, terminating their long migration from the upper Dnieper River. Under Wallia (415-419) they extended their dominion over the greater part of southern Gaul and Spain.[111]

At the battle of Châlons in 451, when Attila's force was annihilated, the Visigoths of southern Gaul and Spain, in alliance with the Franks, slaughtered their own Ostrogothic kinsmen in the Hunnic army. But the remnant of the Ostrogoths then regained their independence of the Huns and were granted permission to settle in Pannonia. Some left later and joined their kinsmen, the Visigoths, in Gaul.[112] Subsequently, under an Amal king, Theodoric the Great, the remainder were commissioned by Emperor Zeno (at Constantinople) to recover Italy from Odovacar. They were successful in this project and then established an Ostrogothic kingdom there. Under Theodoric this Ostrogothic dominion reflected more glory than it did under Hermanaric. It operated in a more civilized environment, but it was not destined to endure long.

Upon the defeat of the Visigoths by the Franks under Clovis near Poitiers in 507, in which campaign the Franks were extending their dominion southward in opposition to the aims of the Visigoths in the opposite direction, the main body of the latter moved to the region south of the Pyrenees, although many remained in southern Gaul. Theodoric, the Ostrogothic king in Italy, aided in preserving this Iberian territory for them, and for a time the Visigoths recognized the suzerainty of the Ostrogoths and were reunited under the dominion of their kinsmen. But, on the death of Theodoric in 526, the two peoples again separated, this time forever. Under Theudis (532-548), the territory of the Visigoths was confined wholly to Spain. During the succeeding centuries, they gradually merged

---

110 C. C. Mierow, *op.cit.*, pp. 93-96.
111 *Ibid.*, pp. 96-97.
112 *Ibid.*, p. 133

into and became one of the basic elements of the present Spanish nation. The Ostrogoths made less durable impress in Italy, and by 555 the name had wholly died out there, only a few leaders of the race being found in Roman service in the east. Their descendants are an important element in the present population of Italy.

Subsequent to the destruction of the Gothic nation on the Dnieper and the passage westward of the Huns, the great Slavic wedge began to move southwestward into central Europe between the Nordic Sarmations in present Poland and their kindred Roxolani in the Ukraine. The Sarmatians will be discussed later.

After the disappearance of the Gothic nation from the upper Dnieper region, all of the Goths in the north, on both sides of the Baltic Sea, were wholly sundered from their kin. They were left to shift for themselves, never again to rejoin the other components of their ancient nation. The latter ultimately became submerged in southwestern Europe, and the Gothic name continues to exist only in Sweden. The separate status of these Baltic Goths and their associated Kimmerians, the earlier Sigynae and later Lithuanians, is an interesting phase of history, narrated below.

---

7. *Fortunes of Goths and Kimmerians at the Baltic Sea.* The Gothic and subordinate Kimmerian population around the Gulf of Riga and the shores of the Baltic as far west as the Vistula River, chiefly at the six ports developed by the Gothic nation, was out of the path of the Huns and maintained itself long afterward as a distinct political entity. Nearly all of this population comprised workmen recruited from the subject Kimmerians (former captive Medians — Sigynae — Lithuanians) on the upper Niemen River.[113] They had been directed in their civil and

---

113 That they were Kimmerians is evident from Tacitus' *Germania*, c. 45, where he states that there was resemblance between the language and customs of these people and those of the Britons in the British Isles. Moreover, the Lettish word *rudze*, for the grain rye, seems to be analogous with the ancient Irish word *ruadan* for a grain, and the Lithuanian word *sora*, for millet, is comparable with the ancient Irish word *scruan* for a grain. (Sullivan, pp. ccclxii-iii).

naval service by a ruling minority of Gothic supervisors; these remained in control after the dispersion of the main Gothic nation and provided the later royal dynasty for Lithuania.[114] Moreover, in the course of time, there was some inevitable infusion of brachycephalic Estonian and Slavic blood from captives of adjoining nations, the on on the north and the other on the east, as proved by linguistic evidence today. A composite race less progressive than the Goths in Sweden was the outcome. They were known as the *Vidivarii*.[114]

These people were the ancestors of the Lithuanians, Latvians, and Borussians (Prussians), represented today by the nations of Lithuania and Latvia and the Prussians of northern Poland.[114] Their present native language is a Kimmerian dialect said to be more primitive than the Slavonic,[115] variously modified by Iranian, Gothic, Estonian, and Slavonian. It also shows some Grecian influence, due to early contact with that nation's colonies on the lower Danube and the Black Sea. Relationship with the Getae (Goths) of northern Thrace is indicated by the fact that the god of some of the Getae was called Gebeleizis,[116] which appears to correspond with the Lithuanian expression Gyva leysis, "the giver of rest."[117] A remarkable affinity between the Siah-pôsh (Kafir) and Sanskrit languages of the Hindu Kush region of central Asia and that of the Lithuanians, Latvians, and East Prussians is recognized.[118] Apparently, this resemblance occurs among the Nordic element of these dialects. In physical features,

---

114 The *Vidivarii*, named in Mierow's Gothic History, pages 60 and 78, are said to have been "a people gathered out of various tribes" that became one nation, for beyond them along the shore of the Baltic dwelt the Aestii. Long since, a Finnic tribe known as the Livs, who may have been Estonians residing east of Lake Peipus, were driven southward by the Slavs and settled in the region subsequently known as Livonia, which is now largely embraced in Latvia. It is possible, of course, for the Livs to have originated even farther north, as in eastern Finland (or Karelia), whence they moved southward in consequence of strife or some other circumstance. East Prussia (the later duchy of Prussia) was conquered by the Teutonic Order in the 13th century and developed by it.

115 W. Z. Ripley, *The Races of Europe*, pp. 340-341.

116 Herodotus, *Hist.*, iv. 94.

117 Gottlieb S. Bayer, *Sinicus Origins*, p. 283.

118 J. C. Prichard, *op. cit.*, vol. 3, page 4. See *post*.

the purest representatives of the three Baltic groups correspond closely to the ancient Nordic type and they are distinguishable from the Poles, the descendants of the ancient Sarmatians, who now are racially mixed.[119] Koumis was made in ancient times by both the Goths and the Lithuanians, whose nobles intoxicated themselves on a fermented beverage prepared from the milk of mares.

In southern Sweden the Gothic kingdom continued to flourish as an independent nation. But that its rulers were alarmed at the success of the Huns in defeating and dispersing the parent nation on the upper Dnieper River in A.D. 376 is proved by their immediate construction of a great fortress on the island of Gotland. Only recently, according to reports, the foundation of this huge structure, consisting of a square floor supported by thousands of oak piles driven into the mud, has been discovered by the Swedish Academy of Antiquities. Jordanes, the Gothic historian, commented about the middle of the 6th century on the still warlike character of the Swedish *Visigauti* (Visigoths or Westgoths). The subsequent greater progress of these Goths than that of the people on the eastern shore of the Baltic is attributable largely to the fact that the former were an alert element, the soldiery. They were free of the more phlegmatic Finnic and Slavic blood and were directed by leaders of noble origin, in whom reposed the learning of the time and the responsibility for the government of this faraway colony. Furthermore, they were in contact with vigorous neighbors, the Swedes on the uplands and the Danes in the south. They continued the trade routes across the Baltic via Visby and the Dvina and other mainland rivers to far eastern and southern destinations, as is proved by the many Roman and Byzantine gold coins and bracteates of the 6th century that have been found in Sweden. Under the leadership of learned members of the nation, they preserved and carried down to posterity the composite tribal and western Asiatic culture that marked the notable civilization of the Gothic nation before its dispersion.

---

119 Herodotus, *Hist.*, iv. 110-117.

These Goths, moreover, subsisted in a salutary environment in Sweden. Except for local quarrels, they were favored by the fertility of the country and by freedom from external disturbing influences. This state of affairs resulted in economic, social, and political stability. Just as the superior culture of the Goths, taken to western Europe by the Skoloti, exerted a marked influence on the cruder social structure in Gaul and other territory on the north and west, so, brought into southern Sweden by the Goths early in the 2nd century, it stimulated and improved the barbarous society of the inhabitants of southern Scandinavia. Detailed information on this subject is as yet largely lacking, but in Sweden, as elsewhere, the Visigothic province apparently was the more progressive division of the Gothic kingdom, and Vestergötland exerted a greater influence than Ostergötland in early times.

Outstanding evidence of the social progress of these Goths is the Westgothic code of laws compiled from their ancient customs and usages and preserved in the manuscript written about 1200 by Aeskil,[120] lawman of Vestergötland. It embodied, among other principles, that of the Conjugal Community, taken by the Goths from the revised and improved Babylonian code of Hammurabi during 634-606 B.C. and adapted to their needs. This principle was impressed upon their subjects, the Skolotic Kimmerians, and continued in effect by the latter in the British Isles[121] and by the Visigoths in Sweden and Spain. The fact that these laws were preserved by the Visigoths rather than by the Ostrogoths presents a parallel with the situation in ancient Rome. The recognition of rights exacted by the rising class (here the Visigoths and in Rome the plebeians) was preserved in specific laws at their insistence, to prevent their oppression by the ruling class. Since a descendant of the regal Amal family of the Royal Scythians continued in Sweden to rule the

---

120 Alfred Bergin, *Law of the Westgoths* (Rock Island, Ill., 1906), *Code of Inheritance*, pp. 49-56.

121 If originally preserved in the Rhine valley, it was lost during the Roman dominance, when most of the local culture was extirpated. It apparently was brought into the *Lex Ripuaria*, c. 37, 2, from Spain during the reign of King Dagobert I (620-639).

Goths, the Ostrogothic division was presumed to know the laws, as in the case of the patricians of ancient Rome, without the necessity of their preservation in written form.

Thus were those ancient laws conserved through the past 2500 years by the Visigoths of both Sweden and Spain, but apparently not in written form by the Ostrogoths who settled in Sweden and in Italy. All the more remarkable is this fact when it is realized that Hammurabi's original code was composed chiefly of laws followed by the ancient Amorites (with probably some customs of the local Sumerians). That code embodies not only their own customary laws but apparently also many customs of the latter's predecessors brought to Mesopotamia about 8000 B.C. from Turkistan, in central Asia, and refined through the succeeding centuries!

Upon the conversion to Christianity of the Goths of Sweden, this nation, under the leadership of the Westgothic dynasty, gained the ascendency over the upland Swedes in the 11th century. About 1133, the Eastgoths elected Sverker, a chieftain and probably a descendant of the royal Ostrogothic family, to be their king. He had married the widow of the last descendant of the royal Steinkil family of the Westgoths and in 1134 became king of all the Goths of Sweden. However, he precipitated strife with the Danes and was dethroned by the upland Swedes in 1155 and their king Eric put in his place. But all the Goths and Swedes united their forces under Karl, son of the deposed King Sverker, in defense of their common country against the invasion of the Danish Prince Magnus, and, when Eric was killed in battle in 1160, Karl, the Eastgoth, succeeded him. He was speedily recognized by the Westgoths and the upland Swedes, which had the effect of forever merging the Goths and Swedes into a single nation in 1161,[122] and today the title of the king of Sweden includes the name of the Goths.[123]

Just as these Goths have become integrated into the modern Swedish nation, it would seem feasible for the

122 Neander N. Cronholm, *History of Sweden* (Chicago, 1902), vol. 1, pp. 132-139.
123 The *Sweden Year-Book*, 1928. see also Calvin Kephart, *The Swedes and Swedish Goths* (1938).

east Baltic lands (except for a Polish corridor along the eastern shore of the Vistula), long occupied by the East Prussians, the Lithuanians, and the Latvians, to be conjoined into a single country under a common constitution that would respect the cultural differences of each. Their modern names might then remain as provincial or cantonal names under a single national name, perhaps that of ancient Sigyna. In such a union, with an over-all unity of purpose, the political influence of these people in world affairs would be greatly increased.

---

8. *Gothic Influence in Southwestern Europe.* It was not long after the Visigoths invaded southwestern Europe in 411 that their influence on the civilization of that region made itself felt. The effect on the pre-existing Roman civilization in Spain was probably more complementary than expansive, since the Roman was more advanced. Greater impress was made on the cruder social state of Gaul.

In their new Spanish home, the Visigoths held largely to their old customs and usages, whereas the subdued people continued to follow chiefly the prevalent native customs and Roman laws in use when the Goths arrived. Euric, one of the most noted Visigothic kings (466-485), directed the first-known written codification of the Visigothic laws, which, unless compiled in some such form while the nation inhabited central Europe, were previously preserved by tradition. This body of Visigothic laws, the Brehon laws (*Feinachus*) of Ireland, and the ancient Welsh codes, along with the Visigothic laws of Sweden, are the earliest-known compilations of statutes of the Nordic peoples. The laws of Euric were intended exclusively for the Goths and not for the Romans.[124] The *Breviarium Alaricanum*, promulgated by Alaric II (485-507), embraced the Roman laws alone and presumably was intended to conciliate his Roman sub-

---

124 Gustavus Schmidt, *Civil Law of Spain and Mexico*, Historical Outline, pp. 24, 25, 29.

jects.[124] The *Fuero Juzgo,* promulgated by Flavius Recesvintus, who reigned over the Visigoths from 653 to 672, was an amalgamation of the Roman and Gothic laws of the kingdom. The latter exercised the greater influence. The coördination and unification of the two systems had been gradual, and finally the combined system that evolved therefrom became the general law of Spain for all subjects. It was adopted by the Visigothic kings prior to the conquest of Spain by the Moors in 710-712. It has preserved its influence to this day and it carried down the same principle of the Conjugal Community that was preserved in the Visigothic laws of Sweden and in the Irish and Welsh codes. As said by S. P. Scott:

> The Goths * * * seems to have wandered farther and to have changed more materially as regards their laws, customs, and religious beliefs than other tribes of migratory barbarians. Distinct from the Germans or Teutons, they have nevertheless often been confounded with them, a fact due to their nomadic tendencies, personal appearance, and general habits * * *. The coincidence of numerous terms of the Gothic language with those of Sanskrit and the identity of many roots of words in both languages have established the origin of the Goths to be Indian[125] and not Scandinavian as was once generally supposed.[126]

The term "barbarian" is relative and of variable meaning. Originally, it implied merely an uncivilized foreigner. It is a long story from the savage and nomadic Gothic barbarians of the Ural and Volga basins about 1600-1000 B.C. to the relatively well-advanced Gothic nation on the upper Dnieper River in A. D. 374. Prior to their supplanting of the Kimmerians in the Ukraine in 634 B.C., they had gained much knowledge of agriculture and their cultural improvement, while not brilliant, must have been

---

125 As already shown, they came from Geté, in Western Turkistan, and not direct from India.

126 S. P. Scott, *The Visigothic Code,* preface pp. vi-vii. Who is meant by the term "Germans or Teutons"? Apparently the Suebi and the Kimmerii.

more real than apparent, for it was reflected in the rapid
progress made from that time to the reign of Hermanaric
(A.D. 351-376). Their contacts with the great western
Asiatic and Grecian civilizations exerted a marvelously
stimulating effect, as is proved by their creation of a monarchial system of government,[127] with its responsive polit-
cal organization[128] and a definite system of laws, despite
a natural repugnance to the adoption of foreign usages.[129]
Increasing attention was given to agriculture,[130] social
customs, and the rights of women.[131] Their former plundering of and later commercial relations with the cities of
Asia Minor undoubtedly exerted an inconspicuous but
more or less continuous influence on their customs. It is
not believed that as a whole they were as inherently
cruel as the various peoples of Asia Minor, who, as
repeatedly related by Herodotus, burned or massacred
their own kin to save them from the cruelty of their
enemies. This belief is substantiated by the comments
of that writer on the reputation of these Scythians for
justness and uprightness.[132]

Consequently, it is safe to say that the Goths who settled
in Sweden and in southwestern Europe were more highly
cultured than is generally recognized. True, their culture
was markedly different in various respects from that found
by them in the Roman provinces. There was a pronounced
temperamental contrast; what had appealed to the one was
given little or no attention by the other. In consequence,
the outstanding traits of the Goths were offset by the
traits developed among the native Iberian, Ligurian, and
Keltic populations. The commingling of these different
peoples on the Iberian peninsula and the interaction of
their complementary characteristics resulted in the later
Spanish nation that established a conspicuous place on
the pages of history.

---

127 Herodotus *Hist.*, iv. 68, 71.
128 *Ibid.*, iv. 66.
129 *Ibid.*, iv. 76.
130 *Ibid.*, iv. 74.
131 *Ibid.*, iv. 75.
132 *Ibid.*, iv. 93, 94.

9. *Gothic Influence on the Franks.* The influence of the advanced Gothic culture on the inhabitants of Gaul was indirect in the north through the Skolotic (or Belgic) Kimmerians and was direct on others in southern Gaul. Aside from their own traditional usages, the Danish Kimmerians brought from Lydia in 606 B.C. other ideas gained while they occupied Lydian territory. Even their own usages may have embodied ideas gained in the repeated raids made by their armies from northern Thrace over western Asia and the Aegean region during the thousand years preceding their emigration across Europe in 606 B.C. The *Lex Salica* of the southern division of the Danish Kimmerians (the Salii), who led the founding of the French nation late in the 5th century A.D., was compiled anterior to the 5th century and supplements were added down to Clovis' time. Thus, all recognized and prevalent usages of these people suitable for codification were reduced to written form upon the emergence of the Salic nation.

The Salic nation had become acquainted with the Visigothic customs and usages in Spain, including the code of Euric promulgated not more than three decades earlier. This code exercised an influence in the evolution of the Frankish legal system during the 5th century and later.[133] The editors of the tribal law codes ordinarily used one or more of the foreign "leges" as a model. Some principles of law and the manner of their arrangement were taken directly from those sources and earlier Visigothic legislation was utilized during Merovingian times.[133] In fact, the Frankish kings, recognizing the superior culture of the Visigoths, habitually profited therefrom in various ways. This tendency was most pronounced in the reign of King Dagobert I (who died in 639), under whom the Merovingian monarchy attained its culmination. He was a patron of the arts and it was under his direction that all of the Frankish laws were redacted and recodified about 625-635 into the digest known as the *Lex Ripuaria*. In addition to preserving customs of the Ripuarian Franks,

---

133 Heinrich Brunner, *Deutsche Rechtsgeschichte*, vol. 1, page 423.

it was greatly influenced by the Salic laws, which were largely incorporated in it. The Visigothic influence in this compilation is directly inferable not only because Dagobert continually intervened in the affairs of the Visigoths but also because the *Lex Ripuaria* included the principle of the Conjugal Community, taken from the Visigothic law,[134] which was not in its predecessor, the *Lex Salica*.

The appropriation in 634-606 B.C. of this principle of law from the revised Babylonian code of Hammurabi by the former Gothic nation of ancient Scythia, its impression on their subjects, the Skolotic Kimmerians, and its transmission by the latter to the British Isles and by the Goths themselves to Sweden, Spain, and France, and finally, through Spanish and French channels to America, is a vivid illustration of the accuracy of Gibbon's assertion that "the laws of a nation form the most instructive portion of history."

---

[134] The Ripuarians, descendants of the Skoloti, like their kin who transmitted this principle of law to the British Isles, knew about it when they settled in the basin of the Rhine in 340 B. C. and could have perpetuated it in the *Lex Ripuaria* instead of having received it from the Visigoths, but the evidence indicates its revival from the latter source. Apparently, it was extirpated during the long strife with the Romans.

CHAPTER IX.

THE SARMATIAN NATION

1. *Origin of the Sarmations (Poles, Iazyges, and Ukrainians).* The *Sarmatians* (or *Sarmatae*) were identified first about 460-450 B.C. by Herodotus, while they were still a young nation and not great in numbers. They inhabited easterly European Scythia, i.e., southern Russia, beyond the Tanais (Don) River, east of the Sea of Azov and north of the Caucasus Mountains, in the modern province of Astrakhan. He reported that they were not pure Scythians, but, *having descended from young Scythian men who had married Amazon women,* they spoke an impure dialect and allowed their women to participate in warfare and to enjoy much freedom.[1] Since the term "Scythia" was a geographical one and that region was inhabited successively by different Nordic nations, the linguistic comparison, of course, was made by Herodotus with that of the inhabitants at the time of his observation. They already have been identified as the Getae (the later Goths). Likewise, the term "Amazon" has been identified as the name of the tribe of Kimmerians who had been pursued through the Caucasus Mountains in 634 B.C. by the Getae, when the latter shattered the Kimmeric nation, and who had evaded their pursuers by turning sharply westward. They settled along the southerly slope of the Black Sea above Cappadocia, between Sinope and the Thermodon River.[2]

Having become troublesome to their neighbors, the younger men of this colony of Kimmerians were massacred and many of the surviving young women were transported back to the northerly shore, where they married young men

---

1 Herodotus, *Hist.,* iv. 110-120.
2 See *ante.*

of the Getae.[3] Whether the Amazon tribe dealt appreciably with their neighbors, chiefly Kelts from Thrace who had settled that region prior to the Trojan War, probably will remain an unsettled question. In any event, it probably did not occur in any marked degree. Nevertheless the difference between the language of the Getae and that of the women of the Kimmeric Amazons, while not great, was sufficient to produce the impure dialect used by the descendants of those intermarriages, who were known as Sarmatians. It was reported by Herodotus, who called them a mixed nation. A place of abode apart from the Getae became desirable, and the young nation then moved beyond the Don River to Astrakhan. Basically, they continued to be predominantly a Nordic people.

———

2. *Amazon Tribe.* The term "Amazon" popularly connotes women who have participated in war and in other activities of men, and the manner in which it was derived deserves consideration here. The fact that the tribe of the Amazons aided the *Albani* of the Caucasus Mountains (who also were Kimmerians) in warfare is confirmation of the same racial origin. The myth that they were a nation of female warriors was dispelled by Plutarch in his life of Pompey (Gnaeus Pompeius, 106-48 B.C.), where he says that a search of the enemy dead after a battle in 65 B.C. failed to reveal any women's bodies among them. However, the myth is readily explicable. After the warriors of the nation south of the Black Sea had been massacred about 550 B.C., it became necessary for the women of the tribe to assume the reins of government and the defense of their homes until enough young men should be reared to assume that duty, probably for a generation or so. This emergency justified the assumption of arms in the meantime by the women still at home and their rule by a queen (doubtless the widow or some other relative

———

3 Herodotus, *ibid.,* i. 103-104, iv. 11-13, vii. 20; Strabo, *Geogr.* xi. 2.5; *Ency. Brit.,* 13th Ed., vol. 6, p. 368, vol. 7, p. 680, vol. 21, p. 206.

of the slain king). The young women then transported across the Black Sea must have been daughters, widows, and sisters of the slain Amazon warriors and, because of their antecedents, they exercised unusual influence in their newly-established homes at the location of the new Sarmatian nation in Astrakhan. Ultimately, the women of this nation willingly left their government to the men as the nation gained strength without interference at their new habitation.

---

3. *Growth and Division of the Nation.* Thus, we may say confidently that the Sarmatian nation had its inception in this manner about 550 B.C.[4] and that the fifth generation of descendants must have become adults at the time of the travels of Herodotus. Further verification of this account is seen in the fact that most of the language of the inscriptions found at the sites of former cities, believed to be Sarmatian, on the northerly shores of the Black Sea, is related closely to the language of the Ossetes of the Caucasus, who descended from seceded Getae, allies of the Thyssagetae.[5] It was 300 years or more before the nation had become so large in numbers that groups began to break away and form new tribes. Apparently, the first such group was the *Iazyges,* who often used the name of Sarmatae. They moved westward prior to 100 B.C. and became allies of Mithradates VI, king of Pontus, early in the 1st century B.C. Mithradates then was engaged in warfare with the Romans on this frontier. After the Roman victory, the Iazyges migrated southwestward from Scythia and by A.D. 50 had settled on the plains east of the Theiss River, in eastern Hungary, on the central Danube.[6] Their subjects revolted against them in A.D. 334 but were repressed with foreign aid. Thereupon, they must have merged with the Kelts and other natives, for

---

4 Strabo, *Geogr.* xii. 3.14; Diodorus Siculus, *Bibl. Hist.,* iii. 12.
5 Hippocrates, *De Aere etc.* 24; *Ency. Brit.,* 13th Ed., vol. 24, p. 220.
6 Tacitus, *Germania,* ch. 43. The Sarmatians named here by Tacitus were the Iazyges.

nothing was heard of them after the subsequent Hunnish invasion, and their name disappeared from history.

The next tribe to break away, evidently not a large throng, was the *Roxolani*. They were first defeated in the Krimea about 100 B.C. by Diophantus, a general of Mithradates, again by the Romans on the lower Danube about A.D. 60, and again by the Romans under Marcus Aurelius Antoninus about A.D. 174. Thereupon, they attempted to settle in the Danube valley, as the Iazyges had, but were driven back. It is said that "they seem finally to have succumbed to the Goths," although nothing is said about the direction in which they retired upon their defeat. Plainly, they did not succumb to any other nation but retreated across the Dniester River to Ukrainia, which then became their permanent seat[7] and where their modern descendants are known as the Ukrainians. At that time, the Gothic nation already had moved northward to the upper Dnieper River basin and in consequence the Ukraine temporarily was left largely uninhabited. It provided a fertile and attractive haven for the Roxolani and they took advantage of their opportunity to settle there. They were joined by other scattered Sarmatians later.[8]

The desertion of the central and lower Dnieper basin by the Goths, moreover, left a pathway of migration and of escape from the Roman armies for the *Sarmatians* proper (the parent nation), who then inhabited the region of the Sea of Azov. Thereupon, they moved northwestward between the Goths and the Roxolani to the upper and central Vistula River basin,[9] in the region subsequently known as *Sarmatia* and now as *Poland (Polska,* meaning 'home on the plains'), where they settled permanently. The vanguard of the Sarmatians already had arrived in this region when Tacitus visited northern Europe about A.D. 90-92, for they still were living a nomadic life, moving

---

7 Strabo, *Geogr.* ii. 5.7, 30, vii. 3.17. The territory of the Roxolani was crossed by the Visigoths when they were pursued by the Huns at the time that the Gothic nation was split assunder and dispersed by their violent attack in A.D. 374-376.
8 C. C. Mierow, *op.cit.*, pp. 79-80.
9 C. C, Mierow, *ibid.*, pp. 71-72, 101, 133-134; Tacitus, *Germania,* ch. 46

about on horseback and in waggons. But they soon must have adopted a settled mode of life, although they unfortunately did not retain their ancient and original national name. The fact that they were only then changing from a nomadic existence to a settled life is the reason for the unfavorable comments made about them by Tacitus. Their condition doubtless was improved after a generation or two.

The territory of the Sarmatians (the later Poles) originally did not extend to the Baltic shores, for the Kimmeric Borussians (or Prussians), who were subjects of the Gothic nation, had been transferred long before by that nation from the upper Niemen basin to the coastal region, between the Vistula and Pregal Rivers, for the development of the ports now called Danzig and Königsberg and for the construction of ships for raids and conquests on the Baltic Sea.[10] The name *Danzig* was applied to this port by the Borussians.

At this time, the Slavic *Wends* (*Venedi*)[11] inhabited central Russia and made predatory raids into the territory of the Roxolani in the Ukraine, that of the Sarmatians in the modern Poland, and that of the Goths on the upper Dnieper and Niemen Rivers.[12] After the dispersion of the Gothic nation by the Huns in 376, the Wends reoccupied their former vast territory toward the upper reaches of the Dnieper River and were in constant contact with the Lithuanians on the north, the Ukrainians on the south, and the Sarmatians on the west. From this region, they later invaded Europe on a broad scale, as described in a subsequent section. Because of their proximity, the two Sarmatian nations could not long escape an increasing intrusion of Slavic blood. This continued through the centuries, in greater degree among the lower classes than among the upper classes, to such an extent that some of their historians today erroneously deem those nations to be of Slavic origin. During medieval times,

---

10 See *Lithuanians, Latvians, and Prussians, ante.*
11 The *Wends* (or *Venedi*) were the former *Neuri* mentioned by Herodotus, *Hist.*, iv. 18, 20, 100, 105-107.
12 Tacitus, *Germania*, ch. 46.

the Poles gained some addition of Suebic population and the Ukrainians gained an addition of Swedish and Danish population. Thus, although fundamentally Nordic in origin, those two nations today include a blend of Slavic blood.

---

4. *Cultural Differences.* The Christian religion and culture of the two Sarmatian nations, however, received their inception and impetus from wholly different directions, that of the Ukrainians from Constantinople and that of the Poles from Rome. The one culture was Greek Orthodox and the other Roman Catholic, both of which grew out of labors by the same missionary, Saint Paul. First the Swedish Vikings and shortly afterward the Danish Vikings under Roerek (Rurik) from Rüstringen drove southward from Novgorod to Kiev after the middle of the 9th century. There the Varangian principality was established under Rurik's dynasty, after which these conquerors boldly overran all of southern Russia, overthrew the Bolgar Khazars, and created a great empire that centered mainly on Ukrainia.. These activities caused the Poles to advance down the Vistula River to the Baltic Sea, through the lands of the Borussians (Old Prussians), kin of the Lithuanians, and many of the natives fled along the coast into Lithuania, Latvia, and Estonia.[13]

Before long, the Varangians invaded Byzantine territory, threatened Constantinople with a fleet of small craft, and won as a consort for their prince, Vladimir I (c. 956-1015), a sister (Anna) of Byzantine Emperor Basil II on condition that the prince should become a Christian and impress it on his people. Accordingly, Vladimir was baptized at Kherson, in the Krimea, in 988, married his

---

13 These and later migrations of Prussians to Estonia explain why such a large proportion of the Finnic Estonians now bear Nordic features. The Prussians who remained behind were subjugated by the Order of Teutonic Knights, aided by Poles, in the latter half of the 13th century. Thus, Polish claims to an outlet to the Baltic historically might well embrace a corridor along the easterly shore of the Vistula, representing her spoils in the conquest of Old Prussian territory, which destroyed its independence.

princess, returned to Kiev in triumph, and readily converted his people to the new faith. The Russian dynasty learned to hold in check the nomadic tribes of the steppes and formed matrimonial alliances with the reigning families of Poland, Hungary, Norway, and France. In short, this land, named from the first syllable of the county (Rüstringen) whence the Danish conquerors had come,[14] became a formidable power in eastern Europe and one of the claimants for the inheritance of the decrepit East Roman Empire. Along with the acquisition of Greek Christianity and culture, the nation continued to operate the great ancient channels of commerce between Scandinavia on the north and the Aegean region and western Asia on the south and east. With Vladimir I the Varangian period of Russian history ceased and the Christian period began.[15]

Poland, which, in the early centuries of the Christian era, lost its ancient and more attractive name of Sarmatia, was out of the path of the Vikings and very little is known of her history from the time of Tacitus until the 10th century. She must have been occupied more or less continually with the task of maintaining her independence against the intrusive Slavs. Christianity was preached first in her territory on the Vistula River by Greek Orthodox missionaries (monks), and Polish Prince Mieszko (Mieczyslaus) I, who reigned during 962-992 was converted by Jordan, chaplain of his Bohemian consort. When Jordan became the first bishop of Posen, the people seem to have followed the example of their prince. But Mieszko's son, Prince Boleslaus I, went considerably further and aimed to secure the independence of the Polish church as an additional guaranty of the independence of the nation. He was the first Polish prince to bear the royal title, which was conferred on him by Emperor Otto III in 1000. But subsequently,

---

14 Calvin Kephart, *Origin of the Name Russia,* magazine *Morskiya Zapiski,* published by Association of former Russia Naval Officers in America, Inc., New York, vol. 4, 1944.

15 It will be noted that the original Russian state comprised practically no Slavic (or Moscovite) territory, for that in the north, centering on Lake Ilmen, was domain for which Slavs, Finns, Swedes, and Danes fought and which the Danes under Rurik incorporated in the Russian state formed by him.

under attacks from her several enemies, Poland became
a ruined country and finally Boleslaus III (1102-1139),
with the aid of Bishop Otto of Bamberg, Upper Franconia, succeeded in the reconversion of most of the
people from near paganism, but this time to the Christianity of the West. However, he partitioned the country
into numerous principalities, which caused the nation to
lose all political significance and to become an easy prey
to her neighbors. The activities of the order of Teutonic
knights, which began in 1201, extended the scope of western Christianity along the shores of the Baltic Sea north of
Poland and beyond the Gulf of Riga. The valor of Duke
Wladislaus Lokietek during 1306-1333 revived and reunited Poland and saved her from disintegration and
conquest by Lithuanians and Suebians. His son Casimir
III the Great continued this constructive service for 37
years longer. Despite all of the strife and devastation that
this country had undergone through the centuries, western Christianity continued to prevail within her borders.

Unfortunately, this difference in culture between the
Poles and the Ukrainians has had a disastrous effect on
their relations and has resulted in a disunion of the
two sister nations. If they should ultimately regain their
independence, the two nations, aggregating about 75 million people of common racial origin, either allied or
united, would constitute a powerful political unit in
possession of one of the richest expanses of territory in the
world. Its influence would be in proportion to the strength
of its union and the height of its cultural evolution.[16]
The kinship of its people with the Kimmeric Prussians,
Lithuanians, and Latvians on the north should be an additional advantage. On their east would be the vast Slavic
nation with which they might coöperate politically, com-
mercially, and culturally upon the disintegration of its
present dictatorship.

16 Since both Greek and Roman Christianity were organized by Saint Paul, the
great missionary to the Gentiles, both nations are on substantial parity insofar as
background of religion and culture are concerned. Mutual respect and tolerance
for their cultural differences are the essential desiderata for greater national stability
in that historic region in the future.

CHAPTER X.

THE SLAVS AND OTHER PEOPLES

1. *The Slavs.* The Slavs, a brachycephalic Aryan subrace, are Neo-Kelts,[1] as is proved by their physical and mental characteristics. They branched from their kin, the so-called Alpine Kelts, after they all had emigrated from the Pamirs and had crossed the Caucasian Mountains about 2300 B.C., as stated before.[1] Instead of following their kin up the Danube River valley in Europe, they moved directly northward and settled in central Russia. The separation may have been caused by strife within the nation. When first reported by Herodotus and other historians, they comprised three nations, the *Neuri,* the *Androphagi,* and the *Melanchleni,*[2] from west to east, whose descendants were known later as the *Wends (Veneli),* the *Slavini (Sclavi),* and the *Antes* respectively.[3] They tended to expand westward through the centuries, and the country of Moscovy centered mainly on the town of Moscow. When in 512 B.C. Darius the Great invaded Scythia in his fruitless attack on the Getae, the Neuri, who then lived north of the Carpathian Mountains, "fled in alarm to the deserts of the north." Apparently, they afterward led a nomadic existence in the region north of the Pripyat River and east of the upper Dnieper River. The Slavini, from whom the Slavs as a whole took their name, inhabited the territory farther southeast, above the Getae in the Ukraine, and the Antes lived in the upper Volga basin.

---

1 "Every trait that can be discovered of the ancient Slavish rites and superstitions tends to confirm the opinion of their Asiatic origin." J. C. Prichard, *op.cit.,* vol. 3, page 428.

2 Herodotus, *op.cit.,* iv. 17, 18, 20, 100, 105-107.

3 Tacitus, *op.cit.,* ch. 46; C. C. Mierow, *op.cit.,* pp. 59, 84-85.

The Wends repeatedly assailed the Getae (Goths) while this nation lived between the Baltic and Black Seas and as often were punished by them. When the Goths were shattered by the Huns in A.D. 376, after many of the Suebic tribes had migrated southward from the Baltic coast, the Wends took advantage of the opportunity to move westward in force along those shores as far as Holstein, near where one of their tribes, the Obodrites,[4] long before had settled; in fact, by 376 the Wends already held the mark of Brandenburg. By 512 nearly all of north Germany was full of them and they were beginning to move southward, pressed from behind by the Slavini. Upper and Lower Lusatia became a Wendish settlement (named *Sorabia*) and under Wendish leadership the Slavini overran Poland and Silesia and conquered and settled in Bohemia *(Czechia)* and *Slovakia* about 550. Tribes of the eastern division, the Antes, one of which was the *Serbes,* crossed the Danube, where they seized the Nordic Alps, Carnolia, Istria, Dalmatia, and western Illyria. In 549 and 550 they began raiding Thrace and eastern Illyria. By 584 they had overrun all of Greece, and by the end of the 7th century they had spread over all of the Balkan peninsula, where their presence has constituted a world problem. Also classified as of the eastern branch of the race are the *Slovenzi* (otherwise termed *Winds)* of Carinthia, Carnolia, Steiermark, and the county of Eisenberg and the Bulgarian Slavs, Serbians, Bosnian Slavs, Dalmatian Slavs, and Croatians.

In the 8th century the Suebians began the gradual and persistent recovery of their ancient territory toward the Vistula River, lower Austria, and most of Styria (Steiermark) and Carinthia, as is reflected by the areas of Suebic domination today. In the north, the Slavs were checked by Charlemagne early in the 9th century at the so-called *Limes Sorabicus.* But in Bohemia, Moravia, and most of

4 Helmoldus. *Chron. Slavorum,* pp. 1-52. Their chief fortress was Michilenburg, the modern Mecklenburg, near Wismar; hence the name of the region. Their ruling family and its present successors, the dukes of Mecklenburg, are the only such rulers of Slavonic origin in Germany, despite the ebb and flow of warfare. They still call themselves princes of the Wends. *Ency. Brit.,* 13th Ed., vol. 17, pages 1019-20.

the basins of the Vistula and Warthe Rivers the Slavs remained and became a large intrusive element of the population. The name of the Wends is preserved in Wendon, a part of Livonia. A portion of Carnolia still retains the name of Windischmarck, derived from the Winds. The Slavic language still prevails over a large part of the country thus overrun. Subsequent to 1359, upon the Turkish reconquest of Anatolia and the consolidation of that nation, many hordes of Turks overran the Balkan peninsula and imparted a marked Turkish strain to the already mixed population of that vast region. The Turkish rule there was terminated by World War I.

About the middle of the 9th century, internal strife among the Slavic tribes that had moved into the region of Lake Ilmen resulted in 859 in their historic call for aid upon the great Danish Viking leader Roerek (Rurik, c. 800-879), then Count of Rüstringen and also Duke of Frisia from 850 in succession to his elder brother Harald Klak (c. 784-850), exiled Skjöldung king of Danmark. Roerek then raised an army of Danish Kimmerians in Rüstringen and proceeded to the Slavic territory, whereupon he was succeeded by Harald's son Godfred as duke of Frisia. By 862 Rurik had achieved his mission; but he soon decided to stay, whereupon he seized Novgorod and became the country's first prince. Russia derived its name from the first syllable of the name of the country whence he had come: Rüstringen.[5] About 885, Rurik's son, Prince Oleg, reduced the power of the kingdom of the Turko-Ugrian Khazars (probably Bolgars) in the east. Rurik's dynasty long endured in Russia.

The Russian nation of today, ironically known as the Union of Socialist Soviet Republics (not republics in the commonly-recognized sense), embraces numerous peoples who are not Slavs. Its ablest constituents are the originally Nordic peoples of the west — the Sarmatian Ukrainians and eastern Poles and the eastern Lithuanians of White

---

[5] Calvin Kephart, *Origin of the Name Russia* in magazine *Morskiya Zapiski*, New York, vol. II, No. 4, November, 1944. Undoubtedly, a motive for Roerek's act was the insistence of Godfred to be given his inheritance of his father's status of duke.

Russia, who have incurred a marked strain of Slavic blood during the Christian era. The descendants of the Swedes and Danes of western Russia have amalgamated mainly with the Ukrainians. The Finnic, Ugrian, and Turkic elements of the Turanian race also constitute large portions of the Soviet nation's present population west of the Ural Mountains. Its population east of those mountains already has been discussed under other titles.

---

2. *Avars, Bolgars, Magyars, Turks and Others.* During the period from the 4th to the 8th century, certain unrelated Turanian peoples, the Avars, Bolgarians, and Hungarians, from the northeasterly direction, penetrated the vast region gained and settled by the Slavs, especially after the dispersion of the Gothic nation. The settlement of the Avars, an Ugrian tribe from Siberia, in Pannonia (Hungary) about 565, separated the northern and the southern Slavs. The Avars had made their way across Slavic territory. Their downfall began with their defeat by Charlamagne in 796 and it was completed by their rout by the Moravians in 827, when the depleted horde returned to its former habitation.

In the later part of the 7th century, many Bolgarians migrated from their kingdom in the upper Volga basin and conquered and superimposed their name on the region now known as Bulgaria. It was then populated largely by Slavs, with whom they have since amalgamated. Submergence usually is the destiny of nomadic people who migrate to and settle in a populated region in which an advanced state of culture prevails, and this has been true of the Turanian Bolgarians. The other Bolgars (the later Khazars) moved southward between the Volga and Don Rivers.

In 895 the Magyars (or Hungarians) under their leader Arpád made their historic incursion from the basin of the upper Volga through the Vereczka Pass into the regions of the Upper Theiss River represented by modern Hungary, where they soon gained control of that country from the Moravian Slavs and other mixed peoples who inhabited it after their annihilation of the Avars. There the Magyars have been dominant for the past millennium, maintaining along with the greatly mixed Romanian population the permanent separation of the northern and the southern Slavs.

In the 7th century the Arabs, a branch of the Aryan Mediterranean race, erected a stupendous Muhammadan kingdom that extended from the Indus River, Lake Aral, and the Caucasus Mountains across Arabia and northern Africa to the Atlantic Ocean. In 711 they completed their conquest of nearly all of the Visigothic kingdom in Spain and southeastern France. Most of these regions they ruled for nearly eight centuries. Finally, in 1492, they were expelled from Spain by Ferdinand and Isabella, but a considerable Moorish strain was left behind in the population. In consequence of this victory and flushed with power, the Spaniards and Portugese then began their memorable explorations and conquests in the American hemisphere and were followed in those pursuits by other European nations. Their discoveries led to the establishment in this hemisphere of the various important nations of European racial origin that exist today, which supplanted the dominance of the numerous Amerind tribes originally from Asia and the non-Turanian tribes of Quichuas of Peru, theretofore the sole inhabitants.

From probably the time of the Slavic penetration of Europe, various Ugrian, Mongolian, Turkish, and mixed peoples have migrated westward from Siberia and Turkistan and northward through the Caucasus Mountains into eastern and southern European Russia, so that that country today comprises perhaps the greatest conglomeration of racial types to be found anywhere. Many are nomadic and migrate from one part of the country to another, as moved by their interest or inclination. While the Turkish element is unnoticeable in the Ukraine, Dacia, and most of the Balkan peninsula, it is preponderant in the Caucasus region and the Russian steppes under the names of Tatar, Kalmuck, and other group names. The broadheadedness of the inhabitants of those districts is attributable to the Tatar and Ugrian strains that penetrated that vast region.

Finally, two centuries ago, large numbers of Indafricans from the west coast of Africa were brought to the western hemisphere to provide cheap labor on the plantations of white people. They now constitute a considerable population in several of the countries, intermarrying with the Indians and with the poorer whites in some of the equatorial Latin countries. In others and in the north there is definite aversion to the amalgamation of races so greatly different in type, mentality, and culture.

A large population of Europeans also has moved into Africa. The northern Europeans have gone to South Africa and the southern Europeans to North Africa. Owing to the unprogressiveness of the Indafrican and his incapacity to govern competently, his territory now is apportioned among the European nations, which rule directly or indirectly practically all of its area except Liberia and Ghana, where local forms of dictatorship prevail. Other areas now are being released.

In addition, the British Commonwealth includes the distant lands of Australia and New Zealand in the South Pacific Ocean, where the native (Indonesian or other) population is small and where modern democracies prevail.

In view of the great contrast between the earth's present population of 2,300,000,000 and the relatively small number, about one-third as many, that existed a few centuries ago, the settled habit of nearly all peoples today and the resultant spirit of nationalism will prevent future mass migrations like those of the past. Migrations of people, except in Russia, now occur under immigration quotas.

CHAPTER XI.

MASSAGETAE AND SAKAE; ORIGIN OF THE SANSKRIT LANGUAGE

1. *Original Habitation*. We already have seen that the habitation of the original Nordic nation shortly after it was driven out of the Tarim Basin, in Eastern Turkistan, about 8000 B.C. by Turks descending from western Tibet over the Kuenlun Mountains was in the foothills and valleys of the western Tien (Celestial) Mountains. About 7700-7500 B.C. they crossed those mountains to the country known anciently as Geté, south and southwest of Lake Balkhash; it comprises the present Russian province of Semiryechensk, in western Turkistan, whose name means the "Land of the Seven Rivers". This province took its name from the streams that flow from the mountains on the southeast into that lake. The Vedic hymns of the Indo-Aryans recite that their ancestors, divided into clans and tribes, once occupied the *Land of the Seven Rivers*. This region is just northeast of ancient Sogdiana, to which the easternmost Nordic tribe or nation, the Sakae, ultimately moved. The descent from the mountains to the steppe in this region is quite steep. The climate is continental and temperate, the winter temperature falling to about 13⁰ Fah. The products of the habitable land are substantially the same as those of Western Scythia, or southern European Russia, to which three of the five recognized later Nordic nations emigrated after 2300 B.C.

From about the time of their settlement in Geté until about 2300 B. C., the Nordic peoples had Turkic neighbors on their south or southwest in Western Turkistan; namely, the Sumerians until about 4300 B.C. and the Hittites thence until about 2300 B.C. Because of the relatively small number of the Nordics during the earlier period, their intercourse and interchange of ideas and customs with the more civilized Sumerians probably were in minor degree, but the evidence indicates that the reverse was true with respect to their relations with the Hittites, who also possessed the superior culture developed earlier by the Turkic people.

During the subsequent centuries in Geté, the original Nordic nation expanded into a greater one, from which different tribes separated later until all ultimately became recognized as five related nations. Three, the *Suebi*, the *Kimmerii*, and the *Getae* (or later Goths) emigrated to Europe, as already explained. The other two, the *Massagetae* and the *Sakae*, remained permanently in Eastern Scythia, and the latter had as neighbors east of the mountains another division of the Turks, the *Issedones*. The Sakae long continued to inhabit the homeland of Geté, but the Massagetae moved westward and southward toward the northerly Iranian escarpment.

The Getae, who emigrated to Europe about 850 B.C., appear to have been the nuclear nation of the Nordic subrace, from which all of the other Nordic tribes separated at different times. In fact, the later Ostrogoths long afterward in Western Scythia were known as the *Royal Scythians* and their dynasty, the later *Amali*[1], was the most eminent one known in early Nordic history. After the Kimmerii had departed toward Europe about 1700 B.C., the Getae moved westward to the region between the Aral and Caspian Seas and the Massagetae broke away and occupied the region between them and the Sakae in Geté. Evidently, rivalry between the Getae and Massagetae increased and a century or so later resulted in strife, whereupon a division of the latter separated and migrated southward to Bactria, where they gained the ascendancy over the indigenous people — probably commingled Pamirians and Iranians. There their Nordic language underwent some modification. Within another century, spurred by the desire for further adven-

---

1 Thus, the geographical name *America*, derived from *Amal-ric*, had its origin in the name of the earliest-known dynasty of the Nordic branch of the Aryan race.

ture, they invaded northwestern India, *where they introduced the Vedic Sanskrit language and literature about 1400 B.C.* and long remained in power in that region. A minority in number, they ultimately were absorbed by the brown native Aryan population.

(a) *Massagetae.* About 750 B. C. the Massagetic nation moved slowly southward east of the Caspian Sea toward Iran. There they were halted by the resistance of the Persian Empire. Their number had continued to increase and, under the impact of the Persian attacks, various detachments separated under recognized leaders and became independent tribes. Among the earliest were the *Dahae*[2] who settled around the southerly end of the Caspian Sea, the name of which was derived later from one of their tribes, the *Caspi.* The main body of the Massagetae subsequently moved eastward and took possession of Bactria. There they expanded into a powerful nation between the Hindu Kush and the Hissar Mountains and up the valley of the Oxus River (the *Amu Darya*), one of the greatest streams of central Asia. Their territory included that part of present Bukhara south of the Hissar Mountains and all together may properly be called *Bactriana*. It is largely a mountainous country, now partly in northern Afghanistan, and possesses a moderate climate. Water was abundant and the land was fertile. Their capital was the city of Balkh, south of the Oxus in Afghanistan.

In their eastward migration, other tribes split off and settled in northeastern Iran, chiefly the *Arii,* the *Chorasmii,* the *Pasiani,* and others. The first of these settled on the Arius River, which took its name from them. Their root-word, *arya* in Sanskrit, is that from which the term *Aryan* was derived. It means "noble" and signified the ruling race. In this eastward movement and the loss of various tribes, the national name of the Massagetae became lost and several tribal names took its place, as happened among the Nordic nations that migrated to western Europe. Sometime after 500 B.C., two divisions of them became known

---

2 *Ency. Brit.*, 13th Ed., vol. 21, page 203.

as the *Tokhari* and the *Ephthalites* (or *White Huns*)[3] and their later dynastic division took the name of the *Kushans*,[3] by which names they will be known in the following pages.

It was this encroachment of these tribes of the former Massagetic nation on the Persian domain that caused Cyrus the Great (of the clan of the *Achaemenidae* of the *Pasargadae*) to wage his several campaigns against them. This strife began even prior to his war in 546 B.C. with Croesus, king of Lydia in Asia Minor, according to the historian Ctesias.[4] Bactriana then became one of the satrapies of that empire, *subject to Persian cultural influence*. Cyrus was slain in battle later, in 528 B.C.,[5] when he attacked the Dahae. The Persians knew that the Dahae and the other Massagetae were kin of the inhabitants west of the Caspian Sea, and in 512 B.C. King Darius the Great, in revenge for the death of his kinsman Cyrus and to secure his northern frontiers on both sides of the Caspian, undertook his historic campaign against the western Scythians (the Getae or Goths) by way of the Bosporus, eastern Thrace, and the lower Danube River. After having marched fruitlessly around the Ukrainian steppes, Darius decided to return.[6]

In 255 B. C., when Diodotus made himself king of Bactriana and tried to expand his dominions, the remnant of the Dahae (tribal name *Parni* or *Aparni*), under a chieftain named Arsaces, fled before him and overran and settled among the Medians (former Nordic Kimmerians) who long before had expanded eastward to the later-known region of Parthia (the present Khorasan). The two elements soon united there, and formed a new and powerful nation named Parthia under the dynasty of the *Arsacidae*. Its resultant language was that known as the *Pahlavi*, which thus was mainly Nordic in origin.[7] It differed from that of the Persians in southern Iran, although it may have been modified by indigenous influence.

---

3 *Ibid.*, vol. 3, pages 180-181 (Bactria); vol. 13, page 526 (Hissar); and vol. 14, page 501 (Indo-Scythians).
4 Herodotus, *op.cit.*, i. 153, vii. 64.
5 *Ency. Brit.*, 13th Ed., vol. 7, pages 707-708. Herodotus i. 214; Justin i. 8.
6 Herodotus, *op.cit.*, iv. 1, 120-142.
7 *Ency. Brit.*, 13th Ed., vol. 20, pages 870-871 (Parthia).

(b) *Sakae*. During the century or so in which the Massagetae thus were moving southward and eastward, were disintegrating into various tribal units, and were settling in the extensive region from the Caspian Sea to the Pamirs along the Iranian escarpment, the Turanian pressure on the north also caused the Sakae to move a short distance southwestward from their homeland of Geté. Upon driving out or subjugating the indigenous population, they took possession of the pleasant and productive region known as *Sogdiana*, just north of Bactriana, where they also separated into two tribes. The principal one retained the national name and the other was known to the Chinese as the *Wu-Sun*.[8] They expanded up the valley of the Jaxartes River (the *Syr Daria*) and that of the Zarafshan River, their domain comprising northern Bukhara, Samarkand, and Ferghana. Their capital was called *Maracanda*, in the valley of the Zarafshan. In its later form, Samarkand, it was applied to the valley of the Zarafshan, which as late as the Middle Ages retained the name *Soghd* (Sogdia). Arabian geographers deemed Sogdiana to be one of the fairest regions of the world. Both Samarkand and Ferghana possessed a temperate and healthful, though dry, climate, well adapted to the Nordic people. While separated on the south by the Hissar Mountains from the territory of their kin in Bactriana, the two different tribal groups or nations maintained close contact at their westerly borders along the course of the Zarafshan River.

———————

2. *Identification of the Massagetae and the Sakae.* Having thus located the final habitations of these five tribes, the Tokhari, Kushans, and Ephthalites and the Sakae and Wu-Sun, all of which later confederated to form a powerful empire, it is necessary next to verify that they actually were blond Nordic peoples. The Tokhari were identical

———————

8 *Ibid.*, vol. 15, page 828.

with the Yue-Chi,[9] who alternatively were called *Getes* (from Getae) by the Chinese, and the blond Nordic Goths were then known as the Getae, so it is self-evident that the former were Nordics. Their easterly neighbors in Bactriana and later affiliates, the Ephthalites, took their name from the fact that they were "white-skinned." Alternatively, the latter were called the "White Huns" by their enemies.[10] According to the Chinese, they actually were a tribe of the Yue-Chi or Getes,[10] which supports the above conclusion. The Kushans were known to have been the primary dynastic division of the Tokhari. A large region in northern Afghanistan, bordering on the Oxus River, long was known as Tokharistan.

Coming now to the inhabitants of Sogdiana, we know that the Sakae and the Wu-Sun were neighbors and were two of the five nations that confederated later in the vast imperial enterprise discussed shortly. Herodotus considered that the Sakae, although Scythians (Nordics), had assumed some of the aspects and customs of the Turanians on the east, perhaps because of long contact with them.[11] These people may have intermarried to some extent and Turanian words thus brought into the language of the Sakae. Their easterly neighbors, the Wu-sun, a branch tribe, are described in Chinese chronicles as "tall, with red hair, green or gray eyes, and fair complexion."[12] Obviously, these are Nordic characteristics. Aeschylus reported that the Sakae were conspicuous for their good laws and were preëminently a righteous nation. They must have appropriated some of their culture from the ancient Hittites and also from the later Issedones, whose descendants were the cultured *Uigurs* of history.

Historical publications are replete with conflicting surmises regarding the homeland of these five easterly Nordic tribes, their ethnography, and their cultural level. Most of the writers have supposed them to have been Turanian,

---

9 *Ibid.*, vol. 3, pages 180-181 (Bactria).
10 *Ibid.*, vol. 9, pages 679-680; vol. 20, page 422.
11 Herodotus, *op.cit.*, i. 201, 215, 216.
12 *Ency. Brit.*, 13th Ed., vol. 15, page 828 (Kirghiz).

probably because much of the information concerning them came from Chinese sources, but those same writers apparently have overlooked the significant facts of their physical description in those sources and of their having taken an Aryan and not a Turanian language into India. Moreover, the country of Geté has been known as the ancient homeland of the Nordic nations for more than two and one-quarter centuries.[13] The cultural level of these people of Bactriana and Sogdiana before they invaded India must have been higher than generally has been supposed, but the quotas that they brought from Geté and that they gained subsequently from the indigenous inhabitants and from the Persian and Grecian invaders are undetermined questions.

3. *Their Importance in History*. These Nordic nations played an important part in Asiatic history, even as their kindred nations did later in Europe, and they deserve greater consideration by historians. The difficulty apparently has been that, despite ample evidence to the contrary, historians have assumed that they belonged ethnically to some other race than the correct one, the Nordic Aryan.[14] Their final habitations were situated along or athwart the primitive caravan routes between central Asia and China, on the east, and Mesopotamia and the easterly Mediterranean region, on the west. These routes were well developed and formerly were flanked by many prosperous cities. It was centuries after the opening of the Christian era until these cities began to disappear, and now nothing is to be seen but a vast desert; all have been buried by shifting sands. Farther east is Kashgar, which from primitive times has been the most important politi-

---

13 Sharifu'd-Din's (Sherefeddin's) history of *Timur*. (Petis de la Croix's French translation to English by J. Darby in 1722), vols. i. and ii.

14 Some even have asserted that the eminent Nordic King Kanishka, of the *Scytho-Indian Empire*, who is known to have used the Sanskrit language, was a Tatar! Descendants of this Nordic population are conspicuous in Afghanistan today.

cal and commercial center at the junction of the routes between the east and the west. The caravan leaders were shrewd traders who knew how to maintain or reëstablish those routes whenever new nations settled athwart their courses. The routes also were followed by explorers or travelers interested in cultural or other pursuits and these Nordic peoples profited by contacts with such foreigners. It should not be overlooked that all this time the inhabitants of Eastern Turkistan and those of Mesopotamia, Assyria, and regions northwestward, except the Akkadians and the Chaldeans and other Aryan Hamites, were kin of the Turkic subrace. They spoke basically the same language, maintained substantially the same cultural level, and exchanged products usable by each other. Consequently, it was necessary for these Turanians to gain and hold the goodwill of the two powerful Nordic nations whose territory they had to cross in their commercial and cultural intercourse.

It is believed that the Sakae, far more than the Tokhari, engaged in more or less regular commerical intercourse with the Turkic nations, chiefly the Issedones (Uigurs), in and beyond the mountains on their east. They may even have intermarried with those Turanians to some extent, as intimated by Herodotus. The Issedones inherited the ancient advanced culture of Turkistan and must have transmitted it in considerable degree to the Sakae, as may be inferred from the preceding remark by Aeschylus.

Of great interest in this connection is the fact that, during the long contact of the Nordics and the Hittites in the region of Geté, the influence of the former on the latter, despite their superior culture (or perhaps in consequence of it), resulted in the transformation of their agglutinative Turanian language to the inflectional form employed by the Nordics. Conversely, one wonders whether the present language of the latter in Europe contains any words or systems derived from the Turkic (Hittite) language.[15] Whether the known subsequent contact of the Sakae with the Issedones was sufficiently intimate to exert an analogous effect on the language of the latter probably is still an undetermined question for philologists.

----

4. *Subjects of the Persians and the Greeks.* The two tribal groups enjoyed the status of independent nations until they suffered defeat at the hands of the Persians and Bactriana became one of the satrapies of the Persian empire in 546 B.C. In 336 B.C., Alexander III the Great (356-323 B.C.), son of Philip II, king of Macedonia, succeeded to the throne of his country. He became the leader of the Hellenes, determined to Hellenize the world, and promptly attacked the Persian Empire, then governed by Darius III. Upon his defeat of Darius, the latter's murderer, his cousin Bessus, satrap of Bactriana, attempted in 330 B.C. to organize a national resistance in the northeast. But Bactriana was conquered without much difficulty and was made a Grecian province, later coming under the rule of the *Seleucid* dynasty. It was only in Sogdiana that Alexander met strong resistance from the Sakae. In 328 he advanced from the Kabul Valley, crossed the Hindu Kush, and invaded Sogdia (northern Bukhara and Samarkand only), even making a raid across the Jaxartes River to impress the inhabitants of the steppe. Until the spring of 327 he moved about Bactriana and Sogdia, beating down recurrent rebellions and planting numerous Grecian cities.[16] Later that year he returned southward across the Hindu Kush on his invasion of Afghanistan and western India. In the spring of 362 he advanced into the Punjab of northwestern India, but when he reached the Hyphasis (Beas)

----

15 Although the Nordic Aryans in Geté had contact during about 7500 to 4300 B.C. with the Sumerians who inhabited Western Turkistan until about the latter date, before the time of the Hittites, it is doubtful whether there was any marked degree of influential interchange of culture between them. Nonetheless, it is not an irrelevant question.

16 Several of these towns bore his own name. The new cities were populated by captives and by those veterans of his army who, because of wounds or fatigue, were no longer able to follow the conqueror in his swift campaign. The language of the conquerors was used among the conquered inhabitants in so far as possible.

River his army refused to go any farther. He then turned southward, imposed governors on the conquered territory east and west of the Indus River, and began his return march near the coast of Baluchistan, finally reaching the cooler region of Media in 324, a year before his death.

A tribe named the *Ariaspae*, living on the Etymandros River, in Seistan (Sijistan), where the Helmund empties into Hamun Lake (or swamp), at the Iranian-Afghanistan boundary, supported Alexander against the Scythians (the Tokhari, former Massagetae). Its members were called *Euergetae*,[17] meaning "Anti-Getae," which further identifies the Getae as then dominant in Bactriana.

The many difficulties encountered by Alexander's successors, the Seleucid kings, afforded Diodotus, Greek satrap of Bactriana, an opportunity to make himself independent (about 255 B.C.) and he then seized western Sogdiana and founded the Graeco-Bactrian kingdom. He assailed the Dahae (Parni) east of the Caspian Sea, perhaps in an attempt to bring those kinsmen of his subjects under his sway. His successors were able to maintain themselves against the Seleucidae, although the latter succeeded in retaining Afghanistan and western India. The campaigns of Alexander had acquainted the Tokhari and the Sakae with the regions and the inhabitants on their south, and the influence of those two nations under their Greek leaders was increasingly felt as far as the Indus. About 190 B.C. the Graeco-Bactrian leader Demetrius, son of Euthydemus, with an army comprised mainly of Nordic Tokhari and Sakae crossed the Hindu Kush and conquered western India from the Macedonians. His power also was extended westward into Afghanistan.

But the Graeco-Bactrian kingdom was torn by dissension and the throne was usurped by Eucratides shortly prior to 175 B. C. This leader greatly extended the conquests of his predecessor over western India and all together ruled over 1000 towns, according to ancient historians. By these wars, the dominant position of the Greeks in India was undermined more rapidly than otherwise would have been the

---

17 Arrian iii. 27,4; Diodorus xvii. 81; Curtius vii. 3.1.

case. After Eucratides' death in 129 B.C., the kings abandoned the Attic standard of coinage and introduced a native standard and at the same time the native (Prākrit) language was used along with the Grecian.[18] On the coins struck in India, the *Brahmi* alphabet, the older form of the *Devanagari*, was used, and on those struck in Afghanistan and in the Punjab the *Kharoshthi* alphabet, derived from the Aramaic, was used.[18] The Aramaic alphabet must have been transplanted to Afghanistan by descendants of one of the tribes of Israel transferred to Iran in 721 B.C., for at the time of the Exile the people of Palestine were bilingual, speaking Aramaic for ordinary purposes while still understanding Hebrew. This element of the Afghan population is known as the *Durani*.[18] *Thus, the Vedic Sanskrit language of the Nordic invaders of about 1400 B.C. had been lost to the general population of northwestern India and the Modern Sanskrit had not yet been introduced there.*

Despite the great power wielded by the Graeco-Bactrian kingdom, it did not endure long and soon was overthrown by native Nordic leaders. Thus, beginning about 190 B.C. the influence of the leaders of the Tokhari and the Sakae in the Graeco-Bactrian armies continually increased, as that of the leaders of the northern barbarians in the armies of the Roman Empire did some centuries later. During 140-130 B.C. the Sakae made an independent invasion of western India. This ambitious tendency of the native leaders culminated in the rise of a new imperial regime in the north, established in 126 B.C.[19] in coöperation with the easterly tribes of the two nations, which may not have been wholly conquered by Alexander. Its ambitions soon reached beyond its borders.

----

18 *Ency. Brit.*, 13th Ed., vol. 3, page 180; vol. 13, page 168b. The *Durani* claim to be Ben-i-Israel and insist on their descent from the tribes carried away captive from Palestine to Media by Nebuchadrezzar. *Ibid,*. vol. 1, pp. 310, 311, 315.
19 *Ibid.*, and vol. 1, page 315, and vol. 9, pages 880-881.

5. *Scytho-Indian Empire.* We come now to an important phase of events that has received only meager treatment in history notwithstanding its marked effect on the subsequent cultural history of the world. The causal force was the final upsurge of Nordic energy in central Asia that resulted in the creation of the epochal *Scytho-Indian Empire.*[20] The status and influence of the strong and virile Nordic nations of the Tokhari and the Sakae and their related and dependent tribes about 200 B.C. should not be underrated. They occupied rich and important regions and were comparable in strength with their kin, the *Suebi,* the *Kimmerii,* and the *Getae* (Goths), in Europe. As adjacent nations, they together constituted an island of blond, energetic, and dominant Nordic Aryans in an ocean of brunet Turanian Turks on their east and north and of mixed Iranians in Bactria and farther south, including Nordics in northern Iran. In addition to the social and cultural intercourse that they long had maintained with the advanced Issedones in and north of the Tien Mountains and with other Turki in Western Turkistan, they had absorbed a considerable measure of the culture and military organization developed on the south by the Persians and Grecians, under whom they long were subjects and in whose armies they served. Consequently, we may accept fully the significant statement by Aeschylus that the Sakae (and doubtless also the Tokhari and the other Nordic tribes) were conspicuous for their good laws and for being preëminently righteous people.

The increasing weakness of the Graeco-Bactrian kingdom finally resulted in the overthrow of its Grecian dynasty by its Nordic subjects under the leadership of the dynasty of the Kushans, the nuclear (or royal) tribe of the Tokhari, who were desirous of regaining their independence. The earliest uprising occurred about 160 B.C., for, according to Chinese sources, their Nordic armies from western Bactriana conquered Sogdiana (including the Wu-Sun

---

20 Sometimes erroneously called the Indo-Scythian Empire. The name *Scythia* was geographical only. History reveals no tribe or nation that ever bore the name Scyth or Scythian or any derivation thereof.

tribe) in 159 B. C. and eastern Bactriana (including the
Ephthalites) in 139 B. C. Thus, a degree of Nordic Aryan
concurrence in central Asia thereby was achieved and by
126 B.C. Grecian authority had been wholly extirpated.
During the next generation, the new confederation terminated Grecian rule over the Nordic tribes in northeastern Iran.[21] Little was heard of the activities of the new
regime during the next 68 years except that Mithradates
II the Great, king of Parthia during c. 120-88 B.C., saved
his kingdom under attacks by the Tokhari.[22] The strife
must have been an attempt by the Nordic federation to
bring the Nordic Parthians under its sway, chiefly those
formerly a part of the parent nation.[22] This period
was one mainly of internal consolidation, but not without difficulties, for it is known that during those years
the five tribes strengthened their federation but had not
yet become a wholly unified nation. Apparently, a foreign adventure was necessary to achieve this result. In this
enterprise, the Kushan dynasty took the lead and by about
58 B.C. the whole of eastern Iran, Afghanistan, Baluchistan, and parts of western India had been brought under
its control and the great Scytho-Indian Empire created.[23]
This form of the dynastic name (Kushan) appeared on its
coins and in Persian writings. In its achievements, the
Kushan dynasty deserves to rank with the later outstanding dynasties of Europe. Its seat was at Balkh, in Bactria,
now northern Afghanistan, which is said to have been a
country "with a thousand cities."

At this stage we are confronted with considerable uncertainty regarding dates. The inscriptions indicate that
the reign of King Kanishka, of the Kushan dynasty, began
in 58 B.C., but whether in the empire or in India then
is undetermined. He established the so-called Vikrama
Era in India, when the great historical epoch began. A
concomitant of this achievement was the extirpation of

---

21 *Ency. Brit.*, 13th Ed., vol. 28, page 944.
22 *Ibid.*, vol. 18, pages 620-621. As stated before, the Parthians were mixed
Kimmerians and Massagetae (Dahae or Parni), perhaps with an underlying Iranian
element.
23 *Ibid.*, vol. 14, page 399.

everything Grecian and the displacement of the Greek language by the *Modern Sanskrit* language of the Nordic conquerors in common use with the native (or Prǎkrit) dialects. *Thus, we may place the introduction of this form of the Sanskrit language into India about the year 58 B.C.*[24]

King Kanishka's successors in sequence were Vasishka, Huvishka, Vǎsudeva, and Godolphernes, who was succeeded about the middle of the 1st century A.D. by another branch of the Kushan dynasty in the person of Kadphises I (c. A.D. 20-85) as king. His successor, Kadphises II (Ooemkadphises), a successful warrior, announced in A.D. 99 his conquest of all of northwestern India.[24]

Some rebellious Sakae, defeated Parthians (Pahlavi), and Grecian followers of the former Graeco-Bactrian kings, driven from the north by Kadphises II about A.D. 98, invaded and conquered the native population of the Indian provinces of Malwa, Gujarat, and Kathiawar about A.D. 100. Their ruler, of the Kshararārta family, was named Bhumaka and he took the Persian title of satrap. "They were hated by the Hindus as barbarians who disregarded the caste system and despised the holy law, and for centuries an intermittent struggle continued between the satraps and the Andhras, with varying fortune. Finally, however, about A.D. 236 the Andhra dynasty, after an existence of some 460 years, came to an end under circumstances of which no record remains and their place in [south] western India was taken by the Kshaharāta satraps, until the last of them was overthrown by Chandragupta Vikramaditya at the close of the 4th century."[25]

The most eminent king of the Kushan dynasty of the Scytho-Indian Empire was another Kanishka, at least the second of the name, who reigned during c. A.D. 123-153 and whose capital in India was situated at Purushapura (Peshwar). He conducted a successful war against the Parthians, conquered Kashmir, and led an army over the Pamirs to the conquest of Kashgar, Yarkand, and Khotan.

---

24 *Ibid.* Few authorities agree on the various dates, so that those used here are subject to ultimate verification.
25 *Ibid.*

He also was an outstanding Buddhist and was noted as the convener of the celebrated Council of Kashmir, whose commentaries were written in the modern Sanskrit language for the benefit of his northern priests, who were uneducated in the Indian vernacular dialects.[26]

In the light of the circumstances just outlined, it would seem that no reasonable doubt can exist regarding the source of the Sanskrit language and the times of its introduction into India. Its elements are well indicated, and this phase of the subject is deserving of more detailed analysis in the light of the facts adduced here. Several modern scholars have intimated that it came into India from Bactriana but that is about all that they have ascertained concerning its antecedents.

After A.D. 225, the history of the Kushan dynasty is one of confusion because of quarrels of rival claimants to the throne. According to Chinese sources, that dynasty was replaced by one called *Ki-to-lo* (Kidara), of the same stock and apparently even a branch of the same family, but which belonged to one of the tribes that had remained in Bactriana when the Kushans marched into India. In A.D. 320 the Gupta Empire was formed in northern India, detaching that region from the Kushan dynasty. In 388 its king conquered the still-ruling Saka satrap of Surashtra (Kathiawar). Thus, the Kushan dynasty was reduced to its northern possessions and the Kshaharãta satraps in southwestern India ceased to exist. But about 450 the dynasty of the Ephthalites, the most easterly tribe in Bactriana, who usually were associated with the Tokhari in warfare and whose leader may have been related to the Kushans, gained the ascendancy in the Scytho-Indian Empire and established itself in Bactria, with headquarters at Balkh and at Bamian. Within five years the new leaders began to assail the Gupta Empire in India, but they were repulsed. About 470 they returned to the attack and by repeated inroads caused the fall of the Gupta dynasty in 480, thereby restoring the power of the Scytho-Indian Empire as far south as the Nerbudda River. In 484 the forces of the empire defeated a Persian king and also ex-

26 *Ibid.*, vol. 14, page 397.

tended its rule in the north as far east as the mountains of Kashgaria. However, this phase of the empire's history is modified by the fact, according to extant reports, that its dominion was largely one of brigandage on an imperial scale. Its monarchs had a reputation for ferocity and cruelty, according to milder Hindu standards. The last Ephthalitic king in India, Mihiragula, a harsh monarch, died about 540. In 557 the nation assailed the Persians, but was defeated by them with the aid of the Turkic Uigurs, who then made their first appearance in western Asia. About 560 the Turks gained all of the territory north of the Oxus River, and in 570 this great Nordic empire collapsed before them. Ultimately, upon the overthrow of the *Sassanian* dynasty in Persia by the Arabs in 637, all of its possessions submitted to the rule of the caliph and of Islam.[27]

In thus creating and maintaining the Scytho-Indian Empire for 628 years, the members of the former five constituent tribes became scattered far and wide over the vast region from the steppe of Western Turkistan, on the north, to the Arabian Sea, on the south, and from central Iran, on the west, to the Pamirs, on the east. They had constantly intermingled with brunet peoples on all sides and had intermarried with them to a considerable extent. Consequently, when the empire disintegrated, its Nordic element was markedly blended with other racial elements. Its people were widely scattered and were unorganized for group migration to distant regions. Before long, its people, always a minority in numbers, were wholly engulfed by and gradually became absorbed in the surrounding darker population. In India the descendants of the Scytho-Indian dynasties and their branches probably became the ancestors of many of the historic rajput clans of northern India, who form the land-owning, fighting, and ruling caste.

Ptolemy reported a tribe named the *Jaxartes* on the lower half of the river of that name, which it doubtless

---

27 *Ibid.*, vol. 3, pages 180-181; vol. 14, page 399.

took from them. This must have been a division of the Sakae. Upon the growth to power of the Turks (Uigurs) in Turkistan, certain tribes of the Tokhari and the Pasiani apparently emigrated to the Aras River basin, in Armenia, where light-complexioned people bearing those tribal names have been found in recent times. Persons with light hair and eyes, descendants of the Tokhari or the Sakae, may still be found in Afghanistan (Kafiristan).[28] Ptolemy reported that some had spread from the Indus Valley to Garawhal, along the Himalaya Mountains.

6. *Sanskrit Language.* Thus, by the foregoing historical outline, the source of the Sanskrit language and times of introduction of its two forms, Vedic and Modern, in India have been clearly revealed. Although definitely a classical language, it was not in even official use there in the 2nd century B.C., for the successors of the Graeco-Bactrian King Eucratides then stamped coins with characters of the native Brahmi alphabet, the ancient parent of all modern Hindu scripts, including on the one hand the Nagari or Devangari and on the other the dissimilar form of the Telugu, Tamil, Kanarese and other southern dialects, whose places of origin still are being sought by scholars. The antecedents and traditions of those leaders in Bactriana were Grecian in origin and obviously such men were not interested in the introduction into India of the modified (or "perfected") language of their Nordic subjects in Bactriana or Sogdiana; *that act was achieved by a member of the Kushan dynasty about 58 B.C., apparently by the first King Kanishka, upon the completion of the conquest of much of northwestern India.* It displaced the Grecian language, formerly used in official circles along with the native dialects. Since the Tokhari, formerly the Massagetae, were a sister nation of the Getae (Goths), we now can readily under-

---

28 *Ibid.*, vol. 1, page 311.

stand the reason why Bopp likened Ulfilas' version of the Bible in the Gothic dialect of the 4th century to Sanskrit[29] and why the Gothic language is said correctly to be the link between the modern western European languages and the Sanskrit language. While both the Vedic and the Modern Sanskrit were the language of the Tokhari, the original Nordic base in each instance underwent considerable modification in Bactriana upon contact with the language of the indigenous inhabitants, apparently commingled Pamirians and Iranians. The Modern form incurred additional modification under the influence of the Persian regime during 546-330 B.C. and the Grecian regime during 330-126 B.C., prior to its introduction in India about 58 B.C.

As the language of the conquerors, each form required time for its acceptance among the literary leaders of the native population. Philological research has established that the so-called Indo-Aryans originally invaded India from the northwest, whence the Kushans came. Their advance from the slopes of eastern Kabulistan down to the Punjab and thence to the plains of the Jumna and the Ganges Rivers can be traced in literary documents handed down by them.[30]

The language found in excavations in Western Turkistan and called *Tocharisch*[31] by its first investigators, appears to be a mixed dialect produced by an intermingling of people speaking an Indo-European language and a language of an entirely different origin. It was not found in the Bactrian region inhabited by the Tokhari, now mainly northern Afghanistan, but apparently was used in the territory inhabited by their kin, the Sakae, affiliated with them in the creation of the Scytho-Indian Empire. As indicated before, there is reason to believe that the Sakae engaged more or less regularly in com-

---

29 Franz Bopp, *Conjugationssystem der Sanskritsprache* (Frankfurt a.M., 1816), preface page x. Ulfilas (c. 311-383) performed this epochal task perhaps about 350-360.

30 *Ency. Brit.*, 13th Ed., vol. 24, page 156.

31 E. Sieg and W. Siegling, *Tocharisch, die Sprache der Indoskythen* (Sitzb. d. Berl. Ak., 1908), pages 915 ff. *Ency. Brit.*, 13th Ed., vol. 2, page 712d.

mercial relations with the enlightened Turanian Issedones in the mountains on their east. Such relations, long continued, invariably have resulted increasingly in intermarriage of members of the two nations and intermixture of their languages. On the other hand, the underlying Iranian influence was weaker in Sogdiana than it was in Bactriana. In the light of these premises, it follows that this so-called Tocharisch language actually was not Tokharian at all but was a compound of the kindred language of the Sakae and of the Turkic language of the Issedones and might well be called the *Saka-Issedon* language. Confirmation is to be seen in the fact that it is not identical with the real Tokharian, although the original (or basic) Nordic Aryan elements of each should correspond closely; in fact, these elements already have been found to depict a *kentum* (usually spelled *centum*) language allied to the Gothic.[32]

---

7. *Christianity in Central Asia.* Evangelical Christianity, under the influence of various eminent personages, made conspicuous advances eastward in central Asia. In 549, only two decades before the collapse of the Scytho-Indian Empire, the so-called White Huns (Ephthalites) of the Oxus River valley in Bactriana sent a request to Aba (c. 500-575), the supreme head (or Catholicos) of the church in Persia, that he ordain a director for them, which was done. A. Mingana gives a list of 21 towns and provinces west of the Oxus River that had spiritual leaders ordained to rule the churches there during the 5th and 6th centuries.[33] Apparently, the majority of the Turkic Uigurs and Keraits farther east also were Christians.[33] This expansion of

---

32 A study of the Sanskrit language from mainly the ethnographical standpoint appears in *Sanskrit Language — Its Origin, Composition and Diffusion*, by this author (Shenandoah Publishing House, Inc., Strasburg, Va., 1949).
33 Alphonse Mingana, *Early Spread of Christianity* in *Bulletin of John Ryland's Library*, vol. 9, pages 304, 305, 316. The Keraits were Mongols.

Christianity was tolerated by the Moslems, who gained the ascendancy in 570, and Christian missions were sent to India, China, and even Japan.[34] Thus, the blood of these eminent Nordic Aryan peoples of Bactriana and Sogdiana continued to exercise marked influence in those regions of central Asia and may even do so today in a less conspicuous manner. Sympathetic investigation of the fate of these people during the long period since the 7th century, when political conditions permit, should be a task of absorbing interest.

It might well be asked to what extent this former Nordic Aryan race was involved in the conquest of Afghanistan and western India by the Great Mogul dynasty in the 16th century. While the leaders of that conquest are reckoned in history (correctly or incorrectly) as Mongolians, many aspects of the invasion and the manner of subsequent domination of India by members of that dynasty suggest that the blood of these former Nordics of Bactriana and Sogdiana may have exerted a substantial, if not dominant, influence in the conquest. The racial aspects of this invasion deserve more consideration by historians.

---

34 Benjamin G. Wilkinson, *Truth Triumphant* (Mountain View, Calif., 1944), where this subject is treated at length.

INDEX

INDEX

INDEX

543

INDEX

INDEX

547

INDEX

INDEX

Getic Secessionists (see Ossetes).
Ghana 519.
Gibbon, Edward 324, 505.
Gibraltar 36, 49, 51, 61, 84, 85, 173, 238, 320.
Gilbert Islands 86.
Gildas Albanius 418, 422.
Giles, J. A. 177, 332, 350, 352, 375-376, 390, 392, 394, 399ff.
Gill, Robert Sutherland 3.
Gilyaks (Siberia) 222.
Gimmira (Gomer, Kimmerians).
Ginnell, Lawrence 424.
Glacial melting 17.
Glacial Stages 12.
Glacial Types 13.
Glamorgan (Wales) 391.
Glismuda (Arnulf's daughter) 461.
God, Divine laws 5-6, 45, 153, 157-158, 199, 372.
Godegisel (king) 452.
Godfred the Bountiful 458.
Godfred (count, Walcheren) 460.
Godfred (duke, Frisia) 260, 460, 461, 516.
Godfred (Generous Usurper) 459, 460.
Godfred (first markgraf) 260, 460, 461.
Godfred (markgraf, duke, Bavaria) 461.
Godley, A. H. 328.
Goetze, Albrecht E. R. 133.
Gog 267.
Goidelic Kimmerians 217, 218, 269, 273, 285, 287, 325, 326, 331, 350-352, 353ff., 390ff., 464.
Gomer (Kimmerians) 267.
Gondi dialect 80.
Gordon, Cyrus H. 127.
Gordon, T. E. 221, 222, 224.
Goshen 152.
Gotama (Buddha) 34, 102, 159.
Goths (see Getae, also Ostrogoths and Visigoths) v, 72, 76-77, 133, 216, 217, 229, 232, 258, 263-264, 266, 275, 298, 307, 315, 330, 333, 337ff., 364, 365, 372, 410, 443, 444, 446, 447, 451, 452, 455, 458, 463ff., 476ff., 496ff., 501ff., 506-510, 514, 515, 521, 531, 536-538.
Gotland (isle) 478, 480, 482, 483, 498.
Gotland (Sweden) 458ff., 476ff., 496ff.
Graeco-Bactrian kingdom 529-530.
Grampian Hills 407, 408, 426, 450.
Graves (see Burials).
Great Bolgary (see Bolgarians) 315, 316, 511.
Great Mogul dynasty 539.
Great Pyramid (Egypt) 190.
Greece 153, 181ff., 193, 198-201, 212, 241, 244, 246, 248, 254, 256, 258, 259, 270, 271, 282-284, 287ff,, 303, 305, 308, 316, 320-322, 345, 348, 355, 357, 368, 375, 402, 470, 474, 476, 490, 494, 497, 515, 528-533, 536-537.
Greek Orthodox Church 160, 161, 511-513.
Greenland 93, 94.
Greutingi (see Ostrogoths) 473.
Grierson, George 213.
Griffins 309.
Griffith, Francis L. 190, 191.
Grimaldi (Negro branch) 48, 49, 51, 52, 53, 84, 85, 174.
Grimm, Jacob 251.
Grimm and Pictet 374.
Guetté, Abbe 430.
Guizot, F. P. G. 390, 393.
Guizot and De Witt 353, 370, 378, 379.
Gunther, John 87.
Günz and Günz-Mindel glacial stages 12.
Gupta Empire 533, 534.
Gutians (Pre-Sumerians) 120.
Guttones (see Goths) 338, 477, 480.
Guyot, Arnold 5, 22, 34, 232, 234.
Gwentian Code 436.
Gwynedd (Wales) 421.
Gyges (Lydia) 272.
Gypsies 476.

Haddington 406.
Haddon, A. C. 61, 81, 205.
Hadramuteans (Arabia) 197.
Hadrian 410.
Hair, bodily 41, 52, 55-56, 65-66, 85-86, 102, 103, 108, 145, 168, 317, 321.
Halfdane (Christian) 459.
Hallins (Hillevions-Halland) 443, 483.
Hallstatt (see Austria).
Hamilton, H. C. 257.
Hamites (Ham) 32, 62, 76, 77, 83, 86, 88, 118ff., 134, 138, 143ff., 165, 167, 178, 180, 187ff., 207, 210, 235, 240, 244-246, 252, 527.
Hammurabi (king) v, 125, 133, 153, 195, 245, 312, 329, 369, 371, 388, 424, 436, 489, 491, 499-500, 505.

INDEX

INDEX

Iamblichus 192, 301.

Iazyges (Sarmatians) 447, 449, 506, 508-509.

Iberia or Iberians 61, 76, 81, 138, 174, 177, 181, 202-203, 218, 227, 259, 292, 303, 307ff., 347, 354, 391, 393, 395-398, 404, 419, 434, 436, 452, 453, 465, 477, 493-495, 501-505.

Ibn al Wardi 314.

Ice Ages 9ff.

Iceni 401.

Iliad 131, 271, 288, 300-301.

Illegitimacy (Negroes) 89.

Illiyahs (see Israelites) 154.

Illyria 281-283, 288, 289, 302, 303, 304, 306, 332, 515.

Inca (Quichua) 103-104, 106, 241.

Indafrican race 22, 30, 34-36, 49-54, 56, 57, 58, 62, 67, 71, 73, 75, 79, 81, 82ff., 91, 142, 162, 163, 168, 187, 194, 204, 205, 233, 237, 240, 246, 518.

India 22, 28ff., 49, 52, 54-55, 57, 58, 61-62, 64, 71, 72, 77, 78ff., 82, 83, 84, 86, 101, 103, 132, 139-141, 165ff., 207ff., 219, 229, 234, 235, 240, 245, 263, 266, 301, 345, 349, 502, 521, 528-530, 532-539.

Indians (American, see Amerinds).

Indo-China 27ff., 49, 52, 53, 54, 64, 75, 78ff., 90ff., 102, 161ff., 221, 235, 236.

Indo-European Languages 2, 72, 135.

Indo-Scythian (see Scytho-Indian) Empire.

Indonesians (Dravidians) 31, 50, 55, 57, 58, 59, 60, 61, 62, 74, 76, 78ff., 82, 85-86, 91, 105, 162, 163, 164ff., 187, 208, 220, 230, 238.

Indus River valley 23ff., 31, 50, 54, 55, 57, 58, 59, 60, 77, 79, 82, 91, 119, 120, 136, 164ff., 187, 189, 204, 212-213, 228, 518.

Insubri 306.

Integration (racial) 89, 90.

Inverness 425.

Iona (Hy) monastery 429.

Ionia (Ionians) 185, 186, 272, 285, 287, 291, 296, 298, 320-322.

Iotuns (primitive Scandinavians) 443.

Iran plateau 23ff., 31, 33, 37, 50-53, 59, 60, 61, 62, 76, 77, 83, 91, 119, 154, 164ff., 172ff., 176, 187, 234, 237, 247, 249, 252, 262, 264, 266, 272, 274, 278, 279, 329, 336, 342, 348, 349, 488, 531, 532, 535.

Iranians 32, 51, 62, 76, 77, 79-80, 93-95, 116, 117, 119, 120, 122, 151, 166ff., 187, 207ff., 234, 235, 239, 243-245, 250, 267, 274, 335, 345, 346-348, 356, 497, 521, 531, 532, 537, 538.

Iraq 56, 117, 164, 268.

Ireland v, 217, 253, 258, 267, 271, 285, 286-287, 293, 326, 348, 354, 355, 362, 365, 370, 371, 375-377, 379, 387, 388, 391ff., 412ff., 432ff.

Irish Church (see Free Church).

Iron Age 128, 137, 139, 282, 336-337, 342, 361, 373.

Iroquois Indians 107.

Irtish River 98, 308, 314.

Isaacs, Nathan 369, 388.

Ishmaelites 151.

Iskanderun (Alexandretta) 139.

Israel 150, 152, 154, 155.

Israelites 152ff., 195, 199, 278, 345, 530.

Issedones (Turki) 98, 143, 231, 254, 255, 262, 263, 268, 308ff., 326, 345, 465, 521, 525, 527, 528, 537.

Istria 515.

Italus (king) 304.

Italy 76, 129, 142, 176, 187, 201, 227, 247, 253, 258, 259, 281-285, 301ff., 307, 308, 333, 335, 354, 364, 382, 389, 452, 458, 486, 494, 500.

Iyrcae (see Bolgarians).

Jacob 151.

Jagog and Magog 314.

James I (king) 424, 432.

Japan and Japanese 71, 76, 77, 91, 95, 96, 101, 102, 114, 163, 235, 247, 539.

Japheth (Aryans) 148.

Java 19, 21, 22, 49, 170.

Jaxartes (tribe) 535-536.

Jebusites (Canaanites) 144, 146, 152.

Jehovah (see Yahweh).

Jeremiah 328.

Jerome, St. 375.

Jerusalem 146, 152, 154, 155, 160, 185.

Jesus the Christ 6, 34, 157-159.

Jews (Hebraic) 155, 157.

Jews (Khazar) 157.

John (Bible) 158, 159.

Joktan (Genesis) 149.

INDEX

INDEX

INDEX

INDEX

INDEX

559

INDEX

INDEX

INDEX

Vegdeg (leader) 361, 362, 365, 366, 441.
Veloscasses 386.
Venedotian Code 436.
Veneti (Italy) 306.
Venturiones 407.
Vernikones 409.
Veromandu 386.
Vespasiana 401.
Vestergotland (West Goths, Visigoths) 480, 498-500.
Vettius Bolanus 406.
Vidivarii 341, 343, 344, 497.
Vikings (see Fomorians) 356, 395, 410, 433, 434, 436, 457ff., 511, 512.
Vikrama Era (India) 532.
Vinili (see Langobards).
Virgil 301.
Visby (Gotland) 480, 948.
Visigauti (see Visigoths) 498.
Visigoths v, 251, 259, 312, 340, 371, 372, 444, 452, 473, 474, 477ff., 489, 490, 491, 493-498, 501-505, 509, 518.
Visimar (king) 452, 484.
Vistula River 256, 322, 337, 338, 439, 441, 455, 469, 471, 476, 483, 496, 509, 510, 512, 515, 516.
Vladimir I 511-512.
Voguls (Hungarians) 107, 317.
Volga River 95, 98, 150, 257, 308ff., 323, 463, 465, 472, 486, 492, 502, 514, 517.
Volsci (Italy) 304.
Voluntii 401-403, 405, 413.
Vortigern (king) 422, 450.
Votiaks 102, 317.

Wade, G. W. 155.
Wakhis (Pamirs) 221, 224.
Wales (see also Cymru) v, 267, 286, 352, 370, 371, 387, 391ff., 435ff., 450, 499, 501, 502, 505.
Wallachs (Romania) 467.
Wallia (king) 495.
Walton, C. S. 474.
Warmund I, II and III (markgrafs) 461. See Wermund.
Warni (Werni, Varini) 354, 360, 440, 445, 453.
Warthe River 447, 452, 516.
Washington, D.C., Negroes 89.
Wasserburg, G. J. 1.
Wasserburg (grafs) 461.
Weapons 39-45, 130, 241-242.

Weatherall, G. H. 1.
Weigall, Arthur 192.
Wends (also see Neuri) 337, 340-341, 442, 444, 455, 463-464, 485, 510, 514-516.
Wermund (count) 260, 460.
Wermund (king) 459.
Werni (see Warni).
Werra River 358, 363, 369, 371, 373, 380, 381, 385, 439, 442, 445, 449.
Weser River 259, 357, 361-363, 365, 369, 373, 380, 383, 386, 398, 425, 439, 441, 442, 445, 449, 450, 460.
West India Islands 108.
Westmoreland 405, 427.
Westphalia 285, 371, 451.
Wheel 114, 122, 130, 142, 208, 243, 250.
White subrace (see Aryan or Nordic Aryan).
Whithorn (Galloway) 412.
Wigton 406, 408.
Wilkinson, Benjamin G. 539.
William the Conqueror 437, 462.
Wilmarth, M. G. 7.
Wilson, Charles W. 268.
Windau 338, 478, 480.
Winds (see Slovenzi).
Wittekind (Widukind) 260, 459.
Wittelsbach dynasty 454.
Wladislaus Lokietek 513.
Woodward, B. B. 375-376.
World War I 516.
World War II 95, 455.
Worms (city) 384.
Writing 150, 182, 183, 188, 200, 210, 244-245, 302-303, 314, 538.
Würm I and Würm II Glaciations 12, 28-32, 35, 40, 42, 44-45, 50-52, 57, 58, 59, 70, 77, 78, 79, 81-85, 90-95, 164ff., 173, 218, 237, 239.
Württemberg 132, 384, 448, 455.
Wu-Sun (Sakae) 211, 230, 345, 524-525, 531-539.
Wynne, W. 435.

Xenophon 128, 268, 290, 299, 307, 321, 327, 402.

Yahweh 155, 199.
Yalta 467.
Yangtze River 92, 94, 95, 100, 170, 221.
Yellow race (see Turanian).

INDEX

D